A Declaration by the Representatives of the [UNITED STATES]

OF AMERICA, in General Congress assembled.

When in the course of human events it becomes necessary for one people to dissolve the political bands which have connected them with another, and to [illegible] -sume among the powers of the earth the separate and equal station to which the laws of nature & of nature's god entitle them, a decent respect to the opinions of mankind requires that they should declare the causes which impel them to the separation.

We hold these truths to be self-evident; that all men are created equal; that they are endowed by their creator with [illegible] [inherent &] inalienable rights; that among these are life, liberty, & the pursuit of happiness; that to secure these rights, governments are instituted among men, deriving their just powers from the consent of the governed; that whenever any form of government becomes destructive of these ends, it is the right of the people to alter or to abolish it, & to institute new government, laying it's foundation on such principles & organising it's powers in such form, as to them shall seem most likely to effect their safety & happiness. prudence indeed will dictate that governments long established should not be changed for light & transient causes: and accordingly all experience hath shewn that mankind are more disposed to suffer while evils are sufferable than to right themselves by abolishing the forms to which they are accustomed. but when a long train of abuses & usurpations [begun at a distinguished period &] pursuing invariably the same object, evinces a design to reduce them under absolute Despotism, it is their right, it is their duty to throw off such government & to provide new guards for their future security. such has been the patient sufferance of these colonies; & such is now the necessity which constrains them to [expunge] their former systems of government. the history of the present king of Great Britain is a history of [unremitting] injuries and usurpations, [among which, appears no solitary fact to contra-dict the uniform tenor of the rest but all have] in direct object

THE GOLDEN BOOK
HISTORY OF THE UNITED STATES

By Earl Schenck Miers
LITT.B., M.A., L.H.D.

GOLDEN PRESS NEW YORK

The paintings in this book are by
ALTON S. TOBEY
unless otherwise credited.
Drawings are by RICHARD P. KLUGA
unless otherwise credited.

Library of Congress Catalog Card Number: 73-88707

 Printed in the U.S.A. Published by Golden Press, New York, N.Y.

Contents

Introduction

To you, as an American boy or girl, history is the story of why you feel, and think, and act the way you do. Long years ago other youngsters like yourself awoke in the morning—glad when they beheld a beaming sun, drowsy when they heard the beat of rain on the roof, gloomy when threatening clouds gathered overhead—but a new day still budged them out of bed.

For being alive was what counted. Going to school, coming home, growing up were wonderful adventures. We can date the age when George Washington or Andrew Jackson or Abraham Lincoln grew from boyhood into manhood, but that fact isn't too important. They were like you, these youngsters of former years —not knowing that they were actors in history, but simply hoping that somehow, despite all their inner doubts, they would make a go of the years ahead.

And of course they did—as you will. Better than any other source, history reveals this truth to us. Great events grow out of average people like you and me—people who do what they think they should, who cling to their own principles and ideals, and who call by the name of freedom their right to do so.

The Golden Book History of the United States begins a long time ago—in the year 986 A.D. A great many people—some of them noble, some of them mean—walk through its pages. Each has something to tell us. Each is somehow part of ourselves. I hope that you will have the same fun I did in making this discovery.

Earl Schenck Miers

EARL SCHENCK MIERS

Carrying the royal banner of Spain, Christopher Columbus lands in the New World—October 12, 1492.

I ~ THE EXPLORERS

from 986 to 1701

Scouts from Leif Ericson's expedition found grapes and wheat in the new land they explored across the Atlantic.

Although Norse ships were small, they were sturdy and seaworthy.

Routes followed by Bjarni Heriulfsson and Leif the Lucky in their voyages to North America.

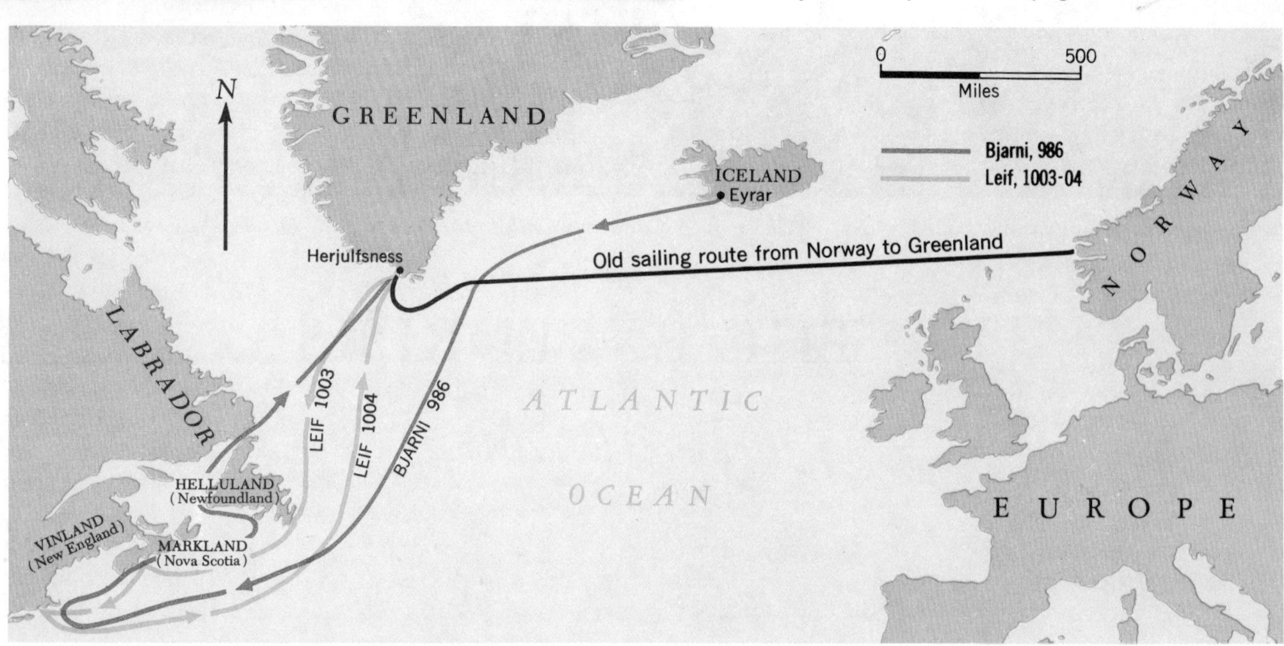

LEIF THE LUCKY SAILS TO NORTH AMERICA

Bold Norsemen from Greenland explore the coast of an unknown land.

A thousand years ago no voyager wanted to sail beyond the sight of land, for dark mystery haunted the open sea. No matter how carefully a navigator set his course, skies could blacken with an unexpected storm. Then rain fell, lightning flashed, thunder grumbled, and towering waves rose like walls around ship and crew. Equally dangerous, a cold night might be followed by a warm morning. At such times fog dropped like a curtain over the water and the winds grew still. In the silence, the sailors pulled on creaking oars. Cautiously their little ships edged ahead.

In the year 986 A.D., Bjarni Heriulfsson, a brave Norseman, left Iceland to join his father in Greenland. Even though Bjarni [pronounced By-arni] never before had sailed these icy seas, old hands at the voyage told him not to worry. Cape Farewell, the southern point of Greenland, could be seen after a few days' sail from Iceland.

For three days, under fair winds, Bjarni and his crew skimmed over the waves toward Greenland. Then all at once the winds died away. That night, all next day, and the day that followed, fog settled over the water. No one knows for certain how many days Bjarni drifted, but long after he had expected to reach Greenland, he was still on the open sea. At last the weather cleared and the following day Bjarni sighted land.

Bjarni now approached a shore that was level and wooded. Small hills rose in the distance. For some reason the Norsemen did not land, although they could not know then that instead of reaching Greenland, they probably were off the coast of Newfoundland. Mystified, Bjarni sailed on, turned north and continued past flat wooded land, then on to shores above which rose glistening ice mountains. The first white man known to have found the continent of North America simply looked and hurried away. Soon afterward Bjarni arrived safely in Greenland.

Years went by, but Bjarni could not forget the new country he had seen. Sometime after the year 1000, Bjarni told his tale to Leif the Lucky, son of famous old Eric the Red. Eager to see this strange land, Leif Ericson begged his father to go with him, for old Eric was the best navigator in the northern seas. Had he not, years ago, won fame as the discoverer of Greenland? Eric shook his head. He was too old now to attempt such an adventure. But Leif was young and strong. Go, Eric told his son. Seek your fame and fortune.

Leif bought a ship from Bjarni and engaged a crew of thirty-five men and women. One was a strange short fellow with a protruding forehead, a small face, and restless eyes. He was Tyrker, a German who had known Leif since childhood and was like a foster father to him. Next to Eric, Leif loved no man so much as Tyrker.

LEIF EXPLORES THE NEW WORLD

Leif the Lucky left Greenland with strong winds filling the sails of his boats. Quickly he voyaged to the new country beyond the North Atlantic. His first sight of land was a bleak coast of many ice mountains (probably Labrador or northern Newfoundland) and from the word *hellur,* meaning large flat stones, he gave the place the name of "Helluland." In a small boat a party went ashore, shivering in the breezes that swept down from the glaciers. There was not a single blade of grass on which to feed the cattle they had brought, and they decided to sail to the south.

The next land Leif saw may have been Cape Breton Island or the neighboring mainland of Nova Scotia. Here the country was level and wooded, the beaches white and sandy, and Leif gave the country the name of "Markland," meaning Forest Land. Once more they set sail, seeking regions Bjarni had not described. Driven by a northeast wind, after two days they again sighted land.

Today no one can say for certain exactly where the Norsemen went ashore. But we do know that Leif and his followers landed upon an island somewhere along the Atlantic coast between northern Maine and southern Massachusetts. There was dew on the grass. When they touched moistened fingers to their mouths, the dew seemed sweeter than any they ever had tasted. They sailed across a sound to another strip of land, and Leif sent the swiftest runners in his party to explore the unknown countryside. These scouts, legend says, were a man and a woman, dressed in a kind of plaid and kilt such as Scottish Highlanders wear. They returned after two and a half days, with a cluster of wild grapes and a sheaf of wheat.

Leif decided to build dwellings and to spend the approaching winter in this land of the sweet dew. He sailed to an island where so many eiderducks nested that the Norsemen found it impossible to step between the eggs. They discovered a river flowing into a lake where hundreds of salmon leaped in the water. Tall grasses supplied excellent food for the cattle, and close by were hillsides to shelter their huts. The year was 1003 A.D.

One day Tyrker the German—Leif's beloved foster father—was missing. Twelve men were sent to search for him, but soon Tyrker returned, shouting that he had come upon hundreds of wild grapevines.

Before Columbus crossed the Atlantic, sailors believed the sea was full of fearful monsters.

Leif embraced his old friend. He ordered the grapes gathered and dried so that they could be carried home. With the coming of the spring the ship was loaded and Leif set sail for Greenland. So ended the adventure of the first white men and women to dwell in North America.

The following year Leif's brother, Thorvald, visited the same land and found the winter dwellings that Leif had built. After this party left, other Norsemen visited these lands. Then mystery once more closed like a fog over the vast continent of North America. Almost five centuries passed, and not another white man appeared on the sandy beaches where Leif the Lucky had made his home.

THE WORLD AWAKENS

As Europe learns more about the world, navigators seek new routes to Asia. Columbus plans a voyage to the Orient.

In this age of jet planes that soar across the ocean in a few hours, it is difficult to imagine how much smaller was the world of a thousand years ago. If you had lived in Europe then, the chances are that from birth to death you would never have traveled more than a dozen miles from your home. Everything you needed to exist would be produced in the town or manor of your birth—all the food you ate, the simple clothes you wore, the crude tools you used. If by luck you had been born a lord, you would have spent your time hunting or jousting or carrying on small wars about boundaries and hunting rights with the owners of neighboring manors. You would have administered the affairs of your castle, conducted its religious life, and depended for your own food upon the labors of the many who were your humble serfs (slaves).

Gradually, however, there came a change, especially in the towns along the sea. Ships appeared from strange lands, bringing war at first, but in time bringing trade. Behind the walls of these growing towns a new class of people called merchants began to appear. In the open squares of the town, daily or weekly markets were held. To acquire goods with which to barter, farmers increased the products they grew. Weavers of cloth, or carpenters, or makers of candles, among others, began to give the world its first manufactures. Men from western Europe, journeying into distant lands, learned from the Moslems new ideas about food and clothing and customs. What a wonder it must have been for the first time to touch materials like muslin or damask, to discover the taste of rice or sugar, of lemons or apricots, or of food seasoned with garlic!

By the time the year 1300 arrived, traders and missionaries, crossing overland to many parts of Asia, had made the world a much bigger, more exciting place in which to live. From the Orient came new wonders: precious stones, fabrics of cotton and silk, rugs, glassware, perfume, dyes, ivory, medicines, spices. Europeans worked longer hours to produce articles of trade: woolen fabrics, wines, furs, sulphur, oil, honey, grain. Travelers told of cities with walls of silver and palaces with roofs of gold. Marco Polo told stories of his fabulous adventures in the strange, mysterious kingdoms of Asia. For the first time Europeans learned of life behind the Great Wall in China. They learned, too, of the islands in the Pacific called Japan, Java, and Sumatra, and of the remote regions of Siberia.

Prince Henry the Navigator of Portugal set up a school for the study of geography and navigation. When he died in 1460, his ships had sailed along two thousand miles of the coast of Africa. Portugal grew wealthy on the gold, ivory, and slaves its sailors found in these jungle lands. Map makers were kept busy charting the new trade routes. The invention of instruments like the compass and astrolabe enabled navigators to set their courses with greater accuracy. Some educated men began to believe that the world was round. If that were true, a ship sailing due west should be able to reach the Orient.

COLUMBUS PLANS HIS VOYAGE

At this time, a boy named Christopher Columbus was growing up in Genoa. The son of a weaver, by day he helped his father at the loom. In the evening he listened eagerly to the exciting tales told by the sailors at the wharves. He longed to go to sea, and he taught himself Latin because that was the language in which all the books on geography were written.

He read and dreamed and awaited his chance. It came when he was about nineteen. He signed aboard a Genoese galley seeking a crew to fight pirates off the Barbary coast of northern Africa.

The more Columbus sailed the sea, the more he loved the life he had chosen. He learned to reef a sail, to steer, to measure distance by eye, to recognize the signs of approaching storms. On one voyage off the coast of Portugal, the Genoese ships with which he was sailing were attacked by a French and Portuguese fleet. Sailors drowned by the hundreds in the bloody battle, and Columbus himself was wounded. He fought on furiously until his ship was rammed, then leaped into the water, grasping an oar that had floated free. Resting on the oar from time to time, he managed to swim the more than six miles to shore. Even this narrow escape did not make him lose his love of the sea, and he went on other voyages, going as far north as Ireland.

Columbus now began to talk about his great dream. He could sail a ship straight west and reach the Orient with its riches of gold, gems, and spices. When friends asked how far he thought the voyage would be from Portugal to Japan he gave the distance at about three thousand nautical miles. This would have placed Japan in the approximate location of the Virgin Islands.

Old sailors laughed, and muttered that he was out of his mind. Undiscouraged, Columbus appealed for help to King John II of Portugal. The king's advisers on navigation called his plan nonsense, and the king himself was shocked by the demands Columbus made. If his voyage should prove successful, Columbus wanted noble rank, the title of admiral, a share of the profits, and governorship of any lands he discovered!

Columbus carried his dream to Spain and at first he did no better in the court of King Ferdinand and Queen Isabella. Spain was at war with the Moors and could spare no money for Columbus. And the Spanish experts laughed as loudly at his wild idea as had the Portuguese.

But Queen Isabella did not laugh. If necessary, she would pawn the crown jewels to fit out an expedition for Columbus. To keep her from taking this step, the royal treasurer somehow raised the money. In round figures, it came to $14,000.

AMERICA DISCOVERED

Sailing west, Columbus finds a new world,
and believes it is Asia.

In the port of Palos before sunrise on August 3, 1492, three ships, carrying ninety men under Columbus's command, hoisted sail. As the wind caught the canvas, the *Santa Maria,* the *Niña,* and the *Pinta* moved toward the open sea. Many were the rewards the king and queen had promised the first man who sighted land, including the sum of 10,000 *maravedis,* an old Spanish coin of considerable value. Putting in at the Canary Islands, off the coast of West Africa, the ships were refitted. When they took to the sea again, the date was September 6, 1492.

Now, if the calculations of Columbus were correct, Japan was 2,400 nautical miles away. The world beyond the horizon was unknown. Who could say that the sea monsters of which sailors sometimes spoke—monsters that could swallow a ship in a gulp—did not exist here? For two weeks the three vessels plunged forward. The men on board, seeing nothing but sky and water, began to grumble among themselves. Pelicans flew over the ships, but a day passed, then another and another, and although other pelicans appeared, there was no sight of land. Masses of seaweed in the water aroused another fear. Sup-

The first map to bear the name America.
Cut this way, it fits over a ball to form a globe.

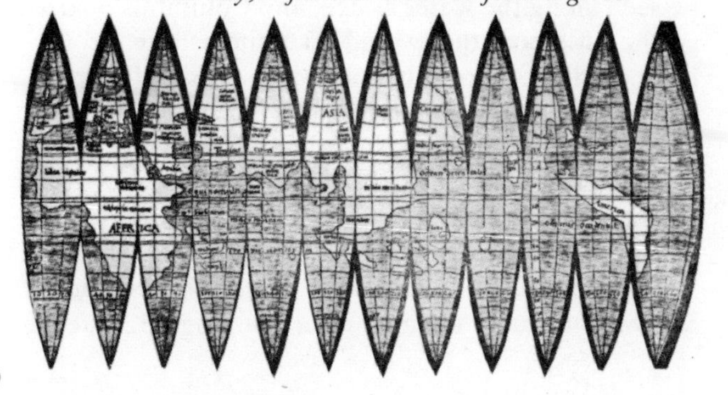

pose the weed should become so thick that the ships stuck in it? And then there was the wind that was blowing them away from Spain. How could they be sure that another wind would blow them home?

The grumbling grew worse. The crews met secretly, declaring that Columbus was risking their lives to carry out his own mad ambitions. Even though land had not been sighted, why should they not turn back? Would they not be honored for the fact that they had sailed farther west from Spain than any men who ever had gone to sea? Some even plotted to heave Columbus overboard and claim he had fallen into the sea.

Late in September a cry rang out aboard the ships, "Land, land, sir!" The men murmured prayers of thanksgiving, but Columbus knew that by morning they would realize they had only seen some storm clouds that resembled an island. Despite the threats of his crew, Columbus kept his vessels plunging westward. So many false cries of land were raised that in early October Columbus issued a harsh order. Anyone who claimed to see land that was not reached within three days would forfeit the reward even if later he was the first to sight a shore.

THE FLEET NEARS LAND

On the afternoon of Thursday, October 11, there came a change. A green branch was sighted in the water, and then a green fish of the kind found near reefs. A stick, skillfully carved, was fished from the sea, and a sailor saw a thorn branch with red berries that seemed to be freshly cut. Even Columbus now believed that land was near, and to the other rewards for the first to sight it he added a velvet doublet.

About two hours before midnight, standing on the deck of the *Santa Maria's* sterncastle, Columbus thought that he saw a light. He called on deck Pedro Gutiérrez, butler to the king, and Pedro, too, said that there had been a light. Then the *Pinta,* speediest of the three vessels, fired a signal. Land had been sighted by a sailor named Rodrigo de Triana.

Throughout that night the ships waited for daylight. The first rays of the rising sun on Friday, October 12, 1492, revealed the treelined coast of Watling Island in the Bahamas. Naked people could be seen along the water's edge, and Columbus boarded the little boat that would take him ashore. Proudly he carried the royal banner with its beautiful green cross that bore the letter F for Ferdinand on one arm and the letter Y for Ysabella (Isabella) on the other.

The sailors knelt in thanks to God. Some could not hold back their tears of joy and others kissed the ground. Columbus gave the island the name of San Salvador and claimed it for the king and queen. The Indians watched the ceremony with gentle good manners. Columbus gave them little red caps and glass beads which they hung around their necks.

Columbus wrote in his journal that the Indians had "very handsome bodies and very good faces." Their hair, he said, was as coarse as a horse's tail, and they wore a braid in back that they never cut. Some painted their faces, some their whole bodies, some only their noses, using shades of black and white, red and blue. All seemed to have very broad foreheads, the result of their custom of flattening the skulls of infants by pressing them between boards. They were highly intelligent and could repeat words that they had heard only once.

Columbus marveled at the boats in which the Indians came to visit the ships. Built all in one piece from the trunks of trees, they sometimes carried as many as forty paddlers. They were "wonderfully made" and skimmed through the water with speed and grace.

A brisk trade developed between the sailors and the Indians, who came loaded down with skeins of spun cotton, parrots, and darts. Everything the Indians offered, Columbus said, was given with "as much love as if their hearts went with it." He could not watch these simple, generous people being cheated by his crew and issued stern orders against offering them in trade "bits of broken crockery" and other worthless items.

Still certain that Japan was near, Columbus sailed to the island Hispaniola (now Haiti and the Dominican Republic). Here he built a fort and left forty-four men while he hastened home with the news of his remarkable discoveries. He was received in triumph at the Spanish court. People stared at the rich and strange prizes from the new-found lands—the cotton, the samples of gold, the strange plants, birds, and animals, the Indians he had brought to be baptized. Plans were made for a second voyage.

Bad news awaited Columbus on his return to Hispaniola. His fort was burned and his colonists has disappeared. Building a second fort and founding the city of Isabella, Columbus made a fresh start as a colonizer. But his love for the Indians was not shared by all. Wealth was what the followers of Columbus were seeking—in gold, in slaves. And Columbus was more a navigator and explorer than a governor. Always he wanted to continue sailing westward until he reached the treasures of the Far East.

In all, Columbus completed four voyages. He discovered the vast continent of South America and many important islands, among them Cuba and Jamaica. When he died on May 20, 1506, Columbus still did not know that he had stumbled upon a new world.

But another Italian navigator of the day, Amerigo

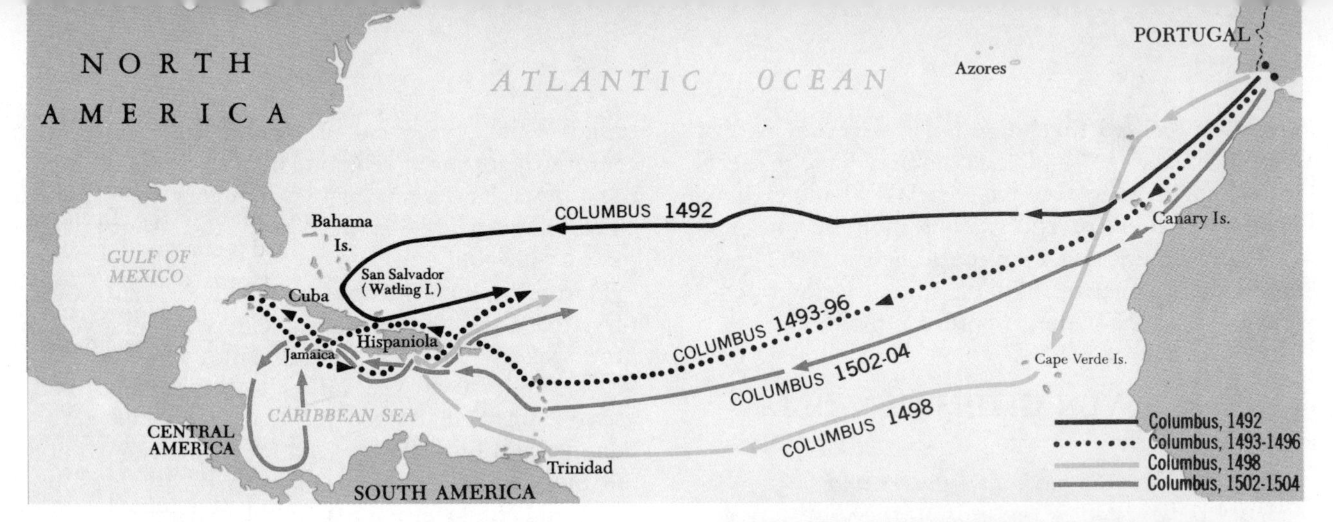

Columbus made four trips to the New World between 1492 and 1502. He explored the West Indies and touched the coasts of Central and South America, but never reached North America.

(Right) *Christopher Columbus*

(Bottom) *Back in Spain after his first voyage, Columbus told King Ferdinand and Queen Isabella of his discoveries in the New World.*

Columbus had his coat of arms made in 1502. The design at bottom left represents the islands he had found.

Vespucci, realized that these lands were not part of Asia. Between 1497 and 1504, he may have made as many as four voyages to the New World and claimed to be the first explorer to set foot upon the continent of South America. A map, published in 1507, gave the name of America to South America. Later geographers gave the name to both continents.

THE SEVEN CITIES OF GOLD

Three Spanish adventurers and a slave follow the trail of a legend.

Six hundred years of war against the Moors had left Spain bankrupt. Some enormous stroke of good luck was needed to save the empire from ruin. The Spanish still believed the legend of a mysterious island in the ocean called Antillia to which, long centuries ago, seven religious men had sailed. Here, the priests had built the Seven Cities of Antillia, cities of such wealth that even the streets were paved with gold.

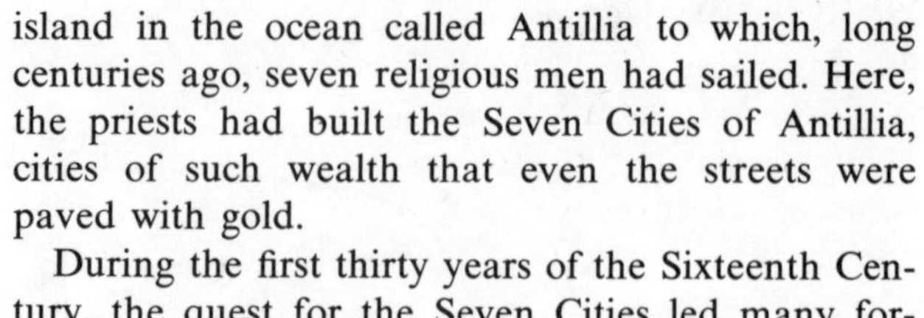

On September 25, 1513, the Spanish explorer Balboa and his followers discovered the Pacific Ocean.

During the first thirty years of the Sixteenth Century, the quest for the Seven Cities led many fortune seekers to follow the sea lanes into the New World. Only seven years after Columbus had died, Vasco Núñez de Balboa led a ragged band across Panama and Europeans gazed for the first time upon the blue waters of the Pacific Ocean. By 1521 the brave and cruel Hernando Cortés had captured Mexico from the Aztec Indians, and in another year the ships of Ferdinand Magellan sailed the globe, proving that the world was round. Yet not all who left for the New World were so lucky. For years mystery surrounded the fate of the more than 250 men who sailed with Alvar Núñez Cabeza de Vaca in 1528.

A hurricane in the Gulf of Mexico wrecked this Spanish fleet off the Texas coast, and those who drowned were more fortunate than those who were eaten by cannibal Texas Indians. The wonder was that any survived. Yet Vaca waded from the stormy sea onto Galveston Island, where the natives made him a slave.

CABEZA DE VACA CROSSES TEXAS

Within a year Vaca escaped into the interior of Texas. Soon he became famous among the natives as a medicine man who achieved remarkable cures by using prayers and the sign of the cross. Five years after the shipwreck, traveling along the Colorado River near the Texas coast, Vaca came upon three other survivors. Dorantes and Castillo, like Vaca, were Spaniards. The other was Stephen, Dorantes' Moorish slave.

In the months that followed, Vaca and his party went up the Colorado River, journeyed west through the mesquite country, and in time crossed the Pecos River. Everywhere in western Texas crowds appeared. Simply to touch the garments of these castaways, the Indians believed, would heal their wounds and cure their illnesses. Stephen, the Moorish slave became an idol, not only because he carried a gourd rattle that the Indians believed possessed mysterious powers, but also because he learned to speak their language. Gifts were showered upon the travelers—beads, buffalo skins, pouches filled with pearls.

Some distance above present-day El Paso, Vaca and his friends crossed the Rio Grande. They saw Indians who lived in permanent homes and ate beans, squashes, and maize (corn). The first Europeans to visit New Mexico and Arizona, the Spaniards and their Moorish comrade heard tales of rich cities to the north where even the arrowheads sparkled like emeralds. Their eyes glittered as they remembered the old legend of Antillia. The Indians must be describing the famous Seven Cities of Gold—in a northern land called Cíbola.

Eight years had passed since Vaca's ship had been wrecked when one day a party of slave hunters, invading the coast of Texas, saw an almost unbelievable sight. Toward them traveled three Europeans and a Moor, accompanied by a band of 600 Indians who treated the four ragged castaways as gods. The slave hunters listened to the stories the party told and their eyes, too, glittered over those wonderful Seven Cities somewhere to the north.

THE SPANIARDS SEARCH FOR WEALTH

Fortune hunters discover the wonders of a new continent, but fail to find gold.

During the eight years that Vaca and his companions had wandered across southwestern America, Spaniards under the mighty Pizarro had seized Peru from the Inca Indians. Yet even the stolen wealth of Peru, added to the captured riches of Mexico, was not enough to satisfy the greedy Spaniards. They listened eagerly to tales about the Seven Cities.

DE SOTO DREAMS OF EMPIRE

No one listened more closely than Hernando de Soto, who had fought with Pizarro in Peru. De Soto talked with a survivor of Vaca's party, and his heart beat faster. He wanted wealth and power. Like Cortés in Mexico and Pizarro in Peru, he would conquer and rule an empire of his own.

In the spring of 1539, de Soto reached Havana and collected nine ships and 620 men for his expedition to capture the Seven Cities. He set sail for Florida—Land of Flowers—discovered years before by Juan Ponce de León. Ponce de León had been searching for "Bimini," where, according to Indian legend, bathing in the waters would give a person eternal youth. Instead, he found the natives becoming more and more suspicious of Spaniards who carried the cross in one hand and the sword in the other. Ponce de León and his men had been driven back to their ships.

But in those days Spaniards believed that heaven intended them to do as they pleased in this land of heathen redskins. De Soto was no exception, and, late in the spring of 1539, he landed his expedition on the shore of Charlotte Bay on the west coast of Florida. He brought ashore his knights and soldiers in armor, more than 200 horses, and hundreds of hogs on the hoof. Two years of nightmare followed. Almost constantly at war with the Indians, he led his men through the wilderness of Florida and up into Alabama, Tennessee, and the Carolinas. They found hunger, sickness, and death rather than gold.

In late April or May of 1541, de Soto stumbled upon a river—the mighty Mississippi—but it meant little to him. At least 200 of the knights and soldiers who had started with him now were dead, and those who survived wore raccoon and wildcat furs under their rusty armor.

The Spaniards had reached the Mississippi some thirty or thirty-five miles below the present city of Memphis, and at this point the treacherous old river was a mile wide. They hollowed out logs to make dugouts or canoes and on June 29, 1541, they landed on the soil of Arkansas near Sunflower Landing, south of Helena.

Still determined to find wealth, de Soto and his tattered band explored the central part of Arkansas. They crossed the Arkansas River and discovered a "very warm and brackish lake" that must have been the now-famous Hot Springs. After two years the Spaniards had not changed their style of conquest. Indians were treated as slaves or fools, and usually as both. De Soto bragged that he was a god who possessed powers making him all-wise. He showed the red men a mirror he carried. In its glass, he declared, was revealed everything they did and thought. But the Indians, far from being fools, played their own game with de Soto. Always they spoke of places of great wealth somewhere in the distance, and by this trick rid themselves of the Spaniards, who pressed on in their search for fortune.

DEATH OF DE SOTO

De Soto and his party wandered down the Ouachita River before camping for the winter. Pitifully weakened, they lived on a little corn, beans, pecans, and dried persimmons grudgingly supplied by neighboring Indians. Malaria broke out and one by one the Spaniards began to die. By May the eyes of de Soto burned with fever. Late that month the captain died and the new captain general of the expedition, Luys Moscoso de Alvarado, feared what the Indians might do when they discovered that the Spanish leader was not an immortal god.

For three days de Soto's corpse was hidden. Then by night it was taken to the middle of the great river de Soto had discovered and buried in the sands of the Mississippi. The Indians, however, were instantly suspicious. They ordered two young Spaniards to be slain, for it was their custom, when any lord died, to kill some persons who should accompany and serve him on the way to the happy hunting grounds. Luckily, the Spaniards avoided this sacrifice by insisting de Soto was not dead but had merely returned to heaven, taking with him all the soldiers he required for that journey.

Although in later months the Spaniards under

Moscoso pushed into Missouri, they never found the Seven Cities. Only 320 survivors—300 less than had started—accompanied Moscoso when in the fall of 1543 the expedition ended in Mexico.

CORONADO SEEKS GOLD

But another Spanish expedition already had discovered the Seven Cities of Cíbola. Francisco Vásquez de Coronado, governor of one of the northern districts of Mexico, also had listened eagerly to the tales Vaca's party brought back. In February, 1540, Coronado set forth with an expedition of 250 horsemen, seventy Spanish footmen, hundreds of friendly Indians, and herds of baggage animals and cattle.

Coronado's band was high-spirited and eager for adventure. Like most Spanish explorers of the time, these soldiers of fortune were young men. Many were still boys outgrowing their teens, and most of the others were in their early twenties. By July they reached the Zuñi River country, close to the present-day boundary between New Mexico and Arizona. A brisk fight one night in Bad Pass was sharp warning that the Spaniards were unwelcome visitors.

The Zuñi tribesmen who watched the approach of Coronado and his soldiers were a proud people. How long they had inhabited this desert country was a mystery. Some experts believe they already had lived in America for at least 10,000 years, and others think 15,000 years may be a more accurate guess. At least ten centuries before Coronado appeared they had built dwellings four and five stories high, containing as many as 1,200 rooms.

The Zuñi Indians, whom the Spaniards would call Pueblos—*pueblo* meaning *village* in Spanish—constructed their homes of desert earth and rock. These first apartment houses in America were set on high cliffs. As a further protection from enemies, there were neither doors nor windows on the first floor. The only entry was by ladders that could be quickly raised in case of attack. When the sun shone on the colored earth and rock of these cliff cities, they sparkled as though made of precious metals—and it was this that fooled Coronado's men.

The Zuni Indians built settlements of sun-dried bricks on the tops of high cliffs.

Catching a glimpse of the Zuñi village of Hawikuh, they cried, *"Albricias! Albricias!"* or, "Reward me! Reward me!"

They were overjoyed. They had found Cíbola! But the Indians fought savagely to save their city. And when, after much bloodshed, the Zuñis finally were subdued, the Spaniards discovered that all they had conquered was a little pueblo of earth and rock. Indeed, there were Seven Cities of Cíbola—seven little pueblos like Hawikuh, all worthless to these treasure seekers.

Coronado quickly forgot the disappointment of Cíbola and led his expedition westward to the Rio Grande. His soldiers explored northeastern Arizona and the Grand Canyon of the Colorado River. Here the Indians streaked their faces with black soot and often wore masks of the same color. They were sun worshippers, and the Spaniards described them in these words:

"Some have their noses pierced, and from them hang pendants, while others wear shells. They also have their ears pierced with many holes, in which they place shells and beads. . . . Their bodies are branded by fire. Their hair is banged in front, but in the back it hangs to the waist."

New stories reached Coronado of a place of untold wealth far to the northeast called Quivira. With spring he was off once more, crossing the plains of Texas and finding nothing. Still hopeful, he retraced his way and marched northward into central Kansas.

At times on the prairies Coronado seemed to be "swallowed up in the sea," for there was "not a stone, nor a bit of rising ground, nor a tree, nor a shrub, nor anything to go by." He passed vast herds of buffalo. The Texas Indians who guided the Spaniards lived on the raw flesh and blood of these animals. Except when they stopped to hunt buffalo, the Indians traveled swiftly behind the dogs they had trained as pack animals.

Reaching Quivira after a weary march of seventy-seven days, Coronado looked with scorn upon the houses of straw in which "barbarous" Wichita Indians lived. Like the Texans, the Wichitas were raw-meat eaters. Yet Coronado could not hide his delight in this Kansas country, calling it "the best I have ever seen for producing all the products of Spain, for besides the land itself being very flat and black and being well watered by the rivulets and springs and rivers, I found prunes like those of Spain and nuts and very good sweet grapes and mulberries."

Coronado's expedition was a failure, and in the spring of 1542 he returned to Mexico.

SPAIN CLAIMS THE NEW WORLD

Half a century had passed since Columbus had discovered the New World. Now two great Continents—North America and South America—were

As the sun shone on the distant pueblo, Coronado thought he had found the city of gold.

(Left) *De Soto had great difficulty in moving his troops and guns through the wild American territory.*

Early explorations of America. The boundaries shown are those of the present day.

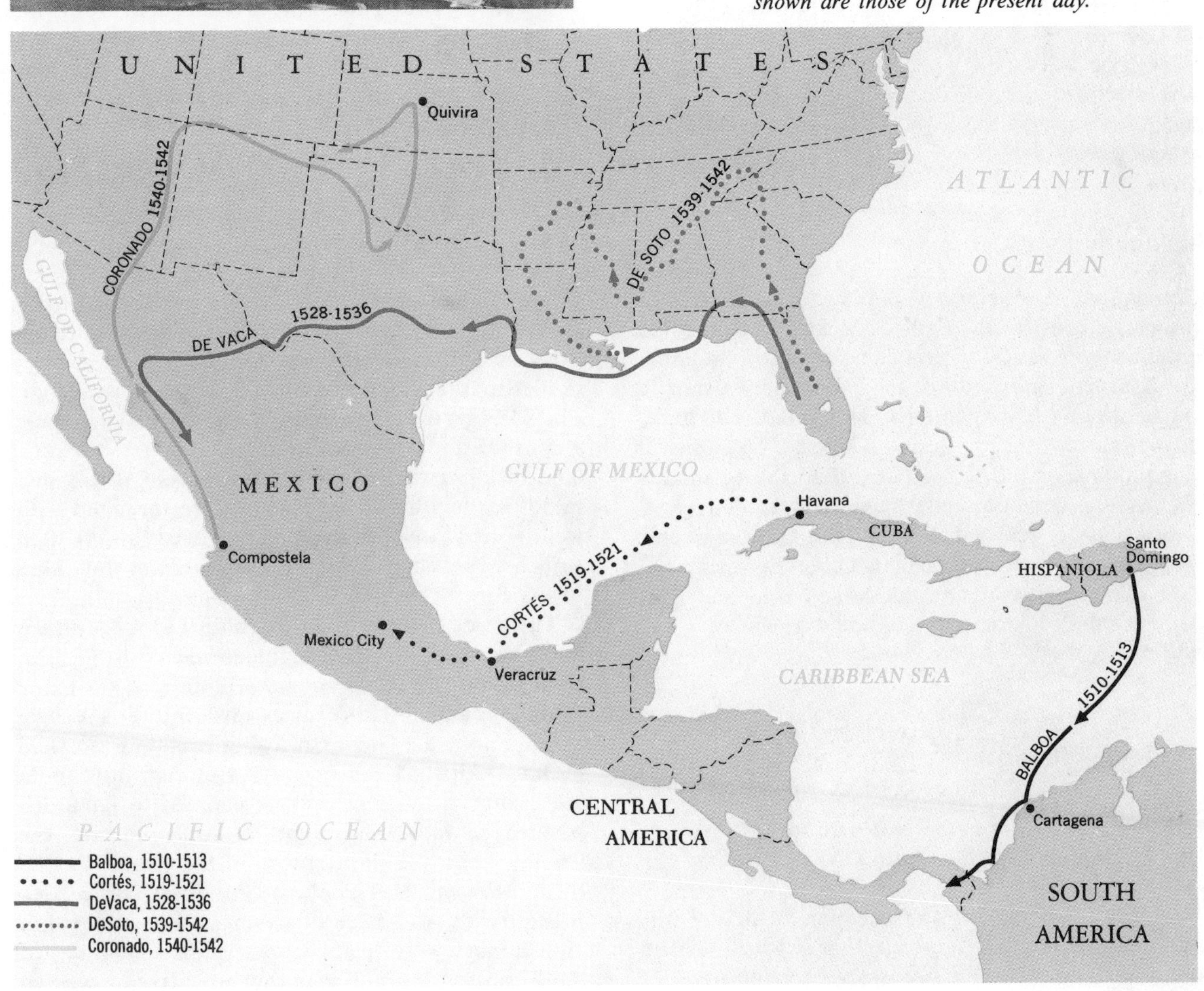

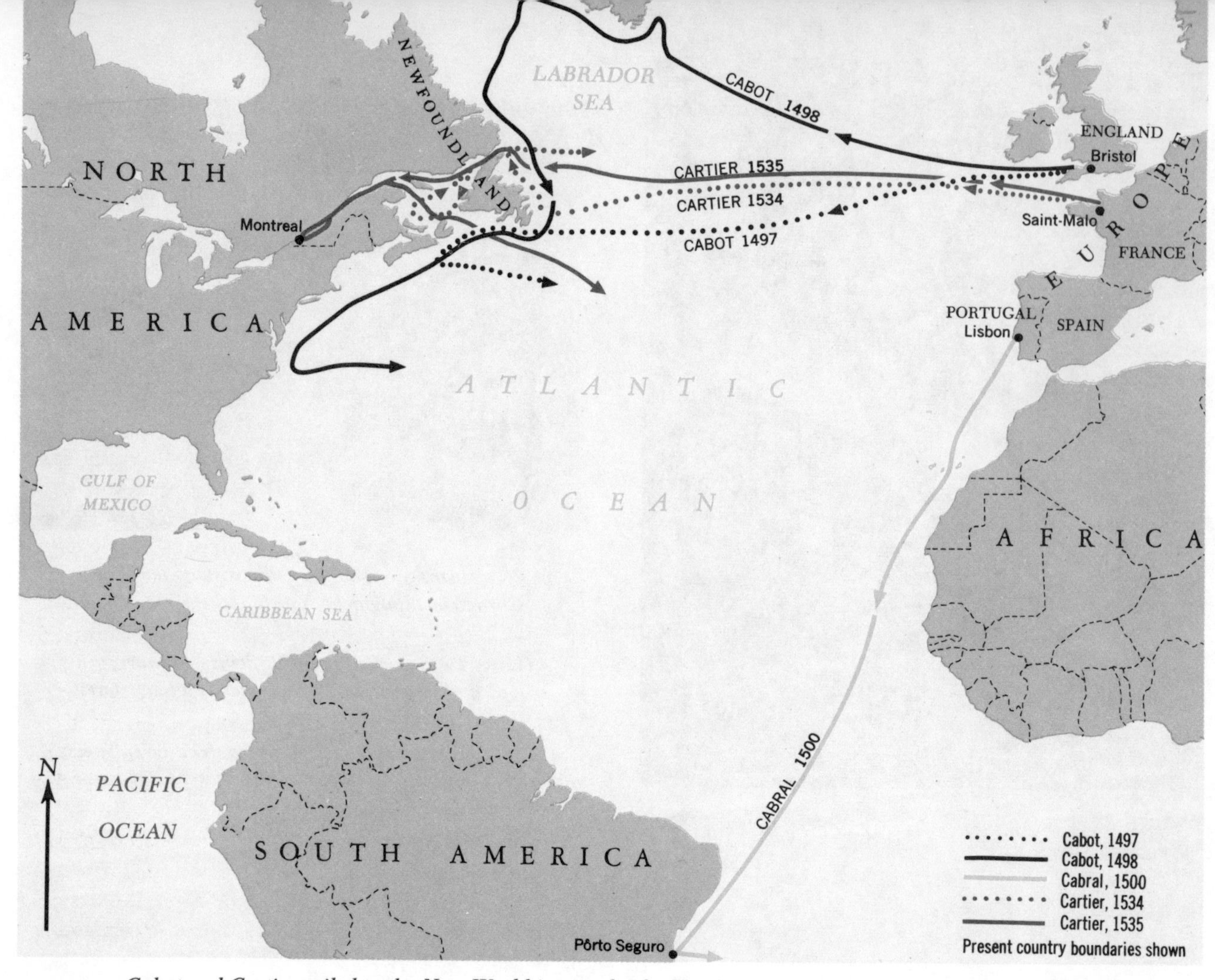

Cabot and Cartier sailed to the New World in search of a Northwest Passage. Cabral reached Brazil.

claimed by Spain. Her navigators were familiar with the entire coast of the Gulf of Mexico and with the coast of the Atlantic at least as far as Newfoundland. De Soto had marched his knights in rusty armor to the banks of the Mississippi and Coronado had hunted buffalo on the prairies of Kansas. The habits of the Indians, as old if not older than the Spaniards themselves, were becoming common knowledge.

Spain never realized that the land and the people were the real wealth it sought. Other European nations would soon invade the New World and fight for an empire. What no one could guess was that, with time, they *all* would lose.

THE SEARCH FOR THE NORTHWEST PASSAGE

France becomes a rival to Spain and Portugal in the New World.

During the 1490's, England's seaport of Bristol was crammed with sailors and merchants who lived by the sea. They were greatly excited by the news of Columbus's first voyage to the West Indies. Merchants who had grown wealthy on trade with the fisheries of Iceland became eager for even greater profits in the lands the Spaniards had discovered. The idea grew that perhaps there was a sea route—a northwest passage—around the newly discovered land blocking the way to the Orient. On a May day in 1497, the wharves of Bristol were thronged with well-wishers who cheered and waved as the first British vessel sailed westward in search of the riches of the East.

The name of this sturdy little ship was the *Matthew* and her crew numbered eighteen men. At the helm stood John Cabot, a native of Genoa and for many years a merchant in Venice. Little more is known about Cabot—or Giovanni Caboto, as he was called in Italy. All that can be said with certainty about his voyage is the fact that he claimed to have discovered in late June what he supposed was the Chinese coast "in the territory of the Grand Chan." In another month Cabot and his crew returned to Bristol, with wild tales of triumph, and in London high honors were heaped upon him. "He is called the Grand Admiral," reported an account written at the time. "He is dressed in silk, and the English run after him like madmen."

The best guess is that Cabot had landed somewhere on Cape Breton Island at the northern tip of Nova Scotia. On a second voyage the following year, Cabot evidently was lost at sea—at least no word was ever heard from him again. Later voyages were made by his son, Sebastian Cabot. Through the exploits of the Cabots, father and son, England could claim to have been the first European nation whose navigators had set foot on the continent of North America; Columbus had landed only in the West Indies.

Meanwhile Pedro Alvares Cabral, a Portuguese explorer, in 1500 discovered Brazil, which he claimed for Portugal.

JACQUES CARTIER SEEKS THE NORTHWEST PASSAGE

Spain and Portugal, with the approval of the Pope, divided the New World between them. They forbade other nations to invade their "sacred rights" as England had done through the voyages of the two Cabots. Then, in 1534, France became a new rival in the struggle for possession of the New World. On April 20, two French ships set sail from St. Malo in search of the Northwest Passage that the Cabots had failed to find. At the head of this expedition was another man of mystery, Jacques Cartier, who left no record of his youth beyond the fact that he was born at St. Malo in France.

Cartier sighted Newfoundland on May 10 and planted the cross of France at Gaspé Bay. The following summer, Cartier returned to North America with a fleet of three ships. He heard of a great river and of a populous island town called Hochelaga, situated hundreds of miles upstream. Although Cartier was sure this river was not the passage he sought to the Orient, he decided to make the journey to Hochelaga.

For two weeks Cartier voyaged up the broad St. Lawrence River, finding a fine harbor at the site of the present city of Quebec. Here he anchored his three ships and continued the journey in small boats. Near where Montreal would one day rise, the Frenchmen landed in early October.

Cartier received a hearty welcome from the Indians. Men, women, and children brought food and danced joyfully.

Next day the Frenchmen marched to Hochelaga along a well-beaten road through a forest of oaks as fine as any in France. Acorns covered the ground. Then the Frenchmen came upon large, cultivated fields "full of grain" and soon were entering the gate of the fortified town of Hochelaga. Within the enclosure were about fifty houses, made of timber frames and covered with bark or strips of timber. Each dwelling had its large center room where the fire was built and the family lived.

The king of these people was named Agohanna, and he wore a red band of porcupine quills around his head as a symbol of authority. But Agohanna was a sick old man who asked Cartier to examine his sore, weakened legs and arms. When Cartier began to stroke these withered limbs with his own strong hands, Agohanna removed the red band and placed it on Cartier's head.

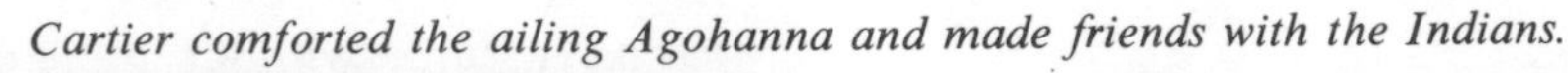

Cartier comforted the ailing Agohanna and made friends with the Indians.

The gesture was a sign to the people to bring forward all who were ill. The blind, the one-eyed, the lame approached, and others "so very old that the lids of their eyes hung down even upon their cheeks." They all begged Cartier to cure them.

For centuries the Indians of North America had had a legend which told how some day palefaced men from across the sea would come as healers. The Spaniards had proved the legend wrong; they were conquerors, not healers. But Cartier was a different kind of man. He gathered the Indians around him, read to them from the Gospel of St. John, made the sign of the cross on the sick and the lame, and offered prayers for their salvation. An eyewitness wrote: "All these poor people kept a great silence and were marvelously good hearers, looking up to heaven and making the same ceremonies that they saw us make."

Afterward Cartier gave tin plates to the women, knives to the men, and hatchets to the chiefs. He threw small rings on the ground and watched the children scampering after them with happy shouts. Cartier knew only one moment of embarrassment, when the Indians heaped food before his party—all of it unsalted and not to French taste. But Cartier thanked the Indians, explaining that his party was not hungry. From the beginning, these Frenchmen knew how to behave in the wilderness.

The voyages of Sir Francis Drake. The map shows present-day boundaries.

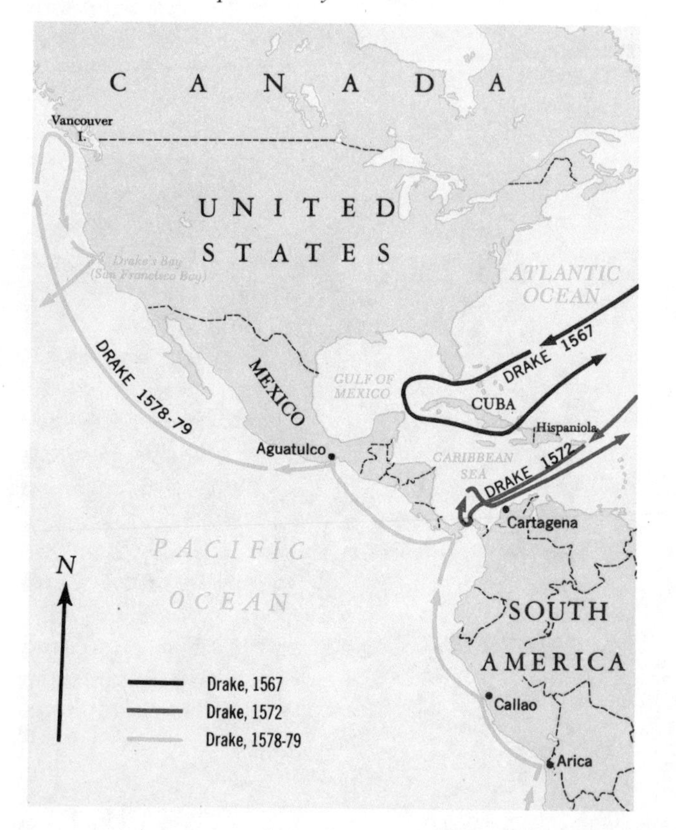

OLD POWERS SEEK NEW EMPIRES

England seeks a place in the New World.
The mystery of the lost colony.

As the years went by, Spain's conquests in the New World made her rich and powerful. She interfered in the affairs of Portugal, Italy, France, and the Netherlands. Even in England, now ruled by Queen Elizabeth I, Spanish spies were hard at work.

Queen Elizabeth was a woman with a quick mind and a strong will, and the spies had many things to report. In the late 1570's Martin Frobisher made three voyages to Labrador in a vain search for gold. Then, in 1577, Francis Drake set off in the *Golden Hind* on a three-year voyage around the world, and Spain realized that England intended to develop into a first-class sea power.

As early as 1542, Juan Rodríguez Cabrillo, a Portuguese navigator employed by Spain, had sailed into San Diego Bay. Cabrillo had explored a considerable length of the coast of present-day California. He had discovered Santa Monica Bay and the three islands of the Santa Barbara group before he died of an illness. Yet Cabrillo's crew brought back no proof of gold in these regions, and Spain was little interested in the lands north of Mexico.

Then troubling reports reached Spain. In 1579, Drake sailed his *Golden Hind* up the west coast of South America and finally into San Francisco Bay. The Indians, bearing gifts of feathers and tobacco, greeted the English as gods. Drake called these native Californians a people of "free and loving nature, without guile and treachery," and gave them "necessary things to cover their nakedness." Drake refused the pleas of the Indians to "take their province and kingdom into his hand and become their king." Instead, he claimed California for England and gave to the land the name of New Albion. He nailed a brass plate to a post "together with her Highness' picture and arms, in a piece of sixpence current English money."

Seeking the outlet of the fabled Northwest Passage, Drake voyaged along the coast of Oregon and as far north as British Columbia. He began to doubt that such a passage existed—or, if it did, that it was navigable—and it seemed to him the land ran continually northwest, "as if it went directly to meet with Asia." Correctly, Drake guessed that Asia and North America must be close together in this area.

Elizabeth greeted Drake warmly on his return to England. She stored away in the Tower of London most of the treasure, worth millions of dollars, that he had brought back with him—treasure he had taken in raids on the Spaniards.

SIR HUMPHREY GILBERT SAILS NORTH

Less successful were the voyages of Sir Humphrey Gilbert. The first, in 1578, had been a secret so well kept that neither the Spanish nor anybody else could learn much about it. The instructions the queen gave Gilbert were "to search, find out and view such remote, heathen and barbarous lands, countries and territories not actually possessed of any Christian people or prince." Sir Humphrey, failing on his first try, sailed again in 1583. If, as some believe, Gilbert actually intended to sail to Florida, he went the wrong way. He took possession of Newfoundland, but misfortune followed him like a school of sharks. On the voyage westward he lost his flagship and the stores for his proposed colony. On the voyage home he was drowned when the bark *Squirrel* went down.

Yet Sir Humphrey Gilbert's voyages were far from complete failures, for they kept alive England's interest in North America. The queen's advisers urged her to plant colonies in the New World. The Spanish and the French were already there, and the Dutch would surely be there, too, as soon as the wars in the Netherlands ended.

What could be gained from colonies in North America? In the northern parts of the continent, the queen's advisers answered, the winters were long and cold, promising a good market for English woolen goods. Furs, which were a great rage in Paris, could be found in abundance in the New World. The fisheries of Newfoundland were another rich source of trade, and the French reported finding large deposits of red copper in the regions they had explored. There was still one more strong argument—Spain. How long should she be allowed to rule the roost, to stir up trouble all over Europe, and even send her spies into Elizabeth's own court?

This was dangerous talk, and Elizabeth kept it secret, for Spain was becoming increasingly warlike toward any nation that challenged her possessions in the New World. To guard against pirates roaming the Florida coast, Spain organized special fleets of armed vessels to escort her treasure ships on their homeward voyages. And Spanish tempers had boiled over in 1564 when the French, growing ever bolder in North America, landed in Florida and planted a colony at Fort Caroline on the St. Johns River.

Under the captain general of the Spanish treasure fleet, Don Pedro Menéndez de Avilés, an expedition was organized to rid Florida of these French invaders. In September, 1565, Menéndez brought his warships up the St. Johns River, but to his surprise the French fleet stood ready to give battle. A game of hide-and-seek between the two naval forces ended disastrously for the French when a storm shipwrecked their vessels. Menéndez at once made an attack on Fort Caroline, killing all the inhabitants of the colony except the women and children. He hunted the survivors of the wrecked fleet and cut them down with his sword.

Sir Francis Drake

FIRST PERMANENT WHITE SETTLEMENT

That same year, at St. Augustine, Florida, the Spanish founded the first permanent white settlement in this country, giving Menéndez a base from which to fight off invaders. Jesuit priests were sent to establish missions among the Indians and by 1571 they had settled as far north as the Potomac River, near the present city of Washington, D.C. Spanish vessels patrolled the coast of Florida and the Carolinas.

Queen Elizabeth knew these facts when she sent two barks to search for a site for a future colony along the southern part of the North American coast. On a bright April day in 1584 these ships left on the journey that carried them to the low-lying coast that now belongs to North Carolina. Here, on an island to which the name of Roanoke would be given, the English believed that they had the ideal spot. They found the Indians on the mainland "most gentle, loving and faithful, void of all guile and treason."

SIR RICHARD GRENVILLE AT ROANOKE ISLAND

The exciting reports these explorers brought home convinced Elizabeth, and a fleet commanded by Sir Richard Grenville was assembled to carry colonists to America. In June, 1585, Grenville landed his colonists on Roanoke Island and wrote a glowing account of what Elizabeth could expect from "her Majesty's new kingdom of Virginia." He had found the mainland "the goodliest soil under heaven." He described the abundance of "sweet trees" and of grapes, which were as fine as those found in France, Spain, and Italy. There were, in addition, "many sorts of apothecary drugs" and among the many kinds of flax was one like silk. In this continent of "huge and unknown greatness" existed many people and towns in a climate so wholesome that he had not seen a single sick person. If Virginia were supplied with horses and cattle, and if Englishmen inhabited this country, no realm in Christendom would compare with it—or so, at least, Grenville reported.

Sir Richard left about a hundred colonists on Roanoke, promising to send a ship with supplies. Instead of cultivating the land, the settlers spent their time searching for gold and picking quarrels with the Indians—not the best way to start a new life in a new world. Then a hurricane struck the coast, making them wish they never had left England.

But relief was closer at hand than anyone dared hope. For weeks Sir Francis Drake had been raiding Spanish ships and towns in the West Indies. Then, unexpectedly, he appeared in the harbor of St. Augustine. He burned that place to the ground while the Spaniards hid in the nearby swamps and swore savage oaths of revenge on these English vandals. Drake sailed on to Roanoke, where he found the colonists still trembling from their experience with the hurricane. He agreed to take them all home.

In a short time the promised supply ship arrived at Roanoke, but when no colonists were found, it turned back to England. Grenville also appeared with three ships and spent days sailing along the coast trying to learn what had happened to his colony. Unwilling to lose possession of the country, Grenville left fifteen men with provisions for two years to hold the fort on Roanoke.

In April of 1587 still another expedition of colonists was sent under the command of John White. He reached Roanoke in June, but found the fort demolished. Of the fifteen men Grenville had left, there was only a single skeleton!

White rebuilt the fort, erected a few houses, and named his new settlement "the Citie of Raleigh in Virginia." That August, his granddaughter, Virginia Dare, became the first child of English parents born in North America. White returned to England, promising a speedy return.

He intended to keep his word, but England was engaged in a long and exhausting war with Spain. In 1588 every good ship England could find was needed to fight off the threatened invasion of the island by the Spanish Armada of 130 vessels, 2,500 guns, and 30,000 men. Storms helped a plucky English fleet to drive off the Armada. "God blew and they were scattered," the English said afterward—and, surely, it must have seemed no less than a miracle.

THE LOST COLONY OF ROANOKE

John White, after four years, at last could carry his promised supplies to Roanoke. A shock—and a mystery—awaited him. Not a single colonist remained. He found chests, books torn from their covers, and armor "almost eaten through with rust." The word "CROATOAN" was carved on one tree and the letters "CRO" on another.

What did it mean? Had the colonists been murdered by Spaniards? Had they been killed by Indians—or, equally possible, had they wandered off to live with the Indians? No one has ever answered these questions.

PLANTING THE TREE OF LIBERTY

After many hardships, the English establish a colony at Jamestown.

In 1603, with the death of Queen Elizabeth, James I became the ruler of England. As he journeyed from his home in Scotland to his court in London, he saw few things to make him cheerful. England had paid dearly for her long years of war with Spain. Beggars filled the streets of the cities and vagabonds roamed country roads. Prices were high and wages were low. Many people awoke each morning without work or hope, and far too often they went to bed hungry. A new life in the New World became their only chance of escaping from these miseries. England decided to make a success of building colonies in North America.

The voyages of Gilbert to Newfoundland and Grenville to Roanoke had taught the English a hard lesson. Starting a new nation in a wilderness was too large an undertaking for one man to run. Now trading companies were organized, with noblemen, merchants, and private citizens investing in them for a share of the profits. A trading company elected its own officers, made its own bylaws, and even coined its own money. It could arm its own soldiers to defend its settlements.

Under James I, two principal companies were chartered to establish colonies in North America, and to each the king granted a tract of land a hundred miles in width and a hundred miles in depth. By December, 1606, the Virginia Company of London was ready to start its colony. When the three ships—the *Susan Comfort,* the *Godspeed,* and the *Discovery*—sailed from Blackwell dock that chilly day, their passengers included two goldsmiths, two refiners, and a jeweler, for the investors still believed that Virginia possessed great quantities of precious ores. They believed, too, that somewhere in the New World was a river that would lead to the South Sea and the riches of the Orient.

The ships carried a strange mixture of people. Among them was Captain John Smith, who told unbelievable tales of fighting in the Netherlands,

The Jamestown settlers built their settlement as a fort. It was surrounded by a wall of heavy logs.

Hungary, and Turkey. He told of his capture by the Turks, of his hardships as a slave in Constantinople, and of his escape across the desert. Another voyager was Captain Bartholomew Gosnold, who had sailed to America in 1602 and landed on the Elizabeth Islands off that strip of Massachusetts coast he named Cape Cod. A third was Edward Brookes, gentleman, who died on the way because—or so it was reported—his "fat melted within him." A fourth was John Layden, carpenter, who would claim a place in history by marrying a maidservant in the first English marriage ceremony on the soil of Virginia.

So they came together—nobleman and peasant, soldier of fortune and craftsman—in all, 144 settlers. They set sail in good spirits, believing that the Indians of Virginia devoted their holidays to gathering diamonds and rubies along the seashore.

Many storms tossed their ships as they sailed to Virginia, but at four o'clock in the morning on April 26, 1607 they sighted the promised land. When they went ashore next day, they were delighted with the tall trees, fair meadows, and streams of sparkling fresh water. But that afternoon, as the explorers were returning to their boats, the Indians attacked—"creeping upon all fours from the hills, like bears, with their bows in their mouths."

Somehow the colonists made peace with the Indians, and they held a great feast. Their bodies smeared with red and black clay, the Indians staged a dance of welcome. One Indian stood in the center of the group, singing and beating one hand against another. The others danced around him, "shouting, howling, and stamping against the ground." They twisted and turned, screwed up their faces, and made a noise "like so many wolves or devils."

Wonderful discoveries filled each day—on the beaches where the mussels and oysters lay "as thick as stones," in the meadows where the strawberries were "four times bigger than ours in England." One day the English saw a strange sight: an Indian boy of about ten years of age with "a head of a perfect yellow and a reasonable white skin." Could he have been a descendant of one of the survivors of the Lost Colony of Roanoke?

By mid-May the colonists agreed upon a site for their settlement, calling the place Jamestown in honor of the king. With good sense, they started at once to build a fort. The beauty of Virginia was all about them. The woods were filled with beech, oak, cedar, cypress, walnut, and sassafras trees. Flowers spread blankets of bright color on the hillsides. Strawberries, mulberries, raspberries, and other fruits grew in abundance, and the rivers teemed with fish. Squirrels raced through the trees and the birds flashed wings of crimson, blue, olive, and white. Nests of turkey eggs seemed to be everywhere and the settlers also found deer, bears, foxes, otters, beavers, muskrats, "and wild beasts unknown."

A FORT IS COMPLETED AT JAMESTOWN

The fort was completed in a month and two days. By late June the ships were ready to return to London for supplies. What followed for the 104 settlers who remained at Jamestown was a nightmare.

Close to the settlement were stagnant swamps which bred mosquitoes and disease during the humid summer months. Storms frequently raised the tides in the river so that its salty water overflowed, spoiling the springs that supplied drinking water. At such times the fish, which had been a main source of food, moved upstream. Canoes were smashed by high tides. Winds tore fishing nets to shreds.

Captain John Smith

In 1614 Pocahontas married John Rolfe, one of the original Jamestown colonists.

The men of Jamestown rejoiced in 1619 when a ship arrived bringing them brides from England.

Worn out from their long journey and the work of building a settlement, the colonists no longer had the strength to fight off this unexpected combination disasters. Within ten days after the ships had sailed back to London, the settlers came down with sicknesses that left them almost too weak to walk or stand. Almost every day someone complained of severe stomach cramps or burning fever. Many died. Quarrels broke out among the leaders of the colony. At the end of five months not five men could be found capable of standing guard at the fort.

But then a miracle occurred. The Indians appeared with bread, corn, fish, and meat to save the starving settlement. Cooler weather dried up the disease-infested swamps. And, just as important, Captain John Smith became the real leader of the colony.

Smith may have told tall tales. He told of his adventures as a soldier of fortune in many parts of the world, but no one could deny that he saved the colony at Jamestown. Perhaps another tall tale was the story of his capture by the Indians and his escape from death when the beautiful princess, Pocahontas, threw her body upon his own to save him from the executioner. But if Smith's stories were astonishing, so also were his achievements. By April, 1609, the colony had begun to prosper. A glassworks produced the first manufactures in North America. A well gave "excellent sweet water," and twenty houses and a church had been built. A blockhouse outside the fort guarded the settlement from surprise attack.

Other ships coming from London during this time increased the population of Jamestown to almost 500. Then John Smith returned to England. Within weeks the colony fell apart.

"THE STARVING TIME"

The dreadful winter of 1609–10—"the starving time"—followed. For each settler who survived in Jamestown, nine others died. The people ate dogs and cats, rats and mice, and hunted in the woods "to feed upon serpents and snakes." Here they were often stalked and killed by hostile Indians. Other settlers fished the rivers, eating anything drawn up in the nets—including boots or "any other leather." In spring the long overdue supply ships, which had been blown off course and partly wrecked in Bermuda, finally reached the settlement. The survivors begged to be taken back to England. They were sailing down the James River, homeward bound, when at Hog Island they sighted another fleet, this one under Lord Delaware, bringing still more supplies to the colony.

Now the weary settlers faced a decision. Should they continue to England or turn back to Jamestown? At last, they agreed to try just once more.

For a colony to succeed in the wilderness, it had to produce some article of trade that the world wanted. So far, Jamestown had no such product. Glassmaking, the growing of silkworms, the cutting of timber, the manufacture of soap from ashes, the shipment of sassafras for medicinal purposes—all had failed to support the colony. But by this time a very remarkable man had reached Jamestown.

His name was John Rolfe. His baby had died after he was shipwrecked in Bermuda and his wife died shortly after he came to Jamestown. There seemed little reason for his staying at all. But John Rolfe would make history twice in America.

On a warm April day in 1614, Rolfe, an English gentleman, and Pocahontas, a "savage" princess, were married in the church at Jamestown. This was the same Pocahontas who was said to have saved the life of John Smith.

From winning the heart of a princess, Rolfe turned to changing the mind of a king. James I liked everything just as it always had been—from old shoes to old ideas. In particular, he stormed against the "filthy novelty" of using tobacco, a fad that was sweeping England. Smoking, James declared in a pamphlet he wrote, was "loathsome to the eye, hateful to the nose, harmful to the brain, and dangerous to the lungs."

Yet, while the king raged against tobacco, John Rolfe was carrying on an experiment that would save the king's settlement at Jamestown. The tobacco grown by the Indians in Virginia was strong and bitter, but Rolfe had brought to the colony seeds of the sweeter varieties of tobacco grown in the Caribbean Islands and South America. These varieties flourished in the soil of Virginia. The demand in Europe for this sweeter tobacco became so great that even the streets between the houses in Jamestown were plowed to grow the "weed." Within a half-dozen years James I saw the "filthy novelty" he hated carry his colony at Jamestown from failure to success.

In the year 1619 three events occurred that changed the future of Virginia colony. In May and June a new kind of shipment arrived from England: a cargo of young women to marry the men who were carving an empire in the wilderness. Also during that spring, a Dutch ship appeared. It was badly in need of provisions, but all the captain could offer in trade were some twenty Negro captives. Thus, without plan, the first slaves were made part of the life of Virginia.

SELF-GOVERNMENT BEGINS IN AMERICA

By far the most important event took place on July 30. In the choir of the church at Jamestown, representatives from all the little settlements that now existed along the James River met in the first legislative assembly in America. One delegate who was not properly entitled to a seat in the assembly was rejected, and so upon a principle of fair representation, self-government started in America. Among the first offenders called before the lawmakers was one accused of using force to make the Indians trade with him. "Such outrages as this might breed danger and loss of life to others in the colony," read the complaint, stating clearly the purpose of self-government.

Laws reveal many things about people: what they want from life, how they live, even how they misbehave. This was true of the laws of those pioneer legislators who planted the seeds of liberty at Jamestown. Among their first acts they urged the adoption of a sensible method of collecting rents, petitioned England for the establishment of a college in the colony, and fixed the price for selling tobacco. Other laws dealt with personal behavior, and one decree ordered "that no injury or oppression be wrought by the English against the Indian whereby the present peace might be disturbed and ancient quarrels might be revived."

Other decrees called for severe punishments for idleness, gambling, drunkenness, the wearing of fancy clothes, and failure to observe religious customs. Another set of laws provided for the money to run the colony through the planting of corn, mulberry trees, silk flax, aniseed, and vineyards, and required the planters of Virginia to air their tobacco thoroughly before storage.

Relations with the Indians were strictly regulated, for, declared the legislators, "they are a most treacherous people and quickly gone when they have done a villainy." So it became unlawful to sell or give an Indian an "English dog of quality," to supply him with arms or gunpowder, or to travel more than twenty miles from a settlement without the governor's permission. Finally a letter was sent to England, urging approval of all these laws.

Only a dozen years after the first colonists had knocked together a fort at Jamestown, only nine years after Lord Delaware had persuaded the miserable survivors of "the starving time" to turn back from Hog Island, two triumphs had been achieved. England had planted its first permanent settlement in America. And the colonists had planted, whether England liked it or not, a tree of liberty.

A BIRD FROM HEAVEN

The Dutch join the struggle for the new land. Hudson explores a river.

Sooner or later, every explorer of the New World met native Americans. The Europeans, believing at first that they had reached India, called these natives Indians.

How the Indians first reached North America, no one can say for certain. The best theory is that a strip of land once linked Asia to Alaska, and the people journeyed by that route as long ago as the last Ice Age. When you look today at the Indian face on the buffalo nickel, you see features identical to those of people living in southwestern Tibet, a fact that perhaps suggests one link between past and present.

All that we can say with assurance is that the first migrations of Indians to our continent occurred tens of thousands of years ago. In time these wanderers from Asia spread across the land, following rivers, valleys, and mountain passes, until they occupied all regions of the continent. They broke into tribes, each group going its own way, until by the time of Columbus more than 400 such tribes existed. Each lived by the nature of the land where it settled—as farmers or hunters or fishermen. Some tribes did not advance much beyond the primitive life of the ancient Stone Age, while others developed highly organized societies.

Tribes had their own habits and customs, but other traits, such as a love of children, they shared in common. And they seemed to share also a kindness toward the white man when he first came to America. Was not this a trait that Columbus reported among the Indians of the West Indies, and Drake noted among the Indians in California, and Cartier found among the Indians in Canada? Grenville, in his first visit to Roanoke, was delighted with the gentleness of the natives of that island, and it was the generosity of the Indians that saved the settlers of Jamestown from starvation during their first wretched summer. With time, however, the white man's actions brought a change in this relationship.

THE PEACEFUL HUDSON VALLEY

In the valley of the Hudson River in 1609, no white man had yet appeared to meet the copper-skinned people who lived there. Giovanni da Verrazano, who explored the coast of North America under the flag of France, may have glimpsed the Hudson in 1524. If so, his visit may well have been the basis for an Indian legend about a bird that descended from heaven and then flew away—a bird so large that it carried men on its back. By 1609, however, almost a century had passed and no other bird from heaven had been seen by the Indians who lived content beside "the stream that flows both ways."

The days of the Indians followed a pattern. Thus, there came for every Indian mother in the valley a day when she went off by herself into the woods. Here, alone, whether the season was sweltering summer or snowy winter, she gave birth to her child. In time, she returned home, carrying her new

Tibetan (right) *resembles the American Indian.*

baby with pride, for a joyous welcome awaited her. Every Indian loved a baby, for it was well known among these valley people that if an infant sensed he was unwanted, he would vanish into the Land of Lost Souls. And there was another danger. A baby that wasn't loved and watched could be carried off by an evil spirit. To safeguard the child from such deviltry, his ankles and wrists were tied to the ground for a time with cornhusks.

INDIAN LIFE IN THE HUDSON VALLEY

For any youngster in the valley, life for the first ten years was a carefree time of learning the customs and lore of his people. He was taught the habits of the animals and how to hunt them. He was shown the great whales in the bay where the river emptied, and where the fish his family ate could be caught. The forest became both friend and foe, for bad spirits as well as good spirits lived here, and he learned to know where to expect each. He was taught which herbs and roots were good for food and medicine, and how to plant corn and make it grow. He watched his mother make the shoes he wore from cornhusks, and he saw her sew deerskin, elk hide, and beaver pelts to make the garments that kept him warm in winter.

Like all people in the valley, he admired the older, prosperous men of the tribe who strutted around in their splendid coats of turkey feathers. His sister prettied herself by painting blue and white rings around her eyes, weaving bands of snakeskin to go around her braided hair, and adorning her arms and neck with copper bracelets.

Wide-eyed, he saw a war party going off in their long canoes. Bonnets of eagle feathers encircled their heads, huge bear claws hung at their necks, and their faces were streaked with every color of the rainbow. He remembered how he had been taught to use a tomahawk, a hunting knife, and a bow and arrow, and he dreamed of the day when he too could go off on such a raid.

Now, with the women, the old men, the other children, he could only wait until shouts announced the party's return. He would dash to the river's edge, counting the scalps on the long poles the warriors held aloft and the captives that had been taken. Sometimes he journeyed with his people to Canoe Place, which was neutral ground for meetings with the Indians from Rockaway, from Canarsie, and from across the bay in the country that one day would be called New Jersey. These were exciting times—for trading pelts and stories.

Then suddenly, in 1609, came the greatest wonder of a lifetime for all the people of the valley. There, coasting up their river, was a bird from heaven, its white wings spread to the wind and men walking upon its back! The Indians stared from their hiding places. The name on the prow of the ship was *Half Moon.*

THE DUTCH ARRIVE IN THE NEW WORLD

The *Half Moon's* arrival meant that still another nation—the Netherlands—was entering the struggle for possession of the New World. The *Half Moon* belonged to the Dutch East India Company. Its crew was part Dutch, part English, which suggests why more than once near mutiny had endangered its voyage to America. The leader of the expedition, Henry Hudson, already was famous in England as a navigator and an explorer. Others had sailed to the north*west* from Europe, looking for a passage to the Orient. Hudson, in two previous voyages for a British trading company, had sailed north*east*, seeking a passage through the ice barrier by way of the North Pole. Hudson's British backers were satisfied to take their profits from the whale fisheries he enabled them to establish at Spitsbergen, an island on the edge of the Arctic Ocean. If Hudson wanted to go on exploring for a northeast passage, he would have to find support elsewhere.

Hudson did—in Amsterdam. The little *Half Moon,* carrying its mixed crew of not more than twenty men, left Holland on April 4, 1609. A month later it rounded the Cape of Norway and Hudson came to a sea full of floating ice. In the bitter cold the crew fell into a quarrelsome mood, and Hudson at last agreed to reverse his course and sail to the northwest. On May 14, the *Half Moon* came about, shaping her course toward the setting sun.

Hudson's hope of new discoveries was based in part on a letter he had recently received from his old friend in Virginia, Captain John Smith. Somewhere in the unexplored regions north of the colony at Jamestown, Hudson reasoned, could be an inland passage to the Orient. On the second of July, the *Half Moon* was off the Grand Banks of Newfoundland with foremast gone and sails torn. Proof that the French already had established themselves in the New World was the sight of a fleet of their ships fishing these waters, but Hudson "spoke with none of them." Mid-July brought him to the coast of Maine and safe harbor in what was probably Penobscot Bay. His crew remained troublesome, and when friendly Indians approached the *Half Moon* in two boats, they were savagely attacked for no reason.

Hudson did not hide his anger. He ordered the *Half Moon* once more to sea, and did not touch shore again until August 3, when his men brought back roses and sweet grapes. Hudson sailed on, believing he had reached the Cape Cod that Bartholomew Gosnold had named seven years before. When he discovered instead that he had entered the James River in Virginia, he was tempted to land and seek out his old friend, John Smith. Had he done so, he would have found that Smith was in England and the inhabitants of Jamestown were dying of dysentery and famine.

Beating north again, the *Half Moon* now embarked on a series of discoveries. Late August found Hudson and his crew rounding the lower capes and entering the body of water we now call Delaware Bay. Shoals of hidden sand scraping the bottom of the *Half Moon* discouraged Hudson from believing that this was the passage he sought to the Orient. Through early September he coasted along New Jersey, seeking shelter from seasonal storms at Sandy Hook. He came at last to the bay that carried him into the river now bearing his name. The *Half Moon* sailed as far up river as what is now Albany before Hudson once more decided he had not yet discovered his northwest passage.

To the staring Indians the little vessel might have seemed like the bird of heaven, but she was more a creature of the devil. Hudson knew that his men were close to mutiny. He headed straight for Ireland before winter closed in around him.

Trouble filled the last years of Hudson's life. First there was resentment in England over the fact that he had sold his services to Holland and carried the Dutch into the New World. The following year, he sailed once more in search of the Northwest Passage, this time for a British company. In the midsummer of 1611, a faithless crew turned on Hudson, forcing him, his son, and several sick sailors to board a frail boat. The party was set adrift. Somewhere in the icy wastes of Hudson Bay, which he discovered, is "his tomb and his monument."

Yet the Dutch did not forget the New World, and soon other birds from heaven were winging their way across the Atlantic. Early in 1614, after a stormy voyage, Captain Adriaen Block reached New York Bay. There his ship burst into flames, and he and his crew passed a peaceful winter living among the Indians while they built a new ship to carry them home. This vessel they named *Onrust,* which in Dutch means "Restless." The name well expressed the spirit of the Hollanders, who in the years to come would sail the Atlantic in increasing numbers and string their trading posts all along the Hudson Valley.

CHAMPLAIN BLUNDERS

By aiding the Algonquin Indians, he earns the hatred of the powerful Iroquois.

France made not only a late but an unlucky start in the New World. Her banner was carried by Samuel de Champlain, a capable man who was the son of a sea captain. Champlain had grown up along the coast of France knowing how to reef a sail and find his way by the stars. His first voyage to the North American continent was made in 1603. He explored the St. Lawrence River as far as the rapids above Montreal, and quickly became a warm friend of the Indians. The following year he explored the North American coast as far south as Cape Cod, and during the summer of 1608 he founded at Quebec the first white settlement in Canada.

But Champlain soon began to meddle in wilderness warfare. The spring of 1609 found the Algonquins and Hurons taking to the warpath against the Iroquois. Champlain chose to join the Algonquins and Hurons. He crossed the lake that would be named after him, and near present-day Ticonderoga pitched into a battle with the Iroquois. Champlain's weapon—an old matchlock gun called an arquebus—could be loaded with four bullets. His first volley, Champlain wrote, killed two Indians and wounded a third. Then a companion fired his arquebus and the battle was over. The astounded Indians "lost courage and took to flight."

Champlain had blundered badly, for the proud and powerful Iroquois remembered him with hatred for a century. They turned first to the Dutch and then to the English for allies. They were determined that the French would never gain a foothold in the land of the Iroquois.

Until the Seventeenth Century, the search for wealth and power had driven the Spanish and the English, the French and the Dutch to sail their little ships across the stormy Atlantic. For the most part these adventurers from Europe brought to the New World old European habits and customs and ideas—and old European jealousies that would in time produce a series of bloody wars. But soon a different kind of colonist would be making the long voyage to America.

BELIEVERS IN RELIGIOUS FREEDOM

English "Separatists" settle in Holland, but soon move to the New World.

In 1607 a violent quarrel broke out between hardheaded King James I and a little group of equally hardheaded English men and women. Anyone who knew James I quickly realized that he could only be happy when having his own way. As king, James I believed that he understood better than any of his subjects what was good for England. Even how the people should worship God, the king insisted, was a matter that he and his bishops alone could decide.

A stubborn group of Christians, called Separatists, challenged the right of the king to tell them how to manage their religious affairs. They said that no one should dictate who should preach to them, or in what manner, or in what company of fellow worshipers. As everyone expected, James I was displeased. The Separatists felt they must either carry on their religion as the king wished, or leave England.

They chose to leave England, and during 1607–08 they went to Holland. For ten long years, as pilgrims in a strange land, they struggled to make a success of life among the Dutch in the city of Leyden. Farmers by training, they were forced to work hard at such city jobs as they could find. This sacrifice they bore cheerfully as long as they could worship God as they pleased. Yet as the Separatists grew older they began to wonder if they had any real future in Holland. Would not their religion disappear as, one by one, they went to their graves? Already their children were copying the ways of the easygoing Dutch. Who would keep them true to the Separatist faith?

Only a few at first suggested going to America and building a settlement in the wilderness where they could bring up their children as they wished. Others argued that the dangers in the New World were too great. But those who held out for making a new start in America spoke up forcefully. Why should they not run these risks? Were they afraid to trust in God to protect them?

In 1617 the Separatists at last decided to establish their own state in the New World. Three years later they finally were able to return to England to begin their voyage. Here they were joined by a "very mixed lot" of other voyagers who were more interested in seeking a fortune than religious freedom. Right at the start one of the two boats they planned to use for the voyage began to leak so badly it had to be left behind. About one hundred in number, they crowded aboard a tiny ship called the *Mayflower*, and with tears and prayers and fearful hearts set

Seeking a Northwest Passage, Hudson sailed up the river that was later to be named for him.

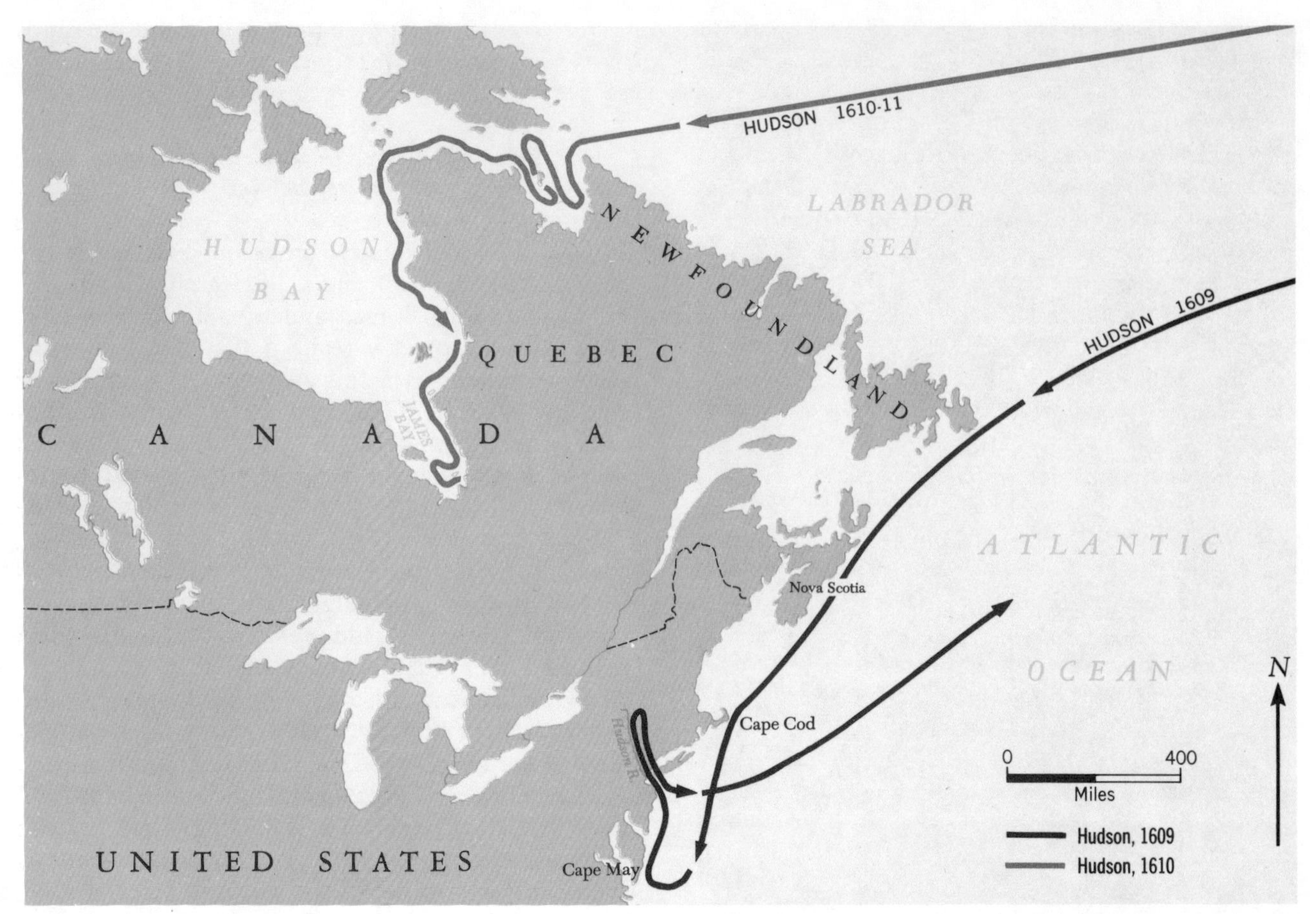

The routes followed by Hudson in his explorations. Present-day boundaries and places are shown.

The Pilgrims looked on the rescue of a man who had fallen overboard as a sign of God's favor.

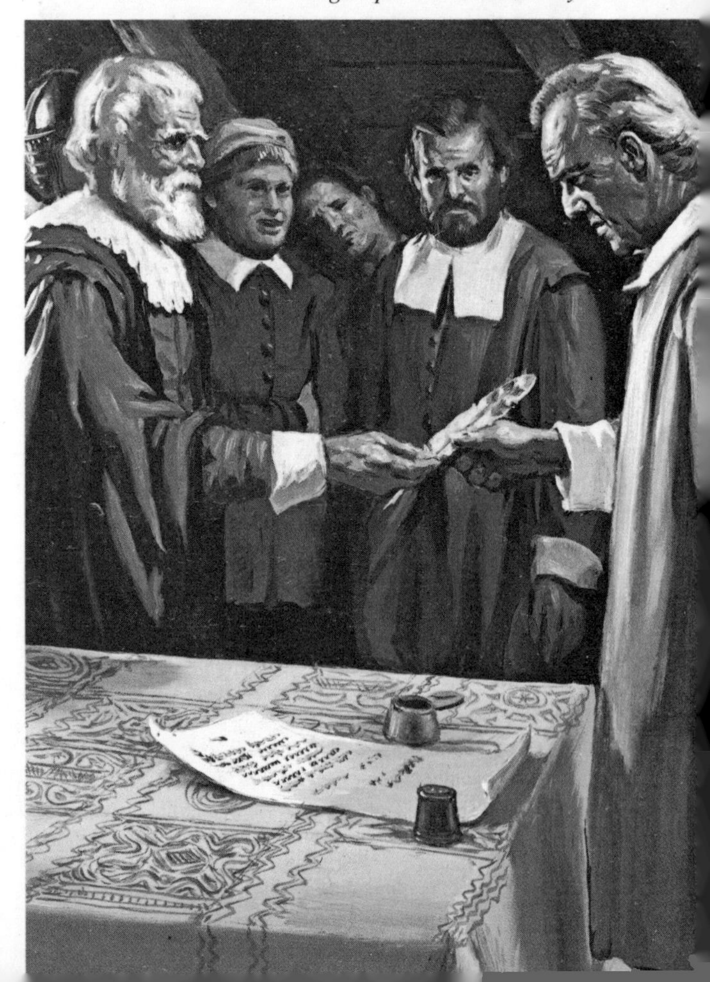

By the signing of the Mayflower Compact, the new settlers took a big step toward democracy.

sail for America on September 6, 1620. Those who were seeking their own religious state in America became known in history as the Pilgrims.

Fair winds at first carried the *Mayflower* across the sea toward her destination in northern Virginia. Then the weather turned. Fierce storms tossed the ship like a cork on the great rolling waves. Blustering winds tore sails to ribbons. Under the blows from the crashing sea, leaks appeared everywhere and one of the main beams cracked and sagged. The Pilgrims put their trust in God, propped up the sagging beam, patched the leaks, and sailed on. They lacked the lemons that would have given them vitamin C, and so they came down with a weakening sickness called scurvy. Yet only one of them died at sea.

That fact seemed a miracle, one of the three miracles by which the Pilgrims reckoned that God *did* bless and guide them. Another such sign was the case of a "proud and very profane" young sailor who cursed the Pilgrims in their misery and told them at least once a day that he hoped to throw half of them overboard before the voyage ended. Instead, it was he who was taken ill, died in great agony, and was thrown overboard. A third sign was the fate of young John Howland, who was swept into the sea by a brutal wave. Howland grabbed a line and hung on until he could be fished back on deck with a boat hook.

After sixty-five troubled days they sighted land—not the coast of Virginia for which they had set sail, but the far-off shore of Cape Cod. They tried for half a day to sail southward, but shoals and roaring breakers drove them back to safe harbor off the coast of Massachusetts. They now faced a bewildering situation, for they had permission to settle in Virginia, not in New England.

As the *Mayflower* rode at anchor, grumblings of mutiny were heard. Some of the passengers, more concerned with finding wealth than religious freedom, threatened to strike off on their own for Virginia. Others spoke up more calmly. They said they must stick together and draw up an agreement under which they would live until they could get permission from England to settle in this new country.

THE MAYFLOWER COMPACT

The document they wrote we now call the Mayflower Compact. Every male passenger signed it, pledging his honor to work with the others in passing and obeying such laws "as shall be thought most meet [fit] and convenient for the general good of the colony." Just as the settlers at Jamestown had planted a seed of liberty when they held their first legislative assembly in 1619, so did the Pilgrims plant a seed of democracy when they signed the Mayflower Compact on November 11, 1620.

For several weeks the Pilgrims searched the sandy New England coast for a suitable harbor and site of settlement. In late December they decided upon a place they called Plymouth, after the city in England where they had boarded the *Mayflower.* On Christmas day they started building their first common house, but in mid-January fire destroyed its thatched roof. This was only one of their many misfortunes.

A good part of their difficulty was the result of their own lack of planning. They had brought neither horses nor cattle, plows nor carts. Even their hooks and nets were too large for the fish that filled the waters all around them. Scurvy, influenza, and pneumonia made the winter months a time of horror. Sometimes two or three men died in a single day, until by spring only half the colony survived. Not more than six or seven of those who lived could be described as being in good health.

One day the Indian chief Massasoit arrived at the settlement with sixty warriors. They could have easily wiped out all the Pilgrims, but they had come to offer their friendship and help. Among them was a remarkable Indian named Squanto, who had been captured by an earlier party of explorers and sold into slavery in Spain. He had escaped to England where he learned to speak the English language. To the Pilgrims he was like a messenger from heaven. Squanto taught the settlers how to plant corn and make it grow. He showed them how to build fish traps and stalk the game in the woods. He taught them how to catch and skin beavers, giving them a source of trade on which the colony at Plymouth would depend for many years.

All through the summer of 1621, with Squanto's help, the Pilgrims worked hard to raise corn. That fall they decided to hold a harvest festival. New England's first Thanksgiving lasted three days, and Indians and settlers alike enjoyed a gay time. The sober black and gray clothes that the Pilgrims wore on the Sabbath were put aside for the garments of bright green and brown that they liked so much. Indians and settlers played games. They filled their bellies, too—on venison, roast duck, shellfish, corn bread, wild fruits, and berries. They drank the wine they had made from wild grapes.

But bleak days were still ahead. In November the little ship *Fortune* arrived with thirty-five settlers but few supplies, so that the colony was burdened with thirty-five more mouths to feed. Winter was hard and crops the following summer were poor. The Pilgrims continued to pray, and they also tried to help themselves—by searching the woods for acorns and wild roots, by prowling the shores to gather clams and crabs.

By the summer of 1623 they were no better than skeletons wandering around in rags, when two more ships arrived with another ninety people to feed. But after a time a warm, gentle rain began to fall. The showers continued for weeks, and in the fields the drooping corn began to stand firm upon its green stalks. That fall the Pilgrims filled their bins with a plentiful harvest.

"THE HEAVENLY LAND"

Peter Minuit buys Manhattan Island for $24, and the Dutch start a colony.

When they saw that there were English settlements firmly planted in Virginia and New England, the Dutch again began to stir. Since 1609, when Henry Hudson had sailed his river in the *Half Moon,* they had been playing a game of hit-and-run in the New World. In 1611, two small trading vessels, the *Little Fox* and the *Little Crane,* became the first of many such ships that sailed into the bay and river that Hudson had discovered. After swapping trinkets for beaver pelts with the Indians, the voyagers seemed eager only to sail away. But Captain Adriaen Block was different. In 1613–14 this brave old sea dog discovered the Housatonic and Connecticut Rivers, Rhode Island, and Block Island.

Eight years later, the Dutch West India Company was chartered for the purpose of trading and colonizing in the areas Hudson and Block had claimed. The first settlers arrived in 1623—some thirty families of French-speaking Walloons from Holland. They were Huguenots (Protestants), and like the English Separatists they were unpopular at home and eager to find religious freedom in the New World. They were a restless group, even when making a new start in America. Some settled at Fort Nassau, the present site of Albany. Others settled on Governors Island, and a few may have made their homes on that island which the Indians called Ma-na-hat-ta, meaning "Heavenly Land."

The first official Dutch settlement on Manhattan Island began three years later when, in May, the little ship *Zee Meeuw* sailed slowly into the harbor. Aboard her was shrewd Peter Minuit, who was empowered by the authorities in Amsterdam to buy the island from the Indians as a site for a Dutch colony. Minuit struck a bargain with the Indian chiefs, who gave him the land in exchange for trinkets worth sixty Dutch guilders (about $24 in our money).

The Dutch quickly established a settlement on the island, naming it New Amsterdam. A strong fort surrounded a colony of some thirty houses and two windmills. A fine sandy road ran along the shore, and across the water rose the wooded hills of Brooklyn. At the wharf was a crane used in unloading the boats from overseas, and here once a week the Dutch gathered for market day. An old trail, sloping up north of the fort, enabled travelers to see on all sides and thus learn if enemies were about. That trail is today known as Broadway. The little Dutch houses of black and yellow brick, each with its gabled roof, large front door, iron knocker, and numerous small windows were set in neat rows. Mops and brooms and scrubbing brushes seemed to be going all day long, for no Dutch woman could be happy unless her home shone with cleanliness.

WEAKNESS OF DUTCH RULE

Cheerful though home life in New Amsterdam appeared, the Dutch were in trouble. The traders who organized the Dutch settlements in the New World simply could not bring themselves to give away land even in the wilderness. The poor were no better off in the New World than they had been in the Old. Then, too, the director-generals that were sent to run the colony were quarrelsome and high-handed. Peter Minuit, who had bargained his trinkets for Manhattan Island, was such a tricky fellow that he was soon out of a job, although that was not the last the New World would hear of him. Wouter Van Twiller, who replaced Minuit, was a conceited chap who lived like an oyster in a shell. William Kiefft, who followed Van Twiller, was an Amsterdam merchant who bungled in his dealings with the Indians and lost their friendship. But the greatest weakness of the Dutch was their inability to give the people any share in government.

JOURNEY TO CONNECTICUT

Unhappy with Puritan religious practices, settlers set up new colonies.

Where the Dutch, through bungling and weakness, failed as colonizers, the English prospered. The Massachusetts Bay Company was organized in 1628 by a religious group called Puritans, and the following year five ships carried settlers to its first town at Salem. Seventeen ships, bringing more than a thousand new colonists, crossed the Atlantic during the next few months. Some settled in Charlestown, but others rowed to the peninsula across the Charles River and laid out the first streets of Boston. All through the 1630's, British colonizing continued. New towns included Medford, Watertown, Roxbury, Dorchester, and Newtown (now Cambridge).

Conditions in England at the time were far from happy. If James I had seemed a stubborn, iron-willed king, Charles I, who followed him to the throne, was even more severe concerning the religious practices of the Puritans.

Peter Minuit bought Manhattan Island from the Indians in exchange for trinkets worth about $24.

But when the Puritans reached the New World, they wished religious freedom only for those who thought as they thought and worshiped as they worshiped. Little groups, dissatisfied with the high-handed manners of their neighbors, struck off on their own, going north, south, and west, in search of homes.

Early in the 1630's more than 200 colonists from the Massachusetts towns of Watertown, Dorchester, and Newtown made the long, weary march to build new homes in the wilderness of Connecticut. These hardy pioneers, setting out on foot, pushed through forests over narrow Indian paths. Women carried young children in their arms and drove the cattle ahead of them. The men lumbered forward like pack animals burdened down with firearms, ammunition, utensils, food. From Massachusetts to the pretty meadowlands along the Connecticut River, where they settled, was a journey of about fourteen days. The first colonists, led by William Holmes, reached Windsor in September, 1633. The following year another party under John Oldham settled at Wethersfield, and in 1635 Thomas Hooker brought a band of followers to Hartford.

Hammers pounded and saws buzzed as forts and houses sprang up along the banks of the Connecticut River. Fields were plowed and corn planted. Oiled paper covered the window openings in the first crude dwellings. All the furniture had to be built by hand. The glow of the fireplace and burning pine knots gave the only light at night.

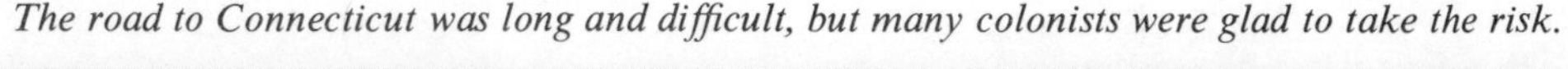

The road to Connecticut was long and difficult, but many colonists were glad to take the risk.

Hunt tricked twenty Indians into boarding his ship, then sold them into slavery.

Yet these Britishers in Connecticut, knowing they were invading land first explored by Adriaen Block and claimed by the Dutch, were determined to work together and hold what they had taken. In 1637 they established the General Court, in which all the towns of Connecticut were represented so that they could act together in case of danger. It was not the Dutch they feared, but the Pequots, the most warlike Indian tribe in New England, who claimed Connecticut as part of their territory.

The leader of this hostile tribe of 3,000 Pequots was Sassacus, an intelligent young chief. He told his people that if the English were allowed to get a foothold in Connecticut, their land would be lost forever. About twenty years before, a trader named Thomas Hunt had sailed up the Connecticut River and had tricked twenty Indians into boarding his boat with promises of presents. Instead, Hunt had carried them off to Spain and had sold them into slavery.

No Pequot had ever forgotten Hunt's treachery. It was an evil act that one day must be avenged. And Sassacus had other proof that no white person could be trusted: the cold-blooded murder of two old Indian chiefs in Massachusetts, and the slaying by a Dutch trader of Totabam, the chief of a small branch of the Pequot tribe. To the Pequots, the white man, with his terrible gunpowder, was an enemy who intended to grab all the land, kill all the animals in the forest, and turn all Indians into slaves.

The situation was not helped by the preaching of Puritan ministers, who spoke of the devil as someone who walked the earth. Anyone who, in the opinion of the Puritans, did not live by the "true" religion could be possessed by the devil. A person who smiled while a minister was preaching could be accused of dealing with the devil. Persons with squinty eyes could easily be branded as witches. Indians, who did not believe in the Puritan faith, were all children of the devil and, therefore, must be watched closely.

In July of 1636, John Oldham, the founder of Wethersfield, was murdered in his boat. In revenge the English burned Indian homes and cornfields. In the following months there were more deeds of violence. A settler named Butterfield was caught by the Indians while cutting hay in his meadow and burned at the stake. Three settlers, off hunting ducks, were brutally killed. Each incident added to the fear that crept through the English settlements in the Connecticut Valley.

On the night of April 22, 1637, a band of 200 Pequots sailed quietly up the river to Wethersfield. They hid their canoes in a small branch of the river and waited for daybreak. It was time for spring planting, and the men, women, and children of Wethersfield were out early that morning, working in their fields. All at once the Indians rushed from the bushes. Tomahawks and scalping knives flashed in the sunlight. The screams of the surprised settlers mingled with the wild yells of the Indians.

Within minutes, the Indians were back in their canoes, shouting as they sailed down-river. With them were two girls they had captured. In the fields of Wethersfield lay the bodies of six men and three women. The survivors stared at the departing Indians, who waved aloft the clothes they had stripped

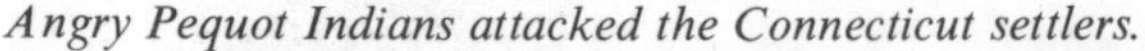

Angry Pequot Indians attacked the Connecticut settlers.

The Connecticut army stormed the Pequot fort, set it afire, and killed most of the inhabitants.

from their victims. The two girls sat terror-stricken in the canoe. The older of them was only sixteen years of age.

In time, through the intervention of the Dutch, the girls were permitted to return home. They had proved a disappointment to the Pequots, who had hoped to learn from them the secret of making gunpowder. But the valley was now aroused. On May 1, at Hartford, the General Court decided to raise an army under an experienced military leader, Captain John Mason.

THE CONNECTICUT ARMY ADVANCES

On the morning of May 26, the little Connecticut army of seventy-seven men advanced upon the chief enemy fort at Pequot Hill in West Mystic. With them that day was Captain John Underhill, who left this account of the fighting:

"Our soldiers were shot, some through the shoulders, some in the face, some in the head, some in the legs. Captain Mason and myself lost each of us a man, and had near twenty wounded. Most courageously these Pequots behaved themselves. But seeing the fort was too hot for us, we devised a way how we might save ourselves. Captain Mason, entering into a wigwam, brought out a firebrand after he had many [of his soldiers] wounded in the house. Then he set fire on the west side, where he had entered. I set fire on the south end with a train of powder. The fires of both, meeting in the center of the fort, blazed most terribly, and burnt all in the space of half an hour. . . .

"Many were burnt in the fort, both men, women, and children. Others forced [their way] out . . . twenty and thirty at a time, which our soldiers received and entertained with the point of the sword. Down fell men, women, and children. . . . It is reported that there were about four hundred souls in this fort, and not above five of them escaped out of our hands. . . ."

So for the first time Englishmen fought Indians for the land of America. But the men of Connecticut were satisfied. They had won the right to live as they pleased in the wilderness.

And they wasted little time in taking advantage of that right. Less than a year after the war with the Pequots ended, about 250 men, women, and children followed Theophilus Eaton, Edward Hopkins, and the Reverend John Davenport into Connecticut to found a colony at New Haven. The laws stating what these settlers could and could not do were printed in a pamphlet bound in blue covers, thus giving to the American language the term "blue laws." Some of the laws were:

"No one shall cross a river on Sunday but an authorized clergyman.

"No one shall run on the Sabbath day, or walk in his garden, except reverently to and from meeting [church].

"No woman shall kiss her child on the Sabbath or fasting day.

"No one shall travel, cook victuals [food], make beds, sweep houses, cut hair, or shave on the Sabbath day.

"Every male shall have his hair cut round according to a cap.

"A man who strikes his wife shall be fined . . .

"No one shall read common prayer, keep Christmas or saint days, make minced pies, dance, play cards, or play on any instrument of music, except the drum, trumpet, and Jew's-harp."

The blue laws allowed the people of New Haven little freedom, but elsewhere in Connecticut freedom was gaining. A sermon preached by Thomas Hooker at Hartford in 1638 led to the famous "Fundamental Orders." Adopted by the settlements of Windsor, Wethersfield, and Hartford, these orders said that "the foundation of authority is in the free consent of the people." In other words, only the people could say how they were to be governed.

The Fundamental Orders were Connecticut's first written constitution. They provided for a form of representative government, and the election of a governor and magistrates (judges). They limited terms of office and gave guarantees of equal representation and taxation.

PURITAN REBEL

Exiled from Massachusetts, Roger Williams founds a colony in Rhode Island.

Roger Williams was a man of strong beliefs. Almost from the moment he reached Boston in early 1631, he was in trouble with the Puritan church rulers. A rebel who had fought for religious freedom in England, Williams went on fighting in America. Like a shuttlecock, he bounced from town to town—from Boston to Salem to the Plymouth colony and back to Salem.

As much as any one person could, Williams soon had Massachusetts in an uproar. Did a court have the right to punish a person who refused to follow the religious customs as ordered by the clergy? Indeed, it had no such right, said Williams. In matters of religion "man is responsible to God alone!" Did

Roger Williams

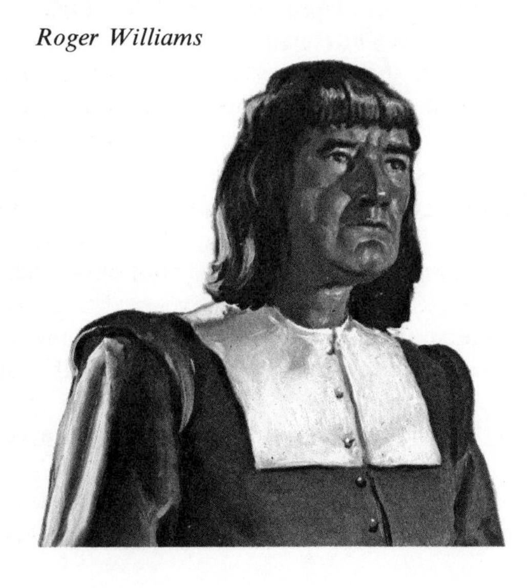

Churches were among the first buildings to be erected by the colonists in the New World.

the king of England have the right to give away land belonging to the Indians? Indeed, the king had no such right, said Williams. He believed that no one should settle in America unless he purchased the land from the original Indian owners. Did the church have the right to run the political life of a settlement? Indeed, it had no such right, said Williams.

Roger Williams was a handsome man, and everyone found him gentle and charming—when he was not arguing for his beliefs. He refused to keep them to himself, and the General Court banished him from Massachusetts in the winter of 1635–36.

Cheerful and determined, he set off on the "narrow Indian path" out of Salem to found his own colony in Rhode Island. In the spring he reached the west bank of the Seekonk River, paid the Indians a fair price for the land he wanted, and in gratitude for "God's providence" in bringing him safely to this place, named his settlement Providence. Under the wise administration of Roger Williams, the colonists of Rhode Island prospered and other settlements sprang up at Portsmouth, Newport, and Warwick.

In Rhode Island no one was placed in the stocks, as had happened in Massachusetts, for failing to attend church regularly. In Rhode Island no one was whipped, as had happened to one planter in Massachusetts, for saying he would rather hear a dog bark than the minister preach. In Rhode Island no one was dipped in the public pond, as happened in Massachusetts, for whispering in church. In Rhode Island anyone could hold whatever religious beliefs he wished, as long as he behaved "peaceably and quietly."

Another colony that grew out of the search for freedom of religion was Maryland. In England, where the Roman Catholic Church was outlawed, Lord Baltimore dreamed of establishing a colony in the New World which would allow Roman Catholics to worship in their own way. The old nobleman died before he could see his dream come true. But his son carried out his plan, and in the spring of 1634, two little ships reached Chesapeake Bay with the first settlers of Maryland. Of the some 200 gentlemen-adventurers, yeomen, artisans, laborers, and servants who crowded the decks of the *Ark* and the *Dove*, less than half were Catholics. Catholic and Protestant would have to live side by side in peace if the colony were to succeed.

THE FIRST GENERAL ASSEMBLY

The settlers soon struck a bargain with the Yoacomico Indians. In exchange for axes, hatchets, farm tools, and bolts of cloth, they received an entire village, which they renamed St. Mary's City. A statehouse was built, and within a year the first general assembly met. In England the laws passed by the colonists were quickly vetoed. But the laws sent over from England were as quickly rejected by the colonists. By 1638 the backers of the Maryland company agreed that the people had a right to self-government.

Meanwhile Catholic and Protestant, living together in Maryland, set an example of how well religious tolerance could work. In 1649 the General Assembly passed an "Act Concerning Religion" which imposed fines and even punishment by flogging if any Christian were disturbed because of his religion.

LIFE IN A CHANGING AMERICA

Farms and villages grow and prosper as colonists arrive from several lands.

Early in 1631, the Dutch founded a settlement in present-day Delaware, near Lewes (pronounced Lewis). They called it Zwannendael, or "Valley of Swans." The Dutch quickly managed to get themselves killed. A tin coat of arms of Holland, nailed to a post, started the trouble. A young Indian chief took the tin plate, wishing to fashion it into a bowl for his pipe. Both the Indians and the Dutch lost their tempers, and when the next Dutch ship arrived at Zwannendael, all that remained was the ruins of houses that had been burned to the ground.

Back into the New World now came Peter Minuit, the man who had bought Manhattan Island. He had organized a colonizing venture for a newcomer in America—Sweden. Minuit's first party of Swedish settlers reached Delaware in 1638, building Fort Christina on the site of present-day Wilmington. Twelve more expeditions were sent from Sweden in the following years. From the start the Swedes were wise colonizers, who scarcely ever spoke a harsh word to the Indians. The Indians watched with admiration as the Swedes brought a new type of dwelling into the wilderness—the log cabin. The hard-working Swedes built mills, houses, boats, and wharves, and set up shops for barrelmaking, brewing, baking, and weaving. In 1640 they shouted a joyous welcome to Reorus Torkillus, the first Lutheran clergyman in America.

THE POPULATION GROWS

By then any sea captain who was an old hand at sailing the Atlantic must have blinked in wonder at how greatly the New World had changed in the last ten years. The Dutch on Manhattan Island and the Swedes on the shores of the Delaware were only a handful of settlers compared to the number of English who came to the New World in the "Great Migration" of 1630 to 1640. In Massachusetts the population of the English was estimated at 14,000. English settlers elsewhere were believed to number 8,000 in Virginia, 2,000 in Connecticut, 300 in Rhode Island, 1,500 in the combined areas of New Hampshire and Maine, and 1,500 in Maryland.

By 1650, the growing population of the English in North America was estimated at 52,000. Ten years later English and Dutch settlers numbered 85,000. In 1671, Governor Berkeley estimated the population of Virginia at 45,000, including 6,000 white servants and 2,000 Negro slaves. Twenty years later, Boston alone claimed 7,000 inhabitants; Newport, Rhode Island, 2,600; New York City (Dutch New Amsterdam) 3,900; Philadelphia 4,000; and Charleston, South Carolina, 1,100.

The settlers' first houses were made of boards driven into the ground like the palings of a fence and contained only a single room. Roofs, slanting front and back, were made of thatch. Chimneys were constructed from branches woven together and plastered with mud or clay. The danger of fire was great, for the heat dried the mud and clay, causing it to fall off and expose the branches to flying sparks. The problem was not solved until limestone beds in Maine and Rhode Island made the use of mortar possible.

HOME LIFE IN AMERICA

As a family prospered, it added rooms for sleeping. About 1650, with the development of an iron industry, hand-wrought nails began to take the place of wooden pegs. Cabinetmakers were kept busy turning out chairs, chests, spinning wheels, and tables, and there were few colonial homes that did not have one high-back chair used by the "head of the family" as a sign of his authority. A wife might stand, or sit on a stool, while her husband settled comfortably in his chair, a king in his own castle.

As early as 1642, the General Court in Massachusetts passed a law that required every parent to teach his children to read and to practice at least one trade. Another law, five years later, required every township of fifty families to support a school that could teach children reading and writing. Each township of one hundred families was required to provide a grammar school that could prepare students for college. Harvard College, founded in 1636, was at the time the only college in the colonies.

THE FIRST PRINTING PRESS

The first printing press in the English colonies was set up by Stephen Day in Cambridge in 1639, and the following year the *Bay Psalm Book* became the first book published in America. But the book New England boys and girls studied most was the *New England Primer.* This included such sections as a "Rhymed Alphabet," and "Dialogue between Christ, Youth, and the Devil." Typical verses in the "Rhymed Alphabet" read:

N *Noah did view*
The old World and new.
O *Young Obadias,*
David, Josias,
All were pious.
P *Peter deny'd*
His Lord and cry'd.

Boston's first bookstore was opened in 1652, and four years later the city established the first public library. During the growing season, the tasks of farming filled the days of the great majority of people. Even children were expected to do their share of the family work. The colonial planter learned to grow three crops in a field, first harvesting his corn, then using the stalks as poles for his beans and permitting the vines of his pumpkins to spread among the hills of his corn.

Other crops introduced by the English into New England were cabbages, turnips, onions, carrots, and parsnips. The Dutch brought to the New World its first beets, spinach, endive, leeks, and herbs like parsley and dill. The Germans in Pennsylvania introduced asparagus, and the Swedes probably brought the first peaches. Wheat, a failure in Plymouth, could be grown with great success along the Connecticut Valley, which became the main wheat and cereal raising center in the colonies by the early 1650's.

EARLY INDUSTRIES

Americans begin to manufacture goods that once had to be brought from Europe.

The first ironworks in America was set up in 1619 on Falling Creek in Virginia, and by the middle of the 1640's ironworks were operating in Massachusetts at Saugus and Braintree. Among the important craftsmen in every village was the blacksmith, who turned out the chains and plows, the axheads and scythe blades, the hoes, pitchforks, and sickles on which the farmer depended. From his shop also came the popular two-wheeled cart.

Other industries sprang up. Maine's first sawmill was operating near York in 1623, and that same year New Hampshire had its first salt works near Piscataqua. Three years later the Dutch at New Amsterdam gave America its first flour mill. In 1629 the first colonial brick kiln was built in Salem and the first New England tannery was set up at Lynn, Massachusetts. Four years later Dorchester had the first water mill for grinding corn. By 1641 Salem had added a glass factory to its industries, and in 1643 twenty families of skilled cloth workers from Yorkshire, England, settled in Rowley, Massachusetts, and opened a woolen mill.

From 1624, when a ship carpenter arrived in Plymouth, shipbuilding played a large part in the life of New England. Boats were needed for fishing, which was itself a major industry, and New England was soon producing its own special kind of vessel known as a shallop. This craft was a simple boat, fitted with both oars and a sail, and almost any boy handy with tools could make one. But ships of greater size were built as well. *The Blessing of the Bay,* a thirty-ton sloop, was launched in 1631, and "a prodigious ship of 300 tons"—almost twice the size of the *Mayflower*—was launched at Salem in 1641. By 1665 it was estimated that 1,300 boats were fishing regularly off the Grand Banks of Newfoundland, while 300 ships from New England traded in every port of North America and Europe.

ROADS AND MAIL

The "narrow Indian path" that Roger Williams followed out of Salem in 1636 when he set off to found Rhode Island was probably no more than eighteen inches wide. Indians always traveled in single file and their trails through the wilderness were narrow ribbons of beaten-down grass. A white man's road was usually a rod (16½ feet) wide, and the work of cutting trees and clearing rocks to build it was a backbreaking job. Even so, in 1639 the General Court in Massachusetts ordered every town to lay out roads connecting it with the next town.

That same year the first "post office" was established in Massachusetts when the General Court selected the home of Richard Fairbanks in Boston as the place where all letters were to be deposited. In 1658 a Virginia law provided that planters must forward a letter from plantation to plantation until it reached its destination. A fine of 350 pounds of tobacco was imposed on any planter who failed to do so. In 1677 the General Court of Massachusetts appointed John Hayward of Boston the first official letter carrier in America.

COLONIAL MONEY

Each colony used its own chief product for money. New York accepted beaver skins in payment for debts, Rhode Island wool, and South Carolina rice. Virginia permitted fines to be paid in tobacco. Indian wampum was also accepted at the rate of three black beads or six white beads for a penny, and the fact that the Indians would accept glass beads for money helped to develop the glass industry. The first mint was established in Boston in 1652. John Hull, a silversmith, was authorized by Massachusetts to turn out the Pine Tree shilling, a crude silver coin about the size of a half dollar. A coin accepted throughout the colonies was the Spanish dollar or "piece of eight." Sometimes this coin was called a "bit of eight," explaining why to this day we refer to a twenty-five cent piece as "two bits."

Peter Stuyvesant

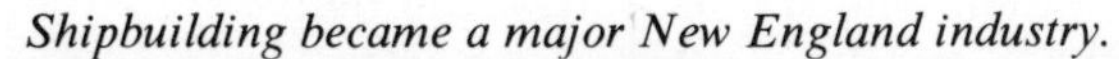

Shipbuilding became a major New England industry.

TWO LITTLE WARS

One-legged Peter Stuyvesant thunders against the British, but the Dutch surrender.

The last director-general of New Amsterdam—and its best—was rawboned, leathery-faced old Peter Stuyvesant. He stomped around on a wooden leg and was called, behind his back, "Peter the Headstrong." In 1655, the Swedes seized a Dutch trading post on the Delaware River at New Castle. Stuyvesant's voice, which sounded as though it came out of a barrel, could now be heard the length of Manhattan Island. He collected a fleet of seven stout sailing ships and set out to teach the Swedes a lesson.

The "war" was over almost before it began, and to the credit of the victorious Dutch, the region prospered under their control. They rebuilt New Amstel (New Castle) into a full-fledged town, greatly increased the trade in furs, and encouraged farming. If they governed in their usual highhanded way, at least they were tolerant of Swedish religious customs.

But unhappy days were ahead for New Amsterdam and headstrong Peter. The English in Connecticut were looking enviously at the Dutch holdings along the Hudson River. They followed the advice of the governor of Connecticut to keep "crowding the Dutch out of those places where they have occupied, but without hostility or any act of violence." Each year more and more Englishmen moved into New Amsterdam. The Dutch, who were peace-loving traders at heart, tried to get along with their English neighbors, but commercial jealousies between England and the Netherlands brought trouble. The first Anglo-Dutch War (1652–54) was a hit-and-run affair that ended in a patched-up peace which lasted ten years. In 1664 the two countries were snarling at each other again, and in late August of that year four British warships appeared off New Amsterdam and demanded its surrender.

Old Peter Stuyvesant thrust two large pistols in his belt and called for a brave defense. His council listened, squirmed at the thought of bloodshed, and then left the meeting (or so Washington Irving declared) "dodging through narrow lanes and alleys, staring at every little dog that barked, mistaking lamp posts for British grenadiers."

Stuyvesant pounded his wooden leg and called for action, but the Dutch only nailed up their doors to keep out the terrible British. They surrendered New Amsterdam "without a blow or a tear."

Under an elm at Shackamaxon (now part of Philadelphia), William Penn made a treaty of friendship with the Indians.

The English turned out to be mild rather than terrible. They did change the names of settlements, so that New Amsterdam became New York and Beverwyck became Albany. The story Washington Irving told of Stuyvesant stomping off to his farm, turning his high-back chair so he would never have to look at the captured city, and cutting down the English cherry trees in his yard was a good tale, but untrue. No better friends could be found on Manhattan Island than old Peter and Governor Richard Nicolls, the man to whom he had surrendered the city. Each dined often at the other's home. And in the same spirit the colonial Dutch and English went on living together peaceably and comfortably.

Briefly, in 1673, with the outbreak of another little war between England and the Netherlands, the Dutch recaptured New York. But when a peace treaty was signed the following year, they gave the city back to the English. After this, the chief worry of New York's Dutch and English was the pirates who were making the city a favorite hangout. The Blue Boar Tavern, on the outskirts of the city, rang with their wild shouts, songs, and fights. Here rough-looking rascals paraded about in fine colored waistcoats and feathered hats, with cutlass and pistols hanging from the sashes around their middles. Whoever saw them had to admit that there was something new in the New World.

WILLIAM PENN COMES TO AMERICA

Unable to practice their religion in England, the Quakers cross the Atlantic.

It was around 1647 that a new religious group, the Society of Friends, began to gain a following in England. They were also known as Quakers. The founder of the movement was George Fox, the son of a weaver and a shoemaker by training. Young Fox wandered through England, seeking a minister in whose preaching he could believe. Simply because a clergyman had been educated at Oxford or Cambridge University, Fox decided, was no guarantee that he had found God. And simply because men erected a building with their own hands and called it a church was no guarantee that the spirit of God dwelt there. Then one day George Fox was struck by a joyous thought. The true "temple of God" was in the heart of each man.

Questioning the right of the educated clergymen of England to speak for God, scorning their elaborate churches was bad enough. But the Quakers went even further. They said that since God lived within each man, it was nonsense to divide people into "ruling" and "lower" classes. God loved all people, and the Quakers addressed everyone as "thee" and "thou" to show that they considered them to be friends. The ruling class of England soon let the Quakers know that they were not wanted.

PERSECUTION OF THE QUAKERS

When the first Quakers reached Boston in 1656, they were thrown into prison and banished from Massachusetts without trial. That same year Connecticut passed a law imposing fines and banishment from the colony upon all members of the Society of Friends, and Puritan clergymen in New England preached sermons upon "the Devil, Quakers and Indians."

The Dutch were just as harsh toward the Quakers. Five Friends arrived in New Amsterdam in 1657. Peter Stuyvesant ordered them severely punished and banished them to Rhode Island. The following year, the New England Confederation, which spoke for the Bay Colony, Plymouth, and New Haven, ordered the Quakers out of all three colonies and threatened them with death if they returned. In 1660 a Quaker named Mary Dyer defied this law and came back to Boston where she was hanged.

But the Quakers would not give up their beliefs, and in 1664 they managed to buy land for a settlement in New Jersey. Meanwhile, in England, William Penn was working for their cause. Penn was an aristocrat, the son of an admiral. While a student at Oxford University, he became a Quaker, shocking his father. Oxford expelled Penn and the admiral sent him on a tour of Europe, hoping that a change of scene would help him to mend his ways.

The result was just the opposite. Penn soon wanted to change everything—religion, government, social manners, and customs. He was sentenced to jail, but it had no effect. He went on preaching his ideas to anyone who would listen and writing pamphlets for anyone who would read them. He traveled through Holland and Germany, winning new converts for the Quakers.

When Penn's father died, King Charles II owed him 16,000 pounds. In payment of this debt, the king gave Penn a royal grant to establish a colony in America. Now at last Penn could put his beliefs into practice. He wrote his famous letter to the Indians, assuring them that when he came to his new colony—Pennsylvania—he wished "to enjoy it with your [the Indians'] love and consent."

He admitted that other colonists had committed injustices against the Indians and caused "the shedding of blood." He added: "But I am not such a man, as is well known in my own country. I have great love towards you, and I desire to win and gain your love and friendship by a kind, just and peaceable life, and the people I send are of the same mind, and shall in all things behave themselves accordingly." He promised that if any inhabitant of his colony should act unfairly against any Indian, he would be speedily tried before a jury of six white persons and six Indians.

Penn spent weeks working out a plan of government for his colony. "Government seems to me a part of religion itself," he said. There were three common ideas of government: "monarchy, aristocracy and democracy, the rule of one, a few and many." For his own government he chose the principle that "any government is free to the people under it" where "the laws rule, and the people are a party to those laws." Again Penn declared: "Let men be good, and the government cannot be bad." Under Penn's plan, there would be guarantees for religious freedom, trial by jury, fair practices between whites and Indians, and payment to the Indians for the land.

Penn's ideas of government brought to America a belief in human decency and dignity. Every man should be free to say and think what he pleased. Every man was a king in his own home. All the people should take part in making and enforcing the laws. A great nation, Penn said, must be a nation of good morals. The laws he framed for his colony forbade corruption, fraud, bribery, extortion, and slander. They also forbade offenses against God, such as swearing, lying, drunkenness, duels, bearbaiting, and cockfights. They forbade anything "which excites the people to rudeness, cruelty, looseness and irreligion."

WILLIAM PENN FOUNDS A QUAKER COLONY

Indians and white settlers alike stood cheering at the water's edge when William Penn landed at New Castle, Delaware, in October of 1682. The very next day he announced that the first court would be held in New Castle in early November. There was to be no delay in beginning his colony on a basis of justice for all. Nor did Penn long delay in dealing with the Indians. Under an elm at Shackamaxon (now part of Philadelphia), he met with chiefs of the Leni Lenapes, the Susquehannocks, and the Shawnees to work out a "treaty of purchase and amity." He was a Quaker, Penn told the Indians, and his religion would not allow him to use "hostile weapons" against them. He had come to America "not to injure others but to do good."

Philadelphia, the capital of Penn's new province, grew quickly. By the end of 1684, it had 357 completed houses and a population of about 2,500.

The Quakers lived peacefully with the Swedes, Finns, and Dutch, the earlier settlers in the region. The people were industrious and developed trade with the other colonies and the West Indies. Shipbuilding soon became an important business. By 1685 Penn's colony had 7,000 inhabitants, and there was a new settlement at Germantown. Five years later William Rittenhouse built America's first paper mill on a branch of Wissahickon Creek. The new community, digging its roots into the wilderness, was busy and prosperous.

But the real strength of Penn's colony was the example it gave to America of how well a true democracy could work.

FLOATING DOWN THE MISSISSIPPI

Marquette and Joliet, followed by La Salle, explore the new continent.

Having lost out in the Iroquois country, because of Champlain's blunder, the French pushed westward and explored the lands bordering the Great Lakes. Here they built forts and trading posts that gave them control of these inland seas. Mackinac and Sault Ste. Marie made the French masters of the junctions of Lakes Huron, Michigan, and Superior, and Fort Radisson protected the far end of Lake Superior. Doggedly the French forged a chain around the inland empire they were building. Fort Frontenac rose on the shores of Lake Ontario. Fort Niagara guarded the passage to Lake Erie. When Detroit was founded in 1701, the French controlled the connection between Lake Erie and Lake Huron.

Jesuit fathers in black robes carried their religion to the Indians of mid-America and revealed to the world new wonders of the wilderness. Father Louis Hennepin was the first white man to look upon mighty Niagara Falls. Stringing their missions deeper into the lake country, the Jesuits heard of a mysterious and mighty river to the south—the Mississippi. No river was quite so great and majestic as this one, the Indians said. Father Jacques Marquette had been in North America seven years when he decided to find this wonderful river. With him on his journey went his good-humored friend, the explorer Louis Joliet.

"We joyfully plied our paddles," wrote Father Marquette of the beginning of that brave adventure in May of 1673. The first Indians they visited were friendly Menominees, who tried to persuade them not to make the trip. "They represented to me that I would meet nations who never show mercy to strangers, but break their heads without any cause," Marquette later recalled. The Indians spoke of monsters that lived in the river and could eat men and canoes together. They spoke of a demon that swallowed all who dared to approach it, and of a country where the heat was so great it could cause death. Father Marquette said he was not afraid. He had been called to carry on God's work and believed he could defend himself against river monsters.

DOWN THE WISCONSIN RIVER

Father Marquette and his small party of seven Frenchmen traveled in two canoes. In early June they were paddling down the Wisconsin River. Vine-covered islands dotted the river. Great forests of oak, walnut, and basswood trees came down to the water's edge. They saw many deer and a place that looked like an iron mine. On they paddled, past forests, prairies, and hills, until on June 17 they reached the Mississippi.

On June 25 they visited a village of Illinois Indians on the west bank of the river. A man standing with his hand stretched toward the sun called a greeting: "How beautiful is the sun, O Frenchman, when thou comest to visit us! All our town awaits thee."

Father Marquette gave the Indians gifts and spoke of God as their Creator. The sachem of the tribe thanked Marquette, calling him "Blackgown."

Afterward Marquette, Joliet, and their French boatmen were entertained at a feast. The Indians served a dish of corn meal boiled in water "and seasoned with grease," which they fed to their guests by the spoonful, as sometimes a small child is fed. Fish and roasted wild ox also were served, as well as "a large dog, which they had just killed, but learning that we did not eat it, it was withdrawn."

The Illinois village contained about 300 wigwams. As Father Marquette's party was shown through the streets, a man went before them, shouting in a loud voice that the palefaced visitors were not to be harmed. Again the Indians spoke of savage tribes that lived to the south and begged the white men

Father Jacques Marquette

Louis Joliet

to turn back while they were still safe. Again Father Marquette replied that he must trust in God to protect them.

Father Marquette and his companion Joliet paddled their canoes to the mouth of the Arkansas River, where the Indians told them they were only ten days' journey from the sea (that is, the Gulf of Mexico). In typical Indian fashion, the Arkansas tribesmen spent the entire day feasting. Father Marquette described their life in the Arkansas wilderness:

"These Indians are very courteous and liberal of what they have, but they are very poorly off for food, not daring to go and hunt the wild cattle [buffalo], for fear of their enemies. It is true, they have Indian corn in abundance, which they sow at all seasons. We saw some ripe, more just sprouting, and more just in ear, so that they sow three crops a year. They cook it in large earthen pots . . .

"The men go naked, and wear their hair very short. They have their nose and ears pierced, and beads hanging from them. The women are dressed in wretched skins. They braid their hair in two plaits, which fall behind their ears. They have no ornaments to decorate their persons. . . .

"Their cabins, which are long and wide, are made of bark. They sleep at the two extremities [ends], which are raised about two feet from the ground. They keep their corn in large baskets, made of cane, or in gourds as large as half barrels. They do not know what a beaver is, their riches consisting in the hides of wild cattle. They never see snow, and know the winter only by the rain which falls oftener than in summer. They eat no fruit but watermelons. If they knew how to cultivate their ground, they might have plenty of all kinds."

Satisfied that they had learned the true course of the mighty Mississippi, Marquette, Joliet, and the boatmen turned their canoes homeward. They took a shorter route by way of the Illinois, Des Plaines, and Chicago Rivers, and thus reached Lake Michigan, the "lake of the Illinois." Here at the water's edge Father Marquette baptized a dying child and that moment repaid him for all the weary days the trip had taken. He walked now on land where one day a great city would rise. Its name would be Chicago.

LA SALLE FINDS THE MISSISSIPPI'S MOUTH

These inland explorations made by Marquette and Joliet were a beginning that no Frenchman could forget. The Spanish, the English, the Dutch, and others had nibbled at the fringes of North America, but the real discoverers of the continent were the French. They had been deep into this wilderness, they had floated on the great river that linked "the Frozen Sea and New Mexico," and now they dreamed of using that river to win a vast empire in the midlands of America. Among them was Robert Cavelier, Sieur de la Salle, who was determined to carry the flag of France down the Mississippi River to the sea.

La Salle was an explorer who had imagination as well as courage. He founded Fort Niagara and built the forty-ton *Griffon,* the first ship of any size to sail on the Great Lakes. In 1680 he established

Explorations of La Salle (map shows present-day borders).

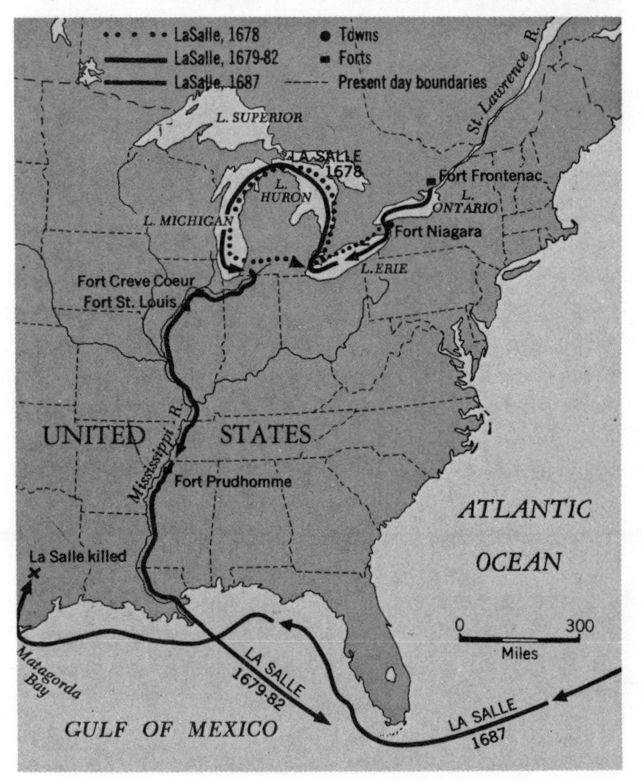

Fort Crèvecoeur (now Peoria) in Illinois and Fort Miami (now St. Joseph) in Michigan.

But La Salle's real triumph came when, on April 9, 1682, he reached the mouth of the Mississippi. He gathered his party on high ground and planted a cross bearing the arms of France. Shouts, volleys of muskets, and the chants of priests rang out as La Salle took possession of all the country. He gave it the name of Louisiana, in honor of the king of France. La Salle claimed not only the territory that the French had already explored, but also all the lands drained by the tributaries of the Mississippi, and a large part of the coast of the Gulf of Mexico.

To protect his new empire, La Salle built Fort Prudhomme on the Arkansas River at Chickasaw Bluffs and Fort St. Louis on the Illinois at Starved Rock. He formed the Indian tribes of Illinois into a federation, then sailed to France to seek permission to establish a settlement at the mouth of the Mississippi. In 1687, he returned to the New World with some 200 soldiers, mechanics, and colonists. That was too small a number to send into a country already occupied by the Spanish. Besides, the soldiers did not know how to fight, nor the seamen how to sail their ships, the mechanics how to handle their tools, the settlers how to get along in a wilderness.

FRANCE LOSES INTEREST

Everything went wrong. The ships were far off course when finally they reached Matagorda Bay on the coast of Texas. Quarrels arose, and La Salle was murdered by two members of his party.

Yet if France lost interest in her new possessions after that, no one was more at fault than La Salle. He had told only his closest friends about his explorations. So little was known in France about the lands he had discovered that people began to doubt their existence. Some said that La Salle had never actually reached the mouth of the Mississippi. Others said that the river simply disappeared into a hole in the ground.

In time, of course, France again became interested in the vast Louisiana Territory. A French expedition under Pierre Le Moyne, Sieur d'Iberville, sailed into Mobile Bay in February, 1698. Journeying overland to the mouth of the Mississippi, Iberville led his party upstream. He reached the site of New Orleans in March of 1699 and erected a cross.

Although Iberville traveled as far north as Baton Rouge, he failed to discover the fortune in gold that the French king, Louis XIV, wanted. Once again the interest of the French faded. But Catholic missionaries and traders kept their claim to the country alive. A dozen years or so later, the French tried to make the Louisiana Territory an important part of their world empire.

JUST A BEGINNING

*In two hundred years much has been done—
but great events are yet to come.*

In round figures, 200 years had passed since Columbus had landed upon the shore of San Salvador, not knowing that he had stumbled upon a new world. First England, then France (and, to a lesser degree, the Dutch and the Swedes) had challenged Spain's claims to half the world. Already many mysteries of the wilderness had been solved. Already a new spirit had risen in this land of mighty rivers and lakes and mountains. People had begun to talk of their *right* to share in their government, their *right* to worship God in their own way, their *right* to a full and happy life.

Yet, really, the story of America was just beginning. It was like a river that starts as a little mountain brook and becomes mightier as it flows on. Many hardships and sacrifices and terrible conflicts lay ahead, and even now there were signs of what was to come. In 1688, the Quakers, meeting in Germantown, Pennsylvania, issued the first written statement in America that protested against human slavery. The following year New Hampshire was torn by King William's War. This was the first of the French and Indian wars that for many years would bring bloodshed to the colonies as France fought England for possession of the vast continent of North America.

There were other events, too, of a quite different kind. In 1690 a single printed sheet, *Publick Occurrences,* appeared in Boston. It was America's first newspaper—although a second issue was never printed. In 1693, Virginia gave the colonies a second institution of higher learning with the founding of William and Mary College, and eight years later Yale College was founded at Saybrook, Connecticut.

By 1700 the population of the colonies was estimated at 262,000, but everyone knew that the New World had just begun to grow. About this time there appeared in London a pamphlet written by Gabriel Thomas, one of the early settlers of Pennsylvania. He told of his life in the colonies where wages were high, taxes low, and work plentiful, where Chesapeake ducks and Pennsylvania cheesecake were the finest in the world. Only beautiful children were born in America, and they were "better natured, milder and more tender-hearted than those born in England."

Of course, there were Londoners who called the proud Pennsylvanian an out-and-out liar trying to trick people into coming to his wretched wilderness. But there were many who did believe him, and they did indeed make the long journey to America, seeking a better life in a new land.

In 1755 British regulars were ambushed by French and Indians along the Monongahela River near Fort Duquesne.

II ∾ GROWTH OF THE COLONIES... THE INDIAN WARS

from 1675 to 1774

In 1676, after a dispute with the governor of Virginia, Nathaniel Bacon burned the settlement at Jamestown.

BLOODY DAYS IN NEW ENGLAND

The Indians strike back at the settlers in King Philip's War.

For nearly forty years New Englanders had lived in peace with the Indians. Now and then a small dispute arose, but it was quickly settled. There were about 4,000 "praying Indians"–Indians who had been converted to Christianity. The red man had learned to live without raids and scalpings–or so New Englanders believed.

Each year the English had pushed their settlements and trading posts deeper into Indian hunting grounds, both to the north and the west. Meanwhile, Dutch traders at Albany and wandering French traders had supplied the Indians with firearms. The tomahawk and fire arrow had been no match for a gun, but with the weapons they had bought, the Indians believed they could meet the white invaders on even terms.

Thus did King Philip, chief of the Wampanoags, talk to his tribesmen in Rhode Island, and later to the Nipmucks and Narragansetts. He told the Indians that they had the power to save their favorite fishing and hunting grounds. And he stirred up their feelings until they shouted with anger at the white man. When in June, 1675, a settler in Swansea, Rhode Island, shot an Indian who had been seen looting houses, King Philip's War exploded. Before the fighting ended, it had left a long and bloody trail from Massachusetts to Connecticut.

CAPTURE OF MARY ROWLANDSON

Typical of the savage assaults that King Philip's warriors made against town after town was the attack on Lancaster, a settlement on the Massachusetts frontier. Mary White Rowlandson later told how the popping of guns was heard as the Indians came howling out of the forest at about sunrise on February 10, 1676. Her minister husband was in Boston on business that day and she faced the trouble alone. From the window she looked out on frightful scenes: houses afire with the smoke rising in thick columns, a child knocked on the head and killed, a man shot while running toward his barn, Indians climbing onto rooftops to shoot down into the town's fortifications.

Then the Indians rushed to the house where Mary was hiding and set it on fire. She tried to escape, with the baby in her arms and her small son and daughter clinging to her skirt. But "the Indians shot so thick that the bullets rattled against the house as if one had taken a handful of stones and threw them." Indians with guns, spears, and hatchets were on every side. Both Mary and her baby were wounded before the Indians seized her.

That night the Indians and their captives camped on a hill overlooking the ruins of Lancaster. While the hungry captives huddled together, the Indians shouted, danced, and feasted in celebration of their victory. Next morning they marched northward and snow added to the misery of the captives. On the ninth night, Mary's baby died.

Mary was sold into slavery to a sachem (chief), who in turn sold her to a Narragansett Indian. Her daughter, she learned, had been sold into slavery by a "praying Indian." The price: one gun. No one would tell what had happened to her son.

For the first week of captivity Mary ate almost nothing. The second week, weakened by hunger, she tried to swallow "the filthy trash" the Indians pushed at her. By the end of the third week she had grown accustomed to the Indian food. Mary's skill at knitting saved her from many hardships. She made a shirt and a cap for King Philip's son, and he invited her to dinner in his wigwam, where she was served a stew made from peas and bear meat. Another Indian gave her a Bible, which she read for comfort during her lonely hours.

But life among the Indians proved hard. Every few days they picked up their camp and moved on, and Mary was loaded down like a pack animal. Sometimes an angry squaw would not feed her or allow her to sleep in a wigwam. Once an Indian tormented her with a story of how her son had been killed and eaten. But unexpectedly, a week later, the boy was brought into camp. Mary embraced him joyously and then combed the lice from his hair.

For eleven weeks, as the Indians wandered through northern Massachusetts and southern New Hampshire, Mary Rowlandson clung to her faith that God would somehow save her. She marched under her heavy loads, waded icy rivers, and knitted caps and shirts. Then, in early May, came wonderful news. The Indians had agreed to sell her back to the English for a ransom of twenty pounds sterling. Her son was sold for seven pounds. In late June, Mary learned that her daughter had escaped from the Indians and had found her way to Providence, Rhode Island. Soon the family was reunited.

Not all who were captured by the Indians were as fortunate as Mary Rowlandson and her children. Many died. Others simply disappeared into the forest and were never heard from again.

Disaster also awaited King Philip. By the spring of 1676, the English had made an alliance with friendly tribes of Naticks and Niantics. In August an Indian traitor guided the English to King Philip's hiding place in a swamp, and the next morning the chief was killed. His head was cut off and sent to Plymouth, where for twenty-five years it could be seen stuck on a pole—a reminder of terror in the wilderness.

BACON'S REBELLION

Virginia planters fight both the Indians and their tyrannical governor.

During the years of King Philip's War in New England, a different kind of war was going on in Virginia. Called Bacon's Rebellion, it is sometimes described as a dress rehearsal for the American Revolution that would come a hundred years later.

Sir William Berkeley, who was then governor of Virginia, seemed to take no notice of the fact that times were hard. The price of tobacco was falling off and taxes were rising. Many poor people who had sold their services for a period of four or more years to pay for their passage to America had now worked out their terms as "indentured servants." Most of these newly freed servants pushed deeper into the wilderness, cleared their own land, and became small planters in the uplands of Virginia. They did not rely on slaves, as the older plantation owners did, but beat back the forests themselves, with the help of their wives and children. Then, in the summer of 1675, a band of Susquehanna Indians, driven south by the Senecas, began stealing livestock along the Virginia frontier. Shootings and Indian raids followed, and the small planters appealed to the governor for soldiers to protect their lives and their property.

Sir William refused to send the militia. The small planters believed it was because he did not want to upset the very profitable fur trade he was carrying on with the Indians. The planters prepared to raise their own army to put down the Indians on the one hand and defy the governor on the other. All they needed was the right leader.

The man they chose was Nathaniel Bacon, Jr., a fact rather surprising in itself. Bacon was as "wellborn" as old Sir William. He had been educated in England before coming to Virginia to build a fine plantation on the banks of the James River. But Bacon was hotheaded, impatient, highly excitable, and he did not like the governor. Moreover, an overseer on Bacon's plantation had been murdered by an Indian, and Bacon wanted revenge. When the upland settlers offered him an army of 300 to command, he gladly accepted.

The war that followed was a strange affair. Bacon and his patchwork army set off to fight the Indians only to learn that the governor had declared him a rebel, had ordered his army disbanded, and had even sent a small force to fight him. Happily, the two armies failed to meet. Bacon stormed into Jamestown, where he was welcomed as a hero. To Sir William's dismay, Bacon was elected to the House of Burgesses, as the Virginia legislative assembly was called. The assembly, taking matters into its own hands, declared war on the Indians and placed Bacon in command of its army.

Sir William refused to accept defeat. In late summer, Bacon marched his army toward the falls of the James River to fight the Indians. Sir William, defying the House of Burgesses, raised his own army and once more declared Bacon in rebellion. Bacon marched to Middle Plantation (later named Williamsburg) and declared Sir William and his council members traitors to the colony.

Bacon sent one of the colony's armed vessels to capture the governor, but failed through no fault of his own. His soldiers, it was recorded, had been drinking too much of "the juice of the grape." Bacon then turned to fighting his *other* foe, and this time he was successful, driving the Indians from their refuge in the marshes along the shores of the York River.

THE BATTLE FOR JAMESTOWN

Meanwhile, Sir William sailed to Jamestown with an army of 600 men. Bacon was willing to meet the old governor more than halfway and marched his own band back to Jamestown. Bacon's rebels arrived, dead tired, and spent the night throwing up defenses "by the help of the moon light." There was a brisk little skirmish at daybreak, but Sir William refused to fire his cannon. He would not be the first to spill blood, he said.

Bacon acted boldly, seizing "the wives and female relations" of the "gentlemen" in the governor's service and placing them before his defenses "in the face of the enemy." Now Sir William did not dare to order a shot fired. So he did the only thing he could—he left town in a hurry.

Next morning the rebels entered Jamestown, and, because it had been a refuge for the governor, Bacon decided to "lay it level with the ground." That night the church and the statehouse were burned, along with all the frame houses.

BACON DIES

Taking over Sir William's home and orchards at nearby Green Spring, Bacon planned many reforms in the government of Virginia. But he soon died of a fever, and his friends buried him in a secret place. Sir William, restored to power by the king, struck back at his old enemies and hanged twenty-three of those who had taken part in the uprising.

By 1685 the statehouse at Jamestown had been rebuilt, and some people may have wondered if Bacon's Rebellion had accomplished anything. The small planters of Virginia thought it had. They had proved that as Englishmen they were entitled to equal protection under the law. And they had shown the ruling class that if it ruled without justice it might some day lose its power.

THE DEERFIELD MASSACRE

The French and Indians attack
an English outpost in Massachusetts.

In 1702, Queen Anne of England began a long and bitter struggle with King Louis XIV of France for the control of Europe. Drums beat as the armies of England and France marched to battle, and soon other drums—Indian drums—were beating in the wilderness of Canada.

By May of 1703, Lord Cornbury, Royal Governor of New York, was receiving reports from his spies among the Mohawk Indians. He learned that the French in Canada were stirring up Indian allies to attack the British frontier settlements of New England. Deerfield, the western outpost of Massachusetts, would be a natural target.

Lord Cornbury warned Governor Dudley of Massachusetts of the coming raid, and Deerfield prepared to defend itself. The fortifications of the town were strengthened. Children under the age of twelve were kept indoors—a hardship during the summer months when their help was needed in farming. Guards watched the edge of the wilderness which stretched for 300 miles between Deerfield and Canada. How near were the French and their Indian allies? When would they strike?

The weeks of summer dragged slowly on. Autumn spread flames of gold and scarlet across the forests. The leaves of the trees turned brown and fluttered to the ground—and still there was no attack.

THE ATTACK COMES

The snow came early that year, piling up deep drifts in the forest. As long as the heavy snow lasted, everyone believed the town was safe. Why, an attacking party would freeze to death trying to cross 300 miles of wilderness in this weather!

Late at night, on the last day of February, 1704, the town watchman was leaning against a house. He could hear a mother singing a lullaby to her sick baby. Perhaps the soft, sweet song put him to sleep, or perhaps he was numbed by the cold. In either case, the watchman never gave an alarm. All at once the French and Indians were there. The snowdrifts piled against the walls of the town made it easy for them to climb over the fortifications.

There were more than 250 of them, and they scattered quickly through the town. In the flickering light of torches they broke down doors. Guns blazed and knives flashed. Houses were set on fire.

Some of Deerfield's people fought back furiously. Some pleaded for mercy and, if they were lucky, were carried off to captivity in Canada. Some hid in dark corners and, if they were lucky, escaped death or capture. Some simply stood, wide-eyed with fear, as Indians carried firebrands through the houses, ate any food they could find, and picked up any articles of clothing or furniture that took their fancy.

An exceptional case was Mrs. Ruth Catlin, who watched a wounded Frenchman carried into her house and laid upon the floor. The man groaned with pain and called for a drink of water.

Mrs. Catlin said, "I will give you a drink." Her shocked neighbors cried: "How can you do that for your enemy?"

"If thine enemy hunger, feed him," Mrs. Catlin

replied quietly. "If he thirst, give him water to drink."

The raiders did not forget Mrs. Catlin's kindness. No harm came to her, and her house was not burned.

When the attack started, there had been 291 persons, ranging in age from eighty-four-year-old Widow Allison to four-week-old John French asleep in their beds. Now 165 had been killed, or captured and forced to march through the cruel wintry weather to Canada.

The Deerfield Massacre was the beginning of a desperate struggle for America that would last, off and on, for fifty years.

THREE WAYS OF LIFE

Colonial life differs in
New England, the Middle Colonies, and the South.

By the year 1700, a traveler from Massachusetts to Virginia could not mistake the fact that British America had three ways of life. They changed sharply as the traveler journeyed through hilly, rock-strewn New England, into the "bread colonies" between the fertile valleys of the Hudson and Potomac Rivers, and on to the plantations of the South.

Anyone who made such a journey in those days needed to be brave. Narrow, dusty roads wound through dank swamps and dark forests. There were few bridges over the creeks and rivers, so that the traveler was often forced to wade the cold, swift streams. At nightfall, when the traveler stopped at a village inn, the best he could expect was a poor place to rest his tired bones.

In New England, the traveler soon realized that this was no region for profitable farming. Much of New England was covered with mountains, and elsewhere the rocky soil made plowing and cultivating crops difficult. Winters were long and hard and summers short. With the exception of the Connecticut, New England rivers could not be traveled by boat for any great distance, so that transportation from farm to market presented a special problem. As a result, New Englanders became merchants, manufacturers, shipowners, shipbuilders, and bankers. New England became a center of trade and shipbuilding. Ships from Newburyport, Ipswich, Gloucester, Salem, Boston, New Bedford, Newport, Providence, New London, and New Haven sailed proudly over the oceans of the world.

As soon as a traveler entered the Middle Colonies, he was in a different world. The fertile valleys of the Hudson and Mohawk Rivers in New York were a farmer's paradise. So were the wide, gently sloping river valleys of New Jersey and Pennsylvania, where wheat took the place of corn as the chief crop. Here the fields also yielded fine harvests of rye, oats, bar-

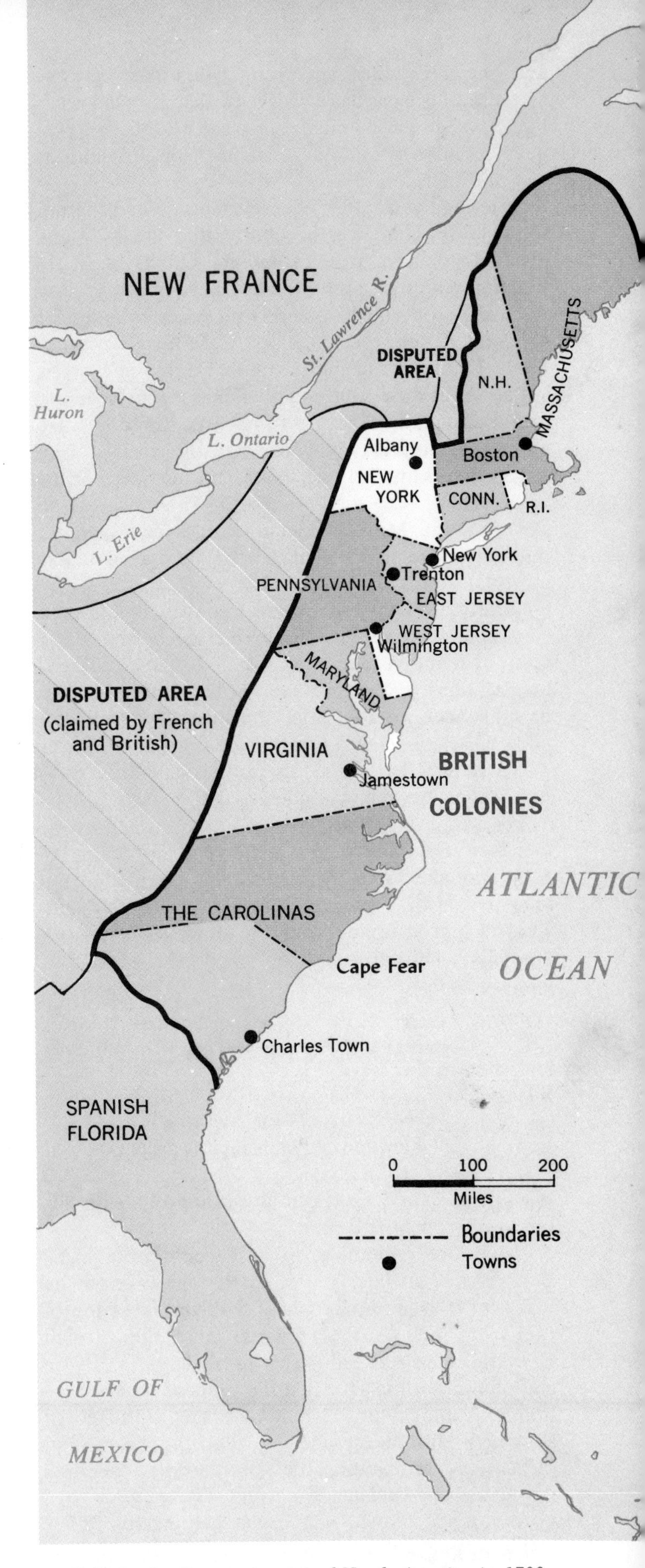

Colonies in the eastern part of North America in 1700.

ley, hay, vegetables, and fruits. Markets were close at hand and easy to reach. With fast-growing cities like New York and Philadelphia, the Middle Colonies gave promise of one day equaling New England as a center of trade.

Entering the South the traveler saw still a different way of life. Here was a country that lived by one product—tobacco, rice, or indigo. Often, in hopes of gaining a quick profit, the Southern planter raised one cash crop and had to rely on other colonies for his food. Often, too, he failed to fertilize worn-out fields. Land was cheap; he simply cleared new acres.

Slaves gave the Southern planter inexpensive labor, and many plantations grew into little kingdoms. He looked on his slave—even when he treated him kindly—the same way he looked on his horse or his plow. They were all "property." There were also slaves in the Middle Colonies and New England, but they were fewer in number and played a less important part.

Clearly, British America was growing without a single plan or pattern. The three regions were going their own individual ways, like so many different little nations. Except for the hardy traveler on foot or horseback, or the sailor touching at the coastal ports of Boston, New York, Philadelphia, and Charles Town (later Charleston), there was very little communication between colonies.

Yet change was coming more quickly than anyone expected. On Milk Street in Boston on January 6, 1706, a maker of soap and candles listened to the lusty howls of a newborn son, his fifteenth child. That red-faced infant would go down in history as "the first civilized American" and "the apostle of modern times."

BENJAMIN FRANKLIN

Franklin sets himself up as a printer in Philadelphia.

Young Benjamin Franklin lived happily with his big family on Milk Street.

"I do not remember when I could not read," Ben recalled in later years. At the age of eight he was sent to a grammar school with the intention of preparing him for the ministry. His father, Josiah Franklin, soon realized that with his large family he could not afford to give Ben the years of long education this calling required. Ben was placed with George Brownell, a private teacher. "Under him," Ben said, "I acquired fair writing pretty soon, but I failed in the arithmetic, and made no progress."

At the age of ten, Ben began helping his father in the business of a tallow chandler and soap boiler. He cut wicks for candles, filled the dripping molds, attended the shop, and ran errands. Ben did not like the trade and wanted to go to sea.

Josiah Franklin would not hear of it, yet he was a good father. For hours man and boy walked the streets of Boston, watching all sorts of craftsmen at work in the hope that the lad could find "some trade or other on land" that he liked.

Always a bookish fellow, Ben was happy when his half brother James returned from England in 1717 with a printing press and type to set up a business in Boston. He was now eleven years old, and he signed papers, agreeing to serve as an apprentice until he reached twenty-one.

Ben fancied himself a poet in those years, and composed and printed two long ballads that he offered for sale. One ballad, *The Lighthouse Tragedy,* telling of the drowning of a captain and his two daughters, was a popular success. Ben was quite proud of himself until his father spoke his mind. A poet? Who could afford a poet in the Franklin family?

Sometimes it was difficult to guess what Ben would do next. He read a book that convinced him he should give up eating meat and live on vegetables—and he persuaded James to give him the board money that was saved on his cheaper diet. This he spent on books.

FRANKLIN LEAVES BOSTON

In 1721, James began to publish a newspaper, the *New England Courant.* Soon a series of articles, signed by "Silence Dogood," was slipped under the door of his office. James liked and published them until he discovered that the author was Ben. These two were quick to quarrel, for James thought of himself more as Ben's master than as his brother.

James never hesitated to criticize civic and religious leaders in his newspaper, and he soon found himself in jail. Ben now forgot the quarrels and carried on the publication of the *Courant.* He was having a wonderful time: "I made bold to give our rulers some rubs in it, which my brother took very kindly, while others began to consider me in an unfavorable light, as a young genius that had a turn for libelling."

Once James was released from prison, he and Ben quickly began quarreling again. "Perhaps I was too saucy and provoking," Ben admitted later. All the same, he decided to strike off on his own.

A three-day voyage brought him to New York. Finding no work there, he pushed on to Philadelphia. The trip across lower New York Bay to Amboy, New Jersey, was long and stormy, and Ben rescued "a drunken Dutchman" who fell overboard by pulling him up by his hair. In three days of weary walking Ben covered the fifty miles across New Jersey to the Delaware River. Hungry, tired, and almost pen-

The colonists feared the pirates who operated off the Carolinas, looting any vessel they could catch.

niless, he reached Philadelphia next morning. It was a day he never forgot:

"I walked up the street, gazing about till near the market-house I met a boy with bread. I had made many a meal on bread, and, inquiring where he got it, I went immediately to the baker's. . . . Not considering or knowing the difference of money, nor the greater cheapness nor the names of his bread, I bade him give three-penny worth of any sort. He gave me, accordingly, three great puffy rolls. I was surprised at the quantity, but took it, and, having no room in my pockets, walked off with a roll under each arm, and eating the other. Thus I went up Market Street as far as Fourth Street, passing by the door of Mr. Read, my future wife's father; when she, standing at the door, saw me, and thought I made . . . a most awkward, ridiculous appearance. . . ."

Ben gave his other two rolls to a mother and her child. Then he attended a Quaker meeting. He fell sound asleep, but the friendly Quakers did not awaken him until the meeting ended.

Ben soon found employment in the printing shop of Samuel Keimer. He roomed at the Reads'—where Miss Deborah decided he was neither awkward nor ridiculous. Such was the nature of this remarkable young fellow that in a very short time he counted among his friends Sir William Keith, the provincial governor.

LIVELY TIMES IN CHARLESTON

Pirates terrorize the seas, but most are caught and hanged.

In the year 1717, James Logan, Secretary of Pennsylvania, reported that 1,500 pirates were sweeping the seas from Newfoundland to Brazil. Driven by the English fleet from their main hide-out in the Bahamas, the pirates made their final stand along the coast of the Carolinas.

One of them was the bloodthirsty Robert Thatch (or Teach), better known as "Blackbeard." In June of 1718 he appeared before Charleston harbor with a forty-gun frigate accompanied by three sloops. His crews numbered about 400 men. He quickly captured several vessels, including one that carried many prominent Charleston citizens who were sailing to London.

Blackbeard chuckled at his good luck. He made out a long list of medicines and other supplies he needed and sent a party to Charleston with a message for the governor. Unless he received these supplies within forty-eight hours he would send the governor the heads of all the Charlestonians he held as prisoners. Charleston had no defense against Blackbeard's frigate. He was given his supplies and the prisoners were released. They arrived home almost naked, for the pirates had even robbed them of their clothes. Blackbeard sailed back to Pamlico Sound, still chuckling.

BONNET THREATENS CHARLESTON

Soon after this, another pirate threatened Charleston—Stede Bonnet. Stede offered the strangest excuse in history for taking up piracy. He said it was the only way he could find to escape from a quarrelsome wife. Stede's dreadful deeds were known—and feared—all the way from Barbados to the coast of Maine. It was no wonder that Charlestonians were worried when, late in the summer of 1718, they heard that Stede Bonnet, aboard his ship the *Revenge,* stood off their harbor.

Robert Johnson, the Governor of South Carolina, decided that he had had enough pirates. He sent two armed ships under the command of William Rhett to deal with Stede. A merry chase followed, ending at the entrance to the Cape Fear River. Here Stede's ships and Rhett's grounded on sand bars.

BONNET IS CAPTURED

The battle now depended on which side the rising tide favored. If Stede's ship broke free first, clearly he would have the colonists at his mercy. Life or death for Charleston depended on every ripple as the tide came in. All at once one of Rhett's ships floated free, coming around and making for Stede's still grounded vessel. The pirates were forced to surrender.

In defeat, Stede was no hero. He whined and begged for his life, trying to invent excuses for the terrible things he had done. Charleston's citizens marched him to Execution Dock and watched as he and his crew were hanged in chains.

The flood tide of piracy was running out in North America. A few weeks after Stede and his rascals swung from the gallows, two stout cruisers from Virginia found Blackbeard and his men lurking in Ocracoke Inlet on the North Carolina coast. A bloody battle was fought and Blackbeard was killed. The colonists hanged the survivors of the crew, and the lead ship returned up the James River with the severed head of Blackbeard decorating her bowsprit.

Bold when attacking the helpless, Stede Bonnet turned coward when facing the gallows.

In 1704, 23 young girls arrived in Mobile to become brides of the French settlers. Many more came later.

THE "MISSISSIPPI BUBBLE"

Many French people invest their savings in the New World, only to lose them.

From the beginning of the Eighteenth Century, France had acted on the belief that the English intended to seize possession of the mouth of the Mississippi River. In 1702, a new and stronger settlement was established at Mobile, replacing Biloxi as the capital of the Louisiana province.

Two years later the excited people of Mobile witnessed the arrival of the *Pelican.* Aboard this snug little vessel were twenty-three young girls who had been brought as wives and home builders for French settlers in the Louisiana wilderness. Each girl was provided with a *cassette,* or trunk, and an outfit of clothing. Within a month twenty-two of the "cassette girls" had found husbands, and the one still unmarried was described as "hard to please." Before the year ended, the first white child was born in the province.

FRANCE BUILDS TRADING POSTS

The French pushed steadily ahead to secure control of the great valley that was the life line of mid-America. Bienville, the new governor of Louisiana, and Cadillac, the founder of Detroit, worked together in exploring the lower Mississippi and Red rivers. French trading posts began to dot the wilderness far up the Missouri River and along the lower Ohio Valley.

In May, 1713, a French frigate brought another shipment of girls in search of husbands—twenty-five this time. Twenty-three more came in 1718, another eighty in 1719, a like number in 1721. Each girl was carefully selected by officers of the church, and nuns watched over them until they had made a good "match."

Another proof that the French were in earnest about developing the Mississippi Valley was the king's selection in 1712 of Antoine Crozat to manage this territory. Crozat was one of the great merchants and bankers of France, and in his hands was placed all the trade of Louisiana.

Crozat had his troubles. The Spanish barred his ships from their ports. The English were unfriendly and looked the other way as pirates took their toll of French ships. By 1717, Crozat was more than willing to give up his dream of making a fortune in gold, silver, mineral ores, furs, and trade with the Indians. Heavily in debt, he surrendered his charter.

A remarkable fellow—some called him a scoundrel—now stepped forward to take over Crozat's unfinished work in Louisiana. His name was John Law. A tricky Scot, Law was a magician at juggling money—usually other people's money. He had risen to high favor with Louis XIV of France.

In 1718—the year New Orleans was founded and France could believe that she had at last secured control of the Mississippi—Law launched his campaign to interest investors in his new company. He spoke of the great riches in gold and silver Louisiana possessed. He told how hundreds of settlers wanted to rush to Louisiana and of the profits his company was certain to earn.

Thousands of Frenchmen believed him. Scrub women, maids, small merchants, and farmers, bank clerks and shopkeepers scraped and saved to buy stock in Law's wilderness empire. The rich also invested heavily and pawned their jewels to buy more stock. All over Paris, the same talk was heard. Everyone would soon be rich.

Then, in 1720, the truth came out. There was no gold or silver, no rush of settlers. So, all at once, the great "Mississippi Bubble" exploded. Hundreds of investors were ruined. And Law, whose bag had long been packed, was already hurrying out of France.

Yet Law's talents for advertising had not been entirely wasted. The legend he had created of the wealth to be gained in Louisiana lingered on, and slowly the population of the region increased. French adventurers continued to push up the Arkansas River (where Arkansas Post had been established), into Illinois country (with settlements at Cahokia and Kaskaskia), and up the Wabash into Indiana (where they built Vincennes). By 1739 they had founded Ste. Geneviève in Missouri. Along the lower Mississippi, French plantations pushed out to the river front, growing tobacco at first, then rice, indigo, and some cotton. By 1751 the planters had introduced sugar as a crop of the Deep South.

RANCHEROS OF THE OLD SOUTHWEST

The Spanish establish missions and ranches in New Mexico and Texas.

The Spanish were strengthening their hold on Texas and New Mexico. A mission was built at San Antonio, Texas, in 1718. In the years that followed, the friars, supported by military forces, established ten more missions and four new towns in Texas.

But the real empire builders in this region were the large landholders, or *rancheros.* Their great cattle ranches and comfortable homes, or *haciendas,* began to spread across this fine range country. The land changed under their control as great ditches were dug to irrigate food and cotton crops. Horsemen looked after great herds of cattle and sheep.

Indian labor was used to produce woven cloth and articles of silver and turquoise in the settlements of Santa Fe and Albuquerque. Spanish traders went northward—up the Colorado and the Arkansas Rivers and into the desert of the Great Salt Lake. Each year the fair at Taos was a time for song, dancing, and hard drinking. Santa Fe was becoming well known to men seeking quick profits—respectable trappers, *rancheros,* merchants, smugglers, thieves.

In the struggle for North America, the French were gaining in the lower Mississippi, the Spanish in Florida, Texas, and New Mexico. Meanwhile, thousands of miles from the New World, another chapter was opening in the story of America.

TOWARD THE ARCTIC SUN

Russian explorers sail east to the northwest coast of the New World.

Peter the Great, Czar of All the Russias, was a man of deep intelligence. He welcomed scholars from France and Germany to his court at St. Petersburg, where they helped to establish the Russian Academy of Science.

Strange reports had been reaching St. Petersburg from across the Ural Mountains. After heavy storms along Russia's Pacific coast line, waves washed up timber unlike the wood of native trees. Often the waves also left on the shores the bodies of strange animals with spears in them. Could this mean that there was inhabited land nearby to the east—land that perhaps joined the continents of Asia and North America? The scholars urged the czar to solve this mystery, and in 1725 he sent an expedition to see whether land linked Russia with America.

To lead this expedition, Peter the Great called to St. Petersburg a Danish-born navigator named Vitus

Jonassen Bering. Now forty-four years of age, Bering had spent half his life on the seas in the service of the British East India Company and the Russian navy. Though stubborn and hot-tempered, he was a capable leader. He and his party traveled for months, at times trapped by howling blizzards. They trudged across hundreds of miles of Arctic land until they reached the coast of the stormy North Pacific. Here they built a ship, the *Gabriel,* and in July, 1727, set off to find a link between the continents. St. Petersburg was 5,000 miles behind them.

For a month, as the *Gabriel* plunged through rolling seas, the days were all alike—a dreary succession of calm and fog, wind and rain. In early August some Siberian Chuckchees appeared, paddling their skin boats, but they could not be talked into coming aboard the *Gabriel.* Two days later Bering and his crew sighted and named St. Lawrence Island. Bucking strong head winds, they passed through the waters now known as the Bering Strait. At one time Bering was at a point where only fifty-four miles separated East Cape, Siberia, from Prince of Wales, Alaska, but fog prevented him from discovering that fact. He decided that an arm of the Pacific Ocean must divide Asia and America, and at last turned back toward Russia.

BERING'S SECOND TRIP

More than five years had passed when Bering returned to St. Petersburg, and Peter the Great was dead. No one was satisfied with Bering's report, and the Empress declared that Bering must again search for the possible land link. He was also to "explore the North American coast as far south as the Spanish possessions in Mexico." It was June of 1741 before Bering was again ready to sail the icy North Pacific in another vessel, the *St. Peter.* At noon on July 16, Bering and his men sighted the mainland of Alaska. Before them rose a majestic mountain that they named Mount St. Elias. Four days later they discovered Kayak Island and a party was sent ashore in two longboats.

Kayak Island held many fascinations for the Russian explorers. Among the plants they saw was Alaska's state flower, the forget-me-not. The people had vanished from the huts of logs and rough planks that they had roofed with bark and dried grass. Inside the dwellings were copper pots and plates, a whetstone, a rattle made of clay, some broken arrows, bits of dried fish, and a strand of rope made of seaweed. Behind them was a mountain covered with a thick forest. The Russians could find no trace of a road. Bering seemed to feel this deserted place was evil and sailed away as soon as he could.

Beating a course to the south-southwest through fog, rain, drenching gales, and pounding waves, the *St. Peter* pushed homeward. Sailors began to come down with scurvy, and in September Bering fell ill. It was a miserable voyage. By November the steersman was so weak that two men had to hold him up as he stood at the helm. Not until December did the *St. Peter* reach the Commander Islands off the Kamchatka Peninsula. There Bering died. He was buried on a sandy hillside with a plain Greek cross marking his grave. Of the seventy-seven men who had sailed with Bering, thirty-one had died by mid-January. But Bering's crew brought back proof that there was a plentiful supply of fur-bearing animals, such as the sea otter, in the region they had visited. And there was money to be made in the fur trade, if a man was willing to take the risks.

THE RUSSIAN FUR TRADERS

In 1745, Michael Novidiskov became the first white man to sail to Attu, the extreme western islet of the Aleutian chain. Soon others followed. They were cruel conquerors, these Russian traders, and it is claimed that many Aleuts committed suicide rather than suffer under the Russians. But the rulers in St. Petersburg were interested in their ten per cent of the profits from each voyage. They had no feeling for the welfare of the people who lived in that far-off country they called "great land" or "mainland"—in Aleut, *Al-ay-ek-sa.*

POOR RICHARD IN PHILADELPHIA

Franklin turns his mind to many projects, including Poor Richard's Almanack.

While the Russians were busy attempting to gain a hold on the far northern regions of the continent, life was changing in the colonies along the Atlantic seaboard. America's first theater was built in Williamsburg, Virginia, in 1716. Five years later Gustavus Hesselius, a Swedish immigrant to Delaware, received the first public grant as an artist when he was commissioned to paint "The Last Supper" for the Church of St. Barnabas in Queen Anne Parish, Maryland.

In 1731, John Bartram established America's first botanical gardens near Philadelphia, and that same year America's first public concert was given "at Mr. Pelham's great room" in Boston. An almshouse (poorhouse) supported by public funds, probably the first of its kind, was established in Philadelphia in 1732, and two years later William Bull of South Carolina became the first American to receive a medical degree. A performance of *Flora, or Hob in the Well* brought the opera to Charleston—and America—in 1735, and in 1737 New York's Trinity Church got the colonies' first organ.

These were also years when that remarkable young man, Benjamin Franklin, began to make his influence felt in Philadelphia. By 1729, Ben had prospered to the point where he had become owner and publisher of the *Pennsylvania Gazette.* Two years later he established the first circulating library in America. No one knew quite what to expect next from Ben's restless mind. He flew a kite in a rainstorm to prove that lightning was a form of electricity. His long list of inventions included the lightning rod, a stove, bifocal glasses, and a rocking chair. He organized the first fire department in Philadelphia, helped to organize the first hospital in America, reformed the city's police system, and founded the school that became the University of Pennsylvania.

From 1732 to 1757, however, Franklin's greatest gift to colonial America was the publication of *Poor Richard's Almanack.* Aside from the Bible, no publication was more popular in the average home. Ben had a way of belonging to Americans. He understood why they believed and acted the way they did. The sayings that he composed for *Poor Richard* were more than catchy phrases, easy to remember.

When Ben wrote, "A penny saved is a penny earned," or "Little strokes fell great oaks," he was speaking of the qualities of thrift and industry a person needed to get ahead in the colonies. Some 10,000 copies of *Poor Richard's Almanack* were sold each year. Colonial America liked Ben's homely advice, agreeing with him that "God helps them that help themselves."

A BLOW FOR FREEDOM

John Peter Zenger, a New York printer, fights for a free press in America.

The growth of newspapers in the colonies was another sign that America was shaping a new life in the New World. Philadelphia's first newspaper, the *American Weekly Mercury,* began publication in 1719. New York followed with the *Gazette* in 1725, as did Maryland, with the *Maryland Gazette* of Annapolis in 1727. The *South Carolina Gazette* at Charleston and the *Rhode Island Gazette* at Newport began publication in 1732.

John Peter Zenger, a poor German printer whose little shop in New York City barely provided for his family, struck the blow that changed newspapers in America. Like many New Yorkers, Zenger watched with displeasure the highhanded actions of William Cosby, who became the royal governor in 1732. Cosby would give no grants of land to settlers unless he was guaranteed a personal profit. He dealt harshly with the Quakers. In order to rule as he pleased, he dismissed the chief justice of the colony's supreme court. Since the publisher of the *Gazette* was also the public printer, no criticism of Cosby was permitted in the columns of the city's only newspaper.

Infuriated citizens appealed to Zenger. Would he publish a rival newspaper if they provided the money? Zenger pointed out that he needed more than money. He was poor in English spelling and grammar. No matter, replied his friends. The articles would be written for him. Under these circumstances the New York *Weekly Journal* appeared. Article after article pictured Cosby and his court party as scamps. New Yorkers read the *Journal* with eyes popping and tongues wagging. Often Zenger had to print extra editions to meet the demand.

Cosby struck back by charging Zenger with having made "seditious libels" which tended to fill the minds of the people with "contempt of His Majesty's government." Zenger was jailed and the bail was set so high that he had no hope of gaining his release. The two attorneys who offered to defend him were disbarred so that they could not handle the case. A young lawyer, no match for Cosby's attorney general, was appointed by the court.

The greatest lawyer in the colonies in thoses days was Andrew Hamilton of Philadelphia. Troubled with gout, Hamilton described himself as "old and weak." The trip from Philadelphia to New York was long and difficult, and no one could have blamed Hamilton if he had begged off defending Zenger. But this grand old man put the principle involved in this case before his personal comfort. Unless the people had a right to complain against "the arbitrary attempts of men in power," what justice did life offer them?

ZENGER STANDS TRAIL

John Peter Zenger stood trial on August 4, 1735. Stirred by the case, people crowded into the little courtroom. Then came the dramatic moment—the door opened and famous old Andrew Hamilton hobbled on his gout-stricken feet into the room. All at once the members of Cosby's official party looked uneasy. With dark glances they followed Hamilton as he slowly lumbered to his seat.

The attorney general presented the charge to the jury—the articles Zenger had published were "false, scandalous, malicious, and seditious." Old Hamilton thundered back that he knew perfectly well Zenger's articles were "libelous." Could the attorney general prove they were "false"? But the governor's party stood by the accepted law of England at the time: Truth was no defense. Persons who made statements that tended "to disquiet the minds of the people" must be punished.

Such law, Hamilton knew was the weapon of tyrants. The only way he could save Zenger—and

The trial of Peter Zenger in 1735, on charges of libeling the governor of New York, was a victory for free speech.

freedom of the press in America—was to convince the jury of this. He spoke brilliantly. If men were denied the right to write and speak their minds about the conduct of men in power, what then? "The next step may make them slaves," said Hamilton. He also said: "The loss of liberty to a generous mind is worse than death. . . . The man who loves his country prefers its liberty to all other considerations, well knowing that without liberty life is a misery."

The jury was out but a few minutes. It gave its verdict: "Not guilty!" Cheers burst from the crowd. Old Andrew Hamilton bowed, having won a victory that would make him remembered forever by freedom-loving men.

A COLONY OF DEBTORS

Oglethorpe colonizes Georgia with settlers from English debtors' prisons.

Another man who struck a blow against injustice was James Oglethorpe. During the Eighteenth Century, anyone in Great Britain who failed to pay money he owed could be thrown into jail. An architect named Robert Castell, imprisoned for this reason, contracted smallpox and died. Castell had been a close friend of James Oglethorpe, who, as a member of Parliament, now made an investigation of English debtors' prisons. His findings created a scandal. Jailers and their deputies, he reported, treated prisoners brutally, made them pay enormous prices for small comforts, and were guilty of many other crimes. Oglethorpe could not forget the misery of these prisoners. They deserved a new life, a better life—and thus he came to the idea of planting the colony of Georgia in the New World.

Hardheaded, practical considerations led the British government to listen to Oglethorpe's plan of bringing debtors to America. There they could "not only gain a comfortable subsistence for themselves and families, but also strengthen our colonies and increase the trade, navigation, and wealth of these our realms." What the king wanted more than anything else was a new buffer land between his now prosperous colony of South Carolina and Spanish and French troublemakers to the south and west. So Georgia was created as a colony that would extend from the Atlantic to the Pacific Oceans, with the Savannah and Altamaha Rivers as its northern and southern boundaries. The king did not worry over the fact that he was claiming parts of Florida, Louisiana, and Texas, and including Albuquerque, Socorro, and other New Mexico settlements in Georgia's territory.

Oglethorpe sailed for America in November, 1732, with 116 settlers. After seven stormy weeks at sea, the voyagers reached Charleston. Oglethorpe plunged at once into building his new state in the wilderness. He was a natural leader and a man who was friendly

Tomochichi, a chief of the Yamacraw tribe, was given a big welcome when Oglethorpe took him to London.

to everyone. Quickly the Indians came to trust and love him. He welcomed to Georgia people of many religious faiths—Protestants from France, Jews from Germany and Portugal, Lutherans and Moravians from the Rhineland districts, Presbyterians from the Scottish Highlands. Georgia also became a colony where Negro slavery was prohibited.

An article in the Charleston *Gazette* described the kind of leader Oglethorpe was: "He's extremely well beloved by all his people. The general title they gave him is *father*. If any of them is sick, he immediately visits them. If any difference arises, he's the person that decides it." Before Oglethorpe returned to England in March, 1734, he had established eleven communities among the forests on the banks of the Savannah River. The largest town was Savannah, with neat gardens, wide streets, and ample provision for houses, churches, and water supply.

Among those who accompanied Oglethorpe when he returned to England were Tomochichi, ninety-year-old chief of the Yamacraw Indians, his wife, his grandnephew, and five braves. Londoners treated the Indians as though they were visiting royalty. They were welcomed with the ringing of bells. They were taken to fairs, to shops, to the theater, and reviews of troops were staged in their honor. The royal household greeted them, for Tomochichi was a dignified old man who changed many British ideas about the so-called savages of America. When it came time for Tomochichi and his party to return home, the chief could not hide his grief at leaving Oglethorpe. The occasion, the old Indian said, "was like the day of death."

Oglethorpe knew how to win new friends and support for his colony. Among the gifts he had brought from America were thirty pounds of raw Georgia-grown silk that he had woven into a dress for the queen, which won her affection for both Oglethorpe and his colony. The king was more interested in a plan to build a chain of twenty forts as a safeguard against the Spanish and French. After a year and a half in England, Oglethorpe was anxious to return to his beloved Georgia.

THE SPANIARDS THREATEN GEORGIA

Troubled years were ahead. The Spaniards at St. Augustine did not like the rapid growth of the colony to the north. They liked it even less when they learned how Oglethorpe was beginning to string his forts along the frontier.

The Spaniards demanded that the British clear out of all of Georgia and South Carolina below Port Royal. Oglethorpe's reply was to prepare for battle. In July, 1742, a Spanish fleet of thirty-six vessels, bringing a land force of 3,000, entered the harbor at St. Simons. Oglethorpe's army, even including friendly Indians, numbered less than 1,000. "I know the enemy are far more numerous than we," he told his soldiers, "but I rely on the valor of our men, and by God's help, I believe we will be victorious."

OGLETHORPE ATTACKS

Oglethorpe planned a sneak attack at night upon the Spanish encampment at St. Simons. Cautiously he moved along a road that was protected by a dense live oak forest on one side and a deep swamp on the other. Nearing the camp, a Frenchman in Oglethorpe's little army fired his musket and deserted to the enemy.

Oglethorpe decided to fight trickery with trickery. He wrote a letter that made the deserter seem to be a spy planted among the Spaniards. The letter told the "spy" to persuade the Spaniards that the Georgian forces were weak and to attack at once. If the Spaniards would not attack, the letter went on, then the "spy" was to persuade the Spaniards to remain at St. Simons three days longer. By then a British fleet with 2,000 land forces would attack St. Augustine. All this "information," of course, was nonsense and, as Oglethorpe had carefully planned, the letter was carried "by accident" to the Spanish commander.

The trick worked and the French deserter was hanged as a spy. Then some vessels from Carolina, appearing by luck, were mistaken for the British fleet sailing to St. Augustine. The Spaniards made a hasty attack along the road flanked by live oak forest and swamp. Oglethorpe and his little army had set a perfect ambush, and almost the whole Spanish attacking force was captured or killed. A second wave of Spaniards, pushing forward to relieve their comrades, also was raked mercilessly by the flaming muskets of Oglethorpe's men. In confusion, the invaders fled to their ships.

Oglethorpe had outgeneraled the Spaniards and had probably saved both Georgia and South Carolina from conquest and ruin. Returning to England in 1743, he lived out his life there; he was almost ninety when he died. He had one deep regret: in later years Negro slavery was permitted in his beloved free colony of Georgia, and by 1760, one third of the inhabitants of the colony of Georgia were slaves.

WAR CLOUDS

British and French interests vie for power in the Ohio River Valley.

In the ancient European city of Aix-la-Chapelle, a famous treaty was signed in 1748 by officials from Great Britain, France, Holland, Germany, Spain, and Genoa. They hoped the treaty would bring at least a hundred years of peace. Yet the ink of their signatures had scarcely dried before those old foes—France and England—began sowing the seed of future war in their colonies in the New World. There trouble began to build up over the rich and undeveloped Ohio Valley.

The members of the Ohio Land Company had no intention of letting the French take any part of the vast regions claimed by the Virginia colony. Although the land originally granted to Virginia had been whittled away to provide for the colonies of Maryland, the Carolinas, and Pennsylvania, Virginia in 1750 remained an enormous empire stretching into the mists of an unexplored wilderness. Virginia territory included what today is the western part of Pennsylvania and also the states of West Virginia, Kentucky, Ohio, Indiana, Illinois, Michigan, and Wisconsin.

What were the possibilities for trade and settlement in these lands? The Ohio Land Company wanted to know the answer, for it was preparing to push westward. In the autumn of 1750 it hired Christopher Gist, a bold woodsman and friend of the Indians, to cross the mountains and report on the country.

Gist was to report on the best mountain passes, explore the land as far as the falls of the Ohio River (at present-day Louisville), search out valleys that could be cultivated, and learn the strength of various Indian tribes. Meanwhile, the company sent to London for goods suitable for trade with the Indians.

GIST STARTS HIS JOURNEY

Gist plunged into the wilderness. He crossed the Blue Ridge Mountains and the Shenandoah Valley, waded through the snowdrifts in the Alleghenies, and swam the Ohio River. At Logstown the Muskingum Indians received him coldly. "You are come to settle the Indians' land," they said. "You never shall go home safe."

Gist was not easily frightened. He went on to meet the Ottawas, who were friendly with the French, and the Wyandots, who seemed glad to see him. At a Wyandot village he came face to face with George Croghan, whom Pennsylvania had sent into the wilderness to establish trade with the Indians of the Northwest. Croghan and Gist were working for rival groups, but they put aside their differences and continued the journey through the Indian territory together.

Across the Muskingum—the "beautiful river"—they traveled among the Delawares and the Shawnees until they came at last to the wonderful country of the Miamis. This confederacy of Indians was even more powerful than the Iroquois, and the British wanted them for allies. Strings of wampum were exchanged and a treaty of peace signed. At that moment four Ottawas appeared with presents from the French, and the chief of the Miamis set up the French flag beside the British flag. Then he spoke bitterly to the Ottawas:

"The path of the French is bloody, and was made so by them. We have made a road plain for our brothers, the English, and your fathers have made it foul and crooked, and have made some of our brethren prisoners. This we look upon as an injury done to us."

The chief of the Miamis turned his back on the Ottawas. The flag of France was taken down.

Gist started home in a happy mood. He traveled through the fine forests of the Kentucky bluegrass region, crossed the mountains, and after seven months reported to Lawrence Washington, a member of the Ohio Land Company, at Mount Vernon. Washington and Gist were pleased with what had been discovered on the expedition, but they knew it would not be easy to keep the French out of this country. They were soon proved right.

YOUNG GEORGE WASHINGTON

Washington warns the French to leave the Ohio River Valley.

On a crisp October day in 1753, a shy and solemn young man rode his horse down Duke of Gloucester Street in Williamsburg, Virginia. Ducks, geese, and pigs scattered across the road. But George Washington, who was then twenty-one years old, took little notice. His mind was on that duty that had called him to Williamsburg.

The Washingtons were well known in Virginia. George's great-grandfather, John Washington, had reached the colony in 1657, settling in Westmoreland County. George's own birth date was February 22, 1732, now that Great Britain had adopted the Gregorian calendar and moved the date ahead by eleven days. His boyhood had been spent at Ferry Farm on the Rappahannock River, opposite Fredericksburg.

AT MOUNT VERNON

For George, these happy years had been filled with rowing and fishing and swimming, with riding and hunting in the green hills. His schooling had been incomplete. He knew a little arithmetic, had his own idea of how to spell English words, and could stumble through a printed page as well as the average reader of the period. His father's death, when the boy was eleven, changed his life. In time George's half brother, Lawrence Washington, brought him to live on his estate at Mount Vernon.

To the end of his days George Washington would love this rich, fertile, tidewater country along the

Three portraits of Washington. The first, the earliest known, was painted by Charles Willson Peale in 1772. Charles' son, Rembrandt Peale, was only 17 when he painted the portrait at center. Later he did the one at right.

Potomac. A well-known man in the region was gruff old Colonel William Fairfax. His disposition was often as prickly as a porcupine, but he took to George. The boy was shy and polite and could ride a horse well—the marks of a gentleman to old Fairfax. He gave George his first job as a surveyor and told him how to invest his money. By the age of eighteen, George was already a landowner and a traveler who had crossed the Blue Ridge Mountains and knew how to get along with frontiersmen and Indians.

Lawrence Washington's health had never been good, and in 1751 he went to the West Indies in the hope that he would grow stronger in the mild climate of the islands. George went with him and came down with the smallpox. The disease left his face marked for the rest of his life.

The climate failed to help Lawrence. Within a few months he was dead, and the management of the estate at Mount Vernon fell to George. From the start, he was equal to the responsibility. Furthermore, he got along well with people, as was shown by his appointment to the rank of major in the Virginia militia.

GOVERNOR DINWIDDIE'S MISSION

George's reputation was growing. Governor Robert Dinwiddie thought highly of him—and that was why on this crisp October day George had come to Williamsburg.

Governor Dinwiddie wanted to send him on a mission, and he did not hide the fact that it was dangerous. The French, who were stringing their forts and trading posts along the Ohio River, continued to dispute British claims to the territory. Occasionally an English frontiersman was driven from his wilderness home. Sometimes he was scalped by an Indian who had drunk too much French brandy. Sometimes he was carried to captivity in Canada. Dinwiddie intended to give the French a stern warning: either stop invading British land along the Ohio or be pushed out.

Carrying this warning to the French was only part of the mission. Washington was also to judge the military strength of French settlements, select sites for British forts, and learn which side the Indians would support in case of war.

The governor admitted that there might be dangers no one could foresee. No one knew how far the party must travel to reach the French commander. It might be anywhere from 500 to 1,000 miles. The journey would be over strange mountains, through silent forests, and across rushing streams in a country best known for its wild Indians, bears, and rattlesnakes. Winter would bring snow and ice, frozen roads in the valleys and drifts in the mountains. But Washington agreed to undertake the job, and left that night for Fredericksburg to start organizing his expedition.

WASHINGTON IN THE WILDERNESS

As his guide, Washington chose Christopher Gist. His interpreter was Jacob Van Braam, a Hollander who had taught Washington how to fence. Four Indians who knew the country were also in the party. By late November the little group reached the forks of the Ohio, on the site of present-day Pittsburgh. From there Washington went on into the country of the Delawares.

Dealing with the Indians was a tricky business. Some were friends of the English; others pretended to be friends but could not be trusted. The sly Chabert de Joncaire, son of a French father and a Seneca mother, tried to get the Indians who accompanied Washington to desert him.

But young Washington handled himself well, and by mid-December he had reached Fort Le Boeuf. There he handed Dinwiddie's letter to Legardeur de St. Pierre, the French commandant. St. Pierre treated Washington with great politeness and gave him a reply to carry back to Williamsburg. It told Governor Dinwiddie that St. Pierre intended to do exactly as the French authorities ordered—which was a polite way of saying that if the English wanted to oust the French from the Ohio Valley, they would have to send soldiers and fight a war.

Gist wondered if Washington had the stamina to make the homeward journey over the mountains and through the snows that fell at this time of year. Gist need not have worried. He would learn that once Washington set himself to a task, he stayed with it until it was finished.

The party traveled on foot most of the way, and once they beat off an attack by Indians. Then, crossing the Allegheny River, cakes of floating ice tipped their raft over. Washington grabbed a raft log and fought his way, half frozen, to a deserted island. Gist now knew the quality of this young fellow.

WASHINGTON'S FIRST BATTLE

Washington heads for the Ohio with orders to drive out the French.

When Dinwiddie read St. Pierre's letter, he decided that Virginia must act. Washington, promoted in rank to lieutenant colonel, was placed in charge of raising a militia force. On his suggestion, plans were made to build a fort at the fork of the Ohio and the Monongahela Rivers. In April the Virginians set out with orders to "drive away, kill and destroy, or seize as prisoners all persons not the subjects of the king of Great Britain, who should attempt to take possession of the lands on the Ohio or any of its tributaries."

The French had also decided to act, as Washington quickly learned in a series of messages from Half King, a friendly Seneca chief. About 1,000 French troops with eighteen cannon had come down the Allegheny to the point where it forks with the Ohio and were occupying the area. Here they were raising a fort named Duquesne.

Washington's men numbered no more than 150, and he had only a few pieces of light artillery. But he pushed ahead until, late in May, he reached the banks of the Youghiogheny, about forty miles from Fort Duquesne. A runner from Half King brought him a warning: "Be on your guard. The French are near, and intend to strike the first English whom they see."

A nearby plain, called the Great Meadows, gave Washington a place to make his stand. Here he threw up a stockade, naming it, with grim humor, Fort Necessity. Gist brought further warning that the French had left their tracks within five miles of the Great Meadows. Another runner from Half King informed Washington that the French were waiting in ambush not far off.

A hard rain fell that night. Taking forty men, Washington started out through the darkness to reach Half King's camp, six miles away. Some time after sunrise, after he had been joined by the Indians, Washington led his troops down a trail through a pile of rocks. Suddenly a French sentry appeared. The battle was on.

Washington threw his own musket to his shoulder, and in fifteen minutes the fight was over. Ten Frenchmen were killed and twenty-two taken prisoner. Only one Virginian had fallen.

Those fifteen minutes of skirmishing on May 28, 1754, drew first blood in the long and costly French and Indian War. On July 3, a strong French and Indian force stormed down on Fort Necessity in a battle that lasted nine hours. Washington knew that his army was too weak to hold off the foe, and at twilight he agreed to surrender.

Next morning, seated on a log outside the stockade, Washington worked out the terms of surrender with De Villiers, the French commander. The French prisoners must be returned. For a period of one year the Virginians must not try to build a fort west of the mountains. In return, Washington was allowed to lead his troops back home. The French had won the opening round.

BRADDOCK FUMBLES A BATTLE

Ignoring Washington's advice, Braddock falls into a French trap.

In June of 1754, twenty-five delegates from seven colonies met in the old city hall in Albany, New York, to try to solve some of their problems. Benjamin Franklin, representing Pennsylvania, came to the meeting with a "Plan of Union" already worked out in his mind. Weeks before, writing in the *Pennsylvania Gazette,* he had spoken sharply of the dangers that would face the colonies unless they agreed upon ways to defend themselves. Beneath a picture of a serpent, divided into as many parts as there were colonies, he had warned: "Join, or Die."

Under Franklin's plan, a grand council or congress would include forty-eight representatives elected by the colonies. Acting within British law, this congress would be responsible for all civil and military affairs. A president general, appointed by the king, would have the power to veto the acts of the congress.

Franklin admitted that his plan was far from perfect, but he felt it was a good start. No one seemed to like his ideas, however—least of all the authorities in England.

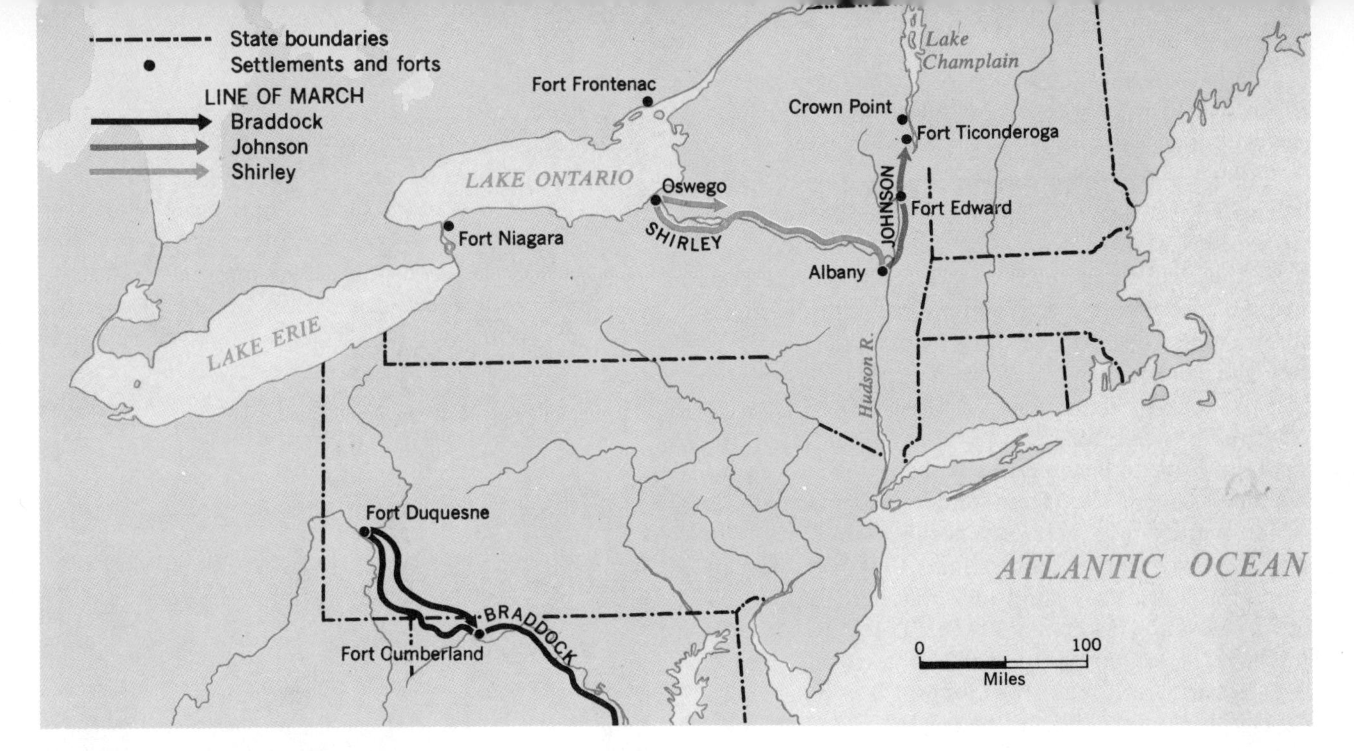

General Braddock planned three assaults on the French and Indians—aimed at Fort Duquesne, Fort Niagara and Crown Point.

Yet some plan of co-operation was badly needed. The French were still stirring up the Indians against English settlers in the wilderness. Governor Sharpe of Maryland was placed in temporary command of all colonial forces. Governor Dinwiddie of Virginia paid no attention to him and handled his own forces as he pleased. Unfortunately, Dinwiddie was no military expert. His Virginia militia became so disorganized that Washington threatened to resign his commission.

England then sent two regiments of regular troops to Virginia under the command of Edward Braddock. He was far from a good choice, for he knew nothing about wilderness warfare. In April of 1755, he called the royal governors of Massachusetts, New York, Maryland, North Carolina, Pennsylvania, and Virginia to a meeting in Alexandria, Virginia.

Hard facts had to be faced. Warm weather was approaching, and no one could doubt that the French and the Indians would soon take to the warpath. General Braddock proposed three expeditions to counter the threat.

The first, which he would lead, would strike at Fort Duquesne. A second force, led by Governor Shirley of Massachusetts, would aim at Fort Niagara at the mouth of the Niagara River, and at Fort Frontenac at the foot of Lake Ontario. A third force, under Sir William Johnson, would seize Crown Point on Lake Champlain.

Everyone was greatly cheered by Braddock's plan, and all but two colonial legislatures voted to support the coming campaigns. Georgia said it could not spare either men or money. The Quakers of Pennsylvania were opposed to all wars and would not take part in this one.

BRADDOCK'S CONCEIT

Braddock had more conceit than common sense. "The savages may be formidable to your raw American militia," he said to men like George Washington and Benjamin Franklin. "Upon the king's regulars and disciplined troops, it is impossible they should make any impression." When supplies were late in reaching Alexandria, Braddock sometimes raved like a madman. The American people, he shouted, were without honor, ability, and honesty.

Not until June 19 did Braddock move with his army. The French had been using the time to rally their Indian allies and were more than ready for the British. Washington, who served as an aide to Braddock, commanded the colonial forces in the lead. He wanted to press on and strike quickly, but the cautious British regulars held him back. At last, on July 8, Washington and his Virginians reached the forks of the Monongahela and Youghiogheny Rivers, about a dozen miles from Fort Duquesne.

The next morning, the British regulars advanced along the southern slopes of the Monongahela. After the fashion of European troops, they marched in neat, solid rows. Washington tried to warn Braddock that this would lead to disaster. There was only one way to fight Indians—in open ranks, man to man. "What!" Braddock said in a burst of anger. "A provincial colonel teach a British general how to fight?"

Refusing to take Washington's advice, Braddock crossed the river and sent his regulars forward in the same solid rows. Under a blistering noonday sun, Braddock and his redcoats plodded on—straight into an ambush. Suddenly bullets and arrows came at them from the woods, while the Indians whooped like demons.

"The Virginia troops showed a good deal of bravery, and were nearly all killed," Washington wrote his mother afterward. "The dastardly behavior of those they call regulars exposed all others, that were inclined to do their duty, to almost certain death. In despite of all the efforts of the officers to the contrary, they ran, as sheep pursued by dogs, and it was impossible to rally them."

Mortally wounded, Braddock was carried from the field. Four bullets pierced Washington's coat and two horses were shot from under him, so that his escape seemed a miracle. But nothing could save the day for the American forces, and they were forced to retreat. Their only good luck was that the French and Indians did not pursue them. Three nights later Braddock was buried by torchlight in the forest, and Washington read the funeral service. Then, wearily, his defeated army began the march home.

THE UNHAPPY ACADIANS

The British expel the Acadians from Nova Scotia.

For twenty years the Acadians in Nova Scotia had accepted British rule. Farming people of French descent, they lived for their families and their church. The Acadians asked only that they be free to follow their own religious beliefs and never be required to bear arms against fellow Frenchmen or their Indian friends.

But the presence of so many French Roman Catholics in Nova Scotia troubled the British. At first they tried to improve matters by bringing in more Protestant settlers from England. These immigrants founded the city of Halifax. French agents meanwhile urged the Acadians to withhold loyalty from England and stirred up the Indians against British rule. This only added to the friction—until fighting broke out in which the British defeated the French at Fort Beauséjour in June, 1755.

The British now demanded an unqualified oath of allegiance from the Acadians. When the Acadians refused, the British decided to take away their lands and expel them.

Despair filled the hearts of the simple Acadians. Some who tried to escape into Canada were hunted down in the woods and shot. An English officer boasted: "Our soldiers hate these French Catholics, and if they can find pretext to kill them, they will." Yet Colonel John Winslow, who was charged with scattering the Acadians among the English colonies, confessed: "The affair is more grievous to me than any service I was ever employed in."

Montcalm ate, danced, and sang with the Indians—and won their respect and friendship.

About 6,000 Acadians were uprooted from their homes. Families were broken up, some never to be reunited. The weeping Acadians were loaded on British ships and dropped along the shores of the Atlantic from the Penobscot to the Savannah Rivers. Many wandered off through the forest, going north into Canada or south into Louisiana. Others set out in open boats, hoping to find their way to Europe. Parents searched through the wilderness for their lost children, and the children wandered sadly from one Indian camp to the next in search of their parents. In later years, Henry Wadsworth Longfellow wrote a poem, *Evangeline,* which told the story of these exiles.

BRADDOCK'S PLANS FAIL

Except for this brutal seizure of the Acadians' land, the British had little to show for their first year of struggle with the French and Indians. None of Braddock's three schemes was successful. Governor Shirley's expedition against Forts Niagara and Frontenac got no farther than Oswego, at the western end of Lake Ontario. The most that could be said for the expedition to Crown Point was that the name of the lake the French called Holy Sacrament was changed to Lake George, in honor of George II, the British king.

The war dragged throughout 1756. The Earl of Loudon, who was sent to the colonies as commander in chief and governor of Virginia, was a tyrant who talked much and accomplished little. He expected to be obeyed without question, and the more foolishly he acted the less he could stand criticism.

FRANCE GAINS POWER

In contrast to Loudon, the French commander, Marquis Louis Joseph de Montcalm de Saint-Véran, knew how to deal with the Indians. When they staged one of their wild war dances, Montcalm danced with them. When they sang their war songs, he sang with them. To the Indians, Montcalm was the sort of general who was worth following.

In 1757 the situation of the English was growing desperate. They had been swept out of the Ohio region, and in northern New York the French and Indians held the upper hand. The French also controlled the St. Lawrence, the Great Lakes, and the valley of the Mississippi. French territory in America was about twenty times greater than British.

The colonies boiled with unrest, and late in the year Bostonians refused flatly to have Loudon's royal soldiers quartered in their city. Loudon acted in his usual way. If the Bostonians did not change their minds in forty-eight hours, he would send troops to force them to obey.

THE TURNING TIDE

Pitt comes to power in England and the colonists raise troops to fight the French.

But Loudon's days were numbered. In England, William Pitt had risen to power. Never would the American colonists find a warmer, more understanding friend in the British government. Pitt promised the colonies troops, money, and a share in their government. In Sir Jeffrey Amherst, General James Abercrombie, General James Wolfe, and Lord George Howe, he chose able military leaders. When aristocrats in England opened their law books and protested that Pitt was giving the colonies more freedom than the British Constitution intended, he replied: "The lawyers are not to be regarded in questions of liberty."

Confidence spread like a freshening breeze across America. When Pitt asked the colonies to raise 20,000 troops for the campaigns of 1758, the Americans did even better than that. New England alone enlisted 15,000. Abercrombie, taking over the supreme command in May, had 50,000 troops, a number almost equal to the entire French population in America.

Colonial soldiers who drilled under Lord Howe could feel that at last they were led by a British commander who understood wilderness fighting. Howe stripped uniforms of unnecessary ornaments. He ordered his men to cut their hair short. He had gun barrels painted black and cut down musket stocks so that they would not glitter in the sunlight and could be handled more easily in the forest. Taking a tip from the Indians, he put his men in leggings as a protection against thorns and insects.

In early July more than 1,000 bateaux (tapering, flat-bottomed river craft) and whaleboats carried Abercrombie's army down Lake George. He then marched his troops through the dense forests of the Adirondacks. He planned to attack Fort Ticonderoga, which guarded the natural trade routes between Lakes George and Champlain.

But Abercrombie's guides were not up to their jobs. Lord Howe, stumbling into an ambush, was killed by a musket ball. With his army in confusion, Abercrombie retreated to re-form his columns.

Within Fort Ticonderoga, Montcalm, with about 4,000 troops, was well prepared for the attack that came on July 8. Abercrombie failed to haul his cannon through the forest—his first mistake. Next he hurled his army against entrenchments too well protected for scaling parties to overcome. At the end of four hours, 2,000 of his soldiers were dead or wounded, and Abercrombie admitted defeat. "What a day for France!" Montcalm wrote afterward. "If I had had two hundred Indians to send out at the head of a thousand picked men . . . not many would have escaped."

Farther south, a British army of about 6,000, including 2,000 Virginians under Colonel George Washington, was marching on Fort Duquesne. General Joseph Forbes, in command of the expedition, was so ill he had to be carried on a litter. Washington advised him to move swiftly by the same route Braddock had taken, but he insisted on building a new road over the Alleghenies. So the army crept rather than marched, and Washington wrote angrily in a letter: "See how our time has been misspent! Behold how the golden opportunity has been lost, perhaps never more to be restored!"

By November, Forbes and his main army were still fifty miles from Fort Duquesne. Forbes wanted to put off the attack until spring, but Washington disagreed. He had heard that the Indians were growing tired and deserting the French. Now was the time to strike. Forbes gave in and Washington pushed ahead with his brigade. He reached a hill overlooking the fort, where the French had left only 500 troops. That night the French set fire to the fort and fled down the Ohio River in their boats.

WASHINGTON LEAVES FORT PITT

Next day Washington marched in and raised the British flag over the ruins. England now controlled the Ohio basin. The Virginians repaired the fort and renamed it Fort Pitt. Nearby, a little village called Pittsburgh sprang up. Washington, who was now twenty-six years old, marched home determined to leave military life forever. He had other plans. He would take his seat in the Virginia assembly, to which he recently had been elected, and he would marry a charming widow named Martha Dandridge Custis.

WOLFE CAPTURES QUEBEC

His victory marks the beginning of the end of French power in America.

William Pitt said that if England wished the co-operation of Americans, "we must be just and allow them freedom." He was a wise statesman, and both the king and Parliament did as he wished.

Now Pitt realized that the victory at Fort Duquesne meant more than winning the gateway to the West, important as that was. The Indians were beginning to wonder about their French friends. Perhaps the French were not so powerful as they claimed. This opened up an opportunity to hit hard at the French strongholds of Ticonderoga and Quebec. And once these were conquered, all of North America would be under British control

In 1759 the British forces began a two-pronged movement. One force, under Sir Jeffrey Amherst, moved up Lake Champlain. A second, under James Wolfe, sailed into the St. Lawrence River. The French, seeing themselves caught like a shell in a nutcracker, retreated from Fort Ticonderoga, and Amherst and his British troops quickly occupied it.

SKIRMISHING FOR QUEBEC

As Wolfe's forces approached Quebec, he must have been concerned at what he saw. The city rose before him on its rock cliff—a neat, tree-shaded community of stone houses, churches, palaces, convents, and gardens. But beyond the city was the loftier height of Cape Diamond. Wherever Wolfe turned, batteries of cannon frowned down upon him. He could also see the tents of Montcalm's army upon the Plains of Abraham, barring the only level approach to the city itself.

The impatient Wolfe was eager for action. The French sent fireboats floating down the Montmorency River, but they were pushed aside before they did any great harm. Wolfe tried to cross the Montmorency and storm the heights to the French camp, but a terrific thunderstorm came up and he was beaten back. When news of this failure reached England, some men said that Wolfe must be mad. "Mad!" King George II said. "Wolfe mad! I wish he'd bite some of the other generals!"

Wolfe was a general any king could admire—he was willing to fight. He might make mistakes, but he would learn by his blunders and he would stick to his job. In time, Wolfe would force the battle. He would make Montcalm risk his army.

Long weeks passed as Wolfe thought through his problem. On September 12, 1759, he was ready to move. As evening came on, he raised his wineglass and sang a little army ditty to his staff:

Why, soldiers, why
Should we be melancholy, boys?
Why, soldiers, why,
Whose business 'tis to die!

WOLFE STARTS THE ATTACK

Toward nine o'clock that night, Wolfe and his army boarded a fleet of flatboats, floating up the St. Lawrence River with the flood tide. To the French they appeared to be retreating, and cheers rang through the streets of Quebec. But Wolfe had carefully selected the cove where he landed. All at once the English were wading ashore and scrambling up the cliffs, 300 feet above the river. Startled sentries were swept aside. As dawn broke, the French looked upon a scene they could hardly believe. There on the open Plains of Abraham before their city stood 5,000 British troops.

Marching forward to meet his English enemies, Montcalm warned his soldiers: "If it is necessary to fight them, it is necessary to crush them." The two armies were about equal in size when they collided with deadly volleys of muskets. The British stood their ground, then charged with their bayonets. Standing in the midst of the charge, Wolfe urged his men on. Then he was struck by bullets in the head, abdomen, and breast.

"Support me," Wolfe cried to an officer nearby. "Do not let my brave soldiers see me drop. The day is ours—keep it."

The dying general was led to the rear. An officer shouted, "They run! They run!"

"Who runs?" Wolfe asked feebly.

"The enemy, sir. They give way everywhere."

Wolfe spoke his last words on earth: "Now, God be praised. I die happy!"

QUEBEC SURRENDERS

Wolfe did not know that his brave foe, Montcalm, had also been mortally wounded and would die the next morning. The retreat of the French from the Plains of Abraham doomed Quebec, and five days later the city surrendered. Other campaigns in 1760

From a cove below the Plains of Abraham, Wolfe's men climbed the forbidding cliffs and surprised the French.

completed the British conquest of Canada. But before the news could be brought to London, King George II died, at the age of seventy-six.

The war with the French and Indians officially ended with the signing of the Treaty of Paris on February 10, 1763. France ceded to England all claims to territory east of the Mississippi River and north of the latitude of the Iberville River (slightly below Baton Rouge). New Orleans and Louisiana were ceded to Spain. Thus France's dream of a North American empire was brought to an end. By the same treaty, Spain, which had been at war with England, ceded all of Florida to Great Britain. The English claimed, at last, almost half of the continent.

THE REVOLT OF PONTIAC

An Ottawa chief battles the British.

On an April day in 1763, in a meadow near Detroit, many Indian tribes gathered. They included the Ottawas, the Miamis, the Wyandots, the Chippewas, the Potawatomies, the Mississaugues, the Shawnees, the Foxes, the Winnebagoes, and the Senecas. The meeting seemed to be a peaceful one. Children romped at their games, men smoked their pipes, and old squaws exchanged gossip.

But the meeting had another purpose. Pontiac, the great Ottawa chief, rose in war dress and spoke of the danger they all faced from the English. But he had a plan. Cunningly, he described how they could win over the English. They must pretend friendship until they gained admission to British forts. Then they would turn on the English and stain the ground with their blood. The other tribes liked the plan and agreed to go on the warpath with the fierce Pontiac.

Using trickery, he soon captured every post west of Oswego, New York, with the exception of the forts at Niagara, Pittsburgh, and Detroit. A good example of his trickery was what happened at Fort Michillimackinack. Here, on the plain outside the fort, the squaws and braves came daily to play a game of ball. It was exciting to watch, and officers from the fort wandered beyond the gates to see the fun. Suddenly the ball sped toward the fort—and the officers. The braves chased after it. Then the braves turned on the officers, while the squaws threw back their blankets and brought out the hatchets they had been hiding. The Indians soon captured the fort.

THE END OF THE REVOLT

Pontiac's terror spread a bloody trail over a wide area, and British forces set out to put down the Indian revolt. On the last day of July, 1763, they planned to take the Ottawa chief by surprise on the outskirts of Detroit. But it was Pontiac who sprang the surprise, striking the British unexpectedly at a little brook, afterward called Bloody Run. Encouraged by their victories, the Indians carried the war to Detroit and Fort Pitt. There was bitter fighting until the British at last gathered enough men to stop the Indians. Pontiac fled, escaping into the country of Illinois, where he tried to rally other tribes to his cause. It was here that the end came. In 1769, Pontiac attended a celebration in Cahokia, Illinois. During the celebration, an Indian who had been bribed with a barrel of whiskey crept up behind him and killed him with a hatchet.

ENGLAND TURNS BACKWARD

George III becomes king and chooses advisers who want to tax the colonists.

The young prince who now became King George III of England was popular with the people. He had many difficult problems to solve, and William Pitt offered his help. But the young ruler turned to the Earl of Bute for advice.

A Scottish nobleman, Bute was the king's tutor and favorite companion. He was gay and handsome, but his good qualities seemed to end right there. He had neither the nimble mind of Pitt, nor his feeling for human rights. The result was that England turned backward in its dealings with the American colonists. Again Americans were treated like distant cousins rather than equal members of the British family.

Bostonians cheered James Otis, foe of the hated tax writs.

It was at Bute's suggestion that George III sent secret agents to America to judge the "character" of the colonists. Bute wanted to force Americans to pay taxes to the mother country. His government imposed upon the colonies "writs of assistance." These were court orders that allowed royal agents to enter the shops and houses of Americans to collect taxes.

The writs, first issued in Massachusetts in 1761, stirred up a storm. James Otis, a fiery lawyer, carried the cause of the colonists to a trial in the town hall in Boston. "A man's house is his castle," said Otis. "This writ, if it should be declared legal, would totally annihilate [destroy] this privilege." With such writs, customhouse officers could enter any house they pleased. Otis declared that he would sacrifice "estate, health, applause and even life" to fight such an unjust law.

When James Otis left the town hall, the people made it clear that they supported him. They cheered and tossed their hats into the air. Although the royal government legalized the issuing of the writs, they were never really enforced.

GRENVILLE REPLACES BUTE

Bute was forced to resign as the King's chief counselor, and George III replaced him with George Grenville. Grenville was Pitt's brother-in-law, but the Americans found that he was no better than Bute. Under Grenville's program, the British House of Commons voted unanimously in 1764 that it had the right to tax the colonists even though they were not represented in Parliament.

The assembly of Massachusetts responded angrily, declaring that "no man can justly take the property of another without his consent." Thus was born the rallying cry of the next ten years—Americans would never agree to "taxation without representation."

But George III and his counselors had a problem. The French and Indian War had cost a great deal, and Britain badly needed money for the army and navy. Why shouldn't the colonists pay their share? But the colonies could not be depended upon to raise the money themselves. The only way out was to tax the people directly.

And so, in 1764, Grenville suggested the Stamp Act. Americans would be required to put certain stamps on all documents, such as contracts and mortgages, as well as on newspapers and pamphlets. The money paid for the stamps would go to the British government.

Once again the colonists cried out against taxation without representation. The assemblies in Massachusetts, Connecticut, New York, Pennsylvania, Virginia, and South Carolina, each took a firm stand against the Stamp Act. But George III was a stubborn man, who insisted that the Stamp Act must be passed to teach Americans "obedience to the laws and respect for the legislative assembly of the kingdom." By March, 1765, the Stamp Act had passed both houses of Parliament.

THE SONS OF LIBERTY

Heeding opposition to the Stamp Act the king recalls Pitt, and the act is repealed.

No one expected the wave of protest that swept the colonies after the Stamp Act was passed. Groups of men called "Sons of Liberty" were formed in widely scattered towns. Men gathered in taverns, in stores, and along the roadsides to speak out against the law. Ministers preached against it on Sundays. In Virginia the fiery backwoods statesman, Patrick Henry, shouted that only Americans could tax themselves. Some members of the Virginia House of Burgesses cried, "Treason! Treason!" Henry answered, "If this be treason, make the most of it!"

Agents appointed by England to collect the taxes due under the Stamp Act ran into trouble. In Boston the Sons of Liberty hanged an effigy, or dummy figure, of the collector from a large elm called the "Liberty Tree." An angry mob roared: "Death to the man who offers a piece of stamped paper to sell!" Another mob in Providence, Rhode Island, forced the collector to resign, and in New York City the Sons of Liberty burned the collector's coach. In New Jersey, Maryland, Virginia—practically everywhere in the colonies—the same kind of thing was happening.

Angered by the Stamp Act, the Sons of Liberty in New York burned the coach of the tax collector.

The Stamp Act took effect on November 1, 1765—a day the colonists called "Black Friday." Church bells rang as though tolling for the death of liberty. Mock funerals paraded through the streets in many cities, towns, and villages. Almost all business was stopped. Rather than buy goods from England, young ladies who called themselves "Daughters of Liberty" met to spin cloth and knit stockings.

In England, George III asked William Pitt to organize a new government. Sick with gout, Pitt hobbled on legs wrapped in flannel to address Parliament. Boldly he declared that, in his opinion, the royal government had no right to tax the colonies without representation. Americans, he said, were "subjects of this kingdom, equally entitled with yourselves to all the natural rights of mankind and the peculiar privileges of Englishmen."

THE STAMP ACT REPEALED

Grenville fought back, calling the colonists rioters on the brink of treason. Pitt spoke against his brother-in-law: "He tells us that America is obstinate—America is in open rebellion. I rejoice that America has resisted. Three millions of people so dead to all the feelings of liberty as to voluntarily submit to be slaves, would have been fit instruments to make slaves of the rest." Pitt called for the repeal of the Stamp Act, and in March 1766 Parliament did as he asked.

When the news reached Boston, the Sons of Liberty gathered under their Liberty Tree to celebrate the victory. Bells rang in New York City, and a petition was sent to the assembly to build statues of Pitt and George III. But on both sides of the Atlantic there were some people who wondered how long this patched-up peace between the mother country and the colonies could last. Some Englishmen said the king had been made to bow to his subjects. If this sort of thing were allowed to go on, the British Empire would soon fall apart.

SAVING THE LIBERTY POLE

Friction between Bostonians and British troops leads to the Boston Massacre.

William Pitt had been known as the "Great Commoner." When the king made him Viscount Pitt and Earl of Chatham, his popularity dropped sharply. People said that in his old age he was seeking honor and comfort. Pitt's health was failing and he was no longer the real leader of the royal government. Again Parliament forced taxes upon the colonies. This time, if necessary, soldiers would see that the law was obeyed.

New taxes were placed on a number of articles—on tea, glass, paper, painters' colors, and various other imports. Britain set up a board of tax collectors which was not under the control of the colonial assemblies.

TROUBLE IN NEW YORK

Trouble began in the spring of 1767. Troops reaching New York City were jeered by the Sons of Liberty, who had put up a Liberty Pole to show that they were against the taxes. It was torn down by

Bostonians jeered at and snowballed the red-coated British troops, calling them "bloody-backs."

the troops, put up again, and once more hauled down. The Sons of Liberty bound their Liberty Pole with iron to resist the axes of the troops, who loaded their muskets. Only the action of the governor prevented bloodshed. The assembly was forbidden to meet until New Yorkers had a "respectful" attitude toward the royal troops.

A wave of protest rolled across the colonies, just as it had during the days of the Stamp Act. One assembly after another sent petitions to Parliament, whose members began to use words like "rebels," "traitors," and "open revolt." Royal troops were sent to Boston in 1768, and as the months went by, tempers on both sides grew shorter. On a January night in 1770 soldiers cut down Boston's Liberty Pole. They sawed it into small pieces and piled them in front of the meeting place of the Sons of Liberty. Another pole was put up on private property, purchased for that purpose.

Most of the people of Boston had decided not to buy any tea until the tax was removed. One Bostonian who opposed this was Theophilus Lillie, a merchant. He found one day that a mob of small boys had put up a post in front of his store. On it was a crudely carved head and a hand pointing out Lillie's store as a place to avoid. A neighboring merchant named Richardson, whose beliefs were the same as Lillie's, rushed out and tried to pull down the post. When a crowd pelted him with dirt and stones, he lost his head, fled into his store for a musket, and fired into the mob. One boy, Christopher Snyder, was killed and another person was wounded.

Boston made a special occasion of Christopher's funeral. A sign on his coffin read: "Innocence itself is not safe." Almost 1,500 persons marched in the procession to the grave as church bells tolled.

BOSTONIANS RIOT

But worse trouble was brewing. Early March brought a wet snow to Boston, and ice covered the ground. In the twilight, people began to crowd the streets. Some of the men carried clubs and, catching sight of the red-coated troops, they said, "Let's drive out these rascals. They have no business here—drive them out!" Others cried: "Town-born, turn out! Down with the bloody-backs!"

Market stalls were torn down to provide clubs. The soldiers pushed the people aside and ran to their barracks. A barber's boy, recognizing a passing soldier, shouted, "There goes a mean fellow, who will not pay my master for shaving him." A sentinel knocked down the boy with his musket.

THE BOSTON MASSACRE

The whole city seemed stirred up. Men were marching on the customhouse on King Street when the barber's boy said, "There's the scoundrel who knocked me down!" Angry voices shouted, "Let us knock *him* down. Down with the bloody-backs! Kill him! Kill him!"

The crowd threw snowballs and pieces of ice at the sentinel, who ran up the steps of the customhouse and called for help. Soldiers appeared, and more snowballs were thrown. A mulatto from Nantucket named Crispus Attucks rallied the mob with wild shouts: "Come on! Don't be afraid! They daren't fire! Kill 'em!"

He rushed forward, struggling to seize a soldier's musket. The soldier fired his gun and Attucks fell dead. Five other soldiers began shooting. Three men were killed and eight more wounded, and the crowd swiftly melted away.

Soon alarm bells were ringing, and drums beat out the call to arms. The streets echoed to the exciting cry: "The soldiers are murdering the people! To arms! To arms! Turn out with your guns!" But there was no more bloodshed. A British captain and eight soldiers were arrested and jailed on charges of murder.

Men like Samuel Adams and John Hancock, who wanted the colonists to break away from English rule, made the most of what happened that day. They called it the Boston Massacre, and they saw that the news was carried to every colony. They distributed an engraving made by Paul Revere, which showed British redcoats firing on defenseless Americans. John Adams, who one day would be President of the United States, later wrote that never was an event in American history more important "than the battle of King Street, on the 5th of March, 1770. The death of four or five persons, the most obscure and inconsiderable that could have been found upon the continent, has never yet been forgiven in any part of America."

To John Adams, however, and to Josiah Quincy, Jr., fell the task of defending Captain Preston and his soldiers against the charge of murder. Adams and Quincy had strong personal feelings, but as lawyers they carried out their duties as well as they could. Preston and six of the soldiers were declared not guilty. The other two, convicted of manslaughter, were branded on the hand with a hot iron.

THOMAS JEFFERSON IN WILLIAMSBURG

Jefferson becomes a lawyer, supports human rights, and opposes British taxes.

No one understood more clearly than John Adams what was happening in America. "The Revolution was effected before the war commenced," he said in later years. "The Revolution was in the minds and hearts of the people." There was another man who also recognized this fact, and who followed John Adams as President of the United States. He was Thomas Jefferson.

Jefferson was seventeen, a rail of a boy standing over six feet, when he arrived in Williamsburg, Virginia, to enroll as a student at William and Mary College. He had hair the color of a carrot, and with his bony arms and spindlelegs he made quite a sight jogging down Duke of Gloucester Street for his daily exercise.

But Jefferson had a mind of his own and was interested in everything that went on around him. He often studied fifteen or sixteen hours a day, and soon he was at the top of his class. Even more important, he attracted the attention of George Wythe.

JEFFERSON STUDIES LAW WITH GEORGE WYTHE

Wythe, whose name rhymes with Smith, was the first professor of law in America. He would count many famous men among his students—men like Henry Clay, Chief Justice John Marshall, and Edmund Randolph. But his favorite was Jefferson, who began to study under him about 1762. Never were teacher and student better suited to each other. Both had brilliant minds, a love for people, a sense of justice. And both were strong-willed, a fact that brought them into court one day on opposite sides of a famous trial.

The belief that the law should protect human rights led Jefferson to take the case of a young mulatto boy named Sam Howell. In Virginia the law said that a child born of a slave woman was also a slave. But Sam was the grandson of a slave, and Jefferson said that there was a law above the law of Virginia. This higher law, under which "all men are free," came from God. Jefferson spoke boldly to the frowning judge: "So that the position as first laid down is proven, that the act of 1705 makes servants of the first mulatto, that of 1723 extends it to her children, but that it remains for future legislation, if any shall be found wicked enough, to extend it to the grandchildren."

As Jefferson expected, he lost the case. But he had come to grips with an important principle. Before long, that principle would be stated in the Declaration of Independence: "All men are created equal."

George Wythe was only one of the men with whom Jefferson formed warm friendships while he was in Williamsburg. Among them were Patrick Henry, George Washington, Edmund Pendleton, Richard Henry Lee, and George Mason.

In 1765 Jefferson heard Patrick Henry speak out against the Stamp Act. He was in the crowd that jeered at the tax collector, who left Williamsburg as quickly as possible. In the spring before the Boston Massacre, Jefferson was a member of the Virginia House of Burgesses that opposed the new taxes ordered by the royal government. With other citizens of Williamsburg, he had stared angrily at Paul Revere's engraving of the Boston Massacre. And so Jefferson came to know the men and events that helped to shape the future of the country.

THE *GASPEE* AFFAIR

A British schooner is lured onto a sandbar and burned.

To avoid paying the taxes on imported goods, some of the colonists turned to smuggling. A favorite place for smugglers was Narragansett Bay in Rhode Island, and in March, 1772, the British decided to do something about it. They sent an armed schooner, the *Gaspee,* under the command of Lieutenant Dudingston, to patrol the bay. Dudingston liked power and did not hesitate to use force. His actions outraged the Rhode Islanders, and John Adams said, "His brutal, hoggish manners are a disgrace to the royal navy and the king's service."

One of Dudingston's orders was that all packet ships must lower their flag as a sign of respect when they passed the *Gaspee.* On June 9, the packet *Hannah* failed to lower her flag, and Dudingston set out after her. But the tide was going out, and the crew of the *Hannah* maneuvered their ship so as to mislead the *Gaspee.* Suddenly the British schooner was scraping bottom, hopelessly grounded.

News of the *Gaspee* quickly spread through the nearby city of Providence. The excited colonists saw that here was their chance to rid themselves of Dudingston. That night, sixty-four armed men, commanded by Captain Abraham Whipple, took their places in eight boats and rowed out to the *Gaspee.* Dudingston was wounded by a shot from one of Whipple's men. Boarding the *Gaspee,* the colonists put the crew on shore and set the ship afire. When the flames reached the powder magazine, there was a tremendous explosion—and that was the end of the *Gaspee.*

The furious British offered $5,000 for the capture of the leader of the Providence rebels. In time, they discovered Whipple's part in the affair, and a British admiral sent him a sharp note:

> *You, Abraham Whipple, on the 10th of June, 1772, burned his majesty's vessel, the* Gaspee, *and I will hang you at the yard-arm.*
>
> *James Wallace.*

The captain replied good-humoredly:

> *Sir,—Always catch a man before you hang him.*
>
> *Abraham Whipple.*

THE BOSTON TEA PARTY

Bostonians disguised as Mohawk Indians dump three shiploads of tea into the harbor.

The refusal of Americans to buy tea was costing the British money. The warehouses of the East India Company were piled high with about 17,000,000 pounds of tea that could not be sold, and in 1773 the company asked the royal government for help. The government agreed that the company's agents

Crowds on Boston Harbor docks cheered as patriots boarded the British tea ships and threw their cargoes overboard.

could sell the tea directly to the people of the colonies, instead of to the merchants. That way the tea would sell at a much lower price, the Americans would rush to buy such a bargain, the government would collect its tax, and the East India Company would be saved.

But as the ships carrying the tea approached the harbors of the colonies, it became clear that there would be no rush to buy. The merchants were angry because they would get no share of the profits, the smugglers had tea of their own to sell, and the ordinary colonist would not buy goods that had been taxed without his consent.

In New York City there was a meeting to thank those "patriotic" merchants who refused to handle the tea. In Philadelphia a large gathering of people in the yard of the State House cheered the declaration that the action of the East India Company was "a violent attack upon the liberties of America." Charleston stood firmly against doing business with the tea-ships. And on November 29, the following notice was posted throughout the city of Boston:

"Friends! Brethren! Countrymen!—That worst of plagues, the detested *tea,* shipped for this port by the East India Company, is now arrived in the harbor. The hour of destruction, or manly opposition to the machinations [plots] of tyranny, stares you in the face. Every friend to his country, to himself and to posterity [his descendants], is now called to meet at *Faneuil Hall,* at nine o'clock THIS DAY (at which time the bells will ring), to make united and successful resistance to this last, worst, and most destructive measure of administration."

The feeling in Boston rose, and on December 16 it boiled over. That evening a town meeting was told that the governor of Massachusetts had refused to send away the tea-ships. Samuel Adams then said that the meeting could do nothing more to save the country, and there was a shout from the gallery: "Boston harbor a teapot tonight! Hurrah for Griffin's Wharf!" As soon as the meeting ended, a number of men, many disguised as Mohawk Indians, hurried through the bright, cold, moonlit night toward Griffin's Wharf. One of them was George Hewes, who later wrote:

"When we arrived at the wharf, there were three of our number who assumed an authority to direct our operations, to which we readily admitted [agreed]. They divided us into three parties, for the purpose of boarding the three ships that contained the tea at the same time. . . . The commander of the division to which I belonged, as soon as we were on board the ship, appointed me boatswain, and ordered me to go to the captain and demand of him the keys to the hatches and a dozen candles. . . . We then were ordered by our commander to open the hatches, and take out all the chests of tea and throw them overboard, and we immediately proceeded to execute his orders, first cutting and splitting the chests with our tomahawks, so as thoroughly to expose them to the effects of the water. In about three hours . . . we had thus broken and thrown overboard every tea chest to be found. . . ."

It was, George Hewes remembered, the "stillest night" Boston had known for several months. Onlookers who tried to snatch up small parcels of tea for their own use had them knocked out of their hands. One old fellow, who tried to hide the tea in his hat, was turned upside down and lost tea, hat, and wig in a single shake. When daylight broke, the harbor was afloat with tea.

A WARNING TO KING GEORGE

Jefferson lists the colonists' grievances.

When word of the Boston Tea Party reached Williamsburg, many people nodded their heads in approval. On June 1, 1774, George III and his counselors punished the Bostonians by closing the city's port. Word of this, too, reached Williamsburg, and Virginians observed a day of prayer to show their sympathy for their fellow colonists in Massachusetts. Stubborn George III and his advisers never seemed to understand that their treatment of the colonies was driving them to act together in common defense. And each act carried them a step closer to breaking with Britain and forming a new nation.

That summer a call went out for all the colonies to send delegates to a continental congress that would meet in Philadelphia in September. Every colony but Georgia responded promptly. Thomas Jefferson had many ideas he wished to place before the Virginia delegates to the congress. But he was too ill to leave his home at the time, so he sent a long document to Williamsburg.

Jefferson's ideas shocked some of his friends. He listed the colonies' grievances against the king and his Parliament. Among them were restrictions on trade, unfair taxes, the dissolving of representative bodies of government, and the sending of armed troops. Jefferson warned the king:

"Open your breast, Sire, to liberal and expanded thought. Let not the name of George the third be a blot in the page of history."

And he also said, "The whole art of government consists in the art of being honest."

Day by day, America was drawing closer to the victory that must come first if ever it would be free—the victory which John Adams described so well and which could only be won within the minds and hearts of the people.

Throughout the night, Paul Revere rode toward Concord, warning the colonists that the British were on their way.

III ~ THE AGE OF REVOLUTION

from 1774 to 1783

ROOST OF REBELS

The colonies help Boston resist the British blockade.

By closing the port of Boston, George III intended to teach the other American colonies a lesson. They could expect the same treatment if they followed Boston's example and defied the royal government.

Bostonians scowled as British redcoats—"bloody-backs"—under General Thomas Gage paraded through the streets. In the harbor British men-of-war rode at anchor, their guns turned on the wharves and homes of old Boston.

The "bloody-backs" had orders to shoot anyone who made the least resistance to the blockade. Even so, General Gage was uneasy. Although the king believed that Gage's four regiments could handle anything that developed, the king did not know much about America. Boston alone had 15,000 inhabitants, and Massachusetts about 400,000. If the New Englanders decided to fight, they could quickly overcome Gage's puny force.

Gage had been in America nine years and had married the daughter of a prominent family in New Jersey. He was governor of Massachusetts as well as general of the army. He knew these people. He had fought with George Washington when Braddock had failed at Fort Duquesne, and he knew how Americans could fight. They were tough, hardy, and strong-minded.

Gage did his job well. Boston became a city of living ghosts. No merchant vessels could enter its harbor. Not one pound of hay, not one sheep or calf, could be landed at any wharf. Not a single passenger could be ferried across the river to Charlestown. Soldiers stood everywhere, and cannon pointed down from every hill, ready to fire at the first sign of an uprising. British warships guarded the harbor.

But the Bostonians soon found that they did not stand alone. Aid poured in from everywhere in the colonies. "Don't pay for a single ounce of tea," said Christopher Gadsden of South Carolina, who sent 200 barrels of rice and promised to send 800 more. Old Israel Putnam, a veteran of the French and Indian War, walked almost a hundred miles from his farm in Connecticut to lead a flock of one hundred sheep to Boston. From Georgia came sixty barrels of rice, from French Quebec 1,000 bushels of wheat, from Wilmington, North Carolina, 2,000 pounds in cash that had been raised within a week. Marblehead and Salem, old rivals in trade, opened their wharves to Boston merchants. From little New England villages came rye, flour, peas, cattle, oil, and fish. In Virginia, George Washington pledged fifty pounds to help the people of Boston.

THE MINUTEMEN TURN OUT

Once Lord North, the king's chief adviser, had called any union of the American colonies a "rope of sand." Now the colonists replied: "It is a rope of sand that will hang him." In every village, men were drilling with guns. Even small boys drilled with broomsticks for the defense of their homes. Forges glowed and hammers beat upon anvils as blacksmiths made guns, swords, and bayonets. On every farm men were making their own gunpowder and lead bullets. Massachusetts had called 12,000 volunteers to arms. They were known as Minutemen, because they stood ready to fight at a minute's notice.

Gage's worries increased. He ordered new fortifications built, but no Boston carpenter would work for him. To be on the safe side, Gage sent his soldiers to seize the gunpowder that the colonists had stored at Cambridge and Charlestown. Rumors spread as far as the Connecticut River that war had started.

Suddenly the roads swarmed with Minutemen marching on Boston. Some came on foot, with muskets slung across their shoulders. Some came on horses or mules, with swords hanging from their saddlebags. Finally convinced the stories were false, they returned home. It was estimated that 50,000 men had turned out. The "rope of sand" was growing sturdier.

THE FIRST CONTINENTAL CONGRESS

Delegates meet in Philadelphia to draw up a list of British wrongs.

In September, 1774, delegates arrived in Philadelphia from every colony except Georgia to organize the First Continental Congress. An argument over voting was settled by giving every colony an equal voice in the debates. The delegates were of various religious beliefs, and a dispute arose over whether each morning session should open with a prayer.

Massachusetts' Sam Adams, a Congregationalist, settled that issue: "I am no bigot. I can hear a prayer from a man of piety and virtue, who, at the same time, is a friend to his country." An Episcopalian minister was selected to give the prayer.

Each morning when the delegates met in Carpenters' Hall, the doors were locked so that their sessions could be kept secret. The delegates might have saved themselves the trouble; Joseph Galloway, leader of the Pennsylvania delegation, was probably a British spy. Otherwise, in the opinion of John Adams, the delegates were "a collection of the greatest men upon this continent in point of abilities, virtues, and fortunes." One thing was certain—they had minds of their own. Some argued that all government in America had ended, others that the situation could still be saved.

On October 8 the delegates resolved:

"That this Congress approve the opposition of the inhabitants of Massachusetts Bay to the execution of the late acts of Parliament; and if the same shall be attempted to be carried into execution by force, in such cases all America ought to support them in their opposition."

THE DECLARATION OF RIGHTS

The delegates drew up a Declaration of Rights, and listed the wrongs that had been done to the colonies by the royal government. They also agreed that the colonies would not use or import British goods, and would not export goods to Britain. This would go on until the government changed its treatment of the colonies. After eight weeks, the delegates decided their work was finished. Sam Adams spoke so that everyone could hear:

"I would advise persisting in our struggle for liberty, though it were revealed from Heaven that 999 men were to perish, and only one of a thousand to survive and retain his liberty. One such freeman must possess more virtue, and enjoy more happiness, than a thousand slaves."

BENJAMIN FRANKLIN IN LONDON

Ben Franklin represents the colonists in England and tells his hosts a fable.

It was soon clear that Americans meant to stand up for their rights, even at the risk of war. In April, another "tea party" took place, this time in New York. When a shipper tried to land a cargo of tea secretly, the Sons of Liberty found out about it and, as in Boston, disguised themselves as Mohawks and dumped it in the harbor. That October, in Annapolis, Maryland, the schooner *Peggy Stewart* was burned because her cargo included seventeen packages of tea. In December, another shipment of tea, this one stored in a warehouse in Greenwich, New Jersey, was set on fire and destroyed.

But the colonists had more on their minds than just destroying British tea. Mills began going up for the manufacture of gunpowder, and Minutemen went out to plow their fields with muskets slung across their backs. Whatever was coming, the colonists were determined to be ready for it.

GAGE SOUNDS THE ALARM

From Boston Gage sent London an alarming report. All New England was preparing for war, he wrote. He did not see how he could be expected to stand off this angry mob with the force he had. Let the mother country cut loose from the colonies. Then the colonies would turn on one another until they were exhausted by their own squabbling. George III answered: "The New England governments are now in a state of rebellion. Blows must decide whether they are to be subject to this country, or are to be independent."

Benjamin Franklin still represented the colonies in London. In a ticklish situation, he wrote a paper entitled, "Hints for Conversation upon the subject of Terms that may probably produce a Durable Union between Britain and the Colonies." Franklin's paper simply suggested that Englishmen in America should enjoy the same rights and privileges as Englishmen in the mother country.

Franklin puzzled the British. He was one of the greatest men of his age—gifted, well educated, quick-witted. He went everywhere in London and knew everyone, and although he made a few enemies, he also made hosts of friends. But the British never really understood Franklin's love of liberty. They were not able to understand how such a man could be so interested in the rights of a few backwoods farmers in America. And although Franklin was a persuasive speaker, he was never able to explain it to them.

By Christmas news of the acts of the Continental Congress reached London, and Franklin's position grew more uncomfortable. When Parliament met in January, 1775, Franklin heard himself described by the Earl of Sandwich as "one of the bitterest and most mischievous enemies this country has ever known." This did not trouble Franklin, who was a skillful diplomat. But as spring came on, he realized that he was wasting his time in London. Entertained by friends one night before he left for America, Franklin made up a fable for them:

THE EAGLE AND THE HARE

"Once upon a time, an eagle soaring around a farmer's barn and espying a hare, darted down upon him like a sunbeam, seized him in his claws, and remounted with him in the air. He soon found that he had a creature of more courage and strength than a hare, for which, not withstanding the keenness of his eyesight, he had mistaken a cat. The snarling and scrambling of the prey was very inconvenient, and, what was worse, she had disengaged herself from his talons, grasped his body with her fore limbs, so as to stop his breath, and seized fast hold of his throat with her teeth.

" 'Pray,' said the eagle, 'let go your hold and I will release you.'

" 'Very fine,' said the cat. 'I have no fancy to fall from this height, and be crushed to death. You have taken me up, and you shall stoop and let me down.'

The eagle thought it necessary to stoop accordingly."

Franklin's listeners had only to put England in the place of the eagle and America in the place of the cat to understand the moral.

THE WAR BEGINS

Paul Revere warns the Minutemen, and the first shot is fired in Lexington.

In February of 1775, some small boys in Boston were angry. Gage's soldiers kept knocking down the snow hills they had built on Boston Common for sledding. The boys complained to the captain, who would do nothing. So they carried their complaint to General Gage, telling him that they had come "to demand satisfaction." Gage accused the youngsters of having been taught "rebellion" by their fathers.

The boys stood their ground. Coming to Gage had been their own idea. For the third time yesterday their snow hills had been trampled down by the soldiers, and the captain had laughed at their complaint. "We will bear it no longer," they said.

Gage shook his head. "The very children here," he told a fellow officer, "draw in a love of liberty with the air they breathe." Then, turning to the boys, he added: "Be assured that if any troops trouble you again, they shall be punished."

Gage could be mild with the boys, but he would have to deal more harshly with their fathers. There was no doubt that the colonists were ready to revolt. Patrick Henry put into words what they all felt when he spoke at St. John's Church in Richmond, Virginia, that spring. He said, "Is life so dear or peace so sweet as to be purchased at the price of chains and slavery? Forbid it, Almighty God! I know not what course others may take, but as for me, give me liberty or give me death!"

By April, Gage had decided to act. He would bag Sam Adams and John Hancock, and ship them to England to stand trial for treason. Then he would march to Concord and seize the materials for war that the patriots were storing there—muskets, cannon, gunpowder in barrels, spades, axes, medicine chests, tents, flour, beef, salt. To do this job, Gage chose his strongest troops, the grenadiers, and his fastest, the light infantry. He would act on the night of April 18, and he tried to keep the date a secret.

But men like Paul Revere, the silversmith, and Joseph Warren, a doctor, had organized a vigilance committee to watch for just such things. On April 15 they saw the British hauling up their rowboats for repairs. They knew that Gage was preparing to move some of his troops. But how—by land or by water? They had to know, so that they could warn Adams and Hancock, who were staying with a friend

Loyalists and patriots often came to blows at town meetings in the days before the Revolution.

in Lexington before leaving for the Second Continental Congress in Philadelphia. And so they arranged with the sexton of Old North Church to give the signal when the time came—two lanterns in the belfry if the British left Boston by water, one lantern if they marched over Boston Neck by land.

Following a day of showers, the night of April 18 was clear and cold. At about ten o'clock 800 British troops marched to their boats from Boston Common and two lanterns flashed in the belfry of Old North Church. Paul Revere leaped onto a horse he had borrowed from Deacon Larkin and rode through the streets of slumbering Charlestown.

The smell of salt marshes rose to greet him as he fled along the road with the Mystic River on his right and the Charles on his left. Two British sentinels challenged him, but Revere spun his horse about, raked the animal's flanks with his spurs, and escaped at a gallop. Soon he was rattling over the bridge into Medford, shouting that the British were coming. He went on, crying the same message at almost every farmhouse, until a little past midnight when he rode into Lexington to warn Adams and Hancock. Revere rode on toward Concord, only to be captured by the British.

THE BATTLE OF LEXINGTON

But already bells were ringing in Lexington. Minutemen were jumping from their beds, snatching up their muskets, and rushing to the Lexington Green. Here Captain John Parker called the roll and ordered them to charge their guns with powder and ball. The men waited in the chilly night air, pounding the ground with their feet to keep warm. Some began to believe the alarm was false and drifted home to bed. Others decided to spend the night in Buckman's Tavern.

Then the alarm bells rang again, and this time there was no mistake. The British redcoats under Major John Pitcairn were less than two miles from Lexington. The Minutemen came back on the run, lining up beside tall Captain Parker.

In the gray light of early morning, April 19, 1775, Major Pitcairn galloped into town at the head of his "bloody-backs." He paused at the sight of the Minutemen, then called out an order:

"Disperse, you villains! Lay down your arms!"

He repeated the order several times, and the Minutemen slowly began to move away, still carrying their guns. Then, suddenly, a shot rang out. Nobody knew who fired it, but it set off a volley from the redcoats. The war had come, with young Jonathan Harrington beating his drum and every man taking care of himself.

The scene on Lexington Green quickly became one of mad disorder. Harrington died there, silent with his drum. A British ball buckled the knees of Jonas Parker, the captain's cousin. John Brown fell at the edge of the swamp, just north of the Green.

The redcoats seemed to go out of hand, firing even after Pitcairn called to them to stop. The Battle of Lexington lasted only minutes. Eight Massachusetts men died, ten were wounded. A slight leg wound to one redcoat was the only British casualty.

Sam Adams, lingering in his flight to freedom, heard the sounds of battle and shouted at the wind: "What a glorious morning for America is this!" Adams and Hancock were well on their way to safety by the time Pitcairn had lined up his victorious troops on the Green. The major waited while his men gave three cheers, then, tight-lipped, led them down the road toward Concord.

VICTORY AT THE BRIDGE

Minutemen swarm into Concord and defeat the British.

The people of Concord awakened at about two o'clock in the morning to the ringing of the alarm bell. Minutemen tumbled out of bed and ran to the Green. Some leaped onto horses and rode to neighboring towns to spread the warning.

There was work for everyone that night. Boys and girls helped to carry supplies into the woods where they would be secure from the redcoats. Walking on each side of the oxen, the youngsters whipped the animals into a trot until the carts were bouncing down the road. Meanwhile, the Committee of Safety—a group of citizens responsible for the defense of the town—huddled together, discussing where to make their stand.

Early morning brought the sounds of fighting at Lexington. Colonel James Barrett, who had proved his qualities as a fighter in the French and Indian War, stationed his Concord forces on a hill near the village.

Men were now coming from surrounding communities—from Lincoln and Acton, Carlisle and Chelmsford, Weston and Littleton. Barrett decided that his position on the hill left him too exposed and moved his force to rising ground beyond North Bridge, a mile or so from Concord Green. Sooner than anyone expected, the British arrived, stepping smartly in two columns, one coming by the main road and the other over the hill that the Americans had just vacated.

Swarming over Concord in search of supplies, the redcoats soon saw how well the citizens had done their work in the hours before dawn. They found some barrels of flour, wooden plates, spoons—and that was about all. They cut down and burned a Liberty Pole and set the courthouse on fire.

Other redcoats rushed to destroy North Bridge. Here the Minutemen surged forward, to be hit by a volley from the "bloody-backs."

"Fire, fellow soldiers," said a Massachusetts major. "For God's sake, fire!"

The Minutemen raised their muskets to their shoulders. They fired, and three British regulars fell dead.

The fire of the Minutemen went on. Dazed and confused, the redcoats fell back, leaving North Bridge in possession of the Americans. The British officers could hardly believe what was happening. The king's best troops were retreating from farmers.

Nor was it an easy retreat. The countryside was alive with Minutemen, and one British officer wrote afterward, "The Americans seemed to drop from the clouds." They were behind every tree, every wall, every barn, every twist and dip in the road. The weary redcoats staggered back into Lexington, saved from surrender by the arrival of reinforcements. By nightfall they limped into Boston.

Every colony in America was stirred by the success at Concord. New Hampshire voted to raise an army of 2,000 to help Massachusetts, Connecticut set its quota at 6,000, Rhode Island at 1,500.

Within Boston, Gage agreed to give safe conduct out of the city to all who surrendered their weapons. But the people who were loyal to the crown—the Sons of Liberty called them Tories—raised an outcry. They wanted Gage to hold those with patriot sympathies in Boston as hostages. Gage agreed.

More unpleasant news was in store for the British. A small force of volunteers—the Green Mountain Boys under Ethan Allen—marched to Lake Champlain and struck suddenly at Fort Ticonderoga on May 10, 1775. They caught the British garrison by surprise. Allen rapped with his sword on the door to the commandant's quarters, and cried: "Come out instantly, or I will sacrifice the whole garrison."

A sleepy-eyed captain opened the door.

"I order you instantly to surrender!" Allen shouted.

The British captain blinked. "By what authority do *you* demand a surrender?" he asked.

"In the name of the Great Jehovah and the Continental Congress!" Allen said.

Wisely, the captain accepted Allen's answer and surrendered.

WASHINGTON TAKES COMMAND

The Continental Congress unanimously selects Washington as army commander.

The Continental Congress mentioned by Allen did not actually meet until a few hours later that same day. This Second Congress was held in Philadelphia. As the delegates crowded into the State House (later called Independence Hall) for the opening session, they were confused men. What authority did they truly have? Whom did they really represent? They had no leader, no program of action, no treasury. How could they deal with the problems of war against the mightiest nation on earth?

But the delegates began to speak, and slowly the confusion cleared away. What if the British did destroy their towns and spread ruin along their seacoasts? "These are inconsiderable objects, things of no moment to men whose bosoms glow with the ardor of liberty," they said in one petition to the king.

News that large British reinforcements were arriving in Boston under the command of three new generals—William Howe, Henry Clinton, and "Gentleman Johnny" Burgoyne—swept away the last feelings of hesitation. Clearly, this was a war that might spread to every settlement. Americans must stand together now and form a "Union of Colonies." (At a later session, the name "Union of Colonies" was changed to the "United States of America.") On the motion of John Adams, the militia forces then assembling at Cambridge were named the Continental army. George Washington was unanimously elected commander in chief. On the morning of June 16, 1775, he rose to speak to the congress:

"Though I am truly sensible of the high honor done me . . . yet I feel distress, from a consciousness that my abilities may not be equal to the extensive and important trust. However, as the Congress desire it, I will enter upon the momentous duty, and exert every power I possess in their service, and for the support of the glorious cause. . . .

"As to pay, I beg leave to assure the Congress, that, as no particular consideration could have tempted me to accept this arduous employment, at the expense of my domestic ease and happiness, I do not wish to make any profit from it. I will keep an exact account of my expenses. Those, I doubt not, they will discharge, and that is all I desire."

REBELS ON BREED'S HILL

American troops fight a battle known as the Battle of Bunker Hill.

As Washington journeyed north to take command of his army, he received news of a fierce battle fought outside Boston.

During the night of June 16, the Americans had seized Bunker Hill and Breed's Hill, two heights north of Boston. When the moon rose about midnight, it shed a pale glow on some 1,000 men on Breed's Hill. They were digging furiously to throw up a small fortress and a line of entrenchments. Below them, in the harbor, river, and ferry slip lay four British men-of-war. The ships were so near that the men on the hillside could hear the sentinels on the decks crying, "All's well."

Colonel William Prescott, a farmer from Pepperell with a froglike voice, led the Americans. Most of them, too, were farmers. Their only weapons were the old muskets and fowling pieces they had brought

In the early dawn, as the men of Concord awaited the British, their wives and children hid supplies in nearby woods.

Their powder and ammunition gone, the Americans on Breed's Hill fought with rifle butts and fists.

from home, their only ammunition the small supply of powder and shot they carried in their powder horns and pouches. As the night passed, the earth piled up higher around their little fort. Then a sentinel aboard one of the British ships spotted the men on Breed's Hill and shouted the alarm.

The big guns of the ship, opening the bombardment upon the hillside, awakened Boston. Soon other men-of-war were firing broadsides at the fort which, as if by magic, had sprouted on Breed's Hill during the night. Scrambling out of their beds, Bostonians rushed to the rooftops, balconies, and steeples to watch what was going on. As the sun came up they could see the Americans coolly completing their work with shells bursting about them.

Within Boston, the British generals debated the next move. Howe said that troops should be landed on Charlestown Neck to pinch off any chance of reinforcements reaching the rebels on Breed's Hill. But Gage decided on a direct attack. His reason was easy to guess. These ragtag rebels would run for their lives once they saw British regulars with fixed bayonets marching on them in a solid mass. By noon Gage had loaded his boats with more than 2,000 troops and twelve pieces of cannon.

The men on Breed's Hill watched the boats crossing the Charles River. Weary, hungry, and thirsty, the Americans pleaded for relief, but there was no one to take their place. Israel Putnam, who had walked to Boston with his flock of sheep during the blockade, called on them to stand firm. Seth Pomeroy of Northampton, seventy years of age, encouraged the younger men. Dr. Joseph Warren said calmly: "It is pleasant and becoming to die for one's country."

At any rate, there was still work to do. Some of the men crawled to a rail fence behind their unfinished fortifications and wove new-mown hay between the rails to screen themselves from the enemy. Others hid behind haycocks, guns ready.

Some time after three o'clock the great British guns opened fire on the American earthworks. The British advanced in two columns, one under Howe, the other under General Robert Pigot. Behind them the guns on the men-of-war continued to hurl shells at the hillside.

Prescott and his farmers waited quietly. The redcoats came on, puzzled by this silence. But Prescott had ordered his troops not to fire until they could see the whites of the enemy's eyes. No American had to be told that ammunition was scarce and every shot must count. The redcoats were almost upon the fort when the command rang out: "Fire!"

A withering volley ran like flame along the length of the American breastworks. The British reeled, swept away as though a great scythe had mown them down. British blood stained the green slopes of Breed's Hill, and British flags fell among the morning lilies. Other redcoats approached what seemed to be a harmless fence. They, too, were shot down, and soon bugles sounded, ordering a full retreat.

Standing on a hillside overlooking Breed's Hill, General Burgoyne saw Howe's redcoats racing down the slope. British guns had now set fire to the town of Charlestown, and the steeple of a church was a pyramid of flame above the burning houses. From the surrounding hillsides, spectators watched the battle. Burgoyne later said, "The roar of cannon, mortars and musketry, the crash of churches, . . . whole streets falling in ruins . . . and the reflection that perhaps a defeat was a final loss to the British Empire in America . . . made the whole a picture and a complication of horror and importance beyond anything that ever came to my lot to be witness to."

THE LAST CHARGE

Once more the British attacked. Once more Prescott stood like a rock—sword buckled to his side, a broad-brimmed hat shading his eyes—waiting for the right moment to cry, "Fire!" Once more the redcoats were thrown back.

Howe couldn't believe what was happening. It was, he said, "a moment that I never felt before." But Prescott's ammunition was all but gone. His men had no bayonets with which to stand off the British in a hand-to-hand fight. After two hours of battle, the end was near, and Prescott knew it as the redcoats advanced a third time.

The Americans had no more powder or bullets and fought with the butt ends of their guns. All at once, said Peter Brown, who fought on Breed's Hill that scorching afternoon, the fight of the Americans "went out like an old candle." Peter wrote his mother: "I was in the fort till the regulars came in, and I jumped over the walls and ran for about half a mile where balls flew like hailstones and cannons roared like thunder." The Americans were forced to retreat. Even so, they fought "from one fence or wall to another," as General Burgoyne admitted, and the retreat was "covered with bravery and military skill."

American losses that day were 100 killed, 267 wounded, and 30 taken prisoner. British casualties numbered 1,054. The Battle of Quebec, which had ended the French and Indian War and won England half a continent, had not cost so much. What had the British gained in this battle that was mistakenly called the Battle of Bunker Hill? The British had won little more than a place to pitch their tents. Franklin, writing to English friends, drew another meaning from the battle: "Americans will fight. England has lost her colonies forever."

MAKING AN ARMY

Washington faces the task of making soldiers out of raw New England farmers.

Washington reached Cambridge, Massachusetts, on July 2, 1775, and the next morning took command of the Continental army. In the following weeks, he had the enormous task of changing farmers into seasoned soldiers. He lacked gunners to handle the few cannon he possessed, but then he lacked almost everything—engineers who could build proper fortifications, ammunition, canvas and sailcloth for tents, money to pay his troops.

Washington found these New England militiamen different from the Virginians who had served under him. They were willing enough to fight, but between battles they wanted to go home and tend to their farms. Washington was used to men who "kept their place" and were respectful to "gentlemen." But New Englanders did not believe in "putting on airs," and a private spoke to a captain as he would to any neighbor.

From the start, discipline was a big problem. Men wandered away from their posts. They used "abusive language" toward officers and fell asleep while on guard duty. Drunkenness and theft were other common offenses.

In a letter, Washington made no secret of his dissatisfaction with one class of New England militiamen: "Their officers generally speaking are the most indifferent kind of people I ever saw." He also wrote: "I daresay the men would fight very well (if properly officered) although they are an exceedingly dirty and nasty people." But some of the New Englanders became trusted generals on his staff. Among them were Israel Putnam, who had been a farmer; Henry Knox, who had been a bookseller in Boston, and Nathanael Greene, the Rhode Island Quaker who became a warrior.

The British sat tight in Boston during the summer and autumn of 1775, and this gave Washington time to whip the easygoing New Englanders into an army. The Reverend William Emerson, who had watched the redcoats at Concord bridge, noticed the change: "Everyone is made to know his place and keep it, or be immediately tied-up, and receive not one but thirty or forty lashes according to his crime," Emerson wrote his wife. "Thousands are at work every day from four till eleven o'clock in the morning. It is surprising the work that has been done. . . ."

With the British strongly entrenched on Bunker Hill, Washington spread his army around them. He was determined to keep the redcoats cooped up on the Boston peninsula and its neighboring islands.

But Howe was willing to wait. Time, he believed,

would wear down the colonists' spirit. The long freezing months of winter would also work in his favor. Tired of the cold and their half-empty bellies, the "rebels" would steal away home and the war would collapse. Nor was Howe altogether wrong. Although the Continental Congress had planned on an army of 20,372 men, divided into regiments of 728 men, enlistments were few. The colonists' leaders could not help wondering how large Washington's army would be when spring came.

ADVENTURE IN CANADA

An American army marches on Canada, but fails to take Quebec.

Most Canadians were in favor of the American patriots, whom they insisted on calling the Bostonians. An attack on Canada would have a good chance of success, and in the fall of 1775 Washington approved a plan to drive a two-pronged assault into Canada and capture Quebec. Ethan Allen had easily taken Ticonderoga; surely he could do as well again.

And so, in November, Ethan Allen crossed the St. Lawrence River to attack Montreal. But his supporting force failed to reach him, and Allen was captured by the British. They remembered him as the conqueror of Ticonderoga, and they ordered him bound hand and foot with irons. He was thrown into the hold of a warship and left there for five weeks without a seat or a bed.

Meanwhile, a second American force under Colonel Benedict Arnold pushed through the winter snow toward Quebec. Their food supply ran so low that one night they were forced to kill a dog and make a soup of it. But, in spite of hunger and cold, they went forward. On November 9 they were near Quebec.

Using the cove and ravine Wolfe had discovered sixteen years before, the Americans climbed to the Plains of Abraham. They believed that the friendly people of Quebec would surrender the city as soon as they heard that the Americans had arrived, but news came that an army of Canadians and Indians under Governor Carleton was ready to go into battle. Colonel Arnold, who was no fool, hastily recrossed the river and withdrew to Point aux Trembles (Aspen Trees Point) to await other American forces under Brigadier General Richard Montgomery.

By December the little American army—about 1,000 ill-clothed, ill-fed men—had returned to the Plains of Abraham. They peered through swirling snow at the walled city, wondering what to do next.

But Montgomery had imagination. He ordered wickerwork baskets filled with snow, over which he poured water. The snow froze into blocks of ice, with which Montgomery soon built a huge mound. On it he mounted six twelve-pound cannon and two short cannon called howitzers. A few shells were lobbed into the city before the Canadians fired back. They scored a direct hit on Montgomery's mound, shattering the ice—and the hopes of the Americans. Montgomery fell as the first shots were fired.

Other schemes for taking Quebec went no better. Before the year ended, it was plain that the American adventure in Canada was a failure.

WASHINGTON'S FIRST VICTORY

Washington besieges the British in Boston and drives them out of the city.

On New Year's Day, "in compliment to the United Colonies," Washington raised a new flag of thirteen red and white stripes with British colors in the upper corner. Spying the strange flag flapping in the breeze on Prospect Hill, the British in Boston believed that Washington wished to surrender. When word of this reached Washington, he smiled. "By this time," he said, "I presume they begin to think it strange that we have not made a formal surrender of our lines."

Washington had no intention of surrendering. He had a plan—a good one—for ousting the British from Boston, but he needed powder and guns to carry it out. Israel Putnam was given the job of getting the powder, and that January a fellow officer wrote: "The bay is open—everything thaws here but Old Put. He is still as hard as ever, crying out for powder—powder—ye gods, give us powder!" Meanwhile, Henry Knox was bringing down the cannon from captured Fort Ticonderoga. Over mountains, through the wilderness that was covered by ice and snow, he hauled the big guns. There were fifty-nine of them, and altogether they weighed 119,900 pounds.

By March Washington had his powder and guns, and had begun to act. For some unknown reason, Howe had failed to seize Dorchester Heights, which overlooked Boston. Washington planned to occupy it. But to keep Howe from learning what he was up to, he bombarded the city from Lechmere's Point, Roxbury, Cobble Hill, Ploughed Hill, and Lamb's Dam. For three days the bombardment went on. Then, at seven o'clock on the night of March 4—the eve of the anniversary of the Boston Massacre—Washington sprang his surprise.

Two thousand men, armed with entrenching tools, swarmed over Dorchester Heights. Three hundred wagons, loaded with fascines (bundles of sticks) and screwed hay (bundles of hay), came in a steady stream. The constant roar of Washington's guns drowned out any sounds made by the men. The

The Americans worked secretly all night to fortify Dorchester Heights unbeknown to the British.

weather was cold, the moon full. The long winter night gave the Americans several more hours of darkness to work in than they had had the previous summer, when they had fortified Breed's Hill.

Under Washington's direction two forts were built. Cannon were rolled into position. Barrels filled with stones were placed where they could be rolled down on troops charging up the hill. Trees from nearby orchards were cut down; the logs were sharpened at the ends and thrust into the ground like giant spikes. By daylight, the whole job was finished.

When Howe saw what the Americans had accomplished on Dorchester Heights, he was astounded. "I know not what I shall do!" he cried. "The rebels have done more in one night than my whole army would have done in a month."

At a staff meeting that morning, Admiral Shuldham told Howe: "If they retain possession of the Heights, I cannot keep a ship in the harbor." Howe tried to cross the river and storm the Heights, but his troops were beaten back by Washington's cannon, aided by rain and a violent wind. Everything had turned against the redcoats. Despite the protests of terrified Tories, Howe decided to leave Boston without fighting a battle.

The British destroyed all the salt and molasses in the city, wrecked the shops of patriotic merchants, and carried off any linen and woolen goods they could find. They left Boston on March 17. Many Americans must have agreed with the newspaperman who wrote that the British withdrawal was due to "the wisdom, firmness, intrepidity and military abilities of our amiable and beloved general, His Excellency George Washington, Esquire."

A PLOT TO MURDER WASHINGTON

Washington escapes death when he is warned not to eat poisoned peas.

With Howe forced out of Boston, George III hit upon a new scheme for strengthening his forces in the colonies. He would hire soldiers from other nations to fight his war in America. The rulers of Russia and the Netherlands turned him down. But the princes of some German provinces, particularly Hesse-Cassel, needed money. They agreed to supply George III with about 17,000 Hessian troops. For each soldier, they received $22.50 plus an annual payment. The soldiers themselves were given no choice. They were farmers and laborers, and many of them had been seized for the army while working in their fields or in their shops, or while they were worshiping in church.

Up to this time, George III might have been able to keep his American colonies. A number of the colonists had no wish to break away from England and form their own nation. They were fighting simply to defend their rights as freeborn British subjects. They would have welcomed a compromise with the royal government. But the king made no offer to compromise, and his hiring of the Hessians angered the colonists and brought them a step closer to declaring their independence.

Even so, there were still many colonists who were loyal to the king. These Tories were especially strong in New York City, where they made up a large part of the population. In those days, the city had 25,000 people and was less than a square mile in size. It was squeezed into an area bounded by the East, the Harlem, and the Hudson Rivers. Beyond the city walls were little settlements known as the Bowery, Bloomingdale, and Harlem. Howe saw that New York had great military importance, and on June 30 he arrived at Staten Island with about 10,000 troops. Twelve days later, his brother, Admiral Lord Richard Howe, sailed a large fleet into New York Bay.

Washington, too, knew the importance of New York, and had been bringing troops to the city. By the end of April a number of forts had been built, and Washington added still others. He built Forts Washington and Independence on the northern boundaries of Manhattan Island, and Fort Constitution (later called Fort Lee) across the Hudson River on the New Jersey shore.

The Tories, encouraged by the arrival of the fleet, decided to help their British friends by plotting against George Washington. A soldier named Hickey, one of Washington's guards at his summer headquarters on Richmond Hill, was bribed to persuade a maid to poison a serving of green peas, one of the general's favorite dishes. But the maid revealed the scheme to Washington, and Hickey ended up dangling from a rope on the nearby farm of Colonel Henry Rutgers.

AN HISTORIC DECLARATION

The Continental Congress meets in Philadelphia and declares independence.

Thomas Paine was an Englishman, the son of a Quaker corset maker. He had worked at various jobs when, in 1774, he met Benjamin Franklin in London. Franklin encouraged him to come to the colonies, and Paine took his advice. Paine was filled with a burning desire for freedom for all men, and in 1776 he wrote a pamphlet entitled *Common Sense,* which sold more than 100,000 copies within several months.

Paine called for American independence, and wrote that "The sun never shone on a worthier cause." His sentences rang like battle cries: "It matters little now what the king of England either says or does. He hath wickedly broken through every moral and human obligation, trampled nature and conscience beneath his feet, and by a steady and constitutional spirit of insolence and cruelty, procured for himself a universal hatred." Paine pleaded with Americans: "A government of our own is our natural right. Ye that love mankind, that dare oppose not only tyranny but the tyrant, stand forth!"

Washington approved Paine's "sound logic, and

George Washington, having dislodged the British at Boston, escaped a Tory plot to poison him in New York.

In a small rented room in Philadelphia, Thomas Jefferson worked at drafting the Declaration of Independence.

unanswerable reasoning." So did thousands of other Americans. As they read *Common Sense,* their doubts and hesitation about independence seemed to fade.

On April 22, 1776, North Carolina took the lead in telling its delegates to the Continental Congress "to concur with those in the other colonies in declaring independence." Massachusetts approved the same action next day. Rhode Island and Virginia hedged somewhat, telling their delegates to *propose* independence. Connecticut's delegates were told to *assent* to independence; so were New Hampshire's. New Jersey left the decision to its representatives. Pennsylvania, Georgia, South Carolina, New York, and Delaware took no official action. Maryland at first opposed independence, then took Virginia's position.

On June 7, 1776, in the spacious meeting room of the State House in Philadelphia, Richard Henry Lee of Virginia rose to address the Continental Congress. A hush fell over the great hall as in a clear voice he offered the resolution:

"That these United Colonies are, and of right ought to be, free and independent States: and that all political connection between us and the State of Great Britain is, and ought to be, totally dissolved."

John Adams seconded the resolution. To protect Lee and Adams from a British charge of treason, their names were omitted from the official record. John Adams, Benjamin Franklin, Roger Sherman, and Robert Livingston were named to a committee to draw up the Declaration of Independence, but most of the work of drafting the document was done by Thomas Jefferson.

DECLARATION OF INDEPENDENCE

Jefferson worked long hours at a folding desk in the room he had rented at 235 High Street. From his window, as he paced and thought, he looked down on sprawling Philadelphia, broiling in the June heat. Nearby stood a stable, from which came the big green horseflies that were a special bedevilment to Jefferson.

The committee was delighted with Jefferson's statement of why the colonies were declaring their independence. Franklin and Sherman, as far as John Adams could recall, did not "criticize any thing." Adams believed that in calling the king a tyrant Jefferson had made the document "too personal."

They were modest men who met that day in Jefferson's room. As representatives of their colonies, they held only *delegated* power. With time they would see where the *real* power of a free people lay. They would invent a way to make sure this power was felt in government, through popular elections. But this would come later.

Jefferson had written into his Declaration of Independence a hard-hitting paragraph condemning

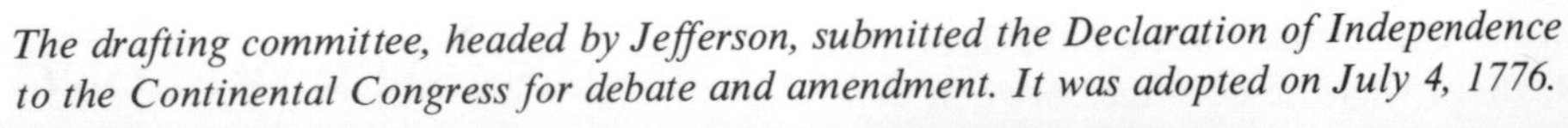
The drafting committee, headed by Jefferson, submitted the Declaration of Independence to the Continental Congress for debate and amendment. It was adopted on July 4, 1776.

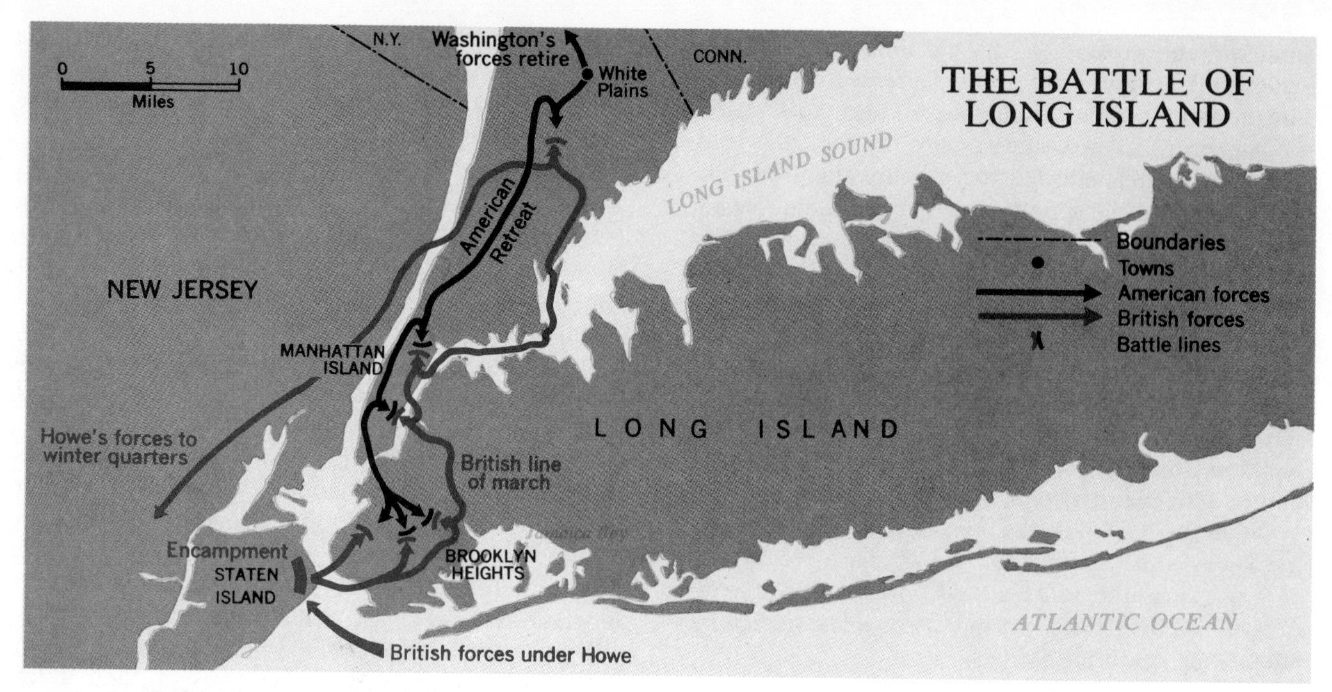

Defeated in the Battle of Long Island, Washington retreated, amid bitter skirmishing, to White Plains.

slavery. John Adams knew that the delegates from South Carolina and Georgia would not allow the paragraph to stand. And while New Englanders owned few slaves, Adams knew they too would be touchy on this subject, since their ships had carried slaves to the South for a neat profit.

So, struggling toward freedom, America already was faced with the great themes that would dominate its history. First, there was the conflict between *delegated* power and *real* power. Out of this, free elections and political parties would grow. Secondly, there was the conflict between *material* interests and *moral* interests that even then made the position of the Negro in America something that haunted the minds of men.

For three days, Congress debated the thoughts and language of the Declaration of Independence. As Adams had predicted, the paragraph on slavery was not accepted. Jefferson was annoyed with some of the delegates, who believed "we had friends in England worth keeping terms with." Parts of the Declaration that criticized the people of England were taken out, but the main body of it remained.

In magnificent language, Jefferson stated: "We hold these truths to be self-evident, that all men are created equal, that they are endowed by their Creator with certain unalienable Rights, that among these are Life, Liberty and the pursuit of Happiness." Again he said: ". . . Governments are instituted among Men, deriving their just powers from the consent of the governed. . . ."

On July 4, 1776, the Declaration of Independence was adopted by the colonies. Four days later the document was read to Philadelphians, who burst into loud cheers. Next day New Yorkers, cheering the Declaration, marched to Bowling Green and pulled down the statue of the king; later they used the lead to make 40,000 bullets. Washington's troops held a celebration, almost forgetting the British fleet off Manhattan Island.

DISASTER ON LONG ISLAND

The Hessians take Long Island and Washington orders his men to retreat.

While news of the Declaration of Independence traveled through the colonies and was celebrated in one town after another, Washington worried over the problem that faced him in New York. The British fleet under Admiral Howe—"Black Dick," the general's seafaring brother—had forced its way past the American batteries and was threatening Manhattan Island. Washington had placed some 8,000 troops under Israel Putnam on Brooklyn Heights to hold off the redcoats. On August 22, 1776, the British moved on Long Island by land and sea.

The Battle of Long Island was fought five days later, and for the first time Americans went into action against hired Hessian soldiers. A German colonel expressed the contempt of the Hessians for their American foes: "These people ought rather to be pitied than feared. They always require a quarter of an hour to load a rifle, and in the meantime they feel the effects of our balls and bayonets."

A British officer later told why the Hessians behaved so savagely: "We took care to tell the Hessians that the rebels had resolved to give no quarter to them in particular, which made them fight desperately, and put all to death that fell into their hands."

Among the Americans who fought on Long Island was fifteen-year-old Joseph Plumb Martin, a farm lad from Massachusetts who was eager to "sniff a little gunpowder." Near the ferry dock, on the Manhattan side of the East River, he loaded his knapsack from the casks of sea bread provided for the troops and then marched aboard the transport.

When they landed on the Brooklyn shore, young Martin saw that the Americans were taking terrific punishment. Wounded men streamed past him, "some with broken arms, some with broken legs, and some with broken heads." To lift his spirits, Martin gnawed on his sea bread and found it "hard enough to break the teeth of a rat."

The call came, "Fall in!" Heart thumping, Martin fell into line. Soon the regiment moved forward toward a creek. Driven into the muddy water, the men thrashed wildly, some swimming, some sinking from view. From a hilltop British fieldpieces poured death upon the outnumbered Americans "like a shower of hail." An American twelve-pounder, opening up, made the redcoats hop for cover.

Washington was heard to exclaim: "Good God! What brave fellows I must this day lose!" And lose them he did—about 1,000 in all. The British force curled around him, crumbling his left flank and piercing the center of his lines. He was pushed into a little corner of the island less than two miles square. One British force was in front of him. A naval force with 20,000 redcoats was behind him.

The men who saw Washington that day, riding his big gray horse, could tell by the dark circles under his eyes that he had gone without sleep for many hours. Yet his mind remained alert, his military judgment sound. It seemed impossible now to snatch men, guns, equipment, and stores from under Howe's blazing guns. But Washington managed to do it, and retreat safely back across the East River to New York. Luck was with him. A Negro servant sent by a Tory lady to tell Howe of the crossing fell into the hands of Hessians. They could not understand a word the poor fellow said. Too late, Howe learned that he had been outwitted.

ON HARLEM HEIGHTS

Washington moves his headquarters to a position close to White Plains.

Now that the Americans had been beaten on Long Island, Admiral Howe felt that this was the right time to offer them peace terms. In September he met on Staten Island with John Adams, Benjamin Franklin, and Edward Rutledge, the American peace commission. The admiral refused to accept either the authority of Congress or the independence of the colonies. Politely but firmly, the Americans ended the peace talks: "You may call us what you please. We are, nevertheless, the representatives of a free and independent people, and will entertain no proposition which does not recognize our independence."

These were unhappy weeks for Washington. Retreats, no matter how skillfully carried out, do not win wars, and the people had much to grumble about. In New York, which had many Tories, the army was behaving badly, plundering houses and annoying residents. Stories were told of surgeons who sold furloughs to able-bodied men for sixpence each. Drunkenness was common. Many people felt that what the American army needed most was a new commander.

NATHAN HALE IS HANGED

Washington ordered an issue of two days' supply of bread and pork to all his troops, proof that he might be forced to march at any moment. His position in New York City was risky, and in September he drew his army north to Harlem Heights. Badly in need of information on what the British would do next, he sent a trusted captain, Nathan Hale, to act as a spy in the enemy's camp.

Captain Hale entered the British encampment dressed as a farmer. He had been making sketches and notes for Washington when a Tory relative recognized him. Betrayed by a member of his own family, Hale calmly accepted his death sentence as a spy. In the morning when young Hale stood beneath a tree, a rope around his neck, spectators crowding around him broke into sobs. According to legend,

On Harlem Heights, Washington repulsed the British. Here the 42nd Highlanders (Black Watch) retreat under fire.

Hale then spoke these last words: "I only regret that I have but one life to lose for my country."

For almost a month Washington waited on Harlem Heights for General Howe to make a move. His entrenchments were strong—especially Fort Washington, rising 235 feet above the tidewater of the Hudson, and Fort Lee, perched across the river on the high cliffs of New Jersey. From the beginning, Washington was troubled. Would his troops, still shaken after the disastrous and exhausting Battle of Long Island, stand up to another assault?

On October 12, Howe used ninety flatboats to carry a large part of his army to Throg's Neck, a low peninsula that juts out from what is today New York's Borough of the Bronx. In a brisk skirmish the Americans repulsed and pursued the British. Howe was forced to take to the heights of New Rochelle. Here, squarely across the road leading to the little village of White Plains, Howe was joined by a number of newly arrived Hessian troops.

Washington moved swiftly, knowing it was time to get off Manhattan Island. Leaving a garrison at Fort Washington, he marched his army up the valley of the Bronx River. Along the heights from Fordham to White Plains the Americans pitched their camps. Every day brought bitter skirmishing. Washington reached White Plains and set up headquarters on high ground to the north of the village. He had chosen a strong defensive position. His restlessness showed that he shared the feelings of the men in the ranks. General and private alike knew that they would soon be engaged in battle.

RACE ACROSS NEW JERSEY

Fort Washington falls, and British and American troops race for Philadelphia.

The fighting at White Plains rose to furious pitch on October 28. The key to the battle was Chatterton's Hill, across the Bronx River, where the Americans were already entrenched. Redcoats and Hessians splashed across the river and up the hill. Artillery raked Washington's entrenchments.

Step by step the Americans gave way, and losing Chatterton's Hill amounted to losing the battle. For days the armies rested within a "long cannon shot" of each other, but Washington knew he must retreat. Rain and wind swept White Plains as the Americans withdrew on November 10.

Washington now had to sprinkle his forces like salt from a shaker. To guard the New York highlands, he sent troops to Peekskill, about eighteen miles above White Plains. Some 7,000 soldiers under General Charles Lee were stationed at North Castle, where they could be called into action when needed. Washington and about 2,000 troops withdrew across the river to Fort Lee.

Even lazy General Howe understood that there was little to keep him from moving through New Jersey to Philadelphia, the seat of the Continental Congress. Howe planned first to storm the American garrison still in Fort Washington. This task he assigned to Scottish Highlander and Hessian troops. In the British general's hands were sketches and reports brought to him by William Demont, a Pennsylvania adjutant turned deserter.

Things were going badly for the small American garrison at Fort Washington. Demont told of the bickering between officers and privates, and the lack of ammunition, food, and clothing. The Highlanders and Hessians attacked, meeting stiffer opposition than they expected. But in the end swamps were waded, cliffs scaled, and earthworks broken through.

The cold, tattered, hungry Americans who fell prisoner amused the British, and one of their officers wrote: "Their odd figures frequently excited the laughter of our soldiers." But there was nothing amusing to an American about the British prison ships, like the *Jersey.* Rancid food, foul air, filth, and vermin were only some of the horrors suffered by the prisoners in the *Jersey's* hold. The living, the dying, and the dead lay huddled together. Each sundown brought the same cry: "*Down,* rebels, down!" And each morning was announced by the same brutal shout: "Rebels, turn out your dead!"

FORT LEE ABANDONED

Washington watched the collapse of Fort Washington from the New Jersey shore. Beside him stood Thomas Paine, the author of *Common Sense.* Fort Lee could not be held now. Washington's only choice was a race with the British across New Jersey toward Philadelphia. General Charles Lee must leave North Castle on the Croton River and quickly bring his forces across the Hudson to Washington's support, and New Jersey citizens must rally to the patriots' cause.

The race between Washington's straggling army and a powerful British force under General Charles Cornwallis began at the little Dutch village of Hackensack. It went on through Newark, New Brunswick, Princeton, and Trenton. The people of New Jersey seemed to lose their patriotism whenever Cornwallis appeared. They almost fell over one another in their eagerness to safeguard their property by swearing oaths of allegiance to the royal government.

"We seem to be playing at Bo-Peep," said a British officer. If the race across New Jersey was a game, it was a frantic one for the ragged Continentals who often marched through freezing rains without stockings and shoes. At each town Washington waited until the redcoats were almost upon him.

David Bushnell hoped to attack British ships in New York harbor in a submarine, but the idea proved unworkable.

Where was Lee? Hourly, the question tormented Washington: "Lee–why doesn't Lee come?" But that strange individual, who had sneered at Washington as "not a heaven-born genius," ambled into New Jersey as if he had all the time in the world. In mid-December he rested in the little mountain village of Basking Ridge, still miles away from his hard-pressed commander in chief. There one day, while Lee was loitering in the local tavern, writing a letter, the British swooped down and captured him.

Bagging Lee added to the cheer of the British as Christmas approached. On December 8, a force of 6,000 redcoats under General Henry Clinton overran Rhode Island and settled around Newport. On that same frosty Sunday, the advance guard of Cornwallis' army entered Trenton, just as the rear guard of Washington's forces was crossing the Delaware River.

Panic swept Philadelphia. The Continental Congress prepared to flee to Baltimore. In those dark hours a new pamphlet by Thomas Paine, *The American Crisis,* again raised the spirits of the Americans. Paine wrote:

"These are the times that try men's souls. The summer soldier and the sunshine patriot will, in this crisis, shrink from the service of his country; but he that stands it NOW, deserves the love and thanks of man and woman. Tyranny, like Hell, is not easily conquered; yet we have this consolation with us, that the harder the conflict, the more glorious the triumph."

TRENTON–"VICTORY OR DEATH"

Washington crosses the Delaware and takes the Hessians by surprise.

"I will not despair," Washington had muttered on leaving New Brunswick. Now, pacing his headquarters in Pennsylvania, he was preparing a surprise for the Hessians under Colonel Johann Rall, who occupied Trenton. Two days before Christmas, Washington ordered rations cooked for three days. The password which he gave his sentries was "Victory or Death."

Washington was gambling on the German habit of holding a big celebration on Christmas Day. The Hessians would drink vast quantities of beer and dance far into the night. Morning would find them drowsy, muddleheaded, careless. It would be the perfect time for an attack.

At twilight on Christmas night Washington's men began boarding boats at McConky's Ferry, a few miles above Trenton. A wintry wind blew, and masses of ice floated in the Delaware River. A swift current swept the ice cakes against the boats. Toward midnight snow began to fall.

"I never have seen Washington so determined as he is now," Colonel John Fitzgerald wrote in his diary at three o'clock that morning. "He stands on the bank of the river, wrapped in his cloak, superintending the landing of his troops. The storm is changing to sleet and cuts like a knife. The last cannon is being landed, and we are ready to mount our horses."

Grimly, the American army marched on Trenton. At eight o'clock, when Colonel Rall was still sleeping off the wine he had drunk the night before, Washington's forces struck. The Continentals quickly overran the town and gained possession of the road to Princeton. Part of the vigorous action was led by Lieutenant James Monroe, a future President of the United States. Rall pulled off his nightshirt, put on

Washington crossed the ice-filled Delaware in December 1776 as snow and sleet fell, then routed the Hessians at Trenton.

a uniform, and tried to rally his flustered troops. It was too late. At noon that December 26, 1776, Colonel Fitzgerald wrote in his diary:

"His men [the Hessians] were frightened and confused, for our men were firing upon them from fences and houses and they were falling fast. Instead of advancing they ran into an apple orchard." The path of retreat toward Bordentown was cut off and by noon Washington had collected nearly 1,000 prisoners, six cannon, over 1,000 muskets, twelve drums, and four stands of colors. Colonel Fitzgerald could not conceal his admiration for Washington. He wrote:

"It is a glorious victory. It will rejoice the hearts of our friends everywhere and give new life to our hitherto waning fortunes. Washington has baffled the enemy in his retreat from New York. He has pounced upon the Hessians like an eagle upon a hen and is safe once more on this side of the river. If he does nothing more, he will live in history as a great military commander."

WASHINGTON BEDEVILS THE BRITISH

Washington takes Princeton, then settles in Morristown for the winter.

It was not a happy New Year's Day for General Cornwallis. He had planned to return to England for a vacation. Instead, he found himself riding from New York to Princeton to take personal command of the British forces. The redcoats now numbered about 8,000, while Washington had 5,000 footsore, hungry men at Trenton. Rain turned the roads into bogs of mud as Cornwallis plunged on toward Trenton, determined to smash Washington forever.

But Washington's riflemen, striking unexpectedly in brisk little skirmishes, made Cornwallis' march a constant misery. Meanwhile, Washington had decided on a bold move. He would march by a round-

But at the Battle of Brandywine the following year, Washington was outflanked by Howe and forced to retreat.

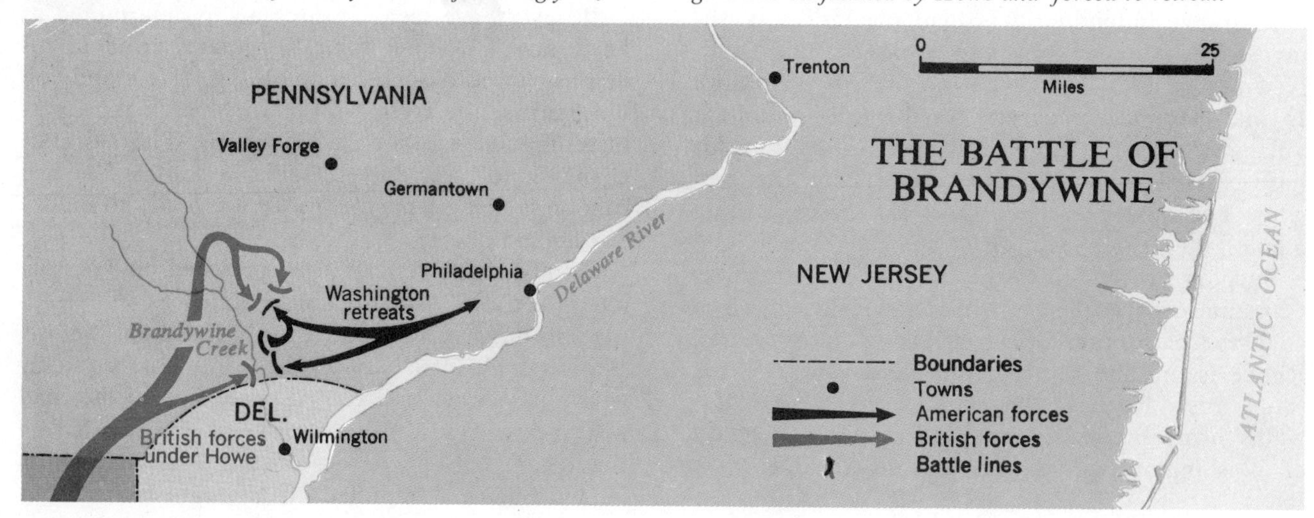

about road and hit suddenly at the British reserves and stores of supplies at Princeton.

Washington's surprise appearance threw the redcoats into confusion. The British retreated into the building of the College of New Jersey (now Princeton University) and were promptly bombarded by an American cannon. After two or three shots the redcoats hung a white flag out the window.

The Battle of Princeton was over in less than an hour. Washington had been in the thick of it, riding a white horse. The prisoners who fell into American hands were described as "a haughty, crabbed set of men." Washington told his staff gaily: "It is a fine fox to chase, my boys."

Cornwallis now fell back to New Brunswick to protect his post there. Washington withdrew into the mountains near Morristown, content to settle down for the winter.

Huts began to dot the countryside as the ragged Americans fought off the chill winds and blustering snow squalls. There were many desertions and few enlistments, so that Washington could almost see his army melting away. Smallpox spread through the camp. It was difficult to tell which the men feared more—the disease or the inoculations Washington ordered.

Yet brighter times were ahead. New Jersey citizens, who had so willingly taken oaths of allegiance to the royal government, now began to support the patriots. They had discovered that the Hessians made no distinction between foe and friend. Houses were broken into, families were robbed of food and clothes, and even young children and old people were shamefully mistreated.

The people of New Jersey daily grew more rebellious against their so-called British protectors. Now they gave any information they could to American horsemen, who spent the good winter days raiding enemy outposts. By the first of March the British and Hessians had drawn back into their strongholds at New Brunswick and Amboy. Washington's riders were "cleaning up" the New Jersey countryside.

In the pleasant little village of Morristown life was not all war and worry for the commander in chief. One day a coach brought a woman "so plainly dressed" that bystanders believed she must be a servant. But she was Martha Washington, and Washington greeted her warmly. She had arrived to spend the winter with the "Old Man," as she affectionately called him.

In "elegant silks and ruffles," the ladies of Morristown visited Mrs. Washington, who received them in "a speckled homespun apron" while knitting a stocking. Polite and smiling, Martha Washington was setting an example of how women must help to win the war by doing without anything they could not make for themselves.

Throughout the winter, the army nipped at the foe. A raid on a British schooner at Elizabethtown supplied badly needed blankets, and a hit-and-run assault on Spanktown (later called Rahway) produced about 1,000 bushels of salt. As spring came, the first of 8,000 fresh American troops reached Morristown, and Washington prepared once more to battle the redcoats.

Even the warm weather did not tempt Howe to leave the gay social life of New York. Surprisingly, one of Howe's closest companions was the captured American, General Charles Lee. Lee obligingly worked out a plan for the British to seize Philadelphia, Annapolis, and Alexandria, which would divide the colonies north and south.

By late May, Washington decided to move down to the first range of the Watchung Mountains, about seven miles from New Brunswick, to counter any move the British might make. But not until June was half over did Howe turn his attention back to the war, and a series of little sparring matches developed between the two armies before the new campaign took shape.

Howe's aim was to lure Washington out of his mountain stronghold, but Washington was too wise to fall into that trap. In July Howe loaded his troops onto British vessels, leaving Washington to guess his intentions. Patriot spies on Staten Island were as mystified as Washington as to which way Howe would move—north or south.

RED FLOWS THE BRANDYWINE

Washington suffers a defeat and retreats, leaving Philadelphia to Howe.

In early August, Washington learned that Howe's vessels were sailing into Chesapeake Bay. It was clear that Howe intended to land somewhere around Wilmington, Delaware, and then swing his columns north to capture Philadelphia.

With recently arrived reinforcements, Washington's forces now totaled about 16,000 men. He was cheered by news of a thumping American victory to the north at Bennington, up in "the New Hampshire Grants" (Vermont), where Americans had routed a British force commanded by two of Burgoyne's officers. And Washington recently had found a new friend—the nineteen-year-old Marquis de Lafayette, who had come from France to offer his services as a soldier without pay.

HOWE OUTWITS WASHINGTON

Washington started after Howe. He reached Philadelphia and treated its citizens to a display of American military strength. On Sunday, August 24, the

American army marched in a three-hour parade—down Front Street, up Chestnut, a turn at the common, then across Middle Ferry to the heights of Darby. Washington's orders were to march in step "without *dancing* along." Twelve deep, the men swung through Philadelphia, but John Adams was not altogether pleased. He said, "They don't hold up their heads quite erect, nor turn out their toes so exactly as they ought."

But dress parades do not win wars. Washington's problem was to stop Howe from taking Philadelphia. Moving to Brandywine Creek, about seven or eight miles northwest of Wilmington, he placed his troops with great skill. Howe could not reach Philadelphia without crossing the Brandywine, and now Washington's troops covered a two-mile stretch of that stream. The center of the American line was at Chadd's Ford, where the British could be expected to try to cross.

Howe had many faults. He was slow, liked personal pleasure too much, and was often overconfident. But he was not stupid. The Battle of Brandywine, opening at daybreak on September 11, 1777, found Howe launching a frontal attack on Washington's strong position at Chadd's Ford.

Too late, Washington discovered he had been tricked. The frontal attack was a bluff. Troops under Cornwallis had taken a road to the left in a long, rapid march. By two o'clock they were across the Brandywine, attacking the Continentals from behind.

When Washington awoke to the bitter truth, he had to pull back his forces to meet the British threat. The result was not very happy. A British officer described the action: "There was a most infernal fire of cannon and musquetry, a most incessant shouting, 'Incline to the right! Incline to the left! Halt! Charge!' etc. The balls plowing up the ground. The trees cracking over one's head."

Washington's losses were between 1,200 and 1,300 killed, wounded, and missing. Those of the British numbered only eighty-nine killed, 488 wounded. More American blood than British had stained the Brandywine red that day. Lafayette, shot in the leg, wrapped a bandage around the wound and helped Washington pull his army back in good order.

Before Howe left for England in 1778, his officers in Philadelphia staged an elaborate farewell parade.

Howe pushed on toward Philadelphia, crossed the Schuylkill River, and on September 26 occupied the city. He had bagged a real prize. The city's residents did not seem disturbed by the British. Indeed, Washington grumbled that they gave Howe information the Americans had never received.

Washington waited his chance to spring at Howe, who had camped at Germantown, some seven miles northwest of Philadelphia. With his own army strung along the hills a dozen miles away, Washington could guess what Howe wanted—possession of the Delaware River, so that supplies could be brought to Philadelphia by water.

Again Washington planned a surprise. On the night of October 3 he sent his men down all four roads leading into the village of Germantown. From the start the American plan was faulty. Seven miles separated the four roads, so that each part of the army never knew what the other three were doing. A heavy fog added to the confusion.

The center of the battle found one American brigade mistaking another for the British. Americans began firing on Americans, but in the panic that followed, Washington once more managed an orderly retreat.

American losses, including prisoners, were 1,100, twice what Howe had suffered.

THE DOWNFALL OF GENTLEMAN JOHNNY

Burgoyne is defeated at Bennington and Saratoga, where he surrenders.

British General John Burgoyne had taken part in driving the Americans from Canada during the campaign of Montgomery and Arnold in 1775 and 1776. Then Gentlemen Johnny had returned to England, where he had talked himself into high favor with the king.

Burgoyne got what he wanted—an army to command. But his orders were strict. He was to do one thing only. Driving down from Canada, he was to push into the Hudson Valley and join with Howe's forces moving up the river.

Burgoyne had ideas of his own about the fighting abilities of Americans. Give the Yankee farmers a tree or stone wall or rail fence to hide behind, he said, and they fought fairly well. But in a great pitched battle they would fall apart.

Gentleman Johnny started from Canada to lay siege to Fort Ticonderoga, his first objective. Here

Crossing a wilderness, the British under Burgoyne reached the Hudson, then headed south—and into disaster.

some 3,500 Americans under General Arthur St. Clair, well warned of Burgoyne's advance, had been busily building Fort Independence on the east shore of Lake Champlain as an added defense. But in front of old Fort Ti stood Sugar Hill, key to the whole American position. It was undefended, for St. Clair did not understand its importance.

Burgoyne did. He dragged a cannon into position on the hilltop and sent St. Clair's troops scampering into the Green Mountains. Part of the loot which the British collected with the capture of Fort Ti was 128 American cannon.

Burgoyne was equally sure that final success was merely a question of time. Faced now with choosing an easy passage across Lake George or pursuing the Americans through dense forests, Burgoyne decided to go by land.

Twenty days of chopping through the woods brought his army only twenty miles to the upper waters of the Hudson River, near Fort Edward. Burgoyne would not think of sitting down to dinner, even in the wilderness, without his bottle of wine, and he needed thirty wagons to carry his personal belongings.

A month at Fort Edward left Gentleman Johnny in a sad fix. He had counted on Tories of the region to supply his army, but most of the people were openly unfriendly. His army faced starvation. Even the hay for his horses had to be hauled in from Canada.

But Burgoyne remembered his strict orders. He decided to push on to meet Howe. (It happened that, at that moment, Howe was on his ship moving south to tangle with Washington for possession of Philadelphia.) Burgoyne then heard that there were mountains of provisions stored at Bennington, a town about twenty-five miles east of the Hudson River—and he badly needed food.

By now Gentleman Johnny appeared to have a talent for doing the wrong thing. Not only did he decide to make the difficult march to Bennington, but he also selected for the expedition 600 Hessians. These were the troops New Englanders hated most. They called them "hired killers" and were sure to fight them fiercely.

THE BATTLES OF BENNINGTON AND SARATOGA

In command of the militiamen from the New Hampshire Grants was rugged old John Stark. This tall, blue-eyed farmer had fought from Bunker Hill to Trenton, then had stomped home when Congress failed to raise his military rank. Now back in service, Stark especially disliked the Hessians.

Burgoyne counted on taking Bennington by surprise, but on August 16, 1777, his troops found Stark's boys dug in and ready for them. The Battle of Bennington was a slaughter. A second American force slipped behind the Hessians and they were caught between two fires. Burgoyne threw in 500 reinforcements but they too were chopped down, bringing the British losses for the day to about 800. The Americans lost seventy men. Staggered by this beating, Burgoyne drew back to Saratoga.

Quickly an American force under General Benjamin Lincoln moved in, cut off Burgoyne's communications with Canada, and attacked Fort Ticonderoga. Isolated on the west bank of the Hudson River, Burgoyne was now met by a strong American force under General Horatio Gates. Gates wore thick-lensed glasses, and some of his men called him "old grandmother." He was no Washington. Cranky and petty, he quarreled with almost everyone. Yet his position outside Saratoga was strong, and there he waited for Burgoyne to attack.

Gentleman Johnny, with his line of retreat to Canada cut, had to move or perish. He threw his

By His Excellency
GEORGE WASHINGTON, Esquire,
GENERAL and COMMANDER in CHIEF of the Forces
of the United States of America.

BY Virtue of the Power and Direction to Me eſpecially given, I hereby enjoin and require all Perſons reſiding within ſeventy Miles of my Head Quarters to threſh one Half of their Grain by the 1ſt Day of February, and the other Half by the 1ſt Day of March next enſuing, on Pain, in Caſe of Failure, of having all that ſhall remain in Sheaves after the Period above mentioned, ſeized by the Commiſſaries and Quarter-Maſters of the Army, and paid for as Straw.

GIVEN *under my Hand, at Head Quarters, near the Valley Forge, in Philadelphia County, this 20th Day of December*, 1777.

G. *WASHINGTON.*

By His Excellency's Command,
Robert H. Harrison, Sec'y.

LANCASTER: Printed by JOHN DUNLAP.

An order by Washington requisitioning supplies of grain during the long winter at Valley Forge.

force against the Americans in a furious assault on September 19. Daniel Morgan, using a turkey call to rally his Virginia riflemen, opened fire from behind the trees of a dense woods. Burgoyne's redcoats fell back, with Morgan's boys howling at their heels. Thus began the battle in which, as one general said, "both armies seemed determined to conquer or die." In the end Burgoyne failed to break out of his trap. His losses came to about 500.

Burgoyne prayed for reinforcements, for he knew that he would have to fight again. The reinforcements never came, but the Americans were having their troubles too. Gates had quarreled with Benedict Arnold. As a result, Arnold resigned his commission as a colonel, but remained on the field when Burgoyne struck once more on October 7.

As a volunteer, Arnold leaped on an iron-gray horse, and one Connecticut soldier believed that he behaved "more like a madman than a cool and discreet soldier." That day Arnold was everywhere—fighting now with Morgan, now with two brigades crashing through the center of the line, now with some Massachusetts regiments routing the Hessians from a pair of stockaded cabins. He fought wildly until a bullet struck his leg and ended his furious one-man war.

By then Burgoyne's army had been torn apart. He retired again to Saratoga, but American sharpshooters gave him no rest. Surrounded by the constant threat of death, deserted by the last of his Indian allies, his food gone and his army beaten, Gentleman Johnny surrendered on October 17, 1777.

ORDEAL AT VALLEY FORGE

The army survives a brutal winter and in spring drills under General von Steuben.

A thirteen-cannon salute was fired in Washington's camp to celebrate the American victory at Saratoga. A little skirmish with Howe at White Marsh next day ended the fighting for 1777. On December 17, Washington marched his tired and ragged army into the bleak hills at Valley Forge, twenty miles from Philadelphia. Both the Continental Congress (which had withdrawn to the little town of York) and the legislature of Pennsylvania then protested Washington's decision to build a winter encampment for his weary troops. Let him keep fighting and drive Howe from Philadelphia, the legislators said, as they warmed themselves before comfortable fireplaces.

Many people criticized Washington at this time. They said he made a habit of failure, and pointed out his defeats at Long Island, White Plains, Brandywine, and Germantown. They called him a dictator, a self-appointed king, a military incompetent.

A group of men were plotting with some army officers to get rid of Washington as commander in chief. Most of the group were New Englanders who wanted to win back control of the army and American politics. Among the conspirators was General Thomas Conway, a soldier of fortune who had joined the American army, and the plotters became known as the Conway Cabal (secret association). The plot failed, and Washington was in an even stronger position than he was before.

After two years as commander in chief, Washington needed no one to tell him the problems of the Continental army. With the thirteen colonies behaving like thirteen separate nations, the Continental Congress was not a very effective legislative body. It had no power to tax, and the paper money it issued had so little value that a wagonload of it was needed to buy a wagonload of provisions. The army lacked decent clothing. Its weapons were often so crude that Benjamin Franklin suggested giving the soldiers bows and arrows, since a man could shoot four arrows as fast as one bullet. Powder and lead for bullets were scarce. Just as scarce was the paper needed as wadding for ramming powder and ball into muskets. To get paper, the soldiers tore apart German Bibles they found in Pennsylvania.

These were a few of the problems on Washington's mind as he watched his shivering soldiers build huts

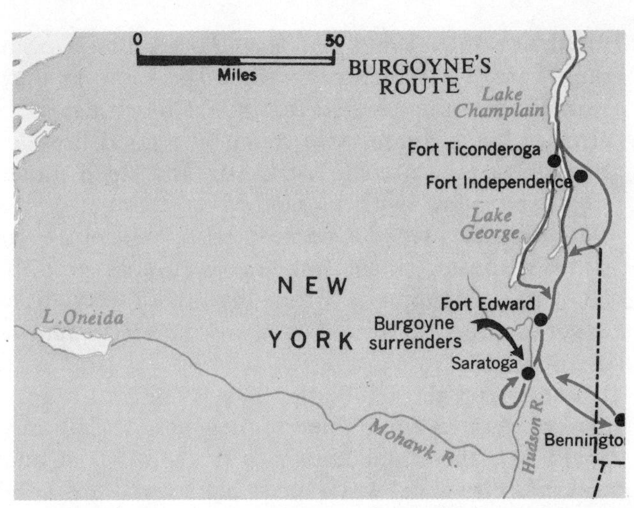

After capturing Forts Ticonderoga and Edward, General Burgoyne was beaten at Bennington, in Vermont, and was finally forced to surrender at Saratoga, N.Y.

Gen. John Burgoyne

During the harsh winter at Valley Forge (1777–78), the American army was badly clothed and almost always hungry. Before spring came, 2,500 men had died.

for their winter camp at Valley Forge. Blood from their bare feet sometimes stained the snow as they worked. Washington said that it was much easier to criticize "in a comfortable room by a good fireside, than to occupy a cold, bleak hill, and sleep under frost and snow without clothes or blankets." He watched sick men die because there was not even straw to protect them from the wet, cold ground. He wrote unhappily: "From my soul I pity these miseries which it is neither in my power to relieve or prevent."

The wintry days at Valley Forge fell into a grim pattern. At mealtime, when soldiers asked what they could eat, the usual answer was: "Fire cake and water." "Fire cake" was a bread baked on a fire without an oven. It was soggy and tasteless. The surprising fact was not that some men deserted from Valley Forge, but that so many stayed. "No pay, no clothes, no provisions, no rum," the soldiers sang out, but they seldom blamed Washington. They looked up to him, and it was he who held the army together that winter.

Spring found its way along the banks of the Schuylkill and into the hills at Valley Forge. Since February there had been a new member on Washington's staff, Baron Friedrich Wilhelm Ludolf Gerhard Augustin von Steuben. He was an old German soldier who knew how to drill discipline into an army. Stout, big-nosed, his head almost bald, he strode before the troops with a greyhound loping at his heels.

He would drill these ragged troops until they were as fine as any fighting force in the world—and drill them he did, day in and day out, with his bright eyes glittering. Sometimes he swore at the men in German, sometimes in French, and sometimes in both languages. When even this failed to get results, he shouted to an aide: "Come and swear for me in English. These fellows won't do what I bid them."

In time, they did as he asked. They came to understand the baron's affection for them and grinned at his roaring outbursts. Soon they were standing, marching, wheeling as soldiers should.

Baron von Steuben, an old German soldier noted for his stern methods, joined Washington's staff at Valley Forge.

BAD NEWS FOR THE BRITISH

After Burgoyne's defeat, France recognizes the U.S. and prepares to enter the war.

During the months of suffering at Valley Forge, Howe and his troops lived comfortably in Philadelphia. A few rugged rebels taunted the soldiers by singing patriotic songs like *War and Washington* and *Burgoyne's Defeat.* But there were many loyalists in the city who shared in the gay times of the invaders. There were elegant dances and dinners, and gambling at the gaming tables. "You can have no idea of the life of continued amusement I live in," wrote one of the many Tory ladies of Philadelphia.

Although the British still had the upper hand, the Americans were about to gain new strength. Their warmest friend in Europe was Count Charles de Vergennes, the French foreign minister. Vergennes looked upon England as a "greedy" neighbor and "the natural enemy of France." Since the closing weeks of 1776, Benjamin Franklin, Silas Deane, and Arthur Lee had been in France, trying to persuade the French government to make an open alliance with America. With Washington driven first from New York and then from Philadelphia, France was cautious. She was willing to help "secretly." She would send ammunition and allow American privateers that raided British shipping to use her ports. But an open break with England seemed too risky.

When Gentleman Johnny surrendered at Saratoga, the situation changed. A British army had been defeated! Now was the time to strike, while England was floundering. The French government signed a treaty of friendship with America on February 6, 1778. The following month, the French ambassador

Americans at Valley Forge drill under von Steuben. His fieriness helped make them soldiers.

in London announced that France had become the first European power to recognize the United States as an independent nation. America now had a strong ally.

These were unhappy days in London. The dreadful defeat of Burgoyne had been a blow to British pride, and Howe, wasting the winter in Philadelphia, aroused scornful criticism. Knowing that a French fleet and French troops would soon come to the aid of America, the British had to change their plans. Philadelphia would have to be abandoned in favor of New York. New York was an island and would be easier to defend against a land and naval assault.

The British government needed someone to blame for all these misfortunes, and in May, 1778, Howe was replaced as commander by Sir Henry Clinton. The men in Howe's army were shocked by the change. Even more shocked were the Tories, who wondered what would happen to them when their British protectors left Philadelphia. Their gay times were over; there was trouble ahead.

GUNS ROAR AT MONMOUTH

Replacing the incompetent Lee,
Washington wins the Battle of Monmouth.

On June 18, the British army marched out of Philadelphia. Thousands of desperate Tories fled with Clinton's soldiers. Carrying what few personal belongings they could, the Tories trudged from the city. Tears ran down their cheeks, for they were leaving homes they loved. But, fearing the American troops who would surely re-enter the city, they preferred broken hearts to broken necks.

In charge of the American occupation forces in Philadelphia was Benedict Arnold, whose bravery had raised him to the rank of general. Arnold moved into the mansion where Howe had lived, and provided himself with a housekeeper, a coachman, a groom, and seven other servants. Soon he was living like a king. He gave extravagant dinners, rode through the streets in a handsome coach, and courted pretty, blonde Peggy Shippen. Peggy's tastes, like Arnold's, were expensive. Moreover, she was a well-known Tory. But Arnold did not seem to care. He married the headstrong Peggy, meanwhile piling up debts. He was falling into a trap that would make him forever remembered in history.

As the redcoats and Hessians under Clinton crossed the Delaware River and marched through New Jersey toward Sandy Hook, another American general was giving Washington trouble. No one had worked harder than Washington to gain Charles Lee's freedom. Washington respected Lee's abilities and had placed him second in command of the forces pursuing Clinton. Lee was a professional soldier who had fought in Portugal, Poland, Turkey, and Hungary. He looked on Washington as only an amateur, and believed himself a far better judge of how Clinton and his forces should be handled.

Clinton's march across New Jersey was a difficult one. The roads twisted through forests, and every mile was a misery. Bridges were down and trees had been felled to block his passage. The British were also hampered by a train of supply wagons that stretched for twelve miles. When the British reached the Raritan River and turned southeastward toward Sandy Hook, the baggage train cut Clinton's forces in two.

On Sunday, June 28, with a sweltering sun beating

down, Washington saw a chance to fall on the rear half of Clinton's army. The redcoats were moving over difficult country toward Monmouth Court House (Freehold). Washington sent repeated orders ahead to Lee—attack, attack! Lee failed to act, and Washington, pushing on to the front, found to his astonishment that the British, not the Americans, were on the offensive.

Lee tried to explain why he had not followed Washington's orders. "Sir," he said, "these troops are not able to meet British grenadiers."

Washington's temper exploded. "Sir," he said, "they are able, and, by God, they shall do it!"

Washington took command. He braced himself to halt the retreat of the confused and disorganized Americans, who were being chased by the British troops. A narrow road, passing through swampy land, gave him a spot to cut off the British assault. His cannoneers rolled up their guns and fired at the redcoats.

Men carried away different memories of the rip-roaring Battle of Monmouth that blistering Sunday, depending on where they fought. One man remembered Washington's calmness: "After passing us, he rode on to the plain [level] field and took an observation of the advancing enemy. He remained there some time upon his old English charger, while the shot from the British artillery were rendering up the earth all around him."

Another man remembered Mary Ludwig Hayes, who carried water to the American cannoneers: "While in the act of reaching a cartridge and having one of her feet as far before the other as she could step, a cannon shot from the enemy passed directly between her legs, without doing any other damage than carrying away all the lower part of her petticoat." History renamed Mary Hayes and made a legend of her as "Molly Pitcher."

Washington (here mistakenly pictured on a dark horse) relieves Lee of command at the Battle of Monmouth.

Wrapped in his cloak, Washington slept on the ground with his troops that night, expecting the battle to begin again at daybreak. But Clinton had had enough. Abandoning his badly wounded and leaving his dead unburied, he stole quietly away in the darkness.

Studying the reports of the Battle of Monmouth, Frederick of Prussia exclaimed: "Clinton gained no advantage except to reach New York with his wreck of an army." The wreck might have been more complete if Lee had acted as ordered. He was arrested, tried by court-martial, and found guilty. In time he was dismissed from the army.

A FRENCH FLEET ARRIVES

But d'Estaing's ships stay out of battle

On July 11, 1778, news of the arrival of a French fleet under Admiral d'Estaing stirred America. A swift move against the British fleet commanded by "Black Dick" Howe could leave Clinton's forces in New York at the mercy of Washington's army. Some Americans believed the end of the war was only weeks away. But d'Estaing was impressed by Howe's great reputation as a naval officer and refused to risk a battle.

Washington saw that there was another way to strike at the British. With the help of d'Estaing's ships and men, he could rid Rhode Island of the British army occupying Newport. But just as d'Estaing's fleet prepared for battle with the British ships protecting Newport, a storm separated the two fleets, and the action was never carried out.

The Americans settled down in New Jersey to camp through the fourth winter of the war. October brought supplies of coats, breeches, and shoes from France. The weather remained extremely mild and everyone was cheerful at Washington's headquarters at Middlebrook. "We danced all night," wrote General Henry Knox, describing one of the many social events that helped to while away the winter months. But elsewhere, in the Indian country, other Americans were passing the time in an entirely different manner.

WAR IN THE WEST

George Rogers Clark leads his rangers against the British and Indians.

The British, who held small forts along the Wabash and Mississippi Rivers, were playing a wicked game in the West. British commander Henry Hamilton had not won his nickname of "Hair Buyer" for nothing. Sending his agents among the Indians who lived north of the Ohio River, he had made clear that the hair he wished to buy should be from the scalps of American settlers. He told London that his aim was to stir up "alarm upon the frontiers of Virginia and Pennsylvania."

Down in the Kentucky country, young, red-headed George Rogers Clark had lived through many Indian raids, and had plans for an attack on the western outposts of the British and their Indian friends. Patrick Henry, who was now governor of Virginia, agreed with Clark. A small band of rangers was outfitted, and Clark plunged into the Illinois country. His rangers quickly captured the Indian settlements of Kaskaskia and Cahokia, but that was only half the job. The British still held Vincennes on the Wabash, and there would be no end to the Indian massacres until this post was taken.

Clark never lacked courage, and now he needed all he could muster. The weather in February, 1779, when Clark and his rangers started for Vincennes, was cold and raw. Eight days out of Kaskaskia the rangers reached the Little Wabash River, at a point where the river divides into two streams with about five miles of land between. Floodwater now covered every inch of that ground to a depth of three feet. Clark might have camped and waited—but he was not the kind of man who waits. He gave the order and his rangers plunged into the water.

Clark's rangers advanced toward the British outpost at Vincennes through miles of icy February floods.

CLARK TAKES VINCENNES

It was a march none of them would ever forget. Water swirled around their hips at each stumbling step. The men groaned as the rifles they held aloft began to feel like the barrels of cannon. Their muscles tightened in agonizing knots. Those who became too sick to walk were towed along in canoes. At last they found a high spot of land where they could camp.

When the sun came up next day, George Rogers Clark suddenly sat upright. Had his ears tricked him? No, that was the sound of a gun. He was within "hearing distance" of the British garrison at Vincennes.

Later the rangers captured five Frenchmen in a canoe. The Frenchmen said that everyone in Vincennes knew that Clark and his boys were coming. The people were very happy and the soldiers were very sad. But Clark could not reach Vincennes that night. The way ahead was too difficult, the floodwater too high.

But Clark intended to try, using his captured Frenchmen as guides. He scooped up a handful of water and mixed it with gunpowder. While the rangers watched, he blackened his face. Then, grinning, he gave a war whoop. They were going to Vincennes! One by one, they followed Clark.

Back in the water, they soon felt their feet grow numb in the slime. Shooting pains in their leg muscles made them cry aloud. Somehow they crawled along. They plunged into a flooded forest, where there were limbs to grasp and logs to keep the shorter men afloat. Finally, the water began to recede. Slowly they realized that they were making it. They were near Vincennes. With colors flying and drums beating, Clark and his boys marched toward town.

The battle that followed was fought viciously, but the rangers would not let anyone stop them after they had come so far. One of them described the fight as "fine sport for the Sons of Liberty." No one knew then how much they had won. But when the war ended, the conquest of Vincennes would give the United States a claim to lands as far west as the Mississippi and as far north as the Great Lakes.

THE WAR AT SEA

John Paul Jones forces the British warship Serapis *to surrender.*

On the high seas, the war reached to distant places as the small American forces challenged the mighty British navy. From 1775 to 1783, British fighting

John Paul Jones carried the naval war to Britain in a series of raids on the British west and east coasts.

The fight between the Bon Homme Richard *and the* Serapis *lasted three hours before the British ship surrendered.*

ships increased from 270 to 468. Some 174 vessels carried sixty cannon or more. During the same period America succeeded in launching about one hundred armed cruisers and managed to sink or capture about 200 British ships. In addition, American privateers (armed ships, privately owned) sank or captured 600 vessels.

America's first naval hero was Jeremiah O'Brien, a New York lad who in 1775 lived in Machias, a town on the coast of Maine. O'Brien led an attack of sloops on the *Margaretta,* a British armed schooner carrying lumber to Gage's troops in Boston, and captured her. It was a hot one-hour battle sometimes called the "Lexington of the Sea."

Other naval heroes were David Bushnell, who built a one-man submarine, the *American Turtle,* and Esek Hopkins, who in 1775 commanded the little fleet that made up the first American navy.

But there was one man who stood out above the others—a Scottish sailor and one-time slave trader whose real name was John Paul. When he joined the Americans as a privateer commander, he added Jones to his name, and let it be known that he preferred to be called Paul Jones.

In late April, 1778, Jones, commanding the *Ranger,* carried the war to Britain when he struck suddenly at Whitehaven on the northwest coast of England. About thirty armed Americans went ashore in two boats. They set fire to houses and ships in the harbor, and a London newspaper spoke of the scene as "too horrible" to describe.

Jones then staged a series of hit-and-run raids along the English coasts. At sunset on September 23, 1779, off Flamborough Head, on the North Sea, he sighted a fleet of forty British merchantmen, escorted by the frigate *Serapis* and a smaller warship.

Aboard his flagship, the *Bon Homme Richard,* Jones turned to give battle to the *Serapis.* The *Bon Homme Richard* was severely battered by the foe. But when the British captain asked if the Americans were ready to surrender, Jones replied, "I have not yet begun to fight."

BATTLE AT SEA

Three hours later the greatest sea battle of the war ended with a victory for Jones. Lieutenant Richard Dale, who commanded a battery of twelve-pounders on the main deck of the *Bon Homme Richard,* wrote:

"The fire from the tops of the *Bon Homme Richard* was conducted with so much skill and effect as to destroy ultimately every man who appeared upon the quarter deck of the *Serapis,* and induced her commander to order the survivors to go below. Nor even under the shelter of the decks were they more secure. The powder-monkeys of the *Serapis,* finding no officers to receive the cartridges brought from the magazines, thew them on the main deck and went for more.

"These cartridges being scattered along the deck and numbers of them broken, it so happened that some of the hand-grenades thrown from the main-

At midnight, under a bright moon, "Mad Anthony" Wayne's men attacked the fort at Stony Point on the Hudson.

yard of the *Bon Homme Richard* . . . fell upon this powder and produced a most awful explosion. The effect was tremendous—more than twenty of the enemy were blown to pieces, and many stood with only the collars of their shirts upon their bodies. . . ."

Midshipman Nathaniel Fanning, who had been stationed as a lookout in the maintop of the *Bon Homme Richard,* described the closing moments of the American ship's victory:

"It was some time before the enemy's colors were struck. The captain of the *Serapis* gave repeated orders for one of his crew to ascend the quarter-deck and haul down the English flag, but no one would stir to do it. They told the captain they were afraid of our rifle-men. . . . The captain of the *Serapis* therefore ascended the quarter-deck, and hauled down the very flag which he had nailed to the flag-staff a little before the commencement of the battle, and which flag he had at that time, in the presence of his principal officers, swore he would never strike to that infamous pirate J. P. Jones."

WASHINGTON AT A STANDSTILL

"Mad Anthony" Wayne takes Stony Point, but winter soon halts the fighting.

The feats of George Rogers Clark in the Indian country and of John Paul Jones on the high seas did not solve Washington's problems in the spring of 1779. Fearing that the British would capture West Point and thus gain control of the highlands to the north, Washington scattered his forces to protect this fortress of the Hudson River.

Washington's idea was to sit tight and wait for Clinton to reveal his plans. Clinton, however, wanted to bring Washington out into the open for a full-scale battle, and the British raided King's Ferry on the Hudson and New Haven, Fairfield, Norwalk, and other Connecticut towns. The object was to tempt Washington to move from his protected position, but he refused to budge.

Meanwhile, British garrisons at Verplanck's Point and Stony Point guarded the two crossings at King's Ferry. In mid-July, after scouting the ground in person, Washington decided that a swift attack might recapture both points.

Veteran troops under Brigadier General "Mad Anthony" Wayne led the attack. The fort at Stony Point was set on a wooded cliff that stretched a half mile into the Hudson River and stood 150 feet above the water. Only a narrow strip of land over a marsh connected the fort with the mainland, and this became flooded at high tide. At midnight on July 16, 1779, with a bright moon shining, Wayne launched his attack.

Waiting inside their works at Stony Point, the redcoats yelled: "Come on, ye rebels! Come on!"

Wayne's boys called back: "Don't be in such a hurry, my lads. We will be with you presently."

The guns blazed and within twenty minutes Wayne had stormed his way almost to the fort. Falling with a scalp wound, Wayne cried: "Carry me up to the fort, boys. Let's go forward."

As Wayne's forces pounced upon the defenders of Stony Point, the redcoats—so said the New York *Journal*—raised a piteous shout: "Mercy! mercy! Dear Americans, mercy! Quarter! Brave Americans, quarter!" At any rate, the fort was quickly won.

Washington visited the fort two days later and ordered the works at Stony Point torn down. Wayne's boys carried off stores worth $158,640—prize money that they divided among themselves. As soon as the Americans left the dismantled fort, the British came back and rebuilt it. Sometimes the war seemed merely to go around in circles.

Benedict Arnold's treason was revealed as Major André, traveling under a false name, was captured by Skinners.

WINTER IN JOCKEY HOLLOW

A raid on Powle's Hook, a spit of sand opposite the lower end of Manhattan Island, ended Washington's campaign for 1779. Again the commander in chief withdrew his army for the winter, this time to settle near Morristown in a section of New Jersey known as Jockey Hollow.

In many ways the winter of 1779–80 was worse than the cruel months at Valley Forge. As badly clad as ever, the men struggled through enormous drifts as one howling snowstorm followed another. Even New Englanders could not remember a colder, more rugged winter than this one. For days, the Hudson River was frozen solid across the 2,000 yards that separated New York from Powle's Hook.

Hunger haunted the soldiers in Jockey Hollow

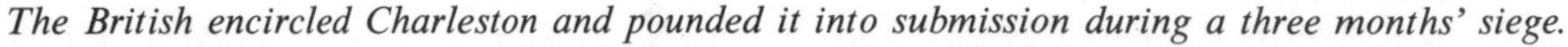

The British encircled Charleston and pounded it into submission during a three months' siege.

and one private declared that he saw several men "roast their old shoes and eat them." A mutinous uprising, though finally controlled, showed how close to the breaking point the men came.

TREASON AT WEST POINT

Benedict Arnold plots with the British to betray the Americans at West Point.

The British had a new plan for winning the war. It went into operation on December 29, 1778, when a strong British force landed two miles below the Savannah River in Georgia. By the end of February, 1779, the redcoats held Augusta and most of Georgia. Other British forces swept into South Carolina. While the British army in New York pinned down Washington, the redcoats were mopping up the southern colonies.

Washington could not afford to lose the South. Yet, if he went to the aid of the small American forces there, the British in New York might overrun his key defenses at West Point, which guarded the Hudson Valley.

Because West Point was so important, Washington had placed its defense in the hands of Benedict Arnold. Arnold had been angered when five junior officers were promoted ahead of him, but Washington thought highly of him. Arnold's new post was a big responsibility, for between New York and the Point there was nothing but a lawless neutral ground terrorized by two bands of armed outlaws. These were the "Cowboys," a gang of loyalist sympathizers, and the "Skinners," who called themselves "patriots."

In this region on a September day in 1780, a lone rider was suddenly stopped on the Tarrytown road by three men.

The rider gave his name as John Anderson and expressed the hope that the three men were Cowboy loyalists.

"We are," one said.

Anderson grinned. "So am I," he said. "I am a British officer on business of importance and must not be detained."

No sooner had he spoken than he realized that he had been trapped. The three men were Skinners. Anderson then said that he was really a patriot and, as proof, he produced a pass signed by General Benedict Arnold. The Skinners were not interested in the pass. They wanted money.

"Gentlemen, I have none about me," Anderson said.

"You said you were a British officer," the others said. All British officers had money. "Let's search him."

In Anderson's boot they found papers, but no money. Before the day ended those papers had been relayed to American officers, and had helped to uncover the ugliest story of the war.

John Anderson was, indeed, a British officer. His name, however, was Major John André. When the three Skinners caught him he was on his way to General Clinton with news that Arnold had agreed to betray West Point to the British. More than that, Arnold would tell Clinton where Washington would be staying on his way to Hartford, Connecticut—an open invitation to the enemy to capture the American commander in chief. For these services Arnold was to receive a British officer's commission and 20,000 pounds in cash.

This unhappy story of treachery went back to the time that the British held Philadelphia. Here André had been a friend of Peggy Shippen and had later come to know her husband, Arnold. When Arnold began to write letters to General Clinton offering to help the British for a price, Major André became the go-between.

Now André was tried by a jury of six generals. He had been captured in civilian dress, and so he was hanged as a spy.

Arnold escaped into Clinton's lines. He was made a British officer and received a traitor's fee, although it was not the 20,000 pounds he had been promised. Americans would despise him forever as the symbol of what General Nathanael Greene called "treason of the blackest dye."

LIVELY TIMES IN THE CAROLINAS

Charleston falls to the British, who fight savagely under "Bloody" Tarleton.

Meanwhile the war in the South boiled like a teakettle. A change came suddenly in early September of 1779, when the French fleet led by Admiral d'Estaing arrived at Savannah. D'Estaing's twenty-two French ships of the line and his eleven frigates were a powerful threat to the British, who had almost no naval support there. The troops of d'Estaing, added to American forces under General Benjamin Lincoln, gave the patriots an army of at least 5,000. The British in Savannah numbered about 3,200.

The French admiral demanded the surrender of Savannah, and the British stalled for time. They put slaves to work strengthening defenses, and reinforcements were rushed up from Port Royal. D'Estaing's guns lobbed shells into the town but did little damage to the British military installations. Rains in early October dampened everyone's spirits and d'Estaing decided that he would either storm Savannah or quit the place.

Francis Marion and his guerrillas staged a series of raids on British supply lines and detachments.

A heavy bombardment on October 9 opened the assault. French and American troops, becoming lost in a swamp, were mercilessly slaughtered. Still others, betrayed by a deserter, fell as they were led into a cross fire. A great friend of America, the Polish Count Casimir Pulaski, who had fought at Brandywine and Germantown, was mortally wounded by a cannon ball while leading a cavalry charge. The Americans lost more than 800 men, the British 150 at most.

D'Estaing, who had been severely wounded, sailed off with his ships and troops. The Americans raced back to Charleston to dig in for the bitter fight they could be sure was coming. Clinton sailed from New York with large British forces and three of his best officers—Earl Cornwallis, J. G. Simcoe, and Banastre Tarleton, who was known as "Bloody" Tarleton. In mid-February Clinton landed his troops on Jones Island, thirty miles from Charleston.

Within Charleston the patriots were in a tight spot. The forts that were intended to guard the city were in bad condition. Except for some cavalry left near Moncks Corner at the head of the Cooper River, General Lincoln drew his entire army inside Charleston. Since only a narrow isthmus, called the Neck, linked the city to the mainland, Lincoln had placed himself in a trap. His force at best numbered 5,000. Clinton had about 10,000 men.

When "Bloody" Tarleton struck savagely at Monck's Corner, routing Lincoln's cavalry, the jaws of the trap drew tighter. By the end of April the British had encircled Charleston so that there were no routes of escape. Three days later the siege rose to its greatest pitch, and General William Moultrie, of the American forces, never forgot what he saw:

"The mortars from both sides threw out an immense number of shells. It was a glorious sight to see them like meteors crossing each other and bursting in the air. It appeared as if the stars were tumbling down. The fire was incessant almost the whole night, cannon balls whizzing and shells hissing constantly amongst us, ammunition chests and temporary magazines blowing up, great guns bursting, and wounded men groaning along the lines. It was a dreadful night! It was our last great effort, but it availed us nothing. After this, our military ardor was much abated. We began to cool, and we cooled gradually . . . on the eleventh of May, we capitulated."

The militia and the armed civilians were free to go home, but Lincoln's soldiers laid down their arms as prisoners of war. During all the years of the Revolution, America would suffer no single loss to equal this.

And now Colonel Tarleton put in his licks. About 350 Virginia cavalrymen, under the command of Colonel Abraham Buford, were leading a supply train toward Salisbury when Tarleton caught up with them in the Waxhaws, a wooded region near the North Carolina border. "With the horrid yells of infuriated demons," Tarleton's men charged and General "Light-Horse Harry" Lee declared afterward, "This bloody day only wanted the war dance and the roasting fire to have placed it first in the records of torture and death in the West."

Buford, seeing he was clearly overwhelmed, raised a flag in surrender. But "Bloody" Tarleton showed no mercy, and wounded men were bayoneted in a scene of savage butchery.

CAMDEN AND KINGS MOUNTAIN

Southern patriots rally to wipe out a British force at Kings Mountain.

After the fall of Charleston, Clinton issued a harsh proclamation. The time had come, he said, when the people of the Carolinas must be either for or against the king. Those who helped the patriots would be hunted down and would be destroyed and their lands and homes seized. Anyone who aided in killing a loyalist would be treated as an enemy of the British crown.

Meanwhile, with the capture of Benjamin Lincoln, Washington urged that the southern armies be placed under the command of that fiery Rhode Island Quaker, Nathanael Greene. But instead Congress chose

Horatio Gates, the victor at Saratoga. General Gates prepared to attack the British at Camden, South Carolina, on the Wateree River, which the redcoats had occupied after the fall of Charleston.

Gates found his army on the verge of starvation, yet he ordered them to make ready to march. Of the two roads that led to Camden, Gates picked the one that offered the least chance to supply his forces. He fed his men on half-cooked meat, green corn, unripe peaches, and molasses. Suffering with weariness and bellyache, the Americans approached Camden.

Now Gates decided on a night march to surprise the Britishers. It happened that at the same time Cornwallis was marching his redcoats to surprise the Americans. The two armies, stumbling upon each other in the darkness, shared the surprise.

By daybreak, Cornwallis had his troops well placed for battle. Gates made the mistake of putting inexperienced militiamen in the center of his line. The fighting was desperate, but the Americans took a terrible drubbing and their losses that August 16, 1780, included about 1,000 casualties, 1,000 prisoners, and nearly all their guns. Gates jumped on a horse and joined his fleeing militia, covering sixty miles before he stopped. He rode himself out of the war.

The defeat and disorganization of the Americans at Camden endangered the patriot cause in the South. For a while, the only opposition to the British came from such daring guerrilla raiders as Francis Marion and Thomas Sumter. There were not enough of them to meet the enemy head on, but they struck hard and fast at British communications, cut up British detachments, and kept the southern loyalists from acting.

Despite the raiders, however, Cornwallis advanced into North Carolina. He sent a force of about 1,000 soldiers under Major Patrick Ferguson to rally loyalist recruits in the western mountains. The patriots learned of this and came riding hard out of the north, south, east, and west.

Ferguson sought safety on a stony ridge between the two Carolinas known as Kings Mountain. He counted on the wooded and boulder-strewn slopes to protect him, but he was fighting woodsmen. These men could scamper nimbly over such ground, and they could drop a squirrel with a single shot at fifty paces.

The Battle of Kings Mountain, fought October 7, 1780, was a stinging blow to British confidence. Among the Americans fighting that day was James P. Collins. The action was hot and it took three assaults for the Americans to gain the top of the cliff. "The enemy," Collins wrote, "was completely hemmed in on all sides, and no chance of escaping—besides, their leader [Major Ferguson] had fallen. After the fight was over . . . the dead lay in heaps

A British force, trapped atop Kings Mountain, fell before the assaults of woodsmen scrambling up the rocky slopes.

The Americans welcomed the French general, Count Jean de Rochambeau, and his trim, disciplined soldiers.

on all sides, while the groans of the wounded were heard in every direction. I could not help turning away from the scene before me with horror and, though exulting in victory, could not refrain from shedding tears. . . ."

British losses that day were 400 casualties, 700 taken prisoner. The American losses totaled eighty-eight.

IN HANNAH'S COWPENS

Morgan prepares a "decent reception" for Tarleton's British army.

Congress now took Washington's advice and put Nathanael Greene in command of the southern army. Arriving at Charlotte, North Carolina, in December, Greene found his fighting force in need of guns, ammunition, wagons, food, and clothes. Opposing them were superior British troops, eager to pay back the Americans for the defeat on Kings Mountain.

During those early weeks, Greene's greatest ally in whipping the Americans into shape was Daniel Morgan, who had used a turkey call to rally his boys in the fighting at Saratoga. Morgan's test came on January 17, 1781, at a place called Hannah's Cowpens, thirty miles west of Kings Mountain.

The British were led by Colonel Tarleton, who was spoiling for revenge. Morgan, whose nickname was the "Old Wagoner," intended to give him a fight he would not forget. "Colonel Tarleton is said to be on his way to pay you a visit," Greene told Morgan. "I doubt not but he will have a decent reception. . . ."

The kind of "reception" that Morgan prepared for Tarleton at Cowpens was important, for it served as a model for a number of later battles fought in the South. Morgan planned his defense with the Broad River at his back, thus cutting off all possible retreat for his men.

Morgan was supremely confident, telling his troops

General Charles Cornwallis

the night before that "as sure as he lived, the Old Wagoner would crack his whip" over Tarleton in the morning. He placed his army in three lines—his raw militia in front, then his seasoned Continentals, and his cavalry in the rear. Each line was to fire two volleys at the British before falling back to the next line of defense.

As Tarleton approached Cowpens, it seemed to him that Morgan was the silliest of fools. Why, a frontal bayonet attack would send those raw militiamen scurrying for their lives! And Morgan's men did indeed begin to fall back under the first British charge. Tarleton believed he had his battle won. He threw in his reserves, and the British charged in wild disorder. But Morgan, knowing exactly what he was about, threw his cavalry across Tarleton's line of retreat. Thomas Young, fighting with the Americans that morning, reported: "The British broke, and throwing down their guns and cartouche [ammunition] boxes, made for the wagon road and did the prettiest sort of running!"

That day 110 Britishers were killed and 702 were taken prisoner. The booty the Americans collected included 800 muskets, one hundred horses, thirty-five wagons of baggage, and sixty Negro slaves. Morgan's loss was twelve killed, sixty wounded.

Tarleton's disaster at Cowpens, said Earl Cornwallis, "almost broke my heart." One third of his British army had been swept away. Meanwhile, Greene was playing his own game, luring Cornwallis northward.

Cornwallis chased Greene grimly, meeting him in battle at Guilford Court House, North Carolina, on March 15, 1781. Although Greene tried to do the same kind of fighting that Morgan had done at Cowpens, he failed to make effective use of his cavalry. As a result, when the day ended, Cornwallis held the field and had captured Greene's guns. Yet British losses had been heavy—about one fourth of the force—so that in London a critic said: "Another such victory will destroy the British army!"

Cornwallis was in a peculiar situation. Greene now had lured him 200 miles from his main base, and Marion's and Sumter's forces were raising hob with attacks on British outposts. Cornwallis appealed to Clinton in New York, begging him to bring all British forces into Virginia.

Meanwhile, Cornwallis had to get back to the sea. If he returned to Camden, he would apparently be admitting defeat. He decided, therefore, to march his army down the Cape Fear River to the port of Wilmington, North Carolina, and from Wilmington into Virginia.

But Greene decided to march south and try to win back South Carolina and Georgia. The British left behind at Camden beat him repeatedly in a series of small battles, but their victories gained nothing.

WASHINGTON AND ROCHAMBEAU

A French army under Rochambeau and a fleet under de Grasse join Washington.

In May of 1781, Washington left his headquarters at West Point to meet in the pleasant little village of Wethersfield, Connecticut, with a most remarkable Frenchman. The previous summer, Count Jean de Rochambeau had reached Newport, Rhode Island, with 5,000 French troops. Now fifty-five years of age, an experienced military leader, and a gentleman of great charm and tact, Rochambeau had quickly won the hearts of the New Englanders.

As Washington journeyed to Wethersfield, he had two problems on his mind—New York and Virginia. Clinton still held New York City, and that winter he had sent a force into Virginia. It was led by Benedict Arnold, the traitor who had changed sides and was now a brigadier general in the British army. Arnold took Richmond, made a number of raids, and then withdrew to Portsmouth. Cornwallis also reached Virginia, and the British were threatening to take control of the state. Meanwhile, Lafayette was moving south at the head of 1,200 American troops.

Washington believed Clinton's position was weak, and he asked Rochambeau to join him in an attack on New York City. Rochambeau felt it might be better to strike at the British in Virginia, but he agreed to do as Washington asked. In either case, the Americans needed the support of the French fleet, now in the West Indies. Washington and Rochambeau sent messages to the commander of the fleet, Admiral François de Grasse. They left it up to him to decide whether to sail to New York or Virginia.

In July Rochambeau's troops joined Washington's at Dobbs Ferry, New York, but by August several important things had happened in the south. Arnold had been replaced by another general, and his force combined with that of Cornwallis. More reinforcements arrived, giving Cornwallis about 7,500 men. Lafayette had only about 3,000 men, even after he had been joined by Anthony Wayne and von Steuben. He wisely refused to let the British get him into a big battle. Instead, he fought small skirmishes.

Cornwallis was also having trouble with Clinton, who remained in New York. Clinton's orders changed from one day to the next. At first he wanted 3,000 troops sent back to New York; then he did not want them; then he wanted them again. At last he told Cornwallis to keep the troops and allowed him to go to Yorktown, off the entrance to Chesapeake Bay.

Washington and Rochambeau were making preparations to attack New York when, on August 14, news came from Admiral de Grasse. He was sailing to Chesapeake Bay with 28 warships and a number of transports carrying 3,000 French troops. Washington immediately decided to attack the British in Virginia. He would swing around New York, hiding his intentions from Clinton, and then race to Virginia to catch Cornwallis in Yorktown. With the French fleet blockading Chesapeake Bay—the only route by which the British could escape or receive reinforcements—Washington would have Cornwallis neatly trapped.

WASHINGTON OUTWITS CLINTON

Pretending to threaten New York, he moves his army to Virginia to trap Cornwallis.

On August 19, Washington began to move his army from Dobbs Ferry. Clinton believed that the American commander was playing the same old game of coming across New Jersey for an attack on New York. Washington was careful to keep his plans secret so that no spy or deserter could reveal them to Clinton.

American and French forces moved through New Jersey in three columns. To make it look as though he were going to attack New York, Washington set up French ovens and warehouses at Chatham. He then pushed his forces ahead, knowing that if his columns could meet at Princeton and Trenton before Clinton awoke to his objective, the race to Virginia was practically won.

The plan worked perfectly. On the last two days of August, the American troops passed through Princeton to Trenton. Washington and Rochambeau, ahead of the armies, were already receiving a hero's welcome in Philadelphia. The Continentals paraded through the streets of the Quaker City on September 2, with drums beating and fifes playing. Next day Rochambeau led his smartly uniformed soldiers through the city. Steadily the Americans and French pressed on to Virginia, and one observer remarked: "General Washington and the army are gone to take Lord Cornwallis in his mousetrap."

Like the pieces in a puzzle, other events fell into place. By the end of August, the French fleet under De Grasse was anchored in Lynnhaven Bay off Hampton Roads. Meanwhile, Lafayette moved quickly to throw a strong defensive line across the peninsula at Williamsburg so that Cornwallis would be tightly sealed into his Yorktown "mousetrap." Early September brought a battle off the Virginia coast between the French fleet and the British under Rear Admiral Thomas Graves. The Britishers, discouraged if not beaten, limped back to New York.

September 9 was a great day for Washington. For the first time since May 4, 1775, he visited his home in Mount Vernon. By mid-September, he reached Williamsburg.

"Men, women and children," wrote Colonel St.

The siege of Yorktown was the last big battle of the Revolution. The British surrender led to peace talks in 1782.

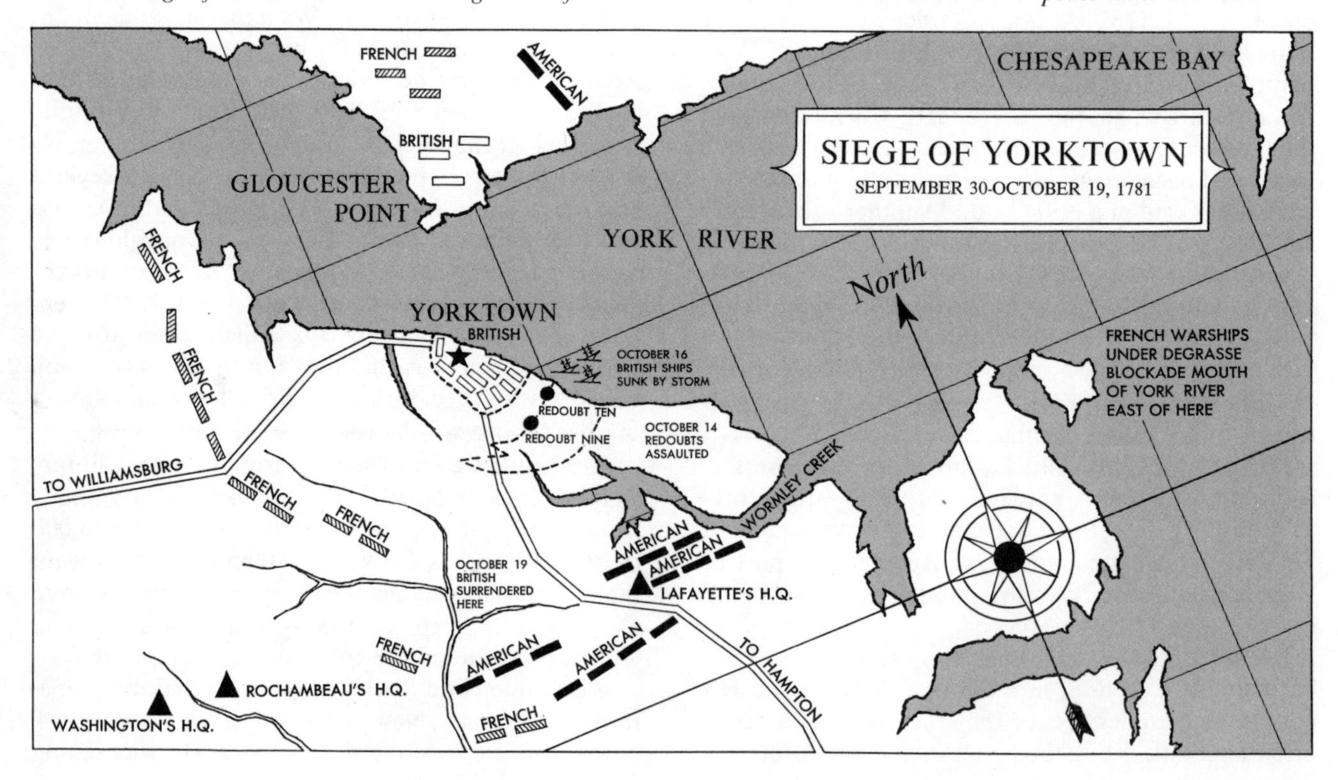

Mount Vernon

George Tucker, who was in command of the militia, "seemed to vie with each other in demonstrations of joy and eagerness to see their beloved countryman." Lafayette rushed forward, "clasped the general in his arms, and embraced him with an ardor not easily described."

Cannon boomed in welcome and Colonel Tucker wrote in his diary: "Cornwallis may now tremble for his fate, for nothing but some extraordinary intervention of his guardian angels seems capable of saving him and the whole army from captivity."

VICTORY AT YORKTOWN

The British and Hessians fight bravely, but Cornwallis is forced to surrender.

On September 28, Washington moved on Yorktown. Cornwallis tried to put up a brave front, but hastily withdrew into his inner lines of defense, and Washington's troops quickly occupied his "outer works." Washington turned to the hard work of building entrenchments and moving up his heavy guns. Joseph Plumb Martin, who had been fighting with the Continentals since the retreat from Long Island in 1776, was amused as he watched Washington strike "a few blows with a pickaxe, a mere ceremony, that it might be said, 'General Washington with his own hands first broke ground at the siege of Yorktown.' "

YORKTOWN BOMBARDED

By October 9, Washington had his big guns in place, and the bombardment of Yorktown began. Quickly the city became a deathtrap. Citizens and soldiers alike rushed to hide against the sand banks of the York River, and there was a report that even Cornwallis was living underground. The diary of a Hessian soldier described the deadliness of Washington's guns:

"During these 24 hours 3,600 shots were counted from the enemy, which they fired at the town, our line, and at the ships in the harbor. These ships were miserably ruined and shot to pieces. Also the bombs and cannon balls hit many inhabitants and Negroes of the city, and marines, sailors, and soldiers. One saw men lying nearly everywhere who were mortally wounded and whose heads, arms, and legs had been shot off. . . ."

Washington's forces, outnumbering those of Cornwallis 16,000 to 7,500, were spread in a semicircle around his foe. As his army dug its trenches ever closer to the enemy, the key to winning Yorktown became two British outposts–Redoubts Nine and Ten.

On October 14, a Sunday night, dark with "a thick fog," a Hessian sentry on Redoubt Ten, hearing a movement, cried out, *"Wer da?"*–"Who's there?" He soon found that it was a French force carrying "long storming spikes." At Redoubt Nine, American troops under Colonel Alexander Hamilton also charged out of the misty night to surprise the enemy.

The fog turned to rain. Shouts, curses, groans filled the night. "As I mounted the breastwork," wrote young Martin, "I met an old associate hitching himself down into the trench. I knew him by the light of the enemy's musketry, it was so vivid." A cry rang out from the French, *"Vive le Roi!"*–"Long live the king!" They had won Redoubt Ten. Soon the Americans were bayoneting their way into the other fort.

THE BRITISH GIVE IN

The end was near for Cornwallis. Sixteen large boats were assembled to ferry his forces across the

Alexander Hamilton led American troops at Yorktown in the assault on Redoubt Nine.

York River to Gloucester, but a violent windstorm sank or dispersed them. Washington's big guns continued pounding the town until a Hessian, viewing a scene "even more horrible than ever before . . . saw nothing but bombs and balls raining on our whole line."

At ten o'clock on the morning of October 16, 1781, a drummer mounted a British parapet. He beat a parley calling for talks between the two opposing leaders. A British officer appeared outside the fort. He waved a white handkerchief. The American guns fell silent. Except for arranging the terms of the surrender, the Battle of Yorktown had ended.

At two o'clock on the afternoon of October 19, Washington rode on his white horse to receive the formal surrender of Cornwallis' army. With him were the beaming Rochambeau, the smiling Lafayette. The sun shone brightly. A Virginia militiaman, gazing at the handsomely dressed French soldiers, realized that they were not, as he once believed, a people who lived "on frogs and coarse vegetables."

As the redcoats came down the road to the doleful piping of their fifes, one American believed that "the British officers in general behaved like boys who had been whipped at school. Some bit their lips, some pouted, some cried." Cornwallis refused to attend the humiliating scene.

The British and Hessians heard the command, "Ground arms and take off cartridge boxes and sabers." Solemnly they obeyed.

"OUR BELOVED GENERAL WAVED HIS HAT"

The war over, Washington bids good-by to his officers.

Washington's "Victory Dispatch" from Yorktown did not reach the Continental Congress until October 24. An old German watchman awakened Philadelphians that morning with the joyous shout: *"Basht dree o'glock, und Cornval-lis isht daken!"* News of the British surrender, traveling through the colonies, produced celebrations everywhere. At Newburgh, New York, the people "hanged and burnt in effigy the traitor Arnold." When information of the disaster was received in London, Lord North, pacing the floor, cried out: "Oh God! It is all over!"

But wars do not end easily. George III seemed as determined as ever to carry on the conflict. Washington was afraid that Americans would grow careless, let down their guard, and lose everything they had gained.

Months went by. The government in England changed, bringing into power persons who favored granting independence to America. Then it changed back and the "war party" once more gained control.

Sir Henry Clinton was removed as commander of British troops in New York. His successor, Sir Guy Carleton, was a genial Irishman who hinted broadly that peace was near.

A year went by. Soldiers quarreled over their idleness, poor provisions, and lack of pay. A cold, bitter winter added to the misery.

Then on April 19, 1783—exactly eight years to the day after the redcoats had fired at the Minutemen on Lexington Green—the army received an announcement. There was to be an official "cessation of hostilities between the United States of America and the King of Great Britain."

On November 25, 1783, with the British gone at last from New York, Washington rode into the city. A dinner in his honor was followed by a "splendid display of fireworks" on lower Broadway. Now free to return home to his beloved Mount Vernon, Washington bade farewell to his officers.

"I cannot come to each of you," he said, "but shall feel obliged if each of you will come and take me by the hand."

General Henry Knox, the Boston bookseller who had fought for freedom since the days of Breed's Hill, embraced his commander in chief with tears streaming down his cheeks. The others came up, each in turn showing his deep affection. The feelings of the occasion were well understood by Lieutenant Colonel Benjamin Tallmadge:

"The simple thought that we were then about to part from the man who had conducted us through a long and bloody war, and under whose conduct the glory and the independence of our country had been achieved, and that we should see his face no more in this world, seemed to be utterly insupportable.

"But the time of separation had come, and waving his hand to his grieving children around him, and passing through a corps of light infantry who were paraded to receive him, he walked silently on to Whitehall, where a barge was in waiting. We all followed in mournful silence to the wharf, where a prodigious crowd had assembled to witness the departure of the man who, under God, had been the great agent in establishing the glory and independence of these United States. As soon as he was seated, the barge put off into the river, and when out in the stream, our great and beloved General waved his hat and bid us a silent adieu."

Home, Washington thought—he was going home at last, to live out his years in peace at Mount Vernon. But only the opportunity to be free had been won—a nation still remained to be built. And so a day would come when Washington would return to this city, stand before other cheering crowds, and, raising his hand, take the oath of office as the first President of the United States.

The Erie Canal, running from the Hudson to Buffalo, opened in 1825. Now goods for the West could be sent up the Hudson.

IV ~ BUILDING THE NATION

from 1783 to 1850

A COUNTRY IN CHAOS

America has won its independence,
but finds that its problems are just beginning.

The Revolution had ended. Now that the army was disbanded and a peace treaty with Britain signed, America settled down in 1783 to living with its newly won independence. After almost ten years of war, the people thought that life would now be easier. But peace, in its way, proved as difficult as war. Sometimes people wondered whether the liberty for which they had sacrificed so much had been worth the struggle.

Compared with nations like Great Britain and France, the infant United States seemed puny. In 1790 it had about 4,000,000 inhabitants. They were so widely scattered that there were fewer than five persons to every square mile. With the exception of perhaps 12,000 pioneers who had made their homes beyond the Appalachian Mountains, the people inhabited a narrow strip of land along the Atlantic seacoast. Roads were few, poorly built, and often dangerous. Cities and towns were small. By the time news of Europe reached America, it was six weeks to three months out of date.

For the most part, the people thought only of their own affairs. Home was the center of their universe. A quarrel with a neighbor could easily become a family feud, a little war. Tories who had fled service in the army during the Revolution were not welcomed by the patriots on their return. Sometimes they were tarred and feathered and driven out of the neighborhood.

The trouble was that the country and its people were penniless. When the French and British troops left and the American forces were disbanded, the farmers lost a major market for their produce.

European merchants flooded America with the surpluses they had built up during the war, selling goods at sacrifice prices to some storekeepers. This cutthroat competition threatened to ruin many other American shopkeepers, who were loaded down with wartime surpluses of their own.

Britain now put heavy duties on Yankee ships that entered British ports, and Spain closed her ports in Europe and America to United States shipping. Without the protection of a strong navy, Yankee vessels sailing into the Mediterranean were forced

At the end of the Revolution, most Americans lived along the eastern seaboard. (Present-day boundaries are shown.)

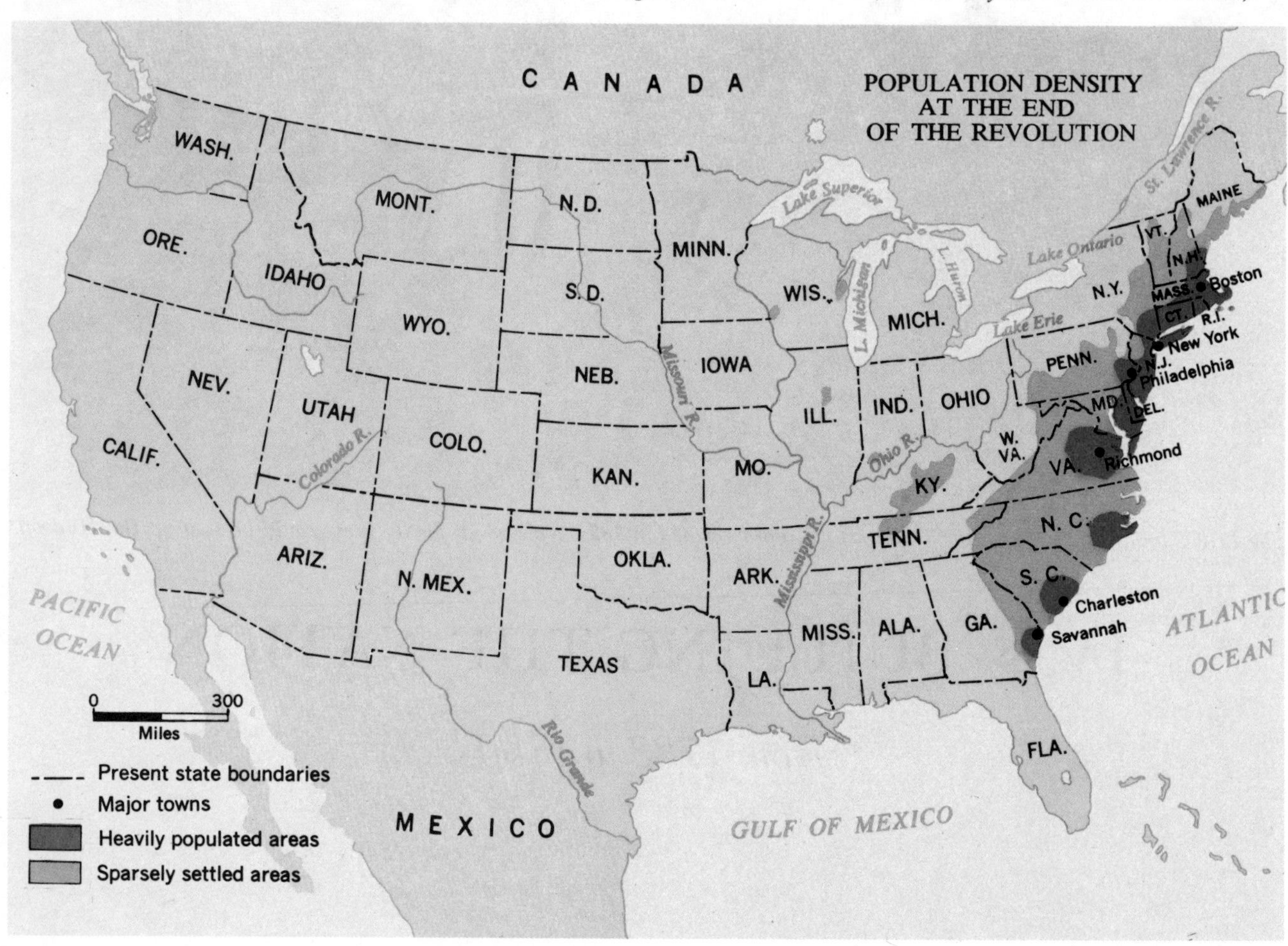

to pay tribute to the Barbary pirates, who swarmed out of the ports of Tunis, Algeria, and Tripolitania on the North African coast.

States often acted more like enemies than partners. Pennsylvania and New York, more prosperous than their neighbors, passed laws to keep foreign goods from their ports. Little New Jersey and Connecticut, however, received such goods freely and closed their eyes to the smuggling that their citizens carried on with Pennsylvania and New York.

What "hard" money remained in America after the Revolution consisted of various foreign coins, and these were rapidly disappearing. People who owned land could not borrow money on it, for land was too plentiful. Paper money had little value and barter (trading goods) became common. To make matters worse, Congress had no power to raise taxes, regulate business, or place duties on imports. To gain that power Congress had to obtain the consent of all the states, a task that was impossible to accomplish at the time.

Something had to give. Too many people were facing poverty and starvation or imprisonment for their debts. More and more people said: "Let the states print more paper money. Make it a law that such money must be accepted in payment of debts."

Paper money has value because something of *real* value—usually gold or silver—backs it up. If a country prints paper money without having gold or silver to back each dollar, that money becomes "cheaper." If there are five paper dollars in circulation and only one dollar's worth of silver as backing in the Treasury, each paper dollar is really worth only twenty cents.

But in everyday business dealings—paying debts and buying goods—people have faith in their currency and a dollar remains a dollar. A $10 debt may be paid with ten one-dollar bills; nobody can say, "You now owe me $50 because the dollar has a *real* value of only twenty cents."

So in times of stress, people who owe money or can't afford to buy things want "cheap" money—more dollars. Those who are owed or who sell things want "hard" money, as close to a hundred-cent dollar as they can get.

In 1786 practically every state in the Union was torn by this struggle over "cheap money." By that time, seven states were issuing more paper money. As a result, there was a flood of paper money that fell quickly in value.

TROUBLE OVER MONEY

In Rhode Island, where the farm vote had made paper money legal, warfare nearly broke out in communities like Providence and Newport. Here many shopkeepers who had paid hard money for their goods refused to sell them for cheap money. Farmers refused to ship their produce into these towns, hoping to starve out the opposition. Shops closed. Skulls were cracked and noses bloodied in street fights. When the court upheld the right of a butcher to refuse to sell meat for paper money, the people's anger turned on the judges. Almost all judges who decided cases in favor of the merchants lost their jobs.

Massachusetts voted against paper money that stormy year of 1786, but the basic financial problem remained. Farms and homes were lost because the owners did not have the dollars to pay what they owed. Feeling rose against lawyers and judges who seemed to be growing rich by foreclosing mortgages. The hard-pressed farmers asked for laws by which they could pay off their debts with personal property —tools, clothes, furniture, real estate—but the legislature ended its meeting in July without providing any form of relief.

Rebellion shook Massachusetts. Mobs prevented the lower courts from meeting at Northampton and Worcester. An armed band seized the court house at Concord and drove the judge out of town. Some 800 rioters went even further at Great Barrington. They opened the jail and freed the prisoners.

Some examples of colonial coins and bills.

Independence Hall, Philadelphia, birthplace of the Declaration of Independence and the Constitution.

In September another force, under tough old Daniel Shays, a veteran of the Revolution, marched on Springfield, where the state supreme court was going to hear cases against debtors. The militia was called out, but Shays kept Springfield in such an uproar that the court could not carry on its business. The militia, firing a cannon into Shays' ragtag army, killed three rebels.

Not until the following February did the militia finally end Shays' Rebellion. It had taken 4,000 men and thousands of dollars to restore law and order in Massachusetts. At the next election the people voted the governor out of office. In his place they put John Hancock, well known as a friend of liberty.

"IN ORDER TO FORM A MORE PERFECT UNION"

Delegates of the new nation meet and draw up a constitution.

The Articles of Confederation, the agreements under which the United States operated, had not made the states into a true Union. There was almost no money with which to pay the national debt. Foreign affairs were loosely and poorly handled, and Indian warfare threatened the frontier. Connecticut and Pennsylvania were having a serious argument over who had the rights to the rich Wyoming Valley of Pennsylvania. New Jersey refused to pay her share of Confederation expenses because Congress could not settle her quarrels with New York and Pennsylvania.

Virginia's statesmen, including George Washington, James Madison, and Governor Edmund Randolph, took the lead in calling a convention to see what could be done. In May of 1787, delegates from eleven states met at Philadelphia in the room where the Declaration of Independence had been signed. New Hampshire was tardy in sending delegates and Rhode Island, always suspicious of her larger neighbors, was never represented.

Many of the delegates wanted to "patch up" the Articles of Confederation and make them more workable. But as the debates went on, the Articles were discarded. To take their place, a new plan of government was created—the Constitution. The British statesman William E. Gladstone would one day call it "the most wonderful work ever struck off at a given time by the brain and purpose of men."

Only twelve of the delegates to the Constitutional convention were past the age of fifty-four. Six were under thirty-one. Many remarkable men took part in the meetings. Among them were George Washington, Benjamin Franklin, and James Madison. Massachusetts sent Rufus King with his "strong expressive eye" and "sweet high-toned voice," and Elbridge Gerry, who "cherishes as his first virtue a love for his country." From Connecticut came Oliver Ellsworth, a judge of the Supreme Court, and Roger Sherman.

Benjamin Franklin spoke up for the Constitution.

From South Carolina came John Rutledge, famous for his oratory, and Charles Pinckney, only twenty-four years of age. New York included among its delegates the gifted and sharp-tongued Alexander Hamilton. Pennsylvania sent Gouverneur Morris, who would have much to do with writing the final draft of the Constitution, and the learned James Wilson. Virginia's delegation included George Mason, a planter who had written most of his state's constitution.

Yet there were some noted men who were absent. Thomas Jefferson and John Adams were abroad on diplomatic missions. Virginia's Patrick Henry and New York's George Clinton were at home. They were distrustful of the gathering and where it might lead the country.

George Washington was elected president of the convention, and Edmund Randolph presented to the delegates the "Virginia plan." It called for a strong national government with three branches—Executive, Legislative, and Judicial. The Legislative branch would be divided into the Senate and the House of Representatives. The plan also called for representation in the legislative branch of government on the basis of population. The smaller states rebelled. They wanted equal representation, which was opposed by "the big three"—Virginia, Pennsylvania, and Massachusetts.

A "New Jersey plan" was proposed, which would simply patch up the Articles of Confederation. This plan gave Congress some additional powers, including that of taxation, but prevented it from vetoing state laws. An executive committee, rather than a president, would be the head of the government.

James Madison attended the Constitutional Convention.

George Washington was elected president of the Convention.

The convention defeated the New Jersey plan. The delegates from the smaller states might have packed up and gone home, but they decided not to take the responsibility for breaking up the convention.

As the hot summer days rolled by, the delegates began to act in the spirit of compromise. Point by point they fought out their differences, carefully working out solutions to the most difficult kind of problems. In the end they created one of the great documents of history. It set up a practical system of government, flexible enough to be adapted to changing conditions. At the same time, it would not sacrifice the democratic principles of liberty and justice on which the nation was based.

With great wisdom, the delegates balanced the various powers of government. No branch was to be too strong or too weak. The executive branch, under the President, could act independently and had command of the armed forces. These powers were checked and balanced by Congress, which controlled the President's appointments and had the power to start all actions concerning taxes and money.

Congress would write the nation's laws, but the President could veto any law he did not approve. Congress could then override the veto by a two-thirds vote. The Supreme Court could uphold the law or declare it unconstitutional.

The President and Vice-President were to be chosen for terms of four years, not by the direct vote of the people but by "electors." Each state was to select as many electors as it had representatives and senators. Meeting in their state capitals, these electors would vote for two men. The candidate receiving the highest number of votes would become President, and the candidate receiving the next highest Vice-President. Each state was given equal representation in the Senate, which was an advantage for the small states. Representation in the House of Representatives was according to population, which was an advantage for large states.

The Constitution was designed to be the law of the land and no state could pass laws conflicting with it. At the same time, many responsibilities were left to the states.

Not all the delegates were satisfied by the work of the convention. They had had to compromise on too many things. Yet they knew that without compromise there could be no democracy. Eighty-one-year-old Benjamin Franklin, whose body was feeble but whose mind was still sharp, pleaded for agreement among the delegates. His voice was too weak to be heard and James Wilson read his statement for him:

"I doubt . . . whether any other convention we can obtain may be able to make a better Constitution. . . . It therefore astonishes me, sir, to find this system approaching so near to perfection as it does. . . . I cannot help expressing a wish that every member of the convention . . . would with me, on this occasion, doubt a little of his own infallibility, and . . . put his name to this instrument."

Of the forty-two delegates present at the time, thirty-nine signed. Then the document was made public—the document which begins with these noble words:

"We the People of the United States, in order to form a more perfect Union, establish Justice, insure domestic Tranquility, provide for the common Defence, promote the General Welfare, and secure the blessings of Liberty to Ourselves and our Posterity, do ordain and establish this Constitution for the United States of America. . . ."

LAUNCHING THE NEW GOVERNMENT

The Constitution is approved and Washington is elected President.

Although the Constitutional Convention was over, there was still a struggle ahead. Before the Constitution was made legal, it had to be approved by at least nine states. Some people voted against the Constitution simply because it was new and different. Others feared that a strong central government would destroy the freedom of the states. And still others opposed the Constitution because it included no "Bill of Rights." They said it contained many safeguards of property rights, but no guarantees for the liberty of individuals. And so two groups sprang up—the Federalists, who favored the new Constitution, and the Anti-Federalists, who were against it.

Washington did much to win support for the Constitution. James Madison, Alexander Hamilton, and John Jay, who was soon to be the first Chief Justice of the Supreme Court, also supported it. They gave their views in a series of brilliant essays known as *The Federalist Papers.* Perhaps most important of

For four months in the summer of 1787 Convention delegates debated the document that was to become the Constitution.

all, defenders of the Constitution won support for it by promising to work for a Bill of Rights as soon as the Constitution was approved by the states.

Delaware, Connecticut, Georgia, New Jersey, South Carolina, Pennsylvania, and Maryland were won over with the least trouble. In Massachusetts, where the farmers believed that the Constitution might favor business, the struggle was especially hard. It was not much better in New Hampshire, but finally, on June 21, 1788, this little state became the ninth to ratify the Constitution, making it the supreme law of the land.

Virginia ratified the Constitution four days later, New York the following month. North Carolina would not agree until 1789, and then only after it was assured that a Bill of Rights would be added. Rhode Island finally signed on May 20, 1790.

Now that the nation had a constitution, it was time to set up the actual government. State legislatures named congressmen and electors to choose a President. Meeting in New York City on April 6, 1789, they made George Washington their unanimous choice for President. John Adams was named Vice-President. Formally notified of his election, Washington borrowed money from friends and started on the long journey from Mount Vernon to New York City.

Everywhere Washington stopped, crowds turned out to cheer him. On April 30, 1789, a barge carried him across New York Bay for his inauguration.

On the deck of a sailboat, a chorus of ladies and gentlemen sang songs. From the Battery, cannon boomed a thirteen-gun salute. The streets were jammed to overflowing. Bands blared.

Finally Washington stood on the balcony of the Federal Building. To encourage the nation's young textile industry, he wore a neat brown suit that had been made in America. He felt ill and faint. But he said: "I do solemnly swear that I will faithfully execute the Office of the President of the United States, and will to the best of my ability preserve, protect and defend the Constitution of the United States."

WASHINGTON AS PRESIDENT

The new government tackles many problems and adopts the Bill of Rights.

When Washington became President of the United States he faced many problems, and one of the most important was that the country needed money. He chose Alexander Hamilton, his aide-de-camp during the Revolution, as his Secretary of the Treasury. The warm friendship between the two men aroused jealousy in other members of the government, and in time caused serious trouble. Nevertheless, Hamilton was a wise choice, for he was truly a genius of finance.

Hamilton went about his difficult tasks with great boldness of imagination. Both the national government and the individual states had borrowed money to carry on the War for Independence. Now Hamilton proposed not only that the national government pay its debts in full to European creditors, but also that it pay the debts of the states. He pushed through his plan by skillful political maneuvering. He won the support of the Southerners by agreeing that the new national capital city should be located in the South, on the banks of the Potomac River.

Whatever Hamilton did, he fought hard and he fought to win. When the tariff of 1790 failed to raise the money he needed, he suggested a tax on whiskey. Congressmen from the South and the West raised a howl. People in their districts used whiskey to trade for manufactured goods, iron, and salt. They said the tax hurt the poor. Besides, it was too much like the English system that allowed agents of the king to snoop into local affairs. Again Hamilton stood his ground, again he won.

Hamilton was no sooner out of one fight than he was in another. When he took office as secretary, there were only three banks in America: in Philadelphia, New York, and Boston. To give the country a sounder banking system, Hamilton proposed the establishment of a Bank of the United States with branches in various cities. It could issue reliable money, collect taxes, and in other ways make it easier for Americans to conduct business.

Opponents called the plan for a government-run bank unconstitutional, and among them was Thomas Jefferson, who was now Secretary of State. For once Washington hesitated in his support of Hamilton. Then Hamilton sent him a brilliantly written memo-

randum justifying the founding of the bank, and the President signed the bill authorizing it.

So Hamilton had won again—but Jefferson's distrust of him grew. The two men were opposites in almost every way. Jefferson was awkward in debate, while Hamilton was quick of speech. Jefferson believed firmly in democracy, while Hamilton referred to the common people as "that great beast." Each was suspicious of the other, and meetings between the two were uncomfortable. Yet both were great men, and Washington needed them both.

The President could have little complaint about the way Jefferson handled the extremely difficult foreign relations of the young nation. Both Britain and Spain dreamed of conquest and expansion beyond the Appalachians, both plotted with the Indians. The British still held illegal fur posts at places like Detroit and Mackinac. The Spanish occupied Natchez on the Mississippi and were pushing farther north. They hoped to stir up so much feeling in Kentucky and Tennessee that these two states, which had only recently become part of the nation, would withdraw from the Union. The British and the Spanish were playing a hardheaded, cold-blooded game. The United States was too weak to protect its borders. What could she do but stand by as rich lands were nibbled away?

But Jefferson took advantage of the rivalries among the European nations. He played the British against the Spanish in a dispute over fur posts on the Pacific coast. The result was that England, who had refused to send a diplomatic envoy to the United States, now changed her mind. When France went to war against Prussia and Austria, Jefferson held Britain and Spain in line by withholding aid from France. In the end, Britain agreed to leave the northwestern fur posts. Spain wanted to make peace with France. Knowing that Britain would not like this, she decided to strengthen her friendship with the United States, to whom she gave free use of the Mississippi and trading privileges at New Orleans.

THE BILL OF RIGHTS

While the United States was making a place for itself among the nations of the world, there was an important development at home. In 1789 the first Congress passed ten amendments to the Constitution, known as "the Bill of Rights." Submitted by James Madison in the House of Representatives, they provided basic guarantees of individual liberties for all the nation's citizens.

The first amendment guaranteed freedom of religion, freedom of the press, and the right peaceably to assemble and to petition the government for "a redress of grievances" (the remedying or correcting of unfair situations).

The next three amendments guaranteed a militia and the right to bear arms, forbade lodging troops in people's homes in time of peace, and declared a citizen's home secure against invasion and search except by permission of a judge—liberties dearly prized by those who remembered the struggles of the Revolution.

Amendments five through eight guaranteed trial by jury, protected citizens against unreasonable arrest or cruel punishment, and provided that no person should be "deprived of life, liberty or property without due process of law."

The final two amendments defined the division of powers between federal and state governments.

By 1791, the amendments were ratified by the states and became part of the Constitution.

VICTORY AT FALLEN TIMBERS

"Mad Anthony" Wayne is sent to put down an Indian uprising.

It was remarkable, really, how much was being accomplished in these first few years. By trial and error, the young nation was moving ahead—in finance, in foreign affairs, in expanding its basic laws. And all the time the country was growing. Vermont became a state in 1791. Kentucky was admitted in 1792, Tennessee in 1796.

But there was serious trouble in the region north of the Ohio River. The Indians, stirred up by the British, were becoming dangerously restless. Washington had kept an old friend, General Arthur St. Clair, as governor of the Northwest Territory, but soon reports suggested that St. Clair might be napping on the job. Indians were massacring settlers. Traders were being killed or driven away.

A force of militia—about 1,500 ragged and poorly trained men—invaded the Territory in October of 1790. Five Indian towns and 20,000 bushels of corn were destroyed. The Indians counterattacked viciously. The militia retreated, and the settlements were open to a new wave of murder, fire, and robbery.

St. Clair now awakened from his nap. With a force of 2,000 men, assembled at Cincinnati, he set off against the Indians. The old general advanced at a snail's pace, stopping often to build forts. The army's food supply shrank to almost nothing; every day more men deserted. In November, 1791, St. Clair and his weary, quarrelsome army were encamped on a branch of the Wabash when the Indians struck. The shriek of their war whoops shook St. Clair from his tent. His defeat amounted to disaster, but for once he moved swiftly. In one day he retreated as far as he had advanced in ten.

All of the region north of the Ohio—and Kentucky

as well—was now threatened with even worse terror. The Indians were led by Joseph Brant, who had a cunning mind and a ruthless heart. When the news of St. Clair's troubles reached Philadelphia, which was now the national capital, the President was furious. Washington loved the frontier and wanted it protected. He turned to "Mad Anthony" Wayne to restore peace to the Ohio country.

Wayne was an efficient officer. First he drilled his men in the fundamentals of fighting. Then in the winter of 1793-94, he moved to Fort Greenville, seventy-five miles north of Cincinnati. With warm weather, Wayne began his advance into the Indian country. He passed one deserted village after another, until he reached a region where a tornado had uprooted the trees.

In this "land of fallen timbers," Wayne met the Indians. There were Miamis, Shawnees, Ottawas, Chippewas, Potawatomis, Sauk and Fox, and a small band of Iroquois. The Americans charged with fixed bayonets. Cavalrymen spurred their horses over the tree stumps. In less than an hour the Battle of Fallen Timbers ended in a complete rout of the Indians. A year later they signed a treaty that gave most of Ohio to the United States.

THE POLITICAL POT BEGINS TO BOIL

The Jefferson-Hamilton feud leads to the formation of America's first political parties.

With peace secure the young nation began stretching its muscles, making progress in many ways. In 1788, *Nicholas Pike's Arithmetic* was first published at Newburyport, Massachusetts. George Washington was among those who endorsed the book, and it became widely used in schoolrooms throughout the country. That same year Noah Webster's *The American Spelling Book* appeared; in time it would sell 70,000,000 copies. In 1792, at Sterling, Massachusetts, Robert Baily Thomas began publishing *The Farmer's Almanac,* which would have a longer life than any other American periodical.

The previous year, George Washington had accepted the services of Pierre Charles L'Enfant, a young French engineer who had served with Lafayette during the Revolution. L'Enfant was to plan a new city on the Potomac, a city which was to be the nation's capital.

It was in this period that two men produced inventions that would change American life and history. One was Samuel Slater. At Pawtucket, Rhode Island, in 1790, he constructed America's first successful power-driven cotton-spinning machine. But cotton was not yet profitable because of the high cost of separating the seed from the fiber. The work was done by hand, and a slave could clean little more than a pound of cotton a day.

Not long after Slater had set up his machine, a young Yankee left New England to take a teaching job in Georgia. His name was Eli Whitney, and when he reached the South he found that his job had disappeared. Although he had never seen cotton or cottonseed before, he turned his mind to the problem of cleaning the fiber. In 1793 he invented the cotton gin, which could clean more cotton in a single day than a slave could in a month. Soon cotton became "white gold" to the South, and plantations began to prosper. Large numbers of field hands were needed to raise the crop, and the South built its future on an increased use of Negro slaves.

Even though America was moving ahead, Washington found his years as President growing more and more unhappy. The feud between Alexander Hamilton and Thomas Jefferson steadily worsened. Each had different views of government, each had his supporters, and this led to the formation of the new nation's first political parties.

Hamilton believed in a strong, centralized government and in encouraging business and industry. In foreign affairs, he favored the British. His views attracted rich merchants, big Northern landowners, and small businessmen. These were the Federalists.

The opposition—the Anti-Federalists—was made up of Southern landowners, of craftsmen, workers, and small farmers. They were against Hamilton's programs of taxation and were pro-French. They sympathized with France's struggle against tyranny, which to them

Alexander Hamilton

seemed much like their own revolution. They found their leader in Jefferson.

First calling themselves the Federal Republicans and later the Democratic-Republicans, they made no effort to oppose Washington for the presidency in 1792. But John Adams, a Federalist running for re-election as Vice-President, was opposed by George Clinton of New York. Although Adams won, he failed to carry five states–Virginia, New York, North Carolina, Georgia and Kentucky–and the Federalists lost control in Congress.

Jefferson's revolt was just beginning. The formation of "Democratic Societies" during the summer of 1793 kept the political pot boiling. All sorts of charges were made against Washington. The Father of the Country was no longer a man who could do no wrong.

Hamilton's excise tax on whiskey outraged many people. In western Pennsylvania, tax collectors were driven off. The men who did this were ordered to cross the Alleghenies and stand trial in Philadelphia. An angry mob awaited the marshal who came to make the arrests. The home of the inspector of excise was destroyed and some of the soldiers guarding it were killed.

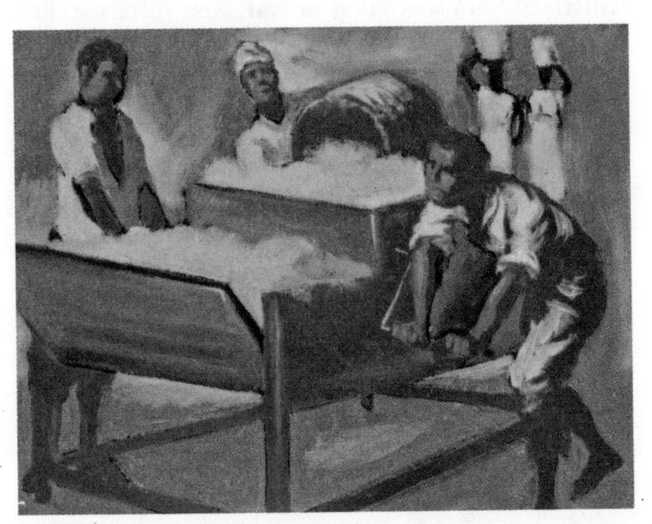

Eli Whitney's cotton gin turned the South's cotton into "white gold" and spurred the use of Negro slave labor.

The Whiskey Rebellion now had flamed into a nasty little civil war. The mails were robbed so that reports on the rebels could not reach Philadelphia. Washington acted vigorously, calling out 15,000 militiamen. In November, 1794, they reached the scene of trouble, but they found no rebel army to fight. A number of suspects were arrested, and two were tried and found guilty. Washington believed he had upheld the spirit of the law, so he immediately pardoned these offenders. The Whiskey Rebellion was over.

President John Adams

JOHN ADAMS SUCCEEDS WASHINGTON

Adams suffers from the political battles around him and loses bid for re-election.

Thomas Jefferson's eye was firmly fixed on the presidential election in 1796, and his followers continued to attack the Federalists as the party of "tyrants, taxes and Tories." Meanwhile, the Federalists were having trouble within their own ranks. There was bad feeling between two of their leaders–John Adams and Alexander Hamilton. Adams was more moderate in his views than Hamilton.

Hamilton was not popular enough to be elected President himself, so he tried to block Adams' election. With the aid of Southern Federalists in Congress, he schemed to divide the electoral college vote evenly between Adams and Thomas Pinckney of South Carolina. Then it would be up to Congress to decide who should become President. But John Adams outmaneuvered Hamilton. Supported by eighteen New Englanders, he won the presidency, while Hamilton's old foe, Jefferson, became Vice-President. The two highest offices in the land were held by men of opposing parties. But this time, Britain and France were at war. Both countries disliked the fact that America was neutral and insisted on the right to seize American ships on the high seas. French diplomats offered to stop these acts of piracy if they were given bribes for themselves and a loan of $12,500,000 for their country.

Adams refused. He substituted the letters X, Y, Z for the names of the diplomats and published their letters. The nation was outraged, and rallied to the

The United States frigate Constellation *acquitted herself well in the undeclared war with France.*

cry: "Millions for defense, but not one cent for tribute!" Washington agreed to take command of the army in case of a war with France. Shipyards turned out a few frigates, marking the beginning of the American navy. The U.S. frigate *Constellation* captured one French frigate and defeated another in a furious battle fought on a stormy sea.

At home, Adams started a different kind of war when he signed the Alien and Sedition Acts. These were set up by the Federalists to make difficulties for people sympathetic to the French—people who were flocking to Jefferson's party. Under the Acts, the President could banish from the country any alien (any person not a citizen) he considered dangerous. Anyone who wrote "scandalous or malicious" articles about the President or Congress could be jailed. More than that, the time a person had to wait before becoming a naturalized citizen was lengthened from five to fourteen years.

Clearly these acts did away with freedom of speech and the press. A congressman from Vermont was jailed and a number of Republican editors brought to trial. Jefferson and Madison led the opposition against this "Federalist tyranny." In a series of resolutions they argued for "states' rights," declaring that whenever the national government assumed a power not granted in the Constitution, "its acts are unauthoritative, void and of no force." In time the Alien and Sedition Acts expired. Although Adams had opposed the Acts, and although he had done little to apply them, he suffered from the political explosion they created.

In the last months of his presidency Adams moved his family into the recently completed White House in Washington, which was now the nation's capital. He complained that the executive mansion was cold, drafty, and uncomfortable. His wife, Abigail, hung her wash in the unfinished East Room. The only interruption in the quarreling that surrounded him came at the death of George Washington on December 14, 1799. Everywhere people mourned this great American who was "first in war, first in peace, first in the hearts of his countrymen."

The interruption was brief, and Adams' political war went on. Hamilton still believed himself the rightful head of the Federalists. He made no secret that he was plotting to rid the party of Adams as its presidential candidate. Adams hit back hard. He dismissed Hamilton's supporters from his cabinet and finally won the nomination. Charles Cotesworth Pinckney, a Revolutionary general and a South Carolina delegate to the Constitutional Convention, was his vice-presidential candidate. The Democratic-Republicans nominated Jefferson for President, with

The Louisiana Territory doubled the size of the nation.

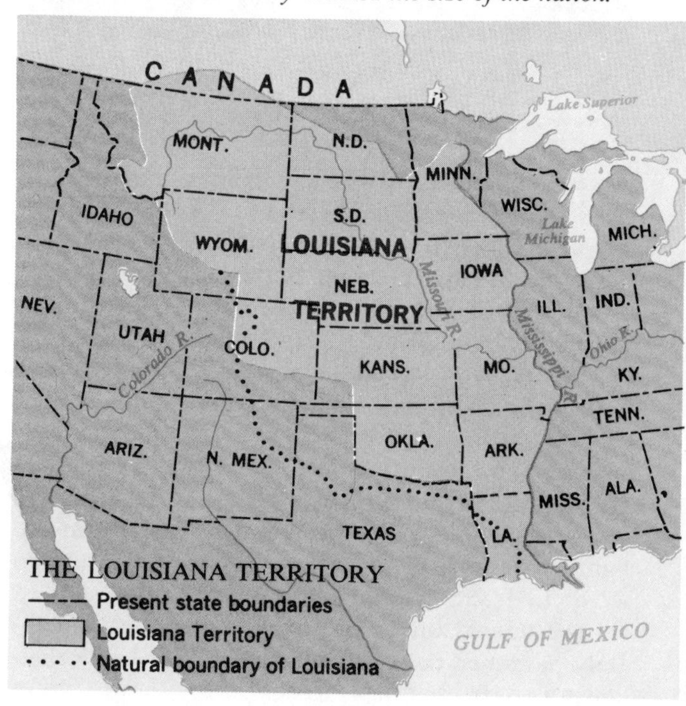

Aaron Burr of New York as his running-mate. Burr had served in the army and in the Senate.

THE ELECTION OF 1800

The country would not soon forget the election of 1800. Hamilton attacked Adams without mercy, and Jefferson called him an enemy of liberty. Federalist clergymen rallied to Adams, calling Jefferson an infidel who would pull down the churches if elected. The campaign divided the nation; New England was for Adams, the South for Jefferson. There was even talk that if Jefferson won, New England might be forced to secede from the Union.

The electors met in December. As expected, New England solidly supported Adams. New Jersey and Delaware also supported him, and he drew a scattering of votes from Pennsylvania, North Carolina, and Maryland. Adams' total was sixty-five, eight less than the Democratic-Republicans', who carried New York and the Southern states. Yet nothing had been decided. Jefferson and Burr had received exactly the same number of votes, and the election was thrown into the House of Representatives.

Congress began voting in mid-February of 1801 in the recently completed north wing of the Capitol. Feelings ran high. Most of the Federalists, who hated Jefferson, wanted to give the presidency to Burr. On the first ballot he received the support of the New England Federalists, Delaware and South Carolina—in all, six states. Maryland and Vermont, unable to make a choice, split their votes. The remaining eight states—or one state short of the number necessary for election—went to Jefferson.

For five days the deadlock continued. Crowds roamed the streets, demanding Jefferson's election. In New York City, Burr remained silent, refusing to make any bargain. Hamilton disliked Jefferson, but he liked Burr even less. Behind the scenes Hamilton worked on his Federalist friends, telling them that Burr could not be trusted, that Jefferson must be the choice. Finally, Hamilton swung the election when the Federalists in divided Maryland and Vermont failed to appear and these states went to Jefferson. News of his victory set off a wave of celebrations. People danced in the streets. In a sour mood Adams left without waiting to see Jefferson inaugurated.

A PRESIDENT IN CARPET SLIPPERS

Buying Louisiana from Napoleon, Jefferson doubles the size of the nation.

Throughout his life Thomas Jefferson had always thought and acted in his own way, and he did not change when he became President. The tall, red-headed Virginian shocked the British ambassador, who appeared at the White House in a splendid uniform and dress sword, by greeting him in a pair of old carpet slippers. Jefferson did not care. He liked the freedom of slouching around in carpet slippers.

As President, Jefferson was willing to make compromises. "Every difference of opinion is not difference of principle," he said in his inaugural address. "We are all Republicans—we are all Federalists." His policies were much like those Adams would have followed if he had been re-elected. By cutting government spending, Jefferson reduced the national debt and lowered taxes. He ended the excise tax on whiskey. He encouraged the expansion of northwestern territory, and in 1803 Ohio became a state.

In Europe, Napoleon Bonaparte was now the ruler of France, and he was planning to build an empire in the New World. He hoped to make Haiti, an island in the Caribbean Sea, a center for growing sugar and other tropical products. He would bring in food for his sugar growers from Louisiana—and the fact that the Louisiana Territory belonged to Spain did not bother him a bit.

Napoleon secretly arranged a deal with Spain. In return for Louisiana, he offered to give to the son-in-law of the King of Spain a principality in Italy, which was then also under French rule. When Jefferson learned of the deal, he was greatly worried. He feared having the French on the borders of the United States. He also feared that the Mississippi would be closed to American trade, and, in fact, in 1802, Americans did lose some of their trading rights in New Orleans. Something had to be done, and in 1803 Jefferson sent James Monroe to France with instructions to purchase New Orleans.

Before Monroe arrived, the American envoy in France received unexpected news. Napoleon was ready to sell not only New Orleans, but all of Louisiana. A revolution and an outbreak of yellow fever in Haiti had ended Napoleon's interest in that island. Besides, he was now plotting a war against England and needed money. He offered the United States a "noble bargain": about 828,000 square miles of land, between the Mississippi and the Rocky Mountains, for $15,000,000.

Jefferson was astonished. But he had a problem—the Constitution gave him no power to make such a purchase. Not too long ago, he himself had attacked the Federalists for taking powers not granted by the Constitution. Yet how could he pass by this opportunity to double the size of the nation? And he had to act quickly, for Napoleon was the kind of man who might very well change his mind. The President decided that the opportunity was more important than the principle and authorized the Louisiana Purchase. The Senate approved it by a vote of 26 to 5 and the House by a vote of 90 to 25.

A political storm arose. The Federalists' strength was mainly in New England. They were afraid that any new states formed of the Louisiana Territory would support the ideas and policies of Jefferson. Again they said that soon New England would be forced to leave the Union. The states of New York and New Jersey would join New England and set up a northern confederacy with its own government.

The Federalists knew that this scheme could not succeed without New York, and for help they turned to Aaron Burr. The Jeffersonians had never forgiven Burr for trying to defeat Jefferson for the presidency in 1801. Burr was quite willing to listen to the Federalists if they would help him become governor of New York.

Once more Alexander Hamilton threw all his political power against Burr, and as a result Burr lost the election. The defeat clearly told the Federalists that their dreams had died. They had failed to win New York, and without it there could be no confederacy. Moreover, the Federalists now had no chance of stopping Jefferson's re-election.

Burr, the man without a party, soon became a man without a country. Furious with Hamilton, Burr challenged his old foe to a duel. Hamilton accepted, and the two met on a misty July morning in 1804 on the banks of the Hudson at Weehawken, New Jersey. Hamilton fired into the air. Burr took careful aim, and Hamilton was mortally wounded.

Guilty of murder, Burr escaped into the Southwest. No one can say for certain what wild schemes filled his mind. He plotted with all kinds of persons, including British and Spanish ministers, and perhaps he did plan to set up his own independent state in Louisiana. Captured as he was sailing a force down the Mississippi, he was brought to trial for treason in 1807. He was acquitted for lack of evidence, but he was in disgrace and fled to Europe.

EXPLORING THE CONTINENT

Lewis and Clark head an expedition to explore the Northwest.

Even before the Louisiana Purchase, Jefferson had wanted to send an expedition to explore the vast wilderness of the West. One of the reasons was the disturbing news about the British in the region west of the Mississippi. American fur traders in St. Louis were complaining of competition from such British-owned organizations as the Hudson's Bay Company and the Northwest Company, which had been operating in this region since 1783. A third company—the Mackinaw Company—also was pushing into the territory that one day would become Minnesota and Wisconsin.

In an historic journey, Lewis and Clark crossed the continent to the Pacific—the first explorers to do so north of Mexico.

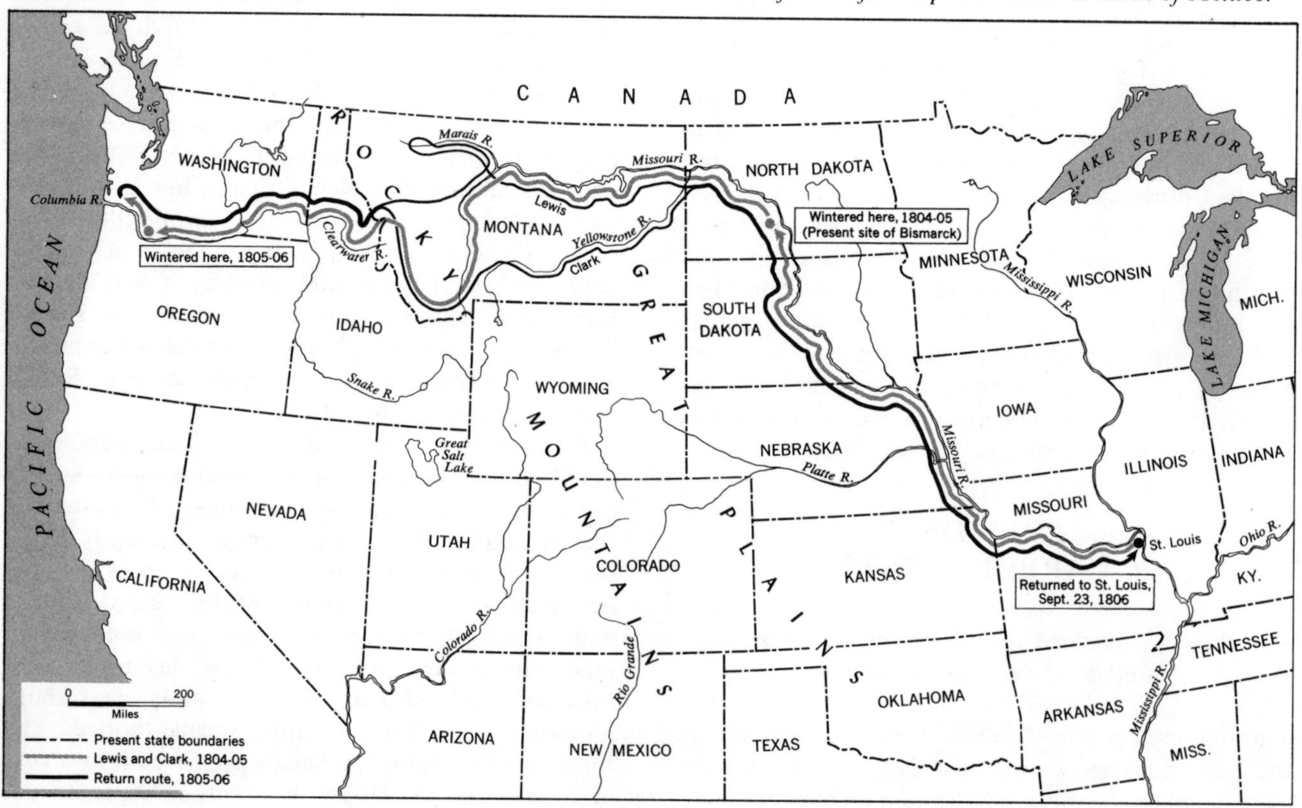

Jefferson wanted to know the facts, and he wanted a survey of the new territory purchased from France. He authorized an expedition under his private secretary, Meriwether Lewis, and William Clark (brother of the famous George Rogers Clark). They were to explore the Missouri River, find the source of the Mississippi, and seek a river leading to the Pacific.

In the summer of 1804, these explorers and their party traveled 1,600 miles into the country of the Mandan Indians. They camped for the winter at the mouth of the Missouri (near the site of present-day Bismarck, North Dakota). Scouts brought back a variety of gifts for Jefferson: the horns of a mountain ram, skins of the red fox, white hare, marten, and yellow bear, articles of Indian dress, a box of plants, "and three cases containing a burrowing squirrel, a prairie hen, and four magpies, all alive."

With spring, Lewis and Clark pushed up the Missouri into Montana. Guided by Sacagawea, the wife of a French guide and the sister of an important Indian chief, they crossed the Rocky Mountains. They talked with Indians of many tribes, who treated the travelers with great friendliness. Their journals became crammed with information about the geography, plant life, and animals in the unknown interior of America. They discovered the source of the Bitter Root River, branched off into other streams, and so came at last to the great Columbia River, which carried them in November of 1805 to their first sight of the Pacific.

On the return journey the party divided. Lewis followed the sources of the Marias River, and Clark the Yellowstone River.

Other explorers, under Lieutenant Zebulon M. Pike, striking out from St. Louis, also were adding to America's knowledge of its continent. Pike pressed up the Mississippi to beyond the mouth of the Minnesota River, talked with Indians, established the authority of the United States government, and selected the site for Fort Snelling. The following year, 1806, he pushed westward and gave his name to snowy Pikes Peak in the Rocky Mountains.

These expeditions showed that the continent was rich in opportunities for new settlements and trade. In time, thirteen states would be formed from America's great bargain—the Louisiana Purchase.

U.S. SHIPS DEFEAT THE BARBARY PIRATES

But warring Britain and France harass American shipping on the high seas.

For years the Barbary states, along the north shore of Africa, had grown rich by demanding the payment of tribute from all vessels entering the Mediterranean Sea. The United States had followed the example of older nations by making payments to these pirate states. But the greedy Pasha of Tripoli grew dissatisfied with this arrangement early in Jefferson's years as President. The United States had a weak navy. If American vessels wished to sail the Mediterranean, they must pay more.

At the Pasha's orders, the United States flag was cut down on the consulate in a declaration of war. Pirate craft from Tripoli boarded American ships, seized cargoes, and imprisoned crews and passengers. For two years such robbery and insult in the Mediterranean simply proved the Pasha right. The American navy was unable to protect its citizens on the high seas.

The bitterest blow came in 1803 when the *Philadelphia* ran aground during a battle. Captain and crew were jailed and the ship was seized as a prize. But on a February night in 1804, a small force under Captain Stephen Decatur entered the harbor of Tripoli. Under the guns of the Pasha's castle, it boarded and burned the *Philadelphia.*

Congress now decided to raise the money to send a squadron capable of handling the Barbary pirates. The harbor of Tripoli was blockaded and the Pasha's vessels constantly attacked. The pirates soon granted freedom to American ships in the Mediterranean.

But the nation's troubles on the high seas were not yet over. By 1806, war between France and England caught American shipping in a squeeze. Britain blockaded the European coast from the French port of Brest to the Elbe River, and France blockaded the British Isles. Each nation seized any American ship suspected of trading with its enemy.

Jefferson knew the United States was not prepared for a war. The British knew it, too, and refused to negotiate any kind of settlement. Arguing that many seamen had deserted the Royal Navy to sign up for higher wages on American ships, Britain declared that she had the right to stop and search American ships and take off sailors suspected of deserting.

On June 22, 1807, off Hampton Roads, the British man-of-war *Leopard* fired upon the American frigate *Chesapeake.* Three American sailors as well as one British deserter were removed.

"British Outrage!" screamed the American newspapers, and Congress had to take action. It passed an embargo act that prohibited any vessel from leaving an American port for a foreign country, and a nonimportation act that said no goods from England and France could be brought into an American port.

These policies, which were supported by Jefferson, crippled the nation's trade. Ships stood idle at the wharves. Sailors roamed the streets, unable to find work. Although there was a great deal of smuggling in Maine and Georgia, trade fell from $108,000,000 in 1807 to $22,000,000 in 1808. The embargoes were no solution to the basic problem of British-American relations. That would not be solved until a war was fought.

THE MANY FACES OF TROUBLE

Madison becomes President and has difficulties both at home and abroad.

Nearing the end of his second term as President, Jefferson faced revolt even within the ranks of his own party. The rebellious Democratic-Republicans were called the "Quids." They were led by John Randolph of Virginia, once one of the President's closest friends. They fought Jefferson's legislative program in Congress. They also hoped to make James Monroe the next President, although Jefferson had already chosen James Madison as his successor.

Meanwhile, the New England Federalists played their old game of threatening secession and even received into their inner circles a British agent from Canada. But many states still relied on their legislatures rather than on a popular vote to select electors for President. Jefferson, as his party's leader, was able to control the legislators and beat off all the opposition. Madison easily won the election of 1808.

James Madison was almost as brilliant as Jefferson, and just as stubborn. A sickly child who received his early education from private tutors, he managed to graduate from the College of New Jersey (now Princeton) at the age of twenty.

Madison was told that he could not hope to succeed in Virginia politics without giving the voters a free drink of whiskey on election day. He replied that then he would rather lose—and he did. Appointed to the governor's council, he fought for religious freedom in Virginia. As a delegate to the Constitutional Convention of 1787, he contributed many ideas, and he became known as the "Father of the Constitution." He was Jefferson's chief lieutenant in the political war between the Democratic-Republicans and Hamilton's Federalists, and then was Jefferson's Secretary of State. Now, as President, he had a thorough grasp of the nation's problems.

At home Madison's troubles wore many faces. In Congress his enemies defeated an effort to renew the charter of the Bank of the United States. If war should come, the government would lack the money and credit it would need. A group of congressmen wanted to take over Florida, which was still owned by Spain, an ally of England. In the Northwest the Indians once more were being stirred to revolt by British agents, and the powerful Shawnee chief Tecumseh could aid these British schemes.

The governor of the Indiana Territory was William Henry Harrison, who had learned how to fight during the Revolution. Harrison summoned Tecumseh to the Ohio state capital at Vincennes, to make peace. The conference began badly on an August day in 1810, when Harrison asked the chief to sit near his "father," meaning himself.

Stiffly, Tecumseh replied: "The sun is my father, and the earth is my mother, and on her bosom I will repose."

Tecumseh offered no hope for peace unless the white men returned all the lands they held along the Wabash and White Rivers. Indian raids the following year ended Harrison's patience. With some 1,100 volunteers, he marched on an Indian village on the Tippecanoe River.

Near here, on a raw day in November of 1811, the Indians asked for a parley. Harrison agreed, but he expected trickery. "Boys," he said to his men while they waited, "if they strike, keep your aim low."

Before dawn, the Indians attacked. Harrison waited for daylight, when he could use his cavalry. "Now ride them down," he ordered. Harrison's cavalrymen fought like frontiersmen, with sabers, clubs, and hunting knives. Tecumseh fled. Next day, in the Indian village, Harrison discovered some guns that had been made in England.

In April of 1812 there was a series of Indian raids from Fort Dearborn (later Chicago) to the Ohio River. Younger men from the frontier had now taken seats in Congress. They became the "War Hawks" who cried that the time had come to settle with England. Massacre along the frontier, the impressment of American seamen, insults to American statesmen—the "War Hawks" built their case against the British point by point.

Finally, Madison asked for a declaration of war against England, and on June 18, 1812, Congress agreed. At that moment in England, the royal government was taking steps to stop many of the acts that had aroused America, but this information reached Washington too late.

THE WAR OF 1812

Again British and American troops and warships meet in battle.

"Mr. Madison's War"—that was what Madison's political foes called the War of 1812. The nation was divided in its opinion of the war, as was shown in the election of that year. De Witt Clinton of New York, supported by a combination of Federalists and Democratic-Republicans, would have won if he had been able to get the electoral college vote of Pennsylvania.

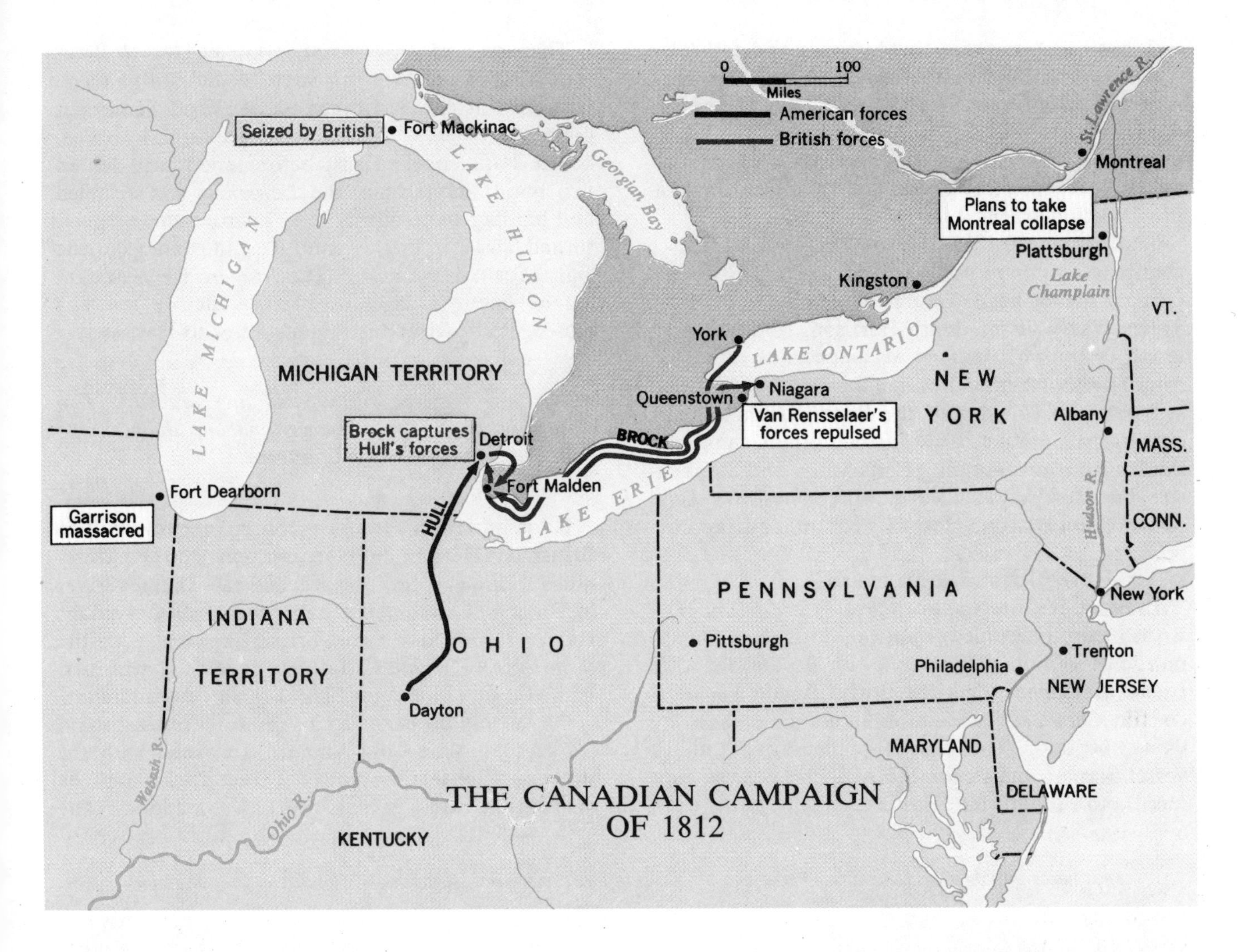

THE CANADIAN CAMPAIGN
OF 1812

Madison was re-elected, mainly because of the support of the "War Hawks." They wanted action, and he planned a campaign to end the British threat along the frontier. The War Department worked out a three-pronged invasion of Canada from Detroit, Niagara, and Lake Champlain. The plan seemed a good one—on paper. In practice, it fell apart.

A force of about 2,000 men under General William Hull, Governor of the Michigan Territory, moved from Detroit into Canada. Overconfident, Hull issued a proclamation inviting Canadians to join him in overthrowing their royal masters. The British only laughed. Seizing Fort Mackinac, they drove Hull back into Detroit. He was frightened by what the Indians might do if he held out, and quickly surrendered. With Detroit captured, the British swept easily to the foot of Lake Michigan and took Fort Dearborn. There, while being evacuated, the American garrison were treacherously massacred by Indians.

British General Isaac Brock, who had bagged Hull, moved next to Niagara. General Stephen Van Rensselaer of New York crossed the Niagara River and attacked Brock at Queenston Heights, in Canada. Van Rensselaer had some 6,000 troops, about half of them regulars. The rest were militiamen from New York. Arguing that they were not required to fight beyond their own borders, they refused to support the regulars. In a disastrous retreat, the Americans were driven across the river. A third force, which was supposed to attack Montreal, did not even budge from its camps.

Meanwhile, the "War Hawks" wanted to annex Florida, which was owned by Spain. But Congress recognized Spain as a "friendly" power and rejected the proposal.

Anyone could see that on the land the war was going badly. But the war at sea was another story. In early August the *Constitution*—"Old Ironsides"—was roaming the Atlantic in search of British prey. She sighted the enemy frigate *Guerrière* and went after her. The *Guerrière* circled, fired two broadsides that fell short, then ran up topsails and jib to make a race to safety. The *Constitution* bore down steadily until she was "within half pistol-shot." Her guns blasted the *Guerrière,* knocking down her masts and tearing her sails into ribbons. The British vessel was scarcely worth towing into port.

Other naval victories that summer and fall filled Americans with pride. The *Essex* captured the British frigate *Alert* south of Chesapeake Bay. The *Wasp* bagged the *Frolic* in southern waters. The British frigate *Macedonian* was captured off the Madeiras, and in December the *Constitution* sank the *Java* off the Coast of Brazil.

The winter of 1812–13 gave American forces a chance to prepare for another campaign against Canada. At the head of troops assembled in the Ohio Valley was William Henry Harrison, who had scattered Tecumseh's Indians at Tippecanoe. Harrison would soon face his old Indian foe again, for Tecumseh was now allied with the British. Although the Americans lost one battle, in two others they kept the British from capturing Forts Meigs and Stephenson. But Harrison realized that the Americans could never regain Detroit unless they controlled Lake Erie.

FIGHTING IN CANADA

Even at sea the war was now going badly. The British navy blockaded American ports from Savannah to New York. Thirty miles off Boston, the U.S. frigate *Chesapeake* met the British frigate *Shannon*. As the *Chesapeake*'s captain, James Lawrence, lay dying, he said, "Don't give up the ship!" But his vessel was no match for the *Shannon*. It was captured and brought into Halifax.

Then, in September, Captain Oliver Hazard Perry set sail on Lake Erie in search of the British navy. He found it on September 10, 1813, off Sandusky, Ohio.

The battle opened just before noon, and within two hours his flagship, the *Lawrence*, was disabled and her flag came down. Perry boarded the *Niagara*, turned away from the painful sight, and gave the signal for "close action." The *Niagara* went straight at the enemy, her guns blazing. Before the day closed, Perry wrote his famous letter to Harrison:

Dear General,

We have met the enemy, and they are ours. Two ships, two brigs, one schooner, and one sloop. Yours with very great respect and esteem.

O. H. Perry

Harrison sent his troops marching northward. The British left Detroit, but Harrison pursued them thirty miles to the east until he reached the Thames River in Ontario, Canada. The battle was a furious affair. Harrison rode down the British regulars with the same sort of reckless, slashing cavalry charge that had won at Tippecanoe. The British surrendered.

On the left, protected by a swamp, Tecumseh stood his ground. When the Americans clashed with the Indians, "the terrible voice of Tecumseh could be distinctly heard, encouraging his warriors." The

In a fierce gun duel on Lake Erie, Perry lost his flagship but transferred to another vessel to continue the fight.

swamp fight turned into a wild tangle—men yelling, clubbing, shooting, slashing with knife and bayonet. The Indians clustered around the gallant Tecumseh. In an instant, it seemed, a hundred bullets hissed about him. Then Tecumseh pitched forward. The Indians fell back, and the Battle of the Thames had ended in a victory for Harrison.

In April, General Dearborn crossed Lake Ontario and captured York (now Toronto) and a month later held control of the Niagara River. But he was an inefficient officer—and by early winter the British not only held the New York side of the Niagara, but had also burned Lewiston and Buffalo. In the South, the month of August brought a frightful massacre by Creek warriors at Fort Mims on the Alabama River. Andrew Jackson rallied the militia in Tennessee and Georgia to deal with the Indians.

British guns battered the Lawrence.

FROM LUNDY'S LANE TO NEW ORLEANS

Americans take the offensive, and win a victory after peace is signed.

After the war had continued for about two years, there were some important changes. Britain had defeated France; she could now send experienced troops to America. But a new kind of leader was rising to the top of the American forces. It included men like Jacob Brown, Winfield Scott, and Andrew Jackson—skilled military men who filled their soldiers with a new fighting spirit.

Proof of this spirit came in July, 1814, in the region around Niagara. Led by Brown and Scott, the Americans won a battle on the banks of the Chippewa River. Scott's men fought especially well. Because of a scarcity of blue cloth, they wore gray uniforms. In their honor, gray uniforms were adopted for the military cadets at West Point.

Scott and Brown pursued the British to Lundy's Lane in Ontario, a mile and a half from Niagara Falls. About 2,600 Americans opposed an enemy force of 4,500 in a battle that stung the British badly. Both Scott and Brown were wounded that day—and, no wonder, for at times the lines were not separated by more than eight or ten paces.

The air blazed with shells and rockets. Scott later said that "though both armies suffered greatly, the enemy suffered most." Yet the Americans were not able to push forward after this victory, and within a few weeks British veterans were marching to invade the United States by way of Lake Champlain. Here Commodore Thomas McDonough, commanding the American fleet on the lake, drove them off.

England acted swiftly to take the pressure off Canada. A British expedition reached Chesapeake Bay in mid-August with instructions to destroy the American fleet and capture Washington and Baltimore. A force of militia, regulars, and sailors, thrown together at the last minute, was brushed aside by the British at nearby Bladensburg, Maryland. With the enemy so near, the nation's capital was in an uproar.

"May God protect us!" wrote Dolly Madison, the President's wife, as the British approached the capital on August 24. "Two messengers, covered with dust, come to bid me fly . . . a wagon has been procured, and I have had it filled with plate and the most valuable portable articles, belonging to the house. Whether it will reach its destination, the 'Bank of Maryland,' or fall into the hands of British soldiery, events must determine. Our kind friend, Mr. Carroll, has come to hasten my departure, and [is] in a very bad humor with me, because I insist on waiting until the large picture of General Washington is secured, and it requires to be unscrewed from the wall. This process was found too tedious for these perilous moments. I have ordered the frame to be broken, and the canvas taken out. It is done!"

Luckily, Dolly escaped the British invaders. For the inhabitants of the capital, wrote a British soldier, "this was a night of terror." Arriving at the White House, he found the table set for forty guests. The soldiers ate the food and drank the wine, and then burned the executive mansion.

The British turned next toward Baltimore. They did not attack the city until September 13, when British men-of-war pointed their heavy guns at Fort McHenry, which guarded Baltimore. Aboard one of the vessels was Francis Scott Key, a Washington lawyer. He was trying to arrange the release of a friend who had been captured by the British. Later he recalled the scene:

"The heavens aglow were a seething sea of flame, and the waters of the harbor, lashed into an angry sea by the vibrations, the *Minden* rode and tossed as though in a tempest. It is recorded that the houses in the city of Baltimore, two miles distant, were shaken to their foundations. Above the tempestuous roar, intermingled with its hubbub and confusion, were heard the shrieks and groans of the dying and wounded. But alas! they were from the direction of the fort. What did it mean? For over an hour the pandemonium reigned. Suddenly it ceased—all was quiet, not a shot fired or sound heard, a death-like stillness prevailed, as the darkness of night resumed its sway. The awful stillness and suspense were unbearable. . . ."

THE NATIONAL ANTHEM

Francis Scott Key looked toward the fort, where by daylight he had seen the flag bravely waving. Had it been pulled down? He waited anxiously through long hours until through smoke in "the dawn's early light" he saw the fort and the flag. Yes, the flag was still there! On the back of a letter he scribbled lines of poetry to express his joy:

> *'Tis the Star-Spangled Banner,*
> *Oh! long may it wave,*
> *O'er the land of the free*
> *and the home of the brave.*

Copies of the poem, struck off as a handbill, were snatched up by the people of Baltimore. A musician, Ferdinand Durang, adapted the words to an old English tune, *Anacreon in Heaven,* and the new song—today our national anthem—was sung all over the country.

Although the British expedition remained in Chesapeake Bay, it did not try to invade Baltimore. Yet Madison was in a desperate situation. The government had neither the money nor the popular support to carry on the war much longer.

New England still talked secession. By the summer of 1814, New England believed that the Federal government would soon collapse. Delegates were invited to Hartford, Connecticut, to consider the question of forming an independent confederation. They met secretly for three weeks, but decided not to take the final step of secession.

At sea, the United States met other setbacks. Her frigates were bottled up within harbors so that they could not fight, and even the *Constitution* was driven off the seas. Yet despite all these discouragements—deadlock along the Canadian border, the burning of Washington, revolt in New England, the overwhelming of the navy—the War of 1812 ended with a triumph. The reason for this triumph was a man who had been born in a log cabin in the Waxhaw settlement between North and South Carolina on March 15, 1767. His name was Andrew Jackson.

A few days after Andy's birth, his father died. Andy was educated in a rural school, where he mastered the three R's of readin', 'ritin' and 'rithmetic. By the time he was thirteen, his mother and two brothers had died from hardships suffered in the Revolution. He was seized by the British and carried to Camden, South Carolina.

Andy refused to shine the boots of a British officer, who lashed out with his sword. Andy's arm was cut almost to the bone. He never forgave the British, even long years afterward when, as a citizen of Tennessee, he had become governor of the state.

"OLD HICKORY AT WAR"

The War of 1812 gave Andy a chance to pay off his grudge. He was so rugged that his soldiers nicknamed him "Old Hickory." His campaign against the Creeks after the massacre at Fort Mims in 1813 was a good example of his toughness. He marched his raw militia through a wilderness, and, at Horseshoe Bend on the Tallapoosa River, fought a bloody battle that crushed the Creek rebellion.

Later, convinced that the British were using Spanish-held Florida as a base of operations, Andy drove the British out. New England Federalists howled that Andy had acted without governmental authority. They were right—but Andy simply pushed on to the next spot where he could strike at his old foe.

In December the British marched on New Orleans with 12,000 troops led by Sir Edward Pakenham. Jackson managed to reach the city eight days ahead of the enemy. The British maneuvered for position, which gave him a month's time to dig in. Although he was outnumbered two to one, Andy was not worried. Let the British advance in neat columns, if they liked. Andy figured that his frontiersmen could take care of themselves.

The Battle of New Orleans was fought January 8, 1815. Jackson knew at once Sir Edward had made a blunder when he launched simultaneous attacks with two widely separated forces. He went along the lines, telling his Tennesseans and Kentuckians: "Look, boys, take them as they come—wait till you get them in range and then give 'em your shot just above the breastplates." Andy's boys understood this kind of fighting. The British counted 700 killed, 1,400 wounded, 500 captured. American losses were eight killed, thirteen wounded.

Great though the victory at New Orleans was, it came after the war was over. The news had not yet reached New Orleans, but about two weeks before, at Ghent in Belgium, the United States and Britain had signed a treaty of peace. Both nations were thoroughly tired of the war.

So the War of 1812 was over. And when Madison left Washington in 1817 to return to his home in Virginia, the United States already was well on the way toward entering a period in history that would be known as "the era of good feeling." The year before Indiana had been admitted as a state, and the first tariff bill imposing a tax on imports had been passed to protect American industries.

AMERICA ON THE MOVE

Settlers move westward from the east and establish homes along the frontier.

James Monroe, who followed Madison as President, was the third Virginian in succession to occupy the White House. A veteran of the Revolution, he had served at Princeton, Brandywine, Germantown, and Monmouth. His political career was shaped by his warm friendship with Jefferson.

As a member of the Virginia assembly and the Continental Congress, Monroe fought steadily for a policy guaranteeing free navigation of the Mississippi River to the people of the West. He had been a bitter opponent of the Federalists in general and of Hamilton in particular.

President James Monroe

When Andrew Jackson fought the Battle of New Orleans in 1815, he did not know that a peace treaty had been signed.

He served under Washington as envoy to France, then was elected governor of Virginia. He helped to negotiate the Louisiana Purchase for Jefferson, and was appointed minister to England and Spain. He served again both as a member of the Virginia Assembly and as governor, then spent six years in Madison's Cabinet as Secretary of State and one year as Secretary of War.

Monroe took the oath of office in a Washington already largely rebuilt from the ashes left by the British invaders in 1814. He made a tour of the country, visiting New York, Providence, Pawtucket, Boston, Buffalo, and Detroit. He saw with his own eyes how America was changing. Everywhere people were on the move—from farms to new factory towns in New England, from older settlements to vacant lands beyond the Appalachian Mountains.

In those days, any region where the frontier existed was called the West. When the Nineteenth Century began, the population of the West was only 386,413, but it grew enormously during the years that followed:

1810—1,078,315 *1830—3,672,569*
1820—2,217,474 *1840—6,376,972*

Many things drove people across the mountains. The poor, the restless, the immigrants seeking freedom from tyranny in Europe, New Englanders whose farms were becoming less fertile every year—all welcomed the chance for a new and better life on the cheap land of the wilderness that lay to the west.

Settlers from New England and the Middle Atlantic states generally traveled the central New York river valley and the Great Lakes, or journeyed by way of western Pennsylvania and the Ohio River, before spilling into Ohio, Indiana, Michigan, and Illinois. Settlers from the South generally used the Cumberland Gap and other mountain passes to reach Kentucky, Tennessee, Mississippi, and Louisiana, or the southern sections of Ohio, Indiana, and Illinois. Each group thus carried its own habits, customs, and beliefs into the wilderness.

Life on the frontier was simple and rough. Home meant a log cabin made tight with clay or mud wedged into the cracks, with shutters or greased paper over the windows, a fireplace of clay and stone, and floors of dirt or puncheons (rough wooden blocks). The early settlers stayed away from the prairies, where there were few building materials and the soil was difficult to plow. They preferred meadows or clearings cut in the forests.

Their furnishings consisted of a table, chairs, a crude bed or two, a spinning wheel, a gun, and an iron crane at the fireplace to hold the pots used in cooking. Men wore deerskin clothes, women dresses of homespun, and youngsters badly fitting hand-me-downs.

The settlers had a constant struggle for food and fuel, and money was scarce. Yet there were gay times, too. Barn-raisings, corn-huskings, and quilting bees brought neighbors together. Preachers traveled

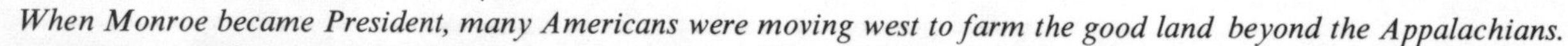
When Monroe became President, many Americans were moving west to farm the good land beyond the Appalachians.

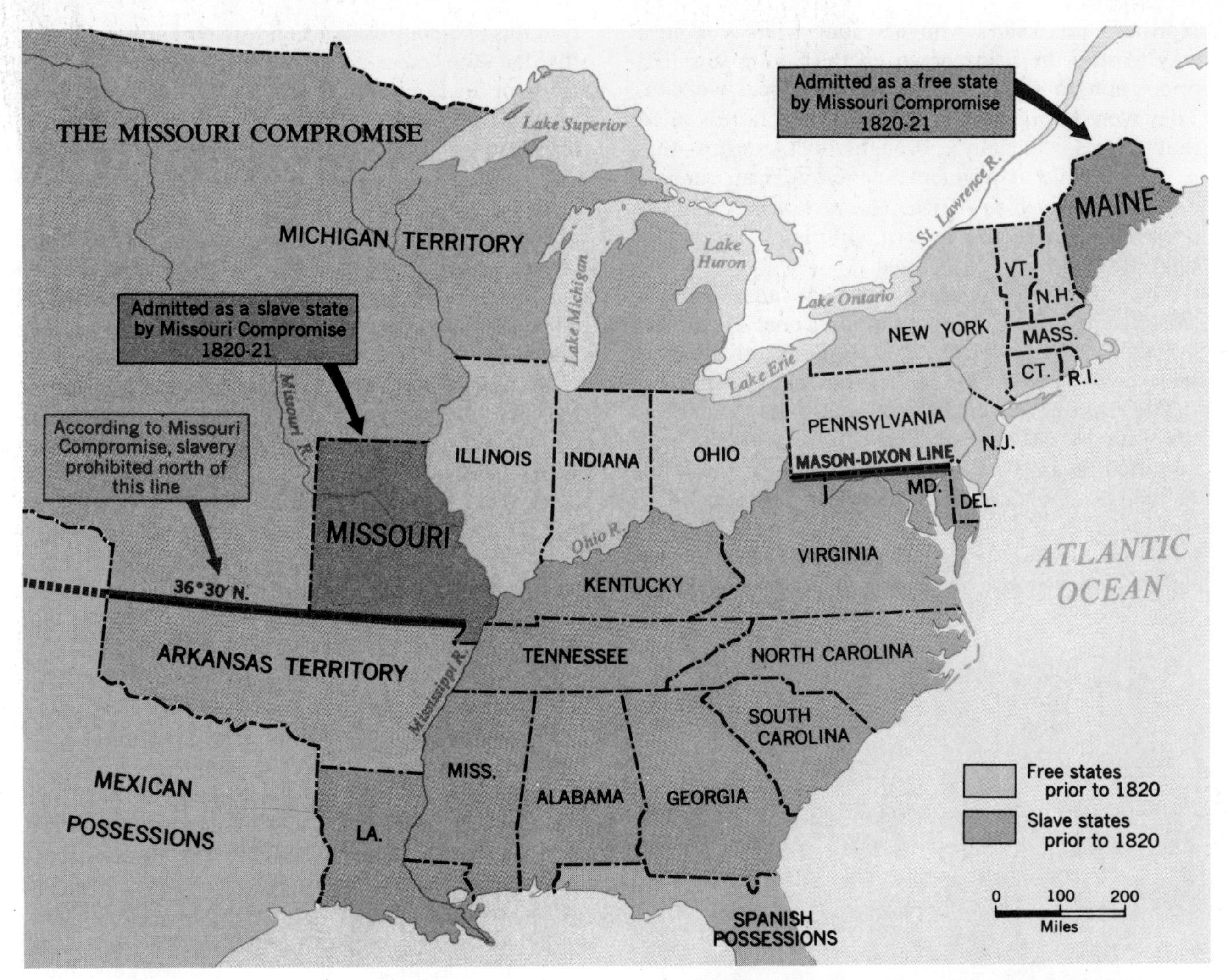

Under the Missouri Compromise, Maine and Missouri were admitted to the Union as the 23rd and 24th states.

through the wilderness, holding "camp meetings." By 1824 there were ninety-eight newspapers in Kentucky, Tennessee, and the old Northwest. Usually these papers took a strong stand on politics, for politics was a serious part of frontier life. Log schoolhouses appeared, and youngsters mastered their three R's or felt the sting of the schoolmaster's switch.

SEEDS OF DISSENSION— THE MISSOURI COMPROMISE

The Union tries to exist half slave and half free, but the slavery issue persists.

Mississippi joined the Union in 1817, Illinois in 1818, and Alabama in 1819. There were then twenty-two states, evenly divided between those that were in favor of slavery and those that were not. Then Missouri, petitioning Congress for admission to the Union as a slave state, threatened to upset this balance.

Many religious groups, especially the Quakers, had long been troubled by the evil of slavery. Benjamin Lundy, a New Jersey Quaker, became the leader of the antislavery movement. As an apprentice in Virginia, he had seen for himself the cruelty with which slaves often were treated.

In 1815 Lundy moved to Ohio, where he founded the Union Humane Society. Among his early converts was Charles Osborn, whose *Philanthropist* became the first antislavery paper in America. Lundy traveled on foot from place to place, speaking against slavery. Soon he won another ally in Elihu Embree, a Quaker in Tennessee, who began publishing the *Emancipator*.

There were some people who believed that the South could never be persuaded to abolish slavery. In 1816 they organized the American Colonization Society for the purpose of sending Negroes back to Africa. By 1820 they had raised the funds to ship back eighty-six Negroes—a drop in an ocean.

But there was no doubt that the antislavery movement would have an enormous effect on the nation.

Northern politicians, who had long been seeking a way to stop the rising power of the South, saw that opposition to slavery could be a political weapon. They were soon proved right. In 1819 Congress ruled that slaves "illegally" brought to America—that is, seized without payment to their African rulers—must be returned to Africa. The next year Congress declared slavetrading a form of piracy for which slave traders could be hanged.

The congressional battle over the admission of Missouri as a slave state was a bitter one. The South insisted on "states' rights," while the North shouted that slavery was a sin and slaveholding a crime.

The dispute about Missouri was at last ended by the famous Missouri Compromise. Missouri was admitted as a slave state and Maine as a free state. A line at the parallel of thirty-six degrees, thirty minutes (which runs between Missouri and Arkansas) divided the remainder of the territory acquired through the Louisiana Purchase. All future territories north of this line would be free. Those south of the line could, if they wished, become slave territories. Congressmen shook hands, believing that they had settled the slavery issue.

Slavery and slavetrading embroiled the nation in controversy. In 1820 Congress held slavetrading to be a form of piracy.

But the issue did not die that easily. The cause of antislavery kept winning new supporters. The gap between the industrial North and the agricultural South slowly widened. The West, too, was becoming divided. It no longer had a single way of life. The Northwest, where land was cheap and labor scarce, was becoming a region of moderate-sized farms operated by a father and his sons. The Southwest, where cotton, sugar, and tobacco were the chief crops, was becoming a region of large plantations operated by slave labor.

THE NATION GROWS AND PROSPERS

Factories rise, transportation improves, and Monroe gives a warning to Europe.

A new development in American life in the Nineteenth Century was the New England factory town. New England's traders and merchants had the money to invest in such enterprises. The many waterfalls in the rivers supplied cheap power to run the machines. Rows of company-owned houses sprang up near the mills to give shelter to the workers. Farm girls, who had learned spinning and weaving at home, were especially needed. Dwellings were provided for them, with house-mothers to look after their personal welfare. Libraries and programs of education and entertainment were set up.

Cotton and woolen textiles were not the only American products. The country was rich in iron ore, and all kinds of metal articles now came from American factories—stoves, steam engines, pipes, beams.

The New England factory town was just one sign of how the North was changing. Another was the flags on the ships that anchored in its ports. America had begun to trade around the world, bringing in tea from China, coffee from Brazil, sugar from Cuba, cocoa from Central America, wines from Madeira and the Canaries. The *Savannah,* partly powered by steam, crossed the Atlantic in 1819. Whaling vessels roamed the seas, and by mid-century, 680 such ships set out in a single year to reap a profit from sperm oil and whalebone.

Since 1807, when Robert Fulton's *Clermont* had made a successful voyage up the Hudson, river travel had changed. At Pittsburgh, in 1811, Nicholas J.

Roosevelt launched the *New Orleans.* The following year this craft chugged down the Mississippi to the port for which she was named. The age of steamboats had begun, and soon steamboats were crossing the Great Lakes.

Men of imagination talked excitedly of what it would mean to the nation if roads and canals could be built to connect the rivers and lakes. Under the leadership of Governor De Witt Clinton, New York acted while others talked. On July 4, 1817, work began on the building of the Erie Canal. Many people laughed at the canal, calling it "Clinton's Big Ditch." But some eight years later it was finished. The canal was four feet deep, twenty-eight feet wide at the bottom, and forty feet at the top. It crossed New York for a distance of 350 miles. Extending from Buffalo on Lake Erie to Albany on the Hudson River, it linked inland America with the sea. Within twenty years, a boat passed through its important locks every seventeen minutes. About 25,000 "canawlers"—men, women and boys—were employed moving its traffic and feeding the passengers who traveled up and down the canal. Five years after it had opened, Cleveland's population had jumped 400 per cent, Detroit's 300 per cent. Other states quickly followed New York's example in building canals.

When on an October day in 1825 the Erie Canal was opened, James Monroe had already ended his second term as President. The Missouri Compromise, the coming of the factory town in New England, and the construction of the Erie Canal had been tremendous events during his eight years in the White House, but Monroe's name would live on for another accomplishment.

THE MONROE DOCTRINE

In his annual message to Congress on December 2, 1823, Monroe stated that North and South America no longer were open for colonization by any foreign power. Should any nation attempt such colonization, the United States would consider its own peace and safety endangered. If any European power should interfere with the independence of governments in North, Central, and South America, the United States would look upon such interference as an unfriendly act. The President said:

"The American continents, by the free and independent condition which they have assumed and maintain, are henceforth not to be considered as subjects for future colonization by any European powers. . . . We owe it, therefore, to candor and to the amicable relations existing between the United States and those powers to declare that we should consider any attempt . . . to extend their system to any portion of this hemisphere as dangerous to our peace and safety . . ."

This policy is known as the Monroe Doctrine.

A HARDHEADED NEW ENGLANDER

John Quincy Adams becomes President, but Congress balks at his program.

Many persons in Washington said that the real author of the Monroe Doctrine was not the President but John Quincy Adams, his Secretary of State. The son of old John Adams, who as a child had watched the Battle of Bunker Hill, John Quincy Adams had grown up knowing such patriots as Washington, Franklin, and Jefferson. He had traveled with his family on diplomatic missions to Europe before graduating from Harvard and entering the profession of law. He was every inch an Adams—hardheaded, sharp-tongued, quick-witted.

Under Washington, Adams was minister to Holland and Portugal. He served a term in the Massachusetts legislature, and then was elected to the United States Senate. He supported the Louisiana Purchase and the embargo against England and France in the crisis leading to the War of 1812. Madison sent him on diplomatic missions to Russia and England.

As Monroe's Secretary of State, John Quincy Adams became widely known. He arranged the treaty by which Spain ceded Florida to the United States in 1819, and set the boundary between Mexico and Louisiana along the Sabine and Red Rivers, the upper Arkansas, the crest of the Rocky Mountains and the forty-second parallel. He was a candidate for President in 1824, but a strong field opposed him, including tough old Andrew Jackson, the hero of New Orleans. The electoral vote gave ninety-nine to Jackson, eighty-four to Adams, forty-one to William H. Crawford (who had served as Monroe's Secretary of the Treasury), and thirty-seven to Henry Clay, the Speaker of the House. No candidate received a sufficient majority. When the election went to the House of Representatives, Clay supported Adams, assuring his election.

Clay became Adam's Secretary of State, and Jackson mistakenly believed there had been a deal between the two men. He watched with satisfaction as Congress turned down bills Adams wanted—bills to build Federal highways and canals, a national university, and Federal weather stations. The country was lining up behind two new political groups, the Whigs and the Democrats. The Whigs supported Adams' program for internal improvements, a national bank, and a high tariff. The Democrats loved Jackson and called all of Adams' measures unconstitutional.

Yet even to his own party Adams was a problem. The politicians of his day believed in the "spoils system"—that is, in rewarding their supporters with

Henry Clay

government jobs and favors. "To the victor belongs the spoils," they said. But Adams refused to play that game. He would not remove men from public office simply because they belonged to a different political party.

Meanwhile, Jackson's popularity grew. Maybe the bankers, the brokers, the contractors, the speculators and the "commercial interests" hated "Old Hickory," but plain people liked his courage and his down-to-earth manner. He seemed to be one of them. In 1828 he was elected President over Adams by an electoral vote of 178 to 83.

SOUTH CAROLINA TRIES "NULLIFICATION"

Jackson uses force to uphold a Federal law . . . Daniel Webster makes a famous speech.

President Andrew Jackson came to the White House a sad and lonely man, for a few weeks after his election his beloved wife Rachel had died. He believed in the "spoils system" and immediately began to rid the government of his enemies. His opponents howled that he was trying to make himself "King Andrew I."

Attacks upon the character of the wife of his Secretary of War brought out another trait in Jackson—his chivalry toward women. He refused to believe the gossips. His Cabinet, which did believe them, resigned, and he appointed another Cabinet. His opponents called it a "kitchen Cabinet," held together by love of the "spoils system" and hatred for Adams and Clay.

When Jackson came to the presidency, he inherited the tariff of 1828. Southerners believed it was unfair to them and called it the "tariff of abominations." They began to use the dangerous word "nullification," which meant the refusal by a state to recognize or enforce a Federal law. Robert Young Hayne, a senator from South Carolina, addressed the Senate on the nature of the Union and the right of a state to "nullify."

Then Daniel Webster of Massachusetts took the floor. In his reply to Hayne he spoke of the Union, of American nationality as a precious heritage, and of faith in national government. He said:

"It is to the Union we owe our safety at home and our consideration and dignity abroad. It is to that Union that we are chiefly indebted for whatever makes us most proud of our country. That Union we reached only by the discipline of our virtue in the severe school of adversity. It had its origin in the necessities of disordered finance, prostrate commerce, and ruined credit. Under its benign influence these great interests immediately awoke us from the dead, and sprang forth with newness of life. Every year of its duration has teemed with fresh proofs of its utility and its blessings, and although our territory has stretched out wider and wider, and our population spread farther and farther, they have not outrun its protection or its benefits. It has been to us all a copious fountain of national, social and personal happiness. . . . Liberty and Union, now and forever, one and inseparable."

"Black Dan" Webster was a great orator, and his speech became famous. But when the tariff law of 1832 included many levies that Southerners found objectionable, a convention in South Carolina on November 24 declared the tariffs of both 1828 and 1832 "null and void." Should the Federal government try to enforce these revenue laws, the convention warned, South Carolina would secede from the Union.

Jackson acted swiftly. A naval force under David Farragut was ordered to Charleston harbor and General Winfield Scott's troops prepared to march into South Carolina. Even a large number of Southern people approved Jackson's stand, and South Carolina backed down.

In a crisis over the banks, Jackson proved how little he knew about money and banking. His attack on the national bank, which had grown steadily stronger since its re-establishment in 1817, brought on one of the stormiest periods of his years in the White House. His opponents tried to limit his power of veto and his right to make appointments. Willing to believe any wild charge against an enemy, Jackson saw himself as "the champion of the people" fighting against the wicked bankers. Unhappily, he won. Public funds were deposited in state banks—Jackson's "pet banks," they were called—and they printed paper money that flooded the country as prices skyrocketed.

"REMEMBER THE ALAMO"

Americans in Texas proclaim independence from Mexico and fight a famous battle.

During Jackson's eight years in the White House, Arkansas and Michigan became states in the Union. The first railroads began operation, and Cyrus McCormick invented his harvesting machine, the reaper. The printing presses developed by Richard Hoe made possible the publication of the first penny newspaper in America.

The Cherokees were moved from their old homeland of northwestern Georgia into the Indian Territory (Oklahoma) and southeastern Kansas, the Seminoles were defeated in Florida, and the Black Hawk War ended the Indians' dreams of remaining on the Iowa prairies. Fur trappers penetrated the Far West, discovering new routes across deserts, plains, and mountains to the shores of the Pacific. In 1836, William Holmes McGuffey, a clergyman, lecturer, and college president, published the first of *McGuffey's Eclectic Readers,* which in time would be read by more than 100,000,000 American boys and girls.

Andrew Jackson

Texas seethed with unrest. The leaders of American colonization in this region were two Connecticut Yankees, Moses Austin and his son Stephen. In 1821, after Mexico had broken away from Spain, Stephen persuaded the new Mexican landlords of Texas to encourage a colony of fighting Americans who would protect the territory if Spain tried to win it back. Land was granted on the Brazos River. It would be tax free for seven years if the Americans would become citizens of Mexico and adopt the Catholic religion. Later, the Mexican government invited Americans to settle in all of the Texas territory on the same conditions.

By 1827, about 12,000 Americans—most of them Southern cotton growers who brought their slaves—had settled in Texas. The Mexicans soon were quarreling with the Americans. To stop the flood of settlers, the Mexican government passed laws abolishing slavery and prohibiting the importation of slaves. Few Americans had kept their promise to become Catholics, and the Mexicans charged them with bad faith. Heavy taxes were levied against the American "intruders."

TEXAS REVOLTS

The most explosive force in this dangerous situation was the rise to power of General Antonio Lopez de Santa Anna. Through various acts this fierce Mexican dictator made clear that he wanted to drive Americans out of Texas. By 1835, the region was in rebellion against Mexico, and in March of the following year Texas declared its independence.

A new Texan army captured San Antonio from General Cos, a brother-in-law of Santa Anna. With a force of many thousands, Santa Anna set out to retake the city. Only a small garrison of Americans had been left to defend San Antonio. They knew they were no match for Santa Anna, but they holed up in the Alamo, an old Spanish mission, and defied the Mexican troops to drive them out.

The defenders of the Alamo, under William Barret Travis, numbered 187. They were a hard-bitten lot—hardy frontiersmen like the old Tennessee Indian fighter Davy Crockett, and Jim Bowie, who had given his name to a heavy-bladed sheath knife designed to be thrown at its target. "If there is anything in the world particularly worth living for," Crockett once said, "it is freedom." Men like Travis and Bowie agreed. They tightened their belts and waited for Santa Anna and his legions to storm the Alamo.

As the Mexicans approached San Antonio in late February, Crockett wrote cheerfully in his diary:

After a 13-day siege, the Mexicans breached the Alamo's defenses and overwhelmed the outnumbered Americans.

"We are up and doing and as lively as Dutch cheese in the dog days." Next morning Santa Anna's troops appeared. Within the Alamo, Travis and his boys raised the flag of the Lone Star Republic. When Santa Anna demanded that the Alamo surrender unconditionally, Travis answered by firing a cannon ball. In a letter addressed "To the People of Texas," Travis explained his position:

"*I shall never surrender or retreat.* I am determined to sustain myself as long as possible and die like a soldier who never forgets what is due to his own honor and that of his country. VICTORY OR DEATH."

For thirteen days, from February 23 until March 6, Santa Anna besieged the Alamo. Food began running low and, peering over the walls, the Alamo's defenders could see that every day Santa Anna received new recruits for a final assault. On March 4, 1836, Mexican guns rained shot upon the Alamo. The next day Crockett wrote the last entry in his diary: "Pop, pop, pop! Bom, bom, bom! throughout the day. No time for memorandums now. Go ahead! Liberty and independence forever!"

The defenders of the Alamo all perished. But the Texan army, under tough Sam Houston, had been given the time to gather its forces for a showdown fight with Santa Anna. That battle came along the banks of the San Jacinto River on April 21. To the cry of "Remember the Alamo," Sam Houston's Texans crushed the Mexicans.

PANIC, POLITICS, AND WAR

Van Buren and Tyler each have a stormy presidency. Polk goes to war with Mexico.

Andrew Jackson would have been more than happy to welcome Texas into the Union. But 1836 was an election year and he was anxious to have his own hand-picked candidate, Martin Van Buren, follow him into the White House. The steadily rising anti-slavery feeling in the North made the annexation of a slave territory like Texas too much of a political bombshell.

The son of a thrifty Dutch tavern keeper from Kinderhook, New York, Van Buren had begun his law career at the age of sixteen. "The Red Fox of Kinderhook," as he was called, was a state senator and the state's attorney general. He was elected to the United States Senate, resigned during his second term to become governor of New York, and then was appointed Secretary of State in Jackson's Cabinet. With Jackson's support, he easily won the presidential election.

Van Buren strolled the streets of Washington in snuff-colored coat, orange cravat, pearl-gray vest, white duck trousers and morocco shoes. He had not

The defenders of the Alamo fought to the last man.

been President long when disaster struck. He had Jackson's foolish banking policies to thank for the Panic of 1837. On May 10, banks in New York City closed; two days later banks in Philadelphia shut their doors. Quickly the panic spread across the country as other banks became unable to meet the demand for payments on their notes in gold and silver.

Stores and factories went out of business, farmers could not sell their produce, and plantation owners could find no market for their cotton. The unemployed roamed the streets.

Van Buren acted sensibly by establishing an independent national treasury. He acted sensibly, too, in settling a Canadian border dispute which saw British troops invading American soil and burning a ship at her dock in Schlosser, New York. This affair could have easily flamed into serious trouble except for Van Buren's firmness and tact. But the people only remembered the hardships they had suffered, and one term was all they wanted of Van Buren.

At last the Whigs had Jackson on the run. Shouting "Tippecanoe and Tyler Too," they swept William Henry Harrison into the White House by an electoral college vote of 234 to sixty. But thirty days after taking office Harrison died of pneumonia.

Now for the first time a Vice-President stepped into the highest office in the land. To make the situation more ticklish, the Whigs had put John Tyler on the ticket only to attract the support of other "turncoat Democrats." Tyler was not the kind of President that New Englanders wanted.

TYLER AS PRESIDENT

Called "Turncoat Tyler" by his enemies and "Honest John" by his friends, Tyler moved into the White House. He had served in the House and the Senate and as governor of Virginia, and his best known trait was putting conscience before politics. Sometimes he seemed to talk on both sides of an issue—as, for example, when he opposed both slavery and any restriction on the extension of slavery. He argued that the wider the area over which slavery was spread the sooner it would disappear.

Kentucky's Henry Clay, a leading Whig, distrusted him from the start. The old issue of the national bank, which Clay supported and Tyler opposed as unconstitutional, gave the pair the chance to bring their feud into the open. Twice Clay forced bills in favor of the national bank through Congress. Twice Tyler vetoed them.

Washington rarely had known such times. Every member of Tyler's Cabinet resigned with the exception of Daniel Webster. An angry mob stormed the White House lawn, hurled stones and insults at the President, and broke windows. A resolution in the House calling for Tyler's impeachment was defeated when Democrats united with Whigs to vote it down.

The annexation of Texas raised another storm. Tyler stood with the South in favor of annexation and concluded a treaty for that purpose with the young republic. A rebellious Senate refused to ratify the treaty. But a new voice was heard when James K. Polk, the Democratic nominee for President in 1844, spoke out strongly in support of annexation.

Tyler was the first man to reach the presidency through the death of another, the first to be threatened with impeachment, and the first President to be married in the White House. Polk was unique, too: he was the first "dark horse" candidate to win the presidency. For seven ballots at their nominating convention at Baltimore in 1844 the Democrats were unable to choose between Martin Van Buren and Lewis Cass of Michigan. Then, to break the deadlock,

President Martin Van Buren

President John Tyler

the little known Polk was nominated to oppose Henry Clay, the Whig candidate.

The chief issue of the campaign was the annexation of Texas. Clay hedged on this question and so managed to reassure neither side. Polk took a firm stand and carried the electoral vote 175 to 105.

THE MEXICAN WAR

Born in Mecklenburg County, North Carolina, and raised in Tennessee, Polk was called by admirers the "Napoleon of the Stump." Aided by his gift of oratory, he was elected to the Tennessee House of Representatives, the United States Congress and the governorship of Tennessee. He was so devoted a Jackson man that he was sometimes tagged "Young Hickory." That nickname won him few friends with the Whigs, or with Northerners who were dead set against seeing slavery spread.

Cries of "Yankee robbers" rang throughout Mexico over the annexation of Texas. With Polk's inauguration, the Mexican minister broke off diplomatic relations and returned home. A special emissary that Polk sent to Mexico was not even received by the angry government. Troops under General Zachary Taylor were ordered to occupy the region between the Nueces and Rio Grande Rivers, and warships were stationed off Vera Cruz.

Those close to Polk realized that he was looking for any excuse to declare war on Mexico. On April 25, 1846, Mexican soldiers, crossing the Rio Grande, clashed with a detachment of Taylor's troops. "American blood has been shed on American soil," Polk said, and on May 13 Congress declared war.

"OLD ROUGH AND READY"

In Mexico, Zachary Taylor wins fame that will carry him to the presidency.

The Whigs protested violently, declaring that "Polk's war" had been started "unnecessarily and unconstitutionally." A young congressman from Illinois named Abraham Lincoln won the nickname of "Spot" for his resolution demanding that Polk identify the exact spot where American blood had been shed. "Let him answer with *facts,* and not with arguments," Lincoln said.

A member of Polk's own party, David Wilmot of Pennsylvania, believed the President was a puppet controlled by the slave interests. He suggested the "Wilmot Proviso" that in any territory acquired through the Mexican War "neither slavery nor involuntary servitude shall ever exist . . . except for crime, whereof the party shall first be duly convicted."

Wilmot attached his "proviso" to many bills that came before Congress. Lincoln remembered voting for it more than forty times. The Democrats doggedly beat down the Wilmot Proviso, but each time it failed to pass, its defeat was like sprinkling salt on the wounds of the antislavery members of Congress.

Polk's worries at home were almost secondary compared to the growing jealousy he felt toward General Zachary Taylor. "Old Rough and Ready," soldiers called Taylor, admiring his style as a fighter. A son of Colonel Richard Taylor, a hero of the Revolution, "Old Rough and Ready" had fought Indians in Indiana, the old Northwest, and Florida. Now, outnumbered at least two to one, he led his army against the Mexican forces under General Mariano Arista. As the Americans approached Fort Brown—and the first battle of the war—officers urged Taylor to wait for reinforcements.

"I shall go to Fort Brown or stay in my shoes," Taylor answered.

Western men knew what Taylor meant. The moment had come "to do or die." Taylor hit the Mexicans at dawn. He pushed through dense tangles of thorn bushes (called chaparral), flung back the Mexicans, snatched blazing cannon from the hands of Arista's gunners, and marched in triumph to Fort Brown. He lost 49 men; the Mexicans lost 1,000.

Taylor then invaded northern Mexico, and by September 28 he had captured Monterrey. Here he agreed to an armistice while he rested his weary army, but Polk ordered him to move on. Reinforced, Taylor pressed forward. By the year's end he practically controlled northeastern Mexico.

"Old Rough and Ready's" conquests made him a national hero. This gave Polk much to think about. Taylor was a Whig, and unless Polk was careful the general would be a winner at the next presidential election. So Polk wanted a new general to win his war in Mexico, but the only logical man, Winfield Scott, also was a Whig. Polk toyed with the idea of sending a political friend like Senator Thomas Hart Benton of Missouri to take command, but he knew that Congress would never allow it.

Volunteers for the war were coming in slowly. To give Scott an army, Polk reduced Taylor's army from 10,000 to 5,000. The wily Santa Anna, capturing the dispatches that ordered this cut of Taylor's forces, leaped at his chance. As soon as "Old Rough and Ready's" veterans had departed to join Scott, Santa Anna struck at the remaining troops in the Battle of Buena Vista on February 22, 1847.

Taylor took the attack calmly. He knew his boys and they knew him. No general on earth could excel Taylor in giving commands so crisply, so clearly. He watched as the fury of the combat mounted, getting his troops and his cannon to the right place at the right moment. Bit by bit, he cut Santa Anna's army to pieces, and the Mexicans retreated to defend their capital, Mexico City. Taylor's popularity increased with every dispatch of victory. Much against his will, Polk had made a future President.

TWO GENERALS

But Winfield Scott fought no less brilliantly than Taylor. A young lieutenant named Ulysses S. Grant, who fought under both Taylor and Scott, understood the difference between these two generals and made this comparison:

"General Taylor never wore a uniform but dressed himself entirely for comfort. He moved about the field in which he was operating to see through his own eyes the situation. Often he would be without staff officers, and when he was accompanied by them there was no prescribed order in which they followed.

"General Scott was the reverse in all these particulars. He always used all the uniform prescribed or allowed by law when he inspected his lines; word would be sent to all division and brigade commanders in advance, notifying them of the hour when the commanding general might be expected . . . On these occasions he wore his dress uniform, cocked hat, aiguillettes [loops of braided cord on a uniform], sabre and spurs. His staff . . . followed, also in uniform and in prescribed order."

In less than twenty years Grant himself was to be called one of the greatest generals of the century, and it would be no secret that he had modeled himself on Taylor rather than on Scott. Yet for all Scott's showiness—he was called "Old Fuss and Feathers"—the old hero of Chippewa and Lundy's Lane had much to teach Grant, just as he had much to teach another young lieutenant on his staff, a brilliant officer named Robert E. Lee.

President James K. Polk

MEXICO CITY FALLS

Approaching Vera Cruz by sea, Scott captured the city on March 29, 1847, after a siege of less than three weeks. He pushed through the valley of Mexico, won three battles, then stormed Chapultepec, a fortress guarding the western approach to Mexico City. On September 14, 1847, he rode into Mexico City as the conqueror of "the Halls of Montezuma."

THE WINNING OF CALIFORNIA

Americans in California revolt, and more territory is added to the United States.

In 1845, the year that James Polk became President, California was still part of Mexico. Here lived the *ranchero,* in comfortable houses built of sun-dried adobe brick. The *ranchero* had helped bring about better government in the territory. But the governors that Mexico sent into California were neither wise nor able. Their mistakes stirred up a spirit of revolt.

American interest in California had begun in the 1820's, when an agent for a Boston firm learned much about the California coast while searching for the sea otter. Soon Yankee traders and whalers in the North Pacific made regular calls at California's seacoast towns.

Fur trappers, crossing the high Sierras, descended into the Sacramento and San Joaquin valleys—men like Jedediah Strong Smith, who discovered the Great Salt Desert, and James Ohio Pattie, who brought the first smallpox vaccine into California. Later, three expeditions by Captain John C. Frémont and his famous guide, Kit Carson, greatly added to the knowledge of the rich natural resources of California. And in his book *Two Years Before the Mast,* Richard Henry Dana told of the exciting life along the California coast.

THE CALIFORNIA REPUBLIC

By 1845 there were perhaps 700 American settlers in California. Increasingly they disliked the high-handedness of the Mexican governors, and at Sonoma in 1846 a band of Yankee rebels ousted the Mexican military commander and seized the *presidio* [fort]. William B. Ide, a farmer, ripped down the Mexican flag from its mast, raising in its place a homespun banner with a star, a bear and the two words, "California Republic."

Texas had not been Polk's only objective when he asked Congress to declare war on Mexico. So, as Taylor marched on the Rio Grande, another American force under Stephen W. Kearny left Fort Leavenworth, on the Missouri, to invade New Mexico and California. Kearny marched his army down the Santa Fe Trail. By mid-August of 1846, he had captured the settlement of Santa Fe without a struggle. Cocky and self-confident, he divided his army and set off for California with 300 cavalrymen.

Crossing the Rio Grande at Albuquerque, Kearny met Kit Carson, who carried dispatches from Frémont to Washington reporting that California already had been successfully conquered. When Frémont had learned that the United States was at war with Mexico, he had become a busy warrior in his own right. By midsummer of 1847 the Stars and Stripes had been hoisted at Monterey, San Francisco, Sutter's Fort, and Sonoma.

KEARNY PUSHES FORWARD

Kearny, listening to Kit Carson, decided on a quick push into California. Sending back his wagons and 200 of his men—and with Carson for a guide—Kearny traveled by pack mule to the Gila River along a trail that even the animals found difficult to cross. The general followed the river through a crisscross of mountain ranges, camped beside giant cactus plants, visited with the peaceful Pimas and Coco Maricopa Indians, and pushed on to the junction of the Gila and Colorado Rivers.

But Kearny's heroic march was far from ended. Another 150 discouraging miles stretched ahead. Kearny's little army desperately needed water and native Californians attacked his battered columns. A relief expedition, sent out from San Diego, finally rescued those who survived. By January 13, 1848, Kearny and Frémont completed the conquest of California.

The Mexican War had fulfilled most of Polk's dreams. A peace treaty was signed in the little town of Guadalupe Hidalgo on February 2, 1848. In exchange for $15,000,000 in cash and claims, the United States secured the Rio Grande as its boundary, Mexico gave up its claims to the territory that today includes California, Texas, Arizona, New Mexico, Utah, Nevada, and part of Colorado. In a later treaty with Mexico, signed December 30, 1853, the United States purchased the land between the Gila River and the present Mexican border. This was known as the Gadsden Purchase.

OVER THE OREGON TRAIL

Britain disputes America over the Oregon Territory.

Before Polk left the White House, the Pacific coastline of the United States would extend from San Diego, California, to Puget Sound, Washington. Some of the territory was gained in the Mexican War, the rest through settlement of a dispute with Great Britain over boundaries in the Oregon country.

The "Oregon Question" really dated from 1792 when an American explorer named Robert Gray discovered the Columbia River. Following international practice, the United States claimed sovereignty over the river's valley and watershed as well as over the nearby coast.

England disputed the claim, declaring that Gray's voyage had been commercial and not official. Then in 1805 the Lewis and Clark expedition, reaching the Pacific, strengthened America's claim to the Oregon country. Six years later fur trappers working for John Jacob Astor established Astoria, an American settlement and trading post, on the site where Lewis and Clark had spent a winter.

The War of 1812 gave the British the chance to force American competitors out of the Oregon fur trade. Although the treaty of Ghent restored Astoria to American ownership, the rivalry between the two nations in this territory was far from ended. In 1818 and 1828, agreements were reached that the country "westward of the Stony Mountains" should be open to the "vessels, subjects and citizens" of both nations. But a strong-willed Englishman, John McLoughlin, was in control of the Hudson's Bay Company, and it looked as though the British would win the race for settlement.

Then something unexpected happened. Jason Lee reached Fort Vancouver in 1834 and settled in the Willamette Valley—the first of the missionaries to enter the Oregon country. Marcus Whitman and Henry Spalding arrived two years later, establishing a mission near Fort Walla Walla. In 1839, under

Wagon trains with as many as 1,000 people traveled over the Oregon Trail from Nebraska across the Rockies.

Fathers Blanchet and Demers, a Roman Catholic mission was set up at Cowlitz, in the present state of Washington. Letters, speeches and pamphlets by these missionaries—and Washington Irving's *Astoria,* a novel romanticizing the expedition of Astor's fur trappers in 1811—helped to spread "the Oregon fever."

"The Great Migration" in 1843 brought about 900 settlers to the Oregon country. In another three years there were some 6,000 American settlers in the territory, outnumbering the 1,000 British. The Americans fought their way over the Oregon Trail. Starting at the Platte River in Nebraska, they drove their wagons up the North Platte into Wyoming. Ten miles a day was a good pace as they followed the Sweetwater River in Wyoming, where they caught their first glimpse of the snow-capped Rocky Mountains. Weeks later they struggled down the western slope of the continent.

FIFTY-FOUR FORTY OR FIGHT

When the Democrats nominated Polk for President, one of their campaign slogans was "Fifty-four Forty or Fight." This meant that they wanted the territorial dispute with Britain settled at the latitude of fifty-four degrees, forty minutes or they would go to war. But Polk wisely avoided a conflict with England by settling upon the forty-ninth parallel of latitude, the present boundary.

Polk had much to show for his four years in the White House. The disputes over Texas and Oregon had been settled, and Wisconsin and Iowa had joined the Union. The United States Naval Academy had been founded at Annapolis, adhesive postage stamps had been used for the first time, and inventions like Elias Howe's sewing machine and new types of farm equipment were making life easier in rural areas. In 1846 came the beginning of the great Mormon migration into Utah, and steamboats traveled the Mississippi. In Barnum's Museum in New York City, people gazed with wonder at oddities assembled from around the world.

Polk wished only one term as President, and the Democratic nomination in 1848 went to a hero of the western men, Lewis Cass. But what Polk most feared came to pass. The Whigs had found a winner in Zachary Taylor.

FILLMORE SUCCEEDS TAYLOR

In 1848, gold was discovered in California. Within twelve months 260,000 Americans had journeyed by land and sea into the territory. The "Forty-Niners" gave colorful names like Git-Up-and-Git and Lazy Man's Canyon to their mining towns. A few struck it rich, attracting the gamblers, the desperadoes, and the dance-hall girls. Bands of citizens known as vigilantes enforced what law there was by a rope slung over the branch of a tree.

Yet not for long could Congress forget the rumble of thunder that echoed through its halls. Friends and foes of slavery were forming like rival armies as the debates began on whether the territory acquired from Mexico should be free or slave.

No one could question where President Taylor stood. He was squarely for the Union and against giving in to the South. His Vice-President, Millard Fillmore, took the opposite position. Within sixteen months after taking office "Old Rough and Ready" ran a high fever, resulting from overexposure to the sun during a Fourth of July celebration. Five days later, on July 9, 1850, he was dead. So Fillmore, the friend of the South, became President and America began its march toward civil war.

In Pickett's charge at Gettysburg, the Rebels fought desperately with the Federals defending Cemetery Ridge.

V ~ DISSENSION AND CIVIL WAR

from 1850 to 1865

THREE OLD GIANTS

Calhoun, Clay, and Webster work out a compromise on the slavery question.

The city of Washington shivered under a wintry sky, and snow flurries scudded along Pennsylvania Avenue from the White House to Capitol Hill. Many men traveled this famous road during the first chilly weeks of 1850, but the nation's interest centered on three—the giants of the United States Senate.

All three of these men were old now. Within two years, all would be dead. Yet the fate of the nation rested in their hands. An angry argument arose over what to do with the territory the United States had gained through the Mexican War. Southerners wanted to carry slavery into the states that soon would be formed from this territory. Northerners wanted free states where slavery would be forbidden.

Old "Black Dan" Webster, although born in New Hampshire, represented Massachusetts in the Senate. As a boy, Daniel Webster had recited poetry and passages from the Bible so well that farmers stopped working in the fields and teamsters reined their horses to listen to his golden voice. The greatest orator in America—that's what people called Webster as he sat in the Senate, waiting to speak his mind.

Almost everyone knew that John C. Calhoun, champion of states' rights and idol of the South, suffered greatly. Tuberculosis had left Calhoun a hollow-eyed wreck, who wheezed beneath the flannel wrappings covering his frail body. So weak was Calhoun at the beginning of 1850 that the speech he had prepared was read for him by Senator Mason of Virginia. Yet none of the fire had gone out of Calhoun's mind or heart, and he argued—as he had for years—that the nation must recognize and protect slavery wherever the flag waved.

The last of these three old giants was Kentucky's Henry Clay, whom Abraham Lincoln called "*the* man for a crisis." Not long before, Clay had declared he was through with politics, but at the age of seventy-three, sick and feeble, he had returned to Washington, believing that the nation needed him.

THE COMPROMISE OF 1850

Since neither the proslavery nor the antislavery forces in Congress wanted to risk a civil war, a compromise was needed to settle the differences. And it was Clay, in large measure, who put through the Compromise of 1850. Its main points were:

First, the speedy admission of California as a free state.

Second, the establishment of territorial governments in New Mexico and Utah, without any restriction on slavery. Whether or not these territories became free states or slave states would be left up to the settlers to decide.

Third, settlement of the boundary between Texas and New Mexico (almost along its present line).

Fourth, no interference with slavery in the District of Columbia, although slave trade would be prohibited there.

And fifth, an effective Fugitive Slave Law would be enforced. Any slave found in a Northern state was to be captured and returned to his master in the South.

THE FUGITIVE SLAVE LAW

How well the Compromise of 1850 would succeed depended finally on "Black Dan" Webster. He was spokesman for a New England that included William Lloyd Garrison and Wendell Phillips, leaders of the abolitionist movement, who wanted to abolish slavery immediately. Webster felt no sympathy toward such "agitators." In his opinion, they did more harm than good. Believing that slavery had spread as far as it could go, Webster threw his support behind a vigorous Fugitive Slave Law. He knew that New England would hate this law. He also knew that without it the compromise would fail.

Through the Compromise of 1850, Clay and Webster believed that they had saved the country and ended the angry debates over slavery. But they were wrong. For the next ten years slavery was the most important question in the nation, driving the North and the South farther and farther apart.

UNCLE TOM STIRS THE NATION

An antislavery novel stirs up feeling between North and South.

In 1851, a small antislavery journal, *National Era,* published in serial form a novel by an unknown author named Harriet Beecher Stowe. Although a Boston firm recognized the appeal of Mrs. Stowe's novel and agreed to issue *Uncle Tom's Cabin,* it had no hope for a large sale.

Before a year ended, the firm's presses were running day and night. At least 300,000 copies of *Uncle Tom's Cabin* were sold the first year. Soon Mrs. Stowe's novel was being read in thirty-six languages, including Javanese. The play based on the novel drew large audiences in hundreds of cities and towns, including New York, Chicago, London and Paris. Song writers, riding the wave of Uncle Tom's popularity, filled the piano racks of America with such sentimental ballads as *Uncle Tom's Glimpse of Glory* and *Little Eva, Uncle Tom's Guardian Angel.*

There was no denying the power of the story told

by Mrs. Stowe. Faithful old Uncle Tom, sold to pay his master's debts, mistreated, torn from his family, an object of property who possessed no human rights, was a tearful argument against "the peculiar institution"—as slavery was called—on which the South depended. Thousands of Americans sobbed over the pages of *Uncle Tom's Cabin,* or wept as his story was enacted on the stage. Slavery was more than the political torment of the nation, they decided. It was a sin against man and God.

The South struck back angrily. Mrs. Stowe was pictured as an old crone out of a fairy tale—the wicked witch or a vampire feasting on her victims. One day, meeting Mrs. Stowe, Abraham Lincoln is supposed to have said: "So this is the little woman who made the big war."

In part, his remark was true. But other acts also sparked the bloody civil war to come—acts in Kansas, Washington, Illinois and Virginia.

TROUBLE IN KANSAS

The Kansas-Nebraska Act does away with the Missouri Compromise.

What happened in Kansas was the result of Missouri's position as a slave state. Not even a prairie brook separated Missouri from the free state of Iowa. To the east, separated from Missouri by the Mississippi River, stood Illinois, another free state. To the west of Missouri stretched the Kansas-Nebraska Territory, soon to be organized into states. If that territory remained free, the slaveholders in Missouri could never move westward. Cotton wore out the land and large slaveholders always needed new fields to grow their crop. Land, at that time, was cheap. Slaves were expensive. To tell a slaveholder that he must stay in a limited area, with his slaves and his cotton, was to tell him that in time he must die.

Strong supporters of slavery in the South—among them such senators as Jefferson Davis of Mississippi and Robert Toombs of Georgia—were determined to avoid this threat to their way of life. Yet they could not bring slavery into Kansas and Nebraska unless they could repeal the Missouri Compromise of 1820, which prohibited slavery in territories situated above the line forming the southern boundary of Missouri.

A senator from Illinois, Stephen A. Douglas, found the answer they sought in his famous Kansas-Nebraska Bill. This act wiped out the Missouri Compromise of 1820 and permitted the settlers of a territory to decide for themselves whether they would be admitted to the Union as a free state or slave state. Congress passed the Kansas-Nebraska Bill in 1854. Douglas, believing he had done the best thing for the country, had created a battlefield.

THE EMIGRANT AID SOCIETY

In New England, antislavery men, led by Eli Thayer of Worcester, Massachusetts, organized the Emigrant Aid Society to encourage others who believed as they did to settle in Kansas. Thayer and his helpers campaigned throughout the northern states, singing the praises of the fertile land of their future free state. Five parties—about 700 settlers—moved into Kansas before the end of 1854.

Meanwhile, the proslavery men in Missouri tramped across the border into Kansas by the thousands. They staked claims, founded towns, and armed their supporters. Feelings ran high on both sides. One plantation owner in Alabama sold hundreds of his slaves to get money for guns the slave staters could use to enforce their will in Kansas. A minister in Brooklyn, New York, said it was more important to send rifles than Bibles to help the free staters win in Kansas. He was Henry Ward Beecher, the brother of Harriet Beecher Stowe, and the rifles sent to free staters became known as "Beecher's bibles."

Yet the extraordinary fact was that despite the creation in Kansas of rival governments, rival constitutions, and rival capitals by proslavery and antislavery forces, not a drop of blood might have been shed except for two persons from Massachusetts—one a senator, the other a fanatic.

THE "CRIME AGAINST KANSAS"

A Massachusetts senator speaks out against slavery.

Charles Sumner, who had graduated from Harvard at the age of nineteen, was a brilliant Boston lawyer. He began his political career late in life, when he

The Negro had no voice in the controversy that split the nation on the question of slavery.

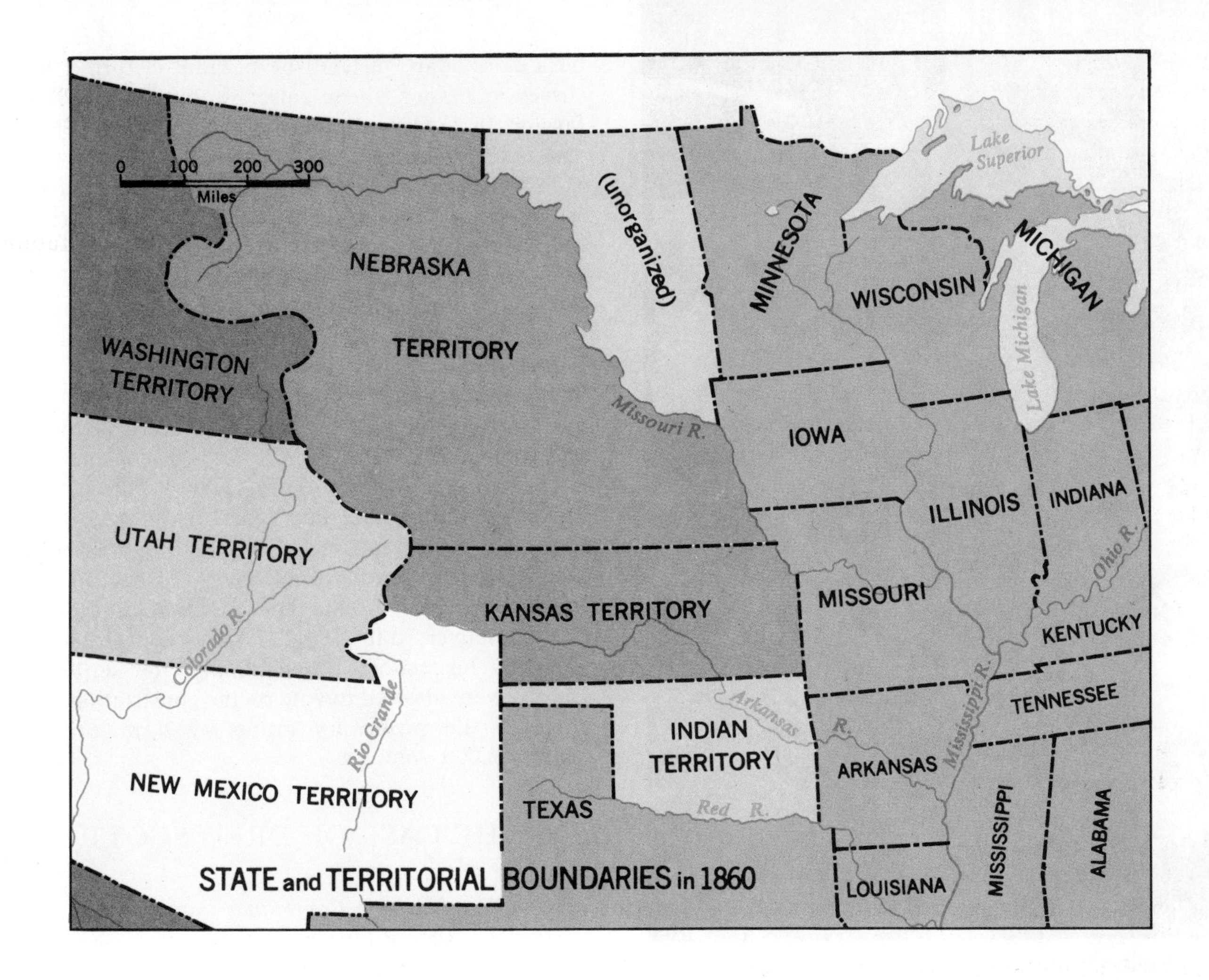

STATE and TERRITORIAL BOUNDARIES in 1860

was elected to the United States Senate in 1851. To Southern hotheads, Sumner quickly became the symbol of all they hated most. For he was not satisfied simply to fight slavery as a political problem. Sumner felt, as did Harriet Beecher Stowe, that slavery must be wiped out completely because it was a great moral evil.

For two days, on May 19 and 20, 1856, Sumner spoke in the Senate on "The Crime Against Kansas," insulting proslavery men in general and South Carolina's elderly senator, Andrew P. Butler, in particular. He accused Butler of wanting to use "the full power in the National Territories to compel fellow men to unpaid toil, to separate husband and wife, and to sell little children at the auction block."

On May 22, Sumner was alone at his desk in the Senate chamber when Congressman Preston Brooks, Senator Butler's nephew, stalked down the aisle. Without warning, Brooks raised his cane and struck the Massachusetts senator on the head. Sumner slumped forward, dazed and blinded. Brooks struck blow after blow until Sumner lay at his feet, insensible and bleeding.

The South made a hero of Brooks, and admirers sent testimonial canes to show they approved of his violent act, but the South lost more than it realized. A half million copies of Sumner's speech were circulated. In the fall of 1856, the young Republican party, running John C. Frémont as its first presidential candidate, showed surprising strength. It polled 1,341,364 votes against 1,838,169 votes cast for James Buchanan, the successful Democratic candidate.

A new political spirit was rising in the North, where there was resentment over the Fugitive Slave Law, the repeal of the Missouri Compromise, and Brooks' brutal assault on Sumner. But Southern politicians seemed simply to grow more stubborn.

ALONG THE POTTAWATOMIE

Violence flares over the slavery issue
but Kansas votes to become a free state.

The stage was set for strange old John Brown to make his first appearance on the national scene. As early as November, 1855, when a free stater named Dow was killed in a quarrel over a land claim, war had threatened to break out in Kansas. But proslavery

Enraged by their hatred of slavery, John Brown and his sons murdered five men in cold blood.

and antislavery forces, coming within speaking distance of each other at Lawrence, happily talked out their differences.

In Washington, President James Buchanan had inherited a bad situation. His predecessor, President Franklin Pierce, had been hostile toward free staters in Kansas. Most of all, Pierce had disliked the agents of the New England Emigrant Aid Society, whom he called unlawful invaders. President Pierce's position encouraged a new wave of trouble in 1856. Sheriff Jones, a proslavery Missourian, came to Lawrence looking for a fight and received what he had least expected—a slap in the face from one of his enemies. Later that same night, an unknown person crept into the sheriff's tent and wounded him in the back. Soon 700 proslavery Missourians—the free staters called them "border ruffians"—stormed down on Lawrence, bringing two cannon. They broke the town's printing press and set fire to the new hotel.

JOHN BROWN STRIKES

On the day after the attack on Lawrence, Brooks caned Sumner, and these two events caused John Brown to strike. Brown's first ambition had been to be a clergyman. Instead, he became in turn a land surveyor, tanner, sheep raiser, wool merchant, and farmer. In 1854, with five sons, he followed the free staters into Kansas.

John Brown and his clan settled near Osawatomie, about thirty miles from Lawrence. The old man's hatred of slavery amounted to insanity, and on the night of May 25, 1856, he and his sons decided that the slavery men in Kansas must be taught a bitter lesson. Sometime after midnight, they reached the Pottawatomie Valley and pulled from their beds five men suspected of being proslavery. All were murdered in cold blood. Then, Brown returned home and went to bed.

The struggle over "Bleeding Kansas" was not to be settled for another two years. In the meantime, President Buchanan tried to force through Congress a state constitution favoring slavery in Kansas. The strong opposition of Stephen A. Douglas defeated this maneuver, but Douglas split the Democratic party by his action. When, finally, the settlers of Kansas were allowed to vote on the constitution, they defeated the proslavery group by a majority of nearly 12,000 votes.

THE CASE OF DRED SCOTT

The Supreme Court finds that slaves are not citizens and rules the Missouri Compromise unconstitutional.

Two days after Buchanan was inaugurated as President, in 1857, the Supreme Court gave its decision on a case that had dragged on for many years. The chief actor in the case was a slave named Dred Scott, who once had been owned by Dr. John Emerson, an army surgeon living in Missouri. In the course of his duties, Dr. Emerson took Dred Scott into the free state of Illinois, and then into that part of the Wisconsin Territory which later became the free state of Minnesota. In 1838, Scott returned with Dr. Emerson to the slave state of Missouri, and was hired out for a time, then sold to another master.

But friends told Dred Scott that since he had lived in a free state, he was a free man, and in 1846 he sued for his freedom. The Circuit Court of St. Louis County gave a verdict in his favor, but the state supreme court reversed that decision. So the case of Dred Scott was transferred to the Federal courts. Finally, it reached the United States Supreme Court.

A NATION DIVIDED

The Supreme Court said that Dred Scott, as a slave, was not a citizen, and, therefore, he did not have the right to sue for his freedom. Then the court went beyond the case and played politics. Almost as though it was trying to save the Democratic party and end all discussion of slavery, it declared that the Missouri Compromise was unconstitutional and that slavery could exist anywhere in the United States. This question had not been before the court, and the decision would be a major cause of the Civil War.

The nation was further divided, not only by the decision that kept Dred Scott a slave, but by the fact that the justices used his case to attack the Missouri Compromise. Opponents of slavery were filled with dark suspicions. They said that the Southern slaveowners had only to whistle and both the President and the Supreme Court danced to their tune. Again there was a feeling in the minds of many men, as there had been after the caning of Sumner, that there must be some kind of change. Something was deeply wrong with the nation, but just what was wrong was something that no one could say in a few words.

And then a lawyer in Illinois found the words—strong, eloquent, stirring words.

LINCOLN DEBATES DOUGLAS

Lincoln runs for the Senate in Illinois.

After Abraham Lincoln had served his one term in Congress, where he had opposed the Mexican War, he returned to Springfield, Illinois, and seemed to lose all interest in politics. He worked hard at his law practice and became one of the most successful lawyers in the state.

But Lincoln could not give up his habit of spending hours with his long nose thrust into the pages of any newspaper that came into his hands. As such things as the Kansas-Nebraska Act, "Bleeding Kansas," and the Dred Scott decision piled up, his frown deepened. Unlike many men of that age, he saw

The Lincoln-Douglas debates made news throughout the nation and brought Lincoln to the fore as a national figure.

what was wrong, and in the summer of 1858, he returned to politics.

In announcing that he would run against Stephen A. Douglas for senator, Lincoln spoke boldly of the crisis facing the nation:

"'A house divided against itself cannot stand.' I believe this government cannot endure permanently half *slave* and half *free.* I do not expect the Union to be *dissolved*—I do not expect the house to fall—but I do expect it will cease to be divided."

Lincoln and Douglas decided to carry their campaign directly to the people in a series of debates. Their first meeting was in the little town of Ottawa, Illinois. In those years, a political rally was also a social event. By wagon, carriage, and buggy, by train and boat, on horseback and on foot, thousands of people poured into Ottawa. Buildings were decorated with bunting, brass bands played, and peddlers hawked badges that read "Lincoln" or "Douglas."

The people chuckled when they saw the two candidates standing side by side—Douglas, whom they had nicknamed "the Little Giant," and Lincoln, whom they called "the Tall Sucker." There they stood, looking like the short and the long of the slavery question they had come to argue. Douglas was about five feet in height, fat, pompous, round-faced, and confident, for he was then one of the most famous men in America. Lincoln's six feet, four inches of skin and bone towered over Douglas, and with his sad face and angular arms, he seemed like a scarecrow who had quit the cornfield to become a prairie lawyer.

But Douglas wasn't fooled by Lincoln's appearance. He had known Lincoln for years, and to a Philadelphia reporter, Douglas gave his opinion of Lincoln: "He is the strong man of his party—full of wit, facts, dates, and the best stump-speaker . . . in the west. He is as honest as he is shrewd."

Douglas hit hard at opponents of slavery, saying that the country was "made by white men, for the benefit of white men," and no Negro could ever be the white man's equal. But Lincoln, wiping his face with a large handkerchief, gave him a sharp answer: "In the right to eat the bread, without leave of anybody else, which his own hand earns, he [the Negro] is my equal and the equal of Judge Douglas, and the equal of every living man."

SLAVERY—"THE REAL ISSUE"

As the two candidates campaigned across the prairies of Illinois, their voices grew scratchier, and sometimes their tempers became short. But Lincoln kept hammering away at slavery as "the dangerous element" which must not be allowed to spread beyond its present boundaries. When after months of argument the debates ended in Springfield, Lincoln swept aside such political considerations as the Kansas-Nebraska Act and the Dred Scott decision. Only a simple issue must be faced, he pleaded—the moral issue. He said:

"That is the real issue. That is the issue that will continue when these poor tongues of Judge Douglas and myself shall be silent. It is the eternal struggle between these two principles—right and wrong—throughout the world. They are the two principles that have stood face to face from the beginning of time; and will ever continue to struggle. The one is the common right of humanity and the other the divine right of kings. It is the same principle in whatever shape it develops itself. It is the spirit that says, 'You work and toil and earn bread, and I'll eat it.' No matter in what shape it comes, whether from the mouth of a king who seeks to bestride the people of his own nation and live by the fruit of their labor, or from one race of men as an apology for enslaving another race, it is the same tyrannical principle. . . ."

Lincoln had known from the beginning he could not win the election. Still, he had gained greatly from the campaign. He had clarified his own ideas and had become a national figure. Soon he would be asked to speak in Ohio, Iowa, Wisconsin, Kansas,

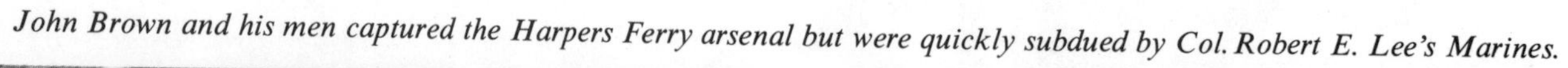

John Brown and his men captured the Harpers Ferry arsenal but were quickly subdued by Col. Robert E. Lee's Marines.

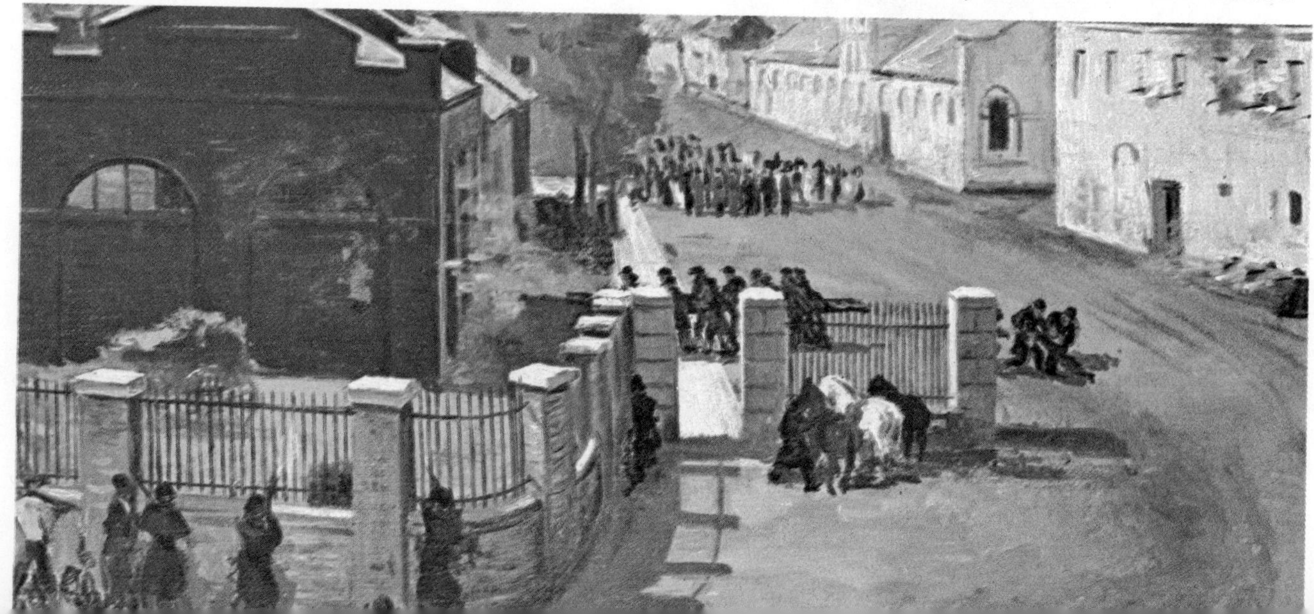

New York City. The image of Abraham Lincoln was spreading across the land.

And so was another image. On October 16, 1859, John Brown struck again.

THUNDER OVER HARPERS FERRY

John Brown tries to start a rebellion, and becomes a martyr to Northerners.

Brown's hatred for slavery kept growing. He raided plantations in Missouri and carried slaves to freedom in Canada. A little band of followers gathered around the old man, believing whatever he told them. And so Brown found supporters for his wild dream. He would capture the United States arsenal at Harpers Ferry, Virginia, and the slaves of the South, realizing that powerful friends had come to help them, would rise in a mass and free themselves from their white masters.

Brown and his handful of followers stormed and captured the arsenal at Harpers Ferry—that much of the old man's scheme succeeded. But not even a hint of a slave uprising followed. Meanwhile, a detachment of marines, under the command of Colonel Robert E. Lee, was hurried to Harpers Ferry to seize Brown and his band of "madmen."

Lee surrounded the arsenal and called for a surrender. Brown refused. Using a heavy ladder for a battering ram, the soldiers smashed open the door. Shots rang out and a marine fell mortally wounded Sunlight flashed on the blades of the bayonets. Brown, trying to escape, was stopped by the sweep of a lieutenant's sword, and the scuffle was ended.

JOHN BROWN IS HANGED

However, the nation was far from finished with John Brown. Convicted of murder, conspiracy, and treason against the state of Virginia, he was sentenced to hang in early December at Charles Town. The crowd that watched the old fellow mount the gallows noticed the proud tilt of his head, the steadiness of his knees. The sheriff's hatchet struck the rope a hard blow, the platform fell away, and with a kind of shiver onlookers muttered: "Well, that does it. John Brown is dead at last."

John Brown was dead, but his spirit seemed to become more alive. New England's literary giants, such as Ralph Waldo Emerson and Henry David Thoreau, spoke of him as "a saint" and "an angel of light." Bells tolled, calling people to services in his honor in Chicago, Philadelphia, Boston, Syracuse, Cleveland, New York City. "History," wrote the poet William Cullen Bryant, "will record his name among those of its martyrs and heroes."

Angry and baffled, Southerners could hardly believe that so many Northerners were making a hero of this murderer and insurrectionist. What could it mean, except that Northerners hated Southerners and would go to any extreme to harm them? From the moment John Brown was hanged at Charles Town, the nation was split and each half would follow its own path. North and South would go their own ways and neither would try to understand the other.

A HOUSE DIVIDED

Lincoln is elected President and South Carolina secedes from the Union.

Within the Democratic party, as the time for nominating a presidential candidate approached, sectional feelings ran high. The clear choice of Northern Democrats was Stephen A. Douglas. But Southerners couldn't forget that Douglas had blocked Buchanan's efforts to admit Kansas as a slave state, and they wanted no part of Douglas. So the Democratic party divided, with the Northern wing nominating Douglas and the Southern wing nominating John C. Breckinridge of Kentucky. By splitting the party, the Democrats were giving the victory to the Republicans, whose surprising candidate for President was that upstart prairie lawyer, Abraham Lincoln.

Most Southerners were thoroughly, but mistakenly, convinced that the Republicans were all wild-eyed abolitionists. So, even before the ballots were counted, Governor William H. Gist of South Carolina wrote a bold letter to the governors of the cotton states. If Lincoln was elected, he said, South Carolina would secede from the Union. He wanted to know what the other Southern states would do.

Gist received a variety of replies. North Carolinians were "very far from being agreed" as to what they should do. Alabama would secede "if two or more States will co-operate with her." Louisiana was a doubtful secessionist state, but Mississippi stood ready to protect her rights should the "Black Republicans" win. Georgia, too, would act for "her safety," and the governor of Florida said his people were willing "to wheel into line" with any state or states "looking to the vindication and maintenance of the rights, interest, honor and safety of the South."

Of course, this correspondence was a carefully guarded secret when in November, 1860, the people voted. Although the two Democratic candidates (Douglas and Breckinridge) had a total popular vote of 2,226,738 against 1,866,452 for Lincoln, Lincoln won the electoral vote by the smashing margin of 180 to 84.

South Carolina began to carry out its threat to

secede. Delegates were elected to attend a secession convention in Columbia, South Carolina, in mid-December, 1860. A smallpox epidemic in Columbia hurried the delegates to Charleston, but no one doubted the outcome when the convention met again on December 19 in St. Andrews Hall. Excited throngs filled the streets and jammed the passages and stairways of the meeting place. Carved in deep black letters on the speaker's gavel was a single word: "Secession." When at last the ordinance that would carry South Carolina out of the Union was put to a vote, not one delegate voted against it.

Church bells rang and cannon thundered as the news spread through the streets of Charleston. South Carolina no longer considered itself part of the United States. All business stopped. Old men shouted and danced like school children. Lights glowed in the big homes along the harbor front and bands played. But when the sun came up next morning, at Fort Moultrie, across Charleston harbor, a bugle sounded and a Federal soldier ran up the Stars and Stripes.

Kentucky-born Major Robert Anderson, in command of the small Federal garrison at Fort Moultrie, was a loyal, intelligent officer. He knew that the old fort he now occupied was tumbling down around him and could never be defended against a vigorous attack. He decided to move to Fort Sumter in Charleston harbor where, with a few repairs, he might be able to put up a defense. On the night after Christmas, without a single Charlestonian suspecting his plan, Anderson transferred his force from Fort Moultrie to Fort Sumter.

Major Robert Anderson

"NO RECONSTRUCTION CAN BE NOW ENTERTAINED"

The South forms the Confederate States of America.

Slavery by itself was not the cause of the Civil War. It was simply an excuse for it. The deeper struggle was political. It arose from the fact that rival forms of democracy had taken root in America. The South, supported by cotton, rice, and sugar as its principal agricultural products, followed the old Greek style of democracy. There, a ruling class looked upon slaves as necessary to its way of life. The North, with numerous rivers and waterfalls to supply cheap power for factories, developed an industrial democracy, where free enterprise became a necessity. The South's democracy looked backward and accepted all changes grudgingly. The North, on the other hand, had a go-ahead democracy, where profits to business meant bigger cities, more schools, better roads, and more food on the table.

The Southern politicians, shouting that their Negro slaves fared far better than the "wage slaves" in the North, fell into two classes. There were the few extremists who wanted to break away from the Union, with or without a good reason. But the second group, the vast majority, depended on control of Congress, the Supreme Court, and perhaps even the President's cabinet to protect their "rights." Unhappily, their system broke down in 1860, when political parties divided in such a manner that the people were forced to favor one of the two rival democracies. When Lincoln was elected in 1860, the South lost its political control and rebelled. And so the war that Lincoln quite properly called "a People's contest" followed.

Once South Carolina seceded, it did not long stand alone. Quickly other states took action—Mississippi on January 9, 1861, Florida the next day, Alabama a day later, Georgia on January 19, Louisiana on January 26, Texas on February 1. Many Southern officers resigned their commissions in the United States army. And in Congress most Southern members closed their desks and started for home. In early February, delegates from the seven seceding states met in Montgomery, Alabama. This convention wrote a constitution that recognized slavery. It elected Jefferson Davis of Mississippi as provisional (temporary) president and Alexander H. Stephens of Georgia as provisional vice-president of a new nation, the Confederate States of America.

A mood of gaiety ran through the South. Look, the people said, at what we have done in only one month. We have formed a new government. With the exception of Fort Sumter in Charleston harbor, Fort Pickens in Pensacola Bay, and two small forts off the coast of Florida, we have seized every Federal

In February 1861, at Montgomery, Alabama, Jefferson Davis was elected head of the Confederate States of America.

fort, arsenal, customhouse and lighthouse in the seven seceding states. Not a drop of blood has been shed and we are already a country! We have acted before Mr. Lincoln and his "Black Republicans" could lift a finger to stop us, and now it is too late for them to undo what has been accomplished.

Jefferson Davis reached Montgomery on February 16. Military companies led the parade as he entered this city, which, like ancient Rome, was set upon seven hills. He spoke briefly, telling the cheering throng that the time for compromise had passed. Now the South must "make all who oppose us smell Southern powder and feel Southern steel." And he said: "No reconstruction can be now entertained."

"THE BETTER ANGELS OF OUR NATURE"

Lincoln still hopes for a peaceful settlement with the South as he gives his First Inaugural Address.

Abraham Lincoln traveled from Springfield to Washington, where on March 4, 1861, he would be inaugurated as the sixteenth President of the United States. Many of his friends were disappointed that during the long journey he had hardly seemed to take any notice of the events in Montgomery. Northern critics of Mr. Lincoln—and there were many—cried that his cautious, standoffish attitude simply showed that he was not qualified for the high office to which he had been elected.

But Lincoln was the sort of man who couldn't be forced to act before he was ready. Often when faced with a problem that seemed to have no solution, he remembered the children of Israel on the shores of the Red Sea. "Stand still and see the salvation of the Lord," Moses had said to them. Lincoln was always willing to wait in that spirit.

March 4 was a gloomy day in Washington, raw and overcast. General Winfield Scott, who feared that some assassin might attempt to take Mr. Lincoln's life, had lined Pennsylvania Avenue, rooftops, street intersections, and the Capitol grounds with expert marksmen, cavalry, and artillery. Lincoln made his inaugural address in a quiet, even voice. He argued against the right of secession, and although he said that his government would "hold, occupy and possess" Federal forts and property, he let it be known that he did not intend to take by force forts and property already seized by the Confederacy.

As Lincoln approached the close of his address, he said:

"I am loath to close. We are not enemies, . . . but friends. Though passion may have strained, it must not break our bonds of affection. The mystic chords of memory, stretching from every battlefield and patriot grave, to every heart and hearth-stone, all over this broad land, will yet swell the chorus of the Union when again touched, as surely they will be, by the better angels of our nature."

PEACE OR A SWORD?

The South threatens a Union garrison at Fort Sumter.

During his first days in office, Lincoln was faced with an unexpected crisis. Supplies were running low at Fort Sumter. He had to decide quickly whether he should abandon the fort or send reinforcements and supplies. Old General Winfield Scott doubted that the fort could be saved, but navy men expressed a more cheerful view. Meanwhile South Carolina raised a cry that unless Anderson and his Federals were withdrawn from Sumter, the people of the proud old Palmetto State would take action to put an end to this "insult" to their sovereignty.

Peace or war? For six critical weeks, while Washington buzzed with rumors, the nation wondered what the spring of 1861 would bring. Secretary of State William H. Seward repeatedly told Confederate "peace commissioners" that Sumter would be surrendered, for the fort wasn't worth a war. But Seward spoke for himself and not for Lincoln. Colonel Rob-

On April 12, 1861, Southern guns bombarded Fort Sumter and started the Civil War that was to last four years.

ert E. Lee was called from his home in nearby Arlington, Virginia, and offered command of Federal forces in the field should war come. Lee had seen years of service in the regular army, and he hated slavery. Yet he was, first of all, a Virginian, and he refused the command for fear that he might be asked to fight against his mother state.

To Lee's relief–and to Lincoln's–Virginia seemed to show no wish to join the Confederacy. Missouri also refused to cut her ties with the Union. Lincoln's hope was that with time the southern people would realize their mistake and the Confederacy would collapse. But the Confederates in Montgomery placed General Pierre G. T. Beauregard in command of the troops in Charleston, and the harbor front began to bristle with cannon aimed at Sumter. Time was running out, Southerners shouted. Their patience was at an end. Sumter must surrender or Southern shells would reduce it to ruins.

At last Lincoln came to a decision. He would send an expedition to the relief of the fort, but the ships would land only provisions. Unless attacked, they would make no attempt to put either men or munitions into Sumter. The report that Federal ships were on their way to Sumter brought quick action from the Confederates. Beauregard was ordered to demand the surrender of the fort. If the Federals stood firm, he was to "proceed in such manner as you may determine, to reduce it."

Major Anderson stood firm and refused to surrender.

STORM OVER SUMTER

Southern forces fire on Fort Sumter, beginning the Civil War.

Shadowy figures moved beside the cannon that lined Charleston's harbor front. The night air echoed with the hoofbeats of galloping horsemen. At street intersections the old men of the city, organized into the Home Guard, stood stiffly at attention.

The time was four-thirty in the morning of April 12, 1861. A flash of light was followed by the boom of a mortar.

Inside Sumter, Sergeant James Chester "followed the burning fuse which marked the course of the shell as it mounted among the stars, and then descended with ever-increasing velocity, until it landed inside the fort and burst."

"It was a capital shot," Sergeant Chester said.

Soon Confederate cannon on all sides opened on the fort until, Chester added, "shot and shell went

In Baltimore, 16 persons were killed when Southerners attacked Federal troops en route to Washington.

screaming over Sumter as if an army of devils were swooping around it." To save ammunition, Major Anderson did not return the fire until after daylight. Even then he ordered only an occasional shot at the Confederates. He knew that he was doomed unless the ships of the relief expedition, then standing off the harbor, reached him. Nature itself seemed against the Federals, for high winds made the dock at Sumter unapproachable.

Charlestonians rushed to their rooftops, some with telescopes. One woman wrote: "We could distinctly see the flames [of the fort] amidst the smoke. All the barracks were on fire."

Sergeant Chester later recalled the satisfied grin of a Federal gunner who lobbed two shells at a hotel and watched the spectators on its rooftop scampering "in a rather undignified manner." Sometime after midnight, a newspaperman wired his paper in Philadelphia: "It will be utterly impossible to reinforce Fort Sumter tonight, as a storm is raging, and the sea is very rough."

FORT SUMTER FALLS

Surgeon Samuel Wylie Crawford described the scene inside Sumter on April 13: "The flames of the burning quarters were still spreading, shooting upward amid the dense smoke as heavy masses of brick and masonry crumbled, and fell with loud noise. All of the woodwork had now been consumed. The heavy gates at the entrance, as well as the planking of the windows on the gorge, were gone, leaving access to the fort easy and almost unobstructed."

That afternoon Anderson surrendered. After thirty-three hours of cannonading, the guns fell silent. Charleston rocked with joy and church bells rang. "It is all over," happy Charlestonians shouted, never guessing how the North was aroused.

"OLD ABE'S BLOOD IS UP"

Lincoln calls for Federal troops, and Southerners riot in Baltimore.

In city and town throughout the North, work stopped. Crowds gathered before newspaper offices, eager for any scrap of news from Charleston. Men cried when they learned that Sumter had surrendered. And as they turned away there was a look on their faces that said clearly: "Whatever Old Abe Lincoln wants, we'll do."

Next day Lincoln called for 75,000 state militiamen to serve in the Federal army for three months. Men rushed to enlist. The President could have had ten times 75,000 soldiers. The spirit of the North was reflected in a Chicago newspaper that said: "Old Abe's Blood Is Up." Singing "John Brown's body lies a-mouldering in his grave, but his soul goes marching on," Northerners prepared to teach Johnny Reb a lesson.

But Johnny Reb was far from idle. Organizing into military companies that took such names as the "Bartow Lincoln Killers," Johnny sharpened his hunting knife, cleaned his squirrel rifle, and reckoned that if Billy Yank wanted another licking he, Johnny Reb, would be willing to oblige. Not a Federal soldier had been killed in the bombardment of Sumter, but next time—well, maybe a little bloodshed would bring Billy Yank to his senses. Actually, the first bloodshed of the war was coming sooner than expected—and in an unexpected place.

VIRGINIA SECEDES

On April 17, Virginia joined the Confederacy. That same day, the 6th Massachusetts Regiment boarded a train for Washington. On the morning of April 19, it reached the Philadelphia and Baltimore Railroad Station in Baltimore. Here the men boarded horse-drawn cars to get to the Baltimore and Ohio Railroad Station, about a mile away.

Many people in Baltimore were in favor of the South. A sullen crowd shouting "Hurrah for Jeff Davis!" scowled as the "Northern invaders" bumped over the cobblestones between stations. Ahead, car rails had been torn up and a barricade thrown across the tracks.

Then one of the teamsters lost his nerve, and his car stopped. Howling with rage, the crowd attacked the Federal soldiers with clubs, paving stones, and other missiles. Still, the troops held their tempers. But when the cars reached the barricade, the soldiers had to get out and march.

The crowd numbered about 10,000 persons, the soldiers about 250. Yelling, swearing, throwing cobblestones, the mob pressed upon the troops. John W. Hanson, chaplain of the 6th Massachusetts, described what happened next:

"At one of the bridges in Pratt Street, a barricade, with cannon to sweep the streets, not quite ready for service, had been arranged. Here the mob supposed the column [of soldiers] would be forced to halt, but . . . before the ruffians could follow over the bridge, or run around to intercept them, the soldiers had succeeded in getting quite a distance up Pratt Street. . . . Cheers for 'Jeff Davis' and for 'South Carolina, and the South,' all sorts of insulting language—such as 'Dig your graves!'—'You can pray, but you cannot fight!' and the like—were heard; but the little battalion went steadily ahead, with no thought of turning back."

Finally the soldiers lost their patience, and shots rang out. The next morning the shocked nation learned that four soldiers and twelve civilians had been killed in the Baltimore riot.

At the Battle of Bull Run, Union troops, after early successes, fled in panic. But both sides lost hundreds in killed and wounded, and hopes of a short war faded.

THE FIRST GREAT BATTLE

Confederates defeat Union forces at Bull Run, near Manassas Junction, Virginia.

Because of the riot, other troops traveling to Washington—the 8th Massachusetts, the 7th New York, the 1st Rhode Island—bypassed the city of Baltimore. This caused a delay, and, in Washington, Lincoln wondered if the troops he so badly needed would ever arrive.

"I begin to believe that there is no North," he cried.

But on April 25, the 7th New York marched into Washington. "The presence of this single regiment," wrote one of Lincoln's secretaries, "seemed to turn the scales of fate. Cheer upon cheer greeted them, windows were thrown up, houses opened, the population came forth upon the streets as for a holiday. It was an epoch in American history. For the first time, the combined spirit and power of Liberty entered the nation's capital."

But North Carolina and Tennessee joined the Confederacy, and now a total of ten states had left the Union. The Confederate capital was moved from Montgomery to Richmond, and the North, eager to end the war, raised the cry of "On to Richmond."

A strong Confederate army under General Beauregard, the hero of Sumter, gathered at Manassas Junction, Virginia, about twenty-five miles west of Washington. The advance guard was almost within sight of the Capitol.

Lincoln was caught in a terrible squeeze. Although General Winfield Scott told him, quite honestly, that the Federal army was not ready for a major battle, the people were demanding action. Lincoln gave in to political pressure, and on July 15, 1861, Union troops marched to battle singing that they would "hang Jeff Davis to a sour apple tree." The Federals stopped to pick blackberries on the way, and ambled along as though they were going to a picnic rather than to a battle.

Three days later, near Manassas Junction, they came to a little stream called Bull Run. Here they exchanged a few random shots with Rebel pickets, who fell back. Confidently, the Federals pressed on into the first great pitched battle of the war. Southerners would call it the Battle of Manassas. Northerners would call it the Battle of Bull Run.

By either name, it was a queer contest. Each commanding general—Beauregard for the South, Irvin McDowell for the North—had the same idea. Each tried to swing his army around the other's right flank. If the maneuver had worked, the Federals might have raced into Richmond and the Confederates might have raced into Washington, which would have made a strange military situation.

"STONEWALL" JACKSON

At first the Federals seemed to be sweeping everything in front of them, but soon the Confederate opposition grew stiffer. A Southern colonel shouted: "Look at Jackson's brigade! It stands there like a stone wall!"

And so, in this first great battle of the war, Thomas Jonathan Jackson won his nickname of "Stonewall." Yet his brigade alone could not have saved the Confederates that day. The Union forces kept pressing forward, while the Rebel lines sagged dangerously.

By midafternoon it looked as though a tremendous Union victory was in the making. But then a second Confederate army, under General Joseph E. Johnston, arrived at Manassas Junction and the situation changed.

Suddenly the battle turned, and the Union boys were running to save their necks. Everyone ran—Federal officers, soldiers, and the politicians who had driven over from Washington to enjoy the show. Colonel Louis Blenker, who fought with the 8th New York, said: "I do not think it is a blame for anybody to lose that battle. There was a panic which nobody can explain."

Out of 28,452 Union soldiers, 481 were dead, 1,011 were wounded, 1,216 were missing. Out of 32,232 Confederate soldiers, 387 were dead, 1,582 were wounded, twelve were missing. Before the Battle at Manassas, the people of both the North and the South had believed that the war would be easily won and soon over. Now they were beginning to realize that the war might be long and hard.

LINCOLN BLOCKADES THE SOUTH

Southerners laugh at Lincoln's plan, but the blockade is effective.

On April 19, 1861, Lincoln declared a blockade of the coast line of all the states in rebellion against the Union. When Southerners heard the news, they laughed. Wherever they gathered, in places like the lobby of the Spottswood Hotel in Richmond, they said things like this:

"That big ape Lincoln—what a fool! You know how many northern ships there are in port now ready for duty? Just three, and old wooden tubs at that. So Lincoln's going to blockade our coast line, eh? With three ships fit for service he's going to patrol 3,549 miles of Atlantic coast and close 180 ports? And how about the Mississippi, with her tributaries? That will give Lincoln another 3,615 miles to patrol."

But the South underestimated Lincoln—which was one of the reasons it finally lost the war. In the spring of 1862, the blockade was already having its effect. The author George Washington Cable, then a youth in New Orleans, described how the blockade had closed in on New Orleans "like a prison-gate . . . the queen of Southern commerce, the city that had once believed it was to be the greatest in the world, was absolutely out of employment."

The blockade depended on ships, and building up the Union navy was one of Lincoln's most remarkable achievements. The statistics from 1861 until the end of the war tell the story:

	1861	*1865*
Ships	*90*	*670*
Officers	*1,300*	*6,700*
Seamen	*7,500*	*51,500*
Budget	*$12,000,000*	*$123,000,000*

General Thomas J. "Stonewall" Jackson

TWO THOUSAND MILES OF TROUBLE

McClellan strengthens the Union army but avoids battle.

By early 1862, the land war had spread from Virginia to Missouri. From Lincoln's point of view, most of it was going badly.

In the East, General George B. McClellan, who had won a small victory over the Confederates in the mountains of western Virginia, had been called to Washington. He was given command of the disorganized Federal forces that had done so badly at Manassas Junction. A capable administrator, McClellan quickly ended the drunkenness, the desertions, and the lack of discipline within the Army of the Potomac, but he showed little desire to fight the Rebels. As the weeks went by, Northern newspapers repeated the same headline: "All Quiet Along the Potomac."

In the West, beyond the Allegheny Mountains, there was trouble.

First, Lincoln had to dismiss General John C. Frémont (who had been the Republican candidate for President in 1856). Frémont would not change

General George B. McClellan

his proclamation freeing the slaves in his military district. Missouri and Kentucky were disturbed by Frémont's proclamation, and Lincoln did not wish to drive these two border states into the Confederacy. Before the year ended, Lincoln would make his own move toward freeing the slaves. But now, he said, such action was the responsibility of the elected government, and not of military authority. The job of a general was to fight battles, and not to run the country.

General Henry W. Halleck, whose nickname was "Old Brains," replaced Frémont in command in St. Louis. Lincoln expected Halleck to cooperate with a second western army under General Don Carlos Buell. But Halleck and Buell were both highly ambitious men, and each wished to win supreme command in the West. Perhaps for this reason each became expert at giving excuses for not cooperating with the other.

Lincoln was worried. What he wanted most was some plan of action that would help the many loyal Unionists in eastern Tennessee. Halleck would do nothing, arguing that the secessionists in Missouri would stab him in the back the moment he weakened his forces there. Then Buell ordered a small force under a Virginia-born Union general, George H. Thomas, to chase the Rebels out of eastern Kentucky. In the Battle of Mill Spring, Thomas sent the Confederates scurrying, and Buell was given more credit than he deserved.

Halleck suddenly came alive. He, too, would act. To fight the battle he planned, he picked an unknown general whose main achievement so far had been upsetting superior officers, like Frémont and Halleck, with his ideas of how to win this war.

His name was Ulysses S. Grant.

THE NORTH FINDS A WINNER

General Grant moves to drive the Confederates out of the West.

Grant's headquarters was in the cheerless town of Cairo, where the southern tip of Illinois rubs against the banks of the Mississippi and Ohio Rivers. In those days, Cairo was a place of mud, disease, and rats, but Grant paid no attention to these things and studied his maps.

This stumpy, awkward little man was perhaps the greatest military leader of his age. He had once thought of being a teacher of mathematics, and he had a quick, clear, and logical mind. There was another thing that helped him now. He had grown up near the Ohio River, and he understood what a river was—nature's best highway to wherever you wanted to go.

Upstream from Cairo, the Tennessee and the Cumberland Rivers emptied into the Ohio. These two rivers were highways into the Deep South. Winning control of them was the first step in pushing the Confederates out of the West. And so, early in February, 1862, Grant began a combined naval and land action against Fort Henry, the Confederate stronghold that guarded the Tennessee River.

FORT HENRY FALLS

Grant expected a bitter fight. But the fort was a bad piece of engineering, set on low ground. High water in the river had almost flooded it when Union Flag Officer Andrew Foote steamed down the river with his ironclads. His guns raked the fort and, even before Grant arrived, the navy had won a victory.

About ten miles away, on the banks of the Cumberland River, stood Fort Donelson, guarding the approaches to Nashville. Grant expected it to fall easily. Again he was in for a surprise—this time an unpleasant one.

First, the weather turned against Grant. When his

men had left Henry, the air was springlike and they had thrown away their heavy coats and blankets. Then a snowstorm came roaring out of the north. The temperature dropped to below zero, and Federal pickets froze to death at their posts.

Donelson proved to be a well-built fort, with batteries that commanded a broad sweep of the Cumberland. Foote's gunboats were soon seriously damaged by the fire of the fort's thirty-two-pounders. Cold and discouraged, Grant feared that the fort would fall only after a long siege.

But General John B. Floyd, the Confederate in command of Donelson, had served as Secretary of War under President Buchanan. He was suspected of having plotted to help the secessionists, and he was afraid of what might happen to him if he should be captured.

On top of this, he was convinced that his army was trapped within the fort. He therefore ordered a massive attack to break open the road to Nashville. He crumbled Grant's right flank, and, if he had pushed on, he might have easily smashed the whole Federal army. But at this point he lost his nerve and pulled his forces back into the entrenchments of Donelson. Grant immediately sealed off the avenue of escape that Floyd had opened.

"UNCONDITIONAL SURRENDER"

That night, Floyd fled from Donelson, with General Gideon J. Pillow. When daylight came, Simon Bolivar Buckner, the general left in command, had to make the best deal he could with Grant. Grant offered him "no terms but immediate and unconditional surrender." Buckner surrendered the fort with more than 14,000 men, and Grant became the North's first real hero. His initials were "U.S.," and people said they stood for "Unconditional Surrender."

"BLOODY SHILOH"

A Confederate attack is beaten back in two days of brutal fighting.

During the next forty-nine days, Grant's reputation rose and fell from one day to the next. Part of the trouble was Grant himself. Most generals then believed that after capturing an objective—as Grant had captured Fort Donelson—it was necessary to stop, call in all forces, and protect the captured territory. But Grant had a different idea. He believed that it was far more important to destroy the enemy's ability to make war than to hold territory. Once a general had an enemy army on the run, he should do everything in his power to keep it running.

So Grant plunged on toward Nashville, reaching the city before the end of February. He did indeed keep the Confederates on the run. They cleared out of Tennessee and did not stop until they reached Corinth, in northern Mississippi.

General Ulysses S. Grant

AT PITTSBURG LANDING

Grant still wanted to destroy the Confederate army at Corinth. As April came on, and the peach blossoms bloomed along the valleys of the Tennessee River, Grant moved his forces to Pittsburg Landing, about twenty miles above Corinth. The result was almost disaster.

There were several reasons for what happened. First of all, Grant's mind was on destroying the Confederate forces; it never occurred to him that he might be attacked by the Rebels. He also expected to be joined at any moment by Buell's army, so that, together, they could make the big push on Corinth.

And then, two days before the fighting started, a horse fell on Grant's leg. Grant went to a mansion ten miles above Pittsburg Landing to rest. He was there on Sunday morning, April 6, 1862, when he heard gunfire down-river. He knew at once that this was no ordinary skirmish.

Grant hobbled aboard his headquarters boat, the *Tigress,* and steamed down the Tennessee to Pittsburg Landing. He could hardly believe what he saw. The Confederates had attacked that morning, taking his men by surprise. The Federals had rushed out of their tents in panic. Hundreds of them were at the riverbank, not knowing where to turn.

THE BATTLE OF SHILOH

The battle that followed came to be known as the Battle of Shiloh, taking its name from Shiloh Meetinghouse, a Presbyterian church that stood on the battlefield. The fighting was the most brutal of the war. An eyewitness wrote: "I hope my eyes never look upon such sights. Men with their entrails protruding, others with bullets in their breasts, and one poor wretch I found whose eyes had been shot away."

Grant had to "look upon such sights" and still keep his head. Although his leg pained him terribly, he moved around the bloody battlefield, ordering ammunition delivered where it was needed, rallying frightened soldiers and re-forming Union lines. He sent message after message to Buell, who was on his way from Nashville with 35,000 men, trying to hurry him along.

Grant's force would probably have been destroyed if it had not been for a small band under Benjamin Prentiss. For hours they held firm, and by the time they surrendered, Grant had rebuilt his lines.

When darkness came, the Federal lines had been pushed to within sight of the river landing. General William Tecumseh Sherman was sure that the Union army was beaten and must retreat next morning. He went in search of Grant and found him under a tree, pacing in the rain.

"Well, Grant," Sherman said, "we've had the devil's own day, haven't we?"

"Yes," Grant replied. "Lick 'em tomorrow, though."

Buell's troops reached Shiloh that night, and next day it was the Confederates who were on the run. Grant had saved his army—a remarkable feat. But the cost of Shiloh in dead, missing, and wounded staggered the nation. Casualties were 13,047 for the North, 10,699 for the South.

THE MONITOR AND THE MERRIMACK

A battle between two strange ships changes the course of naval history.

As early as September, 1861, John Ericsson, a Swede who had become an American citizen, had written to Washington. Ericsson was an inventor. He said he could build a vessel with a revolving gun turret that would "split the rebel fleet at Norfolk into matches in half an hour." No one in Washington

The little Monitor, *with its revolving turret and two guns against ten, proved an easy victor over the* Merrimack.

paid the least attention to him. Then one day a Connecticut industrialist named Cornelius S. Bushnell happened to stop at Ericsson's office, at 95 Franklin Street, New York City.

Bushnell persuaded Ericsson to show him a model of the little ship. After he had seen it, Bushnell put the model in its paper box and hurried to Washington. Navy men laughed and called it "preposterous," but Lincoln remarked, "All I can say is what the girl said when she put her foot in the stocking: 'It strikes me there's something in it.' "

Even so, Ericsson's *Monitor* might never have been built except for one important fact. After Virginia seceded, the Federal government had decided to give up its naval yard at Norfolk. The greatest ship then in the Federal service was the *Merrimack.* (Although frequently called the *Merrimac,* the ship was registered officially as the *Merrimack.*) She was left burned and sunk at the bottom of the Elizabeth River. But the Confederates raised the *Merrimack* from the river mud and completely remodeled her. Cutting the old vessel down to her water line, they raised a new 160-foot-long superstructure of oak and pine on her berth deck. They covered her slanting gun decks with three-inch-thick iron plate, transforming her into an ironclad.

Washington learned that the *Merrimack* had become a new kind of fighting ship and carried a crew of 350. She mounted ten guns capable of handling 150-pound shot. Nobody in Washington knew what the *Merrimack* could do, but if the Confederates could gamble on an ironclad, so must the Union. And so, over the objections of some navy men, John Ericsson was permitted to build his *Monitor.*

The Confederates had the *Merrimack* ready for action on March 8, 1862. Low and ugly, she came steaming out of the Elizabeth River with black smoke pouring from her stack. Immediately ahead was Hampton Roads, a stretch of deep water where the James River, flowing into Chesapeake Bay, empties into the sea. There the Union had anchored its best wooden war sloops—the *Congress,* the *Cumberland,* the *Minnesota*—to guard the approaches to the Atlantic.

Federal sailors had their wash drying in the rigging that morning when a lookout shouted, "That *Thing* is coming down!"

Against the ironclad *Merrimack,* the wooden ships of the Union were helpless. By nightfall, the *Cumberland* had been sunk, the *Congress* burned, and the *Minnesota* grounded.

When the news reached Washington, Lincoln called a special meeting of his Cabinet. The White House was filled with gloom.

Secretary of War Edwin M. Stanton was sure that the *Merrimack* would soon destroy every city in the North. Secretary of State William H. Seward expected at any moment to see the *Merrimack* come steaming up the Potomac and place a cannon shot through the windows of the White House.

But Secretary of the Navy Gideon Welles still believed in John Ericsson. Perhaps the Union's *Monitor* did look like a silly "cheesebox on a raft." But she was on her way to Hampton Roads, and maybe they should wait to see what happened.

Next day—March 9, 1862—the *Merrimack* came back to Hampton Roads to finish her "kill" of the *Minnesota.* But by then, the *Monitor* was there, too, mounting only two guns in her revolving gun turret to the *Merrimack's* ten.

A stranger naval battle was never fought. The *Monitor,* as one reporter said, looked from a distance like "a raft, with an ambulance amidship." But Ericsson's revolving gun turret was a masterpiece. It offered no target at which to shoot. The turret spun around, a port opened, an eleven-inch gun fired, and the port cover closed.

Meanwhile, shot dropped off the turret, so that a Confederate officer on the *Merrimack* said that their fire was "like so many pebblestones thrown by a child." The *Merrimack* limped back into the Elizabeth River that night never to fight again.

The North went wild with joy, and the London *Times* told its readers it would be "madness" for most British men-of-war to try to stand up to the *Monitor.* One battle had changed the entire course of naval history; the day of the wooden warship was over.

ROBERT E. LEE OF THE CONFEDERACY

Lee is given command of the Southern forces and keeps McClellan from bringing the war to an early end.

The war was looking up for President Lincoln. The *Monitor* had given him a victory on the water. In the West, at Donelson and Shiloh, Grant had pushed the war from upper Tennessee to upper Mississippi. April of 1862 brought more good news. A naval expedition under Admiral David G. Farragut captured New Orleans late that month.

Now action in the East might bring the war to an early end. But could McClellan be prodded into moving? Actually, by April McClellan had begun a campaign that might indeed have ended the war before summer—if it had not been for Robert E. Lee.

Up to this point, Lee had not been too active in the field. He had carefully planned the defenses at Manassas Junction and had wanted to be there when the first great battle of the war was fought. But he had remained in Richmond as military adviser to

Jefferson Davis, the president of the Confederacy. Next he had been sent into western Virginia, but there was little anyone could do to keep West Virginia in the Confederacy.

Criticized as a much overrated general, Lee came back to Richmond for a time. Then Union forces took Port Royal, South Carolina, and threatened the Confederate coast line as far south as the Florida keys. Once again Lee was sent to save a hopeless situation. He worked twice as hard as any private in the ranks and stopped the Yankees from ruining ports such as Charleston and Savannah. It was a remarkable achievement.

In the spring of 1862, reports reached Lee of a Federal movement into Virginia. Called back to Richmond, Lee could not hide his alarm. The Army of the Potomac, the Union force under McClellan, had been moved by transports to a strip of land between the York and James Rivers known as the Peninsula. Once this force gained a foothold at Yorktown, the way would be open to Richmond.

Lee worked furiously to avoid disaster. He sent reinforcements to Stonewall Jackson in the Shenandoah Valley, a natural highway to Washington. Soon Jackson had the Federal government fearing for its own safety. The move tied down thousands of Union soldiers who otherwise might have reinforced McClellan, but it did not solve Lee's basic problem.

RICHMOND IN DANGER

Lee urged General Joseph E. Johnston, commander of the Confederates on the Peninsula, to stand firm. His men must hold back McClellan and keep the Union invaders from overrunning Richmond. But Johnston kept giving ground while the Army of the Potomac swept up the Peninsula. By late May, the Union's observation balloons, tied to trees, looked down on the streets of the Confederate capital. Northern newspapers boasted that by June 15 the Federals would occupy the city.

Richmond was in a panic. Its inhabitants stopped complaining about high prices—tea at ten dollars a pound and boots at thirty dollars a pair—they had worse things to worry about. Rumors flew that the Confederate government was preparing to leave the city. Lee told a cabinet meeting that Richmond must not be surrendered.

As May ended, McClellan's forces faced Richmond along the east bank of the Chickahominy River, about six miles from the city. Two Federal corps across the river were dug in along a line from a farm known as Seven Pines to a railroad stop called Fair Oaks station. Heavy rains had flooded the river, endangering the bridges on which McClellan's divided army depended. One wing of his army, anchored at Seven Pines, was dangerously exposed to a Southern surprise attack.

On the last day of May, Johnston struck. The Rebels wore white bands around their hats so that they could tell friend from foe more easily. The Battle of Seven Pines ended in a bloody stalemate. Colonel E. E. Cross, commanding the 5th New Hampshire, wrote:

"In this battle the generalship on the part of the Federals was wretched. Instead of shelling the woods with thirty pieces of artillery as we could readily have done, we allowed the Rebels to choose their own ground, ambush themselves and wait for our attack. . . . As it was we entered a regular trap set for us the night before. I believe an Apache warrior would have arranged our men better. Everything was on the side of the enemy—position, numbers and knowledge of the ground. It is a wonder that we were not defeated."

With heroic courage, McClellan's boys fought their way back across the wobbling bridges of the Chickahominy. General Johnston was severely wounded and was carried off the field by stretcher-bearers. That night, Jefferson Davis chose a new commanding general—Robert E. Lee.

LEE SAVES RICHMOND

Lee forces McClellan to retreat, but fails to destroy his army.

All Richmond became a vast hospital area as ambulances and carts bounced along the streets, bringing the wounded from the Battle of Seven Pines. Yet the Southerners were quietly confident. The Yankee invaders had been beaten back, and Richmond could still be saved.

Lee went quietly to work, doing the best he could. He did not underestimate the task before him. With a force of 80,000 men he must sweep aside McClellan's army of at least 100,000. He already had a plan. He suspected that the right wing of McClellan's army, north of the Chickahominy, remained dangerously exposed. When a Confederate cavalry force under General Jeb Stuart made a bold "ride around McClellan" and found this was so, Lee moved swiftly. Stonewall Jackson was called back from the Shenandoah Valley, and in late June, Lee launched his assault to save Richmond.

The campaign that followed, from June 25 to July 1, 1862, became known as the Battle of the Seven Days. For Lee it began badly, as entrenched Yankee guns beat back the Rebs along Beaver Creek. But at night Lee pulled his forces together. Next morning, on a high bend of the Chickahominy near Gaines' Mill, he went after the Yankees again.

Lee's leadership was steady and intelligent. As the day ran on, McClellan's lines were hammered

General Robert E. Lee at the start of the war.

on right, left, and center, and the Union army was reduced to "a motley mob." Lanky Sam Wilkeson, one of the great reporters of the war, told how the battle ended:

"The scene was one not to be forgotten. Scores of riderless, terrified horses dashing in every direction; thick flying bullets singing by, admonishing [warning] of danger; every minute a man struck down; wagons and ambulances and cannon blocking the way; wounded men limping and groaning and bleeding amid the throng . . . the sublime cannonading, the clouds of battlesmoke and the sun just disappearing, large and blood-red—I cannot picture it, but I see it and always shall."

McCLELLAN ESCAPES

But Lee was still human—he could make mistakes. He was so convinced he had McClellan trapped that he wasted a day. McClellan saw his chance and began one of the boldest maneuvers of the war. Burning his supply base, he fled across the Peninsula for the James River, where his army would be protected by Federal gunboats.

Lee started in pursuit of the retreating Federals, and names like Savage Station, White Oak Swamp, and Malvern Hill now appeared in the battle reports.

Turning at Malvern Hill to gain second wind, McClellan defeated Lee so badly that Confederate General Dan Hill moaned: "It was not war—it was murder!" Next day McClellan reached the protection of the Federal gunboats at Harrison's Landing. He had saved his army.

The cost of the Seven Days was high for both armies. The Union forces counted 1,734 killed, 8,062 wounded, and 6,053 missing (as prisoners or deserters). The Confederate losses were 3,478 killed, 16,262 wounded, and 875 missing. Yet Richmond had been saved and Lee was the hero of the hour—even a new variety of tomato was named in his honor.

THE SQUEEZE IN THE WEST

The North's gunboats help defeat the Southern forces along the Mississippi.

There had been little news from the West that spring and summer to cheer the Confederates. In early April, trying to gain control of the upper Mississippi, the Federals sent the gunboat *Carondelet* to attack fortified Island No. 10, below Columbus, Kentucky.

The *Carondelet* was no beauty—"she looks like a farmer's wagon," her skipper admitted. With hawsers and chain cable wrapped around her pilothouse, and a barge loaded with hay lashed to her side, she looked even more ridiculous. But she came steaming down the Mississippi that April night in 1862, while lightning flashed in the sky. Bugles called Rebel gunners to their posts to defend Island No. 10.

Her guns blazing, the old ship was pounding the Rebel fort to pieces with her deadly fire. Thunder

Confederate wounded were taken to Richmond, where they were cared for at improvised medical stations.

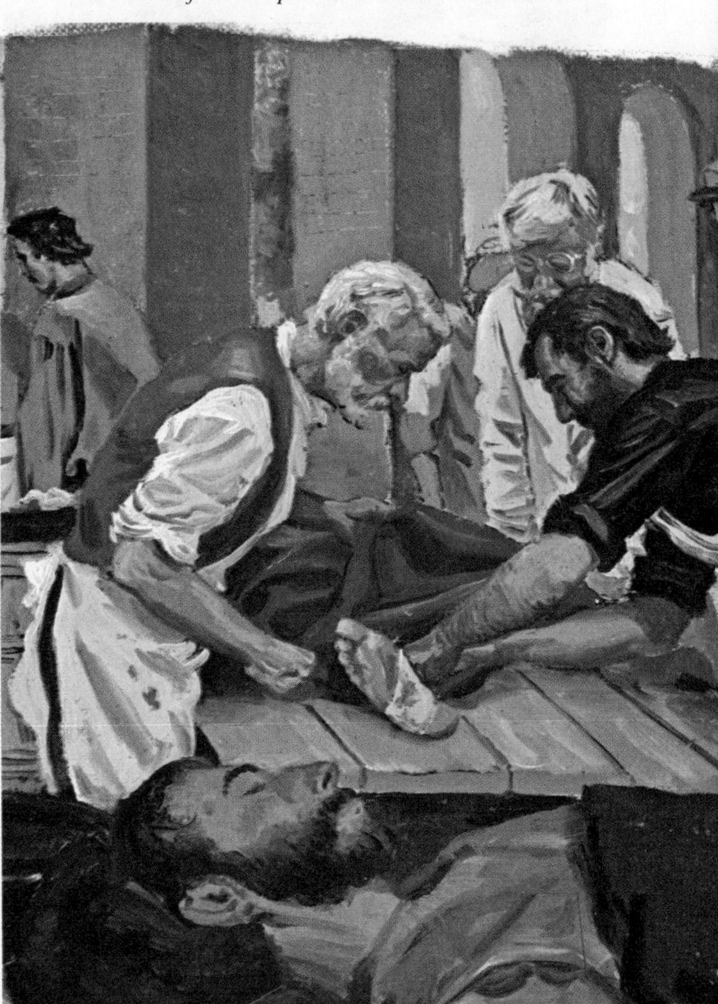

The South's fortified Island No. 10 in the Mississippi River was battered by the Federal ironclad Carondelet.

rolled in waves, and between the thunder there was the boom of the guns on the island and the ship. When three days later a Union force under General John Pope arrived, the *Carondelet* had done so well that the fort surrendered, and the Federals captured 7,000 prisoners.

Pope was the hero of that victory, but the old *Carondelet,* a bit more battered, went on to further glory. Her name would be in the list of Federal gunboats that forced the surrender of Memphis in June.

LEE VERSUS POPE

General Pope is given command of the Union forces.

Lincoln was still trying to find a general who could win in the East. McDowell and McClellan had failed, and now he turned to John Pope.

Pope reached Washington in July, full of bluff and bluster. He was an unusual man. He said to his astonished soldiers: "Let us look before and not behind. Success and glory are in the advance. Disaster and shame lurk in the rear." On July 23, 1862, he ordered his officers to look upon all civilians who refused to take an oath of allegiance to the national government as "spies." He also told them to live off the country (that is, Virginia) without wasting "force and energy . . . protecting private property of those most hostile to the Government."

As a Virginian, Lee was infuriated. He wrote an angry letter to Washington, stating that Pope's order meant making war on civilians. If it were allowed to stand, then "we shall be reluctantly forced to the last resort of accepting the war on the terms chosen by our enemies, until the voice of an outraged humanity shall compel a respect for the recognized usages of war."

More than anything else, Lee now wanted to defeat Pope. And Lee did defeat him, with greater pleasure than he defeated any other Union general during the war. To do so, Lee made a bold decision. He reasoned that, with McClellan's retreat to Harrison's Landing, the fight had gone out of the North's campaign against Richmond. This was the time to carry the war to the North. Lee moved to Manassas Junction, very near the ground where the first great battle of the war had been fought. And here he collided with the Union forces under the command of John Pope.

Pope lost badly. When it was over, the bewildered Pope never quite knew what had struck him. The Battle of Second Manassas (Bull Run), fought from August 28 to August 30, 1862, was called "Lee's masterpiece," which is another way of saying it was Pope's finish.

THE SECRET IN THE DESK

Lincoln considers freeing the slaves, but waits for a Northern victory.

During the spring of 1862, Major Thomas T. Eckert, superintendent of the military telegraph in the War Department, often saw Lincoln trudge across the lawn from the White House. In the War Department building, the President wrote on "some foolscap"—sometimes a phrase, sometimes a sentence, sometimes a paragraph. And many days he did nothing more than gaze in thought. But the pile of notes that Lincoln locked away in his desk steadily grew. It was plain that he was wrestling with an idea.

Then one day in July, riding in a carriage with his Secretaries of State and Navy, Lincoln confessed what was on his mind. If the Rebels did not stop the war, he would issue a proclamation freeing all slaves in those parts of the South still in rebellion against the Union.

Later he brought up the question at a Cabinet meeting. The Secretary of State suggested "that Lincoln postpone its issue, until he could give it to the country supported by a military success, instead of issuing it, as would be the case now, upon the greatest disasters of the war!"

Lincoln nodded. He knew a good argument when he heard one. So, willing to wait, he once more locked the proclamation in a desk drawer.

Lee, of course, knew nothing of this. Flushed with his victory at Second Manassas, and believing that the people of Maryland would rally around the banner of the Confederacy, he struck northward.

"THE BLOODIEST DAY OF THE WAR"

Lee moves into Maryland but is stopped at the fearful Battle of Antietam.

McClellan, who had been put back in command in the East, followed Lee slowly. But it was not the Federals that troubled Lee; it was his own error in judgment. The uprising he had expected in Maryland never came. In fact, the people did not seem to care at all whether the Confederacy lived or died.

Lee forgot this disappointment and planned another bold, hard blow against the Union. He divided his army, sending one wing under Stonewall Jackson to capture the Federal garrison at Harpers Ferry. Then Lee headed north with the other wing, intending to strike at Harrisburg, the capital of Pennsylvania. By destroying the railroad bridge across the Susquehanna River, he hoped to cut communications between the West and the Federal government in Washington.

Despite the risk, Lee's plan might have worked but for a strange accident. John M. Bloss of the 27th Indiana, one of the Federal regiments pursuing the Confederates, was resting in the grass when he noticed two cigars wrapped in a paper. One close look at that paper started Bloss on the run to head-

President Lincoln brooded over the slavery question.

At Marye's Heights, from behind a stone wall, Confederate guns raked Union forces that charged up the hill.

quarters, for it was a copy of Lee's secret order dividing his army. McClellan was joyful.

"If I don't crush Lee now," he declared, "you may call me whatever you please!"

LEE IS TAKEN BY SURPRISE

On September 13, 1862, McClellan caught Lee by surprise. All at once the Federals were where no one expected them to be. They marched over Maryland's Catoctin Mountains and threatened to cut off Lee from the rest of his army at Harpers Ferry. Lee turned and made a stand at South Mountain. The hard-fought battle was undecided when night fell.

Lee was in a terrible situation. Without reinforcements, he could not keep McClellan from taking this mountain pass. He was forced to do what he hated—retreat. In the chilly, misty morning, he led his weary men over the stone bridge of Antietam Creek and began forming for battle along a range of hills between the stream and the little town of Sharpsburg, Maryland.

It was the moment for McClellan to attack. He had Lee exactly where he wanted him. But "Little Mac" hesitated, wasting a day, a day during which Stonewall Jackson rushed to reinforce Lee on the heights overlooking the Antietam. Even then, if he had used all his forces, McClellan might have swept the Rebels from the field. But again he missed his chance.

The Battle of Antietam on September 17, 1862, was afterward called "the bloodiest day of the war." From beginning to end, it was a bruising, dreadful battle. It left its mark on the sunken road later known as "Bloody Lane," on the little white Dunkard Church where the conflict swirled like a bloody whirlpool, and on the cornfield where Yankees and Rebels fell like stalks cut down by a scythe. The losses were staggering to both sides—8,000 for the Confederacy, 12,000 for the Union. When at last Lee led his battered forces back across the Potomac into Virginia, he muttered: "Thank God!"

A WAR BOTH OLD AND NEW

Lincoln's policy changes a "brothers' quarrel" into a war to end slavery.

The Union army had been hammered hard. But Lee was now retreating, and Lincoln had the victory he needed to disclose the secret in his desk.

Five days after Antietam the President issued his first, or preliminary, proclamation of emancipation. It warned that if the sections then in rebellion did not return to the Union by January 1, 1863, he would issue a second proclamation, declaring slaves in these sections "forever free."

Angry Southerners said that Lincoln and his government were pirates, and should be treated as such. But the rest of the world was not impressed with such arguments.

Up to this point, the war could have been called "the war between the states." In a single stroke, the first Emancipation Proclamation changed this brothers' quarrel into "a war to end slavery." The people of the world now believed that a Union victory would benefit humanity. This was particularly true in England and France, where the people would no longer support a government sympathetic to the South.

This new spirit was expressed by Julia Ward Howe in *The Battle Hymn of the Republic:*

In the beauty of the lilies Christ was born across the sea,
With a glory in his bosom that transfigures you and me,
As he died to make men holy, let us die to make men free,
While God is marching on!

Yet, although the character of the war was changing, one of Lincoln's problems remained the same. He still needed a general who could lead the Army of the Potomac to victory. McClellan gave so many excuses for not seeking another battle that Lincoln lost patience.

"I have just read your despatch about sore-tongued and fatigued horses," Lincoln telegraphed McClellan in late October. "Will you pardon me for asking what the horses of your army have done since the Battle of Antietam that fatigues anything?"

BURNSIDE TAKES COMMAND

In early November, Lincoln decided that he was finished with "Little Mac." The army's new commander was bewhiskered General Ambrose E. Burnside, who had been a successful gun manufacturer and railroad executive. He feared that he was not the man for the job, and events proved him right.

December brought snow and chill winds to Virginia. In the hills and valleys around Fredericksburg, where George Washington had played as a boy, Lee had gathered his army in winter quarters. Burnside sent his artillery trains rumbling toward battle on the night of December 10. Bugles next morning awakened Union troops to the urgent work of laying pontoon bridges across the Rappahannock River to get at Lee. It was a murderous business, but by nightfall the Federals had crossed the river and held the streets of the burning town.

MARYE'S HEIGHTS

Lee fell back into the hills beyond Fredericksburg, and Burnside went after him. As the battle raged, with Union boys cut to pieces by Confederate guns, a British reporter was certain he was witnessing "the decline and fall of the American Republic."

The terrible contest reached its climax on December 13 at Marye's Heights. From atop this hill Confederate guns, protected by a stone wall, pointed down the slope up which the Federals must charge.

Six times Burnside ordered his men up that hill. Six times, in the words of Confederate General James Longstreet, "they were swept from the field like chaff before the wind."

"Give me plenty of ammunition, [and] I will kill them all before they reach my line," Longstreet told Lee. Fredericksburg cost the Union 1,284 men killed, 9,600 wounded and 1,769 missing, against Confederate losses of 595 dead, 4,061 wounded, 653 missing. Watching the slaughter, Lee said: "It is well that war is so terrible—we should grow too fond of it." And Union Captain D. P. Conynham wrote:

"And this was war—'glorious war'—with all its pomp and parade—all its glittering attractions. If we could see it in its true colors, it is the most horrible curse that God could inflict upon mankind."

Burnside himself was distressed by the Union losses, but next morning was ready to lead the troops himself in a fresh attack. His officers persuaded him not to try again, and that night the army began its retreat across the river.

A WAR ON MANY FRONTS

Lincoln signs the Emancipation Proclamation and puts "Fighting Joe" Hooker in command of the Northern army.

On New Year's Day, 1863, citizens of Washington tramped to the White House for a public reception. From eleven o'clock until midafternoon, the President shook hands with his guests. At last Lincoln went to his office, his hand so tired that he could hardly hold a pen. Less than a half-dozen persons were present as he signed his name to the Emancipation Proclamation.

The proclamation declared free all slaves in sections then in rebellion against the Union. It also made such persons eligible for service in the armed forces. Nowhere was news of this act received with greater rejoicing than on the islands off the Carolina coast. These had been held by Union forces since November, 1861. At Beaufort garrison, on one island, duty was performed by the first Negro Federal regiment—the 1st South Carolina Volunteers.

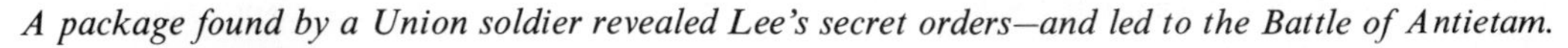

A package found by a Union soldier revealed Lee's secret orders—and led to the Battle of Antietam.

Yet for many Negroes then held as slaves, the proclamation was only a promise of freedom on some distant day when the North won the war. Meanwhile the war was being fought, savagely and bitterly, on many fronts.

BATTLE AT MURFREESBORO

Indeed, on that same New Year's Day two armies were locked in a tremendous battle along Stones River, near Murfreesboro, Tennessee. The fighting decided very little, but 1,667 Union men and 1,294 Confederates were killed.

In the following weeks, the war news might come from almost anywhere:

—From Galveston, Texas, where a Federal naval force was driven off and the port opened again to Rebel blockade runners.

—From the high seas, where Rebel raiders like the *Florida* and the *Alabama* were sinking Yankee merchant ships.

—From Charleston, South Carolina, where a Federal naval force failed to retake Fort Sumter.

—From Kentucky, where John Morgan and his Rebel riders were again raiding as they pleased.

—Or from the Mississippi, where, according to the gossips in Washington, Grant was hopelessly stuck in the mud below the bluffs of Vicksburg.

As the spring of 1863 spread across the land, the pace of the war quickened. Once more Lincoln had switched commanders of the Army of the Potomac, replacing Burnside with General Joseph E. Hooker, who was known to his soldiers as "Fighting Joe."

Hooker was full of confidence. In round figures, his army numbered 120,000 men. Lee had no more than 60,000. Hooker's plan was to cross the Rappahannock River and concentrate one wing of his army on Lee's right at Fredericksburg, and another wing on Lee's left at Chancellorsville, fifteen miles to the west. By pulling these two wings together, Hooker reasoned, he would either crush Lee's army or drive it back into Richmond.

As April passed, Hooker was across the Rappahannock. By May 1, the right wing of his army moved easily on to Chancellorsville. It looked as though Lee, for once, had been outfoxed.

LEE WINS, BUT ALSO LOSES

Lee and Stonewall Jackson stop Hooker, but Jackson is killed.

On the night of May 1, Lee met with his most trusted general, Stonewall Jackson, a mile and a half from Hooker's headquarters at Chancellorsville. For a time, the two battle-weary men slept—Jackson on a pile of straw, Lee at the foot of a tree.

Sometime after midnight, huddled over a little fire of twigs, the generals warmed their hands and talked about the approaching battle. Perched on cracker boxes, Lee and Jackson plotted the destruction of Hooker and his army.

The country around Chancellorsville, known as "the Wilderness," was a jungle fit only for owls, water moccasins, and whippoorwills. Hooker, not knowing the land, would be at a disadvantage. Moreover, Lee's cavalry leader, Jeb Stuart, reported that Hooker's right flank, buried deep in this wilderness, was unsupported.

Jackson spoke of little-known roads through the region. If Lee would divide his army, Jackson believed he could march around and smash that unsupported flank. Of course, Lee would be left with only 20,000 men to stand off Hooker's main assault. The risk was tremendous, but Lee said calmly: "Go on."

Next morning Lee watched Jackson, wearing his battered cadet cap, ride off with his troops into the forest. Lee spread his own men into a thin line of battle, waited, and prayed for victory.

The morning passed, and then the afternoon began to fade. Finally a courier arrived, bringing a note that Jackson had scrawled "near 3 p.m." He was almost on the Federal flank, Jackson wrote, and would attack "as soon as practicable." So Lee returned to waiting, praying, and watching the sun set in the west.

All at once a rumble rolled across that wolf's den surrounding Chancellorsville. Crash upon crash came the sound of Jackson's guns.

"Forward!" shouted Lee, hurling his 20,000 men against the 50,000 Hooker had massed against him.

Lee fought superbly, and as the moon came up, the bright flashes from Jackson's guns glowed in the sky. At last a courier brought word of Jackson's complete success—he had caught the Union boys with their arms stacked, cooking supper. The blare of Rebel bugles bursting from the forest had set the Yankees running in panic.

There would be a great deal of hard fighting before Lee could add Chancellorsville to his victories. For Lee, these were grim days. Word came that Jackson had been mistaken in the dark for a Yankee and had been shot three times in the arm by his own men. Then came even worse reports: Jackson's arm had been amputated—pneumonia had set in—Jackson had become delirious—his death was expected to come at any time.

Lee refused to believe the doctors. "God will not take him from us," Lee said, "now that we need him so much." But death came to Stonewall Jackson, and the entire South grieved with Lee. Chancellorsville had been a costly victory.

Lincoln was shocked when he heard the news from

Chancellorsville—Union casualties were 16,854, against the Confederates' 13,156. Once more his fine Army of the Potomac had been wasted! Those around Lincoln thought he looked "ghostlike." They watched him, hands clasped, pacing the floor. They heard him moan:

"My God! My God! What will the country say! What will the country say!"

GRANT FIGHTS A NEW KIND OF WAR

Grant advances, living off the land.

That spring, many Northerners complained that Grant was stuck in the mud of the Mississippi with no hope of capturing Vicksburg. They understood neither the man nor the situation. True, since taking his army down-river from Memphis, Grant seemed stuck, but the fault was not his.

Vicksburg, Mississippi, was set on high bluffs overlooking a horseshoe bend of the river. With good reason Jefferson Davis called it "the Gibraltar of the Mississippi." This city was almost impossible to take by frontal assault from the river.

To add to Grant's troubles, high water in the Mississippi that spring covered wagon roads to a depth of seventeen feet. Finding dry land on which to pitch the tents of his army was in itself a major problem.

Grant liked to tip back on a campstool, puff on a cigar, and lose himself in thought. The way to take Vicksburg, he decided, was to take his army down-river, and then to get them across. Somehow he had to get at Vicksburg by its "back door." His scheme was to march the army downriver, then load them on transports, which had sailed down under those blazing Confederate batteries, and this way to cross the river.

Before dawn on an April day, Confederate gunners in the city's upper battery made out a mass of "black things"—Grant's gunboats and transports—coming down-river. Instantly their guns roared, giving the alarm. The fire was taken up by one battery after another until, along Vicksburg's four-mile river front, Rebel cannon hurled down tongues of orange flame at the Union flotilla as it went by.

A SHIP IS LOST

Tar barrels, set afire along the shore, lighted the river as though it were midday. Federal gunboats soon set the railway station blazing like a mighty torch in the night. One of Grant's transports was shattered and left to burn. A coal barge sank. But the flotilla got through without losing a man. A week later more ships ran the gantlet. Meanwhile, Grant's army marched down the Mississippi's west bank to a point 30 miles below Vicksburg. At dawn on April 30 it was ferried across the river.

Grant had learned that the Rebel army under General John C. Pemberton, inside Vicksburg, was

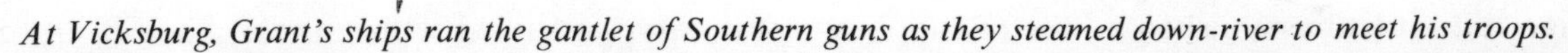

At Vicksburg, Grant's ships ran the gantlet of Southern guns as they steamed down-river to meet his troops.

At Gettysburg the Confederates breached Union defenses at several points before being stopped on Cemetery Ridge.

waiting to be reinforced by another army then being assembled by Joseph E. Johnston. To keep these armies apart, Grant knew he must act swiftly. He also knew that no army was supposed to launch a campaign until it had established a base of supplies, but he saw no reason why he couldn't write his own rules of war. So he decided to live off the land while he cut his way between the armies of Pemberton and Johnston.

The plan worked magnificently. Before the Confederates guessed what was happening, Grant captured Jackson, the capital of Mississippi, and wedged his army between Pemberton and Johnston.

Quickly, Grant turned back toward Vicksburg and met Pemberton's forces in a vicious struggle on the green slopes of Champion's Hills. Then he pursued the Confederates across the Big Black River and up to the back door of Vicksburg. Here deep ravines with Rebel cannon pointing down from every spur faced Grant. Twice in late May he tried to storm these fortifications and was driven back.

There was only one thing Grant could do—besiege Vicksburg and starve out its defenders. Empty bellies would give him the victory he could not win with bullets. For six weeks, shells from Grant's cannon and gunboats rained down on Vicksburg. Houses, churches, schools, stores, hospitals, and factories were smashed into rubble. Civilians dug caves in the hillsides, rushing for them whenever a bombardment began, and the Yankees called Vicksburg "the prairie dog village."

In all American history, there has been no siege like that of Vicksburg. The days dragged on—long, dreary, and filled with hunger. Soon every dog disappeared from the streets; they had all been killed. A baby, William Siege Green, was born twelve feet underground during the siege and lived to be an old man. Toward the end, when food ran out, some claimed to have eaten mule meat and even to have breakfasted on fried rat.

A hot and muggy June gave way to a hotter, muggier July. The people within Vicksburg clung to the hope that Johnston was bringing his army to their relief. But Johnston wasn't coming—Vicksburg and Pemberton's army were doomed.

Meanwhile, up North, another calamity struck the Confederacy.

BATTLE OF GETTYSBURG

Lee invades the North, but is repulsed in a great battle.

Called to a special cabinet meeting in Richmond, Lee was asked a blunt question: Could he send part of his army to rescue Pemberton in Mississippi? Lee gave a blunt answer: No. After two years of war, Virginia could no longer supply his army. His troops needed everything—shoes, food, horses, fodder. He must again carry the war into the North. The rich farms of Pennsylvania offered much that his army needed. Besides, an invasion of the North might loosen Grant's grip on Vicksburg.

Fear raced through the North as Lee's Army of Northern Virginia crossed the Potomac. Washington, Baltimore, Philadelphia—each was certain it was the target at which Lee aimed. In view of the emergency, the governor of New Jersey wrote Lincoln, the experienced McClellan should be restored to command of the Army of the Potomac. After Chancellorsville, the President also was convinced he must replace Hooker, but McClellan was hardly his choice. He chose instead an able Pennsylvania-born general, George G. Meade.

Meanwhile, the Confederates marched through the farm land of Pennsylvania in high spirits. "It's like a hole of blubber to a Greenlander," General Richard S. Ewell wrote home. Lee's chief concern was Jeb Stuart, who had ridden into Maryland and lost contact with headquarters. At the moment, Stuart was having a wonderful time raiding a Federal supply train, but the real job of the cavalry was to act as "the eyes" of the army. Without information from Stuart, Lee was advancing like a blind man.

That was why, at Cashtown, Lee permitted General Henry Heth to take a division to nearby Gettysburg in the hope of getting shoes for his barefooted soldiers. About a mile and a half from the sleepy little village, Heth marched head-on into the Yankees.

A bitter battle soon developed, and Lee, hearing the gunfire, hurried forward from Cashtown. The fight was going badly for the Rebels. But Lee ordered the corps under Ewell, then marching from Fayetteville to Cashtown, to wheel around and come to Gettysburg on the double. The reinforcements swept aside the Yankees, who fled through Gettysburg in panic.

General Ewell was just getting used to a new wooden leg, and tired easily. When he reached the town, where his joyous troops surrounded him and drank toasts to his health with stolen wine, the old general was glad to call the day's work finished. So the Federals escaped to Cemetery Ridge on the other side of town, and fell exhausted among the tombstones.

LEE STANDS AND FIGHTS

Next morning, General James Longstreet saw the slopes which the Union now held. A chill touched his heart, and he pleaded with Lee to get out of Gettysburg. The situation here, Longstreet argued, was Fredericksburg in reverse, with the Yankees holding the upper hand. But Lee, excited by the previous day's success, wanted to stay and fight.

The day wore on, hot, sultry, overcast. Longstreet, facing the Yankees on Cemetery Ridge, saw an old barn, a wheat field, a peach orchard. Beyond were two high hills, called Big and Little Round Top. These looked down on the entire field. How strongly were they held? This was the question in the minds of the Confederate leaders as their troops swept past the barn and locked in a savage fight with the bluecoats. Guns flashed. Bayonet struck bayonet. With a roar, the Rebels pushed forward through the field of wheat.

Yet the two hills were still the keys to the battle. Alabama troops rushed toward Little Round Top and, almost at the same instant, the Federals realized this hill was unprotected. Union men of the 20th Maine set off toward the hill on a run. They fell behind the rocks on the crest of Little Round Top and watched the Rebs scampering up the slopes.

It was a bitter fight from start to finish. No one could deny the Rebels' courage. Up the slopes the Alabama troops came, ducking from tree to tree and boulder to boulder—firing, running, climbing over their own dead, loading, and coming on and on and on until within sight of the ledge at the top of the hill.

A cry ran along the Yankee lines: "Fix bayonets!"

Steel bayonets made a ringing sound as they struck against rifle barrels.

Again a cry: "Charge bayonets, charge!"

With a wild yell, the 20th Maine charged down the slope at the Rebels. The shock of the assault staggered the Alabamians, but they fired and met bayonet thrust with bayonet thrust. The Yankees, reeling back, struck again—and again—and again. Sick at heart, the Rebels knew suddenly that they could not budge these bluecoats from Little Round Top. A shout to retreat sounded. Wrote one Alabamian: "We ran like a herd of wild cattle."

Elsewhere that afternoon, especially in the peach orchard, the Confederates punished the Yankees terribly. Later Longstreet called it "the best three hours of fighting by any troops on any battlefield!" But Big Round Top and Little Round Top were still in the hands of the Federals.

When the stars came out, the lanterns of the ambulances twinkled on the silent fields covered with the dead of both armies. How much had been gained? General Meade was so stunned by the fighting of that second day that he called a council of war and asked his officers if he should withdraw the Federal army. *Stand firm,* his generals advised earnestly. *Fight it out where we are.*

Lee opened July 3 with the most terrific bombardment ever seen on the American continent. A Union colonel described it:

"The thunder and lightning of these two hundred and fifty guns and their shells, whose smoke darkens

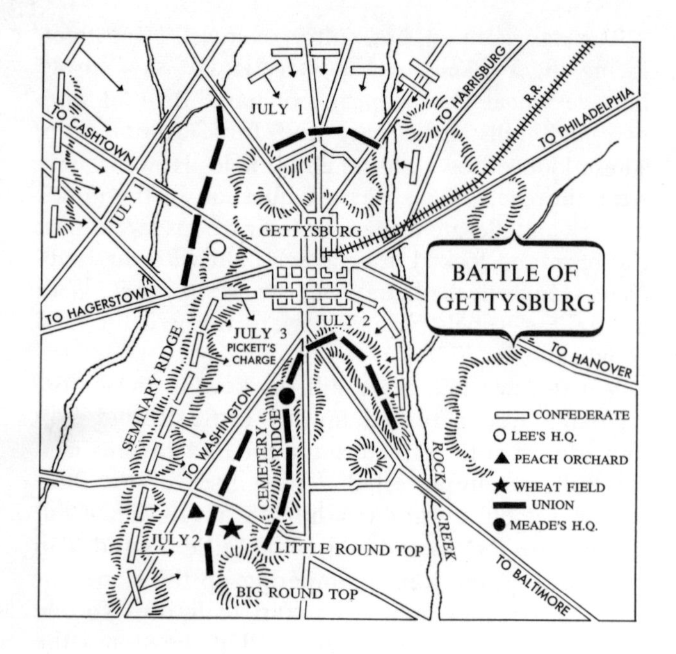

the sky, are incessant. . . . In the air above our heads, on the ground at our feet . . . the projectiles shriek long and sharp. They hiss, they scream, they growl, they sputter. . . . We see the poor fellows hobbling back from the crest, or unable to do so, pale and weak, lying on the ground with the mangled stump of an arm or leg, dripping their life-blood away. . . ."

PICKETT'S CHARGE

Suddenly the cannon fell silent. Now Lee made his supreme effort, and as the smoke cleared the Yankees on Cemetery Ridge saw an incredible sight. Across 1,400 yards of open ground the gray-uniformed soldiers of Pickett's division were marching to storm the Union entrenchments. Row on row the Rebs advanced—steady, heads high, eyes straight. The Yankee guns crackled and a line of flame spread along the crest. The first rows of Rebels seemed to melt away.

But others came up in their place. The advance continued. Again the Yankee guns fired, and again the gray lines melted.

With Pickett's boys that scorching afternoon was young Private John Dooley. He climbed a fence, unable to see the Yankees through the battle smoke clouding the field. With bayonet fixed and heart thumping, he plunged on—over another fence, a ditch, a wall, a little brook, across a meadow and a cornfield.

The Yankees had the range on the Rebels now. A sheet of flame exploded along the length of Cemetery Ridge, and suddenly there were gaps in the Rebel line. But John Dooley, marching shoulder to shoulder with those of his regiment who were still alive, came on toward the wall that shielded the enemy.

Now he could see that wall, and he brought his rifle to his shoulder. He aimed, fired, loaded, fired again. With a buzz, like a swarm of angry hornets, bullets whizzed around him. Thirty yards short of the wall, John Dooley pitched forward. His leg throbbed with pain where a bullet had struck him. Yet he was lucky. He lived to tell the tale of the heroic and hopeless charge of Pickett's soldiers at the Battle of Gettysburg.

THE TIDE TURNS

Just for a moment, ahead of John Dooley, the Rebels reached the wall atop Cemetery Ridge. A few climbed over, letting out a shout of victory. Then the Yankees charged. With a thunderous crash, an artillery battery fired upon the Rebels. They turned and ran, leaping over the wounded and the dead. Tears streaked their faces. Seeing them approach, General Lee said, "Don't be discouraged. . . . It was my fault this time. . . . All good men must hold together now!"

That night Lee began his retreat toward Virginia. His losses for the three days were 3,903 dead, 18,735 wounded, and 5,425 missing. Union casualties were 3,155 dead, 14,529 wounded, and 5,365 missing. The following day, July 4, would bring an even more crushing blow when Pemberton and his entire army surrendered to Grant at Vicksburg.

And yet the war went on. Why? For what purpose? Perhaps the only answer that could be given was spoken by Lincoln when in November he came to Gettysburg for the dedication of a National Cemetery there. The President said:

". . . from these honored dead we take increased devotion to that cause for which they gave the last full measure of devotion—that we here highly resolve that these dead shall not have died in vain—that this nation, under God, shall have a new birth of freedom—and that government of the people, by the people, for the people, shall not perish from the earth."

GRANT COMES ON

Grant takes command of the Union army and places Sherman in charge of the forces in the West.

A great many more honored dead would fall on the battlefields of this war. In September, along the banks of the Chickamauga before Chattanooga, Tennessee, a Confederate army under General Braxton Bragg had struck a harsh blow against the North's Army of the Cumberland under General William S. Rosecrans. The Union army was slaughtered unmercifully, and one eyewitness said: "Chickamauga is as fatal a name in our history as Bull Run." Again

Lincoln needed "a man of success," someone who could rescue the North. This time a call went out to Ulysses S. Grant to hurry to Chattanooga.

Grant arrived, limping from the injury he had received when a frightened horse had fallen on his leg. He found the Federal army cut off from its base of supplies and facing starvation. Veterans in Rosecrans' army, seeing Grant shuffling around on his injured leg, wondered why anyone ever made a fuss over this odd and unmilitary-looking fellow.

But Grant moved quickly to lay a pontoon bridge under heavy artillery fire, thus opening his famous "cracker line" to a base of supplies. Once more food flowed into the Federal camps around Chattanooga. Soldiers with full bellies stopped criticizing Grant. That stump of a general was all right, they said. They'd fight for him—and fight for him they did in November at Missionary Ridge. This engagement is sometimes called the "Battle Above the Clouds" because thunderheads came so low on a mountain above Chattanooga that they hid Yankee from Rebel. Grant's troops charged through deep ravines and up hillsides. They overran the Rebel rifle pits, and left the Confederates—to use Bragg's own words—in "a panic which I never before witnessed."

After Missionary Ridge, Lincoln knew that he had found the general for whom he had been searching so long. Congress revived the rank of lieutenant general—previously given only to George Washington and Winfield Scott. In March, 1864, Grant was called to Washington to receive this rank and to assume command of all the Union armies in the field.

It was a great honor. He now commanded 533,000 soldiers, a fighting force never before equaled in American history. But the responsibility was enormous—he was expected to win the war. Grant left Washington for the West to see his old friend General Sherman. Together they had fought at Shiloh, Vicksburg, and Missionary Ridge, and together they would end the war. Grant told Sherman that they would divide the country between them. While Sherman took command of the western armies and smashed his way to Atlanta, Grant would "handle" Lee.

In early May, Grant started after Lee. The Army of the Potomac, numbering 125,000 men, was now the most powerful fighting organization on the continent. But Lee's 60,000 men were almost all battle-tested veterans who would follow their commander anywhere. Affectionately they called Lee "Uncle Robert." They had watched his beard whiten and the lines deepen in his face as the war went on. But he had never lost faith in their cause.

And Lee's veterans knew they had the advantage when Grant led his Federals back into the Wilderness surrounding Chancellorsville. In this tangle of trees and underbrush, on May 5 and 6, a battle took place unlike any Grant had known. Officers carried compasses so that they could know where they were going. "It was not war," an eyewitness said. "Two wild animals were hunting each other."

When the charges and countercharges were ended and a roaring fire in the thickets threatened to encircle the troops, both armies had been jarred and hurt. Grant's casualties numbered 2,246 killed, 12,037 wounded, 3,383 missing. While Lee's losses were never known, they could not have been less than 8,000—a terrific loss, considering his few reserves.

If Grant tossed that night, realizing that in opposing Lee he had grabbed a bear by the tail, so was Lee to learn Grant was no quitter. At daylight Grant had his troops moving south. He was seeking a new battleground on the other edge of the Wilderness. It was at Spotsylvania Court House, eleven miles southwest of Fredericksburg. Grant's courage raised the spirits of his men. They cheered and shouted:

"Boys, we're on our way to Richmond!"

Not for a moment did Lee intend to let Grant slip through his fingers. Lee, too, wanted to fight. He wanted to knock the starch out of the Federals before they reached Richmond. As the two armies dug in at Spotsylvania, bitter news was in the making for Lee. The Yankee cavalry under Major General Philip H. "Little Phil" Sheridan clashed with Jeb Stuart's horsemen at Yellow Tavern, six miles north of the Confederate capital.

Stuart fought that day as he always did, fearlessly, setting an example of personal courage for his troopers. He saw the Federals breaking his line on the left, and with sword swinging, he spurred his horse to that spot. Soon he had rallied his men, and the Rebel yell rang out as they fought off the Yanks.

JEB STUART IS KILLED

A single Federal, knocked off his own horse, saw Stuart riding hard across the field. The Yankee raised his pistol and fired. Stuart was taken to a tree to rest and that night an ambulance carried him to Richmond. But he had been mortally wounded by that single shot, and a day later he died.

On that sad day for the South, the fighting began at Spotsylvania. On May 12, at a forward point in Lee's line called the "Bloody Angle," the battle reached its height. Men fought hand to hand across the breastworks. The fence rails behind which the Rebels crouched were splintered. Brutal scenes lived in the memory of Colonel Horace Porter, a member of Grant's staff:

"We had not only shot down an army, but also a forest. . . . Skulls were crushed with clubbed muskets, and men stabbed to death with swords and bayonets thrust between the logs in the parapet which separated the combatants. Wild cheers, savage yells, and frantic shrieks rose above the sighing of the wind and the pattering of the rain, and . . . even the darkness of the night and the pitiless storm failed to stop the fierce contest."

Sometime after midnight the fighting ended. No one can be sure how many men fell during those twenty savage hours, but at least 12,000 men were lost in the struggle for one square mile of ground.

Once more Grant moved to outflank Lee—he was "sidling to the left," the reporters said, telling their Northern readers that Grant was still full of fight. But so was Lee, who followed as Grant "sidled"—across the North Anna, the South Anna, the Pamunkey—until the two armies came head on into another battle at Cold Harbor, on June 3.

THE BATTLE OF COLD HARBOR

Lee had fought on this ground during the campaign against McClellan in 1862. He believed that he had caught Grant where he wanted him. In about ten minutes of slaughter Lee proved he was right. In their first charge against the Rebel entrenchments, the Yankees realized that they were doomed, just as they had been on Marye's Heights at Fredericksburg. From about thirty yards away the Rebels opened with their cannon. The Yankees, coming in a solid mass, were shot down mercilessly. They tried to dodge, to lie down, to fall back. A few escaped, but Cold Harbor cost the North 12,000 troops in dead or wounded, while Lee's losses were not more than 1,500. Northerners, angry at these figures, began to call their new general in chief "Grant, the Butcher."

"I was wrong," Grant said, regretting that he had fought the Battle of Cold Harbor. But he was not beaten. On June 15, he started his army across the James River. It was a race with Lee to Petersburg, twenty miles south of Richmond. Through Petersburg passed all but one of the rail lines to Richmond. If the Union forces could take Petersburg, both Lee and Richmond would be cut off from supplies. The two armies dug in within sight of each other for a stubborn siege.

A TIME OF DECISION

Facing re-election, Lincoln is given the victory he needs by Admiral Farragut at Mobile Bay.

That fall Lincoln faced re-election. The Democrats, meeting in August, 1864, nominated McClellan as their candidate. They promised to save the people from "four years of misrule by a sectional, fanatical, and corrupt party" that had led the country to "the verge of ruin."

According to *Harper's Weekly,* Democratic orators called Lincoln a "filthy storyteller, despot, liar, thief, braggart, buffoon, monster, Ignoramus Abe, Old Scoundrel, robber, swindler, tyrant, fiend, butcher and land-pirate."

That August, his "darkest month of the war," even Lincoln doubted that he would be re-elected. Politicians, afraid that the people had tired of the war, tried to get him to call off the election. He refused, saying, "We cannot have free government without elections."

To win a second term as President, Lincoln needed a military success, but Grant was bogged down at Petersburg. Then a Federal fleet under Admiral David Farragut steamed into Mobile Bay, one of the few ports still open to the Confederacy. When the fog lifted, early on the morning of August 5, Farragut ordered his fleet to raise anchor and go into action.

"DAMN THE TORPEDOES!"

A torpedo sent Farragut's lead ship to the bottom of the bay, but Farragut is supposed to have cried: "Damn the torpedoes—go ahead!"

Placing his own flagship in the lead, Farragut took his fleet past the blazing guns of the forts protecting the bay. Then the pride of the Rebel navy, the iron ram *Tennessee,* steamed forth to smash Farragut's wooden ships. The *Tennessee* had eight-inch plates shielding her sides, and iron covers that closed over her gun ports.

Farragut had himself lashed to the rigging. The little Union monitors went after the *Tennessee,* surrounding her like a pack of sea dogs. A shell knocked off the *Tennessee's* stack. Another jammed the cover of her port gun. Another broke her admiral's leg. Farragut called out his commands from his place in the rigging, and all at once the *Tennessee* ran up a white flag.

Mobile Bay was won, and Lincoln had a victory. He would soon have an even more important victory, thanks to the general known as "Crazy" Sherman.

"ATLANTA IS OURS"

Sherman pushes back the Rebels and takes Atlanta. Lincoln is re-elected.

After the Battle of First Manassas (which the North called First Bull Run), William Tecumseh Sherman had been sent to Kentucky. His command was soon taken away from him, and the newspapers called him "Crazy" Sherman. But Grant felt he had the qualities needed for leadership, and Sherman fought at Shiloh and Vicksburg and Missionary Ridge. He fought well, and Grant had called on him again.

In August, 1864, Sherman commanded three great

In a series of bloody battles at Missionary Ridge, the Wilderness and Spotsylvania, Grant pushed on.

Farragut's ships defied Southern guns in Mobile Bay.

Men fought hand to hand across the "Bloody Angle" breastworks at the Battle of Spotsylvania Court House.

western armies—those of the Cumberland, the Tennessee, and the Ohio—which totaled 98,797 men. The previous May, acting on Grant's orders, he had thrown these three armies against a Rebel force of 41,856 men under General Joseph E. Johnston.

Jumping off from Chattanooga, Sherman made a series of brilliant flanking movements. He forced Johnston to fall back, one step after another, to the trenches protecting Atlanta. The Confederate government was so upset that it replaced Joe Johnston with General John Bell Hood.

The change made little difference to Sherman. He would beat either Johnston or Hood. On August 29, the night the Democrats nominated McClellan for President, Sherman launched his assault against Atlanta. Four days later he had the Rebs backed into a last-ditch stand at Rough and Ready, a railroad junction outside Atlanta.

Throw everything into this battle, Sherman told his corps leaders—they had to win for Mr. Lincoln. After a savage fight, Hood surrendered Atlanta. On September 2, Sherman "snapped his fingers, whistled, and almost danced" before telegraphing the President:

"Atlanta is ours, and fairly won!"

The Democrats could no longer say that the war was a failure; Sherman had given Lincoln the military success he needed to win the election. In November the North went to the polls.

Lincoln spent election day alone in the White House. Then he walked across a rain-soaked lawn to the telegraph office in the War Department. Toward midnight, the election was no longer in doubt. Indiana was going for Lincoln—and so, too, was Philadelphia, New York State, Massachusetts, and even the city of Baltimore. In the end, Lincoln would carry every Northern state except Kentucky, Delaware, and New Jersey and pile up a victory in the electoral college of 212 votes to twenty-one.

"WITH MALICE TOWARD NONE"

Lincoln persuades Congress to pass the Thirteenth Amendment.

After capturing Atlanta, Sherman was in high spirits. But the war could never be ended, he said, until the people who supported the enemy's armies were made to feel "the hard hand of war." And so Sherman divided his army into two wings. He sent one wing under General George H. Thomas to pursue the Confederates under Hood into Tennessee. With the other, on November 16, 1864, he began the march from Atlanta to the sea, boasting he would "make all Georgia howl."

Within less than a week Sherman's seasoned troops had tramped into the state capital at Milledgeville. Here they took over the vacant halls of the house of representatives, elected a speaker, declared themselves the "Legislature of the State of Georgia," and passed an ordinance repealing secession. Sherman enjoyed this practical joke. He insisted that his boys debate the issue well and bring Georgia back into the Union "by a fair vote."

General William Tecumseh Sherman

"SHERMAN'S BUMMERS"

To Sherman's soldiers, the march to the sea was "just as much fun as a fox hunt." New words and phrases came into the language. A length of railroad track, torn up, heated, then twisted so that it could never be used again, was known as "Sherman's hairpin." And "Sherman's bummers" were the men who went out every day to raid the plantations for food. "The thousand pounds of meat in my smokehouse is gone in a twinkling," one Southern woman complained. "My eighteen fat turkeys, my hens, chickens and fowls, my young pigs, are shot down in my yard and hunted as if they were Rebels themselves."

On marched Sherman's boys, burning any building that might serve a military purpose—and a great many that could not. Hundreds of slaves trailed after them, singing and dancing around the campfires at night. Each soldier had his camp pet—a dog, a mule, or even a raccoon. Cockfights became a favorite sport, and defeated birds were called "Jeff Davis" or "Bobby Lee."

In early December, Grant was asked where Sherman was. Grant chuckled. Comparing his friend to a ground mole, he said: "You can here and there trace his track, but you are not quite certain where he will come out till you see his head." Later that month Sherman wired Lincoln: "I beg to present you as a Christmas gift, the city of Savannah, with one hundred and fifty guns and plenty of ammunition, and about twenty-five thousand bales of cotton."

THE THIRTEENTH AMENDMENT

Meanwhile, Lincoln was fighting another kind of battle with Congress. The previous spring he had tried to get an amendment to the Constitution that would prohibit slavery. He told a close friend he believed the amendment "would be worth at least a million men." But the House of Representatives failed to give the Thirteenth Amendment the two-thirds majority needed to pass it.

Since then Lincoln had won re-election. The people of the North, he felt, were solidly behind him. Again he urged the passage of the Thirteenth Amendment. He told congressmen that the amendment would "clinch the whole subject" and bring the war to a quick end. Lincoln was known to his friends as "a supreme politician," and he used all his political skill in this fight during the first weeks of 1865.

On the last day of January the Thirteenth Amendment was once more brought to a vote in the House of Representatives. Spectators jammed the galleries and senators crowded the doorway. There was excitement in the air. Many people felt that, if slavery were abolished legally, the country would be headed toward that "new birth of freedom" of which Lincoln had spoken at Gettysburg.

The vote started at about four o'clock. Every time a congressman answered the roll call with an "Aye!" the galleries burst into cheers. Finally the tally clerk leaned over and whispered the result to the Speaker of the House—119 ayes, 56 nays. The amendment had passed by three votes, but the speaker insisted that his own name be called so that he could vote aye before the result was announced.

A terrific cheer came from the galleries, while congressmen danced in the aisles. Outside a hundred cannon boomed, signaling that slavery was dead in America. A crowd surged down Pennsylvania Avenue to the White House, where it serenaded the President.

In early February, Sherman and his "bummers" started through South Carolina in their northward march to support Grant against Lee in Virginia. South Carolina had been the first state to secede, and the troops looked upon its people with hatred. They occupied Columbia, the state capital, on February 17, and that night fire destroyed 1,400 homes and stores. Sherman later gave many reasons why it was not his fault. He blamed the high wind that was blowing, the undestroyed cotton that filled the air with inflammable material, even the wine in Columbia cellars that his soldiers drank too freely. A highly respected Southern novelist, William Gilmore Simms, told another story. Sherman's troops, Simms said, were well prepared with matches and torches for the awful work of that night.

But Sherman simply marched on, leaving behind smoldering ruins. Hate may have brought about the destruction of Columbia, but there was no trace of hate in Lincoln as he approached his second inauguration. Already he was thinking of the tasks that must be faced when the war ended. On a drizzly, blowy March 4, he looked down at the vast throng that was standing in the mud to witness his Second Inaugural. Unexpectedly, the sun broke through the clouds. Standing in a golden glow, Lincoln spoke of the future:

"With malice toward none; with charity for all; with firmness in the right, as God gives us to see the right, let us strive on to finish the work we are in; to bind up the nation's wounds; to care for him who shall have borne the battle, and for his widow, and his orphan—to do all which may achieve and cherish a just and lasting peace among ourselves, and with all nations."

RICHMOND FALLS

Lincoln visits the Confederate capital and instructs his troops to "let the people down easy."

As spring made the countryside green and violets and dogwood blossomed, Grant awoke each morning "expecting to hear that Lee had gone" from Petersburg, Virginia. What was Lee gaining by this senseless defense? Somehow the war had to be ended—but how, where, when? To find the answers Lincoln went to City Point, Virginia, in late March to meet Grant and Sherman.

It was the first and only meeting during the war of the three men who would be most responsible for final victory. Hopefully, Lincoln asked if the war could be ended without another pitched battle. Both Grant and Sherman doubted it. Leaving the conference, Grant said to his aide: "I think we can send him [Lincoln] some good news in a day or two."

Within a week Grant had smashed a hole in Lee's defenses in the Battle of Five Forks. Lee knew that Petersburg was lost—and Richmond with it. Sadly he said, "The line has been stretched until it has broken." The Rebels fell back in disorder before the Yankees, and one Southerner told his general: "I'm running 'cause I can't fly!"

On Sunday, April 2, the news of Grant's breakthrough reached Richmond. It threw the Confederate capital into a panic. Stores were plundered and buildings burned. The people seemed to have gone mad, and it was Yankee troops arriving next morning who put out the fires and restored order. On April 5, Lincoln also reached Richmond.

"Thank God I have lived to see it," Lincoln said. Negroes by the thousands flocked around him, and he said: "Learn the laws and obey them." He visited the Capitol and sat in Jefferson Davis' chair. Asked if he would pardon those who took a pledge of loyalty to the Union, Lincoln answered that he "would save any repentant sinner from hanging." And to General Godfrey Weitzel, commanding the Federal forces in Richmond, he said:

"Let the people down easy."

THE ROAD TO APPOMATTOX

With his troops hungry and lacking supplies, Lee is forced to surrender.

Lee still believed he could escape from Grant and carry on the war. To do so, he must reach North Carolina and join his army with Confederate forces there under the command of Joseph E. Johnston. Foreseeing a move like this, Lee had ordered provisions shipped to the little town of Amelia Court House. With full bellies, his boys might yet teach Grant a few lessons. So Lee rode into Amelia Court House—only to find that the provisions he had ordered had not been shipped.

Lee again showed his great military ability as, holding a hungry army together, he tried desperately during the next five days to escape into North Carolina. He had to watch his soldiers trudging along with their gums bleeding from chewing on parched corn. He saw weary troops throw away their blankets and muskets along the roadside because they no longer had the strength to carry them.

Grant's well-fed, alert soldiers began to close in on every side. His cavalry raided Confederate wagon trains and cut off Confederate stragglers. Pressed at last into a little area surrounding the village of Appomattox Court House, blocked on flank, front, and rear, Lee told his officers:

"There is nothing left me but to go and see General Grant." And, he added: "I would rather die a thousand deaths!"

April 9, 1865, was Palm Sunday. Across America bells tolled and people were going to church as Lee rode into Appomattox Court House to arrange terms of surrender with General Grant. Early in the afternoon, still wearing a mussed field uniform, Grant reached the farmhouse of Wilmer McLean, where the meeting was to take place. Lee was smartly uniformed—he had had more time to get ready.

Lee and Grant shook hands. "I felt like anything rather than rejoicing at the downfall of a foe who had fought so long and valiantly," Grant said afterward.

They agreed on the terms of surrender: Confederate officers could retain their side arms and baggage. Officers and men who had their own horses could keep them. And, in Grant's words, "each officer and man will be allowed to return to his home, not to be disturbed by the United States authorities."

They signed the papers, shook hands again, and Lee walked out on the porch of the McLean farmhouse. It was a hard moment for Lee. Waiting for his horse, Traveller, he pounded his glove against his palm. But at last the horse arrived, and Lee began to ride off. Grant came out on the porch and raised his hat. Lee returned the salute.

As Lee rode back to his own camp, his soldiers rushed out to greet him.

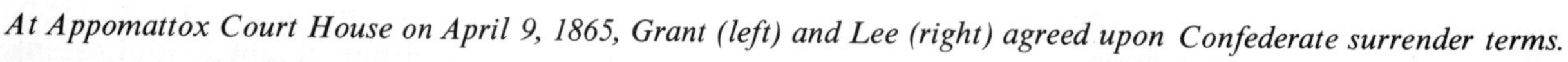

At Appomattox Court House on April 9, 1865, Grant (left) and Lee (right) agreed upon Confederate surrender terms.

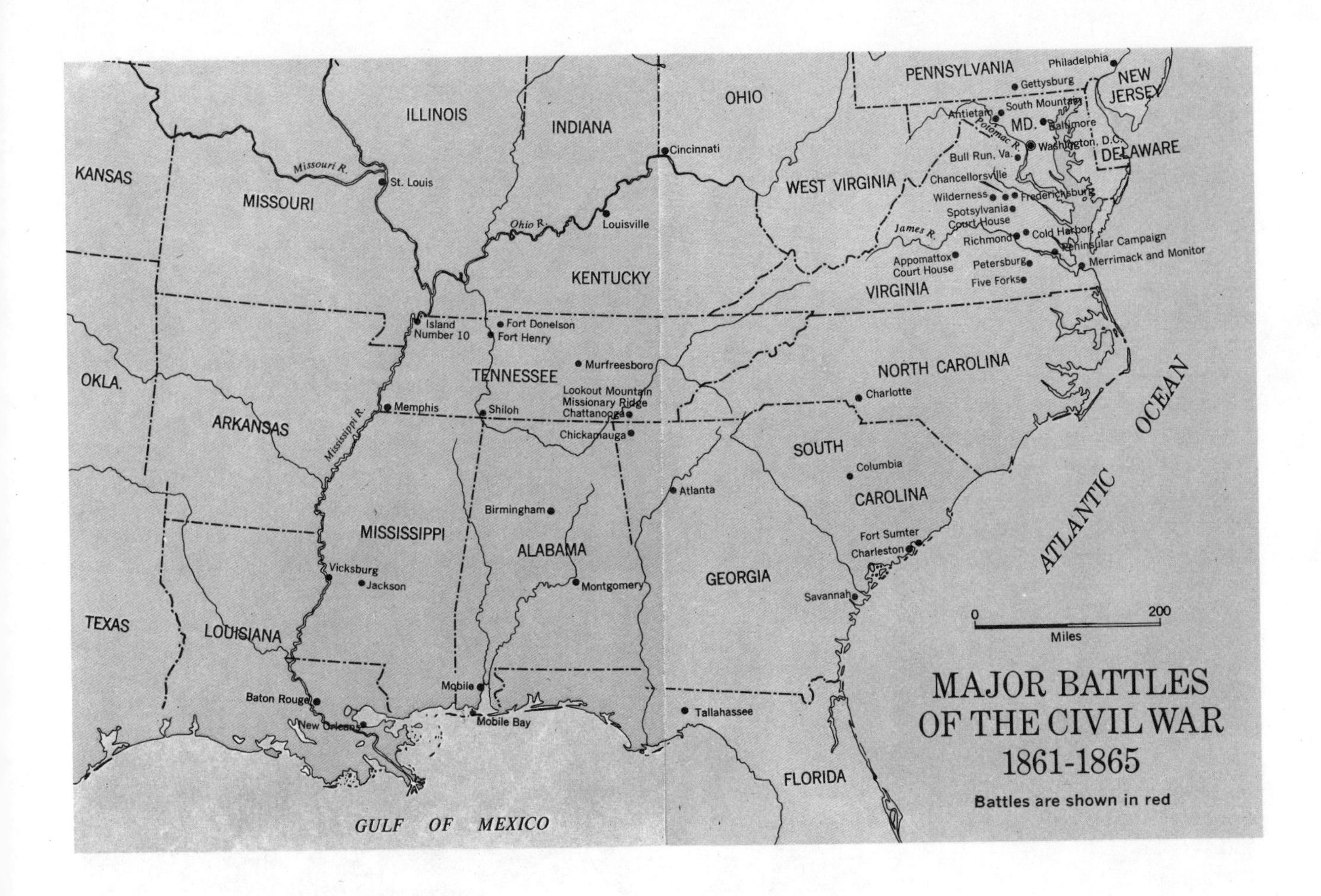

"God bless you, Uncle Robert," they called.

For a few moments, Lee could not speak. Then he managed to say: "Men, we have fought through this war together. I have done the best I could for you. My heart is too full to say more."

"NOW HE BELONGS TO THE AGES"

While the North celebrates its victory,
Lincoln is assassinated.

After Lee's surrender at Appomattox, the Confederacy began to collapse. One by one, other Confederate armies surrendered until at last the Stars and Stripes flew again over one nation.

When news of the surrender at Appomattox reached Washington, Lincoln knew he still faced a battle—a battle against members of his own party who would like a peace of vengeance. But Lincoln wanted to leave to each state, as long as it was willing to return to the Union and abide by the Constitution, the right to work out its own problems. On Good Friday he told the members of his cabinet, "We can't undertake to run State governments in all these Southern states. Their people must do that—though I reckon at first some of them may do it badly."

That night Mr. Lincoln attended a performance of *Our American Cousin* at Ford's Theater. As the play went on, an actor named John Wilkes Booth crept up the stairs to the presidential box and shot Lincoln. The President was taken to a house across the street from the theater where, at twenty-two minutes past seven o'clock the following morning, he died. As he died, Secretary of War Stanton, looking down, said softly:

"Now he belongs to the ages."

In later years many people would write about this war. They would describe it as a vast conflict fought across the face of a vast country. Counting raids, skirmishes, and battles, it had been fought in more than 10,000 places.

They would never be able to estimate its cost in dollars, and they would estimate that 360,222 Union men and 258,000 Confederates had died.

Both North and South would have many disputes over this war—over why it was fought and lost and who was responsible. But when, on the morning of April 15, 1865, Lincoln died, the nation suffered a terrible loss. It no longer had the leader who wanted to make peace in the spirit of his own words:

"With malice toward none; with charity for all."

People in covered wagons, on horseback and afoot raced to claim land in the Oklahoma Territory in April, 1889.

VI ~ WINNING THE WEST

from 1865 to 1907

"BLACK EASTER"

Johnson becomes President as Radical Republicans urge a tough policy toward the South.

The Sunday following Lincoln's death was Easter. Although sunshine flooded Washington, that day became known as "Black Easter." Women put away their new hats and dresses and went to church in mourning clothes. Angry clergymen condemned the South for four years of sinfulness and rebellion that had ended in a mad act of assassination.

At the White House, young Tad Lincoln, who had been his father's favorite, managed at last to hold back his tears. He was sure that his father was now in heaven, and he told a visitor:

"I'm glad he has gone there, for he wasn't happy here. This wasn't a good place for him."

Among those who went to church that Sunday was Andrew Johnson. He had been sworn in as President three hours after Lincoln died, and he knew what was expected of him. There was to be no more talk of "malice toward none." The South must be made to feel the hard heel of vengeance. Senator Ben Wade of Ohio had clasped the new President's hand and said:

"Johnson, we have faith in you. By the gods, we'll have no trouble now in running the country."

THE RADICAL REPUBLICANS

Wade was speaking for the Radicals, the strongest group in the Republican party. Besides Wade himself, they included such important men as Secretary of War Edwin M. Stanton, Charles Sumner of Massachusetts, and Thaddeus Stevens of Pennsylvania. The Radicals were opposed to Lincoln's policy of "charity for all." They wanted no charity for the South. Lincoln had been too soft, too merciful; now that he was dead, the Radicals could come down hard on the South. They meant to make the South pay for what it had done—and pay and pay and pay.

Furthermore, the Radicals were out to prove that Lincoln's assassination was more than a plot hatched in the insane mind of John Wilkes Booth. They said that Booth and his companions had been the tools of Jefferson Davis and the Confederate government. They were determined to hang Jefferson Davis, and General Robert E. Lee with him, and they believed Johnson would not interfere.

Of one thing the Radicals were certain—there was no soft streak in Andrew Johnson. Life had made him hard and tough. Johnson had been born in 1808, in Raleigh, North Carolina. At the age of four, he had seen his father brought home dead. At the age of ten, he had begun to earn his living as a tailor's helper. Fellow workmen taught him the alphabet, and he learned to read from a borrowed book. Later, he moved with his mother and stepfather over the mountains to Greeneville, Tennessee. There he met Eliza McCardle, the girl he would marry. As Andrew worked in his tailor shop, Eliza taught him to write.

President Andrew Johnson

JOHNSON IN POLITICS

Politics in Tennessee was in the control of landowners, and Johnson fought these "aristocrats." His fight was successful; he was twice elected town alderman, and then mayor. His stormy political career carried him to the state legislature, to Congress, to the governorship of Tennessee, and to the Senate. Although he supported a Southerner, John C. Breckinridge, against Lincoln in the election of 1860, Johnson hated secession. At the outset of the war, he attacked the secessionists, saying:

"I would have them arrested and tried for treason, and if convicted, by the eternal God, they should suffer the penalty of the law at the hands of the executioner."

The Radicals remembered this speech. They had no doubt that Johnson would help them run the country their way—but he was not the kind of man they thought he was. As military governor of Tennessee in 1862, he had been fair-minded and moderate. It was true that he had no mercy for Lincoln's assassins, and wanted to see them hanged. But this had nothing to do with any wish for revenge on the South. Johnson had loved Lincoln almost as deeply as the boy in the White House who was glad that his father had gone to heaven.

In his feeling for Lincoln, the new President was closer to the people than the Radicals, as the Radicals would soon discover.

FAREWELL TO LINCOLN

Thousands of mourners watch as funeral train takes Lincoln home to Illinois.

The following Wednesday, a hush fell over Washington. The day before, 25,000 people had crowded into the White House to see Abraham Lincoln in his mahogany coffin. Now they patiently waited for the solemn procession that would start their martyred President on the long journey home to Springfield, Illinois.

The spring sun warmed Pennsylvania Avenue as the church bells began to toll. Then, like an echo, the sound of church bells rose in nearby Georgetown. It was two o'clock. The throng, which lined the sidewalks and rooftops and clung to any toe hold in a tree, had been gathering since daybreak.

Thousands watched as Lincoln's funeral train passed by.

A Negro regiment led the procession, and a hearse, drawn by six white horses, carried the casket. Slowly the procession made its way to the Baltimore and Ohio Railroad Station, and people were trampled as they struggled to catch a glimpse of the marchers. A great sob seemed to shake Washington as the city bade farewell to its sixteenth President—Honest Abe, the Great Emancipator, the Savior of the Union.

At twenty miles an hour the funeral train began its sad journey. Baltimore waited tensely, remembering that, four years ago to the day, troops of the 6th Massachusetts had been stoned and killed in its streets by Southern supporters. Now its buildings were covered with crepe, its church bells rang, its cannon boomed one to the minute. In three hours, some 10,000 weeping Baltimoreans crowded by the casket as it lay in state at the Exchange Building.

The Lincoln train chugged on into Pennsylvania. Farmers, with their wives and children, stood by the rail side. Men took off their hats. Women lifted black veils and stared through tear-dimmed eyes. Children scattered flowers upon the track.

At every station, women brought fresh roses to place upon the casket. Thousands of people waited in a chilling rain at Harrisburg. At Lancaster a lonely old man, ex-President James Buchanan, sat in his carriage on the fringes of the crowd. For miles, as the train approached Philadelphia, the railroad tracks were lined with people. Within the city, 500,000 persons waited to watch the hearse carry the casket to Independence Hall. Some remained standing through the night, hoping for a chance to bid a farewell to their President.

Muffled drums, tolling church bells, rumbling cannon—the story was repeated in every city. In New York, 160,000 persons walked behind the hearse to City Hall.

The funeral train chugged on—to Albany, where 60,000 waited, to Buffalo, where ex-President Millard Fillmore led the procession. Then Ohio had its turn. Cleveland erected a Chinese pagoda for the casket. Columbus built an oriental temple. At every little village in Indiana, arches had been built over the tracks. Rain teemed down on Chicago, and men rushed ahead of the hearse, trying to scoop the mud out of the way.

Next day the Lincoln train started for Springfield. At every town banners read: "Come Home." From across the prairies people poured into Springfield—Lincoln's own people, who remembered him as a lawyer riding the circuit, or as a candidate debating against Douglas.

Now Lincoln was home. On the morning of May 4, 1865, the last procession began, and he was carried to rest in Oak Ridge Cemetery. Leading the march was General Joseph "Fighting Joe" Hooker, whom Lincoln had once removed from the command of

The postwar South was hungry, penniless and ruined. Some women, it was said, even pulled plows in the fields.

an army. At the rear ambled "Old Bob," the bay horse Lincoln had ridden when he journeyed over the prairies as a circuit lawyer. Thrown over "Old Bob" was a red, white, and blue blanket that bore the words: "Old Abe's Horse."

THE DEFEATED SOUTH

Confederate soldiers return to find the South in ruins.

The Confederate soldier returning from the war came back to a ruined South. Almost every face he saw wore a look of despair, almost every mile he traveled was littered with the wreckage left by invading armies. Cities like Richmond, Columbia, and Charleston were ash heaps. Galveston, said a reporter, had become "a city of dogs and desolation," and one Georgian, coming back to burned-out Atlanta, said: "Hell has laid her egg, and right here it hatched."

Travel was slow and hard for the returning Confederate soldier. Railroads had been wrecked, bridges burned or washed away, steamboats captured or destroyed. Horses, mules, wagons, and carriages were difficult to find. The South was almost without money, without food, without hope—but not without outlaws. The number of thieves and cutthroats in Texas alone was estimated at 5,000 and countless highwaymen roamed the roads of Alabama and Mississippi.

Home at last, the Confederate found little to comfort him. Chairs, tables, and beds wobbled on their legs, if they stood at all. Broken dishes had been repaired with cement, and almost every clock had stopped running.

Where to start, what to do, became almost overwhelming problems. Farms were without tools, plows, and seeds. Mills, factories, and mines were either destroyed or shut down. Men sold pies and cakes baked by their wives to the Federal soldiers of occupation. Others peddled the fish they caught. And stories were told of women who hitched themselves to homemade plows and helped their husbands in the fields.

The Thirteenth Amendment freed 3,500,000 Negroes in the South. These former slaves had no leaders, no property, no education, and most of them were bewildered by their new position in life. Some stayed with their old masters, waiting to see what the future would bring. Some became wanderers, a few lived by thievery, and many died of hunger and disease. A number of them believed that the government would soon give them "forty acres and a mule," and that they would have the same opportunities as the white man. Those who wanted to work said that wages they were offered were too low and that they were often cheated.

In late 1865, an Alabamian told the planters' side of the story. Writing of the Negroes, he said:

"They will not work for anything but wages, and few [planters] are able to pay wages. They are penniless but resolute in their demands. They expect to see all the land divided out equally between them and their old masters in time to make the next crop. . . . It cannot be disguised that in spite of the most earnest efforts of their old masters to conciliate [to gain their good will] and satisfy them the estrangement [separation] between the races increases in its extent and bitterness. Nearly all Negro men are armed with repeaters [rifles], and many of them carry them openly, day and night."

It was true that few planters were able to pay wages, and this led to the sharecropping system. The sharecropper would work land owned by the planter, who also furnished him with tools, seed, and farm animals. The sharecropper could buy food and other necessities on credit at the local store. The planter received anywhere from one-half to two-thirds of the crop. The rest went to the sharecropper, and out of this he paid what he owed to the storekeeper. Landless whites as well as Negroes became sharecroppers, and were caught in a system that would go on for many years.

Southerners who were opposed to equality between the races banded together in secret societies. Alabama had its Black Guard and its Men of Justice, Louisiana its White League, Mississippi its White Line, and South Carolina its rifle clubs. At Pulaski, Tennessee, in the fall of 1865, a group of young Confederates organized the Ku-Klux Klan. It took its name from the Greek word *kyklos,* meaning "a circle." Members of the Klan rode at night, wearing masks and flowing white robes. Their object was to frighten the Negroes into behaving the way the whites wanted them to behave.

In 1867 the Klan held a convention at Nashville. Confederate General Nathan Bedford Forrest was made its head, with the title of Grand Wizard. As time went on, lawless men became more and more important in the Klan. These men used violence against the Negroes—beatings and even lynchings. They went so far that in 1869 General Forrest disbanded the original Klan. A new Klan was organized, a Klan which burned fiery crosses in the night, a Klan of terror and violence.

Under the Black Codes, many Negroes were accused of vagrancy, fined, and forced to work off the fine.

ANDREW JOHNSON FIGHTS THE RADICALS

Johnson readmits Southern states and Radicals denounce the "Black Codes."

Before his death, Lincoln had wanted to bring the Southern states back into the Union with his "ten-per-cent plan." A state would be allowed to run its own affairs as soon as ten per cent of its population (based on its voting population in 1860) took an oath to obey the Constitution and the laws of the Federal government.

The Radical Republicans had bitterly opposed Lincoln's plan and argued that no state could be readmitted to the Union without the consent of Congress. The Radicals controlled Congress and intended to see that the Southern states were readmitted only on the Radicals' terms. More than anything else, they wanted the Negroes to have the right to vote. One of their reasons, of course, was the hope that the grateful Negroes would vote for Republicans and help keep them in power.

THE BLACK CODES

After Lincoln's death, the Radicals expected that President Johnson would support them. That would mean the end of Lincoln's "ten-per-cent plan." But Johnson was an old-fashioned Democrat. He cared little about the planters of the South or the Negroes. He was interested in the South's poor farmers—people like those he had known in his boyhood. His plan for readmitting the Southern states was not much different from Lincoln's. And since Congress was not in session during the summer of 1865, and would not meet until December, there was nothing the Radicals could do about it. Acting swiftly, Johnson now readmitted seven Confederate states. Then the Southern states passed a series of laws known as the Black Codes.

The Black Codes varied from state to state, but the purpose of all of them was the same—to limit the freedom of the Negro. The laws on vagrants (homeless wanderers) were especially harsh. Negroes considered vagrants were hauled before a magistrate and fined. They were then assigned to work for the highest bidder until they had worked off their fine.

In Mississippi, Negroes could not own or rent land except in incorporated towns and cities. In South Carolina, Negroes were allowed to become farmers or servants. They were not allowed to enter any other trade or business unless they were licensed and paid a high annual fee.

Horace Greeley, one of the best known newspaper editors in the North, said that the South was seeking "the extermination of the black race."

THE FOURTEENTH AMENDMENT

The Radicals were boiling with anger over Johnson's moves and the Black Codes. When they returned to Washington for the next meeting of Congress, they were determined to strike back at the South. The House and Senate quickly set up the Joint Committee on Reconstruction, which the Radicals controlled. They succeeded in passing the Civil Rights bill over the President's veto. This bill was meant to destroy the Black Codes. It was of great importance, because it was the basis of the Fourteenth Amendment, which was passed in the summer of 1866. Here again the Radicals were successful; included in the amendment were these points:

1. The Negro was a citizen of both the United States and the state in which he lived. He therefore could not be deprived "of life, liberty, or property, without due process of law."

2. If a state denied any group of citizens the right to vote, "except for participation in rebellion or other crime," the number of that state's representatives in Congress could be reduced.

3. All persons, such as army officers and members of Congress, who had broken their oath of allegiance to the United States to fight for the Confederacy were disqualified from holding state or Federal office.

4. The United States government was responsible for its debts, but not for the debts of the Confederacy. All debts of the Confederacy were outlawed, as well as any claims resulting from the emancipation of the slaves.

As Washington sweltered in the hot summer of 1866, the fight between the President and Congress became fierce and bitter. Johnson attacked the Fourteenth Amendment and advised the Southern states not to ratify it. Ten of them—all except Tennessee—took his advice.

James A. Garfield of Ohio, who would someday be President himself, called these states "the sinful ten." Stirring up the Radicals against Johnson, he said, "It is now our turn to act." The Radicals did act, attacking Johnson without mercy in the Congressional elections that fall. They said he was a drunkard and an incompetent. Some even said that he had helped to plan Lincoln's assassination.

JOHNSON LOSES A BATTLE

Radicals force Reconstruction Act on Johnson but are unable to remove him.

When the election returns were in, the Radicals had won large majorities in both houses of Congress. "We've got Andy Johnson on the run," they said, and they intended to keep him running.

The Radicals struck quickly with the Reconstruction Act of March 2, 1867. This abolished the state governments Johnson had recognized and divided the South into five military districts. An officer of the army, not below the rank of brigadier general, was to rule each district. To be represented in Congress now, each state must call a convention and draw up a constitution giving Negroes the right to vote.

Another law forbade Johnson from removing any person from office without the consent of the Senate. Still another law prohibited him from issuing any orders to the army, except through General Grant.

The Radicals were joyful. They were indeed keeping Johnson on the run. He was President in name only. The new laws made it impossible for him to remove any Radical from office, or even to use his constitutional authority as commander in chief of the army.

President Johnson's impeachment trial lasted from March 13 to May 26 in 1868. It was held before the Senate, with the Chief Justice of the Supreme Court presiding. Johnson was acquitted by a margin of one vote.

But stubborn Andrew Johnson did not surrender so easily. He knew that one of the men who was plotting against him was a member of his own cabinet—Secretary of War Edwin M. Stanton.

Few persons in American history are more difficult to understand than Stanton. He had been among those who charged that Lincoln's assassination had been planned by Jefferson Davis and the Confederate government. When he failed to prove this, his hatred for the South became almost insane. He wanted to destroy the South. But to destroy the South he had to destroy President Johnson—or so he seemed to believe.

Johnson suspended Stanton and named General Grant to serve as temporary Secretary of War. When Congress met in December of 1867, the Radicals refused to approve Stanton's suspension. Johnson then dismissed Stanton, but Stanton refused to be dismissed. The law was that he could not be removed from office by the President without the consent of the Senate. Stanton knew that the Radicals in the Senate would support him.

And then something happened for the first and only time in American history. On February 24, 1868, the House of Representatives approved the impeachment of the President of the United States for "high crimes and misdemeanors [misconduct] in office." Eleven charges were brought against Johnson to show that he was unfit to continue as President. The trial, held in the Senate, began on March 13 and ended on May 26.

Most of the charges were rather technical. They were based less on fact than on the wish of the Radicals to be rid of Johnson. But not all the Republicans voted with their party. Seven of them joined with twelve Democrats to vote against Johnson's conviction—just enough to save him. The final vote was thirty-five to nineteen, which was one vote short of the two-thirds majority required by the Constitution to convict a President.

Although Johnson was able to finish out his term, the Democrats nominated Horatio Seymour to run for President in the coming election. The Republicans nominated General Ulysses S. Grant, who became President in 1868.

The South was in for a hard time.

Negroes served in many postwar Southern legislatures. But scalawags and carpetbaggers dominated politics.

SCALAWAGS AND CARPETBAGGERS

New white groups gain power in the South. Negroes are elected to office.

The Radicals were in complete control in Washington, and they were quick to take advantage of it and carry out their plans for the South. They knew they had the support of the freedmen, the Southern Negroes who had been slaves. There were now more Negro voters than white in Alabama, Louisiana, South Carolina, Florida, Mississippi, and Georgia. But political power was soon in the hands of two new groups of white men—the scalawags and the carpetbaggers.

The scalawags were Southerners who had been against secession and were now willing to work with the Republicans. The carpetbaggers were Northerners who had come into the South. They got their name from the handbags made of carpeting in which they carried their belongings. Some of the carpetbaggers had come simply to make as much money as possible. Others had come because they were interested in democracy and wanted to help the freedmen and poor whites of the South.

Uneducated, and with no experience in politics, the Negroes eagerly followed the leadership of the carpetbaggers and the scalawags. These three groups were supported by President Grant, the United States army, and the Radical Republican majority in Congress. Their combined strength was enough to push out of office the Southerners who had governed before and during the war. By the end of 1868, new constitutions had been ratified and new governors and legislators had been elected in North and South Carolina, Georgia, Florida, Alabama, Louisiana, and Arkansas. Two years later, Mississippi, Texas, and Virginia took the same kind of action.

For the first time, Negroes were elected to public office. A newspaperman wrote:

"Seven years ago these men were raising corn and cotton under the whip of the overseer. Today they are raising points of order and questions of privilege. They find they can raise one as well as the other. They prefer the latter. It is easier and better paid. Then, it is the evidence of an accomplished result. It means escape and defense from old oppressors. It means liberty. It means the destruction of prison-walls only too real to them. It is the sunshine of their lives. It is their day of jubilee. It is their long-promised vision of the Lord God Almighty."

While a large number of Negroes were elected to state legislatures, in only one state, South Carolina, were there more Negro legislators than white. And almost all of the important positions in the government were held by whites.

THE RECONSTRUCTION YEARS

The years of Southern Reconstruction were confused and confusing years. The carpetbagger-scalawag-Negro governments were responsible for much that was bad as well as much that was good. They spent huge sums of money. The states soon had enormous debts, and taxes rose higher and higher. To make things worse for the Southern landowners, land values went down as taxes went up.

Dishonesty was common. In South Carolina, the legislature spent $200,000 for furniture to be used in the State House. It was worth no more than $18,000. The speaker of the state's House of Representatives was given $1,000 of public money to make up for a bet he had lost on a horse race. Governor Warmoth of Louisiana said frankly, "Corruption [dishonesty] is the fashion. I do not pretend to be honest, but only as honest as anybody in politics."

On the good side, the carpetbagger-scalawag-Negro legislatures reorganized voting districts on the basis of population rather than wealth. They built railroads, roads, and hospitals, and provided help for the poor, the orphaned, and the insane. The laws they passed in the field of education were especially outstanding. They set up free schools, supported by taxes, for both Negroes and whites. The South had had a very poor public school system, and even that was destroyed in the war. According to some historians, more was done for education in the South during the few years of Reconstruction than had been done by the Southerners themselves in two centuries.

The Southerners struck back at the Radicals with secret organizations like the Ku-Klux Klan, the Knights of the White Camelia, and the Society of the White Rose. Their aim was to frighten the Negroes so that they would not vote for the Republicans or run for office. Anxious to keep the support of the Negroes, the Radicals in Congress passed the Fifteenth Amendment. It became law on March 30, 1871, and prohibited any state from denying the vote to a citizen because of race, color, or previous condition of servitude. The Ku-Klux Klan Act of 1871 set up penalties for preventing citizens from voting. Cases that came under this act were sent to Federal courts, rather than to state courts. The act also allowed the President to proclaim martial law and use Federal troops to put down "conspiracy" in the South.

For the time being, at least, the South was forced to give in to the Radicals.

AMERICA ON THE MOVE

Business and industry grow, and railroad tracks cross the country.

In the years that followed the end of the war, business and industry grew at a terrific rate. So great was the growth that this period is sometimes called "the second American revolution." From 1860 to 1870, the number of factories increased by eighty per cent; 22,000 miles of new railroad track were laid. More and more goods were produced. In the shoe industry, for example, production rose from 5,000,000 pairs of shoes in 1864 to 25,000,000 pairs in 1870. Everywhere America was on the move.

Americans had already realized that they needed a link between the West and the rest of the nation. As early as 1862, Congress had passed an act providing for the building of a transcontinental railroad. The plan was for the Central Pacific to lay tracks eastward from Sacramento, California, while the Union Pacific laid tracks westward from Council Bluffs, Iowa. When the tracks joined, travelers would no longer have to journey by stagecoach or covered wagon.

EAST MEETS WEST

The work went slowly until the war ended, then it went ahead with a rush. Thousands of Chinese and Mexican laborers swung picks and shovels for the Central Pacific; the Irish did the job for the Union Pacific.

"There is nothing concerned with the Union Pacific Railroad that is not wonderful," said a pamphlet published by the company in 1868. It described the rich farm lands over which its tracks crossed: "The

Amid the boom of the 1860's, railroads spanned the land.

grain fields of Europe are mere patch gardens beside the green oceans which roll from Colorado to Indiana. . . . The hills behind sink into the plain until the horizon there is perfect. Those on either side grow fainter, till through the heated air they take on the appearance of low islands seen across many miles of water."

Fighting Indians and weather, bridging rivers, climbing mountains, the railroaders pushed on like an army:

"The boarding cars go in advance. They are pushed to the extremity [end] of the track; a construction train then runs up, unloads its material and starts back to bring another [load]. . . . The trucks, each drawn by two horses, ply between the track-layers and their supplies."

On May 10, 1869, tracks of the Union Pacific met those of the Central Pacific at Promontory, Utah. When the time came to lay the last tie and drive the last spikes, the tracks ran 689 miles eastward and 1,086 miles westward. Nevada sent a silver spike to be driven into the final tie, Arizona a spike of iron, silver, and gold. But to California went the honor of supplying the "last spike" of gold.

Across the land, church bells rang. People shouted. Editors dipped pens into inkwells and wrote long articles about the meaning of this moment. East and West had met at Promontory and were now one country. Distance had been conquered. Soon towns would spring up along these tracks. Soon people would travel the railroad to new homes, new futures.

HOMESTEADING IN THE OLD WEST

Settlers flock to build farms on the free land offered by the government.

Under the Homestead Act of 1862, the Federal Government offered free land from the public lands of the United States. Grants of 160 acres were given to all settlers who would cultivate their land for five years. After the end of the war, a steady stream of homesteaders poured into the West. They came by covered wagon, by train, by boat, and sometimes on foot. In spite of snow and ice, rushing rivers, high mountains, and Indian raids, they pushed on to the low hills of Iowa and the plains of Kansas, Nebraska, and the Dakotas.

The homesteaders were hardy people of many nationalities. There was Gro Svendsen, for example, who settled with her husband in northwestern Iowa. Life in the West was not easy, and at first she was homesick. "Everything is so totally different from what it was in our beloved Norway," she wrote to her family. "One can't make cheese out of the milk because of the flies, bugs and other insects. . . . It's difficult, too, to preserve the butter. One must pour brine over it or salt it; otherwise it gets full of maggots."

Gro was amazed at the long summer days and the violence of the thunder and lightning when the rains fell. Her greatest fear was the "faieren" or prairie fire: "Quite often the scorching flames sweep everything along in their path—people, cattle, hay, fences. In dry weather with a strong wind the fire will race faster than the speediest horse."

But two years later she was able to write:

"We have had a good year, a rich harvest both from the grain that we sowed as well as from the wild fruit and grain. We have plowed and fenced in three acres of new land. On this plot we raised ninety bushels of corn, twenty-four bushels of potatoes, and a plant called sugar cane or sorghum. This sugar cane is pressed and cooked into syrup or molasses. . . . I must tell you something about a fruit called 'watermelon.' We have an enormous quantity of them; I can't compare them to anything I ever saw in Norway. They are as big as a child's head; some are larger. They are sweet and juicy."

Another homesteader, Howard Ruede, settled on the plains of Kansas where wood was so scarce that houses were built of sod. Thousands of homesteaders lived in such dwellings. Usually the sod walls were about two feet thick at the ground, sloping off to about fourteen inches at the top. The inside walls were plastered with sand and a sticky clay. If a sod house was not beautiful, at least it was cheap.

GRASSHOPPERS AND DUST

In 1874, a plague of grasshoppers came to the region of the High Plains, which runs roughly from the Rocky Mountains to the Missouri River. Vast clouds of the insects descended on the land, covering houses, barns, and fields. "In a week," a settler named Stuart Henry recalled, "grain fields, gardens, shrubs, vines, had been eaten down to the ground or to the bark. Nothing could be done. You sat by and saw everything go."

Dry weather followed the plague of the "hoppers" —just as the Indians had predicted. New crops withered in the fields. Farmers had nothing to do and hung around the general store, wondering why they remained. Dust covered everything.

Stuart Henry did not leave. Instead he went to prayer meeting, which was free. He sometimes wondered if "petitions by four-hundred-dollar-a-year ministers had enough breeze behind them to be shot clear up to Heaven so that the yelpings could be heard there." But he stayed, and the following year brought good crops and good prices.

It was faith that made the homesteaders stay on their homesteads—tomorrow would be better. This faith enabled them to endure storm and fire, and the hard work that went into breaking, plowing, seeding, and harvesting a new field of wheat.

And so the people stayed and prospered, and America grew.

THE "LONG DRIVE"

Cowboys drive great herds of cattle across the Plains to the cow towns.

In 1867, the Kansas Pacific Railway began to reach out into the plains. At Abilene, Kansas, J. G. McCoy established the first of the cow towns from which cattle, driven from Texas, could be shipped to the markets of the East. Soon the map of the American West became dotted with trails. Cattlemen from the wild plains of the Southwest followed them as they made the "long drive" to the cow towns on the Kansas Pacific and the Union Pacific railroads. The Chisholm Trail began at the Red River in Texas and crossed the Colorado just below present-day Austin, Texas. It stretched 700 miles to Wichita and Abilene.

A cowboy, or "waddy," led a rugged life on a drive. A trail herd averaged about 3,000 cattle, and a number of men were required to manage it. First came the scout, who usually rode a day's journey ahead, looking for water and safe fords across streams. At the head of the herd, one on each side, jogged the "point men," or lead riders. The "swing riders," or "flank men," came next, and at the rear of the herd were the "drag men," or "tail riders." The leader of the outfit was the "trail boss," and the second in command was the "straw boss."

The Texas longhorn, a descendant of the Andalusian cattle brought into Mexico by the Spaniards in 1519, was an animal of habit. When a herd moved, the strongest longhorn pushed to the front and usually kept this position of leadership throughout the drive. Each day each animal tended to take the same place in the herd that he had the day before. At night, when the herd rested, cowboys stood watch, singing and whistling to soothe the cattle.

An average day's drive, from sunup to late afternoon, covered from ten to fifteen miles. Many dangers threatened the trail rider. Just before dawn he looked for Indians, who liked to steal his horses. A clap of thunder during a storm—even a loud voice at night or the striking of a match—could set off a stampede. Buffalo herds, dry mesa country, and flooded rivers could also mean trouble.

Yet the cowboy, proud and tough, kept the cattle moving. The first summer that the Kansas Pacific reached Abilene, an estimated 35,000 cattle were driven there from Texas. From 1867 to 1884 more than 5,000,000 Texas longhorns followed the trails to shipping points in the North.

When the cowboy reached the end of the trail, he wanted to forget the hardships of the drive and have

Killings were common in the lawless western cow towns.

a good time. He found his fun in the dancing, drinking, and gambling places of such cow towns as Abilene, Dodge City, and Wichita in Kansas, Miles City in Montana, Ogallala and Sidney in Nebraska, and Cheyenne in Wyoming.

Those were the days of the "wild and woolly" West, and there was little law in the cow towns. Often the sound of the six-shooter rang out in the dusty streets. Dodge City, which was known as "the cowboy's capital," counted twenty-five killings in one year. Its cemetery was called Boot Hill, because so many men who were buried there had died "with their boots on."

OUTLAWS AND MARSHALS

The "bad man" became a familiar figure. Later stories were told of outlaws like William H. "Billy the Kid" Bonney, Sam Bass, Johnny Ringo, and Bullwhack Jones—stories that made these men into heroes. But in real life they were simply bandits and thieves and killers, and anything but heroes.

The stories about the "law men," the marshals of the cow towns, were just as inaccurate. Many of the marshals were known killers who were given their jobs because they were quick on the draw. One of them was Wild Bill Hickok, who strode the streets of Hays City and Abilene in a Prince Albert coat and fancy vest.

Wyatt Earp, who cleaned up Tombstone, Arizona, was a bad man who reformed. Bat Masterson, the marshal of Dodge City, was a gunman before he put on his badge. But there were some honest men who enforced the law—marshals like Patrick Floyd Garrett, who hunted down Billy the Kid, and Tom Smith of Abilene, who put aside his guns and went after desperadoes with his bare hands.

Meanwhile, the "cattle kingdom" was growing. By 1876 it had spread over western Texas, Oklahoma, Kansas, Nebraska, Montana, Wyoming, the Dakotas, Colorado, and parts of Utah, Nevada, and New Mexico. Within a few years it brought great changes to the West.

In the early 1870's, for example, a traveler in Montana could have gone miles without seeing so much as a trapper's camp. Huge herds of buffalo "darkened the rolling plains." Every hill, every ravine, every thicket had its antelope, elk, and howling coyotes. By 1883, there were no more buffalo, and antelope and elk were scarce. Instead, 600,000 head of cattle grazed on the range. Montana had become a cattle state.

The cattleman knew both good times and bad. Even when the cattle market was booming, he had to be on the lookout for "rustlers" who stole cattle. It was easy enough for these outlaws to stampede a herd and run off with a good part of it. As homesteaders settled in increasing numbers on the Great Plains, they tried to fence off trails and water holes. Sometimes there were small shooting wars between the cattlemen and the homesteaders.

But the cowboys kept the herds moving, bringing beef to a growing population, helping to build America.

"PIKES PEAK OR BUST!"

Stories of "rich strikes" of gold and silver bring miners rushing to the West.

There were others, too, who were helping to change the West and build America in those years. Among them were the miners who went seeking their fortunes with pick and shovel. Sometimes, to show their determination to reach the mining fields, they would paint a slogan on their wagons, such as: "Pikes Peak or Bust!" And sometimes, when they failed to strike it rich, they would replace the slogan with another: "Busted by gosh!"

Even when a mining boom played out quickly—as it did in the Pikes Peak gold rush of Colorado in 1859—it helped the country grow. Many miners stayed, becoming farmers, ranchers, or businessmen, and new states were formed out of the western territories.

In the years following the Civil War, perhaps as many as 200,000 Americans roamed the West in search of gold or silver. They were restless, determined, and always hopeful. They clambered over the mountains to Nevada when news of the discovery of the Comstock Lode reached the outside world in 1859. A few years later they were tramping into Montana in search of gold. They trudged across the deserts into Arizona and New Mexico for gold, silver, and copper.

A rumor of a new strike was all that was needed to start a rush to "new diggings." In the late summer of 1874, the cry went up: "Gold found in the Black Hills of South Dakota!" Another rush was on, and no one seemed to care that the miners were invading territory belonging to the Sioux and Cheyenne tribes. By December, 15,000 fortune seekers had entered the Black Hills, which the Indians regarded as sacred ground.

The deposits first discovered in the Black Hills' French Creek played out, and the rush turned toward the Deadwood area, where richer deposits had been found. The boom towns of the miners were as lawless as the cow towns of the cowboys. Stories were told of the miners, just as they were of the cowboys. There were stories about Calamity Jane and Poker Alice Tubbs; about Jack McCall, the man who shot down Wild Bill Hickok; about Deadwood Dick Clark, whose feats filled a shelf of novels.

Thousands of homesteaders went west. Many traveled in "prairie schooners," as covered wagons were called.

Settlers feared the sudden fires that often swept across the prairies, destroying everything in their path.

Plagues of grasshoppers sometimes troubled settlers. But those who stayed on found happiness and prosperity.

The miner worked as hard as he played, as shown by the increase in the output of silver. In 1860 the value of the silver produced by the nation was $150,000; by 1873 it was $36,000,000. But soon mining required scientific methods, and the use of expensive machinery. Only large companies could afford the investment. The lone miner, wandering the hills with his burro and his pack, began to disappear. The miner became a man who worked for a large company, who lived in a company-owned house and ate food that he bought in a company store. The boom towns became ghost towns, and the days of "Pikes Peak or Bust!" became a memory.

THE INDIANS FIGHT BACK

Indians whose lands are overrun try to drive the white men from the Plains.

The Indians of the Great Plains grew more and more bitter as they saw the waves of white invaders sweeping into their homelands—the railroad builders with their swinging sledges, the homesteaders with their sod houses, the cattlemen with their bawling herds, the miners with their picks and shovels. During the years of the Civil War, when the whites had been fighting one another, the Indians had struck savagely to rid their hunting grounds of settlers. Little Crow had led 1,300 Sioux warriors in a bloody uprising in Minnesota in 1862. The Arapaho and Cheyenne tribes terrorized Colorado, western Kansas, and Nebraska in a series of raids two years later.

Colorado volunteers, led by Colonel J. M. Chivington, hit back fiercely in November, 1864. Between 500 and 600 Cheyenne and Arapaho Indians, most of them women and children, camped along Sand Creek, believing that they were under the protection of the United States government. Chivington and his volunteers rode down on these Indians, catching them asleep, and the result was the brutal "Sand Creek Massacre."

After the Civil War, Federal cavalry could be sent to the Great Plains. Soon 25,000 men were in the field, covering a vast area from Minnesota and the Dakotas to New Mexico and Arizona. The Indians fought back, under brave leaders like Sitting Bull, Black Kettle, Red Cloud, and Crazy Horse. For twenty years the blood of red man and white man stained the Great Plains.

SLAUGHTER OF THE BUFFALO

Few homesteaders, cattlemen, miners, or cavalrymen appeared to understand what the coming of the white man meant to the Plains Indians. They were wanderers and hunters who depended on the buffalo herds for their existence. Buffalo meat, which they preserved by smoking, provided their food. The clothes and shoes they wore, the tents in which they slept, were made from buffalo skins. Their bows, knives, and hoes were carved from the bones of the buffalo. Its lungs gave them water bags, its intestines supplied thread, its sinews bowstrings.

A demand for buffalo hides in the East brought bands of white hunters to the Great Plains. The buffalo—a slow, clumsy animal with poor eyesight—was easily killed. Colonel R. I. Dodge estimated that as many as 5,500,000 buffalo were shot from 1872 to 1874.

In angry war councils, the leaders of the Plains Indians said:

"Our land is being stolen. Our women and children are being killed while they sleep. Our food is being swept from sight. Our sacred ground in the Black Hills is being overrun by men who worship gold."

It seemed to them that they must either fight—or die.

CUSTER AT LITTLE BIGHORN

Custer's force is wiped out in the Indians' last big victory.

On June 21, 1876, the *Far West,* headquarters boat of General Alfred H. Terry, rode at anchor at the mouth of Rosebud Creek in Montana. Terry spoke earnestly to two fellow passengers, General George Armstrong Custer and General John Gibbon. Both were veterans of the Civil War, as he was. Terry had a plan for smashing Indian resistance. He would catch those red devils between two forces, drive them into the open, and make the plains safe for the white man.

And so Gibbon led the 17th Infantry across the Yellowstone River, then marched up along the Bighorn River to the Little Bighorn. Meanwhile, Custer led the 7th Cavalry up along Rosebud Creek.

Neither Gibbon nor Custer knew that the Indians were gathering at the Little Bighorn in unusual strength. Their camps covered three miles. Among the Indians were the Sioux, under their famous medicine man, Sitting Bull; the Northern Cheyennes, under Chiefs Two Moon and White Bull; the Oglalas, under Chiefs Crazy Horse, Low Dog, and Big Road; the Minneconjous, under Chief Hump; and the Sans Arcs, under Chief Spotted Eagle. The Indians may have numbered as many as 15,000, including about 5,000 warriors.

Custer had been the youngest major general in the Union Army. As he moved up the Rosebud, he

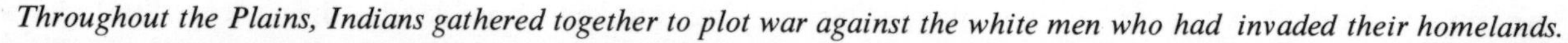
Throughout the Plains, Indians gathered together to plot war against the white men who had invaded their homelands.

was in command of 600 cavalrymen, forty-four Indian scouts, and some packers and guides. On June 24 his scouts warned him of Indian trails turning westward toward the valley of the Little Bighorn. Stubborn and overconfident, Custer pushed on through the night. The next morning, his scouts reported smoke from Indian fires. But when Custer went to see for himself, ground haze made the smoke invisible.

Custer decided to divide his force into three battalions. He sent one ahead to scout. He sent another, made up of three companies under Major Marcus A. Reno, up along one bank of a creek flowing into the valley of the Little Bighorn. Custer himself led five companies up along the opposite bank. When he came within sight of the Indian encampment, his view was partly cut off by bluffs and tall cottonwood trees. He never guessed how many Indians there were.

CUSTER'S LAST STAND

Custer ordered Reno to attack the camp—and then suddenly the Indians were upon them. No one knows exactly what happened, for Custer and all of his 264 men were killed. The only survivor in the Federal ranks was Comanche, Custer's horse.

The Indians continued to fight after the battle of the Little Bighorn, but they had no chance of winning against the might of the United States. With the capture of Geronimo, the warrior-chief of the Apaches, in 1886, the backbone of the Indians' revolt was broken. By then they had no choice but to live in poverty and misery on one of the 171 reservations that Congress had provided for them in twenty-one states and territories.

The Indians were not entirely without friends among the whites. In 1879 Helen Hunt Jackson attended a lecture in Boston where she heard two Indians, Standing Bear and Bright Eyes, tell of the evils that had been done to the Ponca tribe. Helen Hunt Jackson was once described as a combination of "sunshine and fire." Soon after this lecture, she moved to Colorado and wrote to a friend that the Indian was worse off than Negro slaves had ever been. She had found that an agent on an Indian reservation could "order a corporal's guard to fire on an Indian at any time he sees fit."

In 1881, Helen Hunt Jackson published *A Century of Dishonor,* a book that made many Americans realize for the first time how shamefully the Indian was being treated. She sent a copy to every member of Congress at her own expense. Results came quicker than she could have hoped. The Indian Rights Association, founded the following year, was the first of several such groups formed to aid the Indian. Their work led in 1887 to the passage of the Dawes Act, popularly known as the "Emancipation Act of the Indians." This law gave the Indians a homesteader's right to 160 acres of land, citizenship, and the protection of state and territorial laws. The Dawes Act was not perfect, but it was a good beginning, and later other laws to help the Indian were passed.

The Indian had had his land taken away from him without his consent, and he was a tragic figure. But most Americans did not pay much attention to the Indian. In the early 1870's they were far too restless, far too busy, far too anxious to get ahead and build up the country.

THE CHICAGO FIRE

In 1871, Chicago is destroyed by fire, but the city is quickly rebuilt.

In 1831, Chicago was a tiny village clinging to the southwest corner of Lake Michigan. Then, in just forty years, Chicago became a bustling city of 335,000 inhabitants. Important railroads, running east and west, joined at Chicago. Its elevators held grain harvested on the surrounding prairies, and its stockyards already promised to make the city "Hog Butcher to the World."

As Chicagoans strolled the streets on a bright, warm Sunday in October, 1871, they may have spoken of how dry the weather had been during the past three months—no rain, the leaves gone from the trees, the wells drying up. And some may have commented on the fires that had broken out recently in the city. But there was no real warning of the terrible disaster that would strike that evening.

THE FIRE STARTS

No one can say for certain just how the fire started in the O'Leary cow barn at the rear of 137 DeKoven Street. The time was about 8:45 P.M., on October 8. By midnight the fire had raced three-eighths of a mile, and two and a half hours later it had jumped the Chicago River and roared into the city's North Side. Horace White, editor of the Chicago *Tribune,* wrote:

"The fire was moving northward like ocean surf on a sand beach. . . . A column of flame would shoot up from a burning building, catch the force of the wind, and strike the next one. . . . Billows of fire were rolling over the business palaces of the city and swallowing up their contents. Walls were falling so fast that the quaking of the ground under our feet was scarcely noticed, so continuous was the reverberation. Sober men and women were hurrying through the streets from the burning quarter, some with bundles of clothes on their shoulders, others dragging trunks along the sidewalks by means of strings and ropes fastened to the handles, children trudging by their sides or borne in their arms."

A RUSH TO THE LAKE

Horses raced through the streets. Vehicles of every description carried frightened people toward the lake shore. Jail doors were thrown open and prisoners took to their heels.

George Howland, a high-school principal, was another eyewitness. He said: "Engines seemed entirely useless. The long tongues of flame would dart out over a whole block, then come back and lap it all up clean. Iron and stone seemed to come down as in a blast furnace." A woman remembered how people streamed toward the lake: "Some went into the lake itself; some got off in small boats and were out [on the lake] all night before they could get back again."

Mercifully, toward midnight on Monday, rain began to fall. People drifted back next morning to gaze at the ruins. Almost every building in an area of three and a third square miles in the heart of the city had been reduced to smoldering ashes. The property damage was estimated at $200,000,000. Even worse was the human suffering–90,000 left homeless, 300 dead. But already Chicagoans spoke of building a better city–the "fire devils" had destroyed their homes and businesses, but not their spirit. By 1875, only four years later, the city had been so thoroughly rebuilt that few traces of the fire remained. By 1880 the population of Chicago had leaped to 500,000.

THE RISE OF THE CITIES

Cities expand and industry booms, but the "get rich quick" drive brings trouble.

Other cities were growing in the Middle West. St. Louis's 161,000 inhabitants in 1860 had increased to 311,000 by 1870. During the same ten years, Cincinnati's 161,000 grew to 216,000, Cleveland's 43,000 to 93,000 and Detroit's 46,000 to 80,000. In the Far West the liveliest city was San Francisco, with its population of 57,000 in 1860 expanding to 149,000 by 1870. The greatest concentration of growing cities, however, was in that region east of the Ohio River and north of Virginia called the East. Here seven communities were booming:

	POPULATION IN 1860	POPULATION IN 1870
New York City	*806,000*	*942,000*
Philadelphia	*563,000*	*674,000*
Brooklyn	*279,000*	*420,000*
Baltimore	*212,000*	*267,000*
Boston	*178,000*	*251,000*
Washington, D.C.	*61,000*	*109,000*
Pittsburgh	*49,000*	*86,000*

When the Civil War ended, the East was riding high. The expanding West and exhausted South, which was in need of everything, supplied enormous markets for eastern factories. Money was plentiful and a "get-rich-quick" spirit was in the air.

New opportunities for enterprising businessmen took many forms. William Kelley of Pennsylvania invented an air-blast process for burning the carbon out of cast iron so that it could be cheaply converted into steel. This gave new life to the coal, iron, and petroleum industries. It lifted the United States out of the Age of Iron into the Age of Steel. Railroading and steamboating offered other opportunities for quick fortunes. In 1866 Cyrus Field successfully ended his twelve-year struggle to lay the Atlantic cable between the United States and Great Britain, covering 2,000 miles of ocean through water two miles deep. There seemed to be no business project beyong the reach of American know-how.

America's ideas were changing. Where once an American worth $1,000,000 was a rare individual, there were now men worth $10,000,000 and $50,000,000 and $100,000,000. They lived in big mansions and ate dinner with five or six servants serving their meals. Gold plates were set on their tables. Orchestras played soft music while they dined. How had these men grown so wealthy? Who was really paying the bill for such luxury?

No one had to look far for the answer. It was no secret that financiers like Daniel Drew, Jay Gould, and Jim Fisk were reaping millions selling railroad stock not worth the paper it was printed on. It was no secret, either, that graft and corruption were the rule in politics.

New York City had its Tammany "ring" directed by a former chairmaker and volunteer fireman named William Marcy Tweed. "Boss" Tweed and his henchmen skillfully managed to rob the city on a grand scale. A courthouse worth far less cost the taxpayers $8,000,000, and the furnishings for the building added

another $3,000,000. Whatever "Boss" Tweed and his gang controlled—paving contracts, public printing, parks, hospitals, judgeships—brought them millions in graft.

Tweed said to his critics: "What are you going to do about it?" The Tammany politicians knew the source of their strength. American factories, glad to get cheap labor, attracted a steady flow of immigrants from Europe. Tweed had his workers waiting at the docks to meet each boat. There was free beer for every man, a few dollars to tide him over hard times, even help in finding a job. To these people, Tweed was a Robin Hood, robbing the rich to aid the poor. He could count on their votes to keep his own friends in office.

More and more, thoughtful men began to believe that something had to be done about what was happening in America. A few millionaires living in mansions, thousands of poorly paid workers jammed into filthy, run-down tenements—where could this condition lead? Epidemics of smallpox, scarlet fever, and typhoid at one time or another raced through New York, Philadelphia, Boston, Baltimore, and Washington. The workingman began to realize that somehow he must organize if he was to overcome poverty and escape the drab life that surrounded him.

By 1870, labor unions had taken firm root in America, especially among such skilled craftsmen as carpenters and joiners, plasterers, painters, ship carpenters and caulkers, coachmakers, and locomotive engineers. The "Noble Order of the Knights of Labor" was organized in 1869. It represented workmen without regard to skill, occupation, color, citizenship, or sex. A National Labor Reform Party appeared during the political campaign of 1872.

The list of conflicts that would soon tear the nation apart was growing longer from year to year. Debtors were against bankers with their high interest rates. Landless settlers were against speculators and corporation owners on the use of public lands, consumers against manufacturers on the question of tariffs (charges placed on goods produced in foreign countries and brought into the United States) and high prices, and reformers against politicians.

The corrupt Tweed ring in New York City was more the rule than the exception in politics. Americans learned this uneasily during the campaign of 1872, when the Democrats uncovered the scandal of the "Crédit Mobilier." This corporation, formed to control the building of the Union Pacific Railroad, was playing the game of graft by kicking back to those "on the inside" profits they made through governmental help. When members of Congress were shown to be among the insiders, the faith of the public in its political leaders dropped even lower. Clearly, the "get-rich-quick" drive of the nation was heading toward disaster.

During the depression of the 1870's, factories closed, jobs vanished, and the hungry lined up at soup kitchens.

THE PANIC OF 1873

Banks fail, the Stock Exchange closes, and depression grips the country.

The explosion came sooner than anyone had expected. One autumn afternoon in 1873, a newsboy in New York City shouted out the headline that announced the failure of the international banking firm of Jay Cooke and Company.

The prices of stocks and bonds fell like wounded sparrows, and for ten days the Stock Exchange remained closed in the hope of stopping the panic. Yet day by day the dismal truth became clearer. Rare was the businessman who wasn't over his ears in debt. Mortgages were foreclosed, loans called in. Factories shut down or placed their workers on half time. Prices were cut to cost, and often below.

The Panic of 1873 grew into the worst depression the country had known. The city streets were filled with those who could find no jobs. Lawlessness and vice increased. Long lines formed before soup kitchens. In New York City, in mid-January, crowds packed Tompkins Square in a great protest meeting. Young Samuel Gompers, who in future years would become the foremost labor leader in America, was in the throng that morning. He remembered the squadron of police that arrived with nightsticks ready for action:

"Without a word of warning they swept down the defenseless workers . . . using their clubs right and left indiscriminately on the heads of all they could reach.

"Shortly afterward the mounted police charged the crowd on Eighth Street, riding them down and attacking men, women and children without discrimination. It was an orgy of brutality."

But violence could not end a depression. As the years went by, wages fell and the cost of living rose. Misery deepened, especially among those families that depended for their livelihood on such occupations as mining and the making of textiles. The "Molly Maguires," a secret society of workmen, spread terror through the Pennsylvania anthracite coal regions until Federal troops overpowered them. In 1877 trainmen, faced with a ten-per-cent cut in pay, went on strike in Baltimore, Pittsburgh, Buffalo, Chicago, St. Louis, and San Francisco. Again Federal action—this time through the courts—forced them back to work.

PROSPERITY RETURNS

But the young nation was eager to get back to building and growing, to forget the hard times. Gradually, things became better. Businessmen learned to turn waste materials into new products. Foreign markets gave fresh life to many concerns. At a time when Europe's food crops were failing, 1878 and 1879 brought bountiful crops to the United States. The railroads started to build once more. Another flood of immigrants began to pour in.

Proof that Americans were regaining their confidence was the growing interest in sports. The National Baseball League was organized in 1876, roller skating and croquet became national fads, and every town and city had its bicycle club and bicycle races.

AMERICA AND HER WORLD NEIGHBORS

Disputes with Spain and Britain are settled peacefully by diplomats.

Despite the depression, the problems of Reconstruction, and political corruption, during the 1870's America moved steadily toward becoming a world power.

Cubans, long in revolt against Spanish rule, won the warm support of many Americans. A Cuban *junta* (council) in New York City worked openly to outfit expeditions to carry men and war materials to the rebels. However, the Grant Administration, following a policy of not taking sides, declared such acts a violation of international law.

Even so, in late 1873 the United States and Spain came close to war. A Spanish cruiser sighted the steamship *Virginius* flying the American flag off the coast of Cuba. Suspecting that the vessel was carrying men and supplies to the Cuban rebels, the Spaniards forced the *Virginius* into port. Her captain, thirty-six members of the crew, and sixteen passengers were executed.

WAR IS AVOIDED

There was talk of war everywhere in the country. But the governments of Spain and the United States, admitting that there were rights and wrongs on both sides, kept their heads. Spain surrendered the *Virginius* to the United States authorities and made payment for the destruction of American life and property.

Other international disputes were also settled by diplomacy. A difficult argument between Great Britain and the United States for damages to American shipping during the Civil War was decided by arbitration. The United States received $15,500,000 in gold from the British government to make up for losses suffered by American citizens as a result of acts by Confederate raiders, such as the *Alabama,* which had been built in British shipyards. A dispute between Britain and the United States over boundaries on the Pacific coast was referred to the emperor of Germany. Through this settlement, the United States was awarded the San Juan Islands, now part of the state of Washington.

A CENTURY OF FREEDOM

A great world's fair in Philadelphia marks the nation's 100th birthday.

In 1876, Americans looked back with pride on what had been achieved in the century that began with the signing of the Declaration of Independence. In 1776, the Republic had covered an area of 800,000 square miles. Now, only a hundred years later, the nation reached from ocean to ocean, and embraced an area of 3,500,000 square miles of land and water. The population of the colonies had been slightly more than 2,250,000. Now, almost 50,000,000 people lived under the Stars and Stripes.

Americans had many reasons to be proud. Agriculture had become a science. In 1776, cereals, potatoes, flax, and tobacco had been the chief products. In 1876 Americans raised every kind of agricultural product on more than 189,000,000 acres of improved

At the Centennial Exhibition at Philadelphia in 1876, huge crowds admired the exhibits of modern machinery.

Samuel Tilden (left) won the popular vote for president in 1876 but lost to Rutherford B. Hayes (right) in electoral votes.

farm land. American inventors already had greatly reduced the drudgery of farming. Cyrus Hall McCormick had given the farmer a machine to cut grain, and John E. Heath had perfected a machine which not only cut grain but also tied it into bundles. John F. Appleby was working on a threshing machine that would separate the grain from the chaff as the farmer moved along his field. A hundred years ago many an American had plowed with little more than a crooked stick. Now, through the genius of Jethro Wood, the farmer used an iron plow with replaceable parts.

During the same century, an enormous amount mineral wealth had been discovered—coal, copper, petroleum, gold, silver. The Marquette Range of northern Michigan had recently been found to have rich deposits of iron. Coal and iron were the basis of a growing steel industry. The oil wells of northwestern Pennsylvania were creating a new industry of incredible wealth. Lumbering in New England, Michigan, and Wisconsin was still another proof of America's great natural resources.

AMERICAN INVENTIONS

The growth of manufacturing in America had been enormous. Before the Revolution, Great Britain had discouraged any type of industry in order to keep the colonies dependent on the mother country. But once Americans could decide their own way of life, they had moved swiftly ahead. Patent-office records told a dramatic story of how American inventive genius was causing a boom in American industry. In the years from 1790 to 1800, a total of 306 patents was issued; from 1860 to 1870, the total was 79,612. The steamboat, the locomotive, the electromagnetic telegraph, and the sewing machine were all inventions perfected by Americans. Whatever could be made of iron, Americans manufactured. Business houses now carried their customers above the ground floor in the elevator invented by Elisha Graves Otis. Once no two watches in America had been alike, but now watches were manufactured with interchangeable parts, so that they could be turned out by mass production.

American ships, sailing every sea in the world, had increased the value of the nation's exports from $14,262,000 in 1770 to over $600,000,000 in 1875. Once inland travel in America had depended on the pack mule and the canoe, and now railroads and canals linked ocean with ocean. Steamboats had turned the Great Lakes into navigable inland seas.

Education, too, had thrived. In 1776 there had been few colleges in America. Now, a hundred years later, there was 349. The Morrill Act, passed in 1862, offered liberal grants of public land to help states build colleges teaching agriculture and mechanics. The public school population had grown considerably. People read more. In 1776 a printer could produce about 250 newspaper sheets an hour printed on one side; now Robert Hoe's steam-driven "power press" turned out 15,000 complete newspapers an hour, folded for delivery.

CENTENNIAL EXPOSITION

To celebrate these achievements of a century of freedom, a great world's fair was planned. It was held in Philadelphia, where the Declaration of Independence had been signed. Opening in May and closing in November of 1876, the Centennial Exposition drew an attendance of 9,910,965 persons.

In the Main Exhibition Hall, covering twenty-one and a half acres, they visited "the largest building in the world." Here more than thirty countries exhibited products of their science, invention, and industry. One third of the space was required to show the products of America.

In Machinery Hall, covering thirteen acres, they stood before a man-made waterfall thirty-six feet wide and thirty-three feet deep, over which 30,000 gallons of water poured every minute.

In Memorial Hall—also called the Fine Arts Building—they roamed 20,000 feet of floor space to gaze upon an exhibition of paintings and statuary. At the Horticultural Building, surrounded by thirty-five acres of gardens, they gaped at orange and lemon trees and at a century plant about to bloom.

Then they went home—often in luxurious new Pullman cars with a "Hotel Dining Car" and protected by the air brakes that George Westinghouse had invented in 1869. In New York City, they went home to Grand Central Station, completed in 1871, and to the elevated train which, drawn by small steam locomotives, carried passengers up Ninth Avenue.

They went home to the new sports that were now the American's passion—professional baseball, intercollegiate football (first played between Princeton and Rutgers in 1869), lawn tennis (imported from England), and to such farm pastimes as the husking bee, where if a young man happened to find a red ear of corn, he was permitted to kiss any girl present. They went home to pore over the pages of a mail-order catalogue, the first of which was issued by Montgomery Ward & Company in 1873, and to use the typewriter that had been perfected that year.

It seemed that no country could be more wonderful than the one they lived in. They were sure that in the years to come America would be even more wonderful.

THE RETURN OF WHITE SUPREMACY

Tilden loses an election as Republicans and Southern Democrats make a deal.

The year 1876 was also an election year. The Democrats, calling themselves the party of decency and reform, nominated Samuel J. Tilden of New York as their presidential candidate. A corporation lawyer, he had helped to break up the Tweed "ring." The Republican candidate was Rutherford B. Hayes, a Civil War hero, a distinguished lawyer, and a former congressman and governor of Ohio.

The Hayes-Tilden campaign was a vicious one. The Republicans could point to some things that had been accomplished during Grant's eight years in the White House—the adoption of the Fifteenth Amendment (giving the right to vote to all male citizens), the establishment of Yellowstone Park, the completion of the first transcontinental railroad, the admission of Colorado as a state. But Grant had been a weak President. Although he himself was honest, he had done nothing to stop the corruption of other government officials. The Democrats played up the scandals of the Grant administration, blamed it for the long years of depression, and attacked the "Salary Grab Bill of 1873," by which Grant's salary had been raised from $25,000 to $50,000 a year.

Hayes believed that the country was tired of the agitation over Reconstruction and that military rule should end in the South. He was for a sound currency with the government standing behind the paper money, or "greenbacks," it had issued. He supported the small group of Republicans who wanted reforms in the civil service system.

ELECTION DISPUTE

When the votes were counted, they gave Tilden a popular vote of 4,300,590, and Hayes a popular vote of 4,036,298. Tilden had an electoral vote of 184, one short of the number required for election to the presidency, while Hayes had 165. But the election had not yet been decided, for not all the electoral votes were in. Each candidate claimed the twenty votes still due from Florida, South Carolina, Louisiana, and Oregon. The Republicans charged that the voting had been unlawful in the three Southern states, and Congress appointed a special committee to settle the bitter dispute.

Unfortunately for Tilden, this committee played an underhanded game. The Republicans bargained with the Southern Democrats, offering to withdraw Federal troops from the South in return for the electoral votes. This would mean the end of the Reconstruction governments. Negroes would be deprived of their vote, and once more the whites would be supreme in the South. Fifty-six hours before the inauguration, the Democrats agreed. Hayes was given the necessary votes and, in March of 1877, he became the nineteenth President of the United States.

"LEMONADE LUCY"

Hayes and his wife were mild, gentle people. Mrs. Hayes was called "Lemonade Lucy" because she would not serve alcoholic beverages at official functions. But Hayes had a great deal of trouble with his own party during his administration. He believed in making appointments to Federal office on the basis of merit, which angered the politicians who wanted to continue the spoils system. Hayes vetoed a bill that made silver, a less precious metal than gold, the currency supporting greenbacks. The bill was passed over his veto.

Hayes had other troubles, too. Prejudice against Chinese immigrants, who were willing to work for very low wages, led to an outcry against the "Yellow Peril" in the West. Denver was shaken by an uprising against the Chinese, and Congress passed a bill limiting to fifteen the number of Chinese passengers on any ship bound for the United States. Hayes vetoed the bill, but later laws were passed restricting Chinese immigration. A large number of Negroes, seeking escape from the rule of the whites in the South, moved into Kansas and Indiana. The Utes were on the warpath in Colorado. The railroads were paralyzed when trainmen, whose pay had been cut several times, began strikes that led to riots. Some state governors asked for Federal troops to restore order, and Hayes was forced to send soldiers into Pennsylvania and West Virginia.

TWO INVENTORS

The experiments of Bell and Edison lead to great changes in American life.

In the midst of all his difficulties, President Hayes found time to entertain two remarkable men at the White House. They were both inventors, and they were helping to change the pattern of life in America.

One of the two men was Alexander Graham Bell. He had begun his career as an assistant to his father, who had devised a method of teaching the deaf to speak. Bell then taught others how to teach the deaf. His interest in speech and communication led him to experiment with the telegraph, and he invented a telegraphic apparatus that could send a number of messages over a wire at the same time.

Assisted by Thomas A. Watson, a young mechanic, Bell worked at his inventions and experiments for several years. One day, in June of 1873, Bell stood by his receiver trying to hear the signal Watson was sending from the adjoining room. Suddenly the receiver sounded a low twang. Bell rushed into the other room, shouting, "What did you do then? Don't change anything. Let me see."

It turned out that one of the transmitter springs had been stuck, and Watson had plucked the spring to free it. Bell could not hide his excitement. The twang of the spring had come to him over the wire. Then why couldn't other sounds—even the sound of the human voice—be sent over a wire? From there, Bell went on to invent the telephone, which he exhibited at the centennial fair in Philadelphia. On the first day of the fair he demonstrated his invention to the Emperor of Brazil. "My God," said the Emperor, "it talks!"

EDISON'S PHONOGRAPH

President Hayes was fascinated by Bell's story, and he ordered the installation of the first telephone in the White House. The President was just as fascinated by the story of his other famous visitor, Thomas Alva Edison. Edison brought with him his newest invention, the phonograph, or "talking machine." Hayes sat up until three A.M. listening to him.

In 1854, at the age of seven, Edison had moved with his family from Milan, Ohio, to Port Huron, Michigan. His teachers had called him "a dunce," but his mother, who had been a teacher herself, did not agree. The boy was a dreamer, but he was not stupid. He simply liked to work out ideas for himself. Young Tom set up a laboratory in the cellar of his home. To make certain that no one would disturb his equipment, he marked each bottle of his chemicals with the word "poison."

When Edison was twelve, he took a job on the Grand Trunk Railway as a "news butcher," selling newspapers, sandwiches, candy, and peanuts to the passengers. He installed a printing press in a baggage car and issued the *Weekly Herald,* the first newspaper ever published on a moving train. He also cluttered up the baggage car with his laboratory equipment until one day a bottle of phosphorus overturned and set the car on fire.

Out of a job, Edison learned telegraphy, and soon he was an expert at sending and receiving messages. He then began experimenting with electricity, and in 1868 he received his first patent for an electrical vote recorder. He had hoped to sell it to Congress, but he was not successful. Next he built a stock ticker, a telegraphic device that printed on paper tape the results of dealings in the stock market. He sold it for $40,000—twenty times the price he had been prepared to take. By this time he was in his early twenties. He decided to become a "professional inventor" and opened a laboratory at Menlo Park, New Jersey.

Here he often worked eighteen hours a day, forgetting to eat lunch or dinner. Sometimes he slept on a table with a pile of books for a pillow. It was in his laboratory that Edison made a great search for a substance which, when heated by electricity, would give off light without burning to an ash. He tried all sorts of things, from platinum to a hair pulled from the beard of a friend. Finally, on October 19, 1879, he reached the end of his search. A carbon filament shed light for forty hours, and Edison knew he had found the substance he needed.

During his lifetime, Edison would be granted more than 1,200 patents. His inventions, like those of Bell, would help change life in America and the rest of the world.

THE BATTLEGROUND OF POLITICS

Republicans quarrel among themselves, but still manage to get their candidate, James Garfield elected President.

Election campaigns, with their speeches and bands and torchlight parades, were still exciting, but politics had become a routine affair. The Republicans, in power since the elections of 1860, acted as though they expected to occupy the White House forever. Their policies on the tariff, banking, and "sound money" won them the support of businessmen. The Homestead Act won them the support of farmers who raised grain. To Negroes, the Republican Party was the party that had given them freedom. To war veterans, it was the party that had saved the Union. To thousands of other voters, it was the party of Abraham Lincoln. In contrast, the Democrats had only two main sources of strength—the old Confederate states, and the political machines of the big cities of the Northeast.

There were really few issues on which the two parties differed. Though each talked loudly about the tariff, neither changed it to any great extent. Each party had its share of members who favored or opposed the increased use of silver as a basis of currency, and each was equally unwilling to pass laws restricting the activities of "big business."

HALF-BREEDS AND STALWARTS

The real political struggle was largely between two groups within the Republican party itself. They were the Half-Breeds, led by James G. Blaine of Maine, and the Stalwarts, led by Roscoe Conkling of New York. Each group hated the other as much as, if not more than, they hated the Democrats. The dislike did not arise out of any disagreement over policy but out of the division of spoils. To put it another way, to them politics was as much a business as was running a railroad.

Hayes had announced before his election that he would serve only one term as President, and this led to a bitter fight in the Republican convention of 1880. The Half-Breeds rallied behind two candidates—Blaine and Senator John Sherman of Ohio, brother of General Sherman of Civil War fame. The Stalwarts supported a third term for Grant. For more than thirty ballots, neither side could put over a candidate. Then a compromise was reached. Senator James A. Garfield of Ohio, a Half-Breed and a Union veteran, was nominated for President, and Chester Alan Arthur, a Stalwart, for Vice-President. The Democrats also chose a Civil War veteran for their presidential candidate. He was General Winfield Scott Hancock, who had played an important part in the victory at Gettysburg.

Neither party faced up to the issues during the campaign that followed. Each emphasized the war record of its candidate. The decision was close. Garfield received only 9,464 more votes than did his opponent, out of a total of more than 9,000,000 votes cast.

James A. Garfield was the nation's last "log-cabin President." Born in the wilderness of Cuyahoga County, Ohio, he had worked on a farm, driven mules along the towpath of the Ohio Canal, and learned the trade of a carpenter. He paid his own way through Hiram and Williams colleges by teaching English and ancient languages. The working people of America felt that Garfield was one of them. They believed he would stand against big business and fight for the rights of the common man.

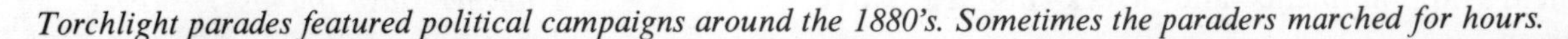

Torchlight parades featured political campaigns around the 1880's. Sometimes the paraders marched for hours.

On July 2, 1881, President Garfield was shot in the railroad station at Washington, D.C. He died ten weeks later.

ASSASSINATION OF GARFIELD

Garfield appoints his political friends to office and is shot by a job seeker.

As Garfield rode down Pennsylvania Avenue on the day of his inauguration, a group of former Confederate soldiers broke through the crowd. They waved the American flag, to show that the wounds of war had healed. On that day Garfield really seemed to be a man of the people

But the people soon found that it was to be "politics as usual" in the White House. Garfield named Blaine as his Secretary of State, and appointed only loyal Half-Breeds to other important Federal offices. The Stalwarts fought back. They threatened to block Garfield's appointments and wreck his legislative program.

Garfield seemed to enjoy this political battle. He was in good spirits as, on a warm July day in 1881, he set off to deliver a commencement address at Williams College. Arm in arm with Blaine, he walked through the waiting room of the Baltimore and Potomac railroad station. He did not notice Charles J. Guiteau, the bearded man who was watching him with wild eyes. Guiteau was a job hunter who had been trying for months to get the President to appoint him as a consul to France. His behavior was strange and he may have been insane.

Guiteau suddenly stepped forward, raised a pistol, and fired two shots. As the President slumped to the floor, Guiteau said, "I am a Stalwart and Arthur is President now." Then, with his pistol still in his hand, he was seized by a group of bystanders.

Guiteau's second shot, entering Garfield's back, lodged deep in his body after fracturing a rib. Alexander Graham Bell was rushed to Washington in the hope that he could locate the bullet with a special electrical device. For ten weeks, while the nation prayed and showered him with gifts, Garfield fought for his life. He was taken to the seashore at Elberon, New Jersey, in the hope that the cooler climate would speed his recovery, but death came on September 19. For the second time in America's history, a President had died from an assassin's bullet. Guiteau was hanged for his crime.

UP FROM SLAVERY

A former slave founds Tuskegee Institute and works to educate his fellow Negroes.

The stories that make headlines in newspapers do not reflect every achievement in a nation's history. In 1881 the headlines told of the death of a President and the battle between the Half-Breeds and the Stalwarts. But 1881 was also the year when Clara Barton founded the American Red Cross. It was the year, too, when a former slave saw a dream come true.

His name was Booker T. Washington. As a boy growing up in Alabama, he had lived in slave quarters where three or four persons slept in a bed. He had eaten enough fat pork and corn bread to hate the sight of them, and he had patiently waited his turn at the table because his family had owned only one fork for five people. Then came the unforgettable day when the boy and his mother were summoned to the "big house." There the Emancipation Proclamation was read to them.

"I am free," young Booker T. Washington thought, enjoying the sound of that wonderful word. But freedom, he believed, had no real meaning without education. Acting on this belief, he walked 300 miles to Hampton Institute in Virginia. In this institution, established in 1868 by the American Missionary Association as a school for Negroes and Indians, Booker T. Washington was an outstanding student.

Returning to Alabama, he dreamed of building a school where other poor Negroes could be educated. He visited typical schools that had been set up for Negroes. They were usually in abandoned log cabins, and taught by teachers who had no training for their jobs. The sight of four or five students sharing one book wrenched his heart. And how could youngsters who ate only fat pork and corn bread develop the strong bodies that should go with alert minds? What these Negroes must be taught, Booker T. Washington decided, was to grow less cotton and more green vegetables.

Despite all the discouragements, the young man planned to open a school that would give Negroes a practical education. Late in 1881, he was ready to receive his first class of thirty students.

His pupils were mainly public school teachers seeking to improve their education, and, Booker T. Washington admitted with good humor, improvement was what they most needed. Many who claimed they had already studied "banking and discount" did not know the multiplication tables. Usually they wanted to take the courses with the longest names and the biggest text books. In a wonderful book about his life, *Up From Slavery,* Washington wrote: "While they could locate the Desert of Sahara or the capital of China on an artificial globe, I found out that the girls could not locate the proper place for knives and forks on an actual dinner table, or the places [where] bread and meat should be set."

Years would pass before Tuskegee Institute would become famous throughout the country as an example of how education could made freedom work for the Negro. But the work began during those last weeks of 1881. Quietly, by stressing the powers of reason, fundamental knowledge, and basic morals, Booker T. Washington was starting a revolution in American education.

Once he needed funds badly and was so discouraged that he was on the point of giving up. Then an old woman entered his office. She was seventy years old, and she hobbled along with a cane. Rags covered her spare shoulders, but they were clean rags. She had no money, but she had brought six eggs she wanted to contribute to the education of Negro boys and girls.

Booker T. Washington never lost heart again. He would go on working night and day—through education he would lead his people up from slavery.

"THE GENTLEMAN BOSS"

Chester A. Arthur becomes President and tries to make government more efficient.

When Chester A. Arthur became President on September 19, 1881, the Stalwarts were overjoyed. Arthur, "the Gentleman Boss," was one of their own kind. He had held an appointment under Grant as collector of the port of New York and had been one of those who had lost their jobs when Rutherford B. Hayes "cleaned house."

But the Stalwarts did not really know their own man. Like Garfield, he refused to take orders from the Stalwarts.

Washington again became a battleground for rival groups within the Republican party. Arthur's triumph came on January 16, 1883, when he signed the Pendleton Civil Service Act. Under this act, a Federal employee who did his job well could not be fired simply because a new President wanted to replace him with one of his own followers. Arthur eliminated fraud from the Post Office Department, and vetoed a rivers and harbors bill that would have provided many new opportunities for graft. He tried also to kill the Chinese Exclusion Bill, which barred immigrants from the Orient, but Congress overrode his veto.

Arthur was a rich man who liked good living and fine clothes. His enemies attacked him for being a dandy and called him a fop for installing the first tiled bathroom in the White House. In spite of their predictions, however, he did not ruin the country.

During Arthur's administration, Brooklyn Bridge, the engineering marvel of the century, was completed. Thousands of people thronged the nation's capital to witness the dedication of the Washington Monument. In 1882, two famous citizens died. One was Henry Wadsworth Longfellow, the poet who wrote *Evangeline* and *Hiawatha.* The other was Ralph Waldo Emerson, the poet, philosopher, and essayist.

Beginning with Lincoln's election in 1860, the Republicans had been successful in putting their man in the White House, but they should have known no political group can hold power forever. They continued to play "politics as usual," and Arthur never had a chance to get the nomination in 1884. After four ballots, the Republicans nominated James G. Blaine.

President Grover Cleveland

CLEVELAND IS ELECTED

The Democrats chose Grover Cleveland. Like Arthur, he was the son of a clergyman. He had been a store clerk, an assistant teacher in an institution for the blind, and a lawyer. In 1863, he was appointed assistant district attorney, then sheriff of Erie County in upstate New York. He later became mayor of Buffalo and governor of New York. He won these offices by fighting stubbornly against the Republicans, who shouted "Shame!" because he had paid $150 for a substitute to fight for him during the Civil War.

"We love him for the enemies he has made," cried the Wisconsin delegate who placed Cleveland's name into nomination at the Democratic convention. Among these enemies was a New York clergyman, who said that a vote for Cleveland was a vote for "rum, Romanism, and rebellion." Many Irish voters took this as an insult to them and their religion, and Cleveland won the election by a majority of 62,683 popular votes. He won the electoral college vote by 219 to 182.

LABOR'S BID FOR POWER

Workingmen join together and fight for their rights with strikes and boycotts.

When Cleveland became President, the working people hoped that he would understand their problems. They were growing restless and dissatisfied. The development of the factory system since the Civil War had made an important change in the way Americans lived.

In earlier times, the American worker had been a craftsman who took deep pride in his work. He owned his own tools. His workshop was often in his own home or in the neighboring cottage of his employer. Worker and employer worked side by side. They knew each other well, and chatted about their families or the small happenings of the day. They were friends who respected each other.

The factory system had no place for pride of craftsmanship or friendship. The worker was no longer a craftsman. He worked at a machine, and had to adapt himself to the pace of the machine. If he quit his job, no one cared. Others could easily be trained to replace him—immigrants who had not yet learned to speak English, Negroes who had been slaves, women, or even children. The working day was long, usually no less than ten hours, and sometimes as much as twelve or fourteen. Wages, on the other hand, were extremely low.

WORKERS AND CORPORATIONS

The worker had lost his independence. He now worked for a corporation owned by stockholders he had never seen. He was directed by men in an office that might be hundreds of miles away—men who had no knowledge of him as a person. The corporation existed only to make profits for its stockholders. When profits fell, wages were cut. A worker who complained too loudly was called a "troublemaker" or an "agitator." If he went on complaining, his name was put on the dreaded "black list." This was a list of "troublemakers" kept by a number of corporations, and they would hire no man whose name was on it.

It was almost impossible for an individual to oppose a corporation. The wealthy corporations were the power behind the politicians, and often they controlled law makers, judges, and juries. The worker did have one weapon with which to fight for better conditions—the strike. But American public opinion in those years was against strikes. Newspapers labeled strikers and strike leaders as dangerous radicals who wanted to destroy the American way of life. The farmer, the businessman, the professional man, and the white-collar worker believed that strikes were a trick of "foreigners" that encouraged the lazy workers and penalized the honest workers. Even the Knights of Labor, an organization of workingmen, sometimes refused to help its own members who had gone on strike.

THE KNIGHTS OF LABOR

Even so, thousands of workers joined the Knights of Labor. Its membership rose from 52,000 in 1883 to 630,000 by October 1886. The principal weapon of the Knights was the boycott—refusing to buy the products of corporations they felt were unfair to workers.

At last, in the late 1800's, all labor was united in a demand for a general law that would limit the working day to eight hours. The workers were no longer afraid to strike, and thousands of them in many trades went on strike for the eight-hour day. A series of demonstrations in a number of cities was set for the first week of May, 1886. Most of them were peaceful enough. In New York City, for example, 20,000 persons gathered to hear the rousing speeches made by their leaders. There was enthusiastic cheering, but no violence. In Chicago, however, the story was different.

THE HAYMARKET RIOT

A protest meeting of workers in Chicago results in violence.

In Chicago, too, the demonstrations began peacefully, with thousands of people parading behind blaring bands. But the workers at the McCormick reaper plant had been on strike for some time, and on May 3 there was a clash between union men and strike-breakers. The police rushed up with nightsticks and pistols, and two men were killed.

A protest meeting was called for the following night, May 4, in a public square known as the Old Haymarket. The newspapers warned that radicals were trying to stir up violence. August Spies, a radical who edited a German-language newspaper, wrote in an editorial: "A war of classes is at hand. Yesterday workingmen were shot down in front of McCormick's factory whose blood cries out for revenge. . . . Whoever is a man must show it today."

A huge crowd was expected at the meeting, but no more than 3,000 persons gathered at the Old Haymarket, and they listened quietly to the speeches.

As the speeches went on, more and more people walked away, until only some 200 persons were left. The meeting was about to break up when 186 policemen marched into the square. The police captain demanded that the crowd instantly disperse.

For a moment nothing happened. Then someone cried out and a bomb burst in the air, killing one policeman and injuring more than 60 people. Wild disorder followed in which six more policemen died and many people were injured. Enraged by these events, the police fired on the crowd, injuring many more people as they fled.

The nation was horrified by the news of the Haymarket riot. No one ever found out who had thrown the bomb. But eight anarchists–radicals who believed in a minimum of government–were arrested and convicted of conspiracy. Four were hanged, one committed suicide, and three were sentenced to prison for life.

Later, in 1893, these three were pardoned by Governor John Peter Altgeld of Illinois. Meanwhile, however, labor had received a crushing blow. The newspapers even attacked the Knights of Labor, which had played no part in the riot. By 1890, its membership had fallen to 100,000.

"BESIDE THE GOLDEN DOOR"

The Statue of Liberty goes up in New York Bay as America continues to grow.

When autumn came in 1886, Americans had something more cheerful to think about–something that filled them with pride. Seven years before, the French sculptor Frederic Auguste Bartholdi had begun work on a colossal statue. It was to be a gift from the people of France to the people of the United States, and the French raised more than 1,000,000 francs to pay for it. Americans raised the money for the construction of the pedestal. Called "Liberty Enlightening the World," the statue was a figure of a woman holding high the torch of freedom. It would stand in New York harbor as "a grand beacon enlightening the waves at the threshold of free America."

Ships filled the harbor, their sirens screaming, when the Statue of Liberty was dedicated on October 28, 1886. President Cleveland, accepting this gift from France on behalf of the American people, said, "We will not forget that Liberty has here made her home." Built of copper, the statue stood 152 feet high on a pedestal almost 150 feet high. Carved

The Statue of Liberty welcomed millions of immigrants.

on the base were these lines by Emma Lazarus that expressed the spirit which had made the country strong and prosperous:

Give me your tired, your poor,
Your huddled masses yearning to breathe free,
The wretched refuse of your teeming shore,
Send these, the homeless, tempest-tossed, to me:
I lift my lamp beside the golden door.

THE WILD WEST SHOW

Not everyone could travel to New York to see the Statue of Liberty, but thousands of Americans saw Buffalo Bill's traveling Wild West show. "Buffalo Bill" was William F. Cody, who had won fame as a scout in the Sioux-Cheyenne country. His star attraction was Annie Oakley, "Little Sure Shot," who at thirty paces could hit a dime tossed into the air.

Thousands, too, were reading Mark Twain's new book, *Huckleberry Finn.* Others were enjoying Frances Hodgson Burnett's *Little Lord Fauntleroy.*

Americans had only to look around them to see how the country was growing and changing. Skyscrapers and apartment houses were going up in cities like Chicago and New York. An electric streetcar was in operation in Cleveland, and a factory with automatic machinery for making tin cans opened in Baltimore. Before 1883, Americans had worked and played on "sun time," but now four standard time zones had been established.

Pittsburgh was no longer the only city that manufactured steel. Birmingham, Alabama, which had been the site of a cotton field in 1870, had grown into a thriving steel center because of the nearby deposits of iron ore and coal. And Grand Rapids, Michigan, was already known as the furniture capital of America.

The nation's inventors were busy, turning out new devices for businesses and homes. William Seward Burroughs invented the adding machine and William L. Brundy the time clock. George Eastman of Rochester, New York, offered for sale the first Kodak camera—price, $250. Printing and publishing were revolutionized by Ottmar Mergenthaler's Linotype machine and Frederic E. Ives' new process of halftone engraving.

A MINORITY PRESIDENT

Cleveland gets a higher popular vote, but Benjamin Harrison becomes President.

The Democrats nominated Grover Cleveland to run for re-election in 1888. The Republicans chose Benjamin Harrison, the grandson of William Henry Harrison, the famous old Indian fighter who had been the ninth President of the United States. Aside from his name and the fact that he had once attended a log schoolhouse, Harrison was not a very colorful candidate. He had been a lawyer and a brigadier general in the army, had failed in a bid for the governorship of Indiana, and had served one term in the Senate.

BUSINESS SUPPORTS HARRISON

Anxious to regain power, the Republicans campaigned for all they were worth. The big issue was the tariff. Cleveland wanted some mild reforms, while Harrison promised high tariffs. The Republicans charged that Cleveland's policies would ruin American business and American labor as well. Businessmen rallied behind Harrison. They contributed large sums of money to his campaign, and warned that if Cleveland were elected they would be forced to close down their factories and throw thousands of people out of work.

On top of this, Cleveland antagonized Union veterans. He approved a recommendation that battle flags captured during the Civil War be returned to the former Confederate states. The flags were national property and could not be returned without an act of Congress; nevertheless, the move cost Cleveland a great number of votes.

Two weeks before the election, the Republicans had a stroke of luck. It seemed that the British minister had written a letter hinting that Cleveland would be more friendly to England than Harrison would. This angered Irish-Americans, who had no love for the British, and cost Cleveland still more votes.

Even so, Cleveland got 100,000 more popular votes than Harrison. But Harrison carried the electoral college vote, 233 to 169, and became the "minority President."

Harrison moved into the White House, where he was afraid to turn off the electric lights and would not push the buttons on the electric bells for fear they would harm him. Harrison himself was honest, but he allowed the Republican politicians to run his administration. They chose his Cabinet; they rewarded their friends and the businessmen who had supported them.

THE McKINLEY TARIFF

Just as they had promised, the Republicans put through a bill for a high tariff. Introduced by William McKinley, a congressman from Ohio, it was called the McKinley Tariff. The best that could be said for it was that it puzzled its supporters as well as its foes. For example, a high duty was placed on tin plate, which was not being manufactured anywhere in the United States. High duties were also placed on butter and eggs, although no one could say when the importation of these products had threatened the American farmer.

Also passed during Harrison's administration was a pension bill which gave a small pension to war veterans incapable of doing hard work, and the Silver Purchase Act. The Silver Purchase Act began to drain the gold from the treasury, but it pleased the farmers and the states that produced silver.

Altogether, Harrison's record as President was not very impressive.

END OF THE FRONTIER

In twenty-four hours, 50,000 settlers claim land in the Oklahoma Territory.

The West was rapidly becoming settled; the frontier was vanishing. During the four years that Harrison was in the White House, six new states—Washington, Montana, North Dakota, South Dakota, Idaho, and Wyoming—were admitted to the Union. And on April 22, 1889, the Oklahoma Territory was opened to homesteaders.

Later, Oklahoma was known as the "Sooner State" and its people were called "Sooners." The reason was that many homesteaders sneaked in to stake out their claims before the official opening of the territory. But there were many more who waited, and they made the Oklahoma land rush a memorable event in American history.

A reporter for the St. Louis *Globe-Democrat,* watching a trainload of homesteaders on that exciting day, told his readers that "what happened when the train began to slacken beggars all description." From the platform of the train leaped boys and old men, all caught up in "a wild rush." Some insisted on carrying the baggage they had brought, but others threw their carpetbags away so that they could move faster. From townsite to townsite, passengers kept jumping off before the train stopped in order to get a head start on their companions. A man with a wooden leg was among those the reporter saw make such a leap—and the man was up and hustling on his way again in the wink of an eye.

In all directions the homesteaders sped, looking for choice lots to claim. A stake driven into the ground, with name attached, established a claim. Then the ground was paced off, and the distance depended on whether the lot was to be used for a home, place of business, or both. The reporter estimated that 6,000 people crowded into the town of Guthrie within three hours after the territory had been legally opened. Hack drivers stood by the railroad sidings, shouting: "This way for lots at a dollar apiece!"

Within twenty-four hours, 50,000 settlers rushed into the Oklahoma Territory. Not for eighteen years, however, did Oklahoma become a state—the forty-sixth in the Union. By that time the Twentieth Century had begun, bringing still more changes to the nation.

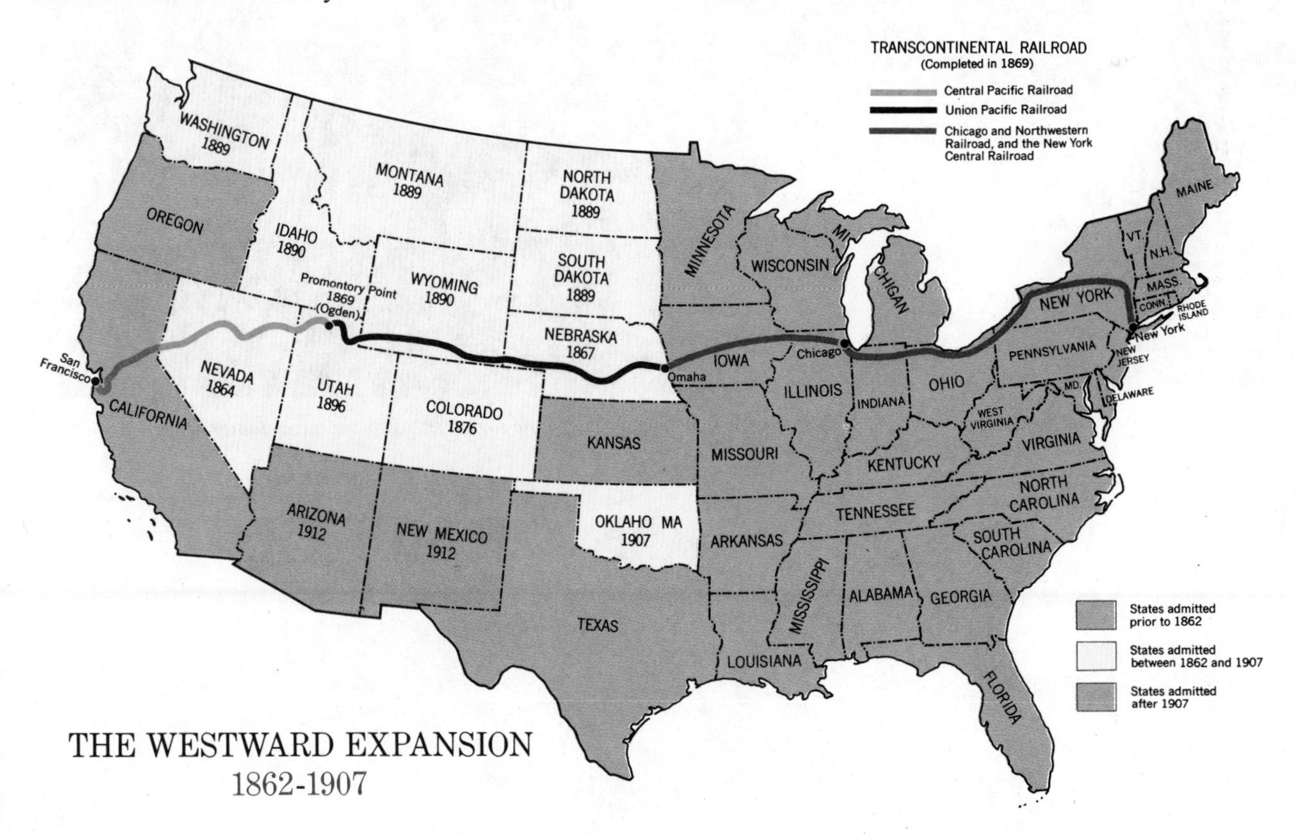

THE WESTWARD EXPANSION
1862-1907

The Panama Canal, opened in 1914, uses a series of locks to raise or lower ships to the next water level.

VII ~ THE AGE OF STEEL

from 1889 to 1917

DISASTER, GHOST DANCERS, AND VIOLENCE

A flood, unrest among the Indians, and labor violence trouble America.

By the 1880's America was like a big, awkward youngster. It was growing, it was increasing in strength, it had a promising future. And, like many growing youngsters, it had problems.

The month of May, 1889, began happily. In New York City there was a celebration of the centennial (one hundredth) anniversary of Washington's inauguration as President. But the closing days of the month brought disaster in Pennsylvania. It struck at Johnstown, a town of rolling mills, steel mills, and wireworks on the banks of the Conemaugh River. In the hills behind Johnstown was a dam than held back a lake three miles long and one mile and a quarter wide. After several days of unusually heavy rains, some people warned that the dam was in poor condition and the town might be in danger. Few inhabitants worried. They had heard such warnings before and nothing had happened.

In the afternoon of May 31, there was a tremendous crash up in the hills. With a great roar, a wall of water forty feet high and an eighth of a mile wide rushed down on Johnstown. "A hundred houses were swept away in a few minutes," one survivor recalled. Another described the scene as the dam gave way: "I looked up and saw something that looked like a wall of houses and trees up the valley. The next moment Johnstown seemed coming toward me. It was lifted right up, and in a minute was smashing against the bridge, and the houses were flying in splinters across the top and into the water beyond."

The Johnstown flood was one of the worst disasters in the nation's history. More than 2,000 persons died in two and a half hours. The wall of water smashed four square miles of houses. The heroines of this frightful day were Mrs. Ogle and her daughter, who managed the local Western Union office. In spite of danger, Mrs. Ogle stayed by her telegraph key, sending warnings of the approaching flood to other communities in the Conemaugh Valley. Finally she clicked out the words: "This is my last message." A few moments later, mother and daughter drowned in the raging water.

By May of the following year, there were reports of a new religion that was spreading among the Indians of the plains. Based partly on Christianity, it taught that the Messiah would soon appear. At the same time, the dead Indians would come back to life in the "Return of the Ghosts." The tribes would get back their old hunting grounds, and once more vast herds of buffalo would roam the plains.

The United States government had made many treaties with the Indians, but had broken one after another. Pushed around by the white man, living lives of hardship in a land no longer theirs, the Indians turned eagerly to the new religion. Hopefully they danced the "Ghost Dance," preparing for the coming of the Messiah and the return of the dead. The old chief of the Sioux, Sitting Bull, used the new religion to stir up feeling against the white man. The Sioux warriors, streaked with war paint, burned and pillaged the cabins of settlers.

The government sent troops after the Sioux, and in December they captured Sitting Bull. More than 200 Indian men, women, and children were slaughtered in the Battle of Wounded Knee, at Wounded Knee Creek, South Dakota. Even worse, the American people failed to realize that they had brought on the tragedy themselves by their shameful treatment of the Indians.

THE HOMESTEAD STRIKE

Violence of another kind broke out in 1892. At Homestead, Pennsylvania, on the banks of the Monongahela River a few miles from Pittsburgh, stood a great ironworks belonging to the Carnegie Steel Company. In June the company announced that wages would be cut because "improvements in the plant enabled the men to make a greater output with the same amount of labor."

The workers at Homestead called a strike, and the company tried to carry on operations with strikebreakers. To protect the strikebreakers, the company hired about 300 armed guards from the Pinkerton Detective Agency in Chicago.

On the night of July 6, the Pinkertons came down the river on barges. Thousands of angry strikers lined the banks of the Monongahela. The Pinkertons tried to reason with the workers, but the conference was broken off by a shot. The firing became general and went on throughout the next day in a somewhat halfhearted manner until the armed guards agreed to surrender on the promise of safe-conduct. Already eleven workmen and six Pinkerton men had been killed and a number wounded on both sides. But the fury of the workers at these imported strikebreakers would not be so easily satisfied. A new burst of rioting shook Homestead, and at least another hundred Pinkerton men were seriously injured.

Poor Benjamin Harrison, living out his last cheerless year in the White House, saw the country swept by labor trouble. State militia restored peace in Homestead, but disorders in the mining regions of Idaho became so serious that the President rushed Federal troops to the scene. Thousands of National Guardsmen were sent to Buffalo, New York, to end a strike called by railroad switchmen. In Tennessee a revolt against the system of employing convicts in mines also had to be put down by military force.

Despite growing dissatisfaction with Harrison even within his own party, he won re-nomination for the presidency at the Republican convention in 1892. The illness of his wife kept him at the White House, away from the last act of his administration that might have given him some pleasure—the dedication of the grounds for the World's Columbian Exposition in Chicago. In place of the President, Vice-President Morton attended the ceremonies held along the shores of Lake Michigan on October 12, 1892, the 400th anniversary of Columbus' discovery of America.

The fair opened on May 1, 1893, and more than 27,000,000 Americans visited the great "White City" that rose on the Chicago lake front. There they were dazzled by the beautiful buildings and landscaping. With its bright lights and twelve great 100-horsepower generators the fair showed how electricity was becoming a servant of America. Visitors who strolled the Midway could enjoy all kinds of amusements, including the Ferris wheel built by an engineer named G. W. G. Ferris. He had been asked to construct a novelty that would equal the Eiffel Tower in Paris, and had succeeded handsomely.

"WE'LL BE IN CLOVER"

The Panic of 1893 and more labor strife mark Cleveland's second term.

When Grover Cleveland left the White House at the end of his first term in 1888, Mrs. Cleveland told a White House attendant: "I want to find everything just as it is now when we come back . . . four years from today."

In 1892, there was at least the chance that she would return to the White House, for Cleveland was nominated for the presidency. As they campaigned for their candidate, the joyful Democrats chanted:

Grover! Grover! Four more years of Grover!
Out they go, in we go; then we'll be in clover!

And when the election returns were in, something had happened for the first and only time in American history. A President who had been defeated after his first term had been re-elected.

Cleveland faced a difficult task, for the country was on the verge of financial panic. Thousands of farmers were losing their farms because they could not repay money they had borrowed to buy machinery, tools, and seed. Railroads were going bankrupt and shutting down. Labor disputes spread.

Cleveland was a "hard money" man who favored gold as the basic support of the nation's currency. He soon found himself in a struggle with the miners, farmers, and businessmen who wanted the government to buy more silver in order to provide "cheap money." They believed that the unlimited use of silver would solve all of the country's problems, as shown by the little verse they liked to chant:

The dollar of our daddies
Of silver coinage free
Will make us rich and happy,
Will bring prosperity.

In June, only a few months after Cleveland took office, the stock market crashed and the Panic of 1893 was on in full swing. Railroads failed, banks closed, and millions of workers lost their jobs. In the West, the jobless seized trains, demanding free transportation to Washington so that they could lay their grievances before Congress. Jacob S. Coxey, a successful businessman of Massilon, Ohio, had some ideas on what should be done to remedy the situation. With 400 followers, who were called "Coxey's Army," he marched to Washington, arriving on April 30, 1894.

Coxey wanted to ask Congress to put the jobless to work on the construction of highways and other public projects at government expense. But Coxey's Army was turned back by the Washington police. People who were unemployed or had had their wages cut complained that "Cleveland and his gang" didn't care if they starved to death. Labor grew more and more restless in 1894, until about 690,000 workers were involved in strikes.

THE PULLMAN STRIKE

The pretty little town of Pullman, on the outskirts of Chicago, became the center of the struggle between workers and employers. Here lived 5,500 people who worked for the Pullman Palace Car Company, which made luxury railroad cars. Pullman was a town of fine public buildings, good schools, churches and playgrounds, and shaded walks and gardens—all owned by the company. Unions were not permitted.

"We were born in a Pullman house," grumbled one resident, "fed from the Pullman shop, taught in the Pullman school, catechized in the Pullman church, and when we die we shall be buried in the Pullman cemetery and go to the Pullman hell."

Although the earnings of the company remained high, in the spring of 1894 the management decided to cut wages by an average of twenty-five per cent. Work schedules were changed to force the men to work shorter hours, cutting their pay still further. When the workers offered to negotiate the cut in wages, the company replied that there was "nothing to arbitrate." On May 11, 1894, the Pullman workers went on strike.

The previous June, a new leader had appeared in

the ranks of labor. He was Eugene V. Debs, and already his new American Railway Union had 150,000 members. Debs said: "The forces of labor must unite. The dividing lines must grow dimmer day by day . . . [we must] march together, vote together and fight together, until working men shall enjoy all the fruits of their toil."

Debs and his American Railway Union supported the strikers at Pullman. Members of the union refused to handle Pullman cars, a decision that affected major railroads in twenty-seven states. The railroad owners, organized into the General Managers' Association, decided to fight back. Workers who refused to handle Pullman cars were fired on the spot. Strikebreakers were hired. On July 7, the Chicago correspondent of the Washington *Post* reported: "War of the bloodiest kind is imminent in Chicago." Mobs burned and looted railroad cars. Violence spread.

The Attorney General in Cleveland's administration was Richard Olney, who had been a lawyer for the railroads. Olney argued that, since the strike interfered with the delivery of the United States mail, Federal troops could be used to break the strike. John P. Altgeld, the governor of Illinois, protested violently. He said that the state militia was fully capable of handling any disorders that might occur. Cleveland shared Olney's attitude toward labor, and he ordered Federal troops into Chicago to put down the strike by force. This was a crushing defeat for labor, and made Cleveland unpopular as he neared the end of his second term.

In spite of the hard times, American inventors were still busy, turning out devices for entertainment and convenience. Thousands of Americans were already finding enjoyment in the stereoscope, a simple optical instrument through which pictures could be viewed in three dimensions. At West Orange, New Jersey, Thomas Edison built the world's first motion-picture studio. And in Detroit, Michigan, people were getting a glimpse of an invention that would have an enormous effect on their future.

The railroad yards at Pullman, Illinois, became the scene of one of the most violent strikes in labor history.

PUTTING AMERICA ON WHEELS

Henry Ford builds a "gasoline buggy" and a new era begins.

In 1893, Henry Ford was thirty years of age, and the only real quarrel in his life had been with his father, who had wanted him to be a farmer. But young Henry wanted to be a mechanic and to do so had struck off on his own.

He was a hard worker, especially when tinkering with any kind of steam engine. He dreamed about steam engines and read about them whenever he could, but his greatest knowledge came through working with them. His ambition in his early years in Detroit, he once said, was "to lift farm drudgery off flesh and blood and lay it on steel and motors." Steam engines could do that, he believed. But after building a steam car, Henry realized he was on the wrong track, for, as he said, "sitting on a high-pressure steam boiler is not altogether pleasant."

Seeking a substitute for a steam boiler, Henry Ford turned to the gasoline-driven cylinder engine. By 1890 he was working on a double-cylinder engine. He planned at first to mount his engine on a bicycle, but when he thought of placing engine, gasoline tank, and controls on such a vehicle, he realized that the idea wouldn't work.

So he constructed a "horseless buggy" instead, and if the job went slowly he wasn't surprised. After all, he worked twelve hours a day for a living, which left him only twelve hours a day to work at home. By 1893, Ford's first automobile was ready for its road test. Although not perfect, it was superior to other American automobiles of that period. With dust flying, it sped along at 25 miles an hour.

"My gasoline buggy," Henry Ford recalled, "was the first and for a long time the only gasoline automobile in Detroit. It was considered to be something of a nuisance, for it made a racket and it scared horses. Also it blocked traffic. For if I stopped my machine anywhere in town a crowd was around it before I could start it up again. If I left it alone for even a minute, some inquisitive person always tried to run it. Finally, I had to carry a chain and chain it to a lamp post whenever I left it anywhere."

Henry Ford's first "gasoline buggy" was an odd-looking contraption, but it ran.

Ford finally sold his first car for $200, and he used the money to build another car. In time, those two cars would become four, then 4,000,000, then 40,000,000. So, as horses reared back and squawking chickens raced across the road, Americans in the 1890's were looking into their future, glimpsing it through clouds of swirling dust.

"CROSS OF GOLD"

William Jennings Bryan makes a famous speech, but McKinley is elected President.

When the Democratic National Convention was held in Chicago in 1896, it looked as though there would be a battle between the "gold" Democrats of the East and the "free-silver" Democrats of the West. The disagreement between the two groups had been growing for years. Throughout much of the Nineteenth Century, the United States had followed a policy of bimetallism—that is, the currency was based on two metals, gold and silver. The nation's paper money could be exchanged for either gold or silver at the United States Treasury. The value of the two metals was fixed by law at a ratio of sixteen to one—sixteen ounces of silver were worth one ounce of gold.

But the law could not fix the value of the metals in the business markets. Silver from the mines of the West was cheap and plentiful, and a man could get more than sixteen ounces of it for an ounce of gold in the open market. He could then take his silver to the Treasury, exchange it at sixteen to one, and make a profit.

"Hard money" men feared that this would drain away the Treasury's gold and weaken the nation's currency. They wanted the money of the United States to be backed up by gold alone. But the people of the western states that depended on silver mining wanted bimetallism continued. In 1900 the United States would indeed abandon bimetallism and go on the gold standard, but in 1896 money was an important political issue.

The "gold" Democrats—the "hard money" men—failed to reckon with William Jennings Bryan. A Nebraska farm boy from the region of the Platte River, he had been a congressman from 1891 to 1895. He was strongly in favor of bimetallism. Bryan was a powerful orator, and standing before the convention in 1896, he made one of his greatest speeches. He said:

"Having behind us the producing masses of this nation and the world, supported by the commercial interests, and the laboring interests, and the toilers everywhere, we will answer their demand for a gold standard by saying to them: You shall not press down upon the brow of labor this crown of thorns, you shall not crucify mankind upon a cross of gold."

Bryan's "Cross of Gold" speech had a tremendous effect on the convention, and on the fifth ballot he became the Democratic nominee for President. The delegates cheered wildly as he promised to stump the country and carry the campaign for bimetallism directly to the people.

In contrast, William McKinley, the Republican candidate, decided on a quiet campaign from the front porch of his home in Canton, Ohio. He said that the country was once more becoming prosperous and that the nation needed conservative policies. The Democrats struck back. They called McKinley the high-tariff candidate who stood for the "rule of the rich" and they alleged that he had sold his soul to Mark Hanna, the multimillionaire political boss of Ohio.

Bryan's "Cross of Gold" speech to the Democratic convention in 1896 won him the presidential nomination.

Stereoscopes, which showed pictures in three dimensions, were popular in the 1880's.

There were certain things about McKinley as a man that appealed to Americans. One was his relationship with his wife. She had epilepsy, and he would not leave her even to campaign for the presidency. And he had worked his way up to the top by his own efforts. He had been a schoolteacher, a post-office clerk, and a struggling young lawyer. At the age of thirty-four he had been elected to Congress, where he served almost twelve consecutive years. He had also served in the Civil War, rising to the rank of major. Veterans of "the bloodiest day of the war" at Antietam would never forget how he had hurried two wagonloads of hot coffee and other refreshments to the hottest spot in the fighting.

Bryan traveled the country and made more than 600 speeches, calling for free silver and an end to "the rule of the rich." But he could not compete with the calm, dignified McKinley. McKinley stood for success and "hard money," and he represented

Fiery smoke billowed into the night air at Havana as an explosion sank the Maine*—and started the Spanish-American War.*

the economic power of the East. Furthermore, the Democrats could raise little money for Bryan's campaign, while Mark Hanna and his friends contributed large sums to the Republicans. The election returns showed a clear-cut victory for McKinley. He won the popular vote by a margin of 601,854, and the electoral college vote by 271 to 176.

The voters were pleased. They were sure that under McKinley they could relax and enjoy prosperity and "the full dinner pail." They did not know that America would soon be at war.

"REMEMBER THE MAINE"

An American battleship is blown up in Cuba, leading to war between the United States and Spain.

On the night of February 15, 1898, the carnival season opened in Havana, the capital of Spain's colony of Cuba. Cubans roamed the streets in gay masquerade costumes. Laughter and music filled the air. Colored lanterns, swaying in a gentle breeze, shed a bright glow upon gardens and courtyards. Cuba seemed a gay and contented land that evening.

But the Cubans, far from being contented, were close to revolt against their Spanish masters. To protect American lives and property from the civil war that could break out at any moment, the United States had sent the battleship *Maine*. All was quiet aboard the ship as she rode at anchor in Havana harbor. The boatswain's mates had "piped down" for the night, and sentries watchfully paced to and fro. The inspection of the ammunition magazines had been completed and the keys handed to the captain. The time was about ten o'clock.

As Havana laughed and sang and danced, a tremendous explosion suddenly shook the city. Broken window glass fell on cobbled streets. Houses rocked on their foundations. Captain Sigsbee of the *Maine* said afterward: "I find it impossible to describe the sound or shock, but the impression remains of something awe-inspiring, terrorizing; of noise, rending, vibrating, all-pervading." Stunned, the people stared at one another. What could it mean? An earthquake? Then a voice, screaming through the night, gave the answer:

"In the harbor. The American battleship. It's blown up!"

Now the sky above the harbor was ablaze with an intense light. Great masses of twisted iron plates and beams, hurled into the air, had crashed down on the deck. A smokestack and the foremast had been swept away. A fire, raging amidships, exploded an occasional shell whose fragments tore through the air.

Quickly the battleship sank, bow first. Men drowned in their quarters. A nearby Spanish warship lowered her boats and rushed to the rescue of Americans clinging to pieces of wreckage. But the casualties aboard the *Maine* that night were terrible. Two officers and 258 sailors were killed.

Next day Americans read of the tragedy in Havana harbor. The more sensational newspapers—the so-called "yellow press"—openly accused Spain of blowing up the ship and called for an immediate declaration of war. President William McKinley kept his head and ordered a thorough investigation of the explosion. An investigating committee of American naval officers concluded that the ship had been sunk by a mine or torpedo exploded under her hull. Yet they could not say who had been responsible for the explosion. The Spanish government reasonably offered to submit the question to arbitration.

The editorial writers for the yellow press would not let up. Did any sane person, they thundered, doubt for an instant that the explosion had been the deliberate act of an agent of Spain? "Remember the *Maine*," they kept repeating. "Remember the *Maine*."

CUBA UNDER SPAIN

For some years, Americans had been disturbed by Spain's oppressive rule of Cuba. Spain held Cuba by force and cared little about what happened to its people. The Cubans paid heavy taxes, and the money was used, not for their benefit, but to support Spanish troops and officials, and to cover the cost of police actions against rebellious villagers. A financial depression in 1893 made conditions still worse. Even the Cubans who had jobs in the cane fields and sugar mills earned barely enough to keep from starving.

Thousands of Cubans joined a movement for independence. Their slogan was *Cuba libre*—"free Cuba." Determined to destroy everything of value to Spain, they burned cane fields and sugar mills to the ground. In 1896, Spain sent more troops and a new captain general, Valeriano Weyler, who soon became known in the United States as "Butcher" Weyler. He put down the rebellion without mercy. Cubans were herded into concentration camps, and famine and disease spread over the land. Americans sent food and medicine through the Red Cross, and Clara Barton, founder of the American Red Cross, went to Cuba to make sure that they reached the people. In 1897, at the insistence of the United States government, Weyler was recalled and a more moderate general took his place.

Conditions improved somewhat, but they were still very bad. American newspapers said that it was the duty of the United States to protect its little island neighbor. Congressmen demanded that the United States intervene in Cuba. This demand was backed by many clergymen, who told their congregations that freeing Cuba would be an act of humanity and Christianity. Grover Cleveland refused to interfere in Cuba, and McKinley continued the same policy. Intervention could mean war, and he felt that the nation was not prepared to fight a war.

The sinking of the *Maine* brought the American people closer to accepting war as the only real solution to the Cuban problem. Whipped up by the newspapers, public opinion in favor of war grew stronger and stronger. At last it grew so strong that McKinley had to take action. He asked Spain to improve certain conditions in Cuba and declare a truce there until October 1. Spain agreed to everything he asked except for declaring a truce. By April 10, Spain had decided to agree to the truce as well, but it was too late. Dropping his policy of caution, McKinley had swung over to the side of those who wanted war and was already preparing a message to Congress. The message was given the next day, and in it McKinley barely mentioned the fact that Spain had agreed to all of his demands. Congress took the message as a call for war, and on April 19 it recognized Cuba's independence. It authorized the President to demand that Spain withdraw from Cuba and to use force if Spain refused. The United States pledged to leave Cuba after independence had been gained.

Spain's answer, on April 24, was to declare war. The next day Congress formally declared that a state of war had existed since April 21.

VICTORY IN MANILA BAY

Commodore George Dewey batters a Spanish fleet in the Philippines.

Quickly the country mobilized for war. Camps at Chickamauga Park (Tennessee), Tampa, Mobile, and New Orleans resounded with the tramp of marching feet and the hoarse shouts of drill sergeants. A squadron of warships steamed out of Key West, Florida, to blockade Havana and the northern coast of Cuba. The American gunboat *Nashville*, overtaking the Spanish ship *Buena Ventura*, fired the first shot of the war on April 22.

But America's first great victory came more than halfway around the world from Cuba. On the first day of May, a naval fleet under Commodore George Dewey arrived at Manila Bay, gateway to the capital of the Spanish-held Philippine Islands. Dewey took his cruisers into the bay under the cover of darkness. The dawn, beginning to break at about half past four o'clock, revealed the American warships strung out in battleline. Aboard the flagship *Olympia,* as the clock ticked toward six o'clock, Dewey turned to the ship's captain and said:

"You may fire when you are ready, Gridley."

A 250-pound shell from one of the *Olympia's* eight-inch guns soared toward Cavite fort. The heavy guns roared on the cruisers *Baltimore* and *Boston.* Answering shots from the fort and Spanish warships in the bay sent the water splashing around the American vessels.

THE SPANISH ARE DEFEATED

Dewey's bluejackets jeered at the poor marksmanship of the Spaniards. The Americans stood by their guns, stripped to the waist. A blazing sun beat down on their naked chests and backs. They watched as the *Olympia* steamed toward a Spanish ship, the *Reina Christina.* No one spoke. The blowers whirred, the engines throbbed. Suddenly a shell burst directly above the *Olympia.* At the after gun, the boatswain's mate gave a shout: "Remember the *Maine*!" Five hundred bluejackets took up the chant.

The engineer watched the battle from the deck of the *Olympia*: "It was something dreadful, the hail of fire that struck and was striking the *Reina Christina.* The *Olympia's* eight-inch guns shot away the bridge, with the Admiral and staff and several young officers. In a few minutes she turned tail, and as she did we sent another eight-inch [shell] through her stern . . . About half past eight the Spaniards were demoralized, so that the *Olympia* pulled out of the fight, but the rest of the fleet made another evolution [circle] before coming out to us. The Spaniards fought bravely, and died to a man with their colors flying and their ships burning about them."

By half past twelve in the afternoon the Battle of Manila Bay was over. The Spaniards had taken enough. Their shore batteries had been silenced, and every ship, as Dewey said, had been "sunk, burned, or deserted." Four hundred of their men were killed or wounded. Amazingly, not a single American had been killed. Dewey then captured Cavite fort and awaited the arrival of U.S. land forces that later took Manila.

The nation went wild with joy when it learned of the smashing victory at Manila Bay. Dewey became everyone's hero. The President made him a rear admiral. Congress unanimously voted its thanks and commendation.

Teddy Roosevelt went on from buffalo hunting in North Dakota to become a national war hero, then President.

TEDDY AND THE ROUGH RIDERS

Theodore Roosevelt leads a famous charge up Cuba's San Juan Hill.

Another man who would soon become a hero was Theodore Roosevelt. Teddy, as everyone called him, had been a frail youngster, suffering from asthma and weak eyes. But he had courage and energy, and he built up his body by exercise. He bounced through Harvard, spent a brief period as a law student, and wrote *The Naval War of 1812,* one of the dullest books in any library. He tried ranching on the Little Missouri River in North Dakota, hunted buffalo, lived as a cowboy, and helped to capture three thieves in the wildest part of the North Dakota Badlands. "By Godfrey, but this is fun!" he said. He wrote another book, *The Winning of the West,* which was filled with high spirits and showed his feeling for the outdoor life.

Roosevelt brought the same kind of energy to his political career. He was a "goo-goo"—that is, a reformer who fought the political bosses. Roosevelt enjoyed the fight. He won a seat in the New York Assembly at the age of twenty-three, but failed in his campaign to become mayor of New York City. He was appointed by both Harrison and Cleveland to the Civil Service Commission, resigning in 1895 to become police commissioner of New York City. He worked hard campaigning for McKinley, who named him Assistant Secretary of the Navy.

When war came, Roosevelt was not satisfied to sit at a desk. He resigned his job and, with Leonard Wood, he organized the First United States Volunteer Cavalry regiment. The men in this famous outfit, known as the Rough Riders, were carefully selected. Roosevelt wanted only "young, good shots, and good riders," and his troops included cowboys and Indians from Arizona, New Mexico, and Oklahoma, football players from eastern colleges, and polo players from Long Island.

The American plan of action in Cuba called for the capture of a Spanish fleet under Admiral Pascual Cervera, which was anchored in Santiago harbor on the southeastern coast of Cuba. The U.S. Navy's North Atlantic fleet waited outside the harbor, challenging the Spanish vessels to come out. Meanwhile, American troops under Major General W. R. Shafter went ashore a few miles east of Santiago. The object was to catch the Spanish fleet between the American land and naval forces.

The landings in Cuba met with little opposition, and the Americans sneered at the Spanish troops. But a stiff little battle to capture an enemy outpost at Las Guásimas taught the Americans that the Spanish were equipped with modern weapons and knew how to use them.

Dewey's route and maneuvers in the Battle of Manila Bay.

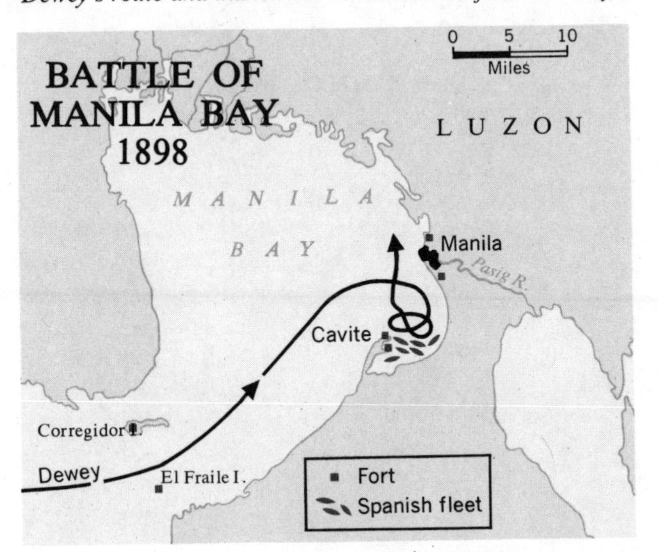

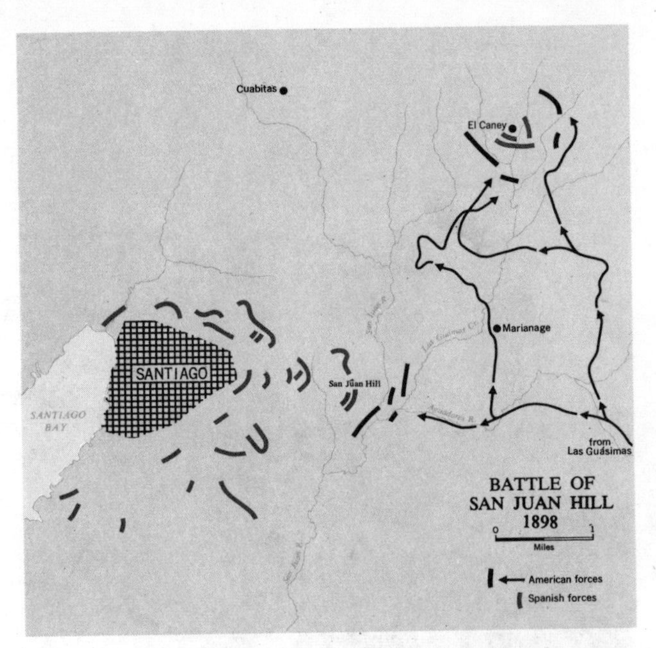

Capture of San Juan Hill and the El Caney heights gave the Americans command of Santiago in eastern Cuba.

THE JUNGLE WAR

Much of Cuba was covered with jungle, which made the movement of troops extremely difficult. The heat drained a man's energy, and as the raw American troops pushed on toward Santiago they discarded their heavy equipment. Rough, sunken roads added to their misery, and heavy showers warned that the torrential rains of the Cuban summer would soon be upon them. Many of the troops were stricken with malaria.

The key to the capture of Santiago was San Juan Hill. It was a nasty place to fight. Smooth, slippery guinea grass covered the slopes. Red flowers of flame trees grew around the blockhouses occupied by the Spaniards. The battle started early in the morning of July 1, and the Rough Riders took part in it, led by Teddy Roosevelt and Colonel Leonard Wood.

Except for Roosevelt, the Rough Riders were dismounted, for this hill could only be taken on foot. Roosevelt knew that horse soldiers hate to be dismounted. It makes them nervous, ill at ease. So he rode along the ranks, asking a single question: "Are you afraid to stand up when I am on horseback?"

The men got the point—it was Teddy who was the easy target. They grinned and clutched their rifles. They would follow wherever Teddy led.

Pistol in hand, Roosevelt stood in his stirrups. He knew that in the blockhouses ahead Spaniards in high-crowned hats were raising their rifles and waiting for the charge. He waved his hand, and the Rough Riders started up San Juan Hill.

Breaking from a cover of woods, Roosevelt found the 9th Division in his way. He said sharply, "If you don't wish to go forward, let my men pass."

In the Battle of Santiago Bay the Spanish gunboat Furor *met heavy American fire and ended up on a reef.*

The Hawaiian "paradise" became a focus of controversy in U.S. politics in the 1890's. Annexation followed in 1898.

As the 19th century ended, the United States acquired territories in the Pacific, including the Philippines, Wake and Guam, and the Hawaiian Islands. Midway had been acquired in 1867 and part of Samoa in 1889. Alaska was purchased from Russia in 1867. Eventually, Alaska and Hawaii would become the 49th and 50th states.

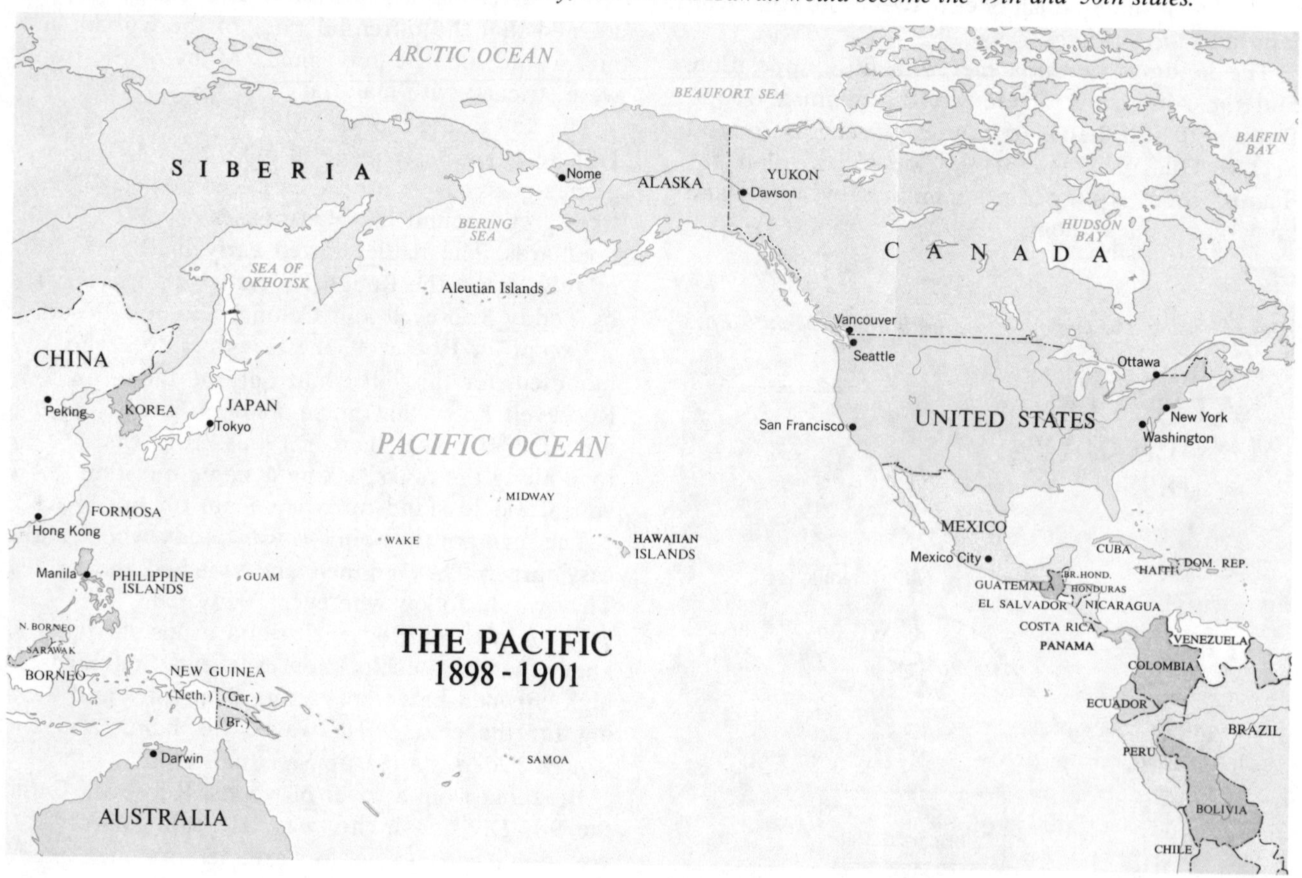

THE PACIFIC 1898 - 1901

The men of the 9th Division looked up. They knew about Teddy—and, all at once, they fell in with the Rough Riders. A famous American reporter, Richard Harding Davis, witnessed the charge.

VICTORY AT SAN JUAN HILL

"Roosevelt, mounted high on horseback, and charging the rifle-pits at a gallop and quite alone, made you feel that you would like to cheer," Davis wrote. Teddy wore a sombrero, and had tied a blue polka-dot handkerchief around his throat.

The battle itself was vicious. The Spanish riflemen knew how to handle their guns. They stood their ground, firing down on the advancing Rough Riders. But the Americans would not stop. They kept coming on—on—on. When their lines broke apart, they formed ranks and plunged ahead until, near the top, they seemed to gather speed. "The Spaniards," wrote Davis, "appeared for a moment outlined against the sky and poised for instant flight, fired a last volley and fled before the swift-moving wave that leaped and sprang after them."

The victory at San Juan Hill, and the capture of the heights at El Caney by other U.S. forces, had several results. American troops now commanded Santiago—and Teddy Roosevelt, who had led the charge up San Juan Hill, was a national hero. Largely because of his war record he was elected governor of New York in 1898.

SMOKE IN SANTIAGO BAY

Spanish warships are destroyed by the American North Atlantic fleet.

The North Atlantic fleet, under Rear Admiral William T. Sampson, waited outside Santiago harbor for Cervera's Spanish warships. July 3 was a clear, hot day with a smooth sea and a light breeze blowing from the northwest. Aboard the *New York,* Sampson's flagship, a shout rose on the signal bridge: "Smoke in the harbor!"

Other bluejackets had also seen the smoke. A gun boomed on the *Iowa,* and a string of little flags signaled: "The enemy's ships are escaping to the westward." Crews rushed to their battle stations. American warships started the chase just three minutes after the gun on the *Iowa* had boomed its warning. Then the bluejackets saw the Spanish ships coming out of the harbor—the flagship *Maria Teresa,* followed by the armored cruisers *Vizcaya, Cristobal Colon,* and *Almirante Oquendo,* and the torpedo-boat destroyers *Pluton* and *Furor.* In about fifteen minutes they had left the harbor.

The Spanish vessels, coming within range, opened their batteries upon the pursuing Americans. But the Spaniards were still flying westward under full speed, trying to escape. They would avoid a battle if they could. The two torpedo boats darted for the *Brooklyn,* which led the chase. The gunners on the *Brooklyn* gave the *Pluton* and *Furor* a demonstration of fast and fancy firing. Shaking off the torpedo boats, the *Brooklyn* sped ahead to take on opponents more her size—the flagship *Maria Teresa* and the cruiser *Vizcaya.* The *Iowa* and the *Texas* hurled their big shells at the enemy. Sampson gave the order: "Not one must get away!"

Aboard the light cruiser *Gloucester,* Lieutenant-Commander Richard Wainwright had a debt to pay that day. Wainwright had been the executive officer of the *Maine,* and he had loved the ship. Wainwright was remembering the *Maine* as he hurled the little *Gloucester* into the battle.

Wainwright made the torpedo boats his personal enemy. His firing was so rapid and so continuous that he swept away one Spanish crew after another. A shell crashed through the *Pluton* and almost broke the vessel in two. The *Furor* tried to find safety behind the cruisers, but the *Gloucester* chased after her, rained a steady fire on her decks, and left her finally to break upon a reef. Of the 140 Spaniards who had been aboard the torpedo boats when Wainwright attacked, only twenty-four survived.

Elsewhere the battle proved equally disastrous for the Spaniards. Flames roared through the *Maria Teresa* and, completely disabled, she ran ashore. The *Oquendo,* also swept by fire, limped ashore. She had been hit sixty-six times. In less than an hour the battered *Vizcaya* turned for the shore.

The *Colon* tried to outrun the *Brooklyn* and the *Oregon,* but she was outmatched. The Americans in the boiler rooms, where the temperature reached 150 degrees Fahrenheit, saw to that. The stokers fainted before the open furnace doors and were carried away. Others took their places. If speed was what the captain wanted, speed he would get.

The guns fired a salvo. The *Colon,* run down, struck her colors. She was scuttled and left sinking. The small cost of the American victory off Santiago harbor seemed incredible—one man killed.

IN DISTANT LANDS

"Manifest Destiny" leads Americans to annex Hawaii and buy Alaska.

After 113 days, the war was ended. A peace treaty was signed at Paris on December 10, 1898. Cuba was freed, and Puerto Rico, the Philippines, and the island of Guam in the Pacific became American possessions. Spain received $20,000,000 for her public property in the Philippines.

Although the United States had won an easy victory over a weak foe, the war still marked a turning point in American history. For years, many Americans had disapproved of "Manifest Destiny"—the belief that the United States had the right to extend its territory. Now the Stars and Stripes waved over islands in the Pacific, and "imperialism" became an exciting game. Americans talked of annexing the Hawaiian Islands, which had been discovered by Captain James Cook in 1778. The first American ship to sail around the world—the *Columbia,* under the command of Robert Gray—visited Hawaii in 1789. But real interest in Hawaii dated from 1819, when New England missionaries sailed from Boston to bring the blessings of the white man's civilization to the half-naked natives of these islands in the Pacific.

The missionaries worked long and hard. They taught the natives to wear trousers and dresses. Wooden houses replaced grass huts, and the villages took on the appearance of New England towns. A printing press was brought to the islands in 1845 and the missionaries published an English-Hawaiian dictionary. For the first time, the natives were exposed to knowledge of the world around them. Ships in the sandalwood trade and whalers from New Bedford made the islands a regular stopping place.

Hawaii prospered. In 1850, under the wise leadership of its native king, Kamehameha III, it adopted the motto: "The life of the land is perpetuated in righteousness." About this time three New Englanders formed Ladd & Company and gave Hawaii its first successful sugar plantation.

The sugar planters steadily gained in influence in the islands, and in 1875 a treaty with the United States allowed Hawaiian sugar and other products to enter American ports duty free. Within the first ten years of this treaty, Hawaii's yearly sugar exports to the United States increased from 17,909,000 to 169,653,000 pounds. The treaty bound Hawaii to America by forbidding it to make similar trade agreements with other governments, and in 1887 the United States was given the right to build a naval base at Pearl Harbor.

"HAWAII FOR HAWAIIANS"

The situation of the sugar planters was suddenly changed by the McKinley Tariff of 1890. Under this act, sugar from other nations, as well as Hawaii, was admitted to the United States without paying duty. The planters, fearing that their profits would drop, began to demand annexation by the United States. But, in 1893, Queen Liliuokalani came to the throne. She believed in "Hawaii for Hawaiians." She tried to end the movement for annexation and destroy the power of the sugar planters.

The planters fought back. With the aid of John L. Stevens, the American minister in Hawaii, they hastily organized a revolution. Although Stevens was not in Hawaii during the ten days before the planters seized the government, he managed to land 160 marines from an American warship in time to ensure the success of the revolution. On February 1, 1893, Stevens announced that an American protectorate had been established. He cabled the State Department: "The Hawaiian pear is now fully ripe, and this is the golden hour for the United States to pluck it."

President Cleveland did not approve of what Stevens and the planters had done, and tried to restore the queen to power. But the whites in Hawaii remained in control of the government, and in 1894 they proclaimed Hawaii a republic. They named Sanford B. Dole, the son of a missionary, its first and only president.

Politicians who were against annexation praised Cleveland; those who were for annexation attacked him. Then Dewey's victory at Manila awakened the United States to its "Manifest Destiny" in the Pacific, and on July 7, 1898, Cleveland signed the resolution annexing Hawaii. On April 30, 1900, it became a territory of the United States.

The American flag now waved in the tropics. It waved in the arctic regions as well, for on March 30, 1867, Secretary of State William H. Seward had purchased Alaska from Russia for $7,200,000. Many Americans had laughed and made fun of "Seward's Folly." Alaska was a frozen waste and good for nothing. Thirty years later the laughter was silenced by the discovery of gold along the Klondike River in the neighboring Yukon Territory of Canada. Not since the Gold Rush of California had news of a gold strike produced such excitement. Miners put on snowshoes and hitched up dogsleds to join the rush into the Yukon area. A second gold strike was made at Nome, Alaska, in 1899.

Then the nation's interest quickly shifted from the frozen North to far-off China. Hundreds of Americans were in China. Some were there for business reasons; others had come as missionaries. Now they faced torture and murder at the hands of the Boxers, a group of Chinese who had organized to defend their country from domination by foreigners. Secretly encouraged by the Chinese empress, the Boxers spread terror among the foreign population until August, 1900, when a combined force of American, British, German, Russian, and Japanese troops restored order.

Peking was captured and the empress dethroned. The sum of $735,000,000 was demanded from China by these foreign countries to pay for the property damaged by the Boxers and for the costs of putting down the rebellion. The American government, believing this amount too large, persuaded its allies to cut it in half. Of the $25,000,000 which was its share of the award, the United States later returned $13,000,000 to China.

THE AGE OF "THE FULL DINNER PAIL"

The country seems calm and peaceful, but labor calls for reforms.

At home, the nation enjoyed the age of "the full dinner pail" that McKinley had promised. Large numbers of Americans lived comfortably in pleasant houses stuffed from wall to wall with heavy Victorian furniture. Women dressed in plumed hats, frilly shirtwaists, and long, billowing skirts. They tried to look like "Gibson Girls," the fashionable ladies drawn by artist Charles Dana Gibson.

Americans were having a good time—at band concerts in the town square, at parades of Union and Confederate veterans, at the Mardi Gras in New Orleans. They rode the "Shoot the Chutes" in New York's Coney Island, or went bathing at fashionable seashore resorts like Atlantic City, New Jersey, and Newport, Rhode Island, or boating on lakes like the one in St. Louis' famous Forest Park.

The sports marvel of the age was Charles M. "Mile-a-Minute" Murphy who, paced by a Long Island Railroad locomotive, rode a mile on a bicycle in sixty-five seconds.

America was changing during these years of "the full dinner pail." The fall of 1900 brought the first automobile show to Madison Square Garden in New York City. Walt Whitman, the poet, predicted that if Americans didn't give up their craze for speed the country soon would be filled with lunatic asylums. But Americans seemed willing to run that risk as steam locomotives sped over the rails at more than sixty miles an hour. Electric trolleys rumbled and clanged in the streets of cities, and New York City had an electric-car cab service.

A miracle was taking place in Florida where Henry M. Flagler was clearing mangrove swamps, jungle, and coral rock to build the city of Miami. More and more Southerners began to wonder if their best friend wasn't the boll weevil. This insect, which destroyed cotton, made them realize how foolish it was to depend on one crop for their income. Alabamians began to cultivate peanuts, for which many uses were discovered by the great Negro scientist George Washington Carver. Peaches from Georgia became a familiar item in northern markets.

Yet elsewhere in America there were serious problems. Floods along the Mississippi River and the heedless cutting of trees by the lumber industry in the Northwest made thoughtful people realize that the nation must develop programs for protecting its natural resources. On September 8, 1900, a tropical hurricane smashed Galveston, Texas, killing more than 5,000 persons. Yellow fever killed a number of American soldiers stationed in Cuba before army medical doctors—a team of six led by Walter Reed—discovered that the disease was passed on to human beings by a certain kind of mosquito.

Labor was struggling with rivalries within its own ranks. A new force in this field was the American Federation of Labor (A. F. of L.), organized in 1886. It had 550,000 members by 1890; 1,500,000 by 1900. Samuel Gompers, who served as president of the A. F. of L. from its founding until his death in 1924, was a "craft union" man who had been a leader in the International Cigar Makers' Union. Negroes, women, and unskilled workers were not permitted to join the A. F. of L. Ignoring politics and "radical" movements, the A. F. of L. concentrated on getting higher wages and a shorter working day.

To millions of American workers, the A. F. of L. seemed a menace. Its refusal, for example, to take an active part in politics meant that it weakened the possibility of gaining labor reforms through state and Federal legislation. Daniel De Leon charged that the leaders of the A. F. of L. were "labor fakers" and called for active political programs to better the lot of the working class.

De Leon, born on the island of Curaçao, educated in Germany, and at one time a teacher at Columbia College, followed the reasoning of Karl Marx, father of modern communism. Marx's "Communist Manifesto" appeared in 1848 and his ideas had begun to circulate in Europe and the United States. De Leon was too rigid in his ideas to appeal strongly to Americans, but in 1897 Eugene V. Debs—already famous for the Pullman strike—and Victor L. Berger gained control of De Leon's movement. Two years later the Socialist Party of America was formed.

In the Rocky Mountain states a militant kind of labor organizer was arising. In the 1890's, when labor and management clashed along the mining frontier, both sides used violence. Mineowners employed strikebreakers and armed guards, and the workers fought back with dynamite and six-shooters, often in the belief that victory in a labor dispute went to the side that was quicker on the trigger. By 1896 the Western Federation of Miners had lost faith in the A. F. of L. and its conservative policies. Delegates from the Western Miners, joining with some socialists, helped to form the Industrial Workers of the World (I. W. W., or "Wobblies") in 1905.

THE "WOBBLIES"

Outwardly America seemed calm and comfortable under William McKinley. But the I. W. W. stood for a rough-and-tumble class struggle "in which

President William McKinley

the bosses were always wrong [and] the 'wage-slaves' and 'working stiffs' always right." This conflict was still not completely in the open when the Republicans renominated McKinley for the presidency in 1900. For Mark Hanna, the boss of the party, there was only one sour note—the nomination of Teddy Roosevelt for Vice-President.

"Don't you realize," Hanna said when Roosevelt was nominated, "that there is but one heartbeat between the White House and this madman?"

William Jennings Bryan was again the Democratic nominee. He hammered hard at McKinley's imperialism, but America decided that it wished another four years of the full dinner pail. McKinley received a popular plurality of 861,459 votes and an electoral college vote of 292 to 155.

"BE CAREFUL HOW YOU TELL HER"

McKinley is mortally wounded by an assassin's bullet.

The men who ran the large corporations cheered McKinley's re-election in 1900. They felt the country was sound and safe for another four years and planned mergers to make big business even bigger. Gold was discovered in Nevada at Goldfield, Tonopah, and Ray, and new oil wells gushed wealth in Texas. A number of steel companies in Pittsburgh were combined to create the United States Steel Corporation, the first American company worth more than a billion dollars. McKinley, convinced that new policies must result from the nation's position as a world power, was willing to support a lower tariff.

In September of 1901, McKinley attended the Pan-American Exposition in Buffalo, New York. When a vast crowd wished to greet the President in person, he said, "Let them come." People formed long lines to shake his hand, and McKinley watched them pushed along by the guards "as logs are propelled down a sluice."

One man who shuffled along in the crowd was Leon F. Czolgosz (pronounced Tchollgosch), twenty-eight years old. Born in Detroit, Michigan, of poor Polish-German parents, he had known bitter years of unemployment and hunger. He saw in McKinley a symbol of "the rule of the rich" that had made life so hard for his parents and himself.

A detective, noticing that Czolgosz had covered one of his hands with a soiled handkerchief, said: "This man has a sore hand." At that moment Czolgosz whipped out a pistol. He fired two shots and McKinley crumpled to the floor, wounded in the breast and abdomen.

The President's first thought was for his sickly wife. "Be careful," he pleaded, "how you tell her—oh, be careful."

For eight days the nation's finest doctors tried to save McKinley's life, but he died on September 14, 1901. Czolgosz was swiftly brought to trial, convicted, and electrocuted. And, just as Mark Hanna had feared, Theodore Roosevelt became President of the United States.

THE "GOO-GOO" AS PRESIDENT

Teddy Roosevelt moves into the White House and the nation moves into the Twentieth Century.

"The McKinley policy is the Roosevelt policy," said the Washington *Post* when Theodore Roosevelt took office as the twenty-sixth President of the United States.

That newspaper soon found out how wrong it was. The Roosevelt policy would be decided by Roosevelt, and no one else. He was a "goo-goo" who made up his mind for himself, flashing his teeth in a smile when things went well, blinking angrily behind his eyeglasses when they didn't. Roosevelt in the White House was an educational force. He talked—and talked—and talked. Basically, he was trying to tell Americans about the big problems of the age in which they lived.

"We woke up every morning wondering what new adventure we were off on when Roosevelt was President," said a member of the White House staff.

Teddy belonged to the Twentieth Century. During

this century, the American people, who numbered just under 76,000,000 in 1900, would see many new things, from Carrie Nation's campaign against the evils of drinking to *The Great Train Robbery,* the first motion picture to tell a story. In the early 1900's, Gimbel's Philadelphia store installed the nation's first escalator, the H. J. Heinz Company revolutionized retail grocery marketing with its "57 varieties," and Henry Ford organized his motor company, starting Detroit on its way to becoming the automobile capital of the world. The new American game of basketball, invented by James Naismith in 1891, was "catching on," and products like Bon Ami and the Ingersoll dollar watch were becoming American institutions.

Teddy Roosevelt himself was one of the most exciting things of the new century. He belonged to a century in which things happened. It was the century of Marconi's wireless and transatlantic radio communication, of the Pure Food and Drug Act, which regulated the sale and advertising of these products, of the St. Louis Fair, which celebrated the one-hundredth anniversary of the Louisiana Purchase, and of the opening of the subway in New York City. It was the century, too, of a memorable event at Kitty Hawk in North Carolina.

THE REMARKABLE WRIGHT BROTHERS

Two young men from Ohio make the world's first successful powered flight.

The story of Wilbur and Orville Wright began in Dayton, Ohio, on an evening in the fall of 1878. On that evening their father brought them a toy called a helicopter. Made of cork and bamboo, and propelled by rubber bands, it gave them an interest in flight that would last throughout their lives. The toy quickly broke, but the Wright brothers constructed helicopters of their own, and then built kites. By 1899 they were writing to the Smithsonian Institution in Washington for information on aviation.

Wilbur and Orville now owned a bicycle repair shop in Dayton. They made their living from bicycles, but flying was what they really loved. In the back room of the shop they built their first glider. To fly it, they went to the beach at Kitty Hawk, on the coast of North Carolina. They built two more gliders, and made a wind tunnel so that they could experiment with models of various kinds of wings. They flew both gliders at Kitty Hawk, making hundreds of

At Kitty Hawk, North Carolina, on December 17, 1903, the Wright brothers made the first powered flights in history.

In Teddy Roosevelt's time, many children went to one-room schools whose "playgrounds" were fields, forests or creeks.

flights over the sand dunes. They learned much from these flights, and in 1903 they were ready to test a plane powered by a gasoline engine. They built their own engine, using an old tomato can for the carburetor.

That same year, another inventor was also ready to test a plane driven by a gasoline engine. He was Samuel Pierpont Langley, who had been experimenting with model aircraft for seventeen years. In October he launched his plane, which weighed 730 pounds, from a catapult on a houseboat on the Potomac River, only to see it fall into the water "like a handful of mortar." Another test in December ended in disaster, and the nation laughed at Langley and his notion of flying through the air.

The nation was still laughing when, nine days later, on December 17, 1903, the Wright brothers decided to test their own plane at Kitty Hawk. They had had all sorts of difficulties—propeller shafts had buckled and sprockets had worn loose on the chain drive—but now they believed they had worked out all the problems.

It was windy at Kitty Hawk that day. The only witnesses as they brought out their plane were four men who lived at the nearby Kill Devil Coast Guard Station and a sixteen-year-old boy. The engine was warmed up and at 10:35 A.M. Orville "got on the machine." He lay flat on his stomach, gazing down the track of two-by-fours they had put down for launching the plane.

The rope that held back the plane was slipped off, and the craft glided down the track. It picked up speed, traveling seven or eight miles an hour, or perhaps as much as nine—and then it lifted into the air. Twelve seconds later it was back on the ground, after flying a distance of 120 feet. On the second flight it flew 195 feet in eleven seconds, and on the third more than 200 feet in fifteen seconds. But on the fourth flight, with Wilbur at the controls, the plane remained aloft for fifty-nine seconds, covering a ground distance of 852 feet. The Wright brothers had made the first powered flights in history.

TEDDY THE TRUST BUSTER

Roosevelt battles big business and plans a canal across Panama.

Just as, in time, Americans became accustomed to airplanes overhead, so did they become accustomed to the "goo-goo" in the White House. True, old Washingtonians complained that the Roosevelt children were turning things upside down in the executive mansion. The President's youngsters roller-skated on the hardwood floor, walked around on stilts greeting visitors, played leapfrog over the furniture, and took their pet pony for rides in the elevator.

But then, their father wasn't much better. He was learning jujitsu. He fought broadsword battles with his old friend General Leonard Wood, and wrestled with Joe Grant, the champion of the District of Columbia.

THE OLD GUARD

Roosevelt had a constant struggle with the conservatives in his own party—the Old Guard or "standpatters," as they were called. At the same time, he realized that a new political movement was rising in the country. It was led by the "progressives" in the Midwest, of whom the most important was Robert M. La Follette of Wisconsin. La Follette had been a congressman and was then elected governor of his home state.

Roosevelt knew that he had to get along with both the Old Guard and the progressives without being captured by either. Sometimes he was forced to give in. For example, he was in favor of a lower tariff, but he knew that if he tried to get it he would be involved in a desperate battle with the Old Guard. So, on this issue, he let the Old Guard have its way.

Usually, however, he jumped into political battles with zest and joy, as he did when he became a "trust buster." Roosevelt was concerned about the "trusts," the combinations of big businesses. The wealthy corporations were combining and gobbling up their weaker competitors. They were growing richer and more powerful, and Roosevelt thought they were getting out of hand. The nation's mounting wealth was controlled by perhaps as little as one-fifth of the population.

In 1901, something happened that gave Roosevelt an opportunity to crack down on the trusts. Edward H. Harriman wanted to extend his Union Pacific railroad to Chicago. To do this, he needed the Chicago, Burlington, and Quincy line. But the Burlington line was part of the Northern Pacific railroad system, which was controlled by James J. Hill and the banking house of J. P. Morgan. Harriman and his group of financiers tried to buy enough stock in Northern Pacific to gain control of it, and so much buying pushed the price of the stock up to $1,000 a share.

Soon both the Harriman group and the Hill group decided that cooperation would be more profitable than competition. Together they set up a new company, Northern Securities, which controlled all their railroads. Harriman stopped buying up stock and prices fell in the stock market, ruining many investors.

Roosevelt began his trust-busting in March of 1902. He started a government suit to dissolve the Northern Securities Company, charging that it stifled competition. The case dragged on for two years before the Supreme Court ruled, five to four, that the company was a trust and must be dissolved. This suit, and thirty-four others begun during Roosevelt's administration, brought results. Congress passed laws strengthening the Interstate Commerce Act and set up the new Cabinet post of Secretary of Commerce and Labor. (In 1913, an act of Congress would divide the duties of this job and provide both a Secretary of Labor and a Secretary of Commerce.)

Roosevelt did not allow his trust busting to interfere with his interest in foreign affairs. In 1850 the United States and Great Britain had signed a treaty which stated that any canal built across the Isthmus of Panama would be under the control and protection of both nations. In 1902 a new treaty was signed, giving the United States a free hand in building a canal. Roosevelt was a navy man and was determined to build a canal. Ships sailing between the Atlantic and Pacific Oceans would no longer have to make the long voyage around Cape Horn, the stormy tip of South America. A canal would shorten the trip by thousands of miles and save many days of sailing time.

To get the land needed for the canal, Roosevelt played a tricky game. When a revolt broke out in the Panama section of Colombia, he quickly took advantage of the situation. Three days after the revolt started he recognized the Republic of Panama. American naval vessels prevented Colombian troops from fighting, and American marines went ashore. "I took Panama without consulting the Cabinet," Roosevelt said. Panama agreed to lease to the United States a ten-mile-wide strip of land across the Isthmus for an endless period of time. Now the canal could be built.

PRESIDENT IN HIS OWN RIGHT

Theodore Roosevelt runs for a full term as President, and wins easily.

The Democratic nominee for President in 1904 was Judge Alton B. Parker of New York. He had become rich from dealings in timber, coal, and railroads, and he was a conservative in his politics. The political situation that year was full of contradictions. The Democrats needed the support of the liberals to win, but they had chosen a conservative candidate. Theodore Roosevelt, on the other hand, was a liberal—but he was backed by the corporations he fought.

The Socialists, Prohibitionists, Populists, and the Social Laborites also ran candidates, but none of them received a single vote in the electoral college. Roosevelt was swept into office by a plurality of more than 2,500,000 popular votes.

"I am no longer a political accident," Roosevelt told his wife. As President in his own right, he was perhaps even more self-confident than he had been. He started construction of the Panama Canal, saying with a grin, "I took the Isthmus, started the canal, and then left Congress—not to debate the canal, but to debate me. [But] while the debate goes on, the canal does too." He went on hunting trips, tramping through the woods and shooting black bears. Always a lover of the outdoors, he called for a program to protect the nation's natural resources. He could be a peacemaker as well as a warrior. He offered to settle a war between Russia and Japan. His offer was accepted, and the peace treaty was signed at Portsmouth, New Hampshire.

The United States had many problems during this period. Slums were increasing, and crime was on the rise. There were no old age or unemployment benefits. Although some states had child labor laws, many children still worked in the fields and factories. Women marched in parades, demanding the right to vote. The Prohibitionists wanted to close the saloons and pour the nation's whiskey into the gutter. Journalists called "muckrakers" wrote articles about political corruption in the cities, the abuses of big business, and the need to help the poor.

And yet, life was pleasant for many Americans, especially in the rural areas. Youngsters fished, swam, hunted, attended one-room schools, and marveled at new farm equipment like the machine-driven multidisc plow and the blow thrasher.

Theatergoers applauded Lillian Russell, Maude Adams, Ethel Barrymore, and Anna Held. Motion-picture theaters, called "nickelodeons" because tickets were priced at five cents, were opening in the poorer sections of cities. The Teddy Bear, a fuzzy stuffed animal inspired by the President's love for big-game hunting, became popular. Automobiles and motor trucks were more common now, as were "rapid-transit interurban" trolley lines, many of which ran between towns and cities in the Midwest.

Disasters made headlines in the newspapers. More than 600 persons died in Chicago's Iroquois Theater fire in 1903. The following year, 1,000 persons died when the excursion boat *General Slocum* sank in Long Island Sound. But the worst disaster of all occurred on the Pacific Coast in the spring of 1906.

THE SAN FRANCISCO EARTHQUAKE

Four square miles of San Francisco are destroyed by earthquake and fire.

On April 18, 1906, just before daybreak, the first gentle tremor of an earthquake was felt in San Francisco. At 5:15 o'clock came "the great shock which did the damage." A reporter for the New York *Sun* wrote:

"It seemed to be two or three minutes after the great shock was over before people found their voices. There followed the screaming of women, beside themselves with terror, and the cries of men. With one impulse people made for the parks, as far as possible from the falling walls. These speedily became packed with people in their nightclothes, who screamed and moaned at the little shocks which followed every few minutes. The dawn was just breaking. The gas and electric mains were all out. But before the dawn was white there came a light from the east—the burning warehouse district. . . ."

And now, following the horror of the earthquake, the stunned people faced a new horror—fire.

"The firemen, making for the nearest point, got their hose out. There was one rush of water; then the flow stopped. The great water main, which carries the chief water supply of San Francisco, ran through the ruined district. It had been broken and the useless water was spurting up through the ruins in scores of places.

"The firemen stood helpless, while fire after fire started in the ruined houses. Most of these seem to have been caused by the ignition of gas from gas mains, which were also broken. The fires would rush up with astonishing suddenness, and then smoulder in the slowly burning redwood, of which three-quarters of San Francisco is built."

Finally, to isolate the fire and keep it from spreading, a number of buildings were dynamited. Soldiers were sent into the city and patrolled the streets to prevent looting. The earthquake and fire destroyed about 28,000 buildings, covering an area of four square miles. Property damage was estimated at $500,000,000. About 500 persons lost their lives, and 250,000 were homeless. But San Franciscans quickly went to work rebuilding their city, and within three years put up 20,000 new buildings.

"BIG BILL" TAFT

Theodore Roosevelt chooses William Howard Taft to succeed him as President.

As the sound of rebuilding echoed across the hills of San Francisco, Theodore Roosevelt was looking forward to a new adventure. With his twenty-two-year-old son Kermit, he was planning to hunt wild animals in Africa. In keeping with the tradition of the Presidency at that time, he had decided not to run for a third term. But he wanted to be sure his policies would be continued, and he chose his own successor in the White House. His choice was William Howard Taft, who didn't want the job.

"Big Bill" Taft was a jolly man who stood over six feet tall and weighed more than 300 pounds. He became the only man in American history to hold the nation's two highest offices—President and Chief Justice of the Supreme Court. Taft was born in Cincinnati, Ohio, on September 15, 1857. His father had served in Grant's Cabinet and had been United States minister to Austria and Russia. But "Big Bill" preferred the law to politics. After his graduation from Yale, he rose from assistant prosecutor of Ohio's Hamilton County to judge of the Federal Court of Appeals.

San Franciscans who had fled the horrors of the 'quake on April 18, 1906, ran from raging fires that followed.

But Taft could not escape politics.

In 1901, President McKinley appointed him the first civil governor of the Philippine Islands. Taft was devoted to the people of the islands, whom he called "my little brown brothers." His administration of the Philippines was a model of colonial government. He did not allow the Filipinos to be treated unfairly because of their color, and he cracked down on army officers who substituted authority for justice. He gave the islands better court systems, better sanitary regulations, better schools.

Taft always put duty above ambition. Twice Theodore Roosevelt offered him what he wanted—a place on the Supreme Court—and twice Taft said no. He had come to the Philippines to do a job and he intended to finish it.

Taft left the Philippines only when Roosevelt called him to Washington to serve as Secretary of War. Taft acted as supervisor of the construction of the Panama Canal and worked out a system of government for the Canal Zone. Roosevelt called him "the most lovable personality" he had ever known. With Teddy's backing, Taft easily won the presidency in 1908 by 1,269,900 popular votes and an electoral college vote of 321 to 162.

Taft may not have been as exciting as Teddy, but in the years that followed he proved to be very much an individual. He was the first President to drive around Washington in an electric car, the first to play golf, the first to receive a salary of $75,000 a year. He found the White House to be "the loneliest place in the world," but he was a vital part of America.

CHANGING AMERICA

It was an America that was still changing, an America that was becoming even more remarkable. New Mexico and Arizona were admitted to the Union, adding the forty-seventh and forty-eighth stars to the national flag. Billy Sunday, the baseball player turned evangelist, drew great crowds to his religious "revivals." Hundreds of horses were turned out to pasture as motorized fire engines came into use, and Henry Ford put automobile production on a mass basis with his Model T, the famous "tin lizzie." Automobiles needed gasoline, and the oil industry boomed.

It was an America where children played with chemical sets and miniature steel beams, reflecting the growing interest in science and engineering. Thousands of people went to the "movies" to see stars like Mary Pickford, Lionel Barrymore, and Sarah Bernhardt. The entire nation was shocked when the liner *Titanic,* sailing from Southampton to America on her maiden voyage, was sunk by an iceberg with a loss of all but 705 of her 2,208 passengers and crew.

On the night of April 14, 1912, the liner Titanic, *on her maiden transatlantic voyage to New York, hit an iceberg and sank with the loss of 1,503 passengers and crew. She had been called "unsinkable" because of her watertight compartments.*

WITH PEARY TO THE NORTH POLE

An American naval officer becomes the first man to reach the North Pole.

Robert Edwin Peary was born in Cresson, Pennsylvania, in 1856. At the age of twenty-five, he entered the United States Navy as a civil engineer. For several years Peary served in Nicaragua, making surveys for a canal that would join the two oceans. But even in this hot climate his chief interest was arctic exploration.

In 1886, Peary made a trip to the interior of Greenland. After that, both in and out of the navy, his only desire was to do what no man had ever done—to reach the North Pole and plant the American flag upon the spot where north meets south and east joins west. Seven times Peary made a "dash" into the arctic wilderness without reaching his goal. In August, 1908, ready to try again, he left a port in Maine aboard the steamer *Roosevelt.* Also aboard the ship were a company of sixty-six men and 140 dogs.

Peary wrote feelingly of his dogs. They were "powerful males, as hard as iron, in good condition." Without these trusty friends he could never succeed. On April 2, thirty-two days after leaving land to cross the arctic ice, he took the third hitch in his belt—for a man lost weight on a trip like this.

Peary pushed on through a biting wind that burned his face and cracked his skin. Another day—April 4—was the same, and so too was the 5th. But he pushed on, knowing his goal was within reach, and on April 6, 1909, he was able to write in his diary:

"The Pole at last. The prize of three centuries. My dream and goal for twenty years. Mine at last! I cannot bring myself to realize it. It seems all so simple and commonplace."

But it wasn't. Peary spent thirty hours at the North Pole, where he planted five flags—the Stars and Stripes, the banner of Delta Kappa Epsilon (his fraternity while a student at Bowdoin College), the

After a number of unsuccessful attempts, Peary was able to lead his party to the North Pole on April 6, 1909.

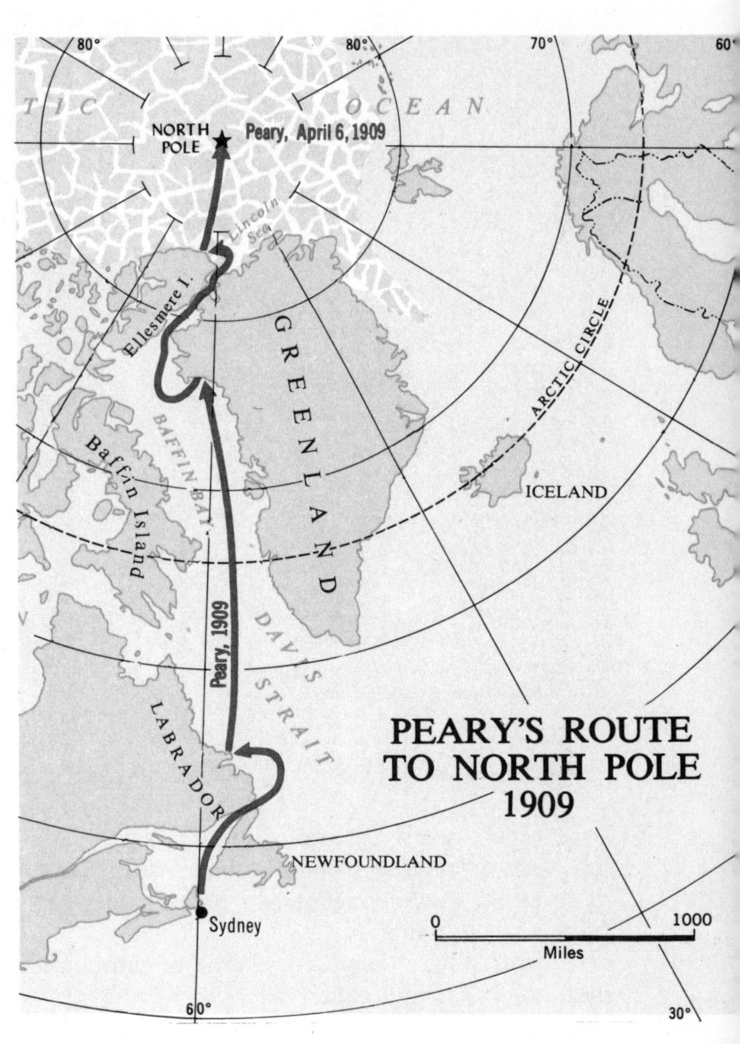

His claim of being the first man to reach the Pole was disputed by Cook, but finally won recognition.

"World's Ensign of Liberty and Peace" (with its stripes of red, white, and blue), and the flags of the Navy League and the Red Cross. He and his comrades gave three cheers. They shook hands. They deposited among the ice blocks a bottle containing a strip of the American flag and their records.

Standing for the first time upon the remotest spot on earth, of what does a man think? "There was not a thing in the world I wanted but sleep," Peary wrote afterward. On the seventh of April, he left the North Pole. "One backward glance I gave—then turned my face toward the south and toward the future."

Shocking news awaited Peary upon his return home. Dr. Frederick A. Cook, who had been a ship's surgeon on one of Peary's earlier expeditions, was being hailed everywhere as a result of his claim of having reached the North Pole almost a year before Peary. A bitter argument developed between Cook and Peary, but Congress finally recognized Peary's claim, voted him its thanks, and promoted him to the rank of rear admiral.

BUILDING THE PANAMA CANAL

Army engineers construct a canal fifty miles across Panama.

Meanwhile, the stupendous work of building the Panama Canal was under way. Called "The Big Ditch" by the engineers who worked on it, the canal was planned to extend from Limon Bay in the Caribbean Sea on the Atlantic side to the Bay of Panama in the Pacific, a distance of 50.72 miles. A series of locks was to be constructed so that, when completed, the canal would be a "bridge of water" rather than an artificial strait. The building of the canal became the task of the United States army engineers under the leadership of Colonel (later Major General) George W. Goethals.

The job was no picnic, as Goethals was willing to tell anybody who would listen. He called the tropical country through which the canal was being dug

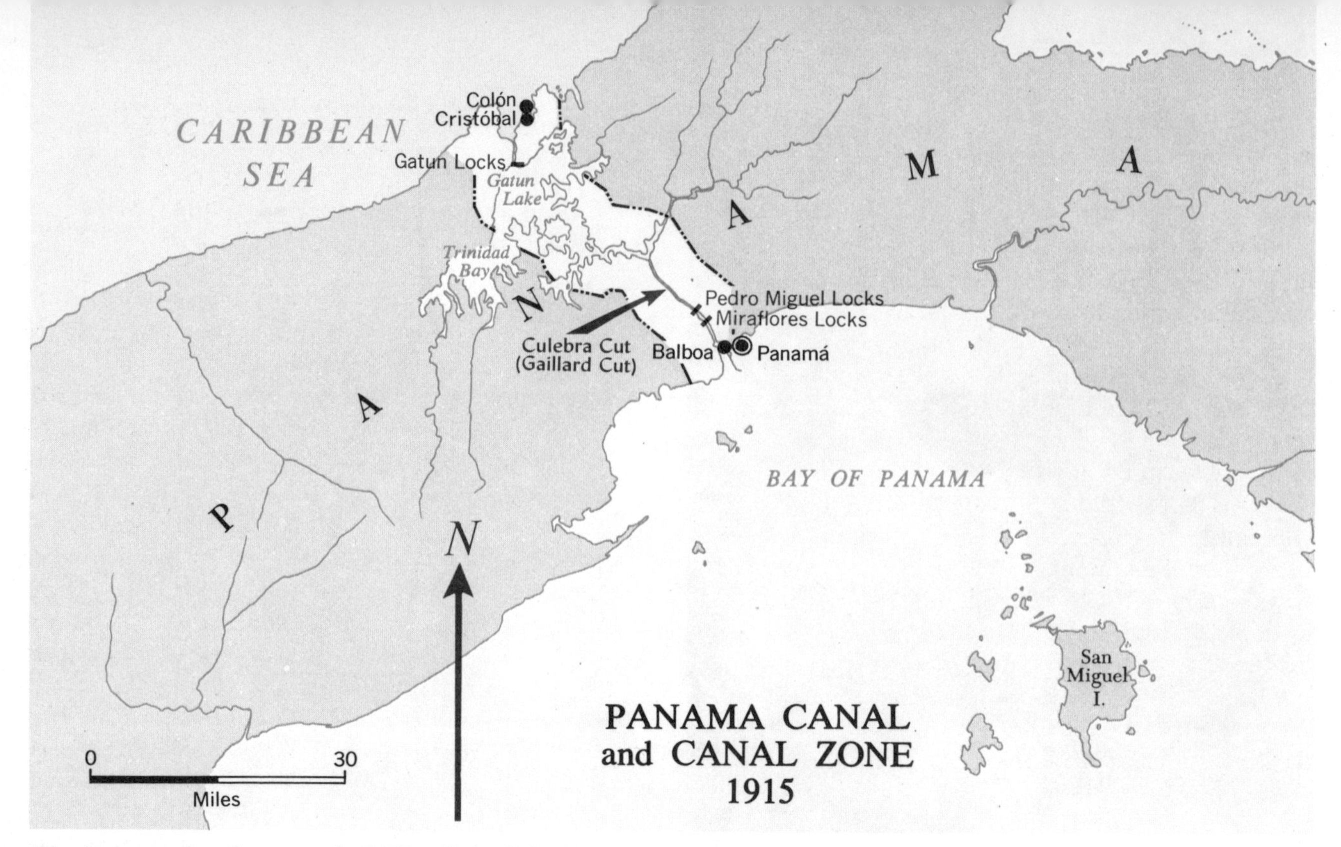

The Panama Canal cut nearly 8,000 miles off the New York-San Francisco run compared with the trip around Cape Horn.

"one of the worst pest-holes of the earth." Sometimes he wondered if men could work here, for diseases like the bubonic plague, malaria, and yellow fever were common.

Colonel W. C. Gorgas, in charge of sanitation in the Canal Zone, became the hero of the project. Gorgas simply refused to believe that anything was impossible, and to prove his point he made medical history. Gorgas found the source of the bubonic plague—flea-bearing rats—and he found the breeding places of the types of mosquitos that carry malaria and yellow fever. He cleared out brush, drained swamps, cut down miles of grass, dug 500 miles of ditches, destroyed some 1,500,000 cans of garbage. When the work began, eight out of every ten patients in Canal Zone hospitals were victims of malaria. Seven years later, as the work neared completion, only one out of ten patients suffered from malaria. Where once seven out of every 1,000 workers died of yellow fever, Gorgas reduced the death toll to less than two out of every 1,000.

Goethals had other headaches. Finding—and keeping—workers was a problem in a project that involved more than 40,000 skilled and unskilled laborers.

Offices, storehouses, living quarters, hotels, mess halls, kitchens, hospitals, and schools had to be built. Panama and Colón, the terminal cities, needed pavements, sewers, running water. The old Panama Railroad, constructed by Americans in 1850–55, was no longer up to the demands placed upon it and had to be largely rebuilt. Since the United States controlled five miles on each side of the canal, laws had to be made, courts set up, police and fire forces organized, schools and hospitals maintained.

There were many discouragements. Landslides and cave-ins hampered the work. There were rocks to dynamite, low-lying marshes to fill in. But Goethals and his men stuck to the task until they reached the great moment on September 13, 1913, when steam shovels Number 226 and 204 took their last bites and the job was done.

THE BULL MOOSER

Teddy Roosevelt forms a new party to run for President, but loses to Wilson

No one took greater pride in what was being accomplished in Panama than President Taft. Perhaps he was not a showman like Teddy Roosevelt, who always insisted that he stood on God's side, fighting the devil. But behind Taft's slow, cautious manner were wisdom and integrity. He had a way of getting things done.

The record of Taft's four years in the White House shows that he actually "out-busted" Teddy as a "trust buster." He avoided involving the United States in a revolution in Mexico. His administration gave full territorial government to Alaska and created the parcel-post and postal-savings systems. It also established the Federal Children's Bureau—the world's first public agency to make investigations and publish reports to advance the welfare of children. Two amendments were added to the Constitution—the Sixteenth, authorizing a Federal income tax, and the Seventeenth, providing for the popular election of United States senators.

In 1910, Roosevelt returned from Africa in a blaze of glory. There were seventeen lions among the 500 animals and birds that he and his son Kermit had bagged during their big-game hunt. Crowds cheered his return and, caught up by the excitement, Roosevelt soon bounced back into politics. Conservative Republicans wished he would go back to Darkest Africa when they heard him say that private property was held subject "to the general right of the community to regulate its use to whatever degree the public welfare may require it." But Roosevelt wasn't easily brushed aside. Although he had chosen Taft as his successor, he now said that Taft had become "useless to the American people."

Clearly, the Republican convention was in for a stormy session when it met in Chicago in 1912. Roosevelt expected to lick the conservatives, but the nomination went to Taft. Undiscouraged, Roosevelt made a rousing speech to his followers, left the Republican party, and formed the Progressive party, which, of course, promptly named him as its presidential candidate. Asked how he felt, Teddy replied: "I am as strong as a bull moose. . . ." So, as the "Bull Moose" candidate, Roosevelt plunged into the 1912 campaign, confident that he could beat Taft and the college president the Democrats had nominated. Roosevelt had never made a worse guess, for Woodrow Wilson also liked to fight.

YOUNG WOODROW WILSON

The Democratic candidate was in his own way as unusual as Roosevelt. Born in Staunton, Virginia, on December 28, 1856, Thomas Woodrow Wilson, one of many children, grew up in a family that felt keenly the disruptions of the Civil War. His schooling began late—at the age of nine—and his weak eyes forced him to drop out of Davidson College before the end of his freshman year. But he had a tough spirit. Two years later he tried again, struggling through a difficult first year at Princeton University. When he was graduated from Princeton, he stood thirty-eighth in a class of 106.

Graduating later from the law school at the University of Virginia, Wilson began practice as a young lawyer in Atlanta, Georgia. But his heart was not in it. He became a graduate student at Johns Hopkins University, preparing for a new career as a college professor in history and politics. His books, *Congressional Government* and *The State,* made his reputation as a scholar. He taught at Bryn Mawr College and Wesleyan University, as well as at Princeton, and turned down many offers to serve as a college president.

WILSON'S RISE TO POWER

A college professor begins a political career that leads to the White House.

Students liked Wilson. He was demanding, but he was fair and he had his streak of fun. He coached football at Wesleyan and enjoyed making up limericks. Offered the presidency of Princeton in 1902, he accepted on one condition. Any university he ran must be something more than a place where "youngsters" performed "tasks." In his opinion, it must be a place "where there are men thinking."

Wilson's years at Princeton became stormy when he attempted to reform the university's eating clubs, which were like fraternities. He believed they were undemocratic. Former graduates raised a rumpus. They wanted the eating clubs left unchanged, whether or not Wilson approved of them. But the public, seeing in the controversy a struggle against snobbery, hailed Wilson as a leader with spirit and "the common touch."

New Jersey was then a Republican state, but the Democratic bosses there knew a winner when they saw one. Where could they find a better candidate for governor than Woodrow Wilson? The people liked him, and he was one of those teaching chaps who would be above meddling with machine politics. Wilson accepted the nomination in 1910 and easily won the election.

Those political bosses simply didn't know their man, and that misjudgment cost most of them their jobs. As governor of New Jersey, Wilson showed the same courage he had when he fought for reform at Princeton. Wilson's political code was simple: The people had elected him, and he intended to account for his actions only to the people.

With the passage of a new election law, Wilson gave New Jersey clean, competent government, and laws to protect labor against the unjust practices of corporations. He reformed the schools and the systems of town and city government. Often the professional politicians balked, but Wilson relied on the people to support him and soon his fame spread beyond New Jersey.

The struggle between conservatives and progressives which had split the Republican convention in 1912 was re-enacted at the Democratic convention in Baltimore. Here the candidate of the conservatives was Missouri's Champ Clark, while the progressives were led by William Jennings Bryan.

Bryan was the moving spirit of the convention. Sixteen years had passed since, as "the Boy Orator of the Platte," he had stampeded the Democrats with his "Cross of Gold" speech. Bryan was heavier, his hair thinner, but he had all of his old vigor as he roamed up and down the convention hall in his alpaca coat, white vest, and wrinkled trousers.

A BATTLE OF GIANTS

From the beginning, the convention was a battle of political giants. The old professionals who played politics as Tammany Hall played it supported Clark. They were against Bryan and the progressives, who believed they had found a winner in Woodrow Wilson. Ballot after ballot the struggle went on. Clark was leading, but Wilson was slowly creeping up.

There was more at stake than just nominating a candidate. The big question was: would the country go progressive or conservative? The answer was important to both business and labor, for it might mean social reform. This was the American way of effecting deep change, not by revolution and bullets, but by political conventions and ballots. And it was this drama, touching everyone's life, that kept the people standing before newspaper offices awaiting the latest bulletins from Baltimore.

The convention dragged on for days with the issue undecided. Then came a break. The Nebraska delegation switched to Wilson. The galleries cheered hoarsely. The people were with Wilson. The Tammany boys and the die-hards from the Solid South tried to rally from the blow. But Wilson kept gaining, inching closer and closer to victory. Toward dawn, after a weary session that had lasted all night, the long-awaited moment drew near. William Allen White, one of the great journalists of the time, who supported the progressives, later remembered:

"It was then, I think, that I danced on my table and yelled to my heart's content. Wilson's strength in the convention slowly mounted until it tipped over the two-thirds majority needed for the nomination."

Wilson accepted the nomination calmly. He campaigned vigorously, hitting hard at the forces of "privilege." With Republican support divided between Roosevelt and Taft, it was almost certain that Woodrow Wilson would become the nation's twenty-eighth President. The popular vote told the story: Wilson, 6,286,214; Roosevelt, 4,216,020; Taft, 3,482,922. By adding the Wilson and the Roosevelt vote, anyone could see that the country was overwhelmingly progressive.

THE AGE OF WILSON

Wilson heads a bustling America, but has trouble with Mexico and a bandit chief.

Few men so influence events that their names become identified with a period in history. George Washington, Thomas Jefferson, Andrew Jackson, and Abraham Lincoln could be called such men. Now there would be an age of Woodrow Wilson. Wilson himself described it as the age of the "New Freedom."

It was an age when suffragettes marched through the streets of Washington, demanding a constitutional amendment that would give women the right to vote. The parcel-post service delivered mail-order catalogues to eager buyers in isolated rural areas. Enthusiastic movie-goers talked of such stars as Mae Marsh, Blanche Sweet, William S. Hart, Flora Finch, Charlie Chaplin, Fatty Arbuckle, Mary Pickford and Douglas Fairbanks, Sr. The first direct transcontinental telephone line was completed between New York and San Francisco, the Panama Canal was opened for traffic, and the Lincoln Highway gave motorists a route from coast to coast. Industrial expansion, a wider use of farm machinery, growing transportation systems, and sprawling cities were other essential parts of the pattern of these years.

President Wilson believed that the real job of government was to serve "humanity." Determined to have his way, he kept Congress in session longer than any other president in history. His achievements were impressive. A new tariff bill lowered duties on products from abroad. An income tax based on the ability to pay was placed on all earnings over $3,000 a year. A new Pure Food and Drug law gave better protection to consumers. The Federal Reserve Act created twelve regional Federal Reserve banks in a system to which all national banks had to belong, and which any state bank could join. The purpose was to strengthen the nation's banks and to set policies affecting money and credit.

Wilson had no patience with Taft's brand of "dollar diplomacy." Wilson believed in an openhanded approach to foreign affairs, but that approach was strongly tested by Mexico.

For years the Mexican government had been in the hands of a dictator. Bandits had ravaged the countryside. A small group, the Creoles, representing about ten per cent of the population, had gained control of that part of Mexico's wealth not controlled by foreign investors. As a result, the average Mexican was poor, downtrodden, resentful. Since the war of 1848 over Texas, it had been easy to convince the Mexicans that the "gringos" to the north were responsible for their troubles. Mexican politicians were quick to use this complaint to hide their own shortcomings.

In 1911 a revolutionary group took over the government of Mexico, only to be overthrown itself two years later. Again Mexico had a dictatorship, and Wilson refused to recognize the government. In 1914, however, he tried something new in American diplomacy. He accepted the offer of the ABC powers—Argentina, Brazil, and Chile—to help settle the differences between the United States and Mexico, and an international conference was held at Niagara Falls. This action won respect for the United States in Central and South America, but even so it could not wipe out Mexico's deeply felt distrust.

For some years Mexico remained a troubled land. In 1916, General Francisco "Pancho" Villa, a bandit chief, raided and looted the border town of Columbus, New Mexico. Wilson acted swiftly. Six thousand troops under Brigadier General John J. Pershing, whose nickname was "Black Jack," were ordered to capture Villa. Pershing pursued Villa through the mountains of northern Mexico. Villa's forces were scattered, but the bandit escaped. Still, peace had been restored. With time and patience, Wilson believed, Mexico and the United States could solve their problems and be good friends.

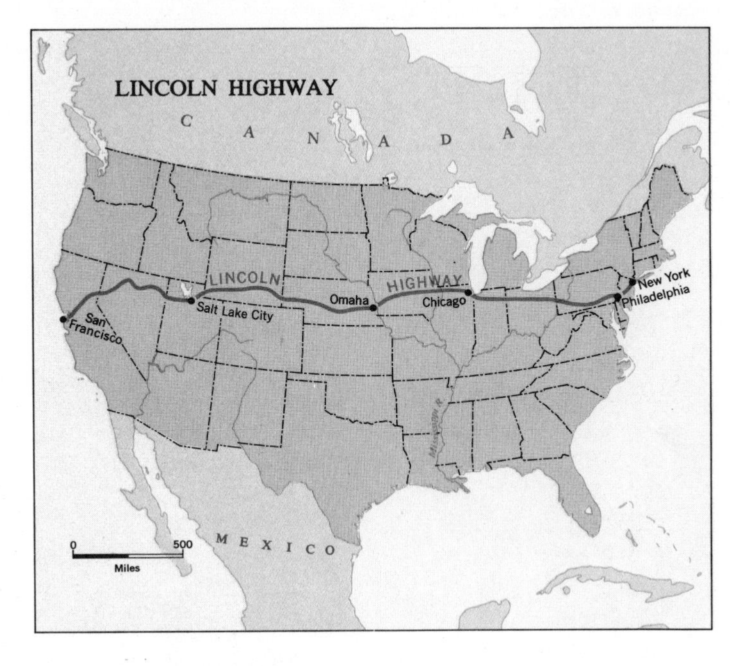

The Lincoln Highway, opened in September 1913, linked New York to San Francisco and was the first transcontinental highway.

"I DIDN'T RAISE MY BOY TO BE A SOLDIER"

War breaks out in Europe, and Wilson promises to keep America neutral.

Always an optimist, Wilson believed that even Europe's difficult problems could be solved by good sense. He sent his old friend Colonel Edward M. House overseas to interest England, France, and Germany in such things as international disarmament, improving health conditions in the tropics, and the improvement of waste areas. But Europe was already divided into two opposing camps. On one side was the Triple Entente of France, Russia, and England; on the other was the Triple Alliance of Austria, Germany and Italy.

Europe was in a dangerous state that could explode into war at any time. There was vicious competition between nations for trade and natural resources. Governments made secret treaties, built up their armies, stirred up race hatreds, and whipped up the patriotic feelings of their citizens. Jealousies and enmities that had arisen centuries ago were still alive. Political boundaries had been shifted, sometimes separating people of the same language and customs.

The bad feeling between two opposing groups, the Serb nationalists and the Austro-Hungarian imperialists, came to a head on June 28, 1914. A Bosnian Serb murdered the Austrian Archduke Ferdinand and his wife, who were visiting Sarajevo, Bosnia (now part of Yugoslavia). Ferdinand was the heir to the Austrian throne, and his assassination set off World War I.

Austria attacked Serbia, and Germany supported the action. Russia went to the aid of Serbia. France joined Russia against Germany. Belgium, a neutral country, was helplessly caught between France and

Pancho Villa stirred up trouble on the U.S.-Mexican border, and President Wilson sent an army under Gen. John J. Pershing to restore order.

EUROPE-1914
0
300
Miles
The Triple Entente
The Triple Alliance
Faeroe Is.
Shetland Is.
Orkney Is.
The Hebrides
SCOTLAND
Glasgow
Edinburgh
Belfast
IRELAND
Dublin
Liverpool
UNITED KINGDOM
ENGLAND
WALES
Birmingham
London
Dover
NORTH SEA
ATLANTIC
OCEAN
English Channel
NORWAY
Bergen
Oslo
SWEDEN
Stockholm
Gulf of Bothnia
WHITE SEA
L. Onega
L. Ladoga
Helsinki
St. Petersburg
Revel
Novgorod
Gotland
Öland
Riga
Moscow
DENMARK
Copenhagen
BALTIC SEA
Bornholm
Kiel
Hamburg
Danzig
Konigsberg
Minsk
Smolensk
NETHERLANDS
Amsterdam
Rotterdam
Brussels
BELGIUM
Cherbourg
Le Havre
Brest
GERMANY
Berlin
Cologne
LUX.
Warsaw
RUSSIA
Breslau
Kiev
Paris
Verdun
Nürnberg
Prague
Brno
Munich
Vienna
Pressburg
Budapest
FRANCE
Loire R.
Bay of Biscay
Bordeaux
Lyon
Bern
SWITZ.
AUSTRIA - HUNGARY
Odessa
CRIMEA
Sevastopol
Milan
Turin
Genoa
Venice
Trieste
Fiume
Belgrade
RUMANIA
Bucharest
Santander
Pôrto
PORTUGAL
Lisbon
Madrid
SPAIN
ANDORRA
Marseilles
Barcelona
Sarajevo
ITALY
Adriatic Sea
MONTENEGRO
SERBIA
BULGARIA
Sofia
Varna
BLACK SEA
Corsica
Rome
ALBANIA
Constantinople
Seville
Málaga
Balearic Is.
Sardinia
Naples
Taranto
Angora
Strait of Gibraltar
Tangier
SPANISH MOROCCO
MEDITERRANEAN SEA
Cagliari
Tyrrhenian Sea
Ionian Sea
GREECE
Aegean Sea
OTTOMAN EMPIRE
Palermo
Sicily
Smyrna
Athens
Algiers
FRENCH MOROCCO
ALGERIA
Tunis
TUNISIA
Malta
Crete
Cyprus (Br.)

Europe before World War I. Below—*In 1917 German U-boats began attacking American ships in the Atlantic.*

Germany. England joined the anti-German forces, now called the "Allies," and Japan, as England's ally, followed. Of the Balkan countries, Greece and Rumania supported the Serbs, while Bulgaria and Turkey joined Germany and Austria in an alliance called the "Central Powers." And so the conflict spread, and the Allies, made up of twenty-eight nations, were at war with the four Central Powers. Italy was at first neutral, but later joined the Allies. Switzerland, Spain, Holland, Denmark, Sweden, and Norway managed to remain neutral.

Americans felt that the war in Europe was none of their business, and Wilson preached strict neutrality. He said that America must be "neutral in fact as well as in name . . . impartial in thought as well as in action." But Germany's ruthless invasion of neutral Belgium turned many Americans against the Central Powers.

THE "LUSITANIA" IS SUNK

Then, on Saturday morning, May 1, 1915, the British liner *Lusitania* sailed from New York for Liverpool. In keeping with United States law, the vessel was unarmed. On May 7, Americans were horrified by what they read in the newspapers. The *Lusitania* had been sunk by a German submarine off the coast of Ireland. Among the 1,198 persons who perished were 128 Americans.

Wilson seemed to stand by his position of strict neutrality. That same May, he said, "There is such a thing as a man being too proud to fight." Meanwhile, fearful of war, women gathered before the White House and sang *I Didn't Raise My Boy to Be a Soldier.*

There was no doubt that Wilson was shocked and shaken by the sinking of the *Lusitania.* So sharp was the note he sent to Germany that Wil-

The torpedoing of the Lusitania *in 1915, with a loss of 1,198 lives, including 128 Americans, shocked the nation.*

"All the News That's Fit to Print."

The New York Times.

EXTRA
5:30 A. M.

VOL. LXIV...NO. 20,928. NEW YORK, SATURDAY, MAY 8, 1915.—TWENTY-FOUR PAGES. ONE CENT

LUSITANIA SUNK BY A SUBMARINE, PROBABLY 1,260 DEAD;
TWICE TORPEDOED OFF IRISH COAST; SINKS IN 15 MINUTES;
CAPT. TURNER SAVED, FROHMAN AND VANDERBILT MISSING;
WASHINGTON BELIEVES THAT A GRAVE CRISIS IS AT HAND

SHOCKS THE PRESIDENT

Washington Deeply Stirred by the Loss of American Lives.

BULLETINS AT WHITE HOUSE

Wilson Reads Them Closely, but Is Silent on the Nation's Course.

HINTS OF CONGRESS CALL

Loss of Lusitania Recalls Firm Tone of Our First Warn-

The Lost Cunard Steamship Lusitania

SOME DEAD TAKEN ASHORE

Several Hundred Survivors at Queenstown and Kinsale.

STEWARD TELLS OF DISASTER

Crashes Into the

...ed for News;
...nia Long in Doubt

...Known Passengers on
...ong Unconfirmed
...eck Details.

List of Saved Includes Capt. Turner;
Vanderbilt and Frohman Reported Lost

Saw the Submarine 100 Y...
and Watched Torpedo as...

Ernest Cowper, a Toronto Newspa...
Attack, Seen from Ship's Rai...
Used in Torpedoes, Say Othe...

Queenstown, Saturday,
May 8, 3:18 A. M.

A sharp lookout for submarines was kept aboard the Lusitania as she approached

ADVERTISEMENT.

NOTICE!

TRAVELLERS intendin... embark on the Atlantic vo... are reminded that a state ... war exists between Germa... and her allies and Great Brita... and her allies; that the zone ... war includes the waters adja... cent to the British Isles; that ... in accordance with formal notice given by the Imperial German Government, vessels flying the flag of Great Britain, or of any of her allies, are liable to destruction in those waters and that travellers sailing in the war zone on ships of Great Britain or her allies do so at their own risk.

IMPERIAL GERMAN EMBASSY
WASHINGTON, D. C., APRIL 22, 1915.

liam Jennings Bryan, who wanted peace at any price, resigned as Secretary of State. As much as Wilson hated war, he hated even more the thought that German submarines were lurking beneath the sea and striking without warning at unarmed merchant vessels. "The rights of humanity" were being destroyed.

And yet, as the 1916 elections approached, the Democrats could still say of Wilson that "he kept us out of war." This fact, plus his programs of social reform, won him the Democratic nomination again. He told the American people:

"I know that you are depending upon me to keep this nation out of war. So far I have done so and I pledge you my word that, God helping me, I will—if it is possible."

For a while, there was a sputter of hope among the progressives that Theodore Roosevelt might be the Republican candidate. But the party's nomination went to Charles Evans Hughes, who resigned from the United States Supreme Court to run against Wilson.

Wilson received the election returns at his summer White House, Shadow Lawn, which was near Long Branch, New Jersey. Early returns showed the President gaining in Colorado and Kansas, but by evening there was bad news. The election was definitely going against Wilson. The New York *World,* one of Wilson's strongest supporters during the campaign, conceded defeat.

The newspapermen who crowded Shadow Lawn asked if Wilson was ready to "throw in the sponge."

An American merchant ship lists heavily to port after being torpedoed in the Atlantic by a U-boat.

To beat the U-boat menace, the Allies organized huge convoys of ships for the Atlantic crossing.

Joseph P. Tumulty, the President's private secretary, answered: "Wilson will win. The West has not yet been heard from."

And then, toward daybreak, the news took a different turn. Ohio, which had been claimed by the Republicans, had gone for Wilson. So had Kansas, and Utah and the Dakotas were "leaning" toward the Democrats. The New York *World* no longer conceded the election.

Charles Evans Hughes had gone to bed believing he was President. He awoke to find that the late vote in his home state of California had gone against him, and that decided the election. The final electoral college vote was Wilson 277, Hughes 254. The election had indeed been a "squeaker."

THE ELECTION AND THE WAR

Wilson's position on the war almost costs him the election in 1916.

Why had Wilson come so close to losing the election? The answer lay in the character of the man himself. Wilson was a scholar, a thinker, a dreamer, an idealist. His schoolteacherish manner may have made him enemies, both in and out of Congress, but this was not the reason he had almost been defeated. Again, big business did not like his social

reforms, but this, too, was not a big issue in the campaign.

It was Wilson's attitude toward the war that almost destroyed him politically. Few men ever hated war more. The use of arms to settle disputes was completely against his nature. God had given man the ability to reason. To Wilson, it was unthinkable not to use reason to settle differences between people or nations. His position of strict neutrality during the early months of the war reflected his hatred of war. He would have no part of it. He would not even encourage the strengthening of American military forces, so that the United States would be prepared if it became involved in the war.

Large groups of Americans supported his position. German immigrants, especially those in the Midwest, hoped for a quick victory for their old "Fatherland." The Solid South was solidly for peace. The Irish, who hated the British, were for any policy which withheld aid to England.

But the war that shook Europe was so great that it made strict neutrality impossible. Both the Allies and the Central Powers needed all kinds of goods, and the result was that business boomed in the United States. England, which had the best navy in the world, declared the seas blockaded to the Central Powers. And if Wilson didn't like it, the British could point out that Lincoln had blockaded Southern ports during the Civil War.

Two things made Americans favor the Allies more and more. One was Germany's brutal invasion of Belgium. The other was that the United States was becoming increasingly prosperous from trade carried on with the protection of the British navy. To many people, Wilson's neutrality made him seem a "pussyfooter," as Theodore Roosevelt called him.

A terrible struggle went on within Wilson after the sinking of the *Lusitania* in 1915. He was still opposed to war—but he could not forget the men, women, and children dead in the cold Atlantic. Convinced that he must act as the moral leader of the world, he would do his duty as he saw it, no matter what it cost him politically.

Wilson might have been defeated in the election if he had run against an aggressive candidate like Theodore Roosevelt. But Hughes did not truly face up to the issue of the war, and when all the votes were counted Wilson remained President. He returned to the White House, still hoping that he could keep the United States off the road to war.

"THE WORLD MUST BE MADE SAFE FOR DEMOCRACY"

Despite many protests, America is slowly drawn into the war.

In his second term as President, Wilson did his best to avoid war. He offered to serve as peacemaker between the Allies and the Central Powers, as he had

A Wilson campaign truck in 1916. In seeking re-election, Wilson's chief slogan was, "He kept us out of war."

done at the outbreak of war. Again his offer was refused. Both sides had gone too far to turn back now. Germany did seem to change her tactics of submarine warfare, and there was still a chance that the United States could stay out of the conflict. But the actions of the German ruling class were killing any hope the Central Powers may have had of sympathy from the United States.

On the last day of January, 1917, the German ambassador to the United States, Count Johann Heinrich von Bernstorff, called on Secretary of State Robert Lansing. He handed Lansing documents announcing that Germany was resuming unrestricted submarine warfare in certain parts of the Atlantic Ocean and the Mediterranean Sea.

Germany now had a fleet of more than one hundred submarines, and her leaders believed that they could cut British imports by forty per cent and end the war within six months. The Germans knew that the use of submarines in this way might bring the United States into the war, but they were willing to take the risk.

Lansing drafted a careful memorandum of his conversation with Bernstorff, then met with Wilson at the White House. Wilson seemed depressed by the entire affair. The two met again the next day, and the following afternoon there was a long Cabinet meeting. Newspapermen realized that something important was happening, and they were tense and excited as they crowded into the halls of the State Department and the anteroom of the White House to await developments.

THE ZIMMERMAN MESSAGE

Behind closed doors, the President and his Cabinet discussed the problem. They had to stand firm and yet leave the way open for a friendly settlement of national differences. On February 3, Wilson took what he believed was the only possible action under the circumstances. Bernstorff was told to leave Washington and the American ambassador to Germany was recalled. By breaking off diplomatic relations, the United States moved a step closer to entry into the war, but there was still hope that war could be avoided.

Germany's decision to resume unrestricted submarine warfare did not catch the British napping. The British Intelligence service had already intercepted a message from German Foreign Secretary Zimmerman to the German ambassador in Mexico. The British turned over the message to the United States Government, and on the first of March, Wilson gave it to the press.

If the United States declared war on Germany, the message said, the German ambassador to Mexico was to try to bring Mexico into the war on the side of the Central Powers. In return, Germany would help Mexico get back its "lost territory" in Arizona, New Mexico, and Texas.

When Americans read the Zimmerman message, they were outraged. Never had their national pride been so deeply insulted. Furthermore, during the months of February and March German submarines sank six American vessels, and forty-eight Americans lost their lives. It appeared as if Germany, confident of victory, was openly challenging the government of the United States to declare war.

For thirteen days Wilson worked on a message to Congress. Washington was full of British agents, who argued behind the scenes that England could not last another six weeks without grain from the United States. Agents of munition manufacturers also flocked to Washington, warning that American investors would lose their money unless England defeated the young, ambitious German Empire.

Meanwhile, senators like W. J. Stone of Missouri and Robert M. La Follette protested sharply that the Allies often seemed to be more autocratic than democratic. Britain as well as Germany had violated America's neutrality. Why was one purer than the other? These senators insisted that the American people did not want war and put enormous pressure on President Wilson to keep America neutral.

But Wilson had reached the point where he could not back down. On April 2, 1917, he calmly went before a joint session of Congress to ask for a declaration of war.

"We must put excited feeling away," he said. "Our motive will not be revenge or the victorious assertion of the physical might of the nation, but only the vindication of right, of human right, of which we are only a single champion."

He reviewed the acts that had brought the United States into conflict with Germany. While Congress and the world listened, he said in memorable words:

"We are glad, now that we see the facts with no veil of false pretense about them, to fight thus for the ultimate peace of the world and for the liberation of its peoples, the German people included; for the rights of nations great and small and the privilege of men everywhere to choose their way of life and of obedience. The world must be made safe for democracy. Its peace must be planted upon the tested foundations of political liberty."

On April 4, the Senate passed the resolution, 82 to 6, and two days later the House passed it, 373 to 50. The United States had entered the war, to fight, as Wilson put it, "for the things which we have always carried nearest our heart—for democracy, for the rights and liberties of small nations, for a universal domination of right by such a concert of free peoples as shall bring peace and safety to all nations and make the world itself at last free."

In the depth of a great economic depression, Franklin D. Roosevelt became President and promised a New Deal.

VIII ~ WORLD WAR I, THE GREAT DEPRESSION, AND THE NEW DEAL

from 1917 to 1940

I WANT YOU
FOR U.S. ARMY
NEAREST RECRUITING STATION

"NUMBER 258"

Americans sign up for the draft.

People remembered Wilson's words. He made Americans feel that in fighting against Germany they were performing a noble duty, crusading in a great cause. And so they were shocked when they learned that the army was to be made up not of volunteers, but of men who were drafted. The Selective Service Act called upon all men between the ages of twenty-one and thirty to register for war service at their regular voting places on June 5, 1917.

Many people were bitterly opposed to the draft. But Wilson's magical phrase, "The world must be made safe for democracy," defeated his critics. Thousands of people, including mayors, clergymen, and heads of chambers of commerce, came to his support. And on Registration Day, 9,500,000 Americans signed up for the draft.

They came from all walks of life. They came from city and country, from cotton fields and college campuses, from farms and factories, from offices and shops. Some were rich and some were poor. Most of them came gladly, feeling that they were taking part in a glorious adventure and helping to keep the world safe for democracy.

The system of selection was simple. There were 4,500 local draft boards. Each man who registered was given a number by his local board, beginning with Number 1. The longest list in the country went up to Number 10,500. In Washington, 10,500 numbered black capsules were placed in a glass bowl. These were to be drawn out by blindfolded officials. Each time a number was drawn it would be flashed to all of the 4,500 local boards, which would check their lists. The men with that number would be called up to the army.

The drawing began on the morning of July 20. Newspapermen waited, ready to dash to telephones and telegraph connections and inform the country of the first number. Secretary of War Newton D. Baker, blindfolded, put his hand into the bowl. He drew out the first number—it was 258. America had begun to select an army. Before World War I ended, the army would reach a strength of 4,000,000 men.

THE YANKS ARE COMING

Training camps are set up all over the nation to turn raw recruits into soldiers.

People in America tried to appear cheerful as the men drafted into the army marched to railroad stations, where trains waited to carry them to training camps. Bands played, often old Civil War tunes—in the North, *Marching Through Georgia,* and in the South, *The Bonnie Blue Flag.* The draftees kissed wives, mothers, and sweethearts good-by and climbed aboard the cars. People waved and yelled and laughed at banners that read: "We're off to lick the kaiser." The train whistle blew, the crowd surged forward for a last wave and cheer, and through the open windows the draftees were showered with candy bars and packs of cigarettes.

Arriving in camp, the draftee exchanged his civilian clothes for olive-drab coat and breeches. He was a soldier—the "doughboy" of 1917. His day began with the sound of the bugle. This sound inspired Irving Berlin, then a sergeant at Camp Upton, New York, to write a famous song, *Oh! How I Hate to Get Up in the Morning!*

Hate it or not, the rookie got up, to drill and work from mess call at six-twenty in the morning to the sounding of taps at ten at night. As the weeks passed, he settled into camp life. He read the camp paper, complained about the food, and laughed at jokes about the officers. He began to speak a language of his own. A friend was a "buddy," a flea or a louse was a "cootie," the regular army ration of canned beef was "bully beef," "canned willy," or "monkey meat," canned salmon was "gold fish," and a German soldier was "Fritz" or "Heinie."

Organizations like the Red Cross, the Y.M.C.A.,

the Salvation Army, the Knights of Columbus, and the Jewish Welfare Board supplied him with theatrical entertainment, movies, Christmas parties, books, and hometown newspapers. He enjoyed camp boxing matches, played baseball and football, and took part in camp track meets.

To keep up his spirits, he sang songs like *Goodbye Broadway, Hello France,* and he expressed his homesickness in songs like *On the Banks of the Wabash Far Away* and *Little Gray Home in the West.* As he prepared to cross the Atlantic to fight in France, he sang *Over There,* one of the best known songs of the war. Written by George M. Cohan, a theatrical star of the day, it announced that "the Yanks are coming" and that they wouldn't be back "till it's over over there."

Before the war ended, 2,086,000 Americans, sailing from ten ports, went "over there." By the end of 1917 they were leaving at the rate of 50,000 a month. By July of the following year, 306,000 men a month were on their way to France.

America's entry into the war produced many volunteers. They were organized into regiments throughout the nation.

ON THE HOME FRONT

Civilians do their bit to help win the war.

Behind the army stood the nation. There were some "draft dodgers" and "slackers." There were some critics who said that the war was not really being fought to make the world safe for democracy. But most Americans were willing to do what they could to help win the war.

Secretary of War Newton D. Baker drew the numbers of the first draftees from a glass bowl.

A man known to few people before the war soon found his name becoming a household word. Herbert Hoover, who had begun life as an Iowa farm boy, became an orphan at the age of ten. Raised by his uncles in Iowa and Oregon, he studied engineering and was a member of the first class to graduate from Leland Stanford University in 1895.

Starting as a clerk in a San Francisco engineering office, Hoover quickly showed his ability. At the age of twenty-three he was off to Australia to take charge of a gold mine. His career as an engineer took him to five continents—to China during the Boxer Rebellion, to South Africa, Borneo, Burma, and Russia. At times as many as 175,000 persons worked under his direction.

When the war broke out in Europe in 1914, Hoover helped the Americans who were stranded in foreign countries. Walter H. Page, the American ambassador in London, was much impressed by what Hoover had done. After the German invasion of Belgium, Page again turned to Hoover for help. Belgium was an industrial country and had to import almost all of its food. Now, overrun by German troops, it faced famine. Holland feared a food shortage of its own and could do nothing to help.

Hungry Belgians gathered in Brussels to receive American food under Herbert Hoover's relief plan.

Beginning in October, 1914, Hoover traveled across Belgium, France, Great Britain, and the United States, gathering food for the hungry Belgians. To carry on his work, he made at least sixty voyages across the Atlantic. Even the Germans came to regard him as a humanitarian. At its peak. Hoover's Commission for Relief in Belgium was raising and spending $25,000,000 a month—more than the budget of the United States during the administration of Grover Cleveland—and Hoover knew where every penny of it went.

FEEDING THE ALLIES

When the United States entered the war, Hoover took on a new job—head of the Food Administration. Besides feeding its own army and civilian population, the United States had to help supply the needs of the Allies. From England, from Italy, from France came the same urgent message: "We are beaten unless you can send us food."

Food could help win the war—and Hoover made sure that it would. Across the country, from Eastport, Maine, to Coronado Beach, California, Americans followed Hoover's plan to save food. They used less wheat and more corn, less meat and more fish and beans, less sugar and more syrups, and they cut down on the use of fats. "To Hooverize"—that is, to waste nothing—became an American custom. "War gardens" were planted in front yards, in parks, and even in window boxes. There were wheatless Mondays and Wednesdays, meatless Tuesdays, porkless Thursdays and Saturdays. No bread until after the first course, only one kind of meat at a meal, no more than one-half ounce of butter to a person, no sugar bowl on the table—by such rules Americans "Hooverized," and it made them feel that they were helping to beat the Germans and win the war.

American industry, under the leadership of Bernard M. Baruch, chairman of the War Industries Board, also played an enormous part in the war. Baruch was born in South Carolina and was a graduate of the College of the City of New York. His investments made him a wealthy man before he reached the age of thirty.

Baruch brought to the task of mobilizing American industry a spirit of optimism and determination. Manufacturers soon learned how to save time, materials, and labor. One way was by standardization. The styles and sizes of automobile tires, for example, were reduced from 287 to nine; shoes were produced in only three colors—black, white, and tan.

Shortly after the United States entered the war, the nation faced the problem of the German submarines, or U-boats, as they were called. On July 16, 1917, the New York *Times* carried a frightening headline:

U-BOATS SINKING 1,600,000 TONS A MONTH, THRICE THE WORLD'S PRODUCTION; DEFEAT THREATENS IF LOSS IS NOT REDUCED.

The United States did not have so many ships that it could afford to lose any. Since the Civil War, the nation had depended increasingly on foreign

Women worked on farms to replace drafted men. Many other women took jobs in factories.

vessels to carry its products overseas. Now, without ships to carry soldiers, food, and munitions to Europe, it could not win the war. A shipbuilding industry had to be developed almost overnight.

Somehow, the job was done. Ships were built of wood, of steel, of concrete. Hulls were made at the steel mills, saving time at the shipyards. On Hog Island, a lonely, marshy strip of land in the Delaware River, rose the biggest shipyard in the world, where fifty ships could be built at one time. On July 4, 1918, 95 ships were launched in a single day.

America had the will to win. This was a good thing, but it sometimes made people go too far. German-born Americans often were suspected of being spies. The word "sauerkraut" sounded too German and was changed to "liberty cabbage." Even German measles was called "liberty measles."

Women left their kitchens to work in factories, shipyards, or offices. Some worked on farms, where they were known as "farmerettes." To raise money to pay for the war, the government sold Liberty Loan Bonds. Stars of the theater and motion pictures spoke on street corners, urging people to buy a bond and drive another nail in the kaiser's coffin.

People who could not afford to buy Liberty Bonds bought war-savings stamps. Children saved their pennies to buy thrift stamps, which sold for twenty-five cents; sixteen of these could be exchanged for a war-savings stamp worth five dollars.

World War I was "a fight for the minds of men," and to reach the minds of men, a Committee on Public Information was set up. It was headed by George Creel, who organized the nation's writers, artists, actors, and public speakers. They produced pamphlets, posters, and motion pictures, and made speeches. A corps of 75,000 "Four-Minute Men" was formed to speak to Americans anywhere, at any time, on such subjects as "Why We Are Fighting" and "The Meaning of America." The pamphlet *How the War Came to America* was read by 7,000,000. Editions were published for the foreign-born in Swedish, Polish, Italian, Spanish, Bohemian, and Portuguese.

Copies of President Wilson's speeches and messages were distributed throughout the world. His war aims became famous as the "Fourteen Points." On January 8, 1918, Wilson made a speech to Congress entitled *A Statement of the War Aims and Peace Terms of the United States.* In it he explained his Fourteen Points, which he felt would bring a lasting peace to the world. He said that there must be no more secret agreements between nations. There must be "absolute freedom of . . . the seas," and landlocked countries like Serbia and Poland must have "access to the sea." Wilson's final point, foreshadowing the formation of the League of Nations, declared:

"A general association of nations must be formed under specific covenants [agreements] for the purpose of affording mutual guarantees of political independence and territorial integrity to great and small states alike."

In this way Wilson held out hope to both small and large nations, and to both friend and foe.

FROM CANTIGNY TO CHÂTEAU-THIERRY

An American army helps stop the German advance toward Paris.

The causes of World War I went far back in history. The struggle among the European nations had begun centuries ago, when America itself was one of the prizes in Europe's race for trade and riches. In time, Britain's strong navy made her the world's greatest colonial power, while Russia and France controlled the European continent. As Germany grew in industrial and military might, she challenged her old rivals. She wanted colonies, and she was no longer satisfied to allow France and Russia to control Europe. The result was World War I.

At the beginning of the war, Germany hoped for a quick victory over France in the west before she moved against Russia in the east. Unexpectedly, Belgium blocked the way. This tiny country's resistance gave the Allies a chance to rally their forces. They made Germany do what she least wanted to do—fight on two fronts at the same time. Even so, the Germans marched through Belgium into France. But they were stopped before Paris, and for two years the western front showed little change.

"LAFAYETTE, WE ARE HERE"

On the eastern front, the story was different. In March of 1917, a revolution overthrew Czar Nicholas II, the ruler of Russia. A second revolution in November put the Communists in control of the government. They were not interested in fighting Germany and the Central Powers. They wanted a quick peace so that they could go about building up a Communist state. Besides, Russia no longer had the strength to fight, and many Russian soldiers were laying down their arms and going home.

When the United States entered the war, the average American citizen had little idea of what was happening on either the western or the eastern front. He believed that America's chief job in the war would be to supply the food, munitions, and money that would carry the Allies to victory. But more than that would be necessary.

The United States had planned to send troops overseas no earlier than March of 1918. Pressure from the Allies made Wilson send soldiers to Europe in the spring of 1917, with the understanding that they would complete their training in France.

The American troops in Europe were called the American Expeditionary Forces, or the A.E.F. They were under the command of Major General John J. Pershing, who was then fifty-seven years old. He had served in Cuba and the Philippines, and had chased Pancho Villa through the mountains of northern Mexico. Pershing had visited France and could speak its language. On July 4, 1917, he was one of a group of Americans who made speeches at the tomb of Lafayette in Paris. A member of his staff, Colonel Charles E. Stanton, spoke the words that became famous: "Lafayette, we are here."

All along the Western front, fighting raged across a desolate, shattered landscape. (Left) *A captured German war painting shows German troops at Verdun in 1916.* (Below) *German Field Marshal Paul von Hindenburg*

Americans were in the fighting sooner than they had expected to be. In October of 1917, the Italian line opposing Austria had crumbled. To bolster it, the Allies shifted some of their forces from the west. The following March, the Communist government of Russia made peace with Germany. Suddenly 500,000 German troops were freed from fighting on the eastern front and could open an assault on the west. Paris was again in danger, and almost a million people fled the city that spring.

The Americans fought their first battle on May 28, 1918. It took place at Cantigny, a little village in northeast France. Although Cantigny was not of much importance, the Germans were anxious to take it. They did not want to admit defeat in their first fighting against Americans. But the Yanks stood firm against the German attacks and won the battle after about forty minutes of furious fighting.

As May ended, American troops were thrown into a gap in the French line on the road between Château-Thierry and Paris. Here the point of assault was a bridge across the Marne River. The Germans had already entered Château-Thierry when, as a British reporter wrote, the Americans attacked "with their habitual courage."

Château-Thierry rocked with the enemy bombardment and the Germans advanced behind a smoke screen. "A surprise, however, was in store for them," the British reporter went on. "They were already crossing the bridge, evidently believing themselves masters of both banks [of the Marne], when a thunderous explosion blew the center of the bridge and a number of Germans with it into the river." About a hundred of the Germans, reaching the southern bank, were captured by the Americans.

The battle swept through street after street. Buildings fell as they were hit by shells from the heavy guns. Machine guns rattled from doorways and street corners. Of the 8,000 Americans in the fighting at Château-Thierry, 1,600 were killed and 2,513 were wounded. This battle, General Pershing said, "stopped the German advance on Paris."

THE NAVY GOES INTO ACTION

American mine layers sow the North Sea with mines to destroy German U-boats.

While American soldiers fought in France, the United States navy set out to destroy the German submarine menace. The most important part of the job was carried out not by the sleek battleships or the perky destroyers, but by the lowly mine layers. Under the command of Admiral William Sowden Sims, they roamed the North Sea. There they dropped explosive mines under the water. Any U-boat that happened to hit one would be destroyed.

Protected by destroyers, the little mine layers left port in the dead of night with no lights showing. Except for the swishing of water against the sides and the churning of the propellers, there was no sound to warn lurking U-boats of the enemy above.

Artists on both sides depicted scenes from World War I. (Below) *A captured German painting of tanks burning on the Western front.* (Right) *American troops advance up a hillside, as painted by W. J. Aylward.*

Camouflaged minesweepers swept across the North Sea, laying a mine barrage from Norway to the Orkneys.

Battleships swept majestically across the horizon, guarding against attack from German dreadnaughts.

In two columns about five hundred yards apart, ten mine layers plunged into the open sea. They had been fitted with underwater outriggers to protect them from German mines, for the North Sea was everybody's battleground. The men stood at their stations, waiting for the signal from the flagship.

Admiral Sims later described the scene:

"Up to this time the ships were sailing in two columns; when they came within seven miles of start point another signal was broken out; the ships all wheeled like a company of soldiers, each turning sharply to the right, so that in a few minutes, instead of two columns, we had eight ships in line abreast, with the remaining two, also in line abreast, sailing ahead of them . . . the officers all had their eyes fixed upon the stern of the flagship for the glimpse of the red flag which would be the signal to begin. Suddenly the flag was hauled down, indicating: 'First mine over.'"

The ships were now going at full speed. Every few seconds, a mine—a huge black object about five feet high—would glide toward the stern, hang there for a moment, and then plunge into the water. The mine layers laid down a barrage of mines from the Orkney Islands, north of Scotland, to the coast of Norway—a distance of about two hundred and fifty nautical miles.

American sailors, under Secretary of the Navy Josephus Daniels, made a proud record in World War I. They took their battle stations on eighty destroyers and laid 56,000 mines in the North Sea blockade of Germany. They guarded about four-fifths of the transports carrying troops overseas, and not one transport was destroyed by torpedoes. Before the war ended, 75,000 American sailors sailed more than three hundred vessels of war in European waters, and Germany lost half her U-boats.

BREAKING THE HINDENBURG LINE

In the Second Battle of the Marne, Americans break through the German defenses, and the tide of war turns.

In the summer of 1918, the German high command, headed by Field Marshal Paul von Hindenburg, planned a great offensive. If it was successful, Paris would fall and the Germans would win the war. But the Second Battle of the Marne, which was fought from July 18 to August 6, proved to be the turning point of World War I.

"BOLDEST STROKE OF THE WAR"

More than 250,000 Americans took part in this action. Among them were the men of the 38th Regiment of the Third Division. They held off almost two enemy divisions after the French, falling back, had left their flanks exposed. The Allies then launched a counteroffensive that was called the "boldest stroke of the war." They struck at the so-called Hindenburg Line, a system of German defenses across northeastern France. The risk was great, for the Germans were stronger in both men and guns, but Pershing argued that taking risks was part of war. Two American divisions—the First and the Second—smashed at the Germans south of Soissons, a city sixty-five miles northeast of Paris.

The fighting was rugged. It took place on open ground, where the men could take cover only in shell holes. The Germans had been taken by surprise, and the Allies had to act quickly if they were not to lose their advantage. There was no time for the artillery to blast out the German machine-gun nests; they had to be overrun by the infantry. The Americans swept ahead in waves, followed by the "mopperups," troops who had the task of rounding up prisoners.

Tanks waddled like turtles across the ground, machine-gun bullets bouncing off their thick sides. Overhead buzzed red-nosed German planes. When darkness came, the planes flew low. They dropped parachutes that floated through the air, carrying great balls of light. The plateau over which the Allies were advancing on Soissons was as bright as day. Then the German bombers went to work, blasting the troops moving up to the front.

At four o'clock in the morning the Yanks were still slugging their way ahead. A hillside before them bristled with nests of machine-gunners who were concealed in the tall grass. Tanks went up the slope, the artillery rolled its guns forward and opened fire with a roar—and the Yanks took the hill. The Germans fought back desperately. Captain Shipley Thomas of the Twenty-Sixth American infantry later said, "There were no prisoners taken in this fierce assault. The Germans fired until they were killed."

In spite of the German resistance, the Yanks came on, taking the ground in a series of little rushes. At dawn on July 21, they felt that victory was near. Every available man was called for the final assault.

The artillery laid down a barrage. The Yanks moved through wooded gullies and across the highway that joined Château-Thierry and Soissons. A hill had to be taken by storm. It was a bloody affair, but the Yanks took it. That day Soissons was captured, giving the Germans the worst defeat they had suffered in a year. The tide had turned in favor of the Allies.

American artillerymen in action on the Marne front.

Captain Eddie Rickenbacker, American World War I ace.

AN AMERICAN VICTORY

The American forces now fought as a separate army. They took over the task of driving the enemy out of St. Mihiel, to the south and east of Verdun. The Germans had held this position since September of 1914. It was a position of great importance, for once the Allies had taken it, they would be able to attack in any direction at any time. General Pershing later described that morning of the twelfth of September when the Yanks attacked:

"The sky over the battlefield, both before and after dawn, aflame with exploding shells, star signals, burning supply dumps and villages, presented a scene at once picturesque and terrible. The exultation in our minds that here, at last, after seventeen months of effort, an American army was fighting under its own flag, was tempered by the realization of the sacrifice of life on both sides; and yet fate had willed it thus and we must carry through. Confidence in our troops dispelled every doubt of ultimate victory.

By September 13 the task had been accomplished. Sixteen thousand German prisoners were captured—a fact which shows how great the American victory was.

THE WAR ENDS

Pershing was eager to push eastward into Germany, but the Allied command decided against it. Instead, the Americans turned north to fight the battle of the Meuse-Argonne. The object was to take Sedan and cut the Sedan-Mézières railroad, the Germans' chief line of supply on the western front. This was part of a larger offensive planned by the Allies to smash the German forces. More than 1,000,000 Americans fought in the battle and 120,000 were killed.

But the end was drawing near for Germany and her allies. In September, Bulgaria was knocked out of the war, followed by Turkey in October and Austria in early November. And, even while the battle of the Meuse-Argonne went on, the Germans were asking President Wilson for terms of peace.

Wilson offered his Fourteen Points as the basis of an armistice. To please Britain and France, however, he was forced to back down on two points. Freedom of the seas could not be guaranteed, and Germany must agree to pay the full cost of the damage caused by her invasion of Allied territory. On November 9, the kaiser fled to exile in Holland. Two days later, the powerful radio of the Eiffel Tower in Paris flashed the news to the world: "Hostilities will cease on all fronts. . . ."

World War I was over.

LOSING THE PEACE

Germany surrenders, but Wilson fails to get the peace treaty he wants.

All over America, in 50,000 cities and towns, people celebrated the end of the war. As one newspaper put it: "In America it has been a people's war throughout. The people made it; they fought it. Why shouldn't they go mad at the thought of German surrender if they want to?"

And the people did go mad—mad with joy. They danced in the streets. They hugged strangers. They started parades, while bands played *Over There* and *When Johnny Comes Marching Home.* Cowboys whooped and yipped in San Antonio, Texas, and soldiers and sailors took over Newport News, Virginia. The mayor of Chicago decreed that saloons could stay open all night, and in San Francisco bonfires burned on the hilltops. Crowds filled New York's Fifth Avenue, while sailors got up a football game in the middle of Forty-Second Street.

Crowds cheered Allied troops on victory parades. All over the U.S. people celebrated the war's end.

WILSON'S HARDEST FIGHT

The war was over—but Woodrow Wilson faced the hardest fight of his life. There was growing opposition in the United States to his Fourteen Points. Many Americans were especially opposed to the formation of the League of Nations, fearing that it would involve the United States too deeply in European affairs. And Wilson had made a serious mistake. He had called upon the people to give him a Democratic majority in Congress when they voted in the November elections. Not only did he not get what he wanted—the Republicans won the election—but he also angered a number of Republican congressmen who had been supporting him.

In December, Wilson sailed for Europe to attend the Peace Conference, which was to be held in the Versailles Palace outside Paris. Again he made a serious mistake. The delegation he chose to go with him included not a single leading Republican. He also failed to include a single senator, which angered senators of both parties. This was important, because the Senate must approve all peace treaties. Wilson was to pay dearly for these mistakes.

Europe gave Wilson a tremendous welcome. Huge throngs greeted him in France, as they did when he journeyed to England and Italy. A sign strung across a street in Paris read: "Honor to Wilson the Just." That summed up the feelings of the people of Europe. To them, Wilson was a great man, almost a saint. He would see that justice was done to minority groups and to small nations as well as to large ones. He would see that there was freedom and independence for all peoples.

But the Allied leaders who met with Wilson had other ideas. Lloyd George had won re-election as prime minister of England by promising to "make Germany pay the whole cost of the war"—and pay to the last penny. Georges Clemenceau, the crafty premier of France, felt it was his duty to look after the interests of France, and no other country but France. Italy's prime minister, Vittorio Orlando, was concerned only with Italy's claim to new territories. On top of this, Wilson received staggering news from the United States. Thirty-nine members of the Senate had signed a letter saying that they would oppose a peace treaty which set up a League of Nations.

WILSON IN PARIS

The Peace Conference was a miserable experience for Wilson. For one thing, its meetings were kept secret—and the Fourteen Points had called for open agreements of peace "openly arrived at." He was weakened by an attack of influenza, and by May one side of his face had begun to twitch. He accepted a number of compromises, in the hope that they would make it possible to set up the League of Nations. And, he believed, once the League was in operation, it would correct the mistakes of the Peace Conference.

Returning to the United States, Wilson threw himself into a vigorous campaign to win support for the League. The Republicans in the Senate fought back with all their strength. They called the League a "super-state" that would swallow up American independence. Against the advice of his doctor, Wilson set out on a coast-to-coast tour of the country, carrying his fight to the people. For twenty-two days he traveled, speaking wherever there were people who would listen. In small towns, he spoke from the rear platform of the train; in cities, he spoke at giant rallies. His opponents continued to make savage attacks on the League.

Wilson was tired and aging, and he was driving himself to a breakdown. Speaking at Pueblo, Colorado, on September 25, he burst into tears. That night he could not sleep. The train was stopped so that he and Mrs. Wilson could walk along a country road. Before daylight, he suffered a stroke, and the rest of the tour was canceled. Wilson was rushed back to Washington, where he had a second stroke in October. In time, he recovered enough to leave his bed and sit in a chair. But he was too feeble to carry on his fight to win the country's support for the League of Nations.

THE SENATE REJECTS THE LEAGUE

The Treaty of Versailles, including the Covenant of the League of Nations, was accepted by twenty-seven nations—but not by the United States. The opposition, led by Senator Henry Cabot Lodge of Massachusetts, was too strong, and the Senate refused to approve it. The final vote, killing almost all hope that the United States would join the League, came on March 19, 1920. This was two months after the League had set up headquarters on the peaceful shore of Lake Geneva in Switzerland and had begun its twenty-six-year experiment in international co-operation.

"IN A SMOKE-FILLED ROOM"

Republicans pick Warren G. Harding as their candidate for president.

After the death of Theodore Roosevelt in 1919, the leading candidate for the Republican presidential nomination was Roosevelt's old friend General Leonard Wood. But when the Republicans held their convention in 1920, they could not decide between Wood and Governor Lowden of Illinois. Harry M. Daugherty, a political boss from Ohio, broke the deadlock. Meeting "at two o'clock in the morning, in a smoke-filled room," the party leaders agreed on a compromise candidate—Warren Gamaliel Harding. They wanted a man who would work with them, and Harding seemed like someone who would.

Daugherty was proud of the job he did in building Harding into a presidential candidate. He once said, "I found him sunning himself, like a turtle on a log, and I pushed him into the water." Harding was born on a farm near Bloomington Grove, Ohio. He attended Caledonia High School, where he played in the band, and was an easygoing student at

Harding did most of his campaigning for the presidency from the front porch of his home in Marion, Ohio.

Ohio Central College. His first job was as a typesetter on the weekly *Democratic Mirror* in Marion, Ohio, at a salary of one dollar a week.

After Harding married Florence De Wolfe Kling, daughter of the town's leading banker, he became a successful newspaper publisher and editor. With Daugherty's support, he was elected to the state senate. He served two terms, then was elected lieutenant governor of Ohio. Although he failed to win when he ran for governor, he was not disturbed. He still enjoyed his Saturday night poker games and took a deep interest in the batting averages of major-league baseball players. In 1914 he was elected to the United States Senate. He was still a senator when his name was brought up in that "smoke-filled room."

"BACK TO NORMALCY"

Harding realized that the nation was tired of wartime sacrifices and keeping the world safe for democracy. People wanted a return of the "good old days." He said, "America's present need is not heroics but healing." By "heroics" Harding meant the League of Nations, which he felt the United States could do without. He also said that what the country needed was "normalcy," coining a new word which he used instead of "normality." Americans did not care what word he used. They agreed with him and elected him President. The defeated Democratic candidate was James M. Cox, the governor of Ohio. Also defeated was the Democratic candidate for Vice-President—Franklin D. Roosevelt of New York, who had served as Assistant Secretary of the Navy during World War I.

THE "RED SCARE"

When trouble breaks out between business and labor, many people blame "Reds" or "radicals."

Woodrow Wilson retired to a house on S Street in Washington. He had hoped that Cox, who supported the League of Nations, would be elected and that the United States would then join the League. But now that Harding was President, Wilson's dream was shattered. He became a shy, lonely man who shunned public appearances, and he died in 1924. Perhaps he blamed Harding and the Republicans in the Senate for the tragedy that darkened his last years—yet the truth was that the American people themselves were just as much to blame. Once the war was over, they felt that they had had enough of Europe and its problems. They were no longer interested in making sacrifices for noble ideals.

"Bring the doughboys home at once," Americans said. They gave no thought to what would happen when 4,000,000 soldiers and sailors were discharged and started to look for jobs. So the soldiers and sailors were brought home. They were cheered wildly as they paraded down Main Street—and then forgotten. They soon learned that while they were draftees at $30 a month some of their friends who had stayed home had earned as much as $10 a day. They joined organizations like the American Legion and the Veterans of Foreign Wars, and demanded that the government pay them a bonus.

Meanwhile, industrial companies were asked to

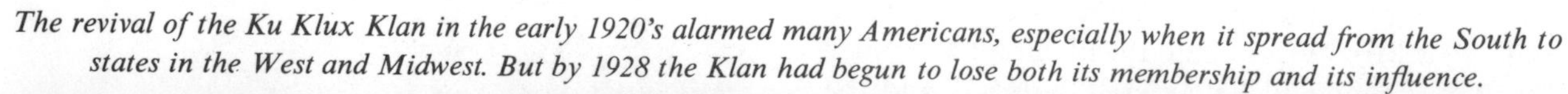

The revival of the Ku Klux Klan in the early 1920's alarmed many Americans, especially when it spread from the South to states in the West and Midwest. But by 1928 the Klan had begun to lose both its membership and its influence.

drop war contracts and go back to production for commercial markets. The businessmen wanted profits, and they said it was time the workers worked longer hours for less pay. The workers had grown accustomed to higher pay and refused to give it up without a struggle. The country was rocked by a series of strikes in one industry after another. Men walked off their jobs in steel mills, coal mines, shipyards, and stockyards, and on railroads and subways.

THE BOSTON POLICE STRIKE

In Boston, even the policemen went on strike. They were paid a minimum of $1,100 a year, out of which they had to buy their own uniforms. They were having a hard time making ends meet, and they decided to form a union that would be part of the American Federation of Labor. Boston's police commissioner ruled that joining a union was against "orders," and suspended nineteen men from the force. Neither he nor the police would back down from their stand. On September 9, 1919, most of Boston's police force went on strike, and there were robberies and disorders in the unprotected city.

The governor of Massachusetts at that time was Calvin Coolidge, who was little known outside his own state. Coolidge insisted that there was "no right to strike against the public safety by anybody, anywhere, any time," and the strike was soon over. Overnight he became a national figure, and a year later he was elected Vice-President of the United States.

Many Americans approved of Coolidge's action in the strike, for a "Red scare" was sweeping the nation. Businessmen charged that there was something more behind all the strikes than just the workers' wish for high pay. The strikes, they said, were caused by foreign "Reds" and "radicals"—anarchists, Bolsheviks, Communists, and Socialists—who were plotting to destroy the American way of life. The hysteria mounted, and government officials said that unless Americans fought back, a Red revolution would break out in the United States.

LOYALTY OATHS

The nation was determined to root out radicals wherever they could be found—in the unions, in politics, in schools and colleges. Between 1917 and 1935, twenty-one states passed laws requiring teachers to take oaths of loyalty to the United States. Textbooks were examined to make sure that they said the right things about "great Americans."

Intolerance bred still more intolerance. As early as 1915, a Georgian named Colonel William Joseph Simmons had revived the old Ku Klux Klan. But it did not really begin to grow until 1920. The Klan was now opposed to radicals and pacifists as well as Negroes, Jews, and Catholics. Any "native white Protestant" could become a member and put on a white robe by paying a fee of $10. Since the local Kleagle, or Klan chief, kept $4 out of the $10 he collected from every new member, prejudice was highly profitable.

By 1924, the Klan was estimated to have more than 4,000,000 members. It was no longer an organization of the South, as it had been in Reconstruction days, but had spread to Oregon, Oklahoma, Arkansas, Indiana, Ohio, and California. The Ku Kluxers, wearing masks and white robes, burned crosses, threatened their neighbors, coated their victims with tar and feathers, and sometimes left them lying beaten to death along the roadside.

But there were a number of Americans who opposed the Klan, and by 1928 it had lost much of its influence. By that time, too, Americans were finding other interests.

AMERICA BEGINS TO RELAX

Listening to radio and watching sports are favorite pastimes in the 1920's.

On November 2, 1920, America's first commercial radio station, KDKA, began operation in East Pittsburgh, Pennsylvania. The broadcast that day gave details of Harding's victory over Cox in the presidential election. Voices came through amazingly well, but music often sounded scratchy and distorted. In time, however, the station put up wall hangings that absorbed distracting studio noises.

Among famous entertainers in early radio days were Billy Jones and Ernie Hare, the "Happiness Boys."

By the winter of 1920–21, radio was a national fad. The simple crystal set, which any bright boy could build in a few hours, became standard household equipment. People forgot about the Red Scare and the Ku Klux Klan and boasted about "getting" Cuba on their radios. In the years that followed, hundreds of radio stations began broadcasting throughout the United States. The names of popular singers became familiar to all Americans, and prominent announcers seemed to be family friends. Soon low-priced vacuum tubes, designed to operate on dry-cell batteries, replaced the crystal detector—the first of many improvements that made listening to the radio more enjoyable.

In the 1920's, America entered a golden age of sports, and great crowds cheered the outstanding performers. In boxing, there was Jack Dempsey, the heavyweight champion. In baseball, there were Babe Ruth, the home-run king, and the New York Yankees. In football, there were Red Grange, the "Galloping Ghost" of Illinois, and the "Praying Colonels" from Centre College who defeated Harvard. In horse racing, there was Man o' War. In tennis, there were Helen Wills and Bill Tilden. And Gertrude Ederle became the first woman to swim the English Channel.

Women made news in other fields than sports. An amendment to the Constitution in 1920 gave them the right to vote. The "flapper" appeared—young women who wore bobbed hair and short skirts, used lipstick, and carried cigarette holders.

THE VOLSTEAD ACT

During World War I, Congress had passed the 18th Amendment prohibiting the manufacture, sale, or transportation of "intoxicating liquors." The Volstead Act, which followed in 1919, set up strict methods of enforcement. It defined as intoxicating any beverage that contained one-half of one per cent of alcohol. By January, 1920, three-fourths of the states had ratified the 18th Amendment, and both Prohibition and the Volstead Act became law. Even wine, which contains about 11 per cent alcohol, was illegal.

Behind Prohibition was a century of struggle. American church groups and women's organizations had steadily campaigned against the "evil of drink." They said drinking wrecked homes and was a cause of poverty. The increasing use of automobiles gave them another strong argument—drunken drivers were a menace on the highways. So, finally, the American tradition that personal habits were no concern of the government was brushed aside.

The people who supported Prohibition were sure that the law could be easily enforced. They soon found that they were mistaken. Saloons were closed, but "speakeasies," which illegally sold intoxicating liquors, took their place. Great quantities of liquor were smuggled in from other countries. It was difficult to stop, for the authorities had to patrol 21,000 miles of coast line and 5,875 miles of land bordering Mexico and Canada. Words like "rumrunner," "bootlegger," and "bathtub gin" soon became part of the language.

Speakeasies replaced saloons during Prohibition.

Bootlegging—the making, selling, and smuggling of illegal liquor—became a big business. Criminals controlled it, and its enormous profits financed the growth of organized crime across the United States. It was also a bloody business in which rival gangs waged war in city streets. Most notorious were the battles in Chicago, begun when gangster Johnny Torrio set out to win control of bootlegging. To do that he needed a strong man who could command a personal army and drive out competing bootleggers. He found him in bull-necked twenty-three-year-old "Scarface" Al Capone, who belonged to the tough Five Points gang in New York City. And so began the rise to power of the best-known gangster of the 1920's.

GANG WARFARE

The other gangs in Chicago had no intention of giving up their share of the rich bootlegging business to Torrio and Capone. The result was the worst gang warfare that had ever been seen in the United States. Capone's "army"—about 700 hoodlums who were experts with sawed-off shotguns and Thompson submachine guns—showed the underworld some new tricks in murder.

Time after time, newspapers told the story of gangsters shot down in the street. Dion O'Banion was killed while shaking hands with a supposed friend. In the St. Valentine's Day Massacre of 1929, gangsters disguised as policemen machine-gunned seven members of the Moran gang in a garage on North Clark Street. "Jake" Lingle, a Chicago *Tribune* reporter who knew too much about the underworld, was shot down. The hotel where

Capone himself lived was sprayed with machine-gun bullets from eight cars. Capone saved himself by stretching out flat on his belly in the hotel dining room.

By 1925, Capone controlled Cicero, a suburb of Chicago, and its 161 speakeasies. He had his own man elected mayor. He went on to win a big share of the illegal liquor business in Chicago itself, where there were 10,000 speakeasies to be supplied. He was now a king of the underworld, who rode through the streets in his own armored car.

Yet the sad fact was that neither Capone nor any other gangster could hold such power without the help of dishonest officials, judges, and police. Chicago became widely known because nowhere else was crime so open, so widespread, and so well protected. But the story of many other cities, such as New York, Detroit, and Toledo, was hardly less shameful.

PROHIBITION REPEALED

Prohibition had made the gangster a real force in American life and was damaging the reputation of the United States in the rest of the world. Herbert Hoover once said that Prohibition was "a great social and economic experiment, noble in motive and far-reaching in purpose." But the "noble experiment" had failed, and in time even stubborn politicians would realize it. In 1933 the 21st Amendment, ratified within ten months, repealed the 18th Amendment, and Prohibition came to an end.

THE UNHAPPY STORY OF HARDING

A friendly, easygoing man becomes President, but dies in mid-term.

Warren G. Harding was one of the most popular men ever to occupy the White House. Wilson had been standoffish and kept the public at a distance. Harding threw open the gates of the White House and invited the people to come in. They found it was easy to like this friendly, handsome man.

But there have been few Presidents who were less qualified for the office than Harding. He did not have the kind of mind to deal with the problems of national government. His method was to trust "the best brains" to work out the problems for him. Sometimes this led to good results, as when Charles Evans Hughes presided over the Washington Conference for the Limitation of Armaments. But not all the men around Harding were as brilliant as Hughes. Some were far from being "the best brains." Moreover, some were as fuzzy in their morals as they were in their thinking.

Slowly and painfully, Harding learned the truth about the men in his administration. On March 4, 1923, he accepted the resignation of Albert B. Fall, his Secretary of the Interior. Fall had taken a bribe to lease naval oil reserves at Teapot Dome, Wyoming, and Elk Hills, California, to private interests. Also involved was Edwin Denby, the Secretary of the Navy. There were other scandals, too, during Harding's administration, but the Teapot Dome affair was the worst.

Harding knew how shocked the nation would be when all the scandals became public. He realized, too, that he had placed too much faith in the friends he had appointed to positions in the government. Worried and weary, he left in June of 1923 for a speaking tour that carried him as far as Alaska. By the time he returned to San Francisco, he was a sick man, and he died there on the second of August. And so ended the life of this unhappy President who had been pushed into a job that was too big for him.

With Harding's death, Calvin Coolidge, the hero of the Boston police strike in 1919, became the nation's thirtieth President. A graduate of Amherst College, he had known lean years as a lawyer in Northampton, Massachusetts. He had willingly taken any political office that came his way. He served as a councilman, as city solicitor, as a representative

President Coolidge on a visit to an Indian reservation.

in the state legislature, as mayor of Northampton, as a state senator, as lieutenant-governor, and as governor. His struggles while a young lawyer had taught him not to waste anything. He did not even waste words, and he became know as "Silent Cal."

Coolidge was President only because of the accident of Harding's death, but he easily won the nomination on his own in 1924. The Republicans could not resist a man who declared that "the business of America is business." The Democrats, on the other hand, were hopelessly split over the Ku Klux Klan and Prohibition.

There were two leading candidates for the Democratic nomination. One was William G. McAdoo, who was a Protestant, a Californian, and a "dry"—that is, he was in favor of Prohibition. The other was Alfred E. Smith, a Roman Catholic, a New Yorker, and a "wet" who was opposed to Prohibition. Meeting in New York City, the Democrats tried for 103 ballots to choose between McAdoo and Smith. At last they compromised on John W. Davis, a former ambassador to Great Britain, not really believing he could win. He didn't.

"KEEPING COOL WITH COOLIDGE"

A trial in Tennessee stirs the nation.
Lindbergh makes the first
nonstop solo flight across the Atlantic Ocean.

Suddenly the United States seemed to find the answer to all its problems in the simple formula of "keeping cool with Coolidge." It was a changing, somewhat giddy world, when for the sake of publicity even congressmen danced the "Charleston" on the steps of the Capitol. In such a world, Coolidge seemed safe and steady. He advised Americans "to spend less than you make, and to make more than you spend."

Not everyone in the country welcomed change. In 1925, the state of Tennessee passed a law that said "it shall be unlawful for any teacher in any of the universities, normals [teachers' colleges], and all other public schools of the State, which are supported in whole or in part by public school funds of the State, to teach any theory that denies the story of the Divine creation of man as taught in the Bible, and to teach instead that man has descended from a lower order of animals." In other words, the law forbade the teaching of Darwin's theory of evolution.

John Thomas Scopes, a young teacher of biology in the Central High School of Dayton, Tennessee, decided to challenge the law. He continued to teach the theory of evolution in his classroom, and for doing so he was arrested and put on trial.

THE SCOPES TRIAL

The Scopes case attracted national attention. Among other things, it involved the teaching of science to American youth. William Jennings Bryan, who had been the "Boy Orator of the Platte" and was now the grand old man of the Democratic Party, helped to plead the case for the state. A group of brilliant lawyers, headed by Clarence Darrow, defended Scopes.

The trial began on July 10, 1925, and went on for eleven days. Newspapermen from all over the world swarmed into Dayton in such numbers that special arrangements had to be made so that they could eat and sleep. There was as much interest in the lawyers as there was in Scopes or evolution. Bryan, an unsuccessful candidate for the presidency on three occasions, was well known to everyone. And Darrow was one of the most famous and colorful lawyers in America.

Like the men who had passed the law, Bryan was a fundamentalist in religion. He believed in the literal truth of the Bible. When he himself took the stand to testify, Darrow questioned him mercilessly. Wagging his finger at Bryan, Darrow thundered, "Do you say you do not believe there were any civilizations on this earth which reach back beyond five thousand years?" Bryan's answer was that he believed the world had been created in the year 4004 B.C.

Again, Darrow asked, "Do you think the earth was made in six days?" Bryan answered, "Not six days of twenty-four hours." The crowd in the little courtroom gasped, for Bryan had been forced to retreat from his position that everything in the Bible was literally true. Nevertheless, the state won the case. But the aging Bryan had been under a severe strain, and less than two weeks after the trial ended he died in his sleep.

EARLY AVIATORS

There were other things, too, that claimed the attention of Americans during this time. There were new heroes in sports—the Notre Dame football team under Coach Knute Rockne, Bobby Jones, who won many titles on the golf links, and Johnny Weismuller, a champion swimmer who later played the part of Tarzan in the movies. And then there appeared a new kind of hero—one who was cheered by all America.

His name was Charles A. Lindbergh, and soon he was known as "Lindy." His father was Charles Augustus Lindbergh, who represented Minnesota in Congress from 1907 to 1917. Young Lindbergh studied engineering at the University of Wisconsin, but left at the end of three semesters to learn flying. By 1925 he was an air mail pilot, flying between Chicago and St. Louis.

Lindbergh piloted his small plane around storms and overhanging clouds, sometimes flying close to the ocean surface.

Aviation had made much progress since the Wright brothers first flew at Kitty Hawk, and there had been a number of notable flights. In 1919, John Alcock and Arthur W. Brown succeeded in flying across the Atlantic Ocean. Seven years later, Richard E. Byrd, who had been a lieutenant commander in the navy during World War I, took off from King's Bay, Spitsbergen, on the first flight to the North Pole. He and his co-pilot, Floyd Bennett, circled the pole several times before returning to their base.

NONSTOP TO PARIS

Now Raymond Orteig, a New York hotel owner, had offered a prize of $25,000 for the first nonstop flight between New York and Paris. Lindbergh was determined to win that prize. Not only did he intend to fly across the Atlantic to Paris—he intended to do it alone. A group of men in St. Louis believed he could do it, and contributed the money for his plane, a Ryan monoplane. In their honor, Lindbergh named his craft *The Spirit of St. Louis.*

In May of 1927, Lindbergh flew his new plane from San Diego, California, to New York City. His time was twenty-one hours and twenty minutes—a new record. Ten days later, on May 20, at 7:52 in the morning, he roared off into the overcast sky. His heavily overloaded plane cleared a tractor by fifteen feet and a telephone wire by twenty feet. Lindbergh dipped to the right to avoid some high trees, then went soaring over Long Island Sound.

All that day, people everywhere in the United States waited for news about Lindbergh. In crowded cities, in small towns and villages, in the country, in shops and offices and homes, in farmhouses, they talked of nothing else. Those who could stayed by their radios. They heard that Lindbergh had passed over Cape Cod, flying not more than ten feet above the trees. They heard that he had been seen by a number of small fishing boats between the Cape and Nova Scotia.

At St. John's, Newfoundland, Lindbergh veered east. He was now over the vast, silent Atlantic, a lone man in a lone plane. Looking down on the ocean, he could see an occasional iceberg floating by.

Fog settled on the sea that night, and at 10,000 feet Lindbergh was just skimming the tops of storm clouds. Now and then he could see a star, but he could not see the moon. Sleet began collecting on his wings, and this meant danger. Suddenly, to his joy, he saw the moon. At about one o'clock in the morning, New York time, the dawn began breaking over the ocean, and he no longer had to fear sleet. The cloud bank broke at sunrise, and afterward the fog came in little patches.

Flying low that morning, Lindbergh saw a boat. He shouted, "Which way is Ireland?" He could not hear the answer, and flew on. Eventually, he sighted Cape Valencia, flew over Dingle Bay on the western coast of Ireland, passed Plymouth and flew over the English Channel. He flew over the city of Cherbourg in France, where the people cheered as they saw the plane overhead, and finally he came in for a landing at Le Bourget Field in Paris. He had made a nonstop solo flight over the Atlantic in thirty-three hours and thirty-nine minutes.

A HERO'S WELCOME

Madly cheering Frenchmen mobbed the field. The news was flashed to America, which went wild with joy. President Coolidge sent a cruiser to France to bring back Lindbergh and his plane. When he arrived in the United States, he was given 55,000 telegrams of congratulation, including one from Minneapolis that bore 17,500 names. Texas named a town after him. The government awarded him the Distinguished Flying Cross and the Congressional Medal of Honor.

Other flights followed Lindbergh's, to Europe and across the Pacific to Hawaii. In 1931, Harold Gatty and Wiley Post flew around the world in less than nine days. The United States was becoming air-minded, and airports were being constructed in city after city.

SACCO AND VANZETTI

A shoemaker and a fish peddler are convicted of murder, but many Americans have doubts about their guilt.

In the year that Lindbergh flew to Paris, a shoemaker and a fish peddler were also in the news. Their names were Nicola Sacco and Bartolomeo Vanzetti. Their story had begun in April of 1920, when a paymaster and his guard were killed during a payroll robbery in South Braintree, Massachusetts. Witnesses described the holdup men as Italians, and suspicion centered on the Morelli gang in Providence.

But it was the time of the Red scare. All alien radicals were under suspicion—and Sacco and Vanzetti were alien radicals. They were charged with the South Braintree slayings and brought to trial the following May. In spite of strong doubts that they were guilty, they were convicted of murder in the first degree.

Nicola Sacco (right) and Bartolomeo Vanzetti

APPEALS DENIED

Eight appeals for a new trial kept their names before America and the world. In 1925, Celestino Madeiros confessed that he had taken part in the killings and that Sacco and Vanzetti were innocent. There was other new evidence. Vanzetti had claimed that he had been selling eels in Boston on the day of the murders. A receipt from the wholesale fish market that delivered the eels to him was found. The court refused to accept any of this as reason for a new trial.

Many people began to believe that the judge was prejudiced, and that Sacco and Vanzetti's only crime was holding beliefs considered un-American.

Felix Frankfurter, who would later be an associate justice of the United States Supreme Court, defended the two radicals in a book, *The Case of Sacco and Vanzetti.* Senator William E. Borah, a power in the Republican party, offered to defend them in court without payment if they were given a new trial.

"IS JUSTICE DEAD?"

Protests came from everywhere in the world—from Casablanca, where the American flag was burned before the American consulate; from Prague, where the Communists called a strike; from London, where British labor leaders cabled the governor of Massachusetts and asked him to show mercy. Noted writers like Romain Rolland of France and George Bernard Shaw of England also sent messages to the governor. He brushed aside these pleas as "unwarranted interference." A number of American writers, including Edna St. Vincent Millay and John Dos Passos, were arrested for picketing the jail where Sacco and Vanzetti were held. Police dragged a woman from Boston Common for wearing a sign on her back that read: "Save Sacco and Vanzetti. Is Justice dead?"

More than one American was asking the same question. Judge Webster Thayer, who presided over the trial and eight times turned down pleas for a new trial, clearly disliked aliens. A committee with the president of Harvard as chairman reviewed the case and refused to recommend mercy. It paid no attention to the later testimony of an eyewitness to the killings who said definitely that Sacco had not fired the fatal shots.

On August 22, 1927, Sacco and Vanzetti were executed. But the case was not really closed. Sacco and Vanzetti continued to be remembered by men who believed that the law must place truth and justice above pride and prejudice. In this way, the nation gained something, as Vanzetti had hoped when he said:

"What I wish more than all in this last hour of agony is that our case and our fate may be understood in their real being and serve as a tremendous lesson to the forces of freedom so that our suffering and death will not have been in vain."

COOLIDGE CHOOSES NOT TO RUN

Herbert Hoover and Al Smith run for President of the country, which is not as prosperous as it seems.

The year 1927 brought many surprises—and they were not over yet. That year America saw Al Jolson in *The Jazz Singer,* the first talking motion picture. And in early August, while vacationing in South Dakota, Calvin Coolidge handed newspaper reporters slips of paper that read: "I do not choose to run for President in 1928."

And so Herbert Hoover, one of the most highly respected men in America, became the Republican candidate for President. The Democrats tried to patch up the differences that had split the party and nominated Alfred E. Smith, "the Happy Warrior." Born a poor boy, Smith had risen from "the sidewalks of New York" to the governorship of the state. He was a Roman Catholic and opposed to Prohibition. To balance the ticket, the Democrats gave the vice-presidential nomination to Joseph T. Robinson, a Protestant and a "dry."

The candidates themselves were the real issue in the campaign. Smith was attacked for the way he spoke, for the way he acted, and for his connection with Tammany Hall, the powerful Democratic political machine in New York. Most of all, however, he was attacked for his religion, particularly in the South. People whispered that if he were elected the country would be run by the Pope in Rome. In the West, the "drys" added another argument. If Smith were elected, Prohibition would be repealed, the country would be flooded with liquor, and there would be drunkenness everywhere.

The Republicans pointed out that never had the country been more prosperous—and the Republicans were responsible. Everyone was eating better, living better, and having more fun. Between the outbreak of World War I and 1929, the total national income had jumped from $34,000,000,000 to $83,000,000,000. That was real prosperity! Under Hoover, the Republicans predicted, things would be even better. There would be "a chicken in every pot and a car in every garage."

Not surprisingly, Hoover won an easy victory. He even carried the Southern states of Virginia, North Carolina, Florida, Texas, and Tennessee—the first time this had been done by a Republican since the days of Reconstruction.

The figures on national income quoted by the Republicans were true enough, but there was much that they failed to show. They failed to show that 60 per cent of the national wealth was falling into the hands of two per cent of the population. They failed to show that the "average" family was borrowing heavily on its future by buying automobiles, radios, washing machines, refrigerators, and furniture on the installment plan. They failed to show that the wages of many workers were not rising as fast as prices. They failed to show that individual shopkeepers were finding it hard to compete against the chain stores.

The figures failed, too, to show the troubles of the farmers. They had lost their wartime markets, and now they had to struggle against tariffs and falling prices for farm products. Meanwhile, too, to make matters worse, windstorms were blowing the topsoil off the land.

So, when Hoover took the oath of office and became President in March of 1929, the people of the nation were divided into three groups. There were a few who were truly prosperous, a great many who believed they were prosperous, and far too many who were living from hand to mouth and had no hope for the future.

Still, on the surface the country seemed wonderfully prosperous, and thousands of Americans invested in stocks. In 1918, a total of 144,000,000 shares had been traded on the New York Stock Exchange; by 1928, the total had risen to 920,000,000. Many of the investors who were risking their money knew little of the stocks they were buying. Often they were buying "on margin"—that is, partly on credit. If the price of their stocks dropped, they would have to put up more money or be wiped out. But they were sure that this was the way to "get rich quick."

THE WALL STREET CRASH

On "Black Thursday," the stock market suddenly collapses.

Thursday, October 24, 1929, was an overcast day. A cool northwest wind blew, and as brokers hurried to their offices on New York's Wall Street, they buttoned their coats against the chill. Although the stock market had been falling sharply for three days, the brokers were in a hopeful mood that morning. After all, business was still "sound," and the market was sure to go up again. In fact, this might be the time to "make a killing" by buying stocks while prices were low and selling later after prices rose.

When trading began at ten o'clock that morning, prices seemed little changed from the day before. Brokers said that the market appeared "steady." But soon large blocks of stock were being offered for sale—20,000 shares of one stock, 25,000 shares of another.

THE BOTTOM DROPS OUT

Within an hour, the market had begun to fall with dizzying speed. From all over the country, as though investors everywhere had lost confidence as they sipped their breakfast coffee, came the same order—sell, *sell,* SELL! Suddenly no one wanted to buy. Good stocks—steel, telephone, copper—fell two points, five points, ten points in scarcely more time than it took to draw a breath. The brokers watched unbelievingly as the bottom dropped out of their world. Leading bankers scurried to a meeting and raised $240,000,000 to buy stocks and try to stop the fall. But the deluge of selling orders was overwhelming.

Elliott V. Bell, a newspaperman, described the scene on Wall Street:

"The animal roar that rises from the floor of the Stock Exchange and which on active days is plainly audible in the Street outside, became louder, anguished, terrifying. The streets were crammed with a mixed crowd—agonized little speculators, walking aimlessly outdoors because they feared to face the margin clerk; sold-out traders, morbidly compelled to visit the scene of their ruin; inquisitive individuals and tourists, seeking by gazing at the exteriors of the Exchange and the big banks to get a closer view of the national catastrophe."

By the time the Stock Exchange closed, more than 16,400,000 shares had been traded, at an average loss of forty points a share—all in a single day.

HOOVER AND THE DEPRESSION

America sinks into a depression and a "Bonus Army" of World War I veterans marches on Washington.

Hoover tried to reassure the nation that business was still sound and that there was no need for panic. Politicians and businessmen tried to keep up the people's morale with cheerful little slogans like "Prosperity is just around the corner." For three years the country drifted along, clinging to the hope that soon things would get better. The truth was that it was sinking deeper and deeper into a depression. By 1932, wages had fallen 55 per cent, and more than 5,000 banks had failed.

Hoover was opposed to using Federal money for direct help to the unemployed. He believed that such help was the responsibility of local communities. Public works projects were put into operation. The idea behind this was that by putting men to work and circulating money, the government could "prime the pump"—that is, start again the normal cycle of production and spending. The most spectacular of these projects was a great dam across the Colorado River. Now called Hoover Dam, it furnishes power and water for irrigation for several states, ensures flood control in California's Imperial Valley, and provides a water supply for the city of Los Angeles.

The depression grew worse, and by the end of 1932, 15,000,000 people were without jobs. America became a land where freight cars stood idle on railroad sidings, where smoke came from the chimneys of few factories, where faded signs on dusty plate-glass windows announced that stores were for rent, and where haggard, hungry men walked the streets asking passers-by, "Brother, can you spare a dime?"

DARK DAYS OF 1932

There were long bread lines in the poorer districts of cities. Many families lost their homes because they could not meet the payments that were due. Little settlements sprang up on the outskirts of cities, where the jobless built shacks from packing cases and other scrap materials. These settlements were soon called "Hoovervilles."

That summer a shocking incident—perhaps the most shocking of the depression years—took place in Washington. Congress had passed a bill calling for a bonus to be paid in 1945 to veterans of World War I. Jobless and hungry, the veterans wanted the bonus paid now. To get Congress to act, they marched on the nation's capital.

The first group of the "Bonus Expeditionary Force" —so called because the men had been in the American Expeditionary Force—arrived in Washington at the end of May. They reached the city by hitch-hiking, or by riding freight cars, or by driving broken-down automobiles called jalopies. Many came with their families, and soon there were about 15,000 of them. Some built "shack villages" on the outskirts of the city. Others occupied old dwellings and empty stores along Pennsylvania Avenue and the Mall between the White House and the Capitol.

In June, after Congress voted down a bill providing for immediate payment of the bonus, most of the veterans were willing enough to return home at the government's expense. But about 2,000 people remained, and when the police tried to force them to leave, four men were killed—two veterans and two policemen. President Hoover then ordered out the Federal troops. A detachment of soldiers commanded by General Douglas MacArthur went into action and drove out the veterans with tanks, tear gas, and bayonets.

The nation was shocked when it read the news and saw the ugly scene in newsreels shown in motion picture theaters. The Washington *News* summed up the feelings of many Americans when it said: "What a pitiful spectacle is that of the great American Government, mightiest in the world, chasing unarmed men, women and children with Army tanks. . . . If the army must be called out to make war on unarmed citizens, this is no longer America."

Herbert Hoover had entered the White House respected as a great humanitarian, but now he had lost the respect of a large number of Americans. His administration, which had begun so hopefully, ended on a note of tragedy and despair.

(Above, left) *When a Cleveland store announced it had 200 jobs open in 1931, 800 applicants showed up.*

(Above, right) *On the outskirts of many cities, the jobless lived in shantytowns called "Hoovervilles."*

(Right) *Brokers feverishly watched ticker tapes as crowds peered through windows during the Stock Market crash.*

(Below) *"Employment Agency," a painting by Isaac Soyer in 1937. Many people hung around such places during the depression, but few jobs were available.*

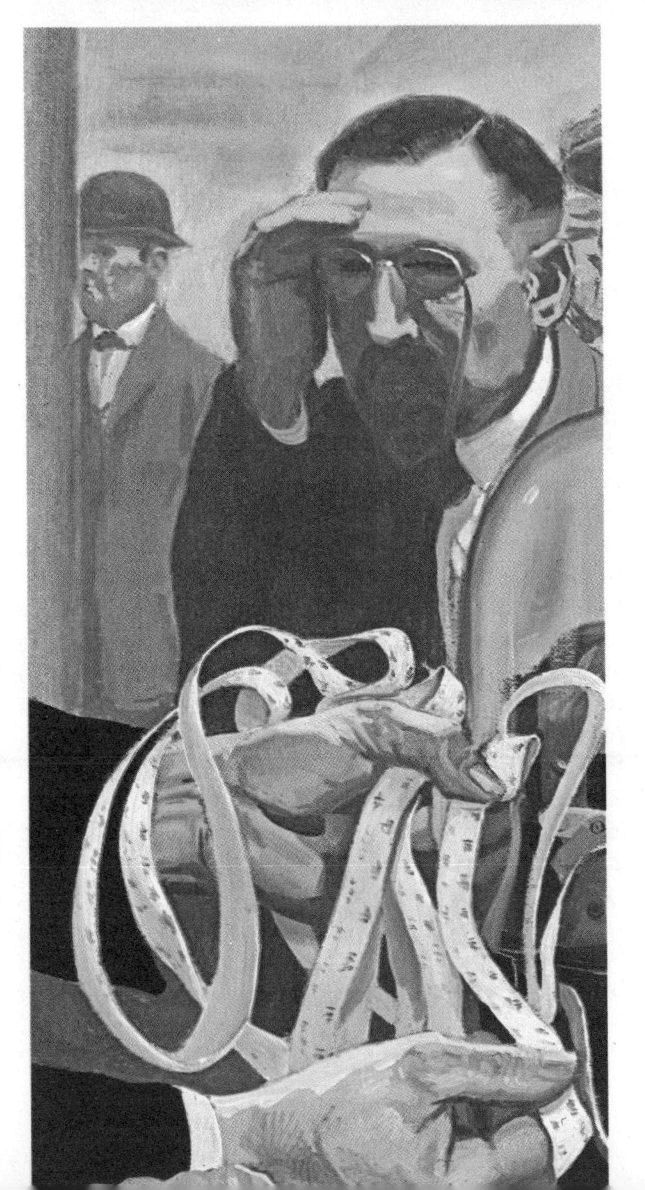

Franklin D. Roosevelt began his political career by campaigning for state senator among neighboring farmers.

FRANKLIN DELANO ROOSEVELT

The governor of New York runs for President and wins a smashing victory over Hoover.

The Republicans renominated Hoover for the presidency; the Democratic candidate was Franklin Delano Roosevelt. There was magic in the Roosevelt name—Franklin D. Roosevelt was Theodore Roosevelt's fifth cousin. And there was magic, too, in F.D.R.'s personality. People saw in him a man of strength and courage—the kind of leader the times required.

The son of a successful railroad executive, Roosevelt started life with every advantage money could buy. He grew up on the family estate at Hyde Park, New York, and was educated by private tutors until he was fourteen. He attended Groton School, where he played football but never won his letter, and Harvard College, where he became editor of the *Harvard Crimson.* He then went on to get a law degree at the Columbia University Law School.

But it was politics that interested him, and in 1910 he began his political career. His friends laughed at his daring when he announced that he was running for state senator from his home district. Roosevelt was a Democrat, and his home district was a Republican stronghold. Roosevelt let them laugh. He conducted his campaign by automobile and talked to the farmers of the neighborhood. When the votes were counted, it was Roosevelt who did the laughing. He had won easily.

In the state senate, Roosevelt soon showed that he was a political leader. He was elected to a second term, served as assistant secretary of the navy during World War I, and was the vice-presidential candidate in the Democrats' unsuccessful campaign against Harding. Then, in the summer of 1921, he was stricken with infantile paralysis. His doctors told him the bitter truth—only after years of exercise and treatment would he be able to move his legs.

"All right," Roosevelt said. "When do we begin?"

In spite of Roosevelt's optimism, it looked as though his political career was over. But Louis Howe, who was Roosevelt's close friend as well as his political manager, believed otherwise. He had faith in Roosevelt's courage and determination. That faith was rewarded on a summer day in 1922. With beads of perspiration glistening on his forehead, Roosevelt pulled back the covers of his bed and shouted, "Look, Louis! I can wriggle my toe!" Later, there were days when Howe watched Roosvelt crawling along a sandy beach to strengthen his muscles. Howe was more sure than ever that nothing could stop Roosevelt from once again living a full, active life.

The time of decision came in 1928, when the Democratic National Convention was held in New York City's Madison Square Garden. Roosevelt had agreed to nominate Al Smith for President. His legs supported by braces, Roosevelt took the arm of his son Jimmy and started on the slow, painful walk to the speaker's stand.

Howe was almost afraid to watch. This was Roosevelt's first important public appearance since his illness. If he fell—as he very well might—it would convince everyone that he was not strong enough to resume his political career. Roosevelt did not seem in the least worried. Jaunty and smiling, he shuffled to the speaker's stand. Then, grasping the edge of the stand, he made his nominating speech. Tears streamed down Howe's cheeks as the hall rocked with cheers.

Roosevelt was elected Governor of New York in 1928 and again in 1930. He won wide approval with his programs for developing water power along the St. Lawrence River, for prison reform, for the establishment of old-age pensions, and for the productive use of public lands. When the depression came, he gave New York its first system of state unemployment relief.

In 1932, nominated to oppose Hoover for the presidency, Roosevelt said in his acceptance speech: "I pledge you, I pledge myself, to a New Deal for the American people." He campaigned vigorously, bringing a spirit of optimism to the country as bands played *Happy Days Are Here Again.* Hoover, on the other hand, warned that if Roosevelt won "the grass will grow in the streets of a hundred cities, a thousand towns; the weeds will overrun the fields . . . churches and schoolhouses will decay."

F.D.R. IS ELECTED

Liberal Republicans climbed aboard the Roosevelt band wagon, seeing in his "New Deal" hope for saving the nation's shattered economy. To the "forgotten men" of the nation, too, the New Deal looked good. Perhaps many Americans did not fully understand what Roosevelt had in mind when he spoke of programs for the "common good" or reforms for the benefit of consumers, farmers, taxpayers, the unemployed, investors, users of electricity, and railroad owners and employees. But they felt that old practices, old habits, and old ways of thinking were no longer effective and must give way to something new. They still believed that their problems could be solved by a firm leader, and in Roosevelt they saw a leader of boldness and optimism. On election day, they gave Roosevelt a smashing victory. He received 22,821,000 popular votes to Hoover's 15,761,000, and he carried the electoral vote by 472 to 59, losing in only six states.

America waited eagerly for March 4, 1933—Roosevelt's inaugural day. Dark rain clouds hung over Washington, and a raw wind blew as Roosevelt stood bareheaded on the platform at the East Front of the Capitol. But when he spoke, his voice rang out clearly and boldly. He said:

"This great Nation will endure as it has endured, will revive and will prosper. So, first of all, let me assert my firm belief that the only thing we have to fear is fear itself. . . . This Nation asks for action, and action now. . . . Our greatest primary task is to put people to work. This is no unsolvable problem if we face it wisely and courageously. . . . I am prepared under my constitutional duty to recommend the measures that a stricken Nation in the midst of a stricken world may require."

Millions of Americans, listening to Roosevelt on the radio, were deeply stirred by his words. Here, they felt, was the man who would find the way to end their troubles.

THE NEW DEAL

Roosevelt tackles the problems of the depression and tries to bring the nation back to prosperity.

Roosevelt's speech had aroused the nation, but words, no matter how stirring, were not enough. The time had come when, as Roosevelt put it, America must stop being "a land stricken by poverty in the midst of plenty." Action was what was needed, action was what Roosevelt had promised—and action was what America got.

Roosevelt's first move came with dramatic suddenness. On March 5 he declared a bank holiday, to begin on the following day. This closed all banks for four days, and gave the government a chance to do something about the bank failures that were taking place all over the country. Special legislation made it possible to reorganize the banks in bad financial condition and to reopen the sound ones. Hoarding was prevented by requiring all private individuals to surrender to the Treasury any gold or gold certificates they possessed.

Roosevelt surrounded himself with advisers who were men with new ideas and new theories. They included some college professors and became known as the Brain Trust. Congress met in special session and quickly gave Roosevelt the laws and powers he asked for. During this period, which became known as the "Hundred Days," Roosevelt succeeded in putting through a great number of emergency and recovery measures. This was part of what is called the "First New Deal," which lasted from 1933 to 1935. Later, during the "Second New Deal," came reform measures. The Roosevelt Administration set up many new agencies to deal with the problems of the depression, and they soon became known by their initials. People grew so accustomed to "government by alphabet" that even Roosevelt was known as F.D.R.

Among the agencies established were:

The FERA—the Federal Emergency Relief Administration—which supplied Federal funds to states for relief of the unemployed.

The WPA—the Works Progress Administration—which helped the unemployed by giving them work

CCC workers on an Idaho conservation job in the 1930's.

on useful projects, such as constructing and repairing public buildings, bridges, and roads. As part of the WPA, the Federal Art Project gave employment to writers, painters, sculptors, actors, and musicians.

The NYA—the National Youth Administration—which helped to keep young people in school by furnishing them with part-time employment.

The CCC—the Civilian Conservation Corps—which set up camps for unmarried men between the ages of seventeen and twenty-three, and war veterans on relief. The men in these camps worked on reforestation, the construction of trails, and the control of pests, floods, fires, drainage, and erosion. Various laws were passed and agencies set up for special groups. For home owners and people who wished to build houses there were the HOLC, the FHA, and FSLA. These initials stood for the Home Owners' Loan Corporation, the Federal Housing Administration, and the Federal Savings and Loan Associations. For farmers, there were the AAA—the Agricultural Adjustment Administration—and the FSRC—the Federal Surplus Relief Corporation. For businessmen, there was the NRA—the National Recovery Administration, which formulated codes of fair competition. The law that established the NRA also guaranteed labor's right "to organize and bargain collectively through unions of their own choosing."

The Supreme Court ruled both the AAA and the NRA unconstitutional. Altogether, aside from the action of the court, neither was entirely successful in accomplishing its aims. However, some of the provisions of these acts became the basis for later laws.

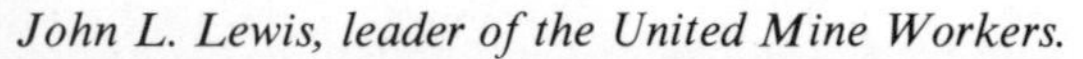

John L. Lewis, leader of the United Mine Workers.

Although in its early days the Roosevelt Administration was concerned mainly with relief and recovery, it did take one important step in foreign affairs. In 1933, Roosevelt officially recognized the Soviet Union, hoping that this would stimulate trade.

In 1935, Congress passed two laws that would have a far-reaching effect on life in the United States. One of these was the Social Security Act. It provided for retirement and other benefits for workers, including unemployment insurance, to be financed by taxes on both employers and workers. The second law was the National Labor Relations Act, often called the Wagner Act, which guaranteed labor the right to organize and to bargain collectively.

Labor made great gains during this period, but, strangely enough, labor itself was divided. The A.F. of L.—the American Federation of Labor—organized workers in craft unions. There were separate unions for carpenters, electricians, and so on, no matter in what industry they worked. This tended to favor the highly skilled workers, and made it difficult to organize the less skilled workers in the mass-production industries.

Some dissatisfied union officials formed the Committee for Industrial Organization—the C.I.O. When the group was expelled from the A.F. of L., it set up the Congress of Industrial Organizations, which was also known as the C.I.O. Under the leadership of John L. Lewis, the bushy-browed president of the powerful United Mine Workers, and Sidney Hillman of the Amalgamated Clothing Workers, the C.I.O. organized industrial unions. These included all the workers in any particular industry, regardless of their skills.

The C.I.O was especially successful in the automobile industry. It used a new kind of strike, the "sit-down" strike, in which the workers refused to leave the plants and made it impossible for their employers to bring in strikebreakers. The most notable sit-down was at the General Motors plants in Flint, Michigan, in 1936. It went on for 44 days. In 1939, after the Supreme Court ruled that sit-down strikes were illegal, labor gave up their use.

Americans were disturbed by some of these developments, but they were also enjoying the lighter side of life. Except for some die-hard "drys," they welcomed the end of Prohibition on December 5, 1933, when Utah became the thirty-sixth state to ratify the Twenty-First Amendment. They amused themselves with the new craze of contract bridge, and listened to "soap operas" on the radio. They gaped at the first sleek diesel-powered trains, and they flocked to motion-picture theaters to laugh at the antics of Mickey Mouse.

"THE NINE OLD MEN"

In 1936, Roosevelt is re-elected, and tries to reorganize the Supreme Court.

In spite of all the measures taken by Roosevelt, there was a growing rumble of dissatisfaction with the New Deal. For one thing, unemployment was still at an alarmingly high figure. And then businessmen were charging that the government was interfering too much with business while it was coddling labor. They were afraid that the "planned economy" of Roosevelt and his brain-trusters would eventually mean the end of traditional American ideas.

At the same time, many Americans feared that the country would become a political battleground. In Louisiana, Governor Huey P. Long gained such control of the state government that he ruled almost as a dictator. The son of a poor farmer, Long had been a traveling salesman and a lawyer before entering politics. The "Kingfish," as Long was called, started a "Share-the-Wealth" movement that won many followers. It called for a minimum income of $2,500 a year for every family. Long was threatening to make a bid for national power in the coming presidential election when his life was ended by an assassin's bullet in September of 1935.

As Roosevelt faced the election of 1936, he felt that Americans who had been hurt by the depression would support him. The Republicans chose Alfred M. Landon, the governor of Kansas, as their candidate. They were encouraged when Roosevelt lost the support of a group of men that included John W. Davis, who had been the Democratic candidate for President in 1924, the publisher William Randolph Hearst, and former Governor Alfred E. Smith. Calling themselves "Jeffersonian Democrats," they attacked the New Deal as the destroyer of individual freedom.

As the campaign went into its last days, members of the National Association of Manufacturers attacked the Social Security law. Workers found messages in their pay envelopes warning them that Roosevelt's legislation would have dangerous results. This made the workers even more strongly in favor of Roosevelt; they did not like the idea of the boss telling them how to vote. The election proved to be a landslide for Roosevelt, who carried the electoral vote in every state except Maine and Vermont.

Roosevelt celebrated his victory with a triumphant good-will visit to Buenos Aires and Rio de Janeiro. On his return, Roosevelt began his battle against the Supreme Court, which had ruled unconstitutional both the Agricultural Adjustment Act and the National Industrial Recovery Act (NRA).

In opposing the Supreme Court, Roosevelt was facing a problem that had plagued other Presidents before him, particularly Jefferson and Jackson. Roosevelt charged that the members of the court had outlived their usefulness in the world of the 1930's. He demanded that Congress increase the number of justices from nine to fifteen, if those justices reaching the age of seventy-five refused to retire.

Roosevelt's supporters rallied behind him, and soon they were calling the members of the court "the nine old men." But there were at least as many people who disagreed with Roosevelt. In fact, not since the controversy over the League of Nations had the country seen such a heated political battle. Roosevelt was accused of threatening the independence of the judicial branch of the government, and Congress refused to pass the laws he requested.

But Roosevelt's moves had their effect. First, the court began making more decisions in keeping with the New Deal. Then death and retirement gave him complete victory. Within four years, Roosevelt appointed seven new members of the court—Hugo L. Black, Stanley F. Reed, Felix Frankfurter, William O. Douglas, Frank Murphy, James F. Byrnes, and Robert H. Jackson. Douglas, who was forty-one years old, was the youngest of the men appointed; Byrnes, who was sixty-two years old, was the oldest.

The battle over the court left wounds that did not easily heal. A bill to reform the executive branch of the government gave Roosevelt's opponents, especially those in the Senate, a chance to once more brand the President a potential dictator. But after the elections of 1938, Congress became more mild. It permitted Roosevelt to make changes in the executive branch of the government which affected every department except the War and the Navy Departments.

In the midst of all the political battles, Americans still found things to amuse and entertain them. They had new sports heroes—Joe Louis in boxing, Joe DiMaggio in baseball, and Jesse Owens in track. Owens' superb running had helped to give the United States another victory in the Olympic games at Berlin in 1936. Americans gathered around their radios to listen to "quiz shows," and to news of King Edward VIII of England, who gave up his throne so that he could marry Mrs. Wallis Simpson of Baltimore. They read *Gone With the Wind,* a novel of life in Atlanta during the Civil War, and they laughed at the Marx Brothers in the movies. Teen-agers were dancing in a new style called "jitterbugging," and people of all ages were interested when, in June of 1939, the King and Queen of England paid a state visit to the United States.

Adolf Hitler

Nazi soldiers parade before the World War I monument at Verdun after the fall of France in 1940.

THE MENACE OF WAR

Hitler and the Nazis come to power in Germany and plunge Europe into war.

During the early days of the depression, Americans were too concerned with their own problems to pay much attention to what was happening in Europe. On January 30, 1933, they were shocked to learn that Adolf Hitler had become chancellor of Germany. He was the leader of the National Socialist German Workers party, who were better known as the "Nazis."

The new master of Germany lost little time in carrying out his threat to rid his country of Jews. Most Americans were horrified and disgusted at his brutal violence. But there were some Americans who supported Hitler, and they formed an organization called "Friends of the New Germany," also known as the American Bundists. On March 17, 1934, waving the swastika banner of the Nazis, they staged a rally in New York's Madison Square Garden. Perhaps this brought home to Americans the fact that they could not close their eyes to events abroad.

For Hitler was not the only Fascist dictator in Europe. Benito Mussolini had been dictator of Italy since 1922, and in 1935 he attacked the little African kingdom of Ethiopia. That same year, to avoid being involved in Europe's conflicts, Congress passed the Neutrality Act. This law prohibited Americans from selling munitions to either side taking part in a war.

There was trouble in Asia, too. Since 1931 Japan had been waging an undeclared war on China. In the summer of 1937, Japanese planes ranged far over the Chinese mainland, dropping bombs on city after city. Japanese troops, wading ashore from ships, occupied Chinese territory. Nanking fell to the Japanese, and on December 12, 1937, their planes sank the United States gunboat *Panay,* which was on patrol in Chinese waters. After a strong protest by Secretary of State Cordell Hull, the Japanese government paid the United States an indemnity of more than $2,000,000.

Three months later, Hitler overthrew the government of Austria, his first step in creating the "Greater Germany." That September he gained control of the Sudetenland, a section of Czechoslovakia, and in the spring of 1939 his troops invaded the rest of the country.

In August, Hitler came to terms with Russia's dictator, Joseph Stalin, and the two nations signed a nonaggression treaty. Almost before the ink was dry on this document, Hitler invaded Poland. Britain and France, living up to their commitments to Poland, then declared war on Germany.

During their undeclared war on China in the 1930's, the Japanese bombed and sank the U.S. gunboat Panay *on the Yangtze River, with a loss of two lives. A U.S. protest brought an apology and payment of a big indemnity.*

By the end of April, 1940, Hitler's troops had seized Denmark and Norway. In May the German armies battered their way through Belgium, the Netherlands, and France. A British force, trapped on the beaches of Dunkirk, a French coastal town, finally escaped across the English Channel.

Throughout the summer and fall, Americans were disturbed by the grim stories they read in their newspapers. German planes were dropping bombs on English ports and towns. Hundreds of English children were brought to America. On Labor Day, speaking at the dedication of the Great Smoky National Park, Roosevelt warned the nation that it could not go on being unprepared for war. The nation could survive, he said, only if the people were willing to "preserve this country and its way of life." Later that month, the Burke-Wadsworth Bill was passed. It provided for the registration for military service of all American men between the ages of twenty-one and thirty-five, and for the conscription and training of two million troops and reserves.

Roosevelt's critics were quick to attack him. They said the United States had no business getting involved in what was happening in Europe, and that Roosevelt was a would-be dictator who was single-handedly dragging the nation into a war. Roosevelt answered them when he spoke to the people in his "fireside chats" over the radio. Again and again he explained that only by helping the British defeat Hitler could the United States hope to save itself from attack by the Nazi warlords.

By this time, most Americans were opposed to Hitler and everything he represented. But they remembered that the United States had entered World War I to save the world for democracy. They remembered, too, what followed—dictatorships rather than democracies had risen in Europe. Would they accomplish anything more by fighting now? Perhaps they should not get involved in Europe's conflicts, look to their own affairs at home, and stay clear of World War II.

But Roosevelt was certain that the United States could not survive if England did not survive. To carry out his program, he decided to do what no American had ever done before—run for a third term as President. This was one of the most important decisions he ever made, for it shattered an American tradition of long standing. More than anything he had done, from the early days of his first administration, when he had closed the banks, to the days of his second administration, when he had fought the Supreme Court, this was a break with tradition.

Again his critics attacked him. Again they accused him of being a "dictator" and a "warmonger." Roosevelt tipped up his cigarette holder and flashed the smile that had become so well known to Americans. He threw around his shoulders the navy cape he had been privileged to wear since he had been Assistant Secretary of the Navy during World War I. He had always enjoyed a good political battle, and he had always campaigned with zest.

Now, once again, Franklin Delano Roosevelt was off to the political wars.

Great fires raged in London during the Nazi blitz of 1940, but St. Paul's Cathedral came through virtually unscathed.

IX ~ WAR CLOUDS...WORLD WAR II

from 1940 to 1945

PEACE AT ANY PRICE

With Europe at war, Americans debate whether or not to stay neutral.

As Hitler's armies overran Europe in 1939 to 1940, many Americans talked as though they still lived in the age of sailing ships. They felt that the United States was protected by two oceans and could remain at peace simply by refusing to fight. Because they were against alliances with other countries, they were called "isolationists."

In 1940 the isolationists formed the America First Committee. Its most famous member was Charles A. Lindbergh, who had been a national hero since his solo flight across the Atlantic in 1927. Through speeches, pamphlets, and articles, the "America Firsters" tried to win the nation over to isolationism. They believed that air power had made Germany so strong it could not be conquered. "In the future," Lindbergh said, "we may have to deal with a Europe dominated by Germany. . . . An agreement between us could maintain peace and civilization throughout the world as far into the future as we can see."

As early as 1935, Congress had passed an isolationist bill forbidding the shipment of arms to nations involved in the wars of Europe and Asia. The following year the isolationists nearly succeeded in putting through a law requiring a popular referendum (vote) before a declaration of war, except in case of invasion. Roosevelt managed to defeat this measure, and in January of 1938 he asked Congress for a billion dollars to build a two-ocean navy. When he was attacked by the isolationists, he told the nation that war was like a contagious disease and could spread. He said, "We are determined to keep out of war, yet we cannot insure ourselves against the disastrous effects of war and the dangers of involvement."

ITALY INVADES FRANCE

After the Allied retreat from Dunkirk in 1940, when England stood alone and German bombs fell on the British Isles, the fight between Roosevelt and the isolationists became even more bitter. The America Firsters predicted that England would fall, and that it would be the United States which would then stand alone. In June of 1940, after the Germans had overpowered the French armies, Italy invaded southern France. Roosevelt made a famous speech to Congress, in which he said that "the hand that held the dagger has struck it into the back of its neighbor."

"In our American unity," Roosevelt went on, "we will pursue two obvious courses; we will extend to the opponents of force the material resources of this nation, and, at the same time, we will harness and speed up the use of those resources in order that we ourselves in America may have equipment and training equal to the task of any emergency and every defense."

As the time for the presidential election drew near, Roosevelt was solidly committed to a policy of giving Britain all aid short of war.

"WE WANT WILLKIE"

Wendell Willkie is a strong candidate but Roosevelt wins the election.

On June 24, 1940, the Republicans met in Philadelphia to choose their presidential candidate. The professionals in the party expected that their candidate would be one of three men. The three were Robert A. Taft of Ohio and Arthur H. Vandenberg of Michigan, both isolationist senators, and Thomas E. Dewey of New York.

But the "amateurs" in the party rallied behind still another man—youthful, vigorous Wendell L. Willkie. A lawyer by training, Willkie was the president of a gas and electric company, the Commonwealth and Southern Corporation. He had been a Democrat until his disagreement with some of Roosevelt's domestic policies led him to join the Republican party. At the same time, he was opposed to the isolationist policies of the Republican Old Guard.

As the voting began at the Republican convention, Willkie's supporters packed the galleries and chanted, "We want Willkie!" Dewey led on the first three ballots, but the galleries never stopped their chant: "We want Willkie! We want Willkie!" On the fourth ballot, Willkie crept into the lead. On the sixth, he won the nomination.

The campaign that followed was a confusing one for anyone who did not understand how Americans thought. Among Willkie's supporters were "Democrats-for-Willkie" and "No-Third-Term-Democrats." Among Roosevelt's supporters were "Republicans-for-Roosevelt" and "Businessmen-for-Roosevelt." The president of the A.F. of L. (the American Federation of Labor) came out for Roosevelt, and the president of the C.I.O. (the Congress of Industrial Organizations) for Willkie.

Willkie proved to be an energetic campaigner. While Roosevelt made few speeches, Willkie stumped the country. He spoke until his voice became so hoarse he could scarcely be heard. Willkie refused to make foreign policy a campaign issue and gave no comfort to the isolationists. He was a firm believer in the need for American preparedness and for aiding Britain and her allies. With certain exceptions, he also approved of the aims of the New Deal. As a result, he was in the difficult position of promising to carry out the Democrats' programs more efficiently than the Democrats.

Early returns on election night favored Willkie, but the final count gave Roosevelt 27,244,160 popular votes, as against 22,305,198 for Willkie. The electoral vote was 449 to 82. A baseball-minded admirer, serenading Roosevelt in front of his home in Hyde Park, New York, held up a sign that read: "Safe on 3rd!"

"MEASURES SHORT OF WAR"

America builds its strength and sends aid to the Allies.

Even during the campaign, Roosevelt had moved swiftly to strengthen America's defenses with "measures short of war." Congress voted huge increases in military spending. The National Guard was made part of the regular army, and the nation's first peacetime draft of men for the armed forces was passed on September 16, 1940. The isolationists could not defeat this bill, but they tacked on to it an amendment prohibiting the sending of drafted men to any area outside the United States and its possessions.

In spite of the isolationists, Roosevelt was determined to aid Britain. He quietly made a bargain with Britain to exchange fifty "over-age" destroyers—that is, vessels used during World War I—for ninety-nine-year rent-free leases on sites for naval bases in the British West Indies and British Guiana. He did this by executive agreement, so that the approval of Congress was not required. When this action was made public in September of 1940, the isolationists bitterly attacked both the agreement and Roosevelt's methods. Even so, Congress voted the money necessary to carry out the agreement. In later months, the United States transferred bombers and some small ships to Britain, and American factories were busy producing war materials.

On January 6, 1941, Roosevelt made an important speech to Congress, outlining what he believed should be the aims of the free nations. He called for "a world founded upon four essential human freedoms." These were "freedom of speech and expression everywhere in the world," "freedom of every person to worship God in his own way everywhere in the world," "freedom from want . . . everywhere in the world," and "freedom from fear—which, translated into world terms, means a world-wide reduction of armaments to such a point and in such a thorough fashion that no nation will be in a position to commit an act of physical aggression against any neighbor—anywhere in the world."

Roosevelt was soon asking Congress to pass the Lend-Lease Bill. This would allow the government to buy any "defense article" for sale, exchange, or lease to any anti-Axis country. In return, the United States could accept "payment in kind or property, or any other direct or indirect benefit which the President deems satisfactory." The intention of the bill was plain. The United States would be cutting through its own red tape in order to supply military materials to Britain.

Roosevelt campaigning in Cleveland, Ohio, in 1940.

Again there was a storm of protest from the isolationists. Senator Wheeler of Montana said lend-lease was a policy "to plow under every fourth American boy." Roosevelt replied angrily that this was "the most untruthful, the most dastardly, unpatriotic thing that has been said in public life in my generation." Most Americans were in favor of lend-lease, and in March, Congress passed the bill and it became law.

That spring and summer the chain of American bases was extended to Greenland and Iceland. American planes and warships that now guarded merchant ships were, in Roosevelt's words, "helping to insure the delivery of needed supplies to Britain."

Germany's submarines struck back. In May, they

sank the merchant ship *Robin Moor,* which was carrying steel rails and automobiles to Cape Town, South Africa. The crew and passengers were set adrift in small boats on the South Atlantic. Four months later, two torpedoes were fired at the American destroyer *Greer* while it was carrying mail to Iceland. In October, another destroyer, the *Kearney,* was torpedoed off the coast of Iceland, and at the end of the same month, the *Reuben James* was sunk while on convoy duty.

"We Americans have cleared our decks and taken our battle stations," Roosevelt said. Warning against the Nazi scheme of world conquest, he said, "They plan to treat the Latin American nations as they are now treating the Balkans. They plan to strangle the United States of America and the Dominion of Canada."

THE ATLANTIC CHARTER

On August 3, 1941, Americans learned that Roosevelt had sailed aboard his yacht *Potomac* from New London, Connecticut, for a few days of fishing and relaxation. There were later reports that he had been seen with rod and reel off Martha's Vineyard—then secrecy covered his movements.

While Americans wondered what had happened to their President, Roosevelt transferred to the cruiser *Augusta,* which headed for Placentia Bay in Newfoundland. Here the British battleship *Prince of Wales* dropped anchor, and Roosevelt and Prime Minister Winston Churchill met in the first of a series of meetings. Aboard the British vessel on Sunday, the President and the Prime Minister joined in singing hymns—*O God, Our Help in Ages Past,* and *Onward Christian Soldiers,* and *Eternal Father, Strong to Save.*

From the meeting in Placentia Bay came the Atlantic Charter, one of the great documents in man's struggle for freedom. The announcement of the Charter did not mean that the United States was ready to enter the war as an ally of Britain, but it did bring the two nations closer together. For now they were informing the world that once Hitler's armies had been defeated and there was peace again, the United States and Great Britain would seek the same objectives. Roosevelt and Churchill stated the aims to which they were committing their countries in an eight-point program:

1. No territorial gains for either country.
2. Boundaries between nations should change only in response to the "freely expressed will of the peoples concerned."
3. The United States and Great Britain "respect the right of all peoples to choose the form of government under which they live," and self-government must be restored in countries which have been forcefully deprived of it.
4. All nations must have equal access to trade and the raw materials needed to insure their prosperity.
5. Economic co-operation among all nations to improve labor standards and social security.
6. The peace to be achieved should enable all men in all lands to "live out their lives in freedom from fear and want."
7. All nations should enjoy freedom of the seas.
8. All nations must give up the use of force, and, to maintain future peace, aggressor nations must be disarmed.

From this meeting in Placentia Bay also came two other developments. In June Germany had invaded Russia. Now Roosevelt and Churchill promised to aid Russia in her struggle against the Axis powers. They also warned Japan that her aggressions in the Far East must stop.

JAPAN ATTACKS PEARL HARBOR

America is suddenly in the war when its Pacific fleet is crippled.

By the spring of 1940, the Japanese were trying to establish what they called the "Greater East Asia Co-Prosperity Sphere." It was clear that they planned to invade French Indochina and the Netherlands East Indies. In September, Japan was granted bases in Indochina by a Nazi-dominated French government. Japan also became a partner of the Axis nations, Germany and Italy. The three nations signed a treaty agreeing to "assist one another with all political, economic and military means when one of the powers was attacked by a power not then involved in the European war or in the Chinese-Japanese conflict."

Officials of the United States government had good reason to be worried about Japan's intentions. Japan was preparing for war, and on July 24, 1941, her troops occupied all of Indochina.

President Roosevelt acted quickly, calling upon Japan to withdraw from Indochina. He ordered a "freeze" on all Japanese holdings and assets in the United States. This meant that Japanese goods and funds could be neither used nor withdrawn, and it put an immediate stop to trade between the two countries. The Japanese depended on this trade for war materials, and they angrily froze American assets in Japan.

Even so, the United States continued to hope that war could be avoided. Throughout the spring and summer of 1941, Kichisaburo Nomura, the Japanese ambassador to the United States, offered suggestions for settling the differences between the two nations. They were unacceptable. Then, in October,

General Hideki Tojo became premier of Japan, and relations between the two countries became even worse.

The following month, a special envoy, Saburo Kurusu, arrived in Washington. Apparently he had come to carry on peaceful negotiations. Kurusu was still in Washington—in fact, he was calling on Secretary of State Cordell Hull—at the very moment on December 7, 1941, when radio stations interrupted their programs with this startling announcement:

"We bring you a special bulletin. At 7:58 o'clock this morning Japanese planes attacked Pearl Harbor."

Pearl Harbor was a United States military base in Hawaii. Americans heard the news with shocked disbelief that quickly turned into anger. They sat by their radios as excited newscasters told of the events of a day which, in President Roosevelt's words, would "live in infamy."

The American forces in Hawaii, caught by surprise, had suffered fearful destruction. Japanese bombers with the rising-sun emblem on their wings had roared over Pearl Harbor in waves. They dropped heavy, armor-piercing shells and torpedoes of high explosive power on the anchored ships of the United States Pacific Fleet.

The battleship *Arizona* was shattered and sunk by an explosion when a bomb struck the forward powder magazine. Several torpedoes sent the *Oklahoma* over on her side. The *West Virginia,* hit by at least six torpedoes, sank with her decks awash. The *California* foundered after being ringed by fire when her fuel tanks were pierced. The *Pennsylvania, Maryland,* and *Tennessee* were damaged. The *Nevada* was so badly damaged while trying to escape from the harbor that she had to be beached. Three light cruisers were seriously damaged, and a destroyer had her bow blown off, and the mine layer *Oglala* was sunk.

The American method of neatly lining up planes wing to wing across an airfield made them particularly vulnerable to a surprise attack. Almost all of the army's 273 planes were wrecked by the first wave of enemy bombers. At the height of the raid, when the commander of the naval air force tried to get his planes off the field, he found that only three of 202 aircraft could still fly.

As a result of Japan's "sneak attack," a good part of the Pacific Fleet was destroyed, and 2,342 American sailors, soldiers, and marines were killed. Next day Congress declared war on Japan and President Roosevelt told the nation, "With confidence in our armed forces, with the unbounded determination of our people, we will gain the inevitable triumph—so help us God."

On December 11, Germany and Italy declared war on the United States. Congress unanimously passed a resolution declaring that a state of hostilities existed with the European members of the Axis.

There were no longer any doubts about what course of action the United States should follow. This was war—total war.

ON THE HOME FRONT

All over the nation, Americans pitch in to help support the war effort.

Total war called for the total effort of the American people. They heard little good news in the days before Christmas 1941. Only three days after the declaration of war against Japan, the Japanese captured the island of Guam from an American force that numbered less than 600. Wake Island, aided by Marine Corps planes, held out until December 23. Americans were encouraged by that gallant stand, but they knew that the nation had not been prepared for war. At the same time, they all stood united

Japan's sneak attack on Pearl Harbor on December 7, 1941, sank several battleships and crippled the U.S. Pacific fleet.

in this struggle for survival. The political conflict of a year ago disappeared overnight.

Americans soon realized that this was a different kind of war from those that had been fought in the past. The government not only drafted men, but also called for women to enlist in the armed forces. The Army had its WACS, the Navy its WAVES, the Coast Guard its SPARS, and the Marine Corps its Women's Reserve.

Never had Americans at home been required to support so many people on the firing line. In 1941 the armed forces numbered fewer than 2,000,000; by 1944-45 the number had risen to more than 11,000,000. And so America went to work. Women of all ages took jobs in war industries—as welders in shipyards or airplane factories, as technicians in engineering plants. They worked in factories and offices, at any job where they could replace men who had gone off to war. Boys still in high school and men over the age of sixty-five also took jobs, for the nation needed the help of every citizen. Unemployment disappeared, and the average weekly wage rose from $25.20 in 1940 to $46.08 in 1944.

Although after Pearl Harbor both the A.F. of L. and the C.I.O. made no-strike pledges, some unions did go on strike. It was true that prices were rising, but the strikers got little sympathy from the press, the public, or Congress. In June of 1943, Congress passed the Smith-Connally Act over President Roosevelt's veto. It gave the President the power to seize any plant or company threatened by a strike and to penalize leaders or "instigators" of strikes against firms working on government contracts. Sooner than expected, the government was taking action authorized by this legislation. It took over the coal mines in November of 1943, when the United Mine Workers threatened to call a strike. A month later the government placed the railroads under the army's authority.

THE COST OF WAR

The amount of money needed to fight a war on a world-wide scale was almost beyond belief. By 1943 the government was spending $8,000,000,000 a month, and from 1941 to 1945 the national debt rose from less than $48,000,000,000 to $247,000,000,000. New and higher taxes were enacted. Stars of the stage and screen and other celebrities took part in drives to sell war bonds. From May, 1941, through 1945, government bond sales amounted to more than $61,000,000,000.

If the cost was enormous, so was the output of war materials. By the middle of 1945, American industry had produced 297,000 airplanes, 6,000 naval vessels, 64,500 landing vessels, more than 17,000,000 rifles, 5,400 cargo ships, 315,000 pieces of field artillery, 4,200,000 tons of artillery shells, and 41,400,000,000 rounds of ammunition.

To keep the economy in balance, the government established the Office of Price Administration, known as the OPA. Its task was to set prices for scarce foods and consumer goods. It also issued ration stamps, so that every family could get its fair share of essential commodities. In 1942, rents were "frozen," so that people could continue to live where they were without rent increases for the duration of the war.

THE GOVERNMENT ACTS AGAINST PRO-NAZI GROUPS

The government took precautions to put down pro-Fascist groups. The German-American Bund and Silver Shirts were disbanded, and enemy-owned businesses in the United States were seized. Fortunately, there was not so much hysteria about minority groups as there had been during World War I. But some 110,000 Japanese-Americans, living on the West Coast, were treated with shocking injustice. Although most of them had been born in the United States, there was fear that some of them might prove to be disloyal. They were removed by the army from their homes and "relocated" inland, away from the Pacific Coast. There they were forced to live in camps until the end of the war.

Negroes, too, were discriminated against; they were especially offended by the army's policy of segregation. At the same time, white Southerners, moving north to take jobs in industry, often resented the economic and social position of the Negro in the North. These whites disliked the Fair Employment Practices Committee, which had been appointed by President Roosevelt in 1941 to prevent racial discrimination in employment.

The worst of several anti-Negro riots took place during June of 1943 in Detroit. Federal troops had to put down a series of street battles in which more than forty persons, including both Negroes and whites, lost their lives.

Europe before the German attack on Russia, June 22, 1941.

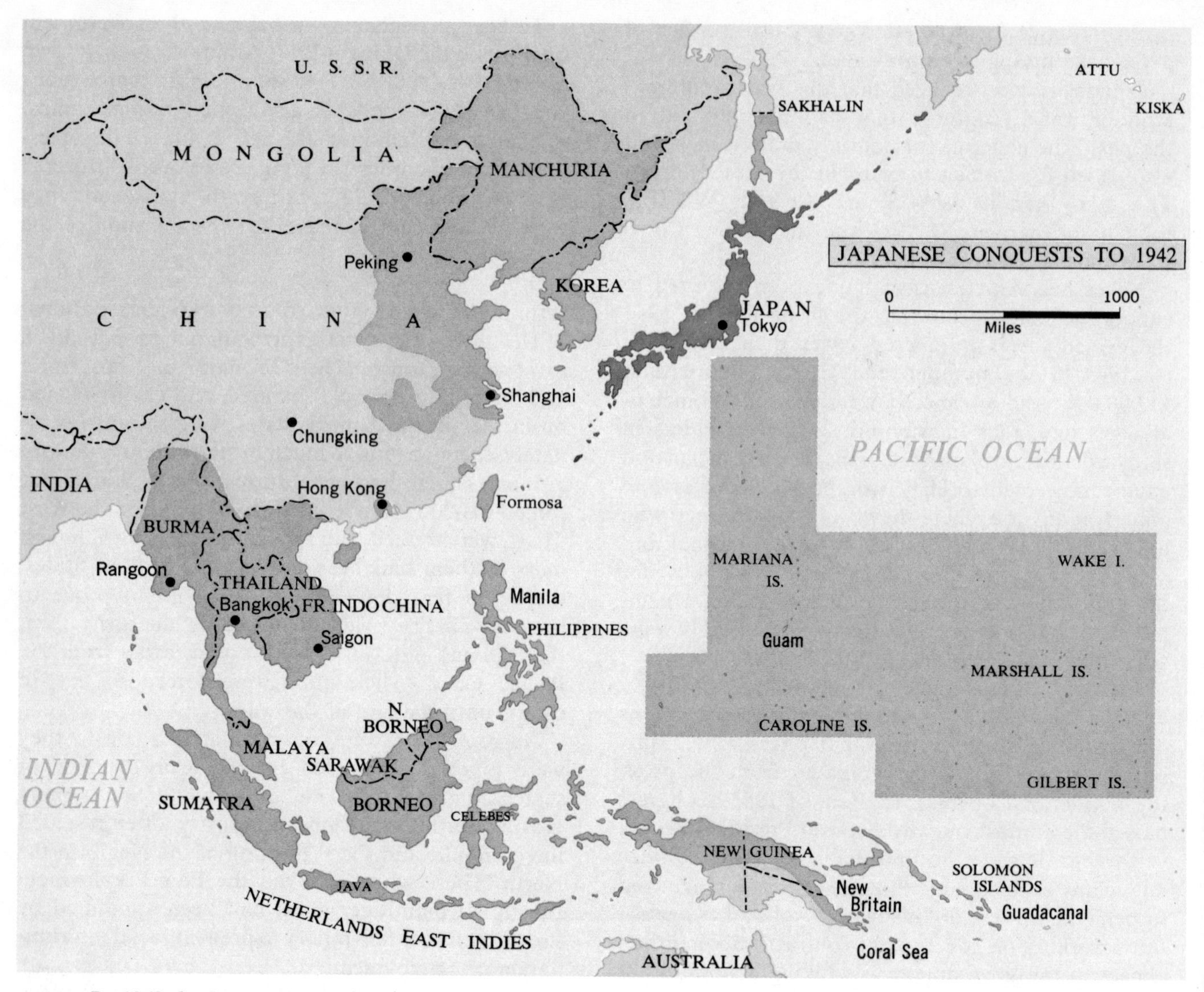

By 1942 the Japanese controlled most of Southeast Asia and the Southwest Pacific, and threatened Australia.

Yet Americans on the home front had much to be proud of. A voluntary system of press and radio censorship worked well. Almost every community supported its United Service Organization (USO), which provided entertainment for servicemen. Stage and screen stars traveled to all corners of the globe to cheer the fighting men. And Irving Berlin, who had written famous songs during World War I, again set America singing with *I Left My Heart at the Stage Door Canteen* and *God Bless America* and *This Is the Army, Mr. Jones.*

"THE NEWS WAS ALL BAD"

The Americans surrender the Philippines as Japanese forces overrun the Pacific.

In the weeks following Pearl Harbor, the Japanese carried forward their campaign of conquest in Southeast Asia and the Pacific. Besides attacking Guam and Wake Islands, they invaded the Philippines, bombed the British base at Singapore, landed on the northern shore of Malaya, and sank the British battleships *Repulse* and *Prince of Wales.*

The Japanese may have landed as many as 250,000 troops in the Philippines. They far outnumbered the Americans and Filipinos under the command of General Douglas MacArthur. Following a plan of defense drawn up several years before by a young staff officer named Dwight Eisenhower, MacArthur clung to the valley that runs from Lingayen Gulf to Manila. Meanwhile, he concentrated forces from other fronts on Bataan peninsula. Although Manila was declared an "open city," or undefended city, Japanese bombers roared overhead. The Japanese chose Sundays, when a great number of people were in church, to make their severest attacks.

By February, 1942, it was clear that trying to defend the Philippines was hopeless. MacArthur was ordered to Australia to take command of the Allied forces in the southwest Pacific. As he escaped by night, in a torpedo boat that crept between islands occupied by the enemy, the defense of Bataan fell to Lieutenant General Jonathan Wainwright.

Bataan was a dismal place at best. On the west, the steep sides of the Mariveles Mountains sloped down to the sea. On the east were boggy rice and sugar fields, surrounded by swamps and mountains. Daily Japanese attacks put constant pressure on the American defenses.

Early in April, the Japanese overran the Bataan peninsula. The battered American force withdrew to Corregidor, an island fortress at the entrance to Manila Bay. There they made another brave stand. By May 6, however, they could hold out no longer, and Wainwright surrendered. Of the 40,000 prisoners taken by the Japanese in the fort and on Bataan, more than half died—some from the long march under the hot sun without food and water, some from mistreatment in the prison camps.

Elsewhere in the Pacific, the Japanese had been sweeping forward with equal success. In January, their paratroopers had seized Tarakan in Borneo and Menado on the tip of Celebes Island. Fighter planes blasted Allied shipping in Macassar Strait. Before the end of February of 1942, all of Malaya, including Singapore, was held by Japan.

Americans at home, reading their newspapers, dug out forgotten geography books. The Japanese seemed to be all over the Pacific, rolling along like a tidal wave. As President Roosevelt said, "The news was all bad." German submarines had sunk ships in Chesapeake Bay. The German invaders had been stopped before Moscow, but the Russians kept pressing for a landing in France to ease the pressure on their homeland. And, in England, German bombers had rained down explosives on London, Coventry, Liverpool, and Bristol.

CORAL SEA AND MIDWAY

Tokyo is bombed. The U.S. Navy turns the tide of battle in the Pacific.

Despite the setbacks, the Allies were learning the lessons of modern warfare. A line of battleships could not win a battle at sea when it was attacked by enemy planes. The answer was the carrier task force —an aircraft carrier surrounded by a group of cruisers. The planes could do double duty. They could spot the approach of the enemy as well as lead an attack. Such a force could move swiftly. It could strike sharply and then move quickly away, like a boxer who lands a stunning blow on his opponent and then dances

General Jonathan Wainwright surrendering the Philippines to the Japanese, as depicted in a Japanese painting.

back out of reach. Successful carrier raids on outposts in the Marshall and Gilbert Islands in the Central Pacific soon proved that this reasoning was correct.

By April of 1942, the American forces were ready for a more spectacular adventure. The new aircraft carrier *Hornet* moved from the Caribbean to San Francisco. Here, in great secrecy, sixteen of the army's two-motored B-25 bombers, under the command of Major General James H. Doolittle, were loaded on the *Hornet's* flight deck. The sailors on the *Hornet* looked with curiosity at the B-25's, which had never before been flown from a carrier.

The *Hornet* put to sea and was joined by the carrier *Enterprise,* flying the flag of Admiral William Halsey. On April 18, when the *Hornet* was 700 miles from the Japanese islands, the planes were launched. The launching took place earlier than was planned, for some Japanese fishing boats suddenly appeared, and there was danger that they might give away the presence of this unusual task force. There was no choice now but to fly—and fly Doolittle's bombers did. They made a surprise attack on Tokyo and then went on to land at bases in China. The damage they did that day was slight. But the bombing of Tokyo made the Japanese realize that their homeland could be attacked and that they might yet lose the war.

The big problem for the Allies at this time was the defense of Australia. In early March, 1942, while American troops tried to halt the Japanese advance in the Philippines, other Japanese forces had captured the north coast of New Guinea. Once there, they had only one way to go—over the jungle-covered Owen Stanley Mountains into Port Moresby, within striking distance of Australia. It would be a complicated action, but if it succeeded the Japanese would take Australia and be able to extend their power through the South Pacific.

The aircraft carrier Lexington *exploded and sank after being bombed in the Battle of the Coral Sea.*

General MacArthur, who had come to Australia to direct the Allied defenses, knew that the Japanese must be stopped. Admiral Chester W. Nimitz, who was in charge of naval operations in the Pacific, also knew this—and so did Rear Admiral Frank Fletcher, task-force leader on the aircraft carrier *Yorktown.*

BATTLE OF THE CORAL SEA

In late April, the *Yorktown* patrolled the Coral Sea. The waters of the sea sweep along the beaches of Guadalcanal and New Britain, and separate the tip of New Guinea from the northeastern coast of Australia. The men on the big flattop waited and watched for the Japanese to move. During the first week of May, there was news. Enemy transports and cargo vessels, guarded by a small carrier, some cruisers and destroyers, were preparing for an invasion. A second Japanese force of two carriers, two cruisers, seven destroyers, and a fuel tanker was getting ready for battle in the Coral Sea.

On May 5, the *Yorktown* was joined by the carrier *Lexington.* By the time the fighting began on May 7, the Allied naval force also included eight cruisers and seven destroyers. American, Australian, and British vessels would all take part in this action.

Things started off well for the Allies. Admiral Fletcher was pleased when he received a message saying, "Scratch one flattop"—which meant that a Japanese carrier had been sunk. But that was only the beginning of a battle unlike any before in naval history. No ship engaged in it ever sighted an enemy vessel. The planes launched from the carriers were the only attacking forces. The ships went on the defensive, maneuvering for position, their guns firing at enemy dive bombers in the sky.

On May 8, at the end of the day, the battle was over. One Japanese carrier had been sunk, another damaged, and forty-three Japanese planes had been downed. The Allied losses were heavier. Three American carriers had been sunk. Two of them were not even supposed to take part in the battle, but they had been near the battle area. The third, the *Lexington,* had fought brilliantly, but had been sunk by an explosion aboard after the battle ended. Thirty-three American planes were lost, and 543 men had been killed. Yet this had been a victory for the Allies. For the first time, they had checked the enemy's advance, and they had probably saved Australia.

American dive-bombers shattered a Japanese fleet at the Battle of Midway, turning back a threat to the U.S. mainland.

Even as repairmen were patching the *Yorktown's* damaged shell, she was driving north. She was needed in another battle.

BATTLE OF MIDWAY

The next point of attack by the Japanese was Midway Island, an outpost of the Hawaiian Islands about 1,200 miles northeast of Wake Island (see map, p. 268). Their striking force included fourteen big transports, for they planned to launch a full-scale invasion. After capturing Midway, they would destroy what remained of the American fleet at Pearl Harbor. As part of the plan, a side attack was to be made on the Aleutian Islands. The Japanese believed the Americans would hurry to defend the Aleutians and leave Midway undefended.

Luckily the Americans had broken the Japanese radio code and knew what to expect. Heavy Flying Fortress bombers, intended for Europe, were sent instead to Hawaii. A group of battleships, heavily armored if old and slow, steamed out of San Francisco. The carriers *Enterprise* and *Hornet,* and later the *Yorktown,* took up positions just east of Midway. Admiral Halsey was ill, and the carriers were commanded by Vice-Admiral Raymond A. Spruance, whose cold, nerveless, thoughtful approach to the problems of battle had earned him the nickname of the "Human Machine."

The Battle of Midway began on June 3, but the real fighting came the next day, when marine fighter planes based on the island staged a furious attack. The marine losses were heavy, but they sent at least one Japanese carrier, and perhaps two, to the bottom. Spruance then launched the planes from his carriers. This was a complete surprise to the Japanese, who believed that the Americans had already sent up all the planes they had. Three Japanese carriers and two battleships were set on fire, and at least one destroyer was sunk.

Planes from the Japanese carrier *Hiryu* found the *Yorktown* and damaged her disastrously. Then American planes sent the *Hiryu* to the bottom. That night two of the burning Japanese carriers sank, and a submarine finished off the third. The *Yorktown,* abandoned by her crew, was nearing her end.

The Japanese had had enough, and they retreated on June 6. They had lost four carriers, two heavy cruisers, four destroyers, and about 300 planes. The American victory not only saved Midway and Hawaii, but also wrecked Japan's war plan. If Midway had been lost, the American defenses in the Pacific would have been of little use. Japan would have controlled important jumping-off points from which to attempt an invasion of the American mainland. Instead, her defeat at Midway gave America the chance to take the initiative.

A sad moment came when the *Yorktown* sank on June 7. She had remained afloat since June 4, but it was impossible to save her. Taps was sounded, and the sailors on the other vessels raised their hands in salute as the carrier settled into the ocean.

Meanwhile, the Japanese attack on the Aleutians had been more successful. By June 7, Japanese troops had occupied the islands of Attu and Kiska. These bases were of little benefit to Japan, however, for they were frequently bombed by American planes flying out of Adak in the Andreanof Islands. By January of 1943 the Americans were at Amchitka, and the following spring the Japanese abandoned Kiska and were driven from Attu.

In Chicago in 1942, an atomic reactor produced the first nuclear chain reaction, forerunner of the atom bomb.

THE "MET LABORATORY"

Fermi produces the first nuclear chain reaction.

Meanwhile, as the war raged in the Pacific and Europe, something was taking place in secrecy at the peaceful campus of the University of Chicago that would eventually decide the war and have an enormous effect on the future of the world.

Each day a group of people gathered in a building on the campus known as the "Met Laboratory." "Met" stood for metallurgy, but no one in the group had much interest in the study of metals. At the head of the group was Dr. Enrico Fermi. An Italian scientist, he had come to the United States in 1939 to escape the tyranny of Mussolini's Fascism. In December of 1942, the people working with Dr. Fermi were warmly congratulating him. It would be many months before the world learned that Dr. Fermi had succeeded in producing the first nuclear chain reaction, which would in time make possible the construction of the atomic bomb.

U.S. TAKES THE OFFENSIVE IN THE PACIFIC

Capture of Guadalcanal protects the lifeline between U.S. and Australia.

The Allied military commanders knew that the victory at Midway would mean little unless a base was established to stop the Japanese from advancing nearer to Australia. Meanwhile, the United States had decided to take part in an invasion of French North Africa. It would be necessary to divert considerable naval strength from the Pacific to this area. And so the United States had to act quickly to check Japan in the South Pacific, and the place chosen for the first American offensive was Guadalcanal.

Before the fall of Bataan and Corregidor, when General MacArthur had been ordered to Australia, he had promised the defenders of the Philippines: "I shall return." In the summer of 1942 he began the long push back, advancing across the Owen Stanley Mountains of southwestern New Guinea. On August 7, American marines waded ashore on the islands of Florida, Tulagi, and Guadalcanal. They were attacking the Japanese bases that threatened the lifeline between Australia and the United States.

The fighting was bitter. The Japanese and American forces on the three islands were fairly evenly matched, and the outcome depended on which side gained supremacy in air and sea power. The Japanese fleet, surprising the Allied naval force that covered the Guadalcanal offensive, sank one Australian and three American cruisers. At the same time, Japanese planes mercilessly bombed the American landing forces. But two weeks later the Japanese lost several ships in a two-day battle.

It was a rough, seesaw fight all the way, on land and sea and in the air. The Americans won an airstrip, lost it, and then regained it, in a jungle where often there was nothing to eat but a few handfuls of captured Japanese rice. Both sides suffered heavy losses. In September the American carrier *Wasp* and five destroyers were sunk in a single day. But October brought an equally serious setback to the enemy. The Japanese merchant fleet trying to carry supplies to Guadalcanal—the so-called "Tokyo Express"—was virtually blasted from the sea.

The climax came in mid-November, at Savo Island, which is also in the Solomon chain. To make a final, determined effort, the Japanese brought to the area four battleships, numerous cruisers, and about thirty destroyers and transports carrying two full divisions of troops. But a large American convoy, escorted by destroyers and cruisers, had just reached Guadalcanal, and a radar station gave warning of the approach of the Japanese. And so the

Americans were ready when a wave of thirty-two Japanese bombers came over Florida Island. Thirty-one of them were downed.

It seemed like madness for Rear Admiral D. J. Callaghan to match his little cruiser force against the oncoming Japanese fleet. And yet he felt he had to take the risk, to keep the Japanese from landing fresh troops on Guadalcanal. As soon as the radar screen showed the Japanese ships to be west of Savo Island, Admiral Callaghan went after them. He paid with his life for his daring, but he left a good part of the Japanese fleet strewn across the ocean floor. Allied lossed were also heavy, but American industry could now build ships more quickly than the Japanese. Never again would Japan's navy seriously threaten the Allied positions in the Solomons. By February 8, 1943, American troops had finally cleared Guadalcanal of the enemy.

U.S. troops crouch low in their landing craft as they approach a Japanese-held island in the South Pacific.

VICTORY IN NORTH AFRICA

An Allied invasion force sweeps across North Africa.

Since late 1940, when the Italians had begun their invasion of Egypt, the fortunes of war had swung back and forth in North Africa. Axis troops attacked, only to be thrown back by the British. Even the German *Afrika Korps,* under General Erwin Rommel, failed to change this pattern.

Allied invaders trap an enemy plane over Algeria.

Then, during the summer of 1942, the *Afrika Korps,* aided by the Italian army, drove deep into Egypt, threatening Alexandria, Cairo, and the Suez Canal. In October, however, the British Eighth Army, led by General Bernard Law Montgomery, attacked at El Alamein and drove back the enemy. Now, for the first time, American forces, under the command of General Dwight D. Eisenhower, were to give active fighting support to the Allies in Africa.

At this time, "Ike" Eisenhower was comparatively unknown. But General George C. Marshall, chief of staff of the army, had a way of knowing everything important about the men he assigned to top command, and his choice was no accident.

Eisenhower was born in Denison, Texas, on October 14, 1890. At the age of two he moved with his family to Abilene, Kansas. Although as a boy he dreamed of becoming a Navy man, he entered West Point. During World War I he became known as a "mechanized nut" who commanded 60,000 men of the Tank Corps at Camp Colt in Gettysburg, Pennsylvania. He ended the war as a major. He remained a major for the next sixteen years, serving in responsible positions at army posts in New Jersey, Maryland, the Canal Zone, and the Philippines.

While in the Philippines, he found in General MacArthur a man who spoke his language. Both men believed that the future belonged to a mechanized army. At the age of forty-five Eisenhower became interested in aviation and qualified for a pilot's license. The organization of the Philippine Air Force, the establishment of the Philippine Mili-

British troops at El Alamein. Their victory here was a turning point in the campaign against the Afrika Korps.

tary Academy, and the designing of secret airfields were among his accomplishments.

Five days after Pearl Harbor, Eisenhower was summoned to Washington from San Antonio, Texas, where he was chief of staff of the Third Army. Soon after that he was on his way to England—and fame. One of his first duties was to command an invasion of North Africa.

In October of 1942, a submarine carried Eisenhower's most trusted staff officer, General Mark Clark, to a secret meeting with French military leaders in Algiers. A month later, Henri Giraud, a French general who had escaped to Algiers from a German prison camp, was brought to Gibraltar to aid in the invasion. On November 7 and 8, a fleet of about 500 transports, escorted by some 350 warships, carried American and British troops to landings at Safi, Casablanca, and Fedala, on the Atlantic coast of Morocco, and at Oran and Algiers, on the Mediterranean coast of Algeria, Paratroopers, flown from England, supported the invading forces.

The Allied forces moved rapidly to occupy Morocco and Algeria and to push eastward into Tunisia. Here the Germans rushed up reinforcements and the fighting became rugged. Allied tank-corps men and infantrymen slugged their way across mine fields, through valleys, and up hills, battling against artillery emplacements and nests of machine gunners. Bizerte, a city in Tunisia, was almost deserted when American tanks finally rolled in on May 7, 1943. The French people who still remained in the city ran from their houses, climbed up on the tanks, and kissed the embarrassed soldiers.

On May 12, 1943, the campaign in Africa came to an end. The remnants of Rommel's *Afrika Korps* surrendered in Tunisia, although Rommel himself escaped. In retaliation, German troops swept through the unoccupied parts of France. The Germans also tried to seize the French fleet at Toulon, but the crews of the ships scuttled and sank about fifty vessels.

THE INVASION OF ITALY

Roosevelt and Churchill meet in North Africa. The Allies move against Italy.

In mid-January of 1943, President Roosevelt and Prime Minister Churchill met with their chief military advisers in the African city of Casablanca. They discussed what action to take after the expected Allied victory in North Africa. At first the Americans favored a landing in France. Then they agreed with the British that the next operation should be an attack on the islands of Sicily or Sardinia, in preparation for a possible invasion of Italy.

Other serious problems were also discussed—the stepping up of the war against Japan, and the conflicts among the leaders of the Free French govern-

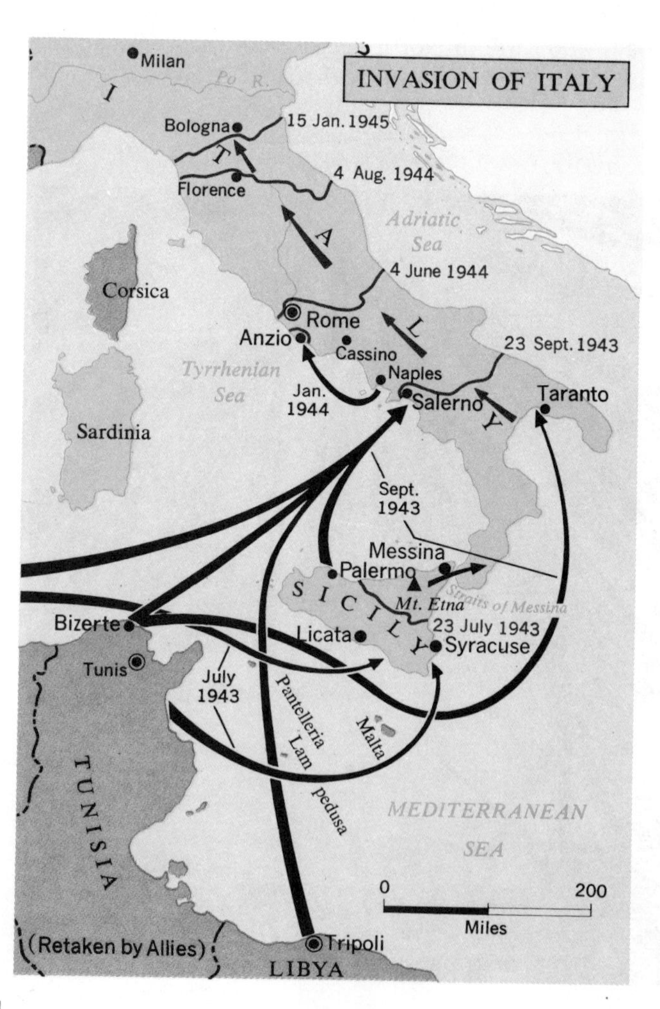

ment. One of the most important things to come out of the Casablanca meeting was the announcement that the Allies would end the war only upon the "unconditional surrender" of Germany, Italy, and Japan.

The Sicilian campaign was planned as a joint operation of British troops under the command of Generals Alexander and Montgomery and American troops under General George Patton, Jr. The entire Allied operation was under the command of General Eisenhower. By June 11, heavy sea and air bombardment by the Allies had knocked out Pantelleria Island, midway across the Sicilian narrows. The next day Lampedusa Island, ninety miles to the southwest, also surrendered.

With the Sicilian channel now clear, the invasion army boarded the 600 ships and 2,100 small craft that were to carry them to the beaches of Sicily. But the weather turned against the Allies. Winds of near-gale force lashed the Mediterranean, and surf pounded the beaches. Paratroopers, sent in advance on July 9 to seize enemy airfields, were swept from thirty to fifty miles from their marks. The Allies also found that the old stone houses in the little fishing villages that dotted the Sicilian coast had been converted to fortresses to fight off the landing forces.

In spite of all the hazards, the British and Americans began wading ashore before dawn on July 10. Allied light cruisers and destroyers pounded enemy tanks and broke up large enemy troop concentrations. The town of Licata was opened to Allied shipping that day, and Syracuse was captured two days later. By July 14, Augusta, north of Syracuse, was occupied. Allied air forces, operating from captured airstrips, flew as many as 1,200 sorties in a single day.

By July 22, the United States Seventh Army had pushed its way through the hills of western Sicily into Palermo. It then turned east along the island's northern coast. In the rugged mountain country, the fighting was vicious. German artillery was mounted on every ridge. Roads were mined and precipices blown away, so that it was extremely difficult to move mechanized equipment. The Allied engineers cursed and sweated and pushed their big guns forward almost inch by inch.

In early August, after hard fighting on the slopes of historic Mount Etna, the German defenses began to give way. The British smashed into Adrano, southwest of Mount Etna, then into Messina, and the Sicilian campaign was over.

Although the Germans managed to withdraw 40,000 men across the Strait of Messina to Italy, the fall of Sicily was a staggering blow. Axis casualties numbered 165,000, including 37,000 Germans, and many guns, tanks, and vehicles were lost as well. The Allied casualties were 31,158.

THE ALLIES TAKE NAPLES

On July 25, even before the fall of Sicily, King Victor Emmanuel of Italy dismissed Mussolini as head of the government. Mussolini was imprisoned and the Fascist party dissolved. The new head of the government was Marshal Pietro Badoglio, who was known to be sympathetic to the Allies. On September 3, he surrendered the Italian army and navy. But six days later the Germans quickly occupied Rome, to insure their control of northern Italy's industries.

On the same September day that the Italians surrendered, the Allies were trying to take full advantage of their success in Sicily. The British under Montgomery went across the Strait of Messina. Their purpose was to bottle up as many Germans as possible to the south of Naples. Once the British could release landing craft, the Americans under General Mark Clark landed troops along the Gulf of Salerno.

By October 1, after bloody fighting, the British and Americans had joined forces, advanced northward, and entered Naples. And yet there were reasons for the Allies to feel discouraged. With the occupation of Rome by the Germans, both King Victor Emmanuel and Badoglio meekly allowed themselves to become powerless. The Germans rescued Mussolini and set him up as the head of a puppet Fascist government in the north. The Allies had hoped for a general uprising among the liberated Italians, but so far there was little sign of one.

THE GUSTAV LINE

The only choice left to the Allies was to fight their way up the Italian peninsula, and this they did, step by step. In the mountain country north of Naples, the German defenses stiffened. After the Allies crossed the Volturno River, the Germans withdrew to prepared defenses known as the Gustav Line, destroying bridges and mining canals and sewers. As winter approached, with its heavy rains and snow, the Allied advance came to a halt 70 miles from Rome.

Late in January, the Allies tried to break through the German defenses. They were successful only at Cassino in central Italy, a key position in the Gustav Line. In a surprise move, the Allies landed troops at the rear of the German forces at Anzio, on the west coast. If the Allies had pressed on into the Alban hills to the north, all might have gone well. But they paused to strengthen their position, and were sealed off by a heavy German counterattack. For four months 50,000 troops were pinned down at Anzio, and not until May 18, 1944, did the Allies finally take Cassino.

But the Allied air forces were busy during the winter months, and German supplies began to run dangerously low. In May the Allies staged a mighty attack, pierced the German lines, and raced northward. Rome fell with little resistance on June 4. The

Allies went on, and on August 4, after heavy fighting, they captured Florence. Again the Germans withdrew to prepared defenses, this time to the Gothic Line, which stretched across the base of northern Italy. Again both sides were at a standstill.

The men on the battleline wrote letters home, telling what it was like to be fighting in Italy. Sometimes the men raged at the cruelty of war, as when they told of the Germans destroying the water supply in Naples and killing civilians with a time bomb planted in the post office. Sometimes the men boasted of that marvel of American inventive genius, the little army jeep that raced swiftly over the roads. Sometimes the men wrote of death, and described how the bodies of their comrades were brought down from the mountains lashed to the backs of mules. "You feel small in the presence of dead men," one soldier wrote, "and you don't ask silly questions."

THE BATTLE OF THE ATLANTIC

German subs take a high toll until the Allies find ways to combat them.

One reason the war slowed down in Italy during the winter of 1943–44 was that the Allies were fighting the Battle of the Atlantic. The German submarine fleet, under Admiral Karl Doenitz, did the most damage in 1942, when it destroyed 1,161 Allied merchant vessels. Eventually, however, the Allies found ways of striking back at the submarines and were able to win the Battle of the Atlantic.

One of the most effective weapons used against the submarines was the destroyer escort. This was a ship about the size of the destroyer used in World War I, but with simpler engines. Fast enough to overtake a large submarine on the surface of the water, it protected convoys at night and chased off submarines by day. It carried a device called a "hedgehog," which fired depth charges in a scattered pattern, in much the same manner as shot fired from a shotgun. These charges exploded only on contact, so that the destroyer escort's sound-locating apparatus could still track down the enemy during a battle.

THE WOLF PACKS

The destroyer escort proved especially valuable against the "wolf packs." These were groups of as many as ten submarines. They strung out in a patrol line that could escape the naval vessels guarding convoys until the destroyer escort was put into use. Also valuable against the wolf packs was the small aircraft carrier. This was no more than a merchant vessel with a flight deck mounted on stilts. It was a cranky little ship, slow and hard to maneuver, but it enabled planes to be launched when and where they were needed.

The airplane, too, played an important part in winning the Battle of the Atlantic. Planes, destroyer escorts, and small aircraft carriers formed "hunter-killer" groups that tracked down submarines. Allied planes also raided submarine launching pens in North Germany, Norway, and France. By September of 1943—the year in which the Battle of the Atlantic was won—the Allied high command could announce that ninety submarines had been sunk in as many days. After the spring of that year, although German submarines still damaged Allied shipping, they were no longer the terrible menace they had been.

THE GERMAN SURFACE NAVY

In contrast to the submarines, the German surface navy was never a serious threat. Its most spectacular success came in May of 1941, when the German dreadnought *Bismarck* ventured into the North Atlantic and sank the British battleship *Hood.* But three days later, after relentless pursuit, the *Bismarck* was sunk. The German pocket battleship *Graf Spee* had been lost in December, 1939, while raiding British shipping in the South Atlantic. Otherwise, the German surface navy did little more than make occasional raids from Norwegian ports. It was small in numbers and was unable to operate effectively over long distances.

WINNING AIR SUPREMACY

Allied planes based in Britain slowly win control of the air from Germany.

An even greater danger to the Allies than the submarines was the German *Luftwaffe,* or air force. The British and the American aircraft industries worked day and night so that the Allies could bring their air strength up to that of Germany. By early 1944, the United States Eighth Air Force, operating from bases in Britain, was able to send as many as 1,000 planes over a German city at one time.

The Americans used "pinpoint bombing," dropping their bombs on specific targets from planes flying at high altitudes. The British preferred "saturation bombing," dropping a large number of bombs in the general area of the target so that the target would be hit by at least some of the bombs. Both methods proved effective.

The Allies never disagreed about what they were trying to accomplish by their bombing campaigns. Their aims were to destroy as much as possible of the German air force, to destroy communications within Germany, to break the will of the German

(Top, left) *American P-51 fighter.*

(Top, right) *U.S. troops in Rome after capturing the city.*

(Left) *Pilots running to man their Lockheed P-38 fighters.*

(Bottom, left) *Bombers ready for action at a British base.*

(Below) *The* Hood *(behind sister ship) was sunk by the* Bismarck.

civilians so that they would no longer support the Nazi war effort, and to smash Germany's chief war industries.

The Allied bombing missions were carefully planned. For example, Schweinfurt was attacked in order to knock out the ball-bearing plant there. Dams were blown up along the Ruhr River, in western Germany, to deprive a number of war industries of their source of power. Hamburg was raided to break up a transportation system. Low-flying bombers blasted railroads, bridges, and locomotive works.

Allied bombs destroyed planes on the ground and left aircraft factories in ruins. By late 1944, the *Luftwaffe* had lost most of its effectiveness. By the end of the war, more than 35,000 German planes had been destroyed, either on the ground or in the air, and almost 1,400,000 tons of bombs had fallen on German-held territory. Perhaps as many as 10,000 American and 12,000 British bombers were lost in the battle to control the air over Europe.

ISLAND HOPPING

Allied forces take key Japanese islands in the Pacific

While the war went on in North Africa, Sicily, Italy, and on the Atlantic, there was war, too, in the far reaches of the Pacific. Japan had bases on islands such as Tarawa, Kwajalein, Truk, Yap, Saipan, and Guam. They served as "unsinkable aircraft carriers" and gave Japan control of thousands of square miles of the Central Pacific.

The Americans fought in the jungles of Pacific islands.

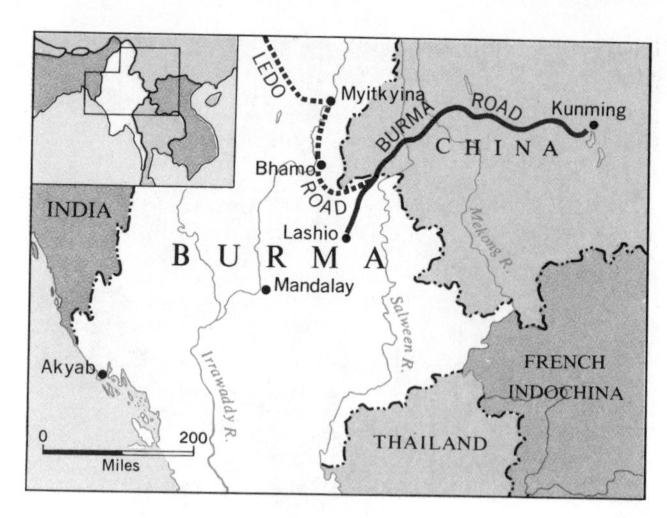

The Ledo and Burma Roads linked India with China.

The Allies decided they could not attempt to capture each island separately; it would cost too much in time, men, and materials. Instead, they adopted a plan of "island hopping." They would seize only key islands and use them as bases from which to attack other important objectives. Allied control of these key islands, and of the sea and air around them, would also make the Japanese bases in the area useless. It would be impossible for the Japanese to bring up reinforcements or supplies.

In November of 1943, Allied naval guns blasted Tarawa, in the Gilbert Islands group of the Central Pacific. Carrier planes roared overhead, dropping tons of bombs on Japanese installations, as Tarawa was softened up for an invasion. On November 22, the marines waded ashore, and many lives were lost because of faulty knowledge of reefs and tides.

The Japanese were well protected by concrete pillboxes and were determined to fight to the last man. Almost 3,000 American marines died in the jungle hell of Tarawa before it fell. In addition, the escort carrier *Liscomb Bay* was torpedoed and went down with about 1,000 men aboard. But the conquest of Tarawa proved to be worth the sacrifice. Allied planes could now bomb and photograph Japanese positions in the Marshall and eastern Caroline Islands, the next steppingstones on the route to the mainland of Japan.

In mid-January of 1944, the largest naval force the world had ever seen sailed out of Pearl Harbor. The heart of this fleet was Task Force 58, which was made up of more than a hundred carriers, battleships, cruisers, and destroyers. There were also transports, landing craft, tankers, small carriers loaded with aircraft replacements, and supply and hospital ships.

The striking point was Kwajalein Atoll in the center of the Marshall Islands. On January 31, shouting infantrymen waded ashore at Kwajalein, and by

February 6 they had captured it. Other troops took Majuro Atoll to the southeast. Bitter fighting took place at Eniwetok Atoll in the northwestern Marshalls, but by the middle of February that, too, had fallen.

Task Force 58 refueled at Majuro and swung into action. Truk, the strongest of all the Japanese bases in the Central Pacific, was hit hard. Saipan, mainstay of the Japanese hold on the Mariana Islands, was raided a few days later.

The United States Fifth Fleet (odd-numbered fleets operated in the Pacific, even-numbered fleets in the Atlantic) also went into action in the Central Pacific. It raided the Palaus, west of the Carolines, and Woleai, Yap, Truk, Kusaie, and Ponape.

The Japanese realized that now not one of their bases in the Central Pacific was safe. Their navy grimly prepared to defend the Marianas, which would certainly be attacked next. Planes from the carriers of Task Force 58 began bombing Guam, Tinian, and Saipan, and on June 15 marines and infantrymen poured onto the beaches of Saipan.

BATTLE OF THE PHILIPPINE SEA

For the first time since 1943, there was opposition from Japanese carriers. But the Battle of the Philippine Sea, fought on June 19 and 20, brought no comfort to the Japanese. American pilots outdid their foes at dogfighting, and more than 400 Japanese planes fell into the sea. Only 27 American aircraft were shot down.

Stripped of its air power, the Japanese fleet tried to run to safety. Four of its carriers, along with several other vessels, were sunk. The Americans lost not a single ship. Before July ended, most of the fighting on Saipan was over, and American troops had landed on Tinian and Guam.

OTHER SIDES OF THE WAR

Spies, engineers, and diplomats all play important parts as the fighting goes on.

More than fighting was involved in a conflict as vast as World War II. The struggle to win the minds of men was as important as a battle to win a mountain ridge in Italy or an island strip in the Pacific.

In occupied France, Belgium, the Netherlands, Denmark, and Norway, members of the underground did everything they could to hinder the enemy's war effort. They staged slowdowns in factories. They blew up railroads and bridges. They published secret newspapers loyal to the Allies, and rescued Allied airmen shot down over Europe.

Secret agents of the Allies were active within Germany, where they gathered valuable information on experiments with rockets. Radio became a weapon that was used by both sides. The Allies tried to bring truthful news to the people of the occupied countries. The Germans, on the other hand, broadcast false stories of Allied disaster and confusion. One of the broadcasters was a traitor named William Joyce, who became known as "Lord Haw Haw." In the Pacific, Japan had its "Tokyo Rose." She played records of songs popular in the United States, and worked upon the homesickness of the fighting men to cause dissatisfaction among them.

Allied statesmen were planning the enemy's defeat. On November 22, 1943, President Roosevelt, Prime Minister Churchill, and Generalissimo Chiang Kai-shek of China met at Cairo, Egypt. They discussed many military matters, including the distribution of forces and equipment in all areas of the war. The most important agreement reached at Cairo was on the Allied war aims in the Far East. Japan was to be stripped of all the Pacific islands she had acquired since 1914. She was to be "expelled from all other territories which she has taken by violence and greed." Manchuria, Formosa, and the Pescadores Islands were to be restored to China, and Korea was to become free and independent.

MEETING AT TEHRAN

Roosevelt and Churchill then journeyed to Tehran, the capital of Iran. There, in late November, they met with Joseph Stalin, the premier of Russia. The military discussions were mainly about plans for an invasion of France sometime during 1944.

Although Stalin would say at the close of the conference that it was certain "our peoples will act together jointly and in friendship both at the present time and after the war," all was not smooth sailing at the Tehran meeting. There were some problems that could not be solved easily, such as the future of Poland and the form of government it should have.

Returning to Cairo in December, Roosevelt and Churchill decided that nothing would block the forthcoming invasion of France. The two statesmen decided that they could not give greater aid to China in its struggle against the Japanese. This was a hard decision to make, especially for Roosevelt, who wanted to give more effective help to Chiang. At this time, a deadlock existed in China. The Chinese lacked the resources to launch a successful counterattack, and Japan had already gobbled up more territory than she could use.

FLYING THE HUMP

As early as 1942, the Americans had been helping China build up its air force so that transports could bring in supplies. The transports flew a dangerous air route across the "Hump"—the Himalaya Mountains between northern Burma and southwest-

Troops waded through shallows to a beach below the Normandy bluffs.

General Eisenhower gave last-minute advice to paratroopers on D-Day.

ern China. Roosevelt persuaded Churchill that at least this program could be stepped up, and results soon followed. The Japanese were so alarmed that they opened a new campaign. They came within 200 miles of China's wartime capital of Chungking before they were finally driven back.

To Roosevelt, it seemed a great pity that more could not be done in the north Burma jungle. He did, however, win agreement on a drive to clear enough territory for a road connecting the Bengal and Assam railway in northeastern India with the Chinese end of the Burma Road. British and American commando troops—notably Orde Wingate's Raiders and Frank Merrill's Marauders—fought the Japanese like the "island hoppers" in the Central Pacific. Using parachutes and gliders, they seized a number of key points.

Meanwhile, Chinese troops under General Joseph W. Stilwell fought their way south toward Mandalay. Behind the advancing infantry came the engineers. They bulldozed and surfaced a track through the jungle, sometimes working within the range of small-arms fire. Eventually, some 400 miles of road were built from Ledo, in northern Assam, to Lashio, the end of the Burma Road. In January of 1945 the first truck convoys reached Kunming, China, from Lashio, with fresh supplies. They had traveled 700 miles.

The Japanese attempted to cut the Bengal and Assam railway, over which supplies began the long trip to China. They were beaten back by Indian troops on the India-Burma border. The heavy "monsoon" rains of summer, disease, and lack of supplies also took their toll of the Japanese. They fell back, and the British followed, retaking Mandalay in March, 1945, and Rangoon in May.

All these events came about, directly or indirectly, as the result of the decisions made at the second Cairo meeting. But the main task before the Allies, as Roosevelt and Churchill agreed, was the invasion of France. They agreed, too, on the man to take charge of the invasion—General Dwight D. Eisenhower.

OPERATION OVERLORD

The greatest invasion force the world has ever seen masses in England to attack the Germans in Normandy.

On Christmas Eve, 1943, General Eisenhower was in Algiers. He was enjoying a Christmas party with members of his staff when he learned that he had been chosen supreme commander of "Operation Overlord," the code name for the invasion of France. Eisenhower knew how much depended on carrying through Operation Overlord with speed. Only weeks before, he had received some important information through Allied underground agents. The Germans were building launching platforms for "buzz bombs" —rocket-propelled glider bombs—at nine different places.

In England, Eisenhower worked furiously to have everything ready for the invasion by a "favorable period of the May moon." The cycle of the moon allowed just six days in each month when tidal conditions along the beaches of Normandy would enable an army to go ashore with some chance of success. Army men wanted to hit those beaches in the predawn darkness, but navy and air force men dis-

Supplies being landed at Omaha Beach. Here many Americans fell in bloody landing clashes.

Saint-Lô, scene of the American breakthrough in Normandy, was pounded to rubble.

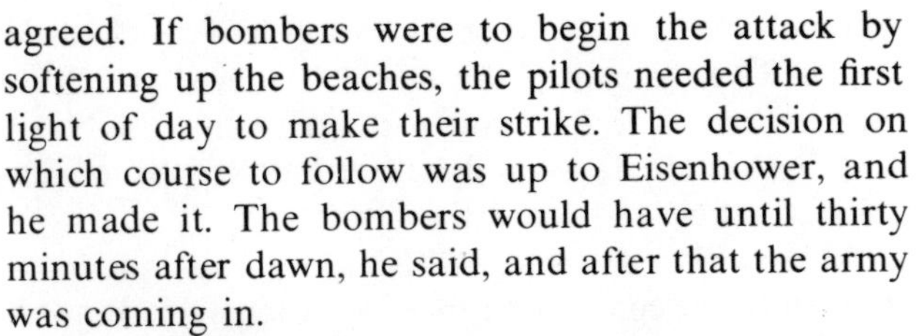

agreed. If bombers were to begin the attack by softening up the beaches, the pilots needed the first light of day to make their strike. The decision on which course to follow was up to Eisenhower, and he made it. The bombers would have until thirty minutes after dawn, he said, and after that the army was coming in.

This was only one of the many difficult decisions Eisenhower had to make during the immense preparations for the invasion. Another was to delay D-Day for Operation Overlord until a "favorable period of the June moon."

Eisenhower faced problems unknown to any other general in history. Four thousand ships of various types would be required for the invasion, and 140,000 troops. To transport airborne troops as well as supplies would require about 1,300 planes and 2,000 gliders. Hundreds of bombers and fighter planes would also be needed.

On June 4, 1944, rain pounded down on the English Channel and the waves rolled high. There were grim faces at Allied headquarters that day. For three days—June 5, 6, and 7—the tide would be right for the invasion. After that, it would be two weeks before the next three favorable days. Again the decision was up to Eisenhower, and again it was a difficult one. With 140,000 men assembling for the invasion, how much longer could Operation Overlord be kept secret?

D-DAY

On June 5, low patches of bad weather spread from Canada to Europe. But even if the skies cleared, conditions would not be right for the invasion. The Channel was still choppy, and the invaders would be seasick by the time they reached the beaches of Normandy. A little later, however, the weather reports were more promising, and Eisenhower reached a decision. The invasion would take place on June 6.

The plan was for the British Second Army under Montgomery to land at the mouth of the Orne River. Airborne troops, dropping on Caen, Le Havre, and Rouen, were to cut communications and confuse the Germans about the true point of assault. The main effort was to be made farther west by American forces under General Omar N. Bradley, landing along a thirty-mile front. Their aim would be to break across the Cotentin peninsula and isolate the important port of Cherbourg. Two beachheads, called Utah Beach and Omaha Beach, were to be established by the American forces. Airborne troops would have the task of capturing the communication points between.

When D-Day came, the bitterest fighting took place at Omaha Beach. Here the Germans were dug into positions along a 100-foot bluff about 200 yards from the beach. Their machine-gun nests were strong and well concealed. An immense V-shaped ditch made it difficult for either men or tanks to cross, and the water itself was filled with various devices to prevent a landing. To make things worse for the Americans, a German infantry division, simply by chance, had been carrying on anti-invasion maneuvers at this point.

Allied bombers thundered over Omaha Beach, dropping their deadly loads. The landing craft bobbed forward. Some made the beach; others blew up as they struck underwater mines. The Allied battleships opened fire with their heavy guns.

DEATH ON OMAHA BEACH

Throughout the day of June 6 and most of June 7, the struggle for Omaha Beach was touch and go. Most of the 7,300 Americans who died during the invasion were killed here. But the Allies were determined to hang on. Ernie Pyle, one of the great American reporters of the war, described the scene after the Allies had succeeded in gaining a foothold:

"As I plowed over the wet sand, I walked around what seemed to be a couple of pieces of driftwood sticking out of the sand. But they weren't driftwood. They were a soldier's two feet. He was completely covered except for his feet; the toes of his GI shoes pointed toward the land he had come so far to see, and which he saw so briefly.

"A few hundred yards back on the beach was a high bluff. Up there we had a tent hospital, and a barbed-wire enclosure for prisoners of war. From up there you could see far up and down the beach, in a spectacular crow's-nest view, and far out to sea.

"And standing out there on the water beyond all this wreckage was the greatest armada man has ever seen. You simply could not believe the gigantic collection of ships that lay out there waiting to unload. Looking from the bluff, it lay thick and clear to the far horizon of the sea and on beyond, and it spread out to the sides and was miles wide.

"As I stood there I noticed a group of freshly taken German prisoners standing nearby. They . . . were looking out to sea—the same bit of sea that for months and years had been so safely empty before their gaze. Now they stood staring almost as if in a trance. They didn't say a word to each other. They didn't need to. The expression on their faces was something forever unforgettable. In it was the final, horrified acceptance of their doom."

By June 12, the beachheads were larger. The British were pushing twenty miles inland, while the Americans were putting sixteen divisions ashore.

Troops advancing up a Normandy hillside.

The invaders had moved across the Channel none too soon, for on June 13 the first of the buzz bombs fell on London. These pilotless, rocket-propelled bombs flew at a speed of more than 400 miles an hour until their fuel was exhausted. Then they nosed down sharply and exploded. By the end of July, the buzz bombs had killed 4,735 Londoners and wounded at least 14,000. The bombs might have done enormous damage if they had fallen on the invading army as it waited to disembark.

During the next six weeks, the hedgerows of Normandy helped to protect the Germans, and the fighting was hard. Even so, the British pushed on Caen and the Americans broke through the German defenses at St. Lô. A tank column raced south into Brittany and down the Loire River. Another column, turning east, made straight for Paris. A German counterattack failed, and the British, breaking through at Falaise, joined with the Americans. In four days the German Seventh Army was smashed, and the road to Paris was open.

Inside Paris, the people learned that on August 19 two columns under General Patton had reached the Seine River, north of the city. The news was like a call to arms. The Parisians rose up against the Nazis, and within six days—and before Patton's Americans arrived—they had freed the city.

Meanwhile, a strong Allied army had landed on the southern coast of France on August 15. It swept northward, capturing the important industrial city of Lyons in less than two weeks. In the north, the Americans advanced—past the Somme River, past the Marne, then across the Belgian border. Eastward along the coast of France the British pushed through Lille and Belgium into the Netherlands. The Americans moved through Luxembourg, and by September 11, they were in Germany. Here they faced the Siegfried Line, a system of fortifications that stretched from Switzerland to Holland. The Allies knew that they might meet strong opposition, but they felt that final victory was not too far away.

RETAKING THE PHILIPPINES

General MacArthur returns at the head of an Allied invasion force.

In the South Pacific, too, things were going well for the Allies. Island hopping was proving to be as successful here as in the Central Pacific. In late 1943, American marines had landed in western New Britain, an island northeast of New Guinea. Since that time, the Allies had been following a plan of encircling the Japanese. The Admiralty Islands fell in February of 1944. When spring came, General MacArthur was able to advance steadily along the coast

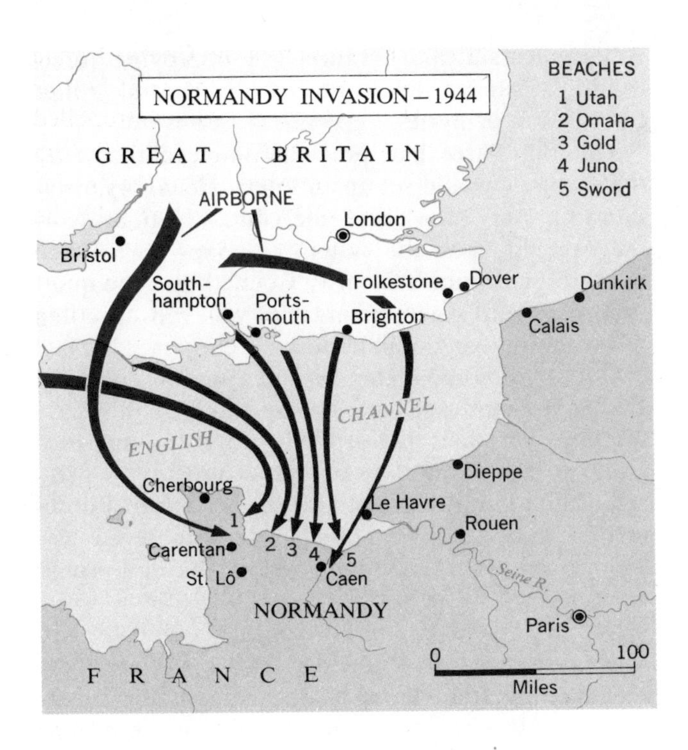

of northern New Guinea. The Allies soon captured bases at Aitape, Wewak, Hollandia, and Biak. "I shall return," General MacArthur had said to the people of the Philippines in the first discouraging weeks of the war. As fall approached, it looked as though he would soon be keeping his promise.

A new United States fleet—the Third—was now operating with its carrier force in the Central Pacific. Japanese resistance was light. American planes soared over Manila, knocking out many Japanese aircraft on the ground. Japanese shipping was also severely damaged.

On September 15, 1944, American troops waded ashore at Peleliu in the Palau Islands and at the Moluccas. Both positions were less than 500 miles from Mindanao, the southernmost of the Philippines. Again Japanese resistance was light, and the Allies changed their plans. Instead of striking at Mindanao, they decided to land on Leyte in the central Philippines. Ulithi Atoll in the western Carolines fell to the Americans on September 20, giving the Allies a base closer to their objective.

By October 20, Americans were on the beaches of eastern Leyte, General MacArthur among them, as he fulfilled his promise to return. The desperate Japanese sent three separate naval forces to oppose the Leyte landings. With these forces came the *kamikazes,* the suicide planes. As part of *kamikaze* tactics, a pilot would steer a plane carrying high explosives directly into an American ship, sacrificing his life in the explosion. Americans called such planes "*baka* bombs," the word *baka* in Japanese meaning "stupid" or "foolish."

The main Japanese force, approaching the Philippines from Singapore, was sighted on October 23. American submarines attacked it unmercifully, sinking a battleship and two heavy cruisers, and damaging a third cruiser. The Americans were led to believe that the Japanese had had enough and were turning back.

Suddenly, however, Japanese planes swooped down on the light carrier *Princeton,* damaging the vessel so badly that it had to be abandoned. But the attack revealed that a second Japanese fleet with carriers was in the area, and Admiral Halsey's Third Fleet steamed north to meet it. Two Japanese carriers and several other vessels were sunk in a single day, and the Japanese force fled back to its homeland.

THE BATTLE OF LEYTE

Admiral Thomas C. Kinkaid, in command of the Seventh Fleet, found the third Japanese force on the night of October 24. It was approaching Leyte Gulf through the Surigao Strait, an arm of the Pacific between Leyte and Mindanao. It was a battered, patched-up force, made up mainly of old battleships, cruisers, and destroyers. In spite of *kamikaze* attacks that took their toll of American vessels, almost the entire Japanese fleet was wiped out.

Meanwhile, the first Japanese force moved on toward Leyte. Steaming through San Bernardino Strait, between Samar and Luzon, on October 25, it entered the open Pacific. Here the Japanese caught a group of American escort carriers protected only by destroyers. Two American carriers, three destroyers, and more than one hundred planes were destroyed in the fight that followed. Again the *kamikazes* took their toll, but in a matter of hours the Japanese were turned back. Their fleet was crippled almost beyond recovery, and the Leyte landings were safe.

Leyte was the decisive battle for the Philippines.

General MacArthur kept his pledge: "I shall return."

On April 12, 1945, Harry S. Truman was sworn in as President as Mrs. Truman and others watched.

American aircraft could now control all the islands. On January 9, 1945, American troops landed on Luzon at Lingayen Gulf, 110 miles north of Manila. This was followed by landings at Subic Bay and Nasugbu, south of Manila. On February 17, despite fierce Japanese resistance, American paratroopers landed on Corregidor, and before the month ended Manila was cleared of Japanese.

A NEW PRESIDENT

Roosevelt dies suddenly, and Harry S. Truman succeeds him.

In November of 1944, Americans went to the polls to choose a President. Roosevelt was running for a fourth term. Running against him was Thomas E. Dewey, the racket-busting attorney from New York. Dewey faced the same problem as most Republican candidates of those years. All he could promise the voters was that he could carry out the nation's present domestic and foreign policies better than his opponent. Roosevelt won a smashing 432-to-99 victory in the electoral college, but his popular majority was only some 3,500,000—the smallest any President had had since World War I.

President Roosevelt attended his last meeting of the Big Three—the United States, Britain, and Russia—in 1945. He met first with Churchill at Malta for preliminary discussions. Then the two went on to Yalta, in the Crimean region of Russia, where on February 4 they began talks with Stalin. During the next five days, the Big Three made plans for the postwar world. They reaffirmed their demand for Germany's unconditional surrender. Once peace was restored, Germany must be disarmed and her war criminals punished. Germany would be divided into four sectors, each to be occupied by troops of one of the four major powers—the United States, Britain, Russia, and France. All occupying forces would be under the control of a central Allied commission in Berlin.

The Big Three had previously agreed that after the war they would set up an international organization to preserve the peace, the United Nations. Now they agreed upon the system of voting to be used in the organization's Security Council. But the question of Poland's new boundaries was still unsettled when the meeting adjourned on February 11.

Only two months later, on the afternoon of April 12, 1945, Americans were shocked to hear this news coming over their radios: "We interrupt this program to bring you a special news bulletin. A press association has just announced that President Roosevelt is dead. . . ." Franklin Delano Roosevelt had died of a cerebral hemorrhage at Warm Springs, Georgia.

Not since the death of Abraham Lincoln had Americans been so stunned. Charles Collingwood, broadcasting from Paris, said: "Tonight the streets are silent. It is not too much to say that the American army is brokenhearted." Later, Anne O'Hare McCormick, writing in the New York *Times,* would call Roosevelt "a man of the world and the world's man," and the Omaha *World-Herald* would say in an editorial: "There are no Republicans in America today, no Democrats, no New Dealers or anti-New Dealers. There are only Americans, united in a sense of national bereavement."

Four hours after Roosevelt's death, Harry S. Truman took the oath of office and became the President of the United States. He told reporters that day: "If you fellows ever pray, pray for me."

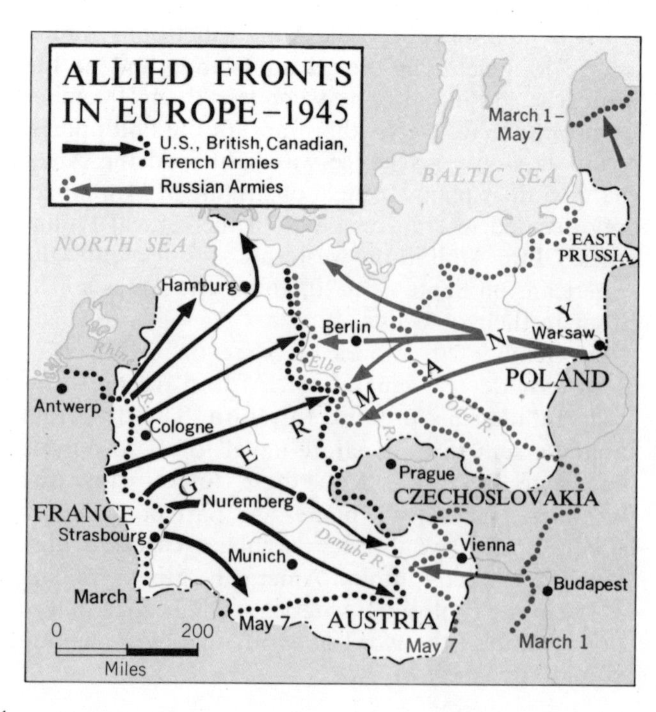

Few Americans knew much about Truman. But, as they saw him on newsreels and heard his nasal twang on the radio, they quickly became accustomed to him. He seemed to fit the description once given of Ulysses S. Grant—an "uncommon common man."

Born in Lamar, Missouri, on May 8, 1884, Truman was a farm boy. Only his weak eyes kept him from entering West Point. He worked as a timekeeper on the Santa Fe Railroad, a wrapper of newspapers for the Kansas City *Star,* a bank clerk, and a bookkeeper. At the age of twenty-two he returned home to run the family farm for his widowed mother.

During World War I, Truman enlisted in the army, fought at Saint-Mihiel, and returned a major in the field artillery. In the years following the war, he came to the attention of Thomas "Big Tom" Pendergast, the shrewd political boss of Kansas City.

With Pendergast's backing, Truman advanced steadily in his political career. He was overseer of highways in Missouri's Jackson County, and then county judge. While serving as judge, he studied nights at the Kansas City School of Law. In 1934 he was elected to the United States Senate. Within six years Pendergast's political machine was bogged down in scandal, but none of it involved Truman. Missourians believed in his integrity, and they re-elected him to the Senate. There, as chairman of the Senate committee investigating the national defense program—known as the "Truman Committee"—he began to win national prominence.

Roosevelt picked Truman as his running mate in 1944, and now, eighty-three days after the election, Harry S. Truman was President of the United States. It was up to him to carry on the war.

VICTORY IN EUROPE

American forces drive across the Rhine and Germany is forced to surrender.

Twenty-six days after his inauguration, President Truman announced the unconditional surrender of Germany. This had come about only after a great deal of fighting. In mid-September of 1944, the American First Army had been halted before the Siegfried Line in Germany. From then until December, the Allies had massed forces, hoping to launch an overwhelming assault north and south of the line. But the Allies' plan weakened the center of their own line, where only four divisions protected a stretch of seventy-five miles.

The Germans, under General Karl Rudolf Gerd von Rundstedt, found that the Allies' weakest spot was at the Ardennes Forest, and prepared to strike at it. Van Rundstedt massed three armies along a 90-mile front to try for a break-through. He also called for the aid of any German plane that could still fly. In the "Battle of the Bulge," which began on December 16, the Germans launched a three-pronged assault that cut through the Allied defenses. They almost succeeded in driving all the way to the sea and the port of Antwerp.

For the American troops, the hardest fighting came at the little town of Bastogne, in southern Belgium. German panzer forces, advancing north and south of the town, isolated the 101st Airborne Division and some armored units. Reinforced but still outnumbered, the 101st hung on until tanks forced their way through the German wedge. After that, the Allies recovered all the ground they had lost within a week.

The Allies then began a push into the Rhineland, and they moved quickly. Cologne was attacked on February 27, 1945, and it fell about a week later. Cologne stood on the western bank of the Rhine River, and, in a kind of frenzy, the Germans tried to destroy every bridge across the Rhine. But they missed one, at the little village of Remagen, and there the American First Army poured across the river. By March 23, four more Allied armies, using boats, were across the Rhine. Two parachute divisions were five miles beyond.

With Russian troops driving from the east and the Americans driving from the west, the end was near for Germany. Now in complete control of the air over Europe, Allied bombers blasted key targets by day and night. On April 22, the Russians were shelling Berlin. Three days later, northwest of Dresden, Russian and American troops met and shook hands at the Elbe River.

The Axis was falling apart, and events followed in rapid succession. On April 28, Mussolini was killed by Italian patriots. The next day, German forces in Italy surrendered. On April 30, Adolf Hitler took his own life in a bomb shelter under the chancellery in Berlin, leaving Admiral Karl Doenitz as the head of Germany. And on May 7, in the schoolhouse at Reims, France, where General Eisenhower had his headquarters, the documents of the German surrender were signed.

Americans cheered and shouted and sang, but fighting still went on in the Pacific.

IWO JIMA AND OKINAWA

With terrific casualties on both sides, the Allies take two islands from which they can invade Japan.

The war in the Pacific was steadily moving closer to the home islands of Japan. American strategy called for the invasion of Iwo Jima, a tiny volcanic island about 750 miles south of Tokyo. Establishing a base here would enable fighter planes to protect the

U.S. Marines took Iwo Jima foot by foot against heavy fire. The battle lasted more than three weeks.

Marines raised the U.S. flag on Mount Suribachi, Iwo Jima.

B-29 bombers on their raids of Japan's main island of Honshu. It would extend Allied control over new areas of the Pacific.

United States marines landed on Iwo Jima on February 19, 1945, in one of the bloodiest battles of the war. There was little room to maneuver on the beaches. The Japanese, counterattacking from well-fortified positions, resisted fanatically. The capture of the island cost the Americans 21,000 casualties, including 4,500 men killed. About 22,000 Japanese were captured or killed.

By early April, American aircraft were flying from a new base on Iwo Jima. Now the Allies turned toward Okinawa, the largest island in the Ryukyus. It lay only 350 miles from Kyushu, the southernmost of Japan's home islands, where the Allies planned to start an invasion of Japan itself.

Okinawa was heavily bombarded from the air and the sea before the first landings on April 1. From the start, it was plain that this would be a fearful struggle. The Japanese knew that losing Okinawa would be a disaster. Allied aircraft based on Okinawa could then attack their homeland from the west, while aircraft based on Iwo Jima struck from the east. Moreover, with Okinawa lost, Japan would be cut off from Formosa, and Allied planes would control the China Sea.

The Japanese allowed about half of the island to be taken rather easily, but the Americans knew that the worst fighting was yet to come. They proved to be right, for inland the Japanese gave up not one inch of ground without the stiffest kind of resistance. In winning Okinawa and the surrounding Ryukyus, about 7,600 men of the Tenth Army were killed and 31,800 wounded; there were also 26,200 non-battle casualties. The Japanese losses were even more horrifying—about 110,000 killed and 7,400 captured.

During the battle, more than 5,000 Japanese aircraft, including *kamikazes,* attacked the Allied invaders. They succeeded in sinking 36 ships and damaging about 200 more. But by June 21 the Allies had conquered Okinawa, and the Japanese grimly braced themselves for the invasion of their homeland. They knew it would come soon.

TRUMAN GOES TO POTSDAM

The Allied leaders meet in Potsdam, Germany, and send a warning to Japan.

With Germany out of the war and Japan tottering, President Truman attended a conference of Allied heads of state at Potsdam, outside Berlin, from July 17 through August 2. "You never saw such pigheaded people as are the Russians," Truman wrote his mother and sister. "I hope I never have to hold another conference with them—but, of course, I will."

The chief military discussions at Potsdam concerned the war with Japan and Russia's part in it, for Russia had promised to go to war against Japan soon. Agreements were also reached on how the German zones of occupation were to be governed, the payment of war debts, the establishment of Poland's borders, and the necessity of bringing Axis leaders to trail as war criminals. But there was still disagreement on a number of things such as Russia's actions in the Balkans and its insistence that it be granted two districts belonging to Turkey. The reports coming from Potsdam suggested that all was harmony among the Allies, but actually there was uneasiness over Russia.

An important document that came out of the conference was the Potsdam Declaration. It warned Japan that she stood on "the threshold of annihilation" and could save herself only by eliminating "for all time the authority and influence of those who had deceived and misled the people of Japan into embarking on a world conquest."

The declaration also said:

"We do not intend that the Japanese shall be enslaved as a race or destroyed as a nation, but stern justice shall be meted out to all war criminals, including those who have visited cruelties upon our prisoners. The Japanese government shall remove all obstacles to the revival and strengthening of democratic tendencies among the Japanese people. Freedom of speech, of religion and of thought, as well as respect for fundamental human rights, shall be established."

Japan had already tried to negotiate a peace through Russia and had been turned down by the Allies, who insisted on an unconditional surrender. Now Japan ignored the Potsdam Declaration.

Britain's Clement Attlee, America's Truman and Russia's Stalin met at Potsdam, Germany, in 1945 to discuss postwar plans.

THE ATOM BOMB AND V-J DAY

Japan surrenders after the most terrible weapon in history hits two of its cities.

The decision on whether or not to drop the atom bomb on Japan was one that only President Truman could make. Secret tests had already demonstrated the terrible destructiveness of the bomb. Consideration was given to the possibility of dropping the bomb on a desert island. When the Japanese learned what this new weapon could do, they might come to their senses and end their hopeless struggle.

In the spring of 1945, a committee of scientists was set up to study the use of the new bomb and advise the President. The committee concluded in its report:

"We can propose no technical demonstration likely to bring an end to the war; we see no acceptable alternative to direct military use." Four cities—Hiroshima, Kokura, Niigata, and Nagasaki—were recommended as suitable enemy targets. All were war production centers of great importance.

On August 6, 1945, the 380,000 inhabitants of Hiroshima, on the island of Honshu, rose early in the morning. Their sleep had been interrupted twice the night before. The Japanese radio had warned that thousands of American B-29's were approaching Japan. The people had gathered up their children and gone to the assigned "safe areas" to wait out a possible raid.

But no bombs had fallen, and in the early sunlight the city looked calm and drowsy. The wooden houses, jammed together, were astir with people rising from their bedrolls, breakfasting on cooked rice and perhaps a handful of peanuts, and setting off to work.

Sometime before six o'clock that morning, the air-raid siren sounded. The people were not greatly disturbed. About this time every morning a lone American weather plane flew over the city, and the siren was sounded. On August 6, the Japanese radar operators detected three planes approaching Hiroshima and supposed them to be on a simple scouting mission. The all-clear signal was given.

But the three B-29's were on no scouting mission. In one of them, the crew was tense. The pilot found a hole in the clouds and nodded. He was going in over the city. The crew reached for their dark arc-welder's glasses and tightened their safety straps.

The plane leveled off, and then a black object dropped from its belly. As the crew watched it falling, they wondered if what they had been told was true. Could this one bomb have the explosive force of 20,000 tons of TNT? They had heard that when this bomb had been tested on the desert in New

American B-29's bombing the mainland of Japan. The same type of plane dropped the atom bomb on Hiroshima.

Mexico, men ten miles away had been knocked down by the rush of air caused by the explosion.

With a roar of its engines, the B-29 swung sharply to get out of range. The bomb exploded, and even through dark glasses the cabin of the plane seemed blazing with light, and the sky around the bomber turned a frightening blue-green. Suddenly the B-29 rocked as though it had been struck by a bomb itself. It was caught in the blast waves of the explosion.

"Look!" cried one of the crew.

In the sky a great ball of fire burst through a white ring of smoke. A pillar of fire, purple in color, rose upward. It reached a height of 10,000 feet within a second, 20,000 feet seconds later—and still it rose. It sprouted a head like a mushroom, then, below, a second mushroom appeared. Looking back 200 miles from the city, the crew could still make out those shapes.

EFFECT OF THE BOMB

The people of Hiroshima—those who lived—would remember a white flash and a roar like 20,000 claps of thunder. Everything seemed to become dust and smoke. Houses disappeared. Eyeglasses were ripped off faces, slippers off feet. The dead in Hiroshima that day numbered 78,150, the missing 13,933, the burned and injured 37,425, the homeless and sick 176,987. The area destroyed was the equivalent of 600 blocks of an average American city.

Still Japan refused to surrender, and three days later a second atom bomb was dropped, this time on Nagasaki.

SURRENDER CEREMONIES

On August 10—the following day—Japan sued for peace. On September 2, aboard the battleship *Missouri,* the Japanese foreign minister and a general representing the Imperial Staff signed the document of unconditional surrender. General MacArthur signed for the Allies. The first two of the five pens he used were handed to General Jonathan M. Wainwright and British General Arthur Ernest Percival, who, in the war's darkest hours, had been forced to surrender at Corregidor and Singapore.

The day was cool and cloudy, and on the veranda deck of the *Missouri* the breeze fluttered the flags of the United States, Great Britain, China, and Russia. General MacArthur finished signing and said:

"These proceedings are closed. The entire world is quietly at peace. A new era is upon us."

V-J Day at last gave Americans the chance to sing and dance and celebrate without restraint. Thousands of people went to church to thank God for deliverance from the worst ordeal mankind had ever known. Even as they celebrated, Americans remembered the millions of Jews who had been slaughtered by the savage Nazis, the homeless and starving in bombed-

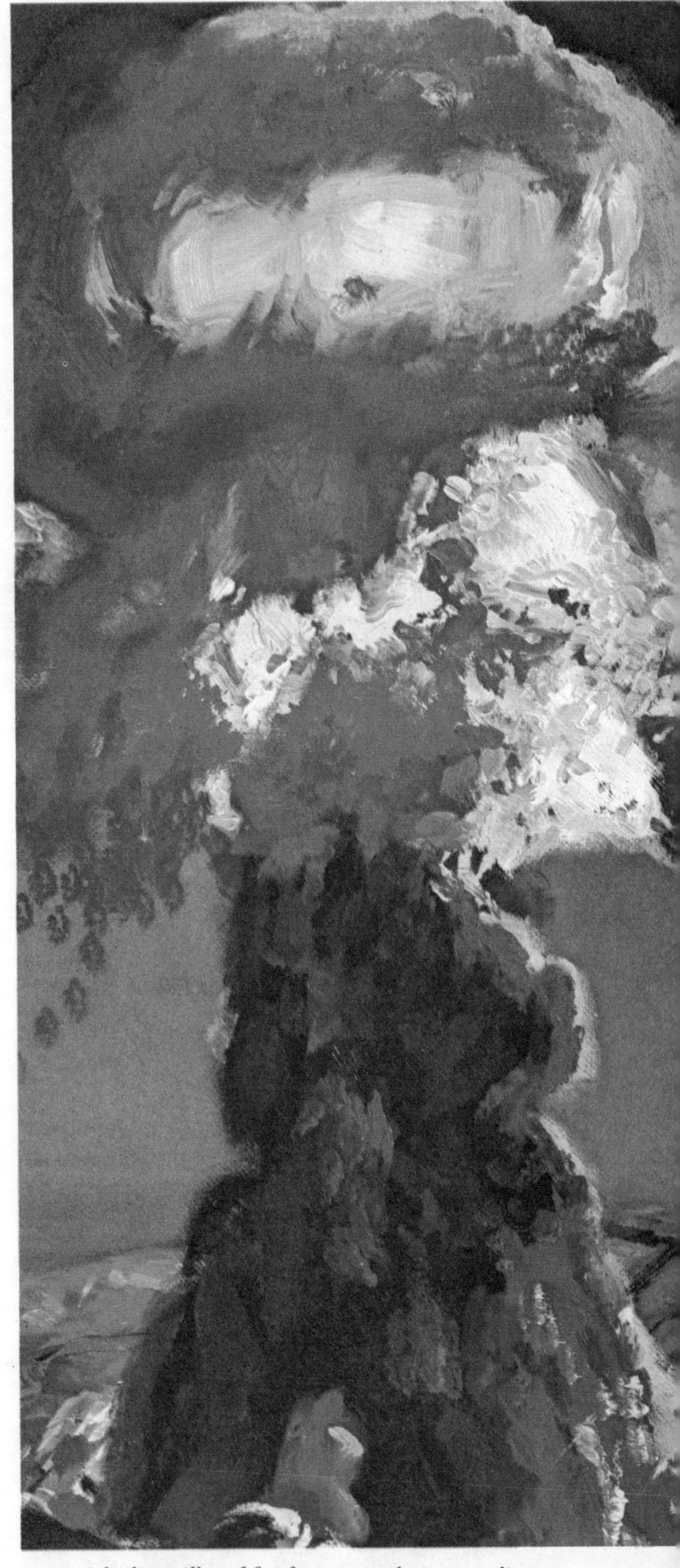

A boiling pillar of fire from an explosion equaling 20,000 tons of TNT rose from the atom bomb at Hiroshima.

Gen. Douglas MacArthur signed the document of surrender by Japan on the battleship Missouri. *Behind him stood Gen. Jonathan Wainwright, who had surrendered Corregidor to the Japanese in May 1942, and British Gen. Arthur E. Percival, who surrendered Singapore in February 1942.*

A flattened landscape of twisted metal and broken masonry spread over atom-bombed Hiroshima.

The Japanese foreign minister and a general of the Imperial staff led the Japanese delegation at the surrender ceremonies aboard the Missouri.

out cities throughout the world, and the dead and maimed victims of Hiroshima and Nagasaki. Americans had their own dead and injured to mourn, too. In all branches of the military service, 353,187 Americans had died, 732,149 had been wounded, and 10,997 were missing. No one could forget their figures.

The war had been won. But the victory would be meaningless unless Americans took up the challenge expressed in the last words written by Franklin Delano Roosevelt before his death:

"We must cultivate the science of human relations—the ability of all peoples, of all kinds, to live together and to work together in the same world, at peace."

THE UNITED NATIONS

Delegates from fifty nations meet in San Francisco and sign the U.N. Charter.

During the war, the Allies had frequently referred to themselves as the United Nations. They implied by this term that they stood together not only to win the war but also to secure the peace that would follow. Americans now realized that their unwillingness to support the League of Nations after World War I might possibly have been one of the many factors that brought on World War II. And so they took the lead in forming a new world organization to be called the United Nations.

"What a great day this can be in history!" President Truman said on June 26, 1945. On that day, delegates from fifty countries, meeting in San Francisco, signed the charter that brought the United Nations organization into being. The main purpose of the United Nations was the keeping of the peace. At the same time, the organization pledged itself to the development of international co-operation in dealing with economic, social, cultural, and humanitarian affairs. The United Nations would try "to develop friendly relations among nations based on respect for the principle of equal rights and self-determination of peoples."

Five agencies were established to carry on the work of the United Nations:

The Security Council. This group was given the chief responsibility for maintaining the peace. Its permanent members were to be the United States, China, France, Great Britain, and the Soviet Union. Six other members were to be elected for two-year terms by the General Assembly. Each member na-

U.S. Secretary of State Edward R. Stettinius signed the United Nations Charter in San Francisco in 1945 as President Truman, Mrs. Eleanor Roosevelt and other American dignitaries looked on.

tion would have one vote, and each of the five permanent members had the power of veto over any proposal brought before the Security Council. This meant that a single vote of "no" by one permanent member could prevent any measure from being adopted.

The General Assembly. All member nations were granted the right to send delegates to the General Assembly, which was to meet regularly once a year unless called into special session. In addition to making recommendations on international problems, the General Assembly was to supervise the budget, decide on the admission, suspension, and expulsion of members, and make studies of problems relating to international co-operation. Routine questions were to be decided by a majority vote, special issues by a two-thirds majority. Freedom of speech in debate would be respected.

The Economic and Social Council. This council was to be made up of eighteen members selected by the General Assembly. The council was to co-ordinate the work of many special agencies, such as the Food and Agricultural Organization, the International Civil Aviation Organization, and the United Nations Educational, Scientific and Cultural Organization (UNESCO). The council was to serve any country, whether or not it was a member of the United Nations, as long as its problem affected the world in the economic, social, intellectual, or humanitarian fields.

The Trusteeship Council. The charter of the United Nations faced the fact that there were parts of the world not yet ready for self-government. The purpose of the Trusteeship Council was to study these regions and to protect them.

The Secretariat. The Secretariat was to do the routine work of administration. Its head would be the Secretary-General of the United Nations, to be appointed by the General Assembly on the recommendation of the Security Council.

In addition, the charter of the United Nations provided for an International Court of Justice to decide on interpretations of treaties and questions of international law. The individual member nations could use its services or not, as they wished.

On January 10, 1946, delegates from fifty-one nations met at Westminster in London to hold the first session of the General Assembly. Two days later, Australia, Brazil, Egypt, Mexico, the Netherlands, and Poland were chosen to serve with the permanent members of the Security Council. On February 2, Trygve Lie, the former foreign minister of Norway, became the first Secretary-General. Among the first acts of the United Nations was the decision to establish its permanent home in the United States. It would soon become a familiar feature of American life.

A NEW WORLD

Although many things are changed by the war, Americans retain their most precious heritage—freedom.

After the dropping of the atom bomb on Hiroshima and Nagasaki, World War II, as terrible as it had been, belonged to the world of yesterday. Nations everywhere—large and small, powerful and weak—recognized this fact, and it was one of the reasons for the establishment of the United Nations.

Late in 1945, the German leaders who still remained alive were tried as war criminals by an Allied court in Nuremberg, Germany. Russia became busy turning the "liberated" countries under her control into satellite states. The Western powers set up the United Nations Relief and Rehabilitation Administration (UNRRA) to help the millions of homeless, hungry refugees in Europe and Asia.

In the United States, war production gave way to the production of goods for peacetime use. Consumers were willing to pay high prices for scarce goods, and businessmen tried to meet the demands of the booming market. Labor wanted its share of the new prosperity, and there were a number of strikes.

Hundreds of thousands of servicemen returned from overseas. Some of them brought home "war brides"—wives from the countries in which they had been stationed. Some of the former fighting men found it difficult to make a fresh start in life. There was a shortage of housing. Some families had to live temporarily in converted army barracks.

Yet, in spite of all the problems that followed the war, the United States was an exciting place to live in, and many things were happening. Jackie Robinson became the first Negro to break into big league baseball. A new method of communication—television—was bringing entertainment into thousands of homes. Factories were turning out all sorts of products made of plastics. Suburban housing developments and shopping centers were springing up beyond the boundaries of cities.

World War II ended with a scientific revolution, brought about by the atom bomb. It was an instrument of death, but it held the promise of peacetime uses of atomic energy. Americans realized that the world had changed, and that there would be even more changes in the years ahead. Americans accepted the scientific revolution as a fact and were confident that they could solve the problems that came with change. For, looking back on their accomplishments during World War II, and looking forward to the future, they knew that one thing had not changed—the most important thing of all.

They were a free people.

Space satellites, then spaceships launched man on one of his greatest adventures—exploration of the universe.

X ∾ INTO THE SPACE AGE

from 1945 to the 1970's

America changes to a peacetime economy, and Truman wins an unexpected victory.

Americans wanted to forget World War II the moment it ended. Parents and wives wanted the men in the armed services to come home. Businessmen wanted to be rid of price controls and other restrictions. Almost everyone wanted to buy the things he hadn't been able to buy for four years.

President Harry S. Truman urged that the change to a peacetime economy be made gradually and in an orderly manner. But most Americans wanted the change to come about as quickly as possible. The armed forces, which had numbered 11,000,000 men in 1944–45, were reduced to about 1,000,000 men by January, 1947.

In 1944, to help veterans of the war get a fresh start in the peacetime world, Congress passed the Servicemen's Readjustment Act, better known as the "G.I. Bill of Rights." It provided money to cover tuition, books, and living expenses for veterans who wished to continue their education. Unemployed veterans could draw $20 a week from the government for a year. Veterans who wanted to buy homes or start businesses could get loans on easy terms.

Happily, the change to a peacetime economy was made more smoothly than the experts expected. Americans were so eager to buy so many things that industry was soon employing a record number of workers. Many items, however, were still scarce, while the demand for them was great. This could cause prices to rise sharply, and the Truman Administration wanted to continue price controls. But too many people were opposed to it, and by autumn of 1946 President Truman had to give up the fight. He announced the removal of all controls except those on rent. And just as had been feared, prices went up.

Americans grew familiar with the word "inflation." This meant that the value of their money was decreasing as prices for the things they bought increased. It was a difficult problem to solve. Workers struck for higher wages, but rising prices soon used up the additional pay they had received. There were labor disputes in many industries, and strikes on the railroads and in the mines.

THE TAFT-HARTLEY ACT

Congress cracked down on labor with the Taft-Hartley Act. The act was named for its sponsors, Senator Robert A. Taft, a Republican from Ohio, and Representative Fred A. Hartley, Jr., a Republican from New Jersey. It was passed over the President's veto on June 23, 1947. Union leaders promptly called it the "Taft-Hartley slave-labor law." Under its provisions, management could sue unions that did not live up to their contracts. The "closed shop"—a shop where all employees had to belong to a specific union—was outlawed. Unions were forbidden to make contributions to political campaigns. Courts could order a "cooling-off" period of sixty days before a strike began, and union leaders were required to sign a statement that they were not members of the Communist party.

The Republicans were in high spirits when their convention met in Philadelphia in June of 1948. Republican leaders believed they knew how Americans felt in this postwar period. Americans were tired of government interference in private business. They had had enough of Roosevelt's and Truman's schemes of social legislation. Once again the Republicans nominated Thomas E. Dewey, the former racket-busting attorney who was now governor of New York. His running mate was Governor Earl Warren of California.

To add to the joy of the Republicans, the Democrats, who nominated Truman for President, were hopelessly split. Many Southern Democrats broke away and formed a rival party, the Dixiecrats. This group was opposed to any civil-rights legislation and believed in "white supremacy"—the right of the white man to rule the country. The Dixiecrats nominated Governor J. Strom Thurmond of South Carolina for President and Governor Fielding Wright of Mississippi for Vice-President.

Still another rebellious group was the Progressive party, which stood for co-operation with Russia and the rights of the "common man." Its candidates were Henry A. Wallace, who had been Secretary of Agriculture and then Vice-President under Roosevelt, and Senator Glenn Taylor of Idaho.

Almost all the experts agreed that Harry Truman did not have a chance to win. No one believed those reports more than Dewey, who campaigned as though it were only a matter of time until he was elected President. Truman did not care what the experts said. He decided to talk to the people, and he traveled the country, talking wherever anyone would listen. He had once said to his fellow politicians, "If you don't like the heat, keep out of the kitchen." Now he proceeded to put on the heat. He made fiery speeches attacking the Eightieth Congress, which he called the "Do-Nothing" Congress. He spoke about civil rights and social legislation.

The result was one of the most surprising political upsets in the nation's history. Truman won easily, receiving 24,105,000 popular vates and 303 electoral votes. Dewey's total was 21,969,000 popular votes and 189 electoral votes. Thurmond carried South Carolina, Alabama, Louisiana, and Mississippi, winning thirty-nine electoral votes. Wallace received no electoral votes and only 1,156,000 popular votes.

THE COLD WAR

Truman takes steps to block the Russians.

Although President Truman had scored a triumph in the election, his troubles were just beginning. A new kind of war had broken out—a "cold war" between the pro-Communist nations and the democracies of the world. It was a war of political and diplomatic maneuvers rather than armed conflict. But it was as important as any war of bloody battles, and the responsibility of leading the free world fell to the United States.

The chief antagonist was the Union of Soviet Socialist Republics, also known as the Soviet Union. This was the communistic nation established by Russia after the Revolution of 1917 had overthrown the czar. The Soviet Union had been an ally of the United States in World War II. Now, however, it appeared that the Russians did not intend to live up to the agreements made at Yalta in 1945 to permit free elections in eastern Europe, or to the agreements made at Potsdam later that same year.

Instead, the Communists were on the move, attempting to extend their influence over other countries. They seized control in Poland, Bulgaria, Romania, Albania, Czechoslovakia, and Hungary. Communists were waging civil war in China. From 1946 to 1949, Communists encouraged guerrilla warfare in Indochina, Burma, Malaya, Indonesia, and the Philippines. Communists were active in Greece and Turkey, and there were strong Communist movements in Italy and France.

Suddenly, in 1948, the cold war threatened to become a hot war. The trouble spot was Occupied Germany. Until that time, Germany had been divided into American, British, French, and Russian zones, and governed by an Allied Control Council made up of the military commanders of each zone. The city of Berlin, deep inside the Russian zone, was also under four-power control.

Immediately following World War II, the Allied powers had agreed that Germany should be punished. But they disagreed on most other issues, such as how much Germany should be forced to pay each nation that had suffered losses in the war. Until those differences were settled, no final peace treaty could be drawn between the Allies and Germany. Disagreement over the conditions of the peace led the Western powers—the United States, Great Britain, and France—to believe that the Russians wished to control all of Germany. To block this, the Western powers began to work together politically and economically.

As a result, the gulf between the East and the West grew wider. In the spring of 1948, the Soviet Union withdrew from the Allied Control Council. Then, in June, the Western powers announced that they would issue a separate currency for use in their zones of Germany, including their sectors of Berlin.

THE BERLIN AIRLIFT

The Soviet Union's next move came quickly. It placed a blockade on all goods being shipped into the Western sectors of Berlin by road, rail, or water. But if the Russians intended to drive the Allies out

Planes crowded Tempelhof airport for the Berlin airlift.

of Berlin, they were disappointed. The Allies refused to give in. Instead, they organized the famous Berlin airlift.

Day and night, American and British planes brought food, fuel, and raw materials into Berlin. When the Russians set up a separate police force and civil government in their sector of Berlin, the Allies began a blockade of their own. All shipment of goods into East Berlin was stopped.

The deadlock lasted until May of 1949, when the Russians agreed to end their blockade if the Allies would end theirs. The test of strength had gone in favor of the Allies. The airlift had kept West Berlin functioning, and the Russians were not prepared to take military action to stop it. Meanwhile, East Berlin had felt the pinch of the Allied blockade.

Normal traffic between the zones was resumed, and the situation became less tense, but major disagreements still remained. The Russians wanted to keep Germany weak and divided. The Allies wanted a revived Germany that could take part in world affairs. They hoped, too, that one day East and West Germany would be reunited, so that Germany would again be one nation.

The Allies' first step toward this goal was to allow some self-government in the West German zones. Elections were held to name delegates to an assembly, and in May, 1949, the Federal Republic of Germany came into being. Konrad Adenauer, an elderly, anti-Nazi lawyer, became chancellor.

THE MARSHALL PLAN

The United States also acted in Greece. When the British withdrew their troops in 1946, the Communists had moved in and tried to overthrow the weak postwar government. In May, 1947, at President Truman's request, Congress voted $300,000,000 for economic and military aid to Greece. This money strengthened the government and enabled it to solve many serious problems—problems which the Communists had taken advantage of. Another grant of $100,000,000 went to aid Turkey, whose geographical position gave it control of Russia's only waterway from the Black Sea to the Mediterranean.

This policy, which later became known as the "Truman Doctrine," temporarily stopped the spread of communism, but it was plain that a more far-reaching plan was needed. Such a plan was suggested by General George C. Marshall, who had been chief of staff during World War II and was now Truman's Secretary of State. In a speech at Harvard, Marshall said that if the leaders of Europe could determine what things they needed to put their countries in good order, the United States would give them financial help. The European Recovery Program—or the Marshall Plan, as it was usually called—was eagerly accepted by Western Europe. In September of 1947, representatives of sixteen European countries met in Paris to work out the details of the program. Eventually, the United States agreed to furnish $17,000,000,000 over a period of four years.

A number of Americans, including some congressmen, were opposed to the Marshall Plan because of its great cost. Most Americans, however, supported it. They pointed out that communism flourished only where there were want and disorder. They were soon proved right. Conditions improved in the countries aided by the Marshall Plan, and a spirit of unity arose among the leaders of the democratic countries.

Talks began between Great Britain and her neighbors in northwestern Europe to consider a plan for mutual defense. The United States joined these talks, and on April 4, 1949, the North Atlantic Treaty Organization (NATO) was formed. Its original members were the United States, Canada, Great Britain, France, Italy, Belgium, the Netherlands, Denmark, Norway, Iceland, Luxembourg, and Portugal. Greece, Turkey, and West Germany joined later. Each agreed to come to the aid of any other NATO member in case of attack. By the following year, these countries were receiving American military weapons.

In the autumn of 1949, a tremendous explosion recorded by scientific instruments in the United States revealed that the Soviet Union now had the atomic bomb. The United States had lost its arms superiority. It was no longer the only country that possessed the mighty weapon that had ended World War II.

WAR IN KOREA

Americans fight on foreign soil as the Communists invade South Korea.

The first direct conflict between the worlds of communism and democracy took place in the Far East, where communism made great gains in the early postwar years. Mainland China had come under the control of the Communists, led by Mao Tse-tung, and the Nationalist government of Generalissimo Chiang Kai-shek had been forced to retreat to the island of Formosa.

Part of Korea, which had been a dependency of Japan, was also controlled by Communists. Under the terms of the settlement between Russia and the Allies, Korea was divided into two zones at the thirty-eighth parallel of latitude. North Korea was occupied by the Soviet Union, South Korea by the United States. In North Korea, the Russians established what they called a Democratic People's Republic. In South Korea, the American army of occupation organized a government based on the principle of self-rule. Later, the United Nations approved plans for an election to establish a single government throughout the country. But the Russians refused to allow Koreans in the zone they controlled to vote.

An uneasy truce existed between the two zones. Then, on June 25, 1950, the North Koreans launched an attack on South Korea. The untrained forces of South Korea were quickly swept aside and their country overrun. Within hours after the war started, the United Nations Security Council met in emergency session. The Soviet Union did not attend. The North Korean Communist forces were accused of breaching the peace, and the council demanded that they pull back north of the thirty-eighth parallel.

President Truman faced a difficult decision. Without military support, the United States could not enforce its demands—and yet the United States was in no mood for another war. By June 27, Truman had made his decision. The United States would fight, together with forces from other nations of the free world. General Douglas MacArthur was called from Japan to serve as commander in chief of the United Nations troops in Korea. Thirteen nations contributed ground forces, and eleven sent air or naval units. The United States, however, made the greatest contribution, as shown by the casualty figures. By the end of the war, American casualties would total 144,173, including 25,604 dead.

The Korean conflict proved to be a hard war to win. Highly mechanized warfare was not very effective, and no amount of planes could stop the Communists. They moved in small groups through the hills, carrying their provisions in packs on their backs. Furthermore, the North Koreans were good soldiers. They knew how to handle modern weapons, and they were willing to fight to the death. The battle for Korea became a lonely, almost personal kind of warfare, with much of the fighting done at night.

BRAINWASHING

Americans captured by the Communists were often subjected to a new technique of psychological warfare known as "brainwashing." The brainwashers believed that if a prisoner were held in jail long enough, and became tired and hungry enough, he might be made to give statements against his own country. The statements might be false, but the prisoner would be too weak to resist the terrific pressure the enemy was putting on him.

By the first week in August, 1950, the United Nations held only the southeast corner of the Korean peninsula. But they stubbornly hung on, neither retreating nor advancing, until mid-September. At that time they were ready to launch an offensive. One United Nations force pressed north, while a second force made a surprise landing on the west coast of Korea at Inchon. The Communists were outflanked and began to retreat. United Nations forces slugged their way north across the thirty-eighth parallel. By November 21, their advance units reached the Yalu River, which marks the border between China and North Korea.

In 1948, Mao Tse-tung's troops marched into Shanghai and clamped Communist control on the Chinese mainland.

It looked as though the war was over—but no one had foreseen that the Chinese Communists would send a great number of troops to help the North Koreans. Only five days later, on November 26, more than 200,000 Chinese troops were thrown into the battle.

The United Nations was forced to retreat all along the front. The hardest kind of fighting followed, and not until mid-January was MacArthur able to pull his lines together some seventy-five miles south of the thirty-eighth parallel. Then, in the western section of the front, some territory was regained, and gradual advances were being made north of the parallel.

Meanwhile, too, there was disagreement between Truman and MacArthur. MacArthur was a fighting man who saw things only in terms of military necessity. He wanted to bomb enemy bases in Manchuria, and called for a complete blockade of the China coast. Truman was against such bold schemes. He felt that the war in Korea should remain a limited war. He wanted to contain the Communists there, but he was determined to keep this local war from becoming an excuse for World War III.

President Truman was following the historical tradition of the United States when he insisted that the civilian government, and not its military leaders, must decide national policy. MacArthur criticized Truman openly, and one or the other had to give in. Truman felt that, as President of the United States, he was responsible for the nation's actions. To maintain order among his generals and the officials of his administration, he dismissed MacArthur. General Matthew B. Ridgway was given command of the forces in Korea. MacArthur was a hero of World War II, and he was invited to address Congress on his return from Korea. Most Americans still considered him a hero, but they accepted the fact that it was up to the President to decide the nation's policy.

By June of 1951, the Communists were willing to talk about a "cease fire" in Korea. Both sides were trying to save face. They wanted to find a way to stop fighting, and at the same time they did not want it to appear as if they had given in to the enemy. A long series of truce talks was held, and finally, on July 27, 1953, the war was ended.

"WE LIKE IKE"

Eisenhower proves to be a popular President during two terms in office.

When President Truman reached the end of his second term in office, he was nearing the age of sixty-eight. He had made some of the most important decisions in the history of the country—to drop the atom bomb on Japan, to stand firm against the Russians in Greece and Turkey, to support the Marshall Plan, to send American forces to fight in Korea. After the Russians exploded their atom bomb, he made another difficult decision—to build and test the hydrogen bomb. Not everyone agreed with what he did, but he was willing to let history decide whether he had been right or wrong.

Four years before, in 1948, the Democrats had been sure that Truman could not hope to beat Governor Dewey in the race for president. They had asked Dwight D. Eisenhower to accept the nomination, but he had refused. Now, as the campaign of 1952 approached, Eisenhower revealed that he was willing to run on the Republican ticket. This upset the plans of Senator Robert Taft of Ohio, who wanted to occupy the White House, as his father, William Howard Taft, had done. Eisenhower won the Republican nomination and ran against Governor Adlai Stevenson of Illinois, the Democratic candidate. The people rallied behind Eisenhower, and the slogan "We like Ike" was heard everywhere. Eisenhower won the election with 33,824,000 votes to Stevenson's 27,314,000; the electoral college vote was 442 for Eisenhower and 89 for Governor Stevenson.

Eisenhower kept his great popularity during his two terms in office. He, too, had to deal with the problems of the cold war. While favoring strong programs for national defense and for financial assistance to the nation's allies, he also worked constantly for peace. He supported the United Nations and was always willing to meet the Russians half way in any move to reduce tensions. He was for gradual disarmament and the control of atomic energy.

At the same time, Eisenhower acted to halt further Communist expansion. Under his leadership, some nations of Southeast Asia were organized into a defensive alliance with the United States. They formed the Southeast Asia Treaty Organization, which was known as SEATO. Eisenhower also had authority from Congress to use force to stop any Communist attack on Formosa, headquarters of Chiang Kai-shek's Chinese Nationalist Government.

In July of 1955, Eisenhower attended a "summit meeting" of world leaders at Geneva, Switzerland. Eisenhower proposed that the United States and the Soviet Union exchange information on their military establishments and allow flights of reconnaissance planes over their military installations. Al-

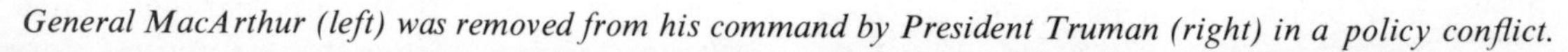

General MacArthur (left) was removed from his command by President Truman (right) in a policy conflict.

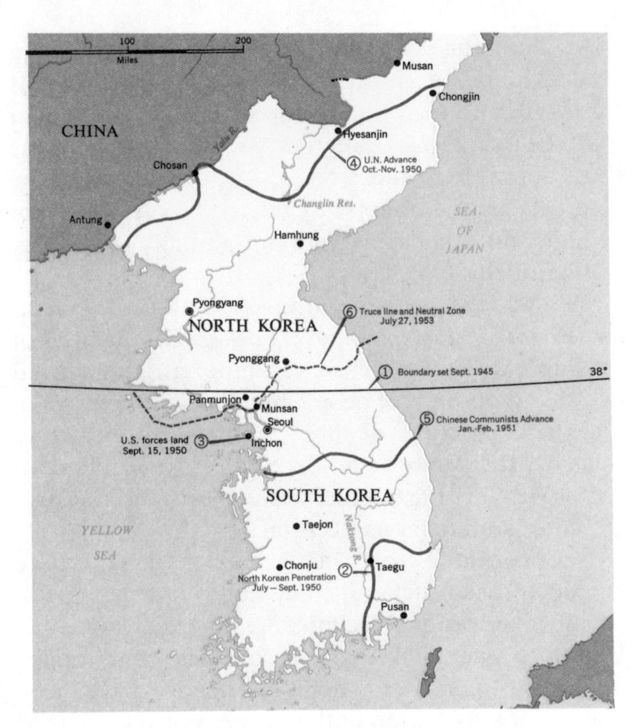

The war in Korea, 1951–1953.

though the meeting was friendly enough, the Russians turned down all of Eisenhower's proposals.

At home, Eisenhower won some of his legislative battles and lost others. He was opposed by the Democrats, who controlled Congress for the greater part of his eight years as President. On top of this, he met opposition from Republican conservatives.

One of these conservatives was Senator Joseph McCarthy of Wisconsin. As a member of a Senate subcommittee investigating government employees, McCarthy charged one official after another with being sympathetic to the Communists. He carried this to such extremes that the word "McCarthyism" became part of the American language. His accusations against leaders of the United States army led him into a bitter dispute with Army Secretary Robert T. Stevens, which ended in a public hearing. The hearing was televised, and for thirty-six days during 1954 Americans watched it with fascination. They saw McCarthy badgering witnesses and arguing with fellow senators who were conducting the hearing. The results were inconclusive, but later the Senate took the unusual step of censuring (officially criticizing) McCarthy for conduct "unbecoming a member of the United States Senate." His actions during the hearing lost him many supporters, and he had lost much of his influence by the time he died on May 2, 1957.

There was little controversy over two other events during Eisenhower's Administration. Alaska was admitted as a state in January, and Hawaii in August of 1959. This increased the total number of states to fifty.

General Eisenhower addressing a crowd from his campaign train during the election of 1952.

Schools in many southern areas resisted integration, but this one in Galveston, Texas, was integrated smoothly.

THE NEGRO FIGHTS FOR HIS RIGHTS

A Supreme Court ruling on schools sets off a major struggle over desegregation.

In 1952 and 1953, the case of *Brown versus the Board of Education of Topeka* was argued before the United States Supreme Court. It was one of a number of similar cases which had come before the court from the states of Kansas, South Carolina, Virginia, and Delaware. Each concerned Negro children who had been refused admission to schools attended by white children. Now the court had to decide whether or not Negro children should be admitted to these schools, and the decision would depend on how the court interpreted the Fourteenth Amendment to the Constitution.

One provision of the amendment guarantees every citizen "equal protection of the laws." But in 1868, when the amendment was adopted, there was little public education in the United States. In the South, there was almost none at all. And so it was years before the question of whether or not the amendment applied to public education was tested in the courts.

In 1896, a case that had to do with the Fourteenth Amendment did come before the Supreme Court. A Negro citizen claimed that he had been denied his right of "equal protection" when he was not permitted to use the transportation facilities used by white citizens. The court ruled that "separate but equal" facilities met the requirements of the law.

As free public education spread, many states were guided by this decision. They built separate schools for Negro and for white children. The states claimed that the schools for Negroes were just as good as those for whites, and were, therefore, "equal." The Negroes argued that segregated schools were not "equal," and that they were not getting "equal protection of the laws."

This was the big issue in the case of *Brown versus the Board of Education of Topeka.* The justices of the Supreme Court knew it was important. It involved not only thousands of people but deeply rooted prejudices and practices of long standing. As the weeks went by, the justices considered all sides of the case.

On May 17, 1954, Chief Justice Earl Warren read the court's unanimous decision:

"We conclude that in the field of education the doctrine of 'separate but equal' has no place. Separate educational facilities are inherently unequal. Therefore, we hold that the plaintiffs and others similarly situated for whom the actions have been brought are, by reason of the segregation complained of, deprived of the equal protection of the laws guaranteed by the Fourteenth Amendment."

In a single stroke the court had changed the pattern of American life. The decision aroused differences of opinion throughout the country. The New York *Times,* for example, said that the court had taken a "monumental and constructive stride in constitutional law and fundamental justice." The Washington *Evening Star,* however, said that the decision was "a blow to fundamental American institutions."

Southerners who disagreed with the decision prepared to fight it by every legal means. The Negroes were just as determined to see that it was carried out. The decision was a victory for which the Negroes had long waited. Some 335 years had passed since their ancestors first reached America as slaves in chains, and it had been some ninety-one years since President Abraham Lincoln signed the Emancipation Proclamation.

In September of 1957, Americans were startled by the news from Arkansas. Governor Orval R. Faubus had used state troops to prevent nine Negro children from enrolling at Central High School in Little Rock. The city's school board, obeying the 1954 ruling of the Supreme Court, had accepted the nine students. It was clear that the governor's action—which he said he had taken to avoid violence—tested the right of a state government to defy the national government. President Eisenhower sent Federal troops to Little Rock to see that the students were admitted and to keep order.

A somewhat similar situation occurred in Mississippi in 1962. Governor Ross A. Barnett denied James Meredith, a Negro, the right to enroll at the University of Mississippi. Again Federal troops were sent to enforce the law. Officials of Prince Edward County in Virginia tried to get around the law in another way. They closed the public schools rather than admit Negro children. In a number of Southern communities, however, the officials obeyed the court's order, desegregated the schools, and there was little trouble.

Although the Negroes welcomed desegregation in the schools, they looked upon it as only a beginning. They wanted to enjoy their full rights as American citizens, and to win them they used many new methods. Under the sponsorship of the Congress of Racial Equality (CORE), Negroes and whites became "Freedom Riders," challenging segregation in interstate buses. Sometimes they were beaten by angry mobs, and often they were arrested by local officials. But the Federal government supported the principle of equality for which they fought.

Negroes used "sit-in" strikes, picketing, and boycotts in their battle against segregation in lunchrooms, in public libraries, in housing, and on beaches. They fought for greater opportunities for employment and for their right to vote. Not all of their efforts were successful; sometimes their progress seemed painfully slow. Yet they were winning increasing respect, and they had reason to be hopeful of the future.

MEN IN SPACE

Russia moves ahead in the race with the United States to conquer space.

In 1957, the world was surprised to learn that Russian scientists, using rocket propulsion, had placed a space vehicle called "Sputnik" into orbit around the earth. The Space Age had begun, and new frontiers of knowledge had been opened to man. At the same time, the Russian feat raised the threat of mass destruction. Rocket-driven intercontinental missiles, carrying nuclear warheads, could wipe out cities and millions of people. Realizing this, the United States government speeded up its own programs of missile design and construction. The United States had to be so strong in striking power that no enemy would risk attacking it. But not until several months after Sputnik, on January 31, 1958, did the United States successfully place a space vehicle, Explorer I, into orbit.

Later in the year, Congress set up the National Aeronautics and Space Administration (NASA). The government stated: "It is the policy of the United States that activities in space should be devoted to peaceful purposes for the benefit of mankind." The program of the NASA had three aims: to carry out scientific investigations in space,

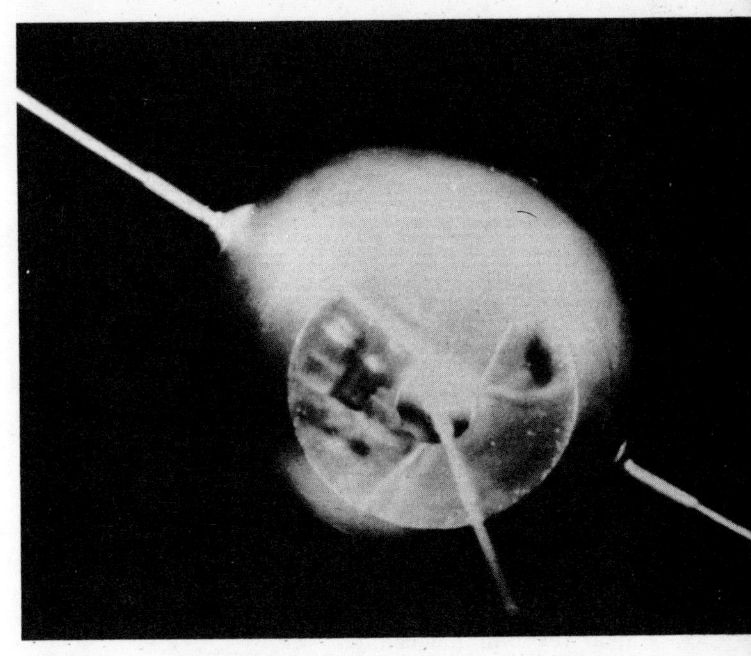

A model of the first Soviet satellite to orbit the earth, photographed in Prague in 1957.

including explorations of the moon and other nearby planets; to apply usefully any information gained by such research; and to develop manned vehicles for flight through outer space.

One of the more spectacular achievements of the United States came on July 20, 1960. The Polaris, an intermediate-range missile, was successfully launched under water from the nuclear-powered submarine *George Washington.* Other results followed. Space vehicles made more accurate weather forecasting possible, and advanced the study of the effect of solar ultra-violet and X-ray radiations. Live television broadcasts between the United States and Europe were made by means of the satellite Telstar. Meanwhile, the Russians was pushing steadily ahead with their own space program. In October of 1959 they photographed much of the far side of the moon with instruments carried on their satellite Lunik III.

In 1960, the fourth year of the Space Age, both Russia and the United States moved closer to the launching of a manned space vehicle. In May, the Russians launched Sputnik IV, which had a pressurized cabin and carried weight equal to that of a man. In August, Sputnik V carried two dogs and a variety of rats, mice, insects, and microbe and plant life into space for experimental purposes.

THE FIRST MAN IN SPACE

The United States had selected seven astronauts who were training for future space flights. In December of 1959, a little monkey named Enos rode a space craft to a height of fifty-five miles above the earth in a flight that covered 200 surface miles.

The race between the United States and Russia

to send a man into space ended on April 12, 1961, when Russia put the world's first satellite spaceship, the Vostok, with a man on board, into orbit around the Earth. The pilot was Flight Major Yuri Alekseyevich Gagarin. Gagarin completed one orbit of the earth and reached an altitude of 186 miles. There he looked upon a sky that was entirely black and an earth that seemed to be surrounded by a blue halo.

The United States was soon ready to launch manned spaceships in two test flights. The first took place on May 5, 1961, at Cape Canaveral (later Cape Kennedy), Florida. Astronaut Alan B. Shepard, Jr., was blasted off in a Mercury space craft, Freedom 7. Americans sat beside their televisions sets, breathlessly watching the launching. Shepard reached a height of 116.5 miles and a speed of more than 5,000 miles an hour. His 302-mile flight lasted fifteen minutes before he parachuted safely into the sea near the Bahama Islands.

Americans felt the same kind of suspense on July 21, 1961. On that day, Astronaut Virgil I. Grissom was lifted from the launch pad at Cape Canaveral in another Mercury space capsule, Liberty Bell 7. Grissom's sixteen-minute flight carried him 118 miles above the earth at a speed of 5,280 miles an hour. His trip covered a distance of 303 miles.

Russia surprised the world again on August 6. The spaceship Vostok II, piloted by Major Gherman Stepanovich Titov, orbited the earth more than seventeen times before landing safely. But American astronauts refused to be discouraged. "We can do it, too," they said.

GLENN ORBITS THE EARTH

The nation cheers a new hero.

There were few Americans who were not at their television sets or listening to their radios on the morning of February 20, 1962. They wished Astronaut John H. Glenn, Jr., good luck as he was strapped into his spaceship and the hatch was fastened. The countdown, delayed for a while by weather conditions over Cape Canaveral, was resumed: ". . . five . . . four . . . three . . . two . . . one. . . ." Columns of vapor rose in steaming clouds from the base of

In July 1962 the satellite Telstar I relayed the first live television broadcasts between the United States and Europe.

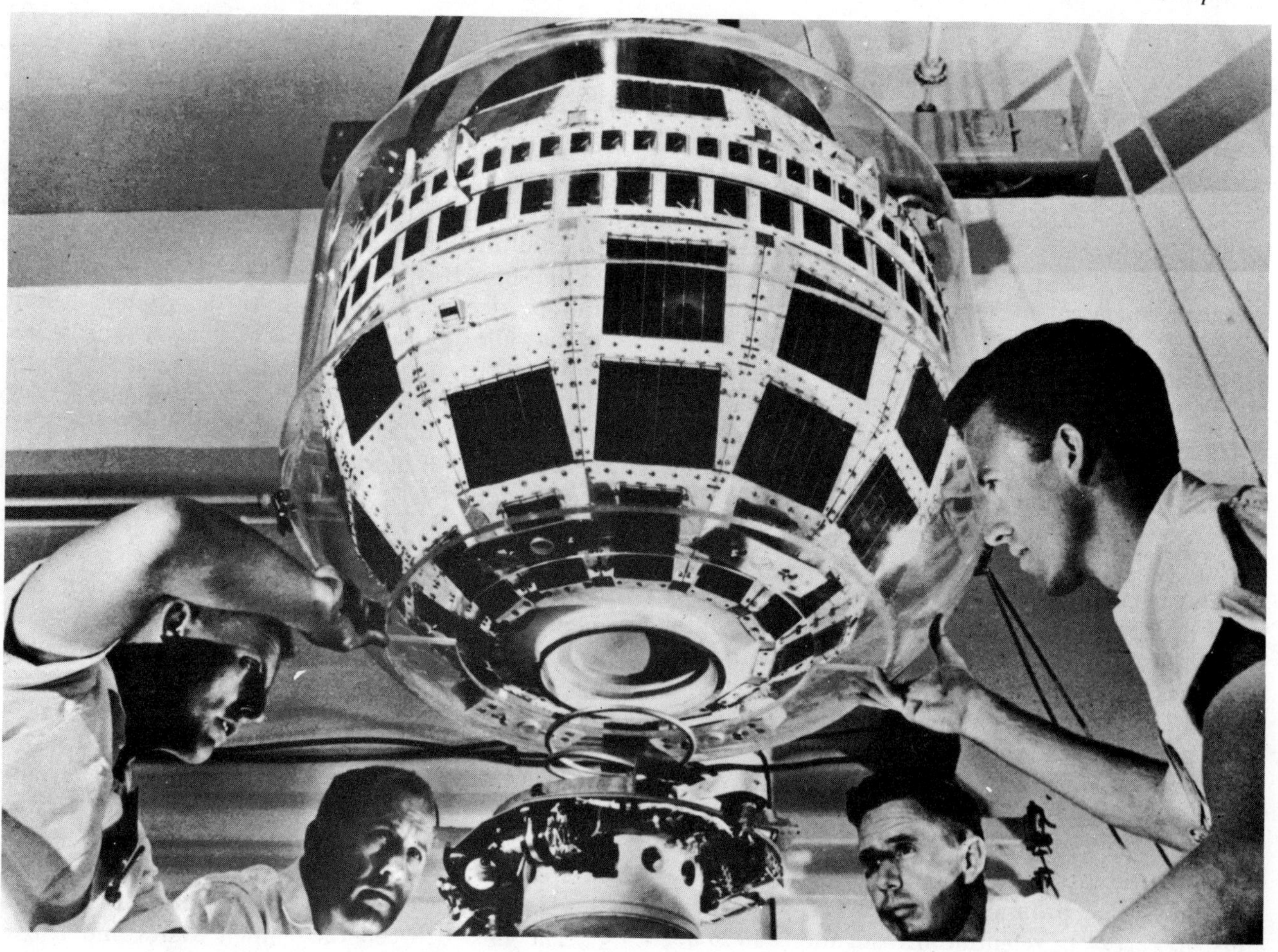

American astronaut John Glenn photographed in his spaceship during his orbital flight of February 1962.

the rocket and it lifted slowly from the ground. A tail of fire marked its path upward. The Friendship 7 disappeared from view, and there was nothing Glenn's well-wishers could do but wait, hope, and pray. Then the control center at Cape Canaveral reported that it had heard from Glenn. He was soaring from day into night at more than 17,000 miles an hour.

"It's a beautiful sight," Glenn said.

Circling the earth, Glenn felt that the sunsets were the most impressive things he had ever seen. "These are of very brilliantly colored hue and the colors stretch out—way out—from the sun to the horizon," he said afterward.

He saw the sun rise, and little yellow-green flecks of light that he could not identify darted by the window of his craft. He described how the stars appeared: "If you've been out in the desert on a very clear, brilliant night when there's no moon up and the stars just seem to jump at you, that's just about the way the stars look."

The continent of Australia lay in the dark of night when he passed over it, but the people of the city of Perth turned on their lights to greet him. He could make out the different patterns of the ocean currents, and when he passed over America the Gulf Stream was particularly clear. He easily identified the irrigated desert north of El Paso, Texas.

Glenn's height above the earth ranged from about one hundred miles to 160 miles. Each of his three orbits around the globe took ninety-nine minutes. At this height, Glenn was weightless, but the sensation he felt was not unpleasant. He released the camera he was using and let it hang in mid-air while he operated instruments, made notes, and threw switches. Then he reached out for the camera, plucking it from the air.

Four hours and fifty-six minutes after blast-off, the Friendship 7 came down safely in the Atlantic Ocean, about 166 miles from Grand Turk Island in the Bahamas. Twenty-two minutes later Glenn was aboard the destroyer *Noa,* and all America looked forward to giving him a hero's welcome. He was the first American to orbit the earth—America's trail blazer through space. Other astronauts would follow him, and it was certain that the future would bring further adventures in space.

KENNEDY BECOMES PRESIDENT

A Democratic victory puts a Roman Catholic in the White House for the first time.

Eisenhower's second term as President ended in 1960, and Americans prepared for a hard-hitting election campaign. Under a constitutional amendment ratified in 1951, while Truman was in the White House, Presidents were limited to two consecutive terms in office. Eisenhower could not run again, and the Republicans were forced to find another candidate. There was little doubt that it would be Richard M. Nixon. He had served for eight years as Eisenhower's Vice-President and was widely known.

Among the Democrats who hoped to be President was Senator John Fitzgerald Kennedy. Born in Brookline, Massachusetts, on May 29, 1917, he was a member of a large family that was constantly involved in politics. Both of his grandfathers had been elected to office, and his father, Joseph P. Kennedy, had served as ambassador to Great Britain.

Young Kennedy's family was wealthy enough for him to enjoy every advantage that money could buy. He attended Canterbury School and Choate School. Although not an outstanding scholar, he did reasonably well. Illness interrupted his first year of study at Princeton University. He later transferred to Harvard, where his work improved considerably. His senior thesis, a study of England's political weaknesses before World War II, he later developed into a book, *While England Slept.*

When World War II broke out, Kennedy was rejected by the army because of a back injury he had received while playing football. But he did exercises to strengthen his back, and in 1942 he was given a commission in the navy.

KENNEDY IN THE PACIFIC

On an August night a year later, Kennedy was commanding a PT boat in Blackett Strait, off the

Kennedy became a hero in World War II when he rescued his crew after an enemy ship sank his PT boat in the Pacific.

Kennedy campaigning on one of his numerous trips around the country in the 1960 election.

Solomon Islands in the South Pacific. In the darkness it was spotted by a Japanese ship, the destroyer *Amagiri.* The ship rammed the PT boat, smashing the hull, and two of Kennedy's crew of twelve men were killed. The survivors, some of them injured, clung to part of the wrecked hull. Kennedy himself was injured, but he had been a strong swimmer since his school days. Towing one of the injured men, he led the rest through the water to a Japanese-held island. After nine days on this island, Kennedy and another officer swam to an island where they found friendly natives. With his knife he carved a message on a coconut shell: "ELEVEN ALIVE NATIVE KNOWS POSIT AND REEFS NAURU ISLAND KENNEDY."

One of the natives set off in a canoe and carried the shell to the New Zealand patrol. The next day, Kennedy and his men were rescued. He was awarded the Navy and Marine Corps Medal for "courage, endurance, and excellent leadership," as well as the Purple Heart. His spine had been injured, and he was retired from active duty in March of 1944.

After the war, Kennedy worked for a time as a newspaper reporter, covering the Potsdam Conference and the United Nations Conference in San Francisco. Then, in 1946, he decided to run for Congress. All the Kennedys loved politics, and they threw themselves into the campaign. Kennedy won the election and served three terms as a congressman. In 1952 he was elected to the United States Senate.

A year later, Kennedy was married to Jacqueline Lee Bouvier. He became a member of a number of important Senate committees, and his future seemed bright. But he was still troubled by his back injury, and in 1954–55 he was twice hospitalized. Even so, he went on working. He wrote a book, *Profiles in Courage,* that won the Pulitzer prize for history. In 1956 he came within a few votes of winning the Democratic nomination for Vice-President, and in 1958 he was re-elected to the Senate.

When Kennedy began to seek the Democratic nomination in 1960, the professional politicians shook their heads. Kennedy had too many things against him. For one thing, he was too wealthy. For another, he was too young. At forty-three, he would be the youngest man ever elected President. Most important of all, he was a Roman Catholic, and the American people would never send a Catholic to the White House.

But Kennedy staged a vigorous campaign in the primaries, and won the Democratic nomination on the first ballot. The outstanding feature of the election campaign was the "television debates." Three times Kennedy and Nixon debated the issues before the television cameras, while millions of Americans watched. When they went to the polls in November, the vote proved to be extremely close—34,227,096 for Kennedy, 34,108,446 for Nixon. But Kennedy won the electoral college vote 303 to 219.

In three television debates viewed by most of the nation, Kennedy and Richard M. Nixon debated the election issues.

Fidel Castro addressing a crowd in Cuba. The Cuban missile crisis in 1962 threatened the world with nuclear war.

CRISIS OVER CUBA

Kennedy makes the Russians remove their missiles from Cuba.

Youth and buoyancy gave John F. Kennedy a deeply revered world image. Along with the toughness without which no President can survive, he was full of sensitivity: ". . . We all inhabit this small planet. We all breathe the same air. We all cherish our children's future."

His first year (1961) began badly in a situation inherited from President Eisenhower. But JFK told the press that he accepted "full responsibility" for the fiasco at the Bay of Pigs, or Bay of Cochinos, as it is called in Cuba. The intention of this invasion was to rid the Western Hemisphere of the threat of Premier Fidel Castro's Communist Cuba. Fifteen hundred soldiers, mostly anti-Castro Cubans, waded ashore, expecting air coverage from the United States. But there were no planes to protect them. No ammunition probably would have been as effective as the little supplied them. An underground army, reported to be opposed to Castro, did not materialize. Castro's tanks, planes and militiamen turned the invasion into a near-slaughter.

Yet Americans were hopeful of an improvement in world conditions when President Kennedy left

An American destroyer inspecting a Soviet freighter bound for Cuba during the missile crisis of 1962.

for summit meetings with European leaders in the fall of that same year. In Vienna, Austria, he met with Premier Nikita Khrushchev of Russia. The meeting, however, brought no improvement and the cold war went on. To add to Kennedy's problems, Russia resumed nuclear testing with the explosion of a huge hydrogen bomb—despite a 1958 U.S.-Soviet-British agreement to refrain from further testing of atomic weapons.

Like most Presidents before him, Kennedy had his troubles with Congress. Although it supported many of his foreign-aid projects, it failed to pass bills for Federal aid to education and medical care for the aged. At the same time, Kennedy could point to some real achievements. "To our sister republics south of the border," he had said in his inaugural address, the United States would offer "a new alliance for progress." In March of 1961, Congress fol-

A vast ball of fire rose into the sky as U.S. scientists exploded a hydrogen device in the South Pacific.

UPI Photo

lowed the President's recommendations and set aside large sums of money for loans to the countries of Latin America. The money was to be used to improve social conditions in those countries. The "Alliance for Progress" program was intended to help friendly nations to help themselves. Boldly the President faced up to civil rights and the challenges of the space age. The nation, he told Congress, should commit itself to achieving the goal, before the decade was out, of landing a man on the moon and returning him safely to earth.

The next time he confronted Cuba he did not fail. Photographs taken by reconnaissance planes clearly revealed missile bases in Cuba supplied and constructed by the Soviet Union. The threat of nuclear attack thus was brought to within ninety miles of our coast. The President ordered a blockade, or "quarantine," thrown around Cuba. He demanded the return to Russia of the missiles already there. Knowing that he risked the possibility of another world war, the President said:

"It shall be the policy of this nation to regard any nuclear missile launched from Cuba against any nation in the Western Hemisphere as an attack by the Soviet Union on the United States requiring a full retaliatory response on the Soviet Union."

Tensely the country—and the world—waited. Twenty-five Russian ships were already at sea, approaching Cuba. If they did not turn back, would our warships sink them? U Thant, Secretary General of the United Nations, labored night and day to avoid a conflict. Meanwhile, in an exchange of messages, JFK and Soviet Premier Khrushchev seemed like a pair of poker players, wondering how many cards to draw. On October 28, 1962, Moscow threw in its hand, ordering its ships home and the Cuban missile bases dismantled.

The resolution of the missile crisis in Cuba was among JFK's greatest triumphs. Another was the conclusion of a nuclear test ban treaty in 1963 between the U.S., the Soviet Union and Britain banning all nuclear tests except those conducted underground. Still another was the creation of the Peace Corps in which thousands of Americans helped 58 nations to build toward a brighter future. But other factors humanized this man. His young children, Caroline and "John-John," pictured dancing around the President's office, revealed that American leadership had passed to a new generation (JFK was twenty years younger than Adlai Stevenson, ten years younger than Lyndon Johnson). He was warm and outgoing, and a trip to West Germany and Ireland, his ancestral land, proved how well liked he was around the world. He resembled one of the characters in his own book, *Profiles in Courage*. Others worked hard, but JFK, despite a disabling physical condition, did not spare himself either.

ASSASSINATION OF JFK

The nation and world mourn the young leader who brought charm and statesmanship to his office.

The big jet plane, bearing the seal of the President of the United States, settled gently onto the runway of Love Field in Dallas, Texas. Roaring crowds waited in the sunshine that Friday, November 22, 1963, for the youthful John F. Kennedy, who as our 35th President was now only 46 years of age. Bareheaded and smiling, JFK appeared with his beautiful wife, Jacqueline Bouvier Kennedy. Texas Governor John B. Connally stepped forward in official greeting and filled the arms of Mrs. Kennedy with red roses.

The President had waved aside advice from Adlai Stevenson that hostile sentiment just then made Dallas a dangerous place to visit. Defiantly, he asked how any Chief Executive could isolate himself from the American people. At Love Field he joined the motorcade that was to carry him to the Trade Mart for a speech at noon, choosing a roofless limousine so that he could wave back at the cheering crowds. Beside him sat Jacqueline, carrying her roses. Police on motorcycles sped ahead as an escort.

The motorcade reached Elm and Houston Streets in downtown Dallas. Here the limousine approached an underpass. Nearby stood the Texas School Book Depository, a drab building. In an open window lurked Lee Harvey Oswald, a former immigrant to Russia and a "loner," who was separated from the wife he had married overseas. Three rifle shots rang out, mortally wounding the President and seriously injuring Governor Connally. That afternoon Oswald

Kennedy's bier, guarded by members of the services, lay in the East Room of the White House on November 23, 1963.

was arrested as the alleged assassin. Two days later, in full view of television viewers across the nation, Jack Ruby, a nightclub owner, worked his way into the crowd-jammed halls of the Dallas jail and shot Oswald. [A commission headed by Chief Justice Earl Warren devoted weeks to investigating both murders and concluded that no conspiracy had existed between Oswald and Ruby.]

The entire world mourned the passing of the young President, who seemed just to be reaching full stride. Dignitaries representing 92 nations participated in the funeral procession, led by a riderless black horse. The martyred President was carried to his final resting place on a gently rolling hillside of Arlington National Cemetery. Weeping Americans, following the procession on television, recognized many familiar faces: the President of France, the Emperor of Ethiopia, Prince Philip of Britain, the Queen of Greece, the King of the Belgians, the Crown Princess and Prince of the Netherlands, the President of Ireland, the Premier of Japan, the President of South Korea, among others.

Upon signing the Civil Rights Bill in July 1964, Johnson handed pens to Dr. Martin Luther King, Jr., and others.

LBJ BECOMES THE NATION'S 36th PRESIDENT

Elected in his own right in 1964, he promises to build the "Great Society."

In a blood-stained dress, on the day of the assassination, Jacqueline Kennedy stood beside Lyndon B. Johnson aboard the presidential plane at Love Field as the tall Texan was sworn into office as our 36th President. "God reigns and the Government at Washington still lives," said James A. Garfield on the morning that Abraham Lincoln died, the first President to become a victim of an assassin's bullet.

Johnson took the presidential oath in an hour of tragedy.

LBJ stood 6-foot-3, or an inch shorter than Lincoln. His political education was gained under two of the strongest, shrewdest men ever to serve in Washington—President Franklin D. Roosevelt and the almost indestructible Speaker of the House, Sam Rayburn—and his basic philosophy was drawn from the Book of Isaiah: "Come now, let us reason together." During the remainder of JFK's term he could do little but carry on the policies of his predecessor. Except for the Washington Monument and the Lincoln Memorial, more people visited Kennedy's grave than any other place around Washington.

Johnson had inherited many difficult problems from Kennedy—civil rights, the plight of the impoverished, a war in Vietnam—and any one of these crises could trip him over the abyss into political oblivion. But the country still believed that he was an extension of JFK (the last thing Johnson wished to be), and so, "running in his own right" in 1964 against a very conservative Republican candidate, Senator Barry Goldwater of Arizona, he carried all but five southern states in one of the most sweeping election landslides in American history. His victory smile must have measured seven inches. What Roosevelt had called the "New Deal" and Kennedy had named the "New Frontier," Johnson now labeled the "Great Society." Declaring "war on poverty," he promised to clean up the slums and revitalize the civil rights program.

From then on Johnson pushed through Congress a massive amount of legislation dealing with health and welfare, job training, education, civil rights, consumer protection, and conservation. Topping the list in 1965 was Medicare, the program to provide medical care for the aged that had been proposed by JFK.

But a gigantic shadow began to eclipse the "Great Society" program—the shadow of Vietnam.

DEATH IN THE JUNGLE

How the Vietnam war drove LBJ from politics

Wrote the Chinese political philosopher, Mao Tse-Tung, in 1937:

"The guerrilla campaigns being waged in China today are a page in history that has no precedent. Their influence will be confined not solely to China in her present anti-Japanese struggle, but will be world-wide."

President Kennedy paid attention to Mao-Tse-Tung. Where, except in Korea, had a war against Communism followed a conventional pattern? A Communist guerrilla war in Malaya had lasted from 1946 to 1957 and involved 400,000 men and caused about 16,000 casualties. In Greece from 1945 to 1950 the struggle against Communist guerrillas had involved about 300,000, nearly half of whom were killed or wounded. Similar wars had broken out in Cuba and Venezuela, the Philippines and Vietnam.

The latter struggle most intimately engaged JFK. Over the opposition of top generals, he ordered the organization of a select corps of guerrilla fighters who would wear green berets as the mark of their distinction. These special forces for the most part were trained in two places—in Panama if their jungle warfare was designed for Latin America, in Okinawa if Asia were their destination. South Vietnam impressed Kennedy as a most suitable area for the Green Berets to operate. His brother Robert, then Attorney General, was asked what was the President's intention in the war in South Vietnam.

"To win it," Robert answered curtly.

"This is a new kind of war," he told a news conference, "but war it is in a very real sense of the word. It is a war fought not by massive diversions but secretly by terror, assassination, ambush and infiltration." By such means and ignoring its pledge signed at Geneva in 1954, the government of North Vietnam intended to conquer the Republic of South Vietnam.

President Kennedy felt that the Communists threatened all Southeast Asia. But JFK tempered firmness with restraint. At his death about 15,000 Green Berets and other U.S. military personnel were in Vietnam as "advisers" to the South Vietnamese forces.

President Johnson put the U.S. into the war on a bigger scale. He did so after North Vietnamese gunboats attacked U.S. destroyers in the Gulf of Tonkin in August 1964 and Congress authorized him to "take all necessary measures" to repel attacks on U.S. forces and "prevent further aggression." Soon

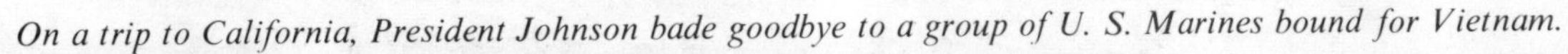

On a trip to California, President Johnson bade goodbye to a group of U. S. Marines bound for Vietnam.

From his lofty perch atop a sandbag bunker, a Green Beret observer scanned a battle area in Vietnam.

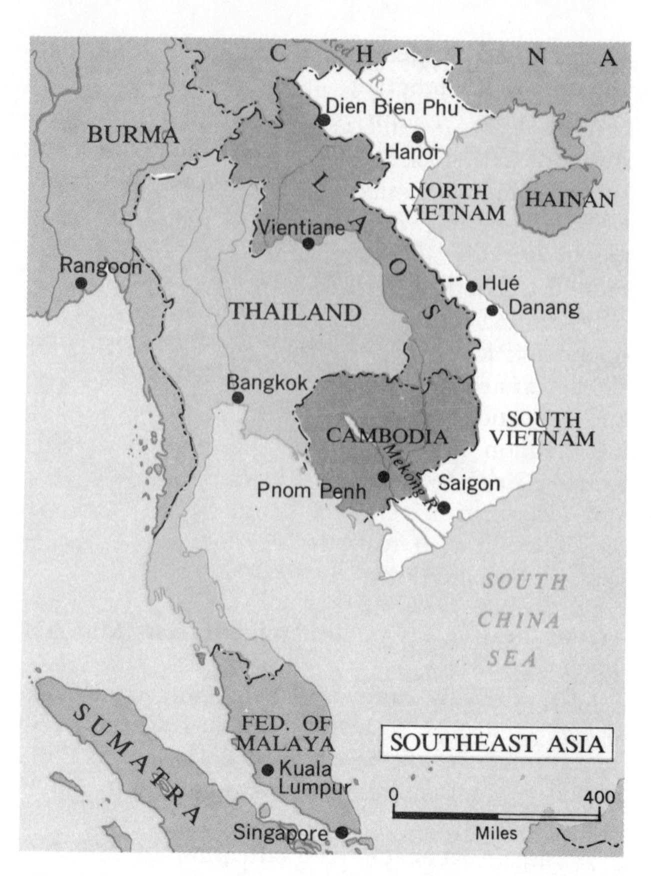

North Vietnam and South Vietnam (divided at the 17th parallel) and neighboring lands of Southeast Asia.

The Americans in Vietnam fought in the watery Mekong delta region, as well as in rice paddies, jungles, mountains.

tens of thousands of American combat troops poured into Vietnam. Fighting spread as the Americans tangled with hit-and-run guerrillas. But Texas-stubborn LBJ stuck to his guns, supporting generals and diplomats who said we were winning as long as we followed American rather than Chinese military tactics. On this basis they demanded ever-increasing numbers of foot troops to die in the jungles.

Dissenting students burned their draft cards in opposition to a war in which they did not believe. They claimed that under the draft law the poor and educationally disadvantaged were being turned into cannon fodder. Bombing raids on "militarily strategic" points in North Vietnam killed civilians, and American hearts were constricted by the view on television of a tear-streaked mother holding in her arms a baby killed by one of our bombs. Congress divided between the "hawks" who supported the war and the "doves" who called for a negotiated peace. Among the doves, the loudest spokesmen were Senator William J. Fulbright of Arkansas, chairman of the powerful Senate Committee on Foreign Relations, and Senator Wayne Morse of Oregon, who insisted that the war never had been declared by Congress and was therefore illegal.

Meanwhile the vital part of LBJ's "Great Society" was falling apart, especially his war on poverty, because of the rising cost of the Asian war. Senator Robert Kennedy, the former Attorney General, now swung over to the "doves," calling for the war to be ended in virtually any way possible. In a stormy White House interview LBJ warned RFK that by supporting critics of the war he strengthened North Vietnam. "The blood of American boys will be on your hands," he said.

News of this interview must have traveled quickly over the "diplomatic grapevine" until it reached a chuckling Mao. Perhaps one day LBJ would learn what this Chinese believed he knew: "Guerrillas are like fish, and the people are the water in which the fish swim. If the temperature of the water is right, the fish will thrive and multiply."

In March 1968, with the war costing heavily in blood and treasure, LBJ announced that he would not seek another term in the White House. By taking himself out of the forthcoming election, he hoped to cool tensions and controversy that had split the nation. In November he halted all bombing of North Vietnam, and a peace conference began in January. But the two sides soon found themselves hopelessly split on the question of peacemaking. For months the weekly talks dragged on with no sign of agreement.

By the time Johnson left office, 550,000 American soldiers were in Vietnam, more than 30,000 Americans had been killed and nearly 200,000 had been wounded.

"I HAVE A DREAM"

Civil rights spark a "revolution" as Dr. King leads a great demonstration in Washington.

The Centennial Celebration of the Civil War, including the one hundredth anniversary of the Emancipation Proclamation, sparked the "Revolution of 1963." Although as a senator John Kennedy had paid little attention to the plight of Black America, as President this Boston millionaire became the Negro's best friend in Washington. Where Congress hesitated, he won gains by executive orders.

He used Federal forces to prevent the governors of Mississippi and Alabama from disallowing eligible Negro students from attending their state universities. At the moment the President was on television pleading with the people of Oxford, the site of the state university of Mississippi, to exercise restraint, the city erupted in riot. Overturned cars were burned. Hundreds were injured and two men killed, one an innocent French journalist.

Ominous storm clouds rolled across America. Negroes attempted to integrate busses and restaurants, believing that the same Supreme Court decision that ordered the desegregation of schools applied to all public facilities. A new term, "Freedom Riders," came into the language, designating white sympathizers who attempted to join black Americans in sharing transportation systems. Often they were cruelly beaten by segregationists.

North or south one could not find a more sadistic "nigger hater" than Eugene "Bull" Connor, commissioner of public safety for Birmingham, Alabama—called "the capital of segregation" by black Americans—who triggered the Revolution of 1963. True, defeated in a recent election, Connor clung to his position by a technicality. But Connor would do anything to continue "disciplining" Negroes.

Connor forgot that press photographs and television cameras would reveal to people across America what was involved in "putting down the nigger." Police dogs snarled at peaceful demonstrators favoring desegregation. Fire hoses swept youngsters off their feet before they were hauled to jail. In time the Negroes fought back, pelting the police with stones and bottles. President Kennedy begged for a truce in this conflict. His wish was respected for three days, then bombs destroyed the home of a civil rights leader and a Negro-owned motel.

Riots rampaged throughout Birmingham. Connor's police felt bricks and bottles batter their heads. Again, overturned automobiles were burned. JFK stationed 3,000 Federal troops, especially trained in riot control, near the city, already grieved by the injury of fifty persons. Order was restored.

Dr. Martin Luther King, Jr., evoked a "dream" of racial harmony in a speech that stirred the nation.

AT THE LINCOLN MEMORIAL

Understandably, Negroes wondered if the Constitution and the Bill of Rights applied to *them.* If so, they wanted their freedom *now.* Three hundred years of "humiliation, abuse and deprivation" were enough, they said.

A. Philip Randolph, President of the Brotherhood of Sleeping Car Porters, a tireless toiler for the rights of black Americans, conceived the idea. With dignity, with drama, Negroes would make a massive descent on Washington, D.C., to demonstrate to the nation that they were real people. Many fears were expressed. What if there were bombings and riots? Suppose Congress was alienated? Or the President embarrassed?

The pessimists were overwhelmed by the enthusiastic approval they received from the white churches. Hundreds of local unions spoke for labor's support. August 28, 1963, was the day set for the ceremonies. Two hundred and fifty thousand workers for civil rights, representing every state in the Union, formed at the Washington Monument for the march down Constitution Avenue to the Lincoln Memorial. Whites walked beside blacks, arms interlocked as they sang freedom songs or carried signs that read:

"Effective civil rights law–Now!"

"Integrated schools–Now!"

"Decent housing–Now!"

But the star of the day was Dr. Martin Luther King, Jr., president of the Southern Christian Leadership Conference, who soon would win the Nobel Peace Prize.

Dr. King possessed possibly the finest ability as an orator in America. His voice had a kind of songlike quality as soft as the breeze on which it floated. And all at once he appeared to be speaking a prose poem:

". . . I have a dream that one day on the red hills of Georgia the sons of former slaves and the sons of former slave owners will be able to sit down together at the table of brotherhood. I have a dream that even the state of Mississippi, a state sweltering with people's injustices, sweltering with the heat of oppression, will be transformed into an oasis of freedom and justice. I have a dream that my four little children will one day live in a nation where they will be judged not by the color of their skin but by the content of their character."

Congressional leaders and President Kennedy met graciously with Dr. King. The crowd dispersed, as it had arrived, by bus, car and train. News commentators spoke rapturously of what had occurred that day. The southern-inspired stereotype of the black American as shiftless, irresponsible and uneducable had been forever destroyed.

Unhappily the commentators spoke too soon.

TRAGEDY AT SELMA

Negro demands for voting rights meet with violence, and disorders spread across the land.

Lyndon B. Johnson was far from being a hard-shelled southerner. As Vice President he had been chairman of the Committee on Equal Employment Opportunity. Following JFK into the Presidency, he told a joint session of Congress: "The time has come for Americans of all races and creeds and political beliefs to respect one another."

But the racial problem was immensely involved. On both sides leaders of weak stature pushed forward, obviously entranced by their sudden prominence. In an effort to dramatize how "literacy tests" were just one of the "barriers to the right to vote," Negro leaders focused on Selma, Alabama, the county seat of Dallas County. More than half of Selma's population of 28,000 people were black Americans, yet only 335 Negroes were registered voters.

Dr. King spent nine weeks in Selma. Negroes marched on the courthouse, demanding that their rights be recognized. Arrests apparently were not enough to satisfy segregationist Governor George C. Wallace. State troopers were told to get tough and "break them up" instead of troubling with arrests. Several Negroes were injured. One died. A proposed march of fifty miles from Selma to the state capital at Montgomery was the Negroes' way of telling the country of their plight.

March 7, 1965 was a hazy Sunday that reeked with mugginess. Still 350 demonstrators started the march. At Pettus Bridge (named for a Confederate general) across the Alabama River, state troopers warned: "You have two minutes to turn around and go back."

Again the nation's television cameras reflected a story of horror. At the harsh order, "Troopers, advance!," the police moved on the marchers. Billy clubs toppled many to the ground. Mounted possemen appeared, wielding nightsticks. Cries for help and mercy brought the throwing of tear-gas bombs. Of eighty-four injured Negroes, seventeen were hospitalized.

Revulsion swept the country. A Federal court order authorized the march from Selma to Montgomery and in an appeal to a joint session of Congress for legislation to "eliminate illegal barriers to the right to vote," an emotionally touched LBJ added: "It's not just Negroes who must overcome the crippling legacy of bigotry and injustice."

On television, in ringing tones, the President told all America:

"We shall overcome!"

From all sections, black and white, came sympathizing Americans until the line of march from Selma to Montgomery swelled to 30,000. They sang "Ain't Gonna Let Nobody Turn Me 'Round." Three white ministers were beaten by hoodlums. One clergyman died of brain injuries. Worse still was the murder of Mrs. Viola Liuzzo, a Detroit housewife and civil rights worker. An Alabama court failed to convict her alleged murderers.

If the reaction to such injustice grew militant, if cries of "Black Power" and "Kill Whitey" rose in Negro areas, if bullying voices called for "guerrilla warfare," the compassionate of heart tried to understand.

Terrible consequences followed. Vicious race riots in Los Angeles (1965), Chicago (1966) and Detroit (1967) were only forerunners to the more than 100 American cities which by 1968 had been similarly inflamed. By mid-August of that year estimates placed the dead at 100, the injured at 2,000, the arrested at 12,000.

The senseless assassination of Martin Luther King, Jr., at Nashville on April 4, 1968 (his assassin was later captured and sentenced to 99 years imprisonment) killed an eloquent voice of non-violence in solving the racial problem. A tough Negro could expect only one response—a white backlash.

Yet hope remained. Appointed by LBJ, Thurgood Marshall became the first Negro justice on the Supreme Court of the United States. The mayor of Washington, D.C., was a Negro, and so were the mayors of Cleveland, Ohio and Gary, Indiana. A black American sat in the United States Senate —from Massachusetts, where the white voters overwhelmingly outnumbered the black.

NIXON FINALLY WINS

A man who quit politics for ever wins his way to the White House.

The decision of Lyndon B. Johnson not to run for a second term virtually shattered the Democratic Party. Two Democrats had already challenged him for the nomination—Senator Eugene J. McCarthy of Minnesota and Senator Robert F. Kennedy of New York, "doves" on Vietnam. Now Hubert H. Humphrey, Vice President and so committed to LBJ's policies, entered the race.

But tragedy lay ahead. Bobby Kennedy's campaign in the primaries fired many voters' imagination. The younger generation, to whom he talked as equals, flocked around him. He asked for their help in saving democracy, and undoubtedly was forging ahead. Thousands lined the streets wherever

Robert Kennedy being mobbed by students in Kansas shortly after announcing his candidacy for president in 1968.

President-elect and Mrs. Nixon with daughters Julie (left, with her fiancé David Eisenhower) and Tricia. Nixon holds a copy of the presidential seal made by Julie.

he appeared, giving credence to the oft-repeated comment that he considered himself the heir apparent to the United States throne. He backed American policy favoring Israel. In Los Angeles on June 5, 1968, while Kennedy was celebrating victory in the California and South Dakota primaries, an alleged assassin of Jordanian Arab extraction, Sirhan Bishara Sirhan, fired eight bullets from a 22-caliber revolver. Three shots struck Bobby, killing him.

Richard M. Nixon, the Republican nominee, had feuded with the press after losing his bid for the governorship of California some years before and had renounced all future office-seeking. But now he appeared in a new, jovial image. During the campaign he answered no questions of consequence. He promised to unify the country, restore respect for the flag, end the Vietnam war "consistent with the requirements of long-range peace in Asia," and help Negroes with "black capitalism." An "independent" candidate George Wallace of Alabama, the former governor, campaigned for "law and order," meaning, as most observers saw it, opposition to integration and civil rights.

Election night showed the lead wavering between Nixon and Humphrey. But Nixon won narrowly:

Popular vote: Nixon, 31,770,237; Humphrey, 31,270,533; Wallace, 9,906,141.

Electoral College vote: Nixon, 301; Humphrey, 191; Wallace, 46.

A "GIANT LEAP FOR MANKIND"

Two astronauts, landing on the moon, become the sensation of a century

From the suborbital missions of Shepard and Grissom in 1961 (see page 302), America mobilized its finest scientists and engineers as it moved steadily forward toward fulfilling President Kennedy's promise of landing men on the moon before the decade ended. The Mercury flights of 1962 and 1963 four times placed manned spaceships in orbit around the earth. The Gemini flights, beginning in 1965 and continuing through 1966, achieved spectacular results. The flight of Gemini 4 found Edward H. White, 2nd, becoming the first American to "walk" in outer space, proving that man could be his own master in a hostile environment. Gemini 7 continued for 206 orbits in 13¾ days, the longest space flight on record. Later Gemini experiments proved that two spaceships could be joined ("docked") in outer space. Now, said the experts, we were ready for the Apollo flights that would land men on the moon.

Tragedy struck quickly. In January 1967 a flash fire on the launch pad cost the lives of astronauts Virgil I. Grissom, Edward H. White, 2nd, and Roger B. Chaffee. Pluckily American scientists found the errors among the two million parts of this type of spaceship. Their reward came in December 1968 when Apollo 8 and its three-man crew raced toward the moon. In ten orbits around the moon the astronauts examined a surface of colorless gray which looked like "a dirty beach." So, link by link, was welded the chain of events that produced moonbound Apollo 11.

Thousands of spectators spent all night on the beaches overlooking Cape Kennedy and by shortly after sunrise as many as a million may have been there, straining their eyes to glimpse Apollo 11 on its launching pad. Three men were aboard the command spaceship, one to fly the main craft while the other two would descend in *The Eagle,* or lunar module, to the desolate, crater-pocked plain selected for a landing site. They were a varied crew, these three—sandy-haired, blue-eyed Neil Armstrong, who had first flown at the age of six; Air Force Colonel "Buzz" Aldrin, whose doctoral dissertation on space travel had baffled his professors at Massachusetts Institute of Technology; and Air Force Lieutenant Colonel Mike Collins, the son of a general, and also a graduate of West Point.

Apollo 11 stood 363 feet high on its pad, and contained 18 million parts. Ahead of it stretched a journey of 238,857 miles to its destination. The feat seemed beyond human imagination. Very likely there was not a television set in America whose tubes did not record the events at Cape Kennedy. Heartbeats all but stopped as the last seconds to blast-off were counted. Then came a roar that made the ground tremble and shock waves were felt for miles around. The time was 9:32 Eastern Daylight Time on July 16, 1969.

The flight, like the blast-off, proceeded perfectly under men who had been training for it since January. News of the adventure flashed around the world. Awed millions at home and abroad could talk of nothing else.

Next day, 148,000 miles away, the astronauts sent America their first evening television entertainment. They described the earth as greenish-blue and "very beautiful."

A cheerful trio—on one broadcast they sang a wobbly chorus of "Fly Me to the Moon"—Armstrong, Aldrin and Collins were seriously businesslike in explaining to viewers how they used a telescope, a sextant, a star chart, a navigational computer and even how they ate. On the third day Apollo 11 rocketed into orbit around the moon. Armstrong and Aldrin crawled into the lunar module, *The Eagle,* in which on the morrow they were to separate from the command craft and land on the moon. The command ship and module must separate on the far side of the moon in this most critical and dramatic phase of their mission. On earth people waited in grim silence. Then came the good news: "*Eagle* has wings." The descent began.

"THE EAGLE" LANDS

Suddenly came the sound of Armstrong's happy voice: "*The Eagle* has landed." Armstrong, first to step on the moon, had discussed for hours with his clergyman what he should say at that historic moment. He touched tentatively the sandlike but firm surface, and declared:

"That's one small step for a man, and one giant leap for mankind."

The men of Apollo 11 before their historic flight. L. to r., Neil A. Armstrong, Michael Collins, Edwin E. Aldrin, Jr.

"Buzz" Aldrin on the moon. Armstrong, taking photo, and Eagle *are reflected in the visor of Aldrin's helmet.*

Before Aldrin descended from *The Eagle,* a television camera was placed so the world could watch the activities of the first earth-men on the moon. They bounced about like kangaroos or two kids with a new plaything. Armstrong brought them back to work. They planted a plaque honoring the five men, including two Russians, who had given their lives in developing space flight. They planted an American flag and various scientific devices intended to send back information from the moon after the astronauts had departed. Once more like hopping kangaroos they gathered samples of the moon's surface and rock formations—substances unlike anything on earth, leading scientists to speculate on new theories of how the universe was created.

Flawlessly *The Eagle* blasted off, redocked with the command ship and started on the long journey home, splashing down in the Pacific only 11 miles from the carrier *Hornet.* For 21 days Armstrong, Aldrin and Collins were quarantined to make sure they had brought back no foreign substances that could contaminate the earth. The nation strained impatiently with plans to honor the heroes from coast to coast.

Meanwhile space scientists planned more moon landings stretching into the 1970's and official Washington talked of the possibility of landing men on Mars in another twenty years.

INDEX

Figures in italics indicate illustrations.

PICTURE CREDITS

Wide World Photos 3, 249, 255 (top left), 264, 270, 274 (top), 280 (right), 281, 282, 283 (bottom), 284 (top), 286 (bottom), 288, 290 (top), 291, 295, 298, 300, 301, 302, 307, 308, 310 (bottom), 312, 313, 314; Collection of Warre 8; Univ. of Minnesota Library, Bell Collection 9; Metropolitan Museum of Art, gift of J. Pierpont Morgan 11 (right center); New York Public Library, Rare Books Division 11 (left center); Historical Soc. of Pennsylvania 57 (left and center), 90; Pennsylvania Academy of Fine Arts 57 (right); Colonial Williamsburg 68; Library of Congress 73, 93, 152, 153, 236, 260 (bottom); Yale Univ. Art Gallery 81; Emmet Collection, New York Public Library 83; J. F. Watson, *Annals of Philadelphia,* 1884 88; New York Historical Museum 89; New York State Historical Assn. 92; Monmouth County Historical Soc. 94; Free Library of Philadelphia 110; National Archives 154, 237 (bottom), 238, 239, 243, 244, 257, 280 (left); Pictorial Parade 231, 232 (bottom left); National Archives, Navy Dept. 232–233 (top); UPI 233 (bottom right), 237 (top), 252, 294, 299 (right), 304 (top), 305, 306, 309; U.S. Army 240, 269, 273 (top—ptg. by Aaron Bohrod, bottom), 277 (top right, bottom right), 278 (bottom—ptg. by Aaron Bohrod), 287, 290 (bottom right), 310 (top left); Smithsonian Institution 241, 260 (top); Brown Brothers 247; Culver Pictures 248; Whitney Museum of American Art 255 (bottom left); U.S. Navy 266 (ptg. by Griffith B. Coale), 271 (ptg. by Griffith B. Coale), 286 (top); U.S. Air Force 277 (top left, center left, bottom left); LIFE 290 (bottom left); Magnum Photos 297; NASA 303, 315; T. Horydczak, from David Studio, Washington, D.C. (rear cover, center).

ABCDEF

Independence Hall, Philadelphia,
*at the time of the Revolution.
Here both the Declaration of Independence
and the Constitution were approved.
Opposite is the opening page
of the Declaration of Independence
in Thomas Jefferson's handwriting,
with revisions by Jefferson, John Adams
and Benjamin Franklin.*

The Free Library of Philadelphia